MW00674607

TRUTH OR CONSEQUENCES

Nuel Belnap

TRUTH OR CONSEQUENCES

Essays in Honor of
Nuel Belnap

edited by

J. MICHAEL DUNN
Department of Philosophy and Department of Computer Science,
Indiana University, Bloomington, U.S.A.

and

ANIL GUPTA
Department of Philosophy, Indiana University,
Bloomington, U.S.A.

KLUWER ACADEMIC PUBLISHERS
DORDRECHT / BOSTON / LONDON

Library of Congress Cataloging-in-Publication Data

```
Truth or consequences : essays in honor of Nuel Belnap / edited by J.
  Michael Dunn and Anil Gupta.
       p.   cm.
  Includes bibliographical references and indexes.
  ISBN 0-7923-0920-0 (acid-free paper)
  1. Logic.  2. Truth.  3. Mathematics--Philosophy.
4. Probabilities.   I. Dunn, J. Michael, 1941-      II. Gupta, Anil,
1949-   . III. Belnap, Nuel D., 1930-
BC71.T78   1990
160--dc20                                               90-5141
```

ISBN 0-7923-0920-0

Published by Kluwer Academic Publishers,
P.O. Box 17, 3300 AA Dordrecht, The Netherlands.

Kluwer Academic Publishers incorporates
the publishing programmes of
D. Reidel, Martinus Nijhoff, Dr W. Junk and MTP Press.

Sold and distributed in the U.S.A. and Canada
by Kluwer Academic Publishers,
101 Philip Drive, Norwell, MA 02061, U.S.A.

In all other countries, sold and distributed
by Kluwer Academic Publishers Group,
P.O. Box 322, 3300 AH Dordrecht, The Netherlands.

Printed on acid-free paper

Printed in the Netherlands

For

Nuel and Gillian Belnap

TABLE OF CONTENTS

PREFACE

The essays in this collection are written by students, colleagues, and friends of Nuel Belnap to honor him on his sixtieth birthday. Our original plan was to include pieces from former students only, but we have deviated from this ever so slightly for a variety of personal and practical reasons.

Belnap's research accomplishments are numerous and well known: He has founded (together with Alan Ross Anderson) a whole branch of logic known as "relevance logic." He has made contributions of fundamental importance to the logic of questions. His work in modal logic, formal pragmatics, and the theory of truth has been highly influential. And the list goes on. Belnap's accomplishments as a teacher are also distinguished and well known but, by virtue of the essential privacy of the teaching relationship, not so well understood. We would like to reflect a little on what makes him such an outstanding teacher.

The following, though true, can only be a partial answer: He understands his subject through and through; he is smart, perceptive, and penetrating. There are two more factors that should be taken into account, if one is to understand Belnap's teaching accomplishments. The first is his attitude towards logic and philosophy: he approaches the subject with a sense of play and a sense of humor. He does not *work* with ideas, he *plays* with them. He doesn't get mired in complicated formulas, he draws pictures. He doesn't construct convoluted proofs, he "arm waves," as he is fond of saying. When things take an unexpected turn, he doesn't fret, he laughs. To do logic and philosophy with Nuel is not like carrying a heavy stone up a steep hill. It is more like exploring an exotic city. He is not content to stay on the main drag; he wants to explore all the alleys and byways. And exploration with him is fun. For he has such infectious enthusiasm, and he is smart, perceptive, and penetrating.

The second factor we need to consider to understand Belnap's teaching accomplishments consists of some of his personal qualities. One important aspect is his informality. In the early sixties, when he first came to Pittsburgh, he even had a nickname "Nuel, call me Nuel" because of his penchant for being on a first name basis with his students. Remember this was well before everyone became a "hippy" and such things became common.

Even more important than this informality, we think, are his intellectual courage, honesty, open-mindedness, and generosity. His office door is always open, and students do not feel silly bothering him with "silly" questions. Never, in all his play and experimentation with ideas, does he exhibit dogmatism. Never is he dismissive or disrespectful of views that are contrary to his own. To play with ideas with such a person is bound to be fun. And when that person is quick to credit you with having taught him something, when he makes you feel part of the enterprise, he becomes an irresistible teacher.

The qualities that make Nuel such a great teacher make him also such an adorable man. It is to this beloved man that these essays are dedicated.

J. Michael Dunn
Anil Gupta

ACKNOWLEDGEMENTS

We wish to acknowledge the help of many people in producing this volume, not the least of whom are our contributors. This book was produced from a camera-ready copy which, in turn, was prepared using Donald Knuth's excellent program TeX. Almost all of our contributors helped by producing either a TeX file or another electronic version of their document that could be massaged (in a few cases "wrestled" is the more appropriate word) into TeX.

André Chapuis deserves special thanks not only for overseeing the entire project, but also for his tireless, skillful, and conscientious work in producing the camera-ready copy. Others who helped in this process are Nancy Garrett, Luzia Martins, and Shirley Roper. Indiana University provided support that was crucial to the preparation of the volume.

We want to take this opportunity to give special thanks to Collie Henderson, Belnap's secretary for many years. The immediate occasion is for her giving to us Belnap's *vita*, list of publications, and a list of his doctoral students. But more generally she has not just been a constant support to Belnap's own work, but a friend and helper to many of his students.

We want to thank the people at Kluwer, particularly Martin Scrivener, for taking on this project. We also wish to thank Scrivener for his helpful cooperation and for his understanding and patience during the delay caused by our complete underestimate of the time needed to perfect the camera-ready copy.

Thanks to Gillian Belnap for the photograph that appears as the frontpiece to this volume.

LIST OF CONTRIBUTORS

Jon Barwise is College Professor of Philosophy, Mathematics, and Logic at Indiana University.

Robert L. Birmingham is Professor of Law at the University of Connecticut.

Aldo Bressan is Professor of Physics at the University of Padua.

Daniel Cohen is Assistant Professor of Philosophy at Colby College.

J. Michael Dunn is Oscar Ewing Professor of Philosophy, and Professor of Computer Science at Indiana University.

Jay L. Garfield is Associate Professor of Philosophy at Hampshire College.

James W. Garson is Professor of Philosophy at the University of Houston.

Dorothy Grover is Professor of Philosophy at the University of Illinois, Chicago.

Anil Gupta is Professor of Philosophy at Indiana University.

A. P. Hazen is Lecturer in Philosophy at the University of Melbourne.

John F. Horty is Assistant Professor of Philosophy at the University of Maryland.

Virginia Klenk is Professor of Philosophy at West Virginia University.

Michael Kremer is Assistant Professor of Philosophy at the University of Notre Dame.

Hugues Leblanc is Professor of Philosophy at Temple University.

Patrick Maher is Assistant Professor of Philosophy at the University of Illinois at Urbana-Champaign.

Ruth Manor is Professor of Philosophy at San Jose State University.

Storrs McCall is Associate Professor of Philosophy at McGill University.

Garrel Pottinger is a Researcher at Odyssey Research Associates Inc.

Peter Roeper is Senior Lecturer in Philosophy in The Faculties at the Australian National University, Canberra.

Alasdair Urquhart is Professor of Philosophy at the University of Toronto.

W. Kent Wilson is Associate Professor of Philosophy at the University of Illinois, Chicago.

Bas C. van Fraassen is Professor of Philosophy at Princeton University.

DOROTHY GROVER

ON TWO DEFLATIONARY TRUTH THEORIES [1]

At one time, debates about truth centered on questions concerning the "nature of truth". Then Ramsey 1927 observed that

> ... 'It is true that Caesar was murdered' means no more than that
> Caesar was murdered, and 'It is false that Caesar was murdered'
> means that Caesar was not murdered.

Such observations have led philosophers to question the assumption that truth has a nature that must be theorized about. So there are now two schools of thought concerning truth: some philosophers argue that truth is to be analysed in terms of either epistemic or metaphysical concepts (as in, "truth is a relational property connecting language with the world");[2] and other philosophers argue that truth is not a substantive relational property. The former are said to advocate a *substantive* analysis of truth, and the latter a *deflationary* analysis.

The development of deflationary theories has meant that substantive theorists must not only give an account of the nature of truth, but also show that a substantive truth property is needed. On the other side, deflationists (who claim the truth predicate need not have an explanatory role) must either provide some other account of the role of the truth predicate, or show the truth predicate is redundant. My project is to provide a comparison of two deflationary theories that claim a role for the truth predicate: the *Disquotational Theory of Truth*[3] and the theory of which Nuel Belnap was a co-founder, the *Prosentential Theory of Truth*.

A Preview. The disquotational and prosentential theories are similar in that both claim the truth predicate has utility in providing us with certain kinds of expressibility. There is some agreement about the expressibility provided, since both claim the truth predicate makes available generalization with respect to sentence positions. However there are differences in their "formal" analyses of this role of the truth predicate. Disquotational theorists utilize first order quantifiers and an explicit truth predicate in their analyses, while prosentential theorists appeal only to propositional quantifiers. This suggests a difference in the "level" of the truth predicate: for the disquotational analysis of generalization seems to treat 'true' syntactically as a metalinguistic predicate, while the prosentential analysis seems to have 'true' operating at the level of the object language. I argue these differences are not as significant as they might first appear.

I will also address some questions that disquotational theorists have left open. Rather than speculating as to how the theory's proponents might answer these

---

[1] I thank Jerry Kapus and Anil Gupta for helpful comments on an early draft of this paper.
[2] For example, Field 1972. For other suggestions see Dummett 1976, especially pp. 115–126, and Putnam 1981, pp. 49–56.
[3] This is the theory that has been generally ascribed to Leeds 1978, Horwich 1982, Soames 1984, and Williams 1986.

1

J. M. Dunn and A. Gupta (eds.), Truth or Consequences, 1–17.
© 1990 *Kluwer Academic Publishers. Printed in the Netherlands.*

questions, I will show that an available option for disquotational theorists is offered by the prosentential theory.

1. THE DISQUOTATIONAL THEORY

The disquotational theory seems to have been inspired by Quine's 1970 remarks about the truth predicate. The account of truth provided by the theory is also said to connect in some way with Tarski's work. I do not know whether Quine subscribes to what is now being recognized as the disquotational theory. But as his brief remarks (pp. 10–13) provide insight others do not provide, I will often rely on Quine's remarks in describing the theory. The key claims of the disquotational theory seem to be the following.

1.1. The truth predicate is a device of disquotation, of semantic ascent and semantic descent. For example,

> Truth is useful, we may say, as a device of (what Quine calls) *disquotation* . . .". (Leeds 1978)

> It is helpful . . . to focus on something that the truth predicate is good for — namely, what W.V.Quine has called "semantic ascent". Soames 1984 (p.412)

Soames gives as an example of semantic ascent, the move from 'Snow is white' to "The sentence 'Snow is white' is true".

1.2. The truth predicate is said to have utility in providing a way of generalizing with respect to sentence positions. For generalization with respect to sentence positions can be achieved via quantifiers binding variables in nominal positions. The truth predicate and semantic ascent facilitate this. Soames illustrates the moves involved in the following passage.

> The importance of semantic ascent is illustrated by cases like (3), in which we want to generalize.
>
> (3) a. Snow is white $\rightarrow$ (Grass is blue $\rightarrow$ Snow is white)
>   b. The earth moves $\rightarrow$ (The sun is cold $\rightarrow$ The earth moves)
>
> . . . . . .
>
> . . . if one wanted to get the effect of asserting all of them, one would have to quantify, replacing sentences with variables. In English such quantification is most naturally, though not inevitably, construed as first order and objectual. Thus, if the variables are taken to range over sentences we need a metalinguistic truth predicate. Semantic ascent gives us

(4)   For all sentences p, q (p is true $\rightarrow$ (q is true $\rightarrow$ p is true))
           (Soames 1984, p.413)

1.3. Disquotational theorists connect their theory in various ways with either Tarski style truth definitions, or the so-called T-sentences of Tarski. Soames thinks of Tarski style truth definitions as legitimizing our use of the truth predicate; so defined,

> the resulting truth predicate is just what is needed for metatheoretical studies of the nature, structure, and scope of a wide variety of theories. (Soames p.425)

And Williams 1986 says,

> We can agree that the "disquotation" schema
>
> "p is true in L iff P"
>
> captures something important about truth. Perhaps in conjunction with some additional conventions to cover cases like "Everything he told you was true", where 'true' is used in connection with statements not directly quoted, it fixes the extension of the truth predicate for language L.

1.4. Soames' talk of "a metalinguistic truth predicate", and the fact that " 'Snow is white' is true" is assumed paradigmatic, both suggest that disquotational theorists think of the truth predicate as functioning syntactically like a metalinguistic predicate.

1.5. The disquotational treatment of the relevant generalizations seems to suggest that the truth predicate also functions semantically as a metalinguistic predicate. However *the* disquotational view on this point is not clear. For consider Quine's explanation of the truth predicate's role in semantic ascent,

> ... The truth predicate is a reminder that, despite a technical ascent to talk of sentences, our eye is on the world. ... By calling the sentence ['Snow is white'] true, we call snow white. Quine 1970 (p.12)

There is a suggestion here, and in other places, that sentences containing the truth predicate are *really* about extra-linguistic things. If that is the case, the truth predicate would function in a way different from (other?) metalinguistic predicates.

1.6. According to disquotational theorists, the concept of truth does not have an explanatory role; it does not require analysis in terms of either substantive metaphysical or epistemic relations. This view is expressed in claims like the following.

> Truth is a useful notion, but it is not the key to what there is, or how we represent the world to ourselves through language. (Soames 1984)

> To explain the utility of disquotation, we need say nothing about the relations between language and the world. ... (Leeds 1978)

2. THE PROSENTENTIAL THEORY

As I can provide only a brief review of the prosentential theory, I will give special emphasis to those parts of the theory that are most relevant to this discussion.[4] The principal claim of the prosentential theory is that the predicates 'true' and 'false' provide prosentential constructions. Prosentences are like pronouns (and other proforms[5]) in that they can be used anaphorically; however, whereas pro*nouns* are atomic and occupy positions nouns occupy, pro*sentences* tend to be non-atomic and occupy the positions that sentences occupy.

My review of the theory will show that the prosentential analysis of sentences containing the truth predicate carries implications regarding both the utility of the truth predicate and how this utility is to be explained.

2.1. A key claim of the prosentential theory is that 'that is true' and 'it is true' function as prosentences. I will illustrate what this can mean in a particular case. When Alan says 'If that is true, then ...' in,

> Mary: Chicago is large.
> Alan: If that is true, then it probably has a large airport.

Alan says, in effect, "If Chicago is large, then ...". For in the simple cases, part of the role of a proform ('that is true') is to "stand in" for its antecedent sentence (Mary's 'Chicago is large').[6] A reason for using the anaphoric 'that is true' (rather than 'Chicago is large') is to make clear that Alan is entertaining what Mary has said, rather than saying something on his own initiative. Anaphoric devices establish such connections. More generally, prosentences (and other proforms) are useful when we need to establish connections between different parts of a discourse. Such facts also explain how it is that 'that is true' can be used to express agreement.

2.2. Prosentences can be modified, as in 'that is false' and 'that may be true'. Since 'that is false', in a given context, can be used to assert the contradiction of an antecedent sentence, it can be used to express disagreement. Thus, in

> Mary: Chicago is large. Alan: That's false.

Alan utilizes the anaphoric overtones of 'that is false', in expressing his disagreement with Mary.

---

[4] The reader is referred to Grover, Camp, and Belnap 1975 (hereafter, GCB) for further details. See also Grover 1977, Grover 1981a, and Grover 1981b.

[5] Included among *proforms* are pronouns, proverbs, proadjectives and prosentences.

[6] Though I call the sentence (or noun) with which a proform is connected its "antecendent", this does not mean that the antecendent has to occur before the proform.

2.3. The prosentential account of the role of the truth predicate in generalization goes roughly as follows. Suppose we want to generalize with respect to the component sentences in

(1)   If Eva says that the reactor is unsafe, the reactor is unsafe.
          If Eva says the guidelines have been satisfied, the guidelines have been satisfied.

In English we would normally say something like

(2)   Everything Eva says (about the safety of the reactor) is true.

Our claim that 'true' has a prosentential role in (2) is based partly on the observation that there are paraphrases of sentences like (2) in which 'true' occurs in a prosentence. In (3), for example, 'true' occurs in the bound prosentence 'it is true'.

(3)   For everything Eva says (about the safety of the reactor), it is true.

This bound use of 'it is true' has an analogue in formal languages. For consider,

(4)   For any p (if Eva says that p then p).

(3) and (4) say roughly the same thing. In fact this pair of sentences illustrate our point that bound prosentences function much as bound propositional variables function in formal languages;[7] what this means, among other things, is that the truth predicate provides the expressibility that propositional variables provide us with in formal languages.

I have ignored (in (4)) the suggested qualifying clause, "about the safety of the reactor". On the assumption that the quantifiers are interpreted substitutionally, and we have a quotation functor,[8] I could incorporate the qualification, as follows

(5)   (If (Eva says that p & Qp is about the reactor's safety) then p)

where 'Qp' stands for " 'p' ".

2.4. It can be seen that the *syntax* of the prosentential truth predicate is a little different from the syntax of those predicates we typically classify as metalinguistic predicates; for we usually think of metalinguistic predicates as combining with terms to form closed sentences. By contrast, in the case of primitive sentences, the prosentential truth predicate combines with terms to form prosentences; furthermore, prosentences might reasonably be said to be "bound" by their antecedents.

---

[7] I refer to variables that occupy sentential positions as *propositional variables*. This is only a grammatical categorization, based on the sentential positions of the variables.

[8] See Grover 1973 for one suggestion regarding the consistent use of propositional quantifiers and quotation, and quantification in and out of quotes. Also Kripke 1976 for further suggestions.

2.5. There are also *semantic* differences between the prosentential truth predicate and predicates we typically classify as metalinguistic. One difference is that the prosentential truth predicate is only a part of a prosentential construction — so it is, in a sense, an "incomplete symbol". Another difference is that the prosentential truth predicate seems to function at the level of the object language. This is something I need to say a bit more about.

What is in question is the semantic content of sentences containing the truth predicate. Many other truth theories assume that a sentence containing a truth predication, e.g., 'That is true', is about its antecedent sentence, ('Chicago is large') or an antecedent proposition. By contrast, the prosentential account is that 'That is true' does not to say anything about its antecedent sentence (e.g., 'Chicago is large'), but says something about an extra-linguistic subject (e.g., Chicago).

In order to see how the sentence 'Chicago is large', itself, need not feature in what is said, it will be helpful to consider the way pronouns function. Consider

(6)   The balloon rises when it is filled with helium.

If we are to understand what is said, we must understand that the words 'the balloon' and 'it' are linked. (They occur in close proximity, and etc.) However, the fact that we must see that there is a link between two expressions, does not mean that when we use 'it' we refer to the words 'the balloon'. Nothing is said in (6) about either the words 'the balloon' or the linking. Similarly, even though a prosentence may be linked with an antecedent expression, we speak only of extra-linguistic objects (e.g., snow, or Chicago) when we use 'that is true'.

Since it is usually at the level of the object language that we talk of such things as balloons and snow, it seems appropriate to characterize truth predications, and modified truth predications, as also functioning — so to speak — at the level of the object language.

2.6. The prosentential theory has assumed that truth does not have an explanatory role,[9] and that truth does not thereby need to be analysed in terms of either substantive epistemic or metaphysical concepts. What the prosentential theory does require, is a theory of anaphora. Such a theory is needed to explain the linguistic and logical aspects of anaphora, so that the semantic and pragmatic features of the utility of prosentences are more adequately explained. A formal theory of the logic of prosentences may also reveal possible options regarding the syntax, semantics, and role in inference, of prosentential constructions in potentially useful formal languages.

---

[9] This is not to deny that the truth predicate may be utilized in our explanations. We frequently need the expressibility that the truth predicate provides.

3. GENERALIZATION — A COMPARISON

The quantifiers used by the two deflationary theories, in their analyses of generalization, are clearly different. For in the one case the bound variables occupy the positions nouns occupy, and in the other, the variables occupy the positions sentences occupy. Quine's followers may hold this difference to be critical; for Quine has argued that quantification which involves bound propositional variables is incoherent — if interpreted objectually. Such a response by "Quine's followers" would be too hasty, however. For even if Quine were right about objectually interpreted propositional quantifiers, it has not been shown that the propositional quantifiers employed by the prosentential theory must be interpreted objectually. Indeed, I will be discussing a version of the prosentential theory according to which the propositional quantifiers are interpreted substitutionally. For it is this version of the prosentential theory that is most similar to the disquotational theory. Let us look at some of the details.

3.1. Soames' example (in 1.2, above) suggests the following as a disquotational analysis of (3)[10]

(7)   For every x, if Eva says x, then x is true.

if we ignore the qualifying clause "about the reactor's safety".[11] The quantifiers are interpreted objectually with the variables ranging over a domain of closed sentences. (So that there is no confusion between the prosentential and disquotational analyses, I am using 'x', 'y', and etc., as variables occupying nominal positions; and I reserve 'p', 'q' and etc., for use as variables that occupy sentential positions.) Since (7) has instances like

(8)   If Eva says "the reactor is unsafe" then "the reactor is unsafe" is true.

"semantic descent" is needed to return such instances to direct speech versions of the instances in (2) above. That is, to restore an instance such as (8), to

         If Eva says "the reactor is unsafe", then the reactor is unsafe.

[12] Note that the disquotational evaluation of sentences like (7) and (8) requires a domain of sentences, D, and an extension for the truth predicate. In the event that

---

[10] Though disquotational theorists make much of the utility of 'true' for generalizing, they give few examples. Note, also, that though both Quine and Soames give examples, their analyses are different.

[11] Another possibility is "For every x, if Eva says that x is true then x is true."

[12] The disquotational theorist will need an operator that produces a that-clause ('that the reactor is unsafe') from the name of a sentence (" 'the reactor is unsafe' ") if the actual instances in (2) are to be recovered, unless that-clauses are treated as names of sentences. An alternative approach would be to adopt.

         For any x, if Eva says that x is true, then x is true

as the disquotational analysis of (3), which has instances like

         If Eva says that 'the reactor is unsafe' is true, then 'the reactor is unsafe' is true.

Semantic descent returns this instance to the original
         If Eva says that the reactor is unsafe, then the reactor is unsafe.

the truth predicate can occur in sentences in D, we might suppose that a Tarski style truth definition[13] is used to determine an appropriate extension for 'true' in a given context.

By contrast, for the prosentential theory, I assume the propositional quantifiers are interpreted substitutionally. So, associated with each quantifier will be a set of closed sentences that I call its *substitution range*, SR. We must suppose the sentences of SR mapped into $\{1, 0\}$. In the event that bound propositional variables occur in the sentences of SR, we should use a "propositional Tarski style truth construction" to determine an appropriate mapping for a given use of a quantifier. By a *propositional Tarski style truth construction* I mean a construction similar to a Tarski style truth construction, except that propositional quantifiers (substitutionally interpreted) and quantification in and out of quotes are featured, rather than the truth predicate and first order quantifiers (objectually interpreted with a domain of sentences).

We know that propositional Tarski style constructions are possible, since it can be shown that sentences of the form

$$\text{For any } x \, (\ldots \, x \, \ldots \, Tx \, \ldots)$$

(hereafter, '$(x)A(x, Tx)$') are provable, just in case sentences of the form

$$\text{For any } p \, (\ldots \, Qp \, \ldots \, p \, \ldots)$$

(hereafter, '$(p)A(Qp, p)$') are provable.[14] Methods of evaluation, similar to those used in Tarski style constructions to determine the extension of the truth predicate, would be used to assign values to the sentences occurring in the appropriate substitution ranges of the bound propositional variables. The value of a sentence like

(9)   For any p, if Eva says that p then p

could then be determined. For (9) will be assigned the value 1, just in case all instances obtained by substituting the members of the appropriate SR for 'p', in 'if Eva says that p then p', have the value 1.

It is clear that if we view 'it is true' in (8) as functioning like the bound propositional variable in (9), then even when used for generalizing, the truth predicate functions semantically at the level of the object language — such universal statements are in effect equivalent to a possibly infinite conjunction of sentences of the *object language*.

---

[13] When I refer to Tarski style constructions I mean to include not only Tarski's but also that of Kripke 1975, Gupta 1982, and etc.

[14] Anil Gupta confirms that it would be a relatively simple matter to systematically replace occurrences of 'x', say, by 'Qp', and 'Tx' by 'p', in his construction.

3.2. These are the two deflationist accounts of the truth predicate's role in generalization. What are we to make of their differences? The first point to be noted is that, if we compare only the assumptions of the quantifiers used in the two analysing languages, the differences are trivial. For in the examples considered above, the disquotational theory assumes a domain of closed sentences, while the prosentential theory assumes a substitution range of closed sentences. In each case an acceptable evaluation derives from an appropriate Tarski style truth construction.

In the one case values of the sentences in the domain are determined by a Tarski style construction, and in the other, values of the sentences in the substitution range are determined by a propositional Tarski style construction. It follows that *for roughly the same expressibility, the two deflationary theories make the same assumptions.*

There are differences, of course, in the underlying explanations of the role of the truth predicate. For example, one theory talks of semantic ascent and T-sentences, and the other theory of proforms and prosentences. I discuss these differences in the next section. Later, I will say more about my supposition that deflationists can appeal to Tarski style truth constructions in their analyses of the role of the truth predicate in generalization.

4. META-LINGUISTIC USES OF THE TRUTH PREDICATE

In our early discussions of the prosentential theory, Nuel was initially concerned that the prosentential theory may not provide an account of 'true' compatible with supposedly metalinguistic uses in model theoretic contexts. Since this is a concern other logicians may share, I will say something about my response.[15] The issue is relevant since it concerns another apparent difference between the two deflationary theories that I have already mentioned: the "level" at which the truth predicate functions.

4.1. I begin with the disquotational theory because the disquotational truth theorists seem to have had their eyes on the logician's employment of the truth predicate.

I have already noted that the truth predicate of the disquotational theory appears to have the syntax of a metalinguistic predicate — the disquotational truth predicate combines with names of sentences to form sentences, and first order quantifiers are used. Given the effective intersubstitutability of '$(x)(A(x, Tx))$' and '$(p)(A(Qp, p))$' in Tarski style constructions, one wonders whether the disquotational truth predicate really behaves like a metalinguistic predicate. What account do disquotational theorists give of the instances of their universal sentences? In particular, what account do they give of primitive sentences containing the truth predicate? Quine is the only person who says anything about what is said when truth is predicated of a sentence. He remarks (p.12)

---

[15] My response persuaded Nuel at the time. I do not know whether he is still persuaded.

> The truth predicate is a reminder that, despite a technical ascent
> to talk of sentences, our eye is on the world. ... By calling a
> sentence true, we call snow white.

Unfortunately Quine does not unpack the metaphors. I read Quine as saying that the truth predicate is not used to say anything about sentences. My reason for thinking this is that his qualification of the "ascent to talk of sentences" as "technical" shows hesitancy; and the ascent seems cancelled when he says that by "calling a sentence true, we call snow white". But then we might ask, if a logician only says something about snow, when she says " 'Snow is white' is true", why does she not simply use 'Snow is white'? One reason offered for mentioning sentences is that semantic ascent is required for generalization with respect to sentence positions.[16] However, even if this were true, this explanation does tell us *what is said* when there is "technical ascent to talk of sentences". Are sentences being talked about, or are they not? Some may claim we do not need to worry about such questions, since all we need know about the truth predicate beyond its syntax, is its logic. Perhaps this is what those who claim T-sentences play a central role in the disquotational theory have in mind. Williams may be one such philosopher. For he says that the "disquotational schema ... captures something important about truth". It is difficult to figure out what Williams' point is, for it is unclear what he thinks is captured. For a start, we need to be told which sentences count as instances of Williams' schema.[17] Can the sentence within quotes contain indexicals, or the liar sentence, and on what grounds should we make these decisions? Note, also, T-sentences alone do not tell us much about the logic of the truth predicate. For, as Sellars 1963 has noted,

'Snow is white' (in our language) is true iff Snow is white

is viewed with the greatest equanimity by pragmatist and coherentist [and deflationist] alike.

Others may claim that Tarski style constructions capture the logic of the truth predicate. But neither does this view distinguish among truth constructions. I believe we need to unpack Quine's metaphors so that we know how the truth predicate interacts with semantic ascent.

In sum, though disquotational theorists focus on a predicate that seems to have the syntax of a metalinguistic predicate, many questions concerning logicians' uses of the truth predicate presently remain unanswered. Only when these questions are answered will we be clearer about the level of the disquotational truth predicate.

4.2. For the prosentential account of the truth predicate as used by logicians, I need to talk about inheritors. The concept of an inheritor is a generic concept that includes within its domain expressions (including proforms) that function much as proforms function.

---

[16] Quine seems to say this, though I think only in a context where he is not considering the possibility of utilizing a substitutional interpretation. Both Leeds and Soames allow that first order objectually interpreted quantifiers are not the only alternative.

[17] Williams does not explain 'p' and 'P'.

4.21. In my discussion of the liar I pointed out that proforms do not always suffice for the anaphoric tasks that we need accomplished.[18] This is because proforms are effective only when they occur in close proximity to their antecedents. For example, we cannot normally use 'she' on p.60 to refer unambiguously to May, if we have not mentioned May since p.1. In such a circumstance, we must establish connections with what was said on p.1 in some other way. We can say, for example,

(10)   The person I referred to on p.1 can pay her own way.

I claim that when 'the person that I referred to on p.1' is used in place of a pronoun, it is used in much the same way that a pronoun is used. So in (10), 'the person I referred to on p.1' is used to refer directly to May. The definite description functions as an *inheritor*. In calling such expressions inheritors my point is that neither the speaker's words, nor the speaker's speech act, feature in the content of what is said in (10); just as neither the links between the words 'it' and 'the balloon', nor the words 'the balloon', feature in the content of

The balloon will rise when it is filled with helium.

We can think of the work done by the various parts of 'the person I referred to on p.1', in identifying the co-referential term on p.1, as being done off to the side — so to speak, in a working column off to the side.

There are also sentential inheritors. Prosentences are included, but there are other kinds of sentential inheritors. For certain combinations of definite descriptions and the truth predicate can stand in for antecedent sentences. For example, there are circumstances where something like,

(11)   If the last indented sentence is true, then . . .

must be used, because

If that is true, then . . .

will not suffice for the task on hand. Let us suppose the speaker wants to acknowledge the antecedent sentence, and 'that is true' cannot be used because the antecedent sentence is not in close proximity. In such a case (11) can function as an inheritor. (Note that in the event the speaker does not know what the last indented sentence is, it might be more appropriate to use quantifiers in analysing (11).)

According to the prosentential theory, sentences like

(12)   'Snow is white' is true.

are also inheritors. Construed as an inheritor (12) says something about snow. In this case the antecedent sentence, 'Snow is white', rather than being picked out with a definite description, is explicitly displayed. Either way, the "semantic ascent" involved would not feature in what is said. In GCB we were grappling with the same issue when we suggested that the following display format

Consider: Snow is white. That is true.

can be used to capture a sentence like (12).

---

[18] See Grover 1977, and Brandom, Section VI.

4.22. It might be objected, "Logicians do not have any use for inheritors, for they talk about languages and sentences, not balloons and snow." I agree, logicians do talk about languages. However there is usually little point in talking about languages if there is no connection with the object languages *in use*. Inheritors facilitate connections between "mention" and "use".[19] For example, in a context where we have been talking about our proof theory, or the syntactical structure of a sentence, we often want to talk about a sentence, or the structural form of a set of sentences of the object language. One reason is that tasks are often made easier if they are reduced to symbol pushing maneuvers. It is in establishing connections between theory and/or symbol pushing maneuvers and language in use that it can be useful to have inheritors. For inheritors provide us with a way of displaying a sentence while in effect *using* it. Consider, again,

'Snow is white' is true

This inheritor provides us with a way of saying that snow is white, while at the same time displaying the sentence. The antecedent sentence of the inheritor

Snow is white

alone, would not do as well. When 'Snow is white' is used, alone, our attention is not usually drawn to the structure of the sentence used. One place where explicit display is useful, is in an explanation of the logical connectives. For example, we customarily explain disjunction using the following format,[20]

> (13)   For any sentences x and y, (xvy) is true just in case x is true or y is true or both x is true and y is true.

Why use this format? Given the prosentential account of the truth predicate, and possible intersubstitutability of '$(x)(A(x, Tx))$' and '$(p)(A(Qp, p))$', it might seem for the prosentential theorist

> (14)   For any p and q, pvq just in case p or q or both p and q.

should do just as well. As (14) does not contain an explicit truth predicate it seems more in the spirit of the prosentential theory. Why do we choose the format of (13) over the format of (14)?[21] A reason (13) is more useful is that the structure of the sentences is explicitly displayed: implicit messages about the structure of the sentences of the object language can be conveyed through such explicit display. (14) is less effective in this regard.

---

[19] For more details see my 1981 papers.

[20] I assume first order objectually interpreted quantifiers, and in the interests of simplicity, an autonomous system of naming expressions of the object language.

[21] Note that, without argument, I cannot assume '$(x)(A(x, Tx))$' and '$(p)(A(Qp, p))$' are intersubstitutable in all contexts. Propositional attitude contexts may be an exception. For, whereas 'Everything Mary believes is true' might reasonably be represented by 'For every p, if Mary believes that p, then p'; this may not be equivalent to 'For every x, if Mary believes x, then x is true.'

Readers may wonder whether this talk of implicit messages does not ascribe a substantive role to the truth predicate in (13). It should be noted that if propositional quantification and quotation are available in the metalanguage, the implicit messages of (13) could have been conveyed without the use of an explicit truth predicate. For consider,

(15)   For any p, q, and r, if Qr is a disjunction such that
            Qp is its first disjunct and Qq its second disjunct,
            then r just in case either p or q, or both p and q.

(15) makes explicit the information implicitly conveyed by (13); yet it has the format of '$(p)(A(Qp,p))$'. The use of propositional quantifiers in (15) suggests only a prosentential role for the truth predicate (in inheritors) in (13). Accordingly, the truth predicate does not seem to have a substantive role in (13) — for it can be "hidden" in prosentential constructions.

Further checking has convinced me that similar accounts can be given of other uses of the truth predicate by logicians.[22] If I am right about all of this, the truth predicate of logicians can be construed as occurring only in prosentential constructions. It functions, so to speak, at the level of the object language. Furthermore, though logicians invariably "mention" sentences in the context of using the truth predicate, the truth predicate does not seem to have a substantive role in what is said about object language sentences. There seems to be little in common, semantically, between the truth predicate in prosentential constructions and those predicates we usually think of as metalinguistic.

5. DISQUOTATION WITH PROSENTENCES

It may now be clear why I think a disquotational theorist has the option of adopting a prosentential explanation of the role of the truth predicate.

5.1. Quine's remark that "by calling the sentence true, we call snow white" agrees with the inheritor account of the content of sentences containing true. Furthermore, my account of the way inheritors function provides one reading of what one might mean by "a technical ascent to talk of sentences". The ascent is "technical" and temporary, since its purpose is to pick out the antecedent sentence of the inheritor in question; and this work is done "off to the side" and does not feature in the content of the inheritor. Hence there is no conflict with Quine's claim that a sentence containing 'true' may be about snow. Also, the intersubstitutability of Tarski style truth constructions that highlight an explicit truth predicate (as in '$(x)(A(x,Tx))$') and propositional Tarski style truth constructions that highlight the prosentential role of the truth predicate (as in '$(p)(A(Qp,p))$'), is consistent with my claim that the disquotational account of generalization can derive from the prosentential account.

---

[22] Consider, for example, our use of 'true' in "There are true sentences that are not provable." This does not have to be represented formally as "There are x's such that x is true and x is not provable." We can say "There are p, such that p and Qp is not provable."

It should be noted that acceptance of prosentential explanations would amount to acknowledging that semantic ascent is *not required* for generalization with respect to sentence positions; since prosentences provide a way of generalizing without semantic ascent. This is not to deny, however, that semantic ascent may be required for other reasons. Note, also, acceptance of prosentential explanations by disquotational theorists would bring explanations of the utility of the truth predicate in those cases where generalization is not an issue. For example, in those cases where the truth predicate is used to establish connections between parts of discourse when expressing agreement, and etc.

The version of the prosentential theory that I have argued a disquotational theorist could endorse, is that version according to which propositional quantifiers are interpreted substitutionally. It would be another matter for a disquotational theorist to adopt a version of the prosentential theory according to which a domain of "propositions" is assumed. The question as to whether a substitutional interpretation suffices is a question I leave open until we know more about the rest of language.

5.2. Without saying how such choices would be made, I assumed in Section 3 that deflationists can choose among alternative Tarski style constructions for a formal account of the logical role of the truth predicate in generalization. However deflationists cannot make such a choice without saying something about such issues as, falsity, the liar sentence (for though inconsistency is clearly a problem for substantive theories of truth, it is not obvious it is a problem for deflationary truth theories), and "neither true nor false". As disquotational theorists have not yet addressed these issues, I will make good on my claim that some understanding of the interaction of the truth predicate and "semantic ascent" can provide at least an intuitive basis upon which to choose among Tarski style constructions.

For suppose the disquotational theorist accepted a prosentential explanation of the truth predicate. Then the prosentential account of the role of 'false' in modified prosentences would follow. So, also, would the following prosentential account of liar sentences.[23] Proforms are parasitic in the sense that they must be appropriately connected to antecedent expressions that can supply content. When a proform is so connected it is *grounded*. In the simplest cases, an occurrence of a proform will be *ungrounded* if it has only another proform as its antecedent. The truth teller ('This is true') is an example of an ungrounded prosentence; and the liar, an example of an ungrounded modified prosentence. Note that an ungrounded proform will not have content when its antecedent is not of a kind that can initially supply content. Ungrounded proforms can be problematic for this reason — we sometimes need to know whether we run the risk of uttering sentences without content. Accordingly, a disquotational theorist would find useful those Tarski style truth constructions that show us how to utilize inheritors that may in some circumstances be ungrounded.

On the other hand, a prosentential account of the truth predicate does not require that Tarski style constructions say anything about philosophers' uses of "neither true nor false". My reasons for this claim have to do with the role of 'not' in "neither true nor false" to reject what is said.

---

[23] See Grover 1977.

We use 'not' or 'no' when we want to reject something. Often the role of 'not' is that of a sentence modifier, as captured in our truth tables — 'not A' is the contradictory of 'A' — but 'not' does not always modify. When 'not' is used as a modifier, 'That is not true' will be a modified prosentence. Suppose 'Snow is white' is our antecedent sentence, then "That is not true" would be equivalent to "Snow is not white", and "That is neither true nor false" would be equivalent to the contradictory "Snow is not white and snow is white."

This reading of "neither true nor false" does not capture most philosophical uses of the phrase, however. We need to consider another way in which 'not' can be used to reject something we find problematic. One reason we need another way of rejecting what someone says is that we cannot always reject something by asserting the contradictory — the contradictory form may be problematic also.[24] For suppose the antecedent is 'The King of France is bald', we get nowhere by responding with 'The King of France is not bald'. A better response might be (as Strawson points out)

(16)   There's a problem with what you say, for there is no King of France.

Or one might say, "I reject both!" or "Neither!", and use display to direct attention to that which one is rejecting.

(17)   Neither!: The King of France is bald. The King of France is not bald.

If it is important that parts of the discourse are connected, prosentences may be used, as in

(18)   Neither!: That is true. That is false.

Because the prosentences are displayed/mentioned rather than used, the truth predicate is only mentioned in such uses of "neither true nor false". And this is why I think Tarski style constructions need not be required to explain philosophers' uses of "neither true nor false".

6. SUMMARY

We have seen that the disquotational and prosentential truth predicates provide for generalization with respect to sentence positions from roughly the same conservative resources. In the one case a domain of sentences is assumed, and in the other a substitution range consisting of the same set of sentences.

The disquotational explanation of the truth predicate's role in generalization is that the truth predicate facilitates semantic ascent. Semantic ascent, in its turn, is said to facilitate generalization with respect to sentence positions. However, until Quine's metaphors relating the truth predicate and semantic ascent are explained, the disquotational truth predicate's role is not adequately explained.

The prosentential explanation of the role of the truth predicate is that it is used in prosentential constructions. A detour through semantic ascent is not required for

---

[24] I have discussed this issue in greater detail in Grover, 1981b.

generalization. However inheritors may sometimes be used to draw attention to the syntax of the language under consideration; in which case, a prosentential theorist can with equanimity exploit the inter-substitutability of '$(p)A(Qp, p)$', '$(x)A(x, Tx)$'.

In conclusion, I have argued that the disquotational theory can be supplemented with prosentential explanations of the underlying role of the truth predicate: I have also demonstrated some advantages of doing this.

BIBLIOGRAPHY

Brandom, R. (1988): "Pragmatism, Phenomenalism, and Truth Talk", in.*Realism and Antirealism*, Midwest Studies, eds., French, Uehling, Wettstein, Minnesota Press.

Field, H. (1972): "Tarski's Theory of Truth", *Journal of Philosophy*, vol. 69, 13 (1972), pp. 347–375.

Grover, D. L. (1973): "Propositional Quantification and Quotation Contexts", in *Truth, Syntax, and Modality*, ed., Leblanc, North-Holland.

Grover, Camp, and Belnap (1975): "A Prosentential Theory of Truth", *Philosophical Studies*, Vol. 27, pp. 73–125.

Grover, D. L. (1977): "Inheritors and Paradox", *Journal of Philosophy*, Vol. LXXIV, pp. 500–604.

Grover, D. L. (1981a): "Truth", *Philosophia*, 10, pp. 225–52.

Grover, D. L. (1981b): "Truth: Do we need it?", *Philosophical Studies*, Vol. 40, pp. 69–103.

Gupta, A. (1982): "Truth and Paradox", *Journal of Philosophical Logic*, 11, pp. 1–60.

Horwich, P. (1982): "Three Forms of Realism," *Synthese*, 51, pp. 181–201.

Kripke, S. (1976): "Is there a Problem about Substitutional Quantification?", in Evans and McDowell, eds., *Truth and Meaning*, Oxford.

Kripke, S. (1984): "Outline of a Theory of Truth", *The Journal of Philosophy*, 72, pp. 690–716.

Leeds, S. (1978): "Theories of Truth and Reference", *Erkenntnis*, 13, pp. 111–129.

Quine, W. V. (1970): The Philosophy of Logic, Prentice-Hall.

Soames, S. (1984): "What is a Theory of Truth?" *The Journal of Philosophy*, vol. 81, pp. 411–29.

Tarski, A. (1956): "The Concept of Truth in Formalized Languages", in *Logic, Semantics, Metamathematics*, Clarendon Press.

Williams, M. (1986): "Do We (Epistemologists) Need a Theory of Truth?", *Philosophical Topics*, 4, pp. 223–42.

W. KENT WILSON

SOME REFLECTIONS
ON THE PROSENTENTIAL THEORY OF TRUTH

The Prosentential Theory of Truth (PSTT) was first put forward in Grover, Camp, and Belnap (1975).[1] The leading idea of the theory is that the forms "it is true" and "that is true" function as (molecular) prosentences in ordinary English — a form of words that stand to sentences as pronouns stand to nouns — and that our ordinary (non-philosophical) concept of truth is to be understood in terms of these expressions. Other uses of "true" are to be understood by assimilating them to its use as a prosentence.

Professor Belnap has avowed that he continues to believe in the idea of GCB that "truth in ordinary language functions as what [Grover] calls an "inheritor", in some respects like a pronoun picking up its meaning from something else in the discourse" ([3], p. 103). At the same time, Prof. Belnap regards Gupta's theory of truth as "the best account we have of how to deploy truth in a property-ascribing way". The aim of this paper is to set him free to accept a theory like Gupta's as an account of how the term is used in ordinary English. I will present reasons for thinking that the prosentential theory of truth (PSTT) does not capture the ordinary use of "true".[2]

The first task is to describe the theory; in the first section, I will do so very briefly. I will describe neither the motivation for the theory nor the philosophical advantages it claims.

In Section 2, I will examine some sentential connectives that PSST introduces. It will be argued that that there is considerable evidence from English syntax to think that PSTT's analysis is not correct.

In Section 3, I examine how molecular prosentences are supposed to work, according to PSTT, and offer some examples to show that English sentences do not work in the way PSTT predicts.

In Section 4, I question whether all occurrences of "true" in English can be satisfactorily translated into a prosentential fragment, English*.

Finally, in Section 5, I present as a conjecture a diagnosis of what has gone wrong.

1. DESCRIPTION OF THE PROSENTENTIAL THEORY OF TRUTH.

A prosentence is understood to be an expression which is like a pronoun but which occupies positions appropriate for sentences rather than positions appropriate for nouns. Specifically, it is the role pronouns play when they occur as anaphora devices (anaphora pronouns) that is taken as the model for prosentences.

---

[1] [8] in the Bibliography. This paper will be referred to in the text as GCB; the authors of GCB will be referred to as the authors.

[2] There are several ordinary uses of "true"; I don't mean to suggest that PSTT captures none of them.

J. M. Dunn and A. Gupta (eds.), Truth or Consequences, 19–32.

An anaphoric occurrence of a pronoun has an antecedent (understood in GCB as always being a linguistic antecedent) from which its semantical value is determined. The authors distinguish two sorts of anaphoric pronoun on which their account of prosentences is modeled: pronouns of laziness and quantificational pronouns.[3] The two sorts are similar by virtue of being anaphors, but work differently semantically.

A pronoun of laziness is described as one that may "stand in" for its antecedent, as one for which its antecedent may be substituted (GCB, 84).[4] It is assumed that the way pronouns of laziness work is that the semantic value they acquire from their antecedent is their reference.

The other sort of anaphoric pronoun that the authors consider is quantificational pronouns. Consider the sentence

(1)   Every person loves his mother.

In the case of quantificational pronouns, the semantic value of the pronoun is determined in the familiar way: the pronoun is taken as a variable bound to the quantified noun phrase (NP) that is its antecedent. The logical form of (1) is

(2)   For every person x, x loves x's mother.

Note that the antecedent can't be substituted for the pronoun in (1) without drastically changing its meaning and even its truth value. The quantificational pronoun doesn't pick up a referent from its antecedent, since the antecedent is not a referring expression.

In analogy with anaphoric pronouns, the authors identify two kinds of prosentences: prosentences of laziness and quantificational prosentences.[5]

First, let's consider pro*sentences* of laziness, an example of which is

I don't know whether Cheech is a Commie, but if so,
I won't vote for him.

In this sentence, "so" is taken to be a whose antecedent is the sentence "Cheech is a Commie". What is essential on the authors' view for "so" to be a prosentence is that it be a pro-form that occupies positions appropriate for sentences; its antecedent need not be a declarative sentence. To see this, consider the following discourse:

A: The Mets will win the pennant again.
B: Heaven forbid!
C: If so, the Pirates will win.

---

[3] The authors do not discuss other uses of pronouns pronoun. GCB seem not entirely satisfied with this classification of pronouns pronoun, which is adopted from Peter Geach.

[4] It is recognized that substitution of antecedent for pronoun may introduce ambiguities not present in the original sentence containing the pronoun of laziness.

[5] It is not clear whether the authors restrict prosentences to only these two kinds or whether they would countenance other prosentential forms and functions, analogous to those of pronouns. For example, they do not consider the question whether there may be deictic occurrences of prosentences in analogy to deictic occurrences of pronouns. It would be implausible to describe deictics as redundant in the sense PSTT claims prosentences to be.

Here, the antecedent is an exclamatory (or perhaps an imperative), and what will replace "so" is the sentence "Heaven forbids the Mets to win the pennant again".[6] As anaphors, prosentences derive their semantic value from their antecedents. In the case of prosentences of laziness, this is taken to mean that their "propositional content" or sense (meaning) is identical to that of their antecedents.

In analogy with pronouns of quantification, GCB suggest that there are prosentences of quantification. A curious feature emerges regarding prosentences of quantification. Let's for the moment set aside examples of anaphora that involve "that is true" and "it is true", where these are taken as prosentences; for it is a principal thesis of PSTT that these are prosentences, the authors' burden being to establish the plausibility of that thesis. (We may also set aside examples involving "thatt", which is a technical device stipulated to be an atomic prosentence.) Except for these examples, then, there is not a single example in GCB of an English quantificational prosentence.[7]

It is difficult to produce clear examples in idiomatic English of the sort we seek.[8] Consider the sentence

(3)   Everything the Pope says is so.

Since "so" does not occupy a sentential position in (3), it can't be taken to be a prosentence according to the criteria set out in GCB. It might be held that, when the logical form of (3) is displayed perspicuously, "so" as it occurs in (3) is represented (perhaps in DS or LF or at whatever level of syntactic representation the authors think appropriate) by a prosentence of quantification whose antecedent is a propositional quantifier (on sentential positions) that represents the underlined quantified NP. The prosentence could then be understood as playing a role in these higher-order quantificational sentences analogous to the role played by pronouns in first-order sentences.[9]

PSTT is a refinement of Ramsey's redundancy theory of truth, by way of some ideas of Prior's, the principal one being that the truth predicate can be eliminated with no loss of expressive power provided our language has propositional quantifiers.

---

[6] It is useful to distinguish the anaphoric pro-form itself, its antecedent, and the expression that the pro-form replaces and that may replace it. Each may be a different expression from the others.

[7] A casual inspection of papers by Grover on PSTT, [5], [6], and [7], failed to turn up any examples of English quantificational prosentences except "that is true" and "it is true" in contexts which Grover claims them to be prosentences of quantification. One would like to discover (an occurrence of) an English form that is clearly a quantificational prosentence on sentential position, for that would provide evidence that there are quantificational prosentences in English and could also provide an independent basis for determining how such forms function grammatically and semantically.

[8] For a discussion of quantificational prosentences, see GCB, pp. 85–92. The form of English prosentences doesn't matter much for my purposes. The authors themselves question whether English contains atomic prosentences that are "generally available" (i.e., that can be put in arbitrary sentential positions); see GCB, p. 88. In this respect, I doubt that English prosentences differ from English pronouns; the latter do not distribute perfectly with respect to every sentential context where a noun or a NP can occur. It isn't too surprising that we are unable to find quantificational prosentences. The history of PSTT is this: having a formal theory of propositional quantification, English readings of the formal wffs were sought. An English lexical category was wanted that is analogous to that of the pronoun, the items of which would play the role for wffs having propositional quantifiers that pronouns were believed to play for wffs having individual quantifiers.

[9] For a discussion of difficulties in interpreting pronouns as bound variables, see [9].

One aim of GCB is to capture Ramsey's (and Strawson's) intuition while avoiding the difficulties that beset redundancy theories. Is truth semantically redundant[10] according to PSTT? The authors present a language, English*, purportedly a fragment of English. In English* there are no occurrences of a truth predicate that make any substantive or predicative semantical contribution to the interpretation of the sentences in which they occur (see GCB, 92). Rather, in English*, "true" occurs only as a part either of a prosentence or of a sentential connective.

According to PSTT, a truth predicate is redundant in the sense that all uses of "true" in English can be represented adequately by prosentential and connective uses in English*: "true" does not provide the means to discuss new topics, to ascribe new (non-composite) properties or relations to things, or to utilize new categories or a new conceptual framework (GCB, 123). But truth is not redundant in that quantificational pro-sentences and the connectives in which "true" occurs are not eliminable from English* without loss of expressive power.

This completes the description of the theory to be examined. I will assess PSTT on whether the theory satisfies some requirements that it itself imposes or that may be plausibly imposed upon it. Does the theory mesh well with syntactical, semantical, and pragmatic data that are generally accepted? Does PSTT make accurate predictions about language usage? These questions will be addressed in subsequent sections of this paper. Many of the arguments will be syntactical; remember, *prosentence* is a category of syntax.

2. "IT IS TRUE THAT"
AND OTHER (PURPORTED) SENTENTIAL CONNECTIVES

One of the strengths of even a crude redundancy theory of truth is its ability to deal with simple sentences such as

(4)   That Bleda is vicious is true.

and

(5)   It is true that Bleda is vicious.

Such sentences are held to have the same assertional content as the sentences that result when the form containing "true" is dropped:

Bleda is vicious.[11]

This sort of example is interesting because it is such an easy case for Ramsey's version of the redundancy theory. According to that theory, "that . . . is true" and "it is true that" may simply disappear, without loss of content, for they are redundant.

Sentences like these pose a problem for PSTT. Within PSTT there are three possibilities for the analysis of sentences containing "it is true that" and "that . . . is

---

[10] I restrict discussion of redundancy to semantic matters here. The authors insist that "true" has pragmatic uses that are not redundant; I agree.

[11] Matters are not quite as simple as presented. In particular, it is simply assumed that everything that isn't part of "Bleda is vicious" must be part of the form that contains "true". The theory looks better that way.

true". If they are prosentences, they must be either prosentences of quantification or prosentences of laziness. Since no quantificational phrase occurs in either sentence, we can rule out that alternative. So if prosentences, they must be prosentences of laziness.

But that can't be correct; the only candidate for an antecedent is "Bleda is vicious", and substitution of that for "is true"in (4) results in

> *That Bleda is vicious Bleda is vicious.[12]

The final alternative, the preferred one,[13] is to treat these expressions as sentential connectives. Logicians intend this to be a category of logical grammar: apply a sentential connective to a sentence and a sentence results. However, no evidence has been offered to support the hypothesis that these English expressions function grammatically as connectives.

I will argue that they are not connectives. An alternative hypothesis is that "is true" functions as a predicate and I will show that it is better supported by the data of English than is the PSTT hypothesis that "it is true that" is a sentential connective in English. If this is correct, then PSTT must find some way to square itself with the syntactical features of English.

Fortunately, no elaborate syntactical analyses need be presented. According to PSTT's hypothesis, a sentence of the form "it is true that S" consists of two major constituents: "it is true that" and "S". According to the hypothesis that I favor, one constituent of sentences of the form "It is true that S" is "that S" and another is "it is true". The evidence presented will show that "that S" is a constituent and/or that "it is true that" is not a constituent.

Sentences of certain forms are widely recognized as grammatically related. An explanation of this is that they are related by rules which move an element in one sentence from one position to another to obtain the other sentence. It is a fundamental assumption of grammatical theory that these rules apply only to constituents. Some of these relations follow.

It is held that (5) is derived from (4) by *Extraposition*. Furthermore, from (5) we can obtain the *cleft*

> It is that Bleda is vicious that is true.

but not

> *It is Bleda is vicious that that is true.

From (5) we can obtain the *pseudo-cleft*

> What is true is that Bleda is vicious.

but not

> *What is true that is Bleda is vicious.

Notice that from

---

[12] I have assumed that the "that" does not go with "is true" to form a constituent. I argue for this assumption later in the text. Even if the assumption is mistaken, an acceptable English sentence is not obtained from the substitution:*"Bleda is vicious Bleda is vicious."

[13] Personal communication from Dorothy Grover.

It is possible that Bleda is kind but it isn't true that Bleda is kind.

we can obtain, by *stripping*,

It is possible that Bleda is kind, but not true φ.

but not

*It is possible that Bleda is kind, but not true that φ.

Additional evidence comes from the possibility of *inserting parenthetical expressions* between "true" and "that", possible usually only at breaks between major constituents:

It is true — as you should know better than anyone — that crimes have been committed.
*It is true that — as you should know better than anyone — crimes have been committed.

Notice also that we have

A: Bill said that Susan is ill.
B: Is it true?/ That Susan is ill?/ *Is it true that?

Some of these relationships show at most that "that S" is a constituent of surface structure. It might be argued that at the level of representation of logical form, "it is true that" is nevertheless a constituent. It remains for the advocates of PSTT to find the syntactical theory that would support their analysis.

I conclude that for our sample sentences (4) and (5), PSTT has no satisfactory account to offer as yet.

There are sentences such as "That is not very interesting, even if it's true", where it appears that "that" and "it" seem to function as pronouns that have the same antecedent. An interesting example the authors consider is (GCB, 105):

(7)   John: Some dogs eat glass. Bill: I believe it.
Mary: You believe it, but it's not true.

(The underlining is my responsibility.) The authors state (GCB, 106) that

> *if* 'it' in 'You believe it' is construed as a separately referring pronoun, its referent will have to be a proposition. And consequently, given the desire to treat the two occurrences of 'it' in Mary's statement as coordinate, we have the makings of an objection to our theory.

The objection is outflanked by proposing to treat "believe it" as "believe that it is true". Thus, where difficulty threatens they propose to restore a prosentential appearance where there was none in English by treating the transitive verb-plus-"that" as another sentential connective. Are these compounds constituents of English sentences at any level of syntactic representation? A plausible theory is needed according to which English has these connectives, a theory that will account for a wide variety of familiar syntactical and semantical facts.

(I see (7) above differently than the authors. The three occurrences of "it" in (7) have John's utterance as their antecedent. On my view, then, they do not have independent reference. Is the authors' worry alleviated? No. Each "it" functions as a pronoun of laziness; what can replace each of them is the complement "that some dogs eat glass". The nature of those complements, it seems, is to denote the propositional content of John's utterance, not simply to express it as PSTT would have us believe.)

Returning to the authors' account of "believes", they propose that all sentences such as

> Johann believes that the canon's theme should be inverted.

should be understood as having a *grammatical constituent* "believes that". A popular alternative to this proposal is to understand such sentences as having a constituent "that the canon's theme should be inverted", understood as having the form[14]

$$S \rightarrow \text{"that"} + S$$

(where it is understood that the grammar allows that a NP can have an S as an immediate constituent.)[15] As in the case of "It is true that" + S versus "It is true" + "that S", I claim that "that S" forms a constituent in sentences of the form

> X believes/knows/hopes/wishes that S.

Which hypothesis does the evidence favor? The authors cite no evidence for their hypothesis. Much the same evidence cited for the earlier case supports the alternative I accept. In addition, application of other rules such as Passive support this constituent structure; simpler phrase structure rules can be obtained when "that" + S is taken as a constituent; there is distributional evidence for "that S" being a constituent; etc.[16] There are moderately strong grammatical reasons to be suspicious of the authors' proposal to take "believes" and other transitive verbs that take sentential complements as linked with "that" to form "believes that", which is to function as a sentential connective. Their problem is to square their proposal with English syntax as well as provide some account of the relation between sentences like

> Umberto believes the CT-thesis.

where the verb is followed by a NP and no complement occurs and sentences where the verb is followed by a "that"-clause, as in

> Umberto believes that what is humanly computable is machine computable.

Viewing these verbs as relations permits a uniform account, even where the verb occurs with a sentential complement; for sentential complements are treated as nominal constructions.

I see no way to integrate the connective treatment into an acceptable theory of English. While the arguments have involved syntax exclusively, they bear on semantics, as we will see in subsequent sections. For within an overall theory of language, syntax and semantics must not conflict.

---

[14] The exact form of the constituent is controversial, but this detail will not affect the argument.

[15] That is, there will be a (phrase structure) rule that permits $NP \rightarrow S$, so the S dominating the "that S" will itself be dominated in these cases by an NP node in the tree structure of the sentence.

[16] Here I follow accounts in [1], pp. 266–97, 316–17; in [2], pp. 138–73; and in [15], pp. 61–73, 539–49. See also [13].

3. HOW DO ANAPHORIC MOLECULAR PROSENTENCES WORK?

In GCB it was maintained that *prosentences* that stand in an anaphoric relation to a linguistic antecedent and where that antecedent is not a quantifier-expression, the prosentence assumes the meaning or propositional content of that antecedent.[17]

The analogy is intended to be with anaphoric pronouns, of course: in the laziness cases, the pronoun takes an antecedent and then assumes the reference of that antecedent (or so the story goes).

I can agree that an anaphor "gets its content from its antecedent" (GCB, 89); I mean by this that its interpretation is context-dependent in certain ways. I do not agree that an anaphor assumes the content of its antecedent. First, we notice a striking apparent disanalogy: pro*nouns* seem to assume the *reference* of their antecedents; why are prosentences different?

Anaphoric devices generally, even lazy ones, do not assume the meaning or content of their antecedents. There are many counterexamples; I'll mention only three. Pronouns (and other nominal anaphors) typically have meaning that their antecedents may not have:

> <u>Leslie</u> was a wonderful colleague, but <u>he/ she</u>was a very private person.
> <u>My accountant</u> has stolen money from <u>other</u> people.
> We're not leaving <u>the Chancellor's</u> office until <u>the bastard</u> talks with us.

It can be seen, further, that anaphoric proforms of laziness do not invariably take the *reference* of their antecedents, as is demonstrated by the famous "paycheck" examples:

> The man who gave <u>his paycheck</u> to his wife was wiser than the man who gave <u>it</u> to his girlfriend.

If the reference is different, can the sense be the same?

It is easy to see what is going on here. In the paycheck example, "it" stands in for *the words* that are the words of its antecedent. But how those words will be interpreted depends, in part, on the context in which they occur. The context in which "it" occurs is sufficiently different that a different interpretation is imposed on the words as they occur in that context.

If "it is true" were a prosentence, analogous examples could be constructed:

> The car salesman who admitted to his wife that <u>he knew nothing about cars</u> was not as forthright as the one who admitted that <u>it is true</u> to his customers.

Now consider an example that is still more problematic:

> A: Colorless green ideas sleep furiously.
> B: That's not true.

---

[17] In subsequent work by by Dorothy Grover, [6] and [7], the mechanism is different but the result is the same. I argue against the result; a mechanism yielding the result will be incorrect if my argument is sound.

I understand what B has said; I think what B has said is true. I don't understand what A has said; A's utterance is anomalous. Consider the PSTT account of B's utterance. In English*, it would be parsed as "It-is-not-true-that that is true". This expression consists of two major constituents: "that is true", which is a prosentence having the same content as its antecedent, and "It-is-not-true-that", which is a modifier that yields the contradictory of the content that it modifies. How can a nonanomalous utterance be the contradictory, that is, "have exactly the opposite truth conditions" (GCB, 98), of another utterance, when that other is anomalous and therefore has no truth conditions? PSTT fails to provide an answer.

PSTT requires prosentences to be declarative, i.e. to occupy discourse positions appropriate for declarative sentences. That requirement is natural if one is going to take "it is true" and "that is true" as prosentences, for they are declarative sentences.[18] But PSTT doesn't restrict the antecedents to being declarative sentences, for that restriction would exclude quantifier expressions as antecedents and PSTT would collapse. Let's look at a few examples to see what PSTT would predict. I will assume that forms besides declarative sentences have propositional content. In each example, PSTT will predict that the utterance of the prosentence should be normal, whereas I think that the utterance of the prosentence is (not necessarily grammatically) anomalous.

A. Performatives. (I don't suggest that a prosentential response to a performative is always anomalous.)

> A: I wonder what time it is.
> B: *It's true.

> A: I apologize for burping at the table.
> B: *That's true.

B. Imperatives.

> A: Eat your liver!
> B: *That's true.[19]

The antecedents in these examples have propositional content. On PSTT, a prosentential response should pick up that content. So PSTT predicts that the responses are acceptable. The problem can't lie in the wrong form of words occurring in the antecedent, for there are examples where a can occur acceptably. Rather, the particular use of the antecedent makes the use of "true" inappropriate.

---

[18] On the authors' model, forms such as "Do it!" and "Do so!" look like complex prosentences of imperative form.

[19] Anil Gupta has pointed out to me that PSTT may offer an explanation of the oddity of these examples in terms of the pragmatics of truth. Following Strawson, "true" is taken to be used to acknowledge or to assent to an assertion that has occured in the linguistic context. The details of this explanation remain to be developed, but I expect to cavil. Space does not permit an examination of the pragmatics of truth here.

4. ENGLISH* AND PROBLEMS OF TRANSLATION

A. English*.   A major argument on behalf of PSTT is that English truth talk can be translated without loss into English*, presented as being a fragment of English that contains no truth predicate that can be used ascriptively. In English*, "true" only occurs either as part of a prosentence like "that is true" (treated as atomic); or as part of forms that are interpreted as atomic sentential connectives such as "it is not true that", "it might be true that", etc. These are used to translate tense, modals, and other modifiers.[20]

This argument would be compromised if English* were not a fragment of English, but rather an enhancement of English. I doubt that English* is a fragment of English. Besides the availability of connectives which I regard as questionable (as to their syntax, for reasons given above, and as to their semantics representing satisfactorily the corresponding English expressions), English* has propositional quantifiers over sentential positions. If English* is a fragment of English, then English will have such quantifiers. But no evidence has been offered that English has propositional quantifiers of this sort.

We saw in Section 1 that it is difficult to find examples (independent of the claims of PSTT) of English propositional quantifiers binding English prosentences. In the absence of positive evidence, this is evidence to doubt the assumption.

There is one other reason that might be cited against the assumption. It is known that quantification over individuals allows the phenomenon of crossing coreference, manifested in the Bach-Peters sentences, an example being

The pilot who shot at <u>it</u> hit <u>the MIG that chased</u> **him**.

Following Lakoff [10], McCawley [12] has argued that Bach-Peters sentences can't be formed from sentential pronominalizations. I once thought that Bach-Peters sentences could be generated using propositional quantifiers, but I have been persuaded that the results have no coherent interpretation. A sample follows for the reader to judge:

> Any axioms for arithmetic that jointly imply that it is true are falsified by a statement that they are all true.

In sum, it remains unclear whether English* is a proper fragment of English or whether it incorporates devices not found in English.

B. Translation Problems.   Whether or not English* is a fragment of English, a host of translation problems beset the PSTT claim that all English truth talk can be translated into English* without loss. I can mention only two sorts of problem here. First, with regard to translation, all of us have beliefs that have the form

> The color of Carrie's hair was _____
>
> he last music that was played at my father's went _____

---

[20] English* requires these connectives because its grammar prohibits modifiers to occur inside of prosentences.

where the blanks cannot be filled by words at all but by sensory images or memories of exact shades of colors or sounds. Many of these beliefs are true. Yet PSTT cannot translate a sentence that affirms this:

> My belief about how the last piece of music played at my father's funeral went is true.

There is no *S* that does the job. Much of our everyday truth talk concerns belief. PSTT fails to address the problems associated with such talk.

The other translation problem I will take up concerns modification, a matter discussed in some detail in GCB.

There are a number of adverbs that modify "true" in ordinary English: "almost", "very", "barely", "merely", etc. It has been observed that adverbs like "certainly" modify sentences, whereas adverbs like "completely" are Verb Phrase (VP) modifiers. The latter cannot acceptably occur in positions where they would be directly attached to an S node, or to other constituents. Compare:

> Certainly/*completely that is true.
> That certainly/*completely is true.
> That is certainly/completely true.
> That is true *certainly/completely.

The semantics coheres with this result. What could "completely" be doing in English* according to PSTT? Syntactically, it would not fit as a sentential modifier, and semantically that wouldn't make sense. But if truth is essentially empty, a prosentential mirror reflecting only the contents of its antecedents, then it is difficult to know what to make of the adverb as it occurs in:

> A: Tom left to go home to his wife.
> B: That's not completely true.

Does B's utterance mean

> Tom didn't completely leave to go home to his wife?
> Tom didn't leave to go completely home?
> Tom didn't leave to go home completely?

We can anticipate yet another sentential connective, "It-is-not- completely-true-that"; the difficulty for PSTT will be to provide a sensible analysis of this sentential connective when "completely" makes no sense as a sentential modifier; "completely" modifies "true". Again, compare "Everything Lloyd said is almost true" with "Almost everything Lloyd said is true": the two have different truth conditions. David Lewis's discussion of "true enough" bears on the same point (See [11]).

In ordinary English we have "nearer to the truth" and "truer than", and "sort of true". PSTT will have to move the comparatives into the structure of the sentences said to be truer. How this will be done in a systematic way remains to be seen.

This brings me to the final section of the paper.

Section 5. Diagnosis

In GCB, the authors emphasize that our interest is in the world: to describe to others how it is; to tell them how we want it to be; to inquire of them how it is. PSTT treats "true" as an instrument to assist us in accomplishing these tasks. I do not deny that it is.

Part of the world has to do with what humans say and believe: witness cultural anthropology and linguistics. What PSTT denies, and what I affirm, is that "true" plays a role in describing this part of the world. PSTT treats metalinguistic uses of language as "technical" or as philosophical devices. But metalinguistic uses of language are widespread;[21] perhaps we're all philosophers at heart.

Tarski turned the focus of considerations on the nature of truth to language and semantics; in particular, to formal languages. There were good reasons for this: formal languages were better understood than natural languages or belief systems, for example. But now we are obsessed with the truth of linguistic entities, to the neglect of a broader picture of the applicability of truth. (This is not entirely a bad thing, for that broader picture continues to involve intolerable vagueness.)

As an account of ordinary truth talk, proponents of PSTT would do well to look at what people say: "Tyler's novel is true to life"; "imagine a true red"; "Rodney flew false colors".

There is one theme common to many ordinary uses of "true", but it is one that I can express only vaguely. Language, belief and thought, some art, maps and diagrams, and perhaps much else, are presently understood as being (or being used as) representational systems. The sentences and utterances that concern PSTT typically represent the world. This is explicit in the emphasis in GCB in the claim that utterers of "That's true" are talking about the ordinary world things — the dogs and fire hydrants mentioned in the antecedent — and not about sentences or propositions. Language may be understood, in part anyway, as a representational system; semantic theories exploit this, as does PSTT. The common theme in the use of "true" with respect to representational systems just is: how good is the representation? A representation is true if it is faithful to the world or to an appropriate object in it, or to some standard envisaged or accepted, in certain respects (not in every respect, of course), respects which are often only tacitly understood.

It is the nature of a representational system that the system itself contribute to the character of a given representation within it. That is, given a set of representations within a representational system, we may inquire which aspects of these representations correspond to reality (certain conventions being understood) and which aspects are artifacts of the representational system itself. Truth primarily concerns the former.

Many humans have a need to have things said explicitly. In the case at hand, the need to say that a particular representation — a belief, someone's testimony, whatever — is a faithful representation. What PSTT offers is, at most, the ability to show that an utterance is faithful to the world. Try as you like, if PSTT is correct,

---

[21] For discussion of a broad sample of the phenomenon, see [4], 78–80; [16]; and [14], 52–3.

you cannot say of Guido's testimony, that it is false, and have Guido's testimony be the subject of your claim. All you end up doing is uttering the negation of whatever Guido said. In doing so, you thereby show (exemplify) that Guido did not represent the world accurately (if your own claim is taken as correct), but you don't say it. It is troubling to suppose that we can't talk about our own talk, our own beliefs, in terms of their being representations of something else.

Some considerations make me wish PSTT were correct. For if it were, I would assert with full conviction that everything that Prof. Belnap says in the next papers he publishes (with possibly one or two exceptions) will be true. Then while I may not have claim to being co-author, at least I could lay claim to having made independently the discoveries that Nuel will have made. By this means, my professional reputation could change dramatically with very little effort on my part.

But just remember, you didn't hear it here first![22]

---

[22] I thank Dorothy Grover, Alan and John Richardson, Brian Skyrms, and Anil Gupta for helpful comments on PSTT.

BIBLIOGRAPHY

[1]   Akmajian, A. and Heny, F. (1975): *An Introduction to the Principles of Transformational Syntax*. Cambridge, Mass.: The MIT Press.
[2]   Baker, Carl L. (1978): *Introduction to Generative-Transformational Syntax*. Englewood Cliffs: Prentice-Hall.
[3]   Belnap, N. D. (1982): "Gupta's Rule of Revision Theory of Truth", *Journal of Philosophical Logic*, 11, pp. 103–116.
[4]   Gardner, H. (1983): *Frames of Mind*. New York: Basic Books.
[5]   Grover, Dorothy L. (1977): "Inheritors and Paradox", *Journal of Philosophy*, LXXIV, pp. 590–604.
[6]   Grover, Dorothy L. (1981): "Truth", *Philosophia*, 10, pp. 225–252.
[7]   Grover, Dorothy L. (1981): "Truth: Do We Need It?", *Philosophical Studies*, 40, pp. 69–103.
[8]   Grover, Dorothy L., Camp, J.L. and Belnap, N.D. (1975): "A Prosentential Theory of Truth", *Philosophical Studies*, 27, pp. 73–125.
[9]   Heny, F. and Schnelle, H.S. (eds.) (1979): *Syntax and Semantics 10: Selections from the Third Gronigen Round Table*. New York: Academic Press.
[10] Lakoff, G. (1976): "Pronouns and Reference", in J. D. McCawley, ed. *Syntax and Semantics 7: Notes from the Linguistic Underground*. New York: Academic Press, pp. 273–335.
[11] Lewis, D. (1983): "Scorekeeping in a Language Game", in *Philosophical Papers*, vol.1, Oxford: Oxford Univ. Press, pp. 233–249.
[12] McCawley, J. D. (1973): "External NPs versus Annotated Deep Structures", *Linguistic Inquiry*, IV, pp. 221–240.
[13] McCawley, J. D. (1988): *The Syntactic Phenomena of English*, vol. 1, Chicago: The Univ. of Chicago Press.
[14] Ong, W. J. (1982): *Orality and Literacy*. London: Methuen.
[15] Soames, S. and Perlmutter, D. (1979): *Syntactic Argumentation and the Structure of English*. Berkeley: Univ. of California Press.
[16] Stubbs, M. (1983): *Discourse Analysis*. Chicago: The Univ. of Chicago Press.

MICHAEL KREMER

PARADOX AND REFERENCE [1]

Since the publication of Kripke's "Outline of a Theory of Truth" in 1975, we have seen a flood of work on the Liar paradox. However, only more recently have there been efforts to extend the results of these investigations to contexts in which structurally similar paradoxes arise. In this paper I aim to contribute to our understanding of paradox by showing how the techniques and ideas of Kripke can throw light on paradoxes associated with the idea of *reference*. I will presuppose familiarity with the basic ideas of Kripke, 1984; notation will be congruent with that in Kremer, 1988.

1. INTRODUCTION

It has long been known that paradoxes that are very similar in structure to the Liar paradox arise in many other contexts. The shared structure may be brought out as follows: we have in our language terms, e.g. 'true', whose meaning is intimately tied up with certain patterns of inference, e.g. the principle that any sentence A is equivalent to the sentence $T'A'$ predicating truth of A. Yet combined with other patterns of inference that we wish to endorse, e.g. the rules of classical logic, these rules of inference lead us to arrive at conclusions that we wish to reject, e.g. that the sentence displayed on p. 33 is not 'The sentence displayed on p. 33 is not true':

> The sentence displayed on p. 33 is not true.

It is convenient to group the contexts which share this structure into three kinds (no special significance should be attributed to this grouping):

(1)   terms that, like 'true', can be thought of as predicates of sentences, or as relations between sentences and other objects — in this class we find, among others, modal and epistemic terms;[2]

(2)   terms that, while not predicates of sentences, can be thought of as "semantic", in particular, satisfaction and denotation; and

(3)   set-theoretic terms, especially set membership.

---

[1] This paper is based on parts of chapter 5 of my doctoral dissertation, *Logic and Truth*, University of Pittsburgh, 1986. The inspiration for that work was a seminar on the topic of truth given by Nuel; without his encouragement and direction it would never have been completed. In the course of that seminar he also set the problem to which this paper is a direct response. I am privileged to be able to contribute to a volume of papers dedicated to the best teacher of logic I have known, and a good friend.

[2] I do not mean to pronounce on the issue of whether sentences, or propositions, or some other things are the proper objects of belief, knowledge, etc. If propositions are the proper objects then I may be understood to be mentioning such relations as 'believes the proposition expressed by', 'knows the proposition expressed by', and so on.

J. M. Dunn and A. Gupta (eds.), Truth or Consequences, 33–47.
© 1990 *Kluwer Academic Publishers. Printed in the Netherlands.*

The traditional classification of the paradoxes, due to Ramsey, into "semantical" (or "epistemological") and "logical" paradoxes, corresponds to the second and third of the above groups (Ramsey, 1978b). Ramsey's idea that the paradoxes could be dealt with by a divide-and-conquer strategy has lost favor recently, perhaps in part because of the inability of his scheme of classification to deal with paradoxes in the first of our groups. As a result, some recent work has endeavored to extend ideas and techniques initially developed in response to paradoxes of truth to concepts in our first and third groups, the hope being to develop a general theory of paradox. However, less attention has been paid to the paradoxes associated with the concepts in our second group, although these concepts, among all those with which paradoxical phenomena are associated, are the most closely related to the concept of truth.

The relation of *satisfaction* generates the famous "heterological" paradox of Grelling, which was known to both Russell and Tarski. One can also produce paradoxes, closely analogous to the Liar paradox, using the notion of the *denotation* of singular terms; in Russell's day Berry's paradox of "the least integer not nameable in fewer than 19 syllables" was a well known example of this type. (Russell, 1956b, p. 60.) Closely related to Berry's paradox is Richard's paradox, which involves the class of those real numbers which can be *defined* by means of a finite number of words, and which Tarski considered to be a close cousin of the Liar. (Russell, 1956b, p. 60; Tarski, 1983c; p. 402, Tarski, 1944, p. 346.) More recent discussions of the semantic paradoxes, however, have largely ignored the notion of reference.[3] It is these paradoxes of reference which will be the main topic of discussion in this paper. Hence this paper can be seen as a small contribution to our understanding of the general phenomenon of paradox. My discussion will begin with some motivational remarks; then I will show how to apply Kripke's ideas to the concept of denotation, and explore some complications which seem special to this case; finally, I will sketch a *logic* of denotation based on this Kripkean approach, patterned after the logic of truth presented in Kremer, 1988. My emphasis throughout will be on philosophical motivation rather than on formal proof; detailed proofs of the results claimed here can be found in Kremer, 1986.

2. DENOTATION AND PARADOX

In this section we will present a simple example of a paradox of denotation, which highlights the similarity between the present problem and that of the Liar paradox. We will work with a first-order language L^4 with both predicates and function symbols. For each closed term t of L, L will contain a quotation name 't' of t; and L will also be equipped with a special function symbol δ, where δx is to be

---

[3] Chihara, 1979, pp. 599–602, is an important exception — in the context of a general analysis of the semantic paradoxes, on which my description of the "general structure" exhibited in the paradoxes is loosely based, Chihara discusses Berry's paradox at some length. A second notable exception is Brandom, 1984, where the general problem of paradoxes of reference is raised in the context of a pronominal account of reference, in the spirit of a redundancy theory of truth.

[4] We take $\sim$, & and $\forall$ as primitive; the other connectives and the existential quantifier may be defined in the usual way.

understood as "the denotation of x." We can define a relation of reference in terms of δ and $=$: $xRy \equiv_{df} \delta x = y$. Our functional notation builds in the fact that each term has exactly one referent. Moreover, the use of a function symbol for denotation is in exact parallel with the use of a predicate for truth. Just as a predicate results in a sentence when applied to the name of a sentence, a function symbol results in a term when it is applied to the name of a term. Intuitively, we want t and $\delta't'$ to be co-referential. Proof-theoretically, they should be intersubstitutable, at least in extensional contexts, just as A and $T'A'$ are. The schema $t = \delta't'$ is the analogue of the Tarski biconditional schema $A \equiv T'A'$.

Now let's consider an intuitive case of a "paradox of denotation:"

> The successor of the denotation of the longest term displayed on p. 35 is one.

Letting s stand in for 'successor' and t for 'the longest term displayed on p. 35', we can represent the above sentence as $s\delta t = 1$. Also, we see that the longest term displayed on p. 35 is 'the successor of the denotation of the longest term displayed on p. 35'; we represent this empirical fact as $t = 's\delta t'$. Using this "empirical premiss" together with the laws of logic and arithmetic, and a "δ-rule" representing the intersubstitutability of t and $\delta't'$, we can show that the sentence displayed above is false:

1	$t = 's\delta t'$	empirical premiss
2	$s\delta t = 1$	assumption
3	$\delta t = 0$	2, arithmetic
4	$\delta's\delta t' = 0$	1, 3, logic
5	$s\delta t = 0$	4, δ-rule
6	$s0 = 0$	3, 5, logic
7	$s0 \neq 0$	arithmetic
8	$s\delta t \neq 1$	$2 - 7$, reductio.

This is not yet a paradox, but it is already quite close. For we can also use the "empirical premiss" to prove $\delta t = s\delta t$:

1	$t = 's\delta t'$	empirical premiss
2	$\delta t = \delta's\delta t'$	1, logic
3	$\delta t = s\delta t$	2, δ-rule.

From this result we can see that δt cannot denote *any* natural number, since no number is its own successor. But now suppose that we adopt the convention that if x is not a number, then the successor of x is zero. Then we will have $\forall x(x \neq sx)$, by virtue, it would seem, of the meaning of s. Using this principle we can refute our "empirical premise:"

$$\begin{array}{ll}
1 & \forall x(x \neq sx) \\
2 & \quad t = \text{`}s\delta t\text{'} \qquad \text{assumption} \\
3 & \quad \delta t = \delta\text{`}s\delta t\text{'} \qquad 2, \text{logic} \\
4 & \quad \delta t = s\delta t \qquad 3, \delta\text{-rule} \\
5 & \quad \delta t \neq s\delta t \qquad 1, \text{logic} \\
6 & t \neq \text{`}s\delta t\text{'} \qquad 2-5, reductio.
\end{array}$$

Yet we should not be able to disprove the empirical fact that $t = $ '$s\delta t$'. I call this paradox the "Anti-Butler,', since the term $s\delta t$ here seems to say of itself that it is "another thing," in opposition to Butler's famous maxim that "a thing is what it is, and not another thing." This paradox is closely analogous to the Liar paradox as presented in Tarski, 1983b, p. 158. If we let l stand in for 'The sentence displayed on p. 33', we get as an empirical premiss $l = $ '$\sim Tl$', and refute this by using the intersubstitutability of $T\text{`}A\text{'}$ and A, and the logical principle $\sim(Tl \equiv \sim Tl)$, which is analogous to step 5 in the proof above:

$$\begin{array}{ll}
1 & l = \text{`}\sim Tl\text{'} \qquad \text{assumption} \\
2 & Tl \equiv Tl \qquad \text{logic} \\
3 & Tl \equiv T\text{`}\sim Tl\text{'} \qquad 1, 2, \text{logic} \\
4 & Tl \equiv \sim Tl \qquad 3, \text{T-rule} \\
5 & \sim(Tl \equiv \sim Tl) \qquad \text{logic} \\
6 & l \neq \text{`}\sim Tl\text{'} \qquad 1-5, reductio.
\end{array}$$

But again, we should not be able to *refute* an empirical fact like $l = $ '$\sim Tl$'.

3. FIXED POINTS AND DENOTATION

Like the Liar paradox, the "Anti-Butler" paradox constructed in the last section may be given a model-theoretic presentation as well. Suppose we are given a "base model" $\langle D, I\rangle$, where I assigns classical interpretations to all the non-logical constants of **L** *except* δ, D contains all the closed terms of **L**, and $I(\text{`}t\text{'}) = t$ for each closed term $t$ of **L**. Can we find an interpretation $Y : D \to D$ which suits $\delta$'s intuitive role as a denotation-sign? As noted before, we would like $t$ and $\delta\text{`}t\text{'}$ to be coreferential for each closed term t; this motivates a *fixed point* requirement on Y. We require that $Y(t) = DV_{\langle D,I,Y\rangle}(t)$ for each closed term t, where $\langle D, I, Y\rangle$ is the model obtained by adding to $\langle D, I\rangle$ the interpretation Y of δ, and $DV_M(t)$ is the denotation value of the closed term t in the classical model M.

As in the case of truth, for some choices of the base model $\langle D, I\rangle$ there will be no *classical* fixed points, i.e. fixed point interpretations Y of δ where $Y : D \to D$. For example, suppose that s is a one-place function symbol of **L**, $I(s)(d) \neq d$ for each $d \in D$, t is an individual constant of **L**, and $I(t) = s\delta t$. Then $\langle D, I\rangle$ models the two conditions which led to our Anti-Butler paradox, namely $\forall x(x \neq sx)$ and $t = {}'s\delta t'$. Let Y be *any* interpretation of δ, with $Y : D \to D$; we can show that Y is not a fixed point. Let $Y(s\delta t) = d \in D$. Then: $DV_{\langle D,I,Y \rangle}(s\delta t) = I(s)[Y(I(t))] = I(s)[Y(s\delta t)] = I(s)(d) \neq d$. Hence $Y(s\delta t) \neq DV_{\langle D,I,Y \rangle}(s\delta t)$.

In the case of truth, Kripke allowed the interpretation of the truth predicate T to be *partial*; in general, while all closed sentences of **L** are members of D, some sentences are neither in the extension nor the "anti-extension" of T. It is convenient to represent this state of affairs slightly differently by introducing a third "truth-value," $*$, and letting the interpretation of T be a function $X : D \to \{t, f, *\}$. We now extend this idea to the case of denotation, letting # be an "additional denotation-value," where it is stipulated that $\# \notin D$. We then let δ be interpreted by any function $Y : D \to D \cup \{\#\}$. Just as, in the case of truth, sentences took values in $\{t, f, *\}$, terms will now take values in $D \cup \{\#\}$. In particular, we should expect "paradoxical" terms, like the Anti-Butler $s\delta t$, to take the denotation-value #.

Thus, we let a model M be a triple $\langle D, I, Y \rangle$, where D includes all the closed terms of **L**, $\# \notin D$, I assigns a classical interpretation to each non-logical constant of **L** other than δ, $I({}'t') = t$ for each closed term t of **L**, and $Y : D \to D \cup \{\#\}$. Y will be called a "denotation-concept." An assignment of values to variables is a function $a : Var \to D$.[5] A valuation scheme is a function V such that, for any model M, assignment a, and term t, $V_{M,a}(t) \in D \cup \{\#\}$, and for every formula A, $V_{M,a}(A) \in \{t, f, *\}$.[6] Given an assignment a, variable x and $d \in D$, $a(d/x)$ is that assignment which is exactly like a except perhaps in assigning d to x. As usual, $V_{M,a}(\forall x A)$ should depend systematically on the range of values $\{V_{M,a(d/x)}(A) : d \in D\}$.

In the three-valued logic used in Kripke's theory of truth, there is a natural ordering on the set $\{t, f, *\}$ of truth-values: $* < t$ and $* < f$. This reflects the idea that * is really a *lack* of a "real" truth-value. Similarly, we can order $D \cup \{\#\}$, by $\# < d$ for every $d \in D$. For Y and $Y' : D \to D \cup \{\#\}$, let $Y \leq Y'$ if and only if $Y(d) \leq Y'(d)$ for every $d \in D$. Given this ordering we can define *monotonicity*: a valuation scheme V is monotonic if and only if for every base model $\langle D, I \rangle$, assignment a, $Y \leq Y'$ and term t, $V_{\langle D,I,Y \rangle,a}(t) \leq V_{\langle D,I,Y' \rangle,a}(t)$.[7]

We can also define a fixed point, relative to V, to be any model $M = \langle D, I, Y \rangle$ such that for any closed term t of **L**, $V_M(t) = Y(t)$. We are now in a position to state the analogue of Kripke's central fixed point result.

THEOREM (MINIMAL FIXED POINT). *Given any base model $\langle D, I \rangle$ and monotonic valuation scheme V, there is a $Y : D \to D \cup \{\#\}$ such that $\langle D, I, Y \rangle$ is a fixed point relative to V.*

---

[5] Note that the range of a does not include #. The variables of **L** are taken to range only over D.

[6] The continued presence of the "third truth value," *, will be discussed below.

[7] Note that this definition says nothing about the values of *formulas*. This will be discussed further below.

Proof Sketch. As in Kripke's discussion of truth, construct a sequence Y_α where:

$$Y_0(d) = \# \text{ for all } d \in D.$$

$$Y_{\alpha+1}(d) = V_{\langle D,I,Y_\alpha \rangle}(d) \text{ if } d \text{ is a closed term of } \mathbf{L};$$

$$\# \text{ otherwise.}$$

When λ is a limit ordinal,

$$Y_\lambda(d) = d' \in D \text{ if } \exists\alpha\forall\beta(\alpha < \beta < \lambda \Rightarrow Y_\beta(d) = d');$$

$$\# \text{ otherwise.}$$

We can then show that for some ordinal σ, $Y_\sigma = Y_{\sigma+1}$, exactly as in Kripke's original proof. Then $\langle D, I, Y_\sigma \rangle$ is a fixed point. □

As in the case of truth, the construction of the minimal fixed point can be generalized; if Y_0 is any *fixable* denotation-concept, i.e. $V_{\langle D,I,Y_0 \rangle}(t) \geq Y_0(t)$ for each closed term t, then for some ordinal σ, $\langle D, I, Y_\sigma \rangle$ is a fixed point, which we can call the fixed point generated by Y_0. We can then show that the minimal fixed point is not, in general, the only fixed point relative to a given base model $\langle D, I \rangle$ and valuation scheme V. Consider, for example the following analogue of the "truth-teller:" suppose that t is a constant of $\mathbf{L}$, and $I(t) = \delta t$. We may call δt a "Butler" term, since intuitively it says of itself that it is what it is, and not another thing. In the minimal fixed point δt has the value #, but for each $d \in D$ there is a fixed point in which it denotes d, generated by the setting $Y_0(\delta t) = d$, and $Y_0(d') = \#$ for every $d' \neq \delta t$.

In general, Kripke's technical concepts can be transferred directly to the present context. Given a base model $\langle D, I \rangle$ and monotonic valuation scheme V, we can define the grounded closed terms to be those which take a value in D in the minimal fixed point and the paradoxical closed terms to be those which do not take a value in D in any fixed point. The "Anti-Butler" term is paradoxical; the "Butler" term is ungrounded but not paradoxical. We can also define the notion of an intrinsic fixed point, and of a term's having an intrinsic denotation value. Given a base model $\langle D, I \rangle$ and a valuation scheme V, two denotation-concepts Y_1 and Y_2 are incompatible if and only if there is some $d \in D$ so that $Y_1(d), Y_2(d) \in D$ and $Y_1(d) \neq Y_2(d)$. A denotation-concept Y is intrinsic if and only if Y is compatible with every fixed point. If Y is also a fixed point then Y is an intrinsic fixed point. A closed term t has an intrinsic denotation value $d \in D$ if and only if it has that value in some intrinsic fixed point. We can prove that the intrinsic fixed points form a complete lattice, and so there is a largest intrinsic fixed point; the proofs transfer directly from the case of truth.[8]

---

[8] For example, if s is an individual constant with $I(s) = \delta s + (-\delta s)$, then $\delta s + (-\delta s)$ will have the intrinsic denotation-value 0 under the strong Kleene scheme for evaluating complex terms, discussed in the next section.

4. MORE ON MONOTONICITY

In order to apply Kripke's apparatus to the concept of denotation, we must choose a *monotonic* valuation scheme. This requirement, as noted in footnote 7 above, places no restrictions on the semantic values of the *sentences* of **L**. However, the natural extensions to the case at hand of the most important three-valued logics discussed by Kripke introduce truth-value gaps as well as denotation gaps. The three schemes may be understood intuitively as follows: the weak Kleene (WK) scheme evaluates expressions involving semantic "gaps" according to the principle "(any) garbage in, (all) garbage out." The strong Kleene (SK) principle is more complex. We consider the result of allowing the "gaps" to be filled in all "possible" ways (with t or f or with objects $d \in D$ as the case may be). If this process yields a constant unambiguous value, that value is assigned the whole expression; otherwise it too is evaluated as a gap. The supervaluation scheme (SV) employs a similar idea; however, only consistent ways of "filling the gaps" are considered in this case, in the sense that where one expression is responsible for several "gaps" they must all be filled in the same way.

In the next section it will be technically convenient to exploit a valuation scheme (WS) which mixes the Weak and Strong Kleene ideas. This scheme evaluates complex *terms* and *atomic* sentences in accordance with the weak Kleene principle; but it uses the strong Kleene rules for the connectives and quantifiers to evaluate *complex sentences*.

Some examples will help make clear how these schemes work. Suppose that t is a non-denoting term, D includes the positive and negative integers, and $0, 1, \cdot, <, +$ and $-$ have their usual interpretations. We would expect to get the following values:

Scheme	$-t$	$t + (-t)$	$0 \cdot t$	$t < 0$	$t \cdot t < 0$	$0 < 0 \cdot t$
WK	#	#	#	*	*	*
SK	#	#	0	*	*	f
SV	#	0	0	*	f	f

WS will yield the same results as WK in all these cases.

If we focus on the weak Kleene scheme, we see that, although we have non-denoting singular terms in **L**, the idea, common to most free logics, that many sentences involving such terms should have a definite truth-value is not forced on us here. There is however one motivation, linked directly to the concept of denotation, for wanting *some* such sentences to have a determinate truth-value. We have introduced a functor δ into **L** intending δx to mean "the denotation of x". What happens to δt when t does not name a closed term of **L**?

An analogous problem occurs for Kripke in his theory of truth; Kripke's solution is to build into the definition of a fixed point that all non-sentences are in the anti-extension of the truth-predicate. In our terms, if $d \in D \backslash \textbf{Sentence}$, then $X(d) = f$, where X is the interpretation of the truth-predicate. This has the consequence that Tt is false when t does not name a sentence of **L**. Analogously, since the domain D corresponds on the side of denotation to the set $\{t, f\}$ on the side of truth, we might be led to the Fregean solution of choosing some designated object $a \in D$ and stipulating that $Y(d) = a$ whenever $d \in D\backslash \textbf{Term}$; however, there is no one value a which seems "right" in this case as f does in the other. Moreover, such a stipulation would have the consequence of making $\exists x \delta t = x$ true even when t does not name a term of $\textbf{L}$. If we think of $\delta t = x$ as saying "t refers to x" we might expect $\exists x \delta t = x$ to be false in this case, by analogy to the falsity of Tt when t does not name a sentence of $\textbf{L}$. The only way to achieve this would be to set $Y(d) = \#$ when $d \in D\backslash \textbf{Term}$, *and* to employ a valuation scheme V^* in which the sentence $\exists x t = x$ is evaluated as *false* when t is a "gap." For example, V^* could assign denotation values in accordance with the weak Kleene principle, assign the value f to *any* atomic sentence in which a term with denotation $\#$ occurs, and assign the values of complex sentences in accordance with the strong Kleene rules for the connectives and quantifiers. So defined, V^* is monotonic for the same reasons that WK is — the requirement of monotonicity puts *no* constraints on the interpretation of sentences.

We will not take such a course in this paper. Rather, we will only require of fixed points that they assign the same value to t and $\delta't'$ for each closed term t of $\textbf{L}$. The advantage of this procedure will be to allow some generality which the adoption of a scheme such as that defined in the previous paragraph would preclude.[9] For there is a clear sense in which the scheme V^* defined in the last paragraph is not monotonic. Consider a slightly more general problem than the one we have been discussing. Suppose that in $\textbf{L}$ we have both a denotation functor δ and a truth predicate T; that we have quotation names for both the sentences and the closed terms of $\textbf{L}$; that we are given an interpretation $\langle D, I \rangle$ of all the non-logical constants of $\textbf{L}$ except T and δ; and that we wish to construct fixed point interpretations X and Y of T and δ respectively. It is natural to use the orderings on $\{t, f, *\}$ and $D \cup \{\#\}$ to define an ordering on the pairs $\langle X, Y \rangle$, where X is a truth-concept and Y is a denotation-concept — $\langle X, Y \rangle \le \langle X', Y' \rangle$ if and only if $X \le X'$ and $Y \le Y'$. Let us call a valuation scheme V "pairwise monotonic" iff for any $\langle X, Y \rangle \le \langle X', Y' \rangle$, $V_{\langle D,I,X,Y \rangle}(A) \le V_{\langle D,I,X',Y' \rangle}(A)$, for every formula A, and $V_{\langle D,I,X,Y \rangle}(t) \le V_{\langle D,I,X',Y' \rangle}(t)$, for every term t. Let us call V "T-monotonic" iff whenever $X \le X'$, $V_{\langle D,I,X,Y \rangle}(A) \le V_{\langle D,I,X',Y \rangle}(A)$, for every formula A. Finally, let us call V "δ-monotonic" iff whenever $Y \le Y'$, $V_{\langle D,I,X,Y \rangle}(t) \le V_{\langle D,I,X,Y' \rangle}(t)$, for every term t.

If V is T-monotonic, then given D, I, and Y we can construct a fixed point interpretation X of T. If V is δ-monotonic, then given D, I, and X we can construct a fixed point interpretation Y of δ. However, if V is pairwise monotonic, we can simultaneously construct fixed point interpretations of both T and δ, by defining an ordinal sequence $\langle X_\alpha, Y_\alpha \rangle$.

Now V^* is δ-monotonic and T-monotonic; but it is not pairwise monotonic. In contrast, SK, WK, SV, and WS are all pairwise monotonic. One might conclude that V^* will prove useless in a simultaneous treatment of δ and T, while the other

---

[9] An alternative approach would be to set $Y(d) = \#$ when $d \in D\backslash \textbf{Term}$ and to use a scheme like WS, on which $\exists x t = x$ will have the value $*$ when t does not denote. This approach would not run afoul of the considerations proferred in the rest of this section. However, it would introduce some complexity into the logic of the next section.

valuation schemes will retain their usefulness. This conclusion should not be drawn too quickly, however. Under V^*, it is true, there will be base models $\langle D, I \rangle$ for which one cannot simultaneously construct fixed point interpretations of δ and T. However, given such a base model, one can adopt a two-stage approach, which reflects the two-stage grammar of our language $\mathbf{L}$ — the terms of $\mathbf{L}$ constituting the first stage, and the formulas the second. One can first construct a fixed point interpretation Y of δ, and then use the expanded base model $\langle D, I, Y \rangle$ to construct a fixed point interpretation X of T. Note that one cannot proceed in the other order. If one first constructs a fixed point interpretation X of T, while keeping the interpretation of δ fixed, and then constructs a fixed point interpretation Y of δ, relative to $\langle D, I, X \rangle$, the changes in the interpretation of δ will result in changes in the semantic values of some of the sentences of $\mathbf{L}$, and X will not necessarily be a fixed point relative to $\langle D, I, Y \rangle$. The source of the difference is this: we have in our language ways of forming formulas out of terms — predicates — where the semantic value of the resulting formulas depends on the semantic values of the terms in question. We do not have in our language any ways of forming terms out of formulas, except quotation; and the semantic value of a quotation name does not depend on the semantic value of the quoted sentence.

In fact, if our language contained subnectors,[10] that is, operators which are like quotation in that they form terms out of formulas, and where the semantic values of the terms so formed depend on the semantic values of the formulas in question, then pairwise monotonicity would be necessary for a simultaneous treatment of denotation and truth. It is a mere happenstance that we did not include any subnectors in the vocabulary of $\mathbf{L}$; there is no reason to develop a theory which could not deal with that possibility. So we have good reason to prefer valuation schemes which are pairwise monotonic over those which are not.

A natural example of a subnector is the definite description operator i, which forms the term ixA from the formula A. It is worth pausing briefly to consider how we would have to modify our theory if we added the definite description operator to $\mathbf{L}$. First it should be noted that the appropriate semantics for i is the following:

$$\mathrm{WS}_{M,a} ixA = d \in D \text{ if } \mathrm{WS}_{M,a(d/x)}(A) = t, \text{ and for every } d' \neq d,$$
$$\mathrm{WS}_{M,a(d'/x)}(A) = f;$$
$$\# \text{ otherwise.}$$

If we weakened the first clause of this definition, letting a definite description ixA denote $d \in D$ just in case A is true when d is assigned to x, and A is *not true* otherwise, pairwise monotonicity would fail. The present definition insures that $ixAx$ denotes a member of D just in case the sentence $\exists x(Ax \ \& \ (\forall y Ay \supset y = x))$ has the value t.

Second, it is only the presence of variable-binding operators like i that force the construction of the minimal fixed point to proceed beyond the first infinite ordinal ω. This is just as in the case of truth. For example, suppose that P is a one place predicate, b and c are individual constants, $I(c) = d_1$, $I(b) = d_2$, $d_1 \neq d_2$, and

---

[10] The term 'subnector' is due to Curry; see Curry, 1976, p. 33.

$I(P)$ is the set consisting of $c, b, \delta`b', \delta`\delta`b'', \ldots, \delta^n b$, and so on, where $\delta^n b$ has the obvious meaning. Then consider the term $t = ix(Px \,\&\, \delta x = c)$. In the minimal fixed point this term will denote the individual constant c; but at every finite stage in the construction of the minimal fixed point it will denote #. Hence the minimal fixed point will not be attained at ω; for $Y_\omega(t) = \#$.

Third, we can make use of the definite description operator to give a plausible reconstruction of the most famous paradox of denotation: Berry's paradox of the least integer not nameable in fewer than 19 syllables. Let $\langle D, I \rangle$ be a base model such that the natural numbers are elements of D. Suppose that P is a one-place predicate whose interpretation is some *finite* set of terms (think of P as standing in for 'is a term with less than 19 syllables'), N is a one place predicate whose interpretation is the set of natural numbers, and $\leq$ is a two-place predicate whose interpretation is the set of all pairs $\langle x, y \rangle$ of natural numbers such that x is less than or equal to y. The reasoning in Berry's paradox goes roughly as follows. Since $I(P)$ is a finite set, there must be some natural number which is not named by any of the terms in $I(P)$ — so we have:

(1) $\exists x(Nx \,\&\, \forall y(Py \supset \delta y \neq x))$.

But any non-empty set of natural numbers has a least element; so there is a least number not named by any of the terms in $I(P)$. Thus:

(2) $\exists x(Nx \,\&\, \forall y(Py \supset \delta y \neq x) \,\&\, \forall z((Nz \,\&\, \forall y(Py \supset \delta y \neq z)) \supset x \leq z))$.

By the laws of arithmetic the x asserted to exist in (2) is unique, so we can speak of "the" least natural number which is not named by any member of $I(P)$. We thus expect (3) to denote a number:

(3) $ix(Nx \,\&\, \forall y(Py \supset \delta y \neq x) \,\&\, \forall z((Nz \,\&\, \forall y(Py \supset \delta y \neq z)) \supset x \leq z))$.

But now suppose that (3) is a member of $I(P)$; then we are immediately landed in trouble, for whatever number we take (3) to denote, we find that (3) cannot denote it!

On the Kripke approach to paradoxes of denotation outlined in this paper we would expect (3) to denote #. This can happen without violating the principle that if there is a natural number n such that $A(n)$, then there is a least natural number n such that $A(n)$. In the present example, we find that since (3) denotes # and (3) is a member of $I(P)$, (1) and (2) have the truth value *, rather than t.

Thus it seems there is some interest to the study of the definite description operator i in the context of a fixed point approach to denotation. Nonetheless, in the next section we will not add the operator i to the vocabulary of **L**, in order to keep things simple.

5. A LOGIC OF DENOTATION

In Kremer, 1988, fixed point models are used to define a logic of truth. The same idea will suffice to provide a logic of denotation. Fix a valuation scheme V and a class of models K. For Γ and Δ sets of formulas of **L**, define:

$\Gamma \models_{V,K} \Delta$ iff

for every $M \in K$ and assignment a, $V_{M,a}(A) = t$
for every $A \in \Gamma \Rightarrow V_{M,a}(B) = t$ for some $B \in \Delta$; and

for every $M \in K$ and assignment a, $V_{M,a}(B) = f$
for every $B \in \Delta \Rightarrow V_{M,a}(A) = f$ for some $A \in \Gamma$.

We will be primarily interested in the relations $\models_{V,F}$ (I will usually drop the subscript 'F') and $\models_{V,S}$ where S is the class of all models and F is the class of all models which are fixed points relative to V.

In the case of truth, as is shown in Kremer, 1988, quantification over the class of minimal fixed point models, or over the class of largest intrinsic fixed point models, results in a logic which is not compact. This same phenomenon recurs in the present context, under any of the valuation schemes discussed above. Thus let Mi be the class of all models $\langle D, I, Y \rangle$ such that Y is the minimal fixed point relative to $\langle D, I \rangle$; and let Li be the class of all models $\langle D, I, Y \rangle$ in which Y is the largest intrinsic fixed point relative to $\langle D, I \rangle$. Let $\{a_n : n \in \omega\}$ be a collection of distinct constant symbols, and let F be a one place predicate. Let $\Gamma = \{a_n = \text{'}\delta a_{n+1}\text{'} : n \in \omega\} \cup \{\exists x Fx, \exists x \sim Fx, F\delta a_0\}$; let $\Delta = \{a_n \neq \text{'}\delta_{n+1}\text{'} : n \in \omega\} \cup \{\forall x Fx, \forall x \sim Fx, \sim F\delta a_0\}$. Then $\Gamma \models_{V,Mi} \Delta$ and $\Gamma \models_{V,Li} \Delta$, while for any finite subsets Γ' and Δ' of Γ and Δ respectively, $\Gamma' \not\models_{V,Mi} \Delta'$ and $\Gamma' \not\models_{V,Li} \Delta'$; hence the relations $\models_{V,Mi}$ and $\models_{V,Li}$ are not compact.[11]

I shall presently give an axiomatization in a Gentzen sequent-calculus for the relations $\models_{WS,F}$ and $\models_{WS,S}$. The choice of the valuation scheme WS is primarily for convenience' sake. The supervaluation scheme yields a cumbersome logic, and the WK rules for the connectives and quantifiers seem less natural than the SK rules. However, the SK treatment of atomic formulas and complex terms leads to some peculiar results. For example, if F is a *one place* predicate, the sequent $\forall x Fx \vdash Ft$ is valid under SK. But in general the sequent form $\forall x A \vdash A[t/x]$ is not valid under SK; in particular if F is a two-place predicate symbol, $\forall x Fxx \vdash Ftt$ is not valid for some choices of t, though $\forall x \forall y Fxy \vdash Fts$ is valid. Under the WK treatment of atomic formulas and complex terms, the logic of inferences involving identity and the quantifiers is simplified. WS allows us this simplification while retaining the more natural SK rules for the connectives.

Before turning to the actual presentation of the sequent-calculus axiomatization of $\models_{WS}$, I will define some useful syntactic notions. For any term t, we define the set

---

[11] Similarly, if we let $N\#$ be the set of fixed points in which $Y(d) = \#$ for all $d \in D\backslash \textbf{Term}$, $\models_{V,N\#}$ is not compact. This problem can be solved though, as suggested by Anil Gupta for the case of truth, by revising the definition of $\models$ to quantify over all languages containing Γ and Δ.

$G(t)$ of terms, by induction: if t is a variable, individual constant, or quotation-name, $G(t) = \emptyset$; if t is δs, $G(t) = \{\delta s\} \cup G(s)$; and if t is $ft_1 \ldots t_n$, $G(t) = \cup_i G(t_i)$. The intuitive significance of the set $G(t)$ (the "guarantors" of t) is this: in any model, t denotes (a member of the domain) if and only if every member of $G(t)$ denotes. This fact, which can easily be proved by induction, exploits the WK interpretation of complex terms. We will also make use of the following fact: a term t denotes just in case the identity $t = t$ is true.

For atomic formulas and negated atomic formulas, A, we will also define a set of "guarantors" $G(A)$: $G(t = s) = G(t \neq s) = G(t) \cup G(s)$; and $G(Pt_1 \ldots t_n) = G(\sim Pt_1 \ldots t_n) = \cup_i G(t_i)$. The WK treatment of atomic formulas implies that an atomic (or negated atomic) formula A has a definite truth-value (in $\{t, f\}$) just in case every element of $G(A)$ denotes (a member of D).

We may now define the relations $\vdash_S$ and $\vdash$ in accordance with the following rules.

(1)   Identity: $A \vdash A$.

(2)   Weakening: $\Gamma \vdash \Delta \Rightarrow \Gamma, A \vdash \Delta; \Gamma \vdash \Delta \Rightarrow \Gamma \vdash A, \Delta$.

(3)   Cut for identities: $\Gamma \vdash t = s, \Delta$ and $\Gamma, t = s \vdash \Delta \Rightarrow \Gamma \vdash \Delta$;
        $\Gamma \vdash t \neq s, \Delta$ and $\Gamma, t \neq s \vdash \Delta \Rightarrow \Gamma \vdash \Delta$.

(4) $A, \sim A \vdash B, \sim B; A, \sim A \vdash s = s; t \neq t \vdash B, \sim B; t \neq t \vdash s = s$.

(5)   If $t, s \in$ **Term** and $t \neq s$, 't' $=$'s' $\vdash$ and $\vdash$ 't' $\neq$'s'.

(6)   If A is atomic or negated atomic, and $s \in G(A)$, then $A \vdash s = s$;
        $s \neq s \vdash A$.

(7)   If A is atomic or negated atomic and $G(A) = \{s_1, \ldots, s_n\}$,[12] then
        $\Gamma \vdash A, \Delta \Rightarrow \Gamma, \sim A \vdash s_1 \neq s_1, \ldots, s_n \neq s_n, \Delta; \Gamma, A \vdash \Delta \Rightarrow$
        $\Gamma, s_1 = s_1, \ldots, s_n = s_n \vdash \sim A, \Delta$.

(8) DN-intro: $\Gamma, A \vdash \Delta \Rightarrow \Gamma, \sim\sim A \vdash \Delta; \Gamma \vdash A, \Delta \Rightarrow \Gamma \vdash \sim\sim A, \Delta$.

(9)   &-intro: $\Gamma, A \vdash \Delta \Rightarrow \Gamma, A \& B \vdash \Delta; \Gamma, B \vdash \Delta \Rightarrow \Gamma, A \& B \vdash \Delta$;
        $\Gamma \vdash A, \Delta$ and $\Gamma \vdash B, \Delta \Rightarrow \Gamma \vdash A \& B, \Delta$.

(10) $\sim$&-intro: $\Gamma, \sim A \vdash \Delta$ and $\Gamma, \sim B \vdash \Delta \Rightarrow \Gamma, \sim(A \& B) \vdash \Delta$;
        $\Gamma \vdash \sim A, \Delta \Rightarrow \Gamma \vdash \sim(A \& B); \Gamma \vdash \sim B, \Delta \Rightarrow \Gamma \vdash \sim(A \& B)$.

(11) $\forall$-intro: If t is free for x in A, $\Gamma, A[t/x] \vdash \Delta \Rightarrow \Gamma, \forall x A, t = t \vdash \Delta$.
        If y is not free in Γ, Δ, or A, and y is free for x in A, $\Gamma \vdash A[y/x], \Delta \Rightarrow$
        $\Gamma \vdash \forall x A, \Delta$.

(12) $\sim\forall$-intro: If y is not free in Γ, Δ, or A, and y is free for x in
        A, $\Gamma, \sim A[y/x] \vdash \Delta \Rightarrow \Gamma, \sim\forall x A \vdash \Delta$. If t is free for x in A,
        $\Gamma \vdash \sim A[t/x], \Delta \Rightarrow \Gamma \vdash t \neq t, \sim\forall x A, \Delta$.

(13)   Identity axioms: If $G(t) = \{s_1, \ldots, s_n\}$,[13] then $s_1 = s_1, \ldots,$
        $s_n = s_n \vdash t = t; t \neq t \vdash s_1 \neq s_1, \ldots, s_n \neq s_n$.

---

[12] $G(A)$ may be empty — the rule still applies.
[13] $G(t)$ may be empty — the rule still applies.

(14)   =-intro: If t and s are free for x in A, $\Gamma, A[t/x] \vdash \Delta \Rightarrow$
         $\Gamma, A[s/x], t = s \vdash s \neq s, \Delta; \Gamma, A[t/x] \vdash \Delta \Rightarrow \Gamma, A[s/x],$
         $s = t \vdash s \neq s, \Delta; \Gamma \vdash A[t/x], \Delta \Rightarrow \Gamma, t = s \vdash t \neq t, A[s/x], \Delta;$
         $\Gamma \vdash A[t/x], \Delta \Rightarrow \Gamma, s = t \vdash t \neq t, A[s/x], \Delta.$

(15) $\neq$-intro: If t and s are free for x in A, $\Gamma, A[t/x] \vdash \Delta \Rightarrow$
         $\Gamma, A[s/x], t = t \vdash t \neq s, \Delta; \Gamma, A[t/x] \vdash \Delta \Rightarrow \Gamma, A[s/x],$
         $t = t \vdash s \neq t, \Delta; \Gamma \vdash A[t/x], \Delta \Rightarrow \Gamma, s = s \vdash t \neq s, A[s/x], \Delta;$
         $\Gamma \vdash A[t/x], \Delta \Rightarrow \Gamma, s = s \vdash s \neq t, A[s/x], \Delta.$

(16) δ-intro: If t is a closed term, then $\Gamma, A[t/x] \vdash \Delta \Rightarrow \Gamma, A[\delta\text{'}t\text{'}/x] \vdash$
         $\Delta; \Gamma \vdash A[t/x], \Delta \Rightarrow \Gamma \vdash A[\delta\text{'}t\text{'}/x], \Delta.$

The relation $\vdash$ between finite sets of formulas of **L** is given by rules (1) to (16); the relation $\vdash_S$ is given by rules (1) to (15). If Γ and Δ are *arbitrary* sets of formulas then $\Gamma \vdash \Delta$ if and only if there are finite subsets Γ' and Δ' of Γ and Δ such that $\Gamma' \vdash \Delta'$, and similarly for $\vdash_S$.

A few remarks on these rules may be helpful.

1.   Rules (1), (2), (5) and (8) to (12) are taken directly from the rules for the Strong Kleene valuation scheme given in Kremer, 1988.

2.   Rules (6), (7) and (13) reflect the Weak Kleene treatment of atomic formulas and complex terms, which we have adopted. Rule (13) corresponds to the usual identity axiom, which has the form: $t \neq t \vdash$ and $\vdash t = t$. This simpler rule is no longer sound in the present context. For example, $\nvDash s\delta t = s\delta t$, since if $s\delta t$ is an "Anti-Butler" term with denotation value #, the sentence $s\delta t = s\delta t$ has the value *.

3.   The introduction rules for the quantifiers and for identities introduce certain self-identities, or negated self-identities, as side conditions. We exploit here the fact that a term t will denote an element of the domain — over which the variables range in quantification — just in case the sentence $t = t$ is true. In each case the rules given for the quantifiers and identity in Kremer, 1988 are not sound in the present context. For example, the old rule for introducing a universal quantifier on the left of the turnstile was: $\Gamma, A[t/x] \vdash \Delta \Rightarrow \Gamma, \forall x A \vdash \Delta$. In conjunction with an instance of identity, $Fs\delta t \vdash Fs\delta t$, this rule leads us to the conclusion $\forall x Fx \vdash Fs\delta t$; but this conclusion is not sound, since the term $s\delta t$ might be an "Anti-Butler" paradoxical term. The revised rule (15), on the other hand, only allows us to prove the sequent $\forall x Fx, s\delta t = s\delta t \vdash Fs\delta t$, which is sound.

4.   Rule (3) represents a little bit of cut. I have endeavored to rid the proof system given here of cut, but my success has not been complete. I believe that it is possible to prove the eliminability of rule (3) from a system of rules adapted from the present system by the introduction of further complications into the quantifier rules and the identity rules. However, I have not been able to prove this so far, so this is an open question.

5.   Straightforward Henkin-style completeness proofs will suffice to
          prove the following soundness and completeness results: for any
          Γ and Δ, $\Gamma \vdash_S \Delta$ iff $\Gamma \models_S \Delta$; and $\Gamma \vdash \Delta$ iff $\Gamma \models \Delta$. Detailed
          proofs may be found in Kremer, 1986. It should be noted that the
          argument is simpler than that given for the case of truth in Kremer,
          1988, because of the presence of the rule of "cut for identities".

6.   This completeness result implies that the introduction rules for δ
          produce a conservative extension of the language $\mathbf{L}'$, where the rules
          for $\mathbf{L}'$ are (1) to (15), the vocabulary of $\mathbf{L}'$ does not include δ, and
          $\mathbf{L}'$ contains quotation names of all the closed terms of $\mathbf{L}$, including
          those closed terms involving δ.[14] On the other hand, if $\mathbf{L}''$ is just
          like $\mathbf{L}'$ except that its rules are the rules of classical logic, then the
          rules for δ do not yield a conservative extension of $\mathbf{L}''$. For example,
          the sequent $t = \text{`}s\delta t\text{'} \vdash \exists x(x = sx)$ would not be provable in $\mathbf{L}''$,
          but would be provable with the addition of the δ rules. This provides
          a proof-theoretical explication of the significance of Kripke's fixed
          point theorem.[15]

6. CONCLUSION

We have shown that the framework developed by Kripke in response to the problem
of the Liar paradox extends readily to the concept of denotation. This extension
has yielded some interesting results, as well as some (perhaps) unexpected complications. It is my modest hope that this exercise has thereby contributed to our
understanding of paradox in a more general way.

---

[14] The argument given in Kremer, 1988, for the case of the truth predicate works just as well here.

[15] See Kremer, 1988, for a detailed discussion of this point in the case of truth.

BIBLIOGRAPHY

Brandom, Robert, (1984): "Reference Explained Away," *Journal of Philosophy*, 81, pp. 469–492.

Chihara, Charles, (1979): "The Semantic Paradoxes: A Diagnostic Investigation," *Philosophical Review*, 88, pp. 590–618.

Curry, Haskell B., (1976): *Foundations of Mathematical Logic*, second edition, Dover, New York. First edition published in 1963.

Feferman, Solomon, (1984): "Towards Useful Type-Free Theories I," in Martin, 1984, pp. 237–288. First published in 1984.

Kremer, Michael, (1986): *Logic and Truth*, Ph.D. dissertation, University of Pittsburgh.

Kremer, Michael, (1988): "Kripke and the Logic of Truth," *Journal of Philosophical Logic*, 17, pp. 225–278.

Kripke, Saul, (1984): "Outline of a Theory of Truth," in Martin, 1984, pp. 53–81. First published in 1975.

Martin, Robert L., ed., (1984): *Recent Essays on Truth and the Liar Paradox*, Oxford University Press, Oxford.

Ramsey, Frank P., (1978a): *Foundations*, D.H. Mellor, ed., Humanities Press, Atlantic Highlands, N.J.

Ramsey, Frank P., (1978b): "The Foundations of Mathematics," in Ramsey, 1978a, pp. 152–212. First published in 1925.

Russell, Bertrand, (1956a): *Logic and Knowledge*, Macmillan, New York.

Russell, Bertrand, (1956b): "Mathematical Logic as Based on the Theory of Types," in Russell, 1956a, pp. 59–105. First published in 1908.

Tarski, Alfred, (1944): "The Semantic Conception of Truth," *Philosophy and Phenomenological Research*, 4, pp. 341–376.

Tarski, Alfred, (1983a): *Logic, Semantics, Metamathematics*, Hackett Publishing Co., Indianapolis.

Tarski, Alfred, (1983b): "The Concept of Truth in Formalized Languages," in Tarski, 1983a, pp. 152–268. First published in 1933.

Tarski, Alfred, (1983c): "The Establishment of Scientific Semantics," in Tarski, 1983a, pp. 401–408. First published in 1936.

ANIL GUPTA

TWO THEOREMS CONCERNING STABILITY [1]

Dedicated to Professor Nuel Belnap on the occasion of his sixtieth birthday

I

The theory of truth developed by Nuel Belnap, Hans Herzberger, and myself views the concept of truth as governed by a rule of revision. It interprets the truth-concept via a rule that determines the extension of truth, not absolutely, but relative to an antecedent *hypothesis* concerning this extension. And it attempts to explain the behavior of truth in terms of this rule. One finds, when one repeatedly revises a hypothetical extension of truth, that sentences like the Liar ('this very sentence is not true') always oscillate in the resulting revision process. Whatever we hypothesize the truth-value of the Liar to be, the rule revises it to something different. Sentences like the Truth-Teller ('this very sentence is true') do not oscillate, but the value they acquire in the revision process depends on the initial hypothesis. Ordinary, intuitively unproblematic, sentences, on the other hand, exhibit a perfect stability: whatever the initial hypothesis of revision, these sentences always stabilize at the same value (after perhaps some initial oscillations).[2]

Viewing the concept of truth in terms of a rule of revision promises to give us, I believe, some understanding of how a language can contain its own truth-concept. But it also raises a question. The theory uses certain concepts, e.g., "stability in L", to explain the notion "true in L", but these concepts are excluded from the languages (L) that have been studied so far. This exclusion, it seems to me, is justified: in studying anything as complex and perplexing as the concept of truth, it is best to begin with the simplest possible languages. Nonetheless, the question whether — and how — a language L can contain notions such as "stability in L" is a natural one and needs to be addressed.

I propose in this paper one way of adding "stability in L" to L, and I prove two theorems that lend plausibility to the proposal. In general terms, the proposal is to interpret "stability in L" via a rule of revision. It is shown that this rule has the following desirable property: under certain conditions it exhibits perfect convergence and stability. No matter what we take as the initial hypothesis, the revision process invariably stabilizes at, and converges to, the same classical interpretation

---

[1] This paper was written while the author held an NEH Fellowship for University Teachers. The result it reports was obtained, however, several years earlier.

[2] For motivation and details of the revision theory see the papers by Belnap, Herzberger, and me in *Journal of Philosophical Logic*, vol. 11, no. 1 (February 1982), pp. 1–116. [Herzberger's and my papers are also reprinted in Robert L. Martin (ed.), *Recent Essays on Truth and the Liar Paradox*, (Oxford and New York: Oxford University Press, 1984), pp. 133–235.] A more extended presentation of the theory will be given in a book that Belnap and I are writing.

49

J. M. Dunn and A. Gupta (eds.), Truth or Consequences, 49–60.
© 1990 *Kluwer Academic Publishers. Printed in the Netherlands.*

for "stability". It is shown that sometimes the rule for "stability" behaves in this way even though the concept of truth exhibits all kinds of pathologicality.

II

A revision semantics for a predicate may be viewed as consisting of two parts. The first specifies the rule of revision associated with the predicate — a rule that tells us what the extension of the predicate would be under various hypotheses concerning this extension. The second part articulates, in terms of this rule, the objects to which the predicate applies (or fails to apply) unproblematically, and the objects on which its application is problematic. The first part of the semantics is specific: the rule of revision it provides will vary from predicate to predicate. The second is general: it is the same for all predicates that are given a revision semantics. Let us begin with a brief review of the second part.

Let ρ be a rule of revision. We suppose that

$$\rho : \{\mathbf{t}, \mathbf{f}\}^D \to \{\mathbf{t}, \mathbf{f}\}^D,$$

where $\mathbf{t}$ and $\mathbf{f}$ are the truth-values and D is a nonempty set.[3] Let S be a sequence of members of $\{\mathbf{t}, \mathbf{f}\}^D$, where the length of S, $lh(S)$, may either be an ordinal or the class On of all the ordinals. If α is an ordinal $< lh(S)$ then S_α is the αth member of S and $S{\upharpoonright}\alpha$ is the sequence S restricted to α. The central notions we need to define are those of a *revision sequence for ρ* (intuitively, this is a sequence obtained by repeated applications of ρ), and of *stability in* a sequence.

Given a sequence S of member of $\{\mathbf{t}, \mathbf{f}\}^D$ and an object $d \in D$, we say that

> d is *stably* $\mathbf{t}(\mathbf{f})$ *in* S iff there is an ordinal $\alpha < lh(S)$ such that for all $\beta \geq \alpha$ if $\beta < lh(S)$ then $S_\beta(d) = \mathbf{t}(\mathbf{f})$; d is *stable in* S iff it is either stably $\mathbf{t}$ or stably $\mathbf{f}$ in S; otherwise, it is *unstable in S.*

A *revision sequence for ρ* is a sequence S that satisfies the following condition: for all ordinals $\alpha < lh(S)$

(i)   if $\alpha = \beta + 1$ then $S_\alpha = \rho(S_\beta)$;
(ii)   if α is a limit ordinal then for all $d \in D$ if d is stably $\mathbf{t}$ ($\mathbf{f}$) in $S{\upharpoonright}\alpha$ then $S_\alpha(d) = \mathbf{t}$ ($\mathbf{f}$).

Finally, an object $d \in D$ is *stably* $\mathbf{t}$ ($\mathbf{f}$) *for ρ* iff d is stably $\mathbf{t}$ ($\mathbf{f}$) in all revision sequences of length On for ρ; d is *stable for ρ* iff it is stably $\mathbf{t}$ or stably $\mathbf{f}$ for ρ. Intuitively, the revision rule ρ yields a definite verdict on the stable objects: the objects that are stably $\mathbf{t}$ for ρ fall under the predicate, whereas those that are stably $\mathbf{f}$ do not. The

---

[3] This supposition is convenient (and adequate for our purposes), but inessential. A more general conception of "revision rule" is possible and is sometimes useful.

application of the predicate is problematic on the unstable objects. The unstables can be further sorted into such categories as "paradoxical", "Truth-Teller-like", etc., in terms of their behavior in the revision sequences. See the papers cited in note 1.

Our goal is to provide a semantics for a language L equipped with two distinguished predicates T and S that have, respectively, the intuitive interpretations "true in L" and "stable in L". We assume that, apart from these two predicates, L is a classical first-order language. By a *ground* model M for L we understand an ordered pair $\langle D, I \rangle$ such that D contains all the sentences of L and I provides a classical interpretation for all the nonlogical constants of L *excluding* T and S.[4] So, for example, I assigns to a one-place predicate G a function from the domain D into the truth-values $\{t, f\}$. Let g_1 and g_2 be possible interpretations in M of a one-place predicate, i.e., let $g_1, g_2 \in \{t, f\}^D$. Then, $M + g_1$ is a model just like M except that it assigns to the predicate S the interpretation g_1. Such models we shall call *intermediate* models of L, and we use the variables $M, M', \ldots$ to range over them. Similarly, $M + g_2$ will be the model just like M except that it assigns to the predicate T the interpretation g_2. Such models we shall call *standard* models of L, and we use the variables $\mathcal{M}, \mathcal{M}', \ldots$ to range over *them*. The notion "true sentence of a language L in a standard model $\mathcal{M}$" is familiar from the Tarskian semantics for classical languages. Its definition can be found in virtually any logic book and will not be reviewed here. The notion "stable sentence of L in an intermediate model M" is explained by the revision semantics.[5] These are sentences that are stable (in the sense explained in the previous paragraph) for the rule that the revision semantics associates with the predicate T. This rule, τ_M, is defined in the following way. Let D be the domain of M. Then, τ_M is an operation on $\{t, f\}^D$ such that for all $g \in \{t, f\}^D$ and $d \in D$,

$$\tau_M(g)(d) = t \text{ iff d is a sentence of } L \text{ that is true in the}$$
$$\text{standard model } M + g.$$

The core intuition underlying our semantics for S is this: Given the language L (with its distinguished predicates T and S) and a ground model M for L, we can determine the extension of S, *provided that we have a hypothesis concerning this extension*. For once we have a (hypothetical) interpretation — say g_1 — for S,[6] we can determine the revision rule τ_{M+g_1} for T in the intermediate model $M + g_1$, and this yields the sentences that are stable in M relative to the hypothesis g_1. We thus obtain a new revised hypothesis concerning the interpretation of S. The revision rule for S, σ_M, is then this: σ_M is an operation on $\{t, f\}^D$ such that for all $g \in \{t, f\}^D$ and $d \in D$,

---

[4] I does not provide any interpretations for T and S.
[5] The papers mentioned in note 1 define closely related, but distinct, notions of stability. We follow the definition given by Belnap, *op. cit.*
[6] Since we are working within a classical context, we can recover the interpretation of a predicate from its extension (and conversely).

$$\sigma_M(g)(d) = \textbf{t} \text{ iff d is a sentence of } L \text{ that is stable in the}$$
$$\text{intermediate model M} + g, \text{ i. e., d is a}$$
$$\text{stable sentence for } \tau_{M+g}.$$

Note that the definition of σ_M — and its motivation — is parallel to that of τ_M. In both cases, the extension of the predicate can be determined only on the basis of a prior hypothesis concerning this extension.[7] Note also that there is a sense in which the semantics given for S is at a higher level than that for T: the definition of σ_M makes reference to the entire revision process for T.[8] This difference in level does not imply, however, that the language which contains "stability" has to be different from the object language.

    A full presentation of the semantics of S requires an explanation of many more notions. As these are not absolutely essential to the main result we wish to prove, we pass over them in silence.

Some Examples

Let L be a language with quotational names for all its sentences. Let M ($= \langle D, I \rangle$) be a ground model for L that interprets the quotational names in the intended way and assigns to the names a and b the following interpretations:

$$I(a) = Ta$$
$$I(b) = {\sim}Tb.$$

Intuitively, then, Ta is a Truth-Teller, and ${\sim}Tb$ is a Liar sentence of L. Clearly, these sentences are bound to be unstable in the revision process for T, irrespective of the interpretation assigned to S. Hence, if S is a revision sequence for σ_M and α is an ordinal such that $0 < \alpha < lh(S)$ then

$$S_\alpha(Ta) = \textbf{f},$$
$$S_\alpha({\sim}Tb) = \textbf{f},$$

but

$$S_\alpha(Ta \ \& \ {\sim}Ta) = \textbf{t}.$$

Set:

$$A_0 = {\sim}Tb$$
$$A_{n+1} = S(`A_n\text{'}) \lor A_0.$$

---

[7]   For an extended discussion of τ_M, see my "Truth and Paradox", *loc. cit.*

[8]   If we were giving a semantics for a language with, for instance, a truth-predicate and a denotation-predicate this difference in levels would not have occurred. The semantics for "stable truth" sketched by Belnap, *op. cit.*, attempts to keep its level the same as that of truth.

Suppose S is a revision sequence of length $\geq \omega$ for σ_M such that

$$S_0(\sim Tb) = \mathbf{t}.$$

Then, for all $n < \omega$,

$$S_n(A_n) = \mathbf{t}, and$$

$$S_{n+1}(A_n) = \mathbf{f}.$$

III

Let M be a ground model, and **M** an intermediate model, for L. We say that S is a *revision sequence of* M (**M**) iff S is a revision sequence of length On for the rule σ_M (τ_M). *The revision process is stable in* M (more briefly, M is *stable*) iff for every revision sequence S of M there is an ordinal α such that

$$S_\alpha = S_{\alpha+1}.$$

Thus, each revision sequence S of a stable model M reaches a fixed point of σ_M, i. e., a point g such that $\sigma_M(g) = g$. Note that once a revision sequence reaches a fixed point g, all its subsequent values are also g.

The revision process is convergent in M (more briefly, M is *convergent*) iff there is a g $\in \{\mathbf{t}, \mathbf{f}\}^D$ such that for all revision sequences S of M there is a revision sequence S' and an ordinal α satisfying the condition

$$S_0 = S_0' \text{ and } S_\alpha' = \text{g.}^9$$

It is an immediate consequence of the above definitions that M is both stable and convergent iff there is fixed point g of σ_M satisfying the condition that for all revision sequences S of M there is an ordinal α such that

$$S_\alpha = \text{g.}$$

We show below that ground models exist that are both stable and convergent.

Let L be a language with quotational names 'A' for each of its sentences A, and let U be a set of its sentences. We say that a ground model $M(= \langle D, I \rangle)$ of L is *U-neutral* iff the quotational names have their intended interpretations in M and the interpretations of the remaining constants do not distinguish amongst the members of U.[10] Finally, the notion of *the degree of* an expression X ($deg(X)$) is understood

---

[9] The notions of convergence and stability for intermediate models can be defined in a parallel way. As we do not need these notions in the arguments given below, we do not give explicit definitions for them.

[10] More precisely: if a is a non-quotational name in L then $I(a) \notin U$; if G is an n-place predicate then for all d_m and $d_m' \in U$ ($1 \leq m \leq n$), $I(G)(d_1, \ldots, d_m, \ldots, d_n) = I(G)(d_1, \ldots, d_m', \ldots, d_n)$; and if f is an n-place function symbol then the range of $I(f)$ is disjoint from U and for all d_m and $d_m' \in U$ ($1 \leq m \leq n$), $I(f)(d_1, \ldots, d_m, \ldots, d_n) = I(f)(d_1, \ldots, d_m', \ldots, d_n)$.

in the following way.[11] The degree of any formula or term that does not contain any occurrences of S (including those within quotational names) is 0. The degree of the *remaining* expressions X is determined by these rules:

(i)   If $X = $ 'A' then $deg(X) = deg(A) + 1$.

(ii)   If $X = G(t_1, \ldots, t_n)$, where G is any n-place predicate of L (including =, T, and S), then $deg(X) = $ the maximum of 1, $deg(t_1), \ldots, deg(t_n)$. Similarly for function symbols.

(iii)   If X is $(\forall x)A$ or $\sim A$ then $deg(X) = deg(A)$.

(iv)   If $X = (A \ \& \ B)$ then $deg(X) = $ the maximum of $deg(A)$ and $deg(B)$.

THEOREM 1. *Let L be a language that has quotational names for all its sentences, and U the set of sentences of L of degree > 0. Let $\mathrm{M}(= \langle \mathrm{D}, \mathrm{I} \rangle)$ be a U-neutral ground model for L such that for some name a*

$$\mathrm{I}(a) = Ta.$$

Then, the revision process is both stable and convergent in M.[12]

Proof. Let L, M, U be as above, and let S and S' be arbitrary revision sequences of M. We show

Claim. For all ordinals α and for all natural numbers m, n if $\alpha, m > n+1$ then for all sentences A of degree n, $S_\alpha(A) = S'_m(A)$.

This claim suffices for the theorem, for it implies that

$$S_\omega = S_{\omega+1} = S'_\omega.$$

We establish the claim by a transfinite induction on α.

Induction Hypothesis I. For all ordinals $\alpha_0 < \alpha$ and all natural numbers m, n if $\alpha_0, m > n+1$ then for all sentences A of degree n, $S_{\alpha_0}(A) = S'_m(A)$.

Let m, n be arbitrary natural numbers and A an arbitrary sentence of degree n. Suppose that $\alpha, m > n + 1$. We need to show that

(1) $S_\alpha(A) = S'_m(A)$.

This is easy if α is 0 or limit. (The interesting case is when α is a successor ordinal.) The former case is trivial since by hypothesis $\alpha > n+1$. For the latter case we need only appeal to Induction Hypothesis I. Suppose, for example, that

$$S'_m(A) = \mathbf{t}.$$

---

[11] Expressions of L consist of the terms and formulas of L.

[12] An analogous claim (for classical languages with truth-predicates) is established in §2 of "Truth and Paradox". The proof of the present theorem is more complex, however, because L has not only a truth-predicate T but also a stability-predicate S. For an informal discussion of this theorem, see the remarks at the end of the paper.

Induction Hypothesis I yields that for all ordinals β such that $n + 1 < \beta < \alpha$,

$$S_\beta(A) = \mathbf{t}.$$

Thus A is stably $\mathbf{t}$ in the sequence $S{\restriction}\alpha$. Hence, by the definition of revision sequence, we have

$$S_\alpha(A) = \mathbf{t}.$$

The other half of the argument is exactly parallel.

The proof of (1) is equally trivial if $m = 0$. We may suppose, therefore, that m and α are successor ordinals. Let $\alpha = \gamma + 1$ and $m = p + 1$. Consider the intermediate models

$$\mathbf{M}_1 = \mathbf{M} + S_\gamma$$
$$\mathbf{M}_2 = \mathbf{M} + S'_p.$$

To establish (1) we need to show that A is stable for $\tau_{\mathbf{M}_1}$ iff it is stable for $\tau_{\mathbf{M}_2}$. To this end we show that given a revision sequence T of length On for $\tau_{\mathbf{M}_1}$, we can construct a revision sequence T', also of length On, for $\tau_{\mathbf{M}_2}$ satisfying the condition

(2) A is stably $\mathbf{t}$ $(\mathbf{f})$ in T iff A is stably $\mathbf{t}$ $(\mathbf{f})$ in T'.

The argument for the "converse" claim (in which the roles of $\tau_{\mathbf{M}_1}$ and $\tau_{\mathbf{M}_2}$ are switched) is exactly parallel.

Let T be a revision sequence of length On for $\tau_{\mathbf{M}_1}$. We construct a sequence T' of members of $\{\mathbf{t}, \mathbf{f}\}^D$ thus:

$$T'_0 = T_1$$
$$T'_{\delta+1} = \tau_{\mathbf{M}_2}(T'_\delta)$$

If δ is limit, then $T'_\delta(\mathrm{d}) = \mathbf{t}$ iff either d is stably $\mathbf{t}$ in $\langle T'_\mu \rangle_{\mu < \delta}$ or d is unstable in $\langle T'_\mu \rangle_{\mu < \delta}$ and $T_\delta(\mathrm{d}) = \mathbf{t}$.

It is easily seen that T' is a revision sequence for $\tau_{\mathbf{M}_2}$. In order to establish (2), we show:

Subclaim. For all ordinals ϑ, the standard models

$$\mathcal{M}_{1+\vartheta} = \mathbf{M}_1 + T_{1+\vartheta} \qquad [= (\mathbf{M} + S_\gamma) + T_{1+\vartheta}]$$
$$\mathcal{M}'_\vartheta = \mathbf{M}_2 + T'_\vartheta \qquad [= (\mathbf{M} + S'_p) + T'_\vartheta]$$

are *n-isomorphic* (symbolically: $\mathcal{M}_{1+\vartheta} \cong_n \mathcal{M}'_\vartheta$) in the sense that they are isomorphic when restricted to the language $L{\restriction}n$ containing only sentences of degree $\leq n$.[13]

---

[13] Thus, if $n > 0$, $L{\restriction}n$ is like L except that it does not contain any quotational names of degree $> n$. If $n = 0$, $L{\restriction}n$ does not contain the predicate S and quotational names of degree > 0.

We prove this claim by transfinite induction on ϑ.

Induction Hypothesis II. For all ordinals $\mu < \vartheta$, $\mathcal{M}_{1+\mu} \cong_n \mathcal{M}'_\mu$.

We show that $\mathcal{M}_{1+\vartheta} \cong_n \mathcal{M}'_\vartheta$.

Since $\alpha, m > n + 1$, we know that $\gamma, p > 0$. Hence all sentences of the form

(3) $(Ta \ \& \ B),$

(4) $\sim(Ta \ \& \ B),$

where B is a tautology, fall outside the extension of S in the models $\mathcal{M}_{1+\vartheta}$ and $\mathcal{M}'_\vartheta$. All contradictions and tautologies, on the other hand, fall in the extension of S in these models. Further, all tautologies fall within, and all contradictions fall outside, the extension of T in the models $\mathcal{M}_{1+\vartheta}$ and $\mathcal{M}'_\vartheta$. (For this we appeal to the facts that T and T' are revision sequences for $\mathbf{M}_1$ and $\mathbf{M}_2$ respectively and that $T'_0 = T_1$.) Similarly, either formulas of the form (3) or of the form (4)–but not both–fall within the extension of T in these models. Since for all natural numbers q

$$|\{C : C \text{ is a tautology } \& \ deg(C) \geq q\}| = |\{C : C \text{ is a sentence}\}|,^{14}$$

we conclude that

$$|\{C : \mathcal{S}_\gamma(C) = T_{1+\vartheta}(C) = \mathbf{t} \ \& \ deg(C) \geq q\}| = |\{C : \mathcal{S}'_p(C) = T'_\vartheta(C) = \mathbf{t} \ \& \ deg(C) \geq q\}|.$$

That is, the cardinality of sentences of degree $\geq q$ that fall within the extension of both T and S in the model $\mathcal{M}_{1+\vartheta}$ is the same as the cardinality of those in the extension of T and S in the model $\mathcal{M}'_\vartheta$. Similar claims hold for the other three possibilities.[15]

Construct an operation Ψ on the domain D thus: Let Ψ be the identity operation on the nonsentences in D and on the sentences of degree $< n$; if $n = 0$, make Ψ an identity operation on the sentences of degree 0 also; on the remaining sentences choose Ψ so that it respects the interpretations of T and S in $\mathcal{M}_{1+\vartheta}$ and $\mathcal{M}'_\vartheta$. By the observations made in the previous paragraph, such a Ψ exists.

We claim that Ψ is an isomorphism between the restrictions of $\mathcal{M}_{1+\vartheta}$ and $\mathcal{M}'_\vartheta$ to $L{\restriction}n$. For:

(i) Ψ respects the interpretation of all the quotational names in $L{\restriction}n$ since it is an identity on all sentences of degree $< n$ and, if $n = 0$, on those of degree 0.

(ii)   Because of the U-neutrality of the ground model M, Ψ respects the interpretation of all the nonquotational names, function symbols, and predicates other than T and S.

---

[14] Notation: $|Z|$ = the cardinality of Z.

[15] That is, for (i) sentences of degree $\geq q$ in the extension of T but not that of S; (ii) those in the extension of S but not that of T; and (iii) those in the extension neither of T nor of S.

(iii) Concerning S: If $n = 0$ then S does not belong to $L \upharpoonright n$ and can be ignored. If $n > 0$, then by Induction Hypothesis I the interpretations of S in $\mathcal{M}_{1+\vartheta}$ and $\mathcal{M}'_\vartheta$ (i.e., S_γ and S'_p respectively) agree on sentences of degree $< n$. So Ψ respects the interpretation of S in the two models. (By definition it respects the interpretation of S on sentences of degree $\geq n$.)

(iv) Concerning T: Set $q = n$, if $n > 0$; otherwise, set $q = 1$. Then, Ψ respects, by definition, the interpretation of T on sentences of degree $\geq q$. For sentences of degree $< q$, we appeal to Induction Hypothesis II and argue by cases. If $\vartheta = 0$, we have the desired result in virtue of the fact that $T'_0 = T_1$. If $\vartheta = \mu + 1$ then Induction Hypothesis II yields that $\mathcal{M}_{1+\mu} \cong_n \mathcal{M}'_\mu$. Hence the same sentences of degree $\leq n$ are true in the models $\mathcal{M}_{1+\mu}$ and $\mathcal{M}'_\mu$. This gives the desired result. If ϑ is limit, the result follows from Induction Hypothesis II and the construction of T'.

Hence, $\mathcal{M}_{1+\vartheta} \cong_n \mathcal{M}'_\vartheta$.   □

The above proof (more particularly, the argument for the Subclaim) yields the following corollary.

COROLLARY. *Let L be a language that has quotational names for all its sentences, U the set of sentences of L of degree > 0, and $M (= \langle D, I \rangle)$ a U-neutral ground model. Then, for all sentences A of degree 0 and all g_1 and $g_2 \in \{t, f\}^D$*

$$\sigma_M(g_1)(A) = \sigma_M(g_2)(A).$$ □

That is, the stability and instability of sentences of degree 0 in the intermediate model M + g does not depend upon g. The following lemma will be useful in the proof of the next theorem.

LEMMA. *Let S be a revision sequence of length On for a rule ρ. Then, there is an ordinal α such that for all elements d that are stable in S, and all $\beta \geq \alpha$,*

$$S_\beta(d) = S_\alpha(d).$$

The least such α will be called, following Herzberger, the stabilization ordinal for S.

Proof. If d is stably t (f) in S then, by definition, there is an ordinal β such that for all $\gamma \geq \beta$

$$S_\gamma(d) = t \ (f).$$

Let β_d be the least such β for d, and let α be the supremum of $\{\beta_d : d \text{ is stable in } S\}$. Then, α is the stabilization ordinal for S.   □

Define g_t to be the member of $\{t, f\}^D$ such that for all d $\in$ D,

1. $g_t(d) = t$, if d is a sentence of L;
2. $g_t(d) = f$, otherwise.

THEOREM 2. *Let L, U, M, D be as in the Corollary. Suppose that for all sentences A of degree 0*

(5) $\qquad \sigma_M(g_t)(A) = t.$

Then for all $g \in \{t, f\}^D$,

$$\sigma_M(\sigma_M(g)) = g_t.$$

(Hence, M is both stable and convergent.)

Proof-Sketch. Let S, S' be arbitrary revision sequences of length On for $\tau_{M+\sigma_M(g)}$. And let α, β be the stabilization ordinals for S, S' respectively (cf. the Lemma above). Define

$$\mathcal{M}_\mu = (M + \sigma_M(g)) + S_\mu$$
$$\mathcal{M}'_\mu = (M + \sigma_M(g)) + S'_\mu.$$

We show

Claim. For all ordinals ϑ and all natural numbers n if $\vartheta > n$ then

$$\mathcal{M}_{\alpha+n+1} \cong_n \mathcal{M}'_{\beta+\vartheta}.$$

This claim suffices to prove our theorem. It implies that all sentences stabilize in S' and, as S' is arbitrary, that they stabilize in the same way in all revision sequences: a sentence is stably t in S' iff it is stably t in S'', where S'' is an arbitrary revision sequence of length On for $\tau_{M+\sigma_M(g)}$.

The claim can be proven by an inductive argument similar to that used in the proof of the Subclaim (cf. the proof of Theorem 1). The argument goes through in virtue of the following facts:

(a)   The extension of T in $\mathcal{M}_{\alpha+n+1}$ agrees with that in $\mathcal{M}'_{\beta+\vartheta}$ as far as the sentences of degree 0 are concerned. This is so in virtue of the hypothesis (5), the Corollary, and the fact that α and β are the stabilization ordinals for S and S' respectively.

(b)   The extension of T in $\mathcal{M}_{\alpha+n+1}$ agrees with that in $\mathcal{M}'_{\beta+\vartheta}$ on sentences of degree $< n$ also. For this we appeal to the induction hypothesis.

(c)   The induction hypothesis yields also that the extension of T in $\mathcal{M}'_{\beta+\vartheta}$ is a maximally consistent set, even if ϑ is a limit ordinal. For every sentence is bound to be stable in the sequence $S' \restriction \beta + \vartheta$. (The extension of T in $\mathcal{M}_{\mu+1}$ (also, $\mathcal{M}'_{\mu+1}$) is also bound to be maximally consistent, regardless of the value of μ.)

(d)   If $\sigma_M(g) \neq g_t$ then the cardinality of the set of sentences of degree $> p$ (p an arbitrary natural number) that fall outside the extension of

S in $\mathcal{M}_{\alpha+n+1}$ $(\mathcal{M}'_{\beta+\vartheta})$ is bound to be the cardinality of the set of sentences of the language. Further, if A falls outside this extension then so does $\sim A$.

The requisite isomorphism Ψ is now easily constructed. Set $p = n$, if $n > 0$; otherwise, set $p = 1$. Let Ψ be identity over nonsentences and sentences of degree $< p$. On the remaining sentences let it preserve the interpretations of T and S in $\mathcal{M}_{\alpha+n+1}$ and $\mathcal{M}'_{\beta+\vartheta}$. If $\sigma_M(g) \neq g_t$ then such a Ψ exists by observations (c) and (d) above. On the other hand, if $\sigma_M(g) = g_t$ then the interpretation of S is preserved by any operation on the sentences of degree $\geq p$. And clearly there are operations that will preserve the interpretation of T. In this case we do not need to appeal to (c) and (d).

In view of observations (a) and (b), and the U-neutrality of the ground model M, Ψ is an isomorphism of the required sort. Hence $\mathcal{M}_{\alpha+n+1} \cong_n \mathcal{M}'_{\beta+\vartheta}$. □

Remarks

(1) Theorem 2 shows that if there is no vicious self-reference for T and the ground model is U-neutral then the revision rule yields a classical interpretation for S. Theorem 1 shows that the same phenomenon occurs even if there is all kind of vicious reference for T, provided that there is a Truth-Teller in the language.

(2) The proviso in Theorem 1 that there be a Truth-Teller in the language can be weakened. I do not know whether it can be completely eliminated. (In one special case its elimination is easy: if we confine ourselves to revision processes in which the extension of truth at limit stages is required to be maximally consistent.)

(3) The condition of U-neutrality can also be considerably weakened: we can allow the language to contain certain kinds of self-referential sentences involving S. If, for example, the language has a name a that denotes

$$\sim Sa,$$

and is otherwise U-neutral, then the arguments given above go through: the revision process for S converges to, and stabilizes at, a fixed point. Note that the value of $\sim Sa$ in this fixed point is **t**.

(4) If the notion of "stability in L" is added to L in the above manner then we can express within L such claims as "The Liar is not stable", " 'The Liar is not stable' is true", "some sentences are stable", etc. We do not have to see these claims as formulated in a metalanguage. Presumably, notions such as "paradoxical in L", "Truth-Teller-like in L" can be added to L in a parallel way.

(5) The notion of "stability" we have added is really that of "first-order stability". In the presence of vicious reference, this notion can itself exhibit a higher-order instability. If L has a name a that denotes A, where

$$A = \sim Sa \vee \sim Ta,$$

then A oscillates in the revision process for S. If at one stage it is in the extension of S then at the next stage it falls out of the extension. And at the next, it is back in. A higher-order notion of stability that captures this fact can be added to the language: we need only follow a procedure analogous to the one followed above for S.

Note that distinctions of *orders* in the notions of stability do not imply distinctions in the *languages* to which these notions can belong.

(6) There are models that are stable but not convergent, and the other way around. If the denotation of a name a in M is

$$Sa \lor {\sim}Ta,$$

and this is the only vicious reference for S, then M is stable but not convergent (assuming a Truth-Teller exists in the language). On the other hand, had a denoted

$$\sim Sa \lor {\sim}Ta,$$

then M would have been convergent but not stable. Presence of both kinds of vicious reference implies that the model is neither stable nor convergent.

ALASDAIR URQUHART

THE COMPLEXITY OF DECISION PROCEDURES
IN RELEVANCE LOGIC

1. INTRODUCTION

Relevance logic is distinguished among non-classical logics by the richness of its mathematical as well as philosophical structure. This richness is nowhere more evident than in the difficulty of the decision problem for the main relevant propositional logics. These logics are in general undecidable [22]; however, there are important decidable subsystems. The decision procedures for these subsystems convey the impression of great complexity. The present paper gives a mathematically precise form to this impression by showing that the decision problem for $R_\rightarrow$, the implication fragment of R, is exponential space hard. This means that any Turing machine which solves this decision problem must use an exponential amount of space (relative to the input size) on infinitely many inputs.

The first-degree fragment common to E, R and most other well-known relevance logics has a simple decision procedure. The details of the Anderson-Belnap decision procedure are to be found in [4, Chapter III]. A four-valued matrix is characteristic for this fragment; since the decision problem for the two-valued propositional calculus can be reduced efficiently to the decision problem for this fragment, the complexity of the decision problem is the same as that for the classical two-valued propositional calculus (that is to say, the problem is co-NP-complete).

The decision problem for the pure implicational fragments of E and R is much harder. It was solved by Saul Kripke in a *tour de force* of combinatorial reasoning, which was published only as an abstract [13]. Belnap and Wallace extended Kripke's decision procedure to the implication-negation fragment of E in [5]; an account of their decision method is to be found in [4, pp. 124–139]. The decision method extends immediately to R. In fact, in the case of R we can go farther; Robert Meyer in his thesis [16] showed how to translate the logic LR, which results from R by omitting the distribution axiom, into $R_{\rightarrow\wedge}$, so that the decision procedure can be extended to all of LR. This decision procedure has been implemented as a program Kripke by Thistlewaite, McRobbie and Meyer [21]. The program is not simply a straightforward implementation of the decision procedure; finite matrices are used extensively to prune invalid nodes from the search tree.

The decision methods of Kripke, Belnap and Wallace are of a truly marvellous complexity. In fact, they are so complex that it is not clear how to compute an upper bound on the number of steps required by the procedures for an input formula of a given length. The key combinatorial lemma of Kripke which forms the basis for all these decision procedures [4, pp. 138–139] simply asserts the finiteness of the search tree without giving an explicit bound on its size.

J. M. Dunn and A. Gupta (eds.), Truth or Consequences, 61–76.
© 1990 *Kluwer Academic Publishers. Printed in the Netherlands.*

Is this complexity inherent in the logics in question, or could there be a more efficient decision method? The lower bound proved in this paper provides a partial answer to this question. It is proved by adapting a method used by Mayr and Meyer [15] to show that the word problem for finitely presented commutative semigroups is exponential space complete. The method used here is a simplification of Mayr and Meyer 's, and provides an alternative proof of their lower bound.

In the last part of the paper we discuss the complexity of the Kripke decision method, and show, by adapting some ideas of McAloon [14], that the size of the search tree produced by the method is primitive recursive in the Ackermann function. It is not clear whether the large lower bound or the monstrous upper bound is closer to the truth.

2. MODEL THEORY FOR IMPLICATIONAL LOGICS

The lower bound is proved for a fixed logical system, for the sake of convenience; we shall indicate later how the proof can be adapted to a more general class of systems. The logic we discuss is the system $R_{\to \wedge \circ}$, which contains the fusion connective $\circ$ in addition to $\to$ and $\wedge$ (the fusion connective is dubbed "co-tenability" by Anderson and Belnap [4, pp. 344–346]). We also include the constant t. Employing the conventions of Church [6] for replacing parentheses by dots, we state the axioms for the system as follows:

1. t
2. $t \to .A \to A$
3. $A \to B \to .B \to C \to .A \to C$
4. $(A \to .B \to C) \to .B \to .A \to C$
5. $(A \to .B \to C) \to .A \to B \to .A \to C$
6. $(A \wedge B) \to A$
7. $(A \wedge B) \to B$
8. $(A \to B) \wedge (A \to C) \to .A \to (B \wedge C)$
9. $A \to .B \to .A \circ B$
10. $(A \to .B \to C) \to .(A \circ B) \to C$

The rules of the system are *modus ponens* and *adjunction*:

From $A \to B$ and A infer B (*modus ponens*);
From A and B infer $A \wedge B$ (*adjunction*).

It is an easy exercise to prove from these axioms that fusion is associative, commutative and square-increasing, and that t forms the semigroup identity. Thus, using $(A \leftrightarrow B)$ as an abbreviation for $((A \to B) \wedge (B \to A))$, the following are theorems:

$$((A \circ B) \circ C) \leftrightarrow (A \circ (B \circ C))$$
$$(A \circ B) \leftrightarrow (B \circ A)$$
$$A \to (A \circ A)$$
$$(t \circ A) \leftrightarrow A$$

We now state the model theory for the system, which is due to Richard Routley and Robert Meyer [19]. A *model structure* is a triple $\langle 0, K, R \rangle$, where K is a set, $0 \in K$, and R is a ternary relation on K satisfying the postulates:

(a) $R0aa$
(b) $Raaa$
(c) $(Rabc \wedge Rcde) \rightarrow \exists x(Radx \wedge Rxbe)$
(d) $(R0ax \wedge Rxbc) \rightarrow Rabc$
(e) $(Rabc \wedge R0cd) \rightarrow Rabd$

If $M = \langle 0, K, R \rangle$ is a model structure, then a *valuation* in M is a function V that assigns to each propositional variable P a set $V(P) \subseteq K$, and which satisfies the condition: if $a \in V(P)$ and $R0ab$ then $b \in V(P)$. A *model* consists of a model structure, together with a valuation.

If $\mathcal{M}$ is a model, we define truth relative to a point in $\mathcal{M}$ by the following recursive definition (writing $x \models A$ for "A is true at point x in $\mathcal{M}$"):

(a)   For a variable P, $x \in K$, $x \models P \Leftrightarrow x \in V(P)$;
(b) $x \models t \Leftrightarrow R00x$;
(c) $x \models (A \rightarrow B) \Leftrightarrow \forall yz((Rxyz \,\&\, y \models A) \Rightarrow z \models C)$;
(d) $x \models (A \circ B) \Leftrightarrow \exists yz(Ryzx \,\&\, y \models A \,\&\, z \models B)$;
(e) $x \models (A \wedge B) \Leftrightarrow x \models A \,\&\, x \models B$.

A formula A is *valid* if $0 \models A$ in all models $\mathcal{M}$. It is not difficult to verify that all theorems of $R_{\rightarrow \wedge \circ}$ are valid (see [19] for details).

3. MODELS CONSTRUCTED FROM SEMI-THUE SYSTEMS

Let Σ be a finite alphabet, Σ^* the set of all finite strings over Σ. We define a *semi-Thue system* to be a finite set of pairs of strings in Σ^*; if $\langle \alpha, \beta \rangle$ is such a pair of strings, we write it in the form $\alpha \longrightarrow \beta$, and refer to it as a *production* of the semi-Thue system.

We say that $\gamma \alpha \delta \Rightarrow \gamma \beta \delta \; (S)$ if γ and δ are words in the alphabet of S, and the production $\alpha \longrightarrow \beta$ belongs to S. The relation $\alpha \overset{*}{\Rightarrow} \beta \; (S)$ is defined to hold if (1) $\alpha = \beta$ or (2) there is a sequence $\alpha_1, \cdots, \alpha_k$ so that $\alpha = \alpha_1$, $\beta = \alpha_k$ and $\alpha_i \Rightarrow \alpha_{i+1}(S)$ for $1 \leq i < k$.

A semi-Thue system over an alphabet Σ is *commutative* if it includes all productions of the form $xy \longrightarrow yx$, for $x, y \in \Sigma$; it is *contractive* if it includes all productions of the form $xx \longrightarrow x$ for $x \in \Sigma$. If S is a commutative contractive semi-Thue system, we say that a production belonging to S is *proper* if it is not of the form $xy \longrightarrow yx$ or $xx \longrightarrow x$.

We now show how to construct a model for $R_{\rightarrow \wedge \circ}$ from a commutative contractive semi-Thue system. The basic idea for the construction is derived from Meyer and Routley [18].

Let S be a semi-Thue system over the alphabet Σ. Define a ternary relation on Σ^* by: $R\alpha\beta\gamma$ if and only if $\alpha\beta \overset{*}{\Rightarrow} \gamma \; (S)$. The relational structure $M(S)$ is defined as $\langle 0, \Sigma^*, R \rangle$, where 0 is the empty string.

LEMMA 1. *If S is a commutative, contractive semi-Thue system, then $M(S)$ is a model structure.*

The relation $R0\alpha\alpha$ clearly holds since 0 is defined as the empty string; the relation $R\alpha\alpha\alpha$ holds for all strings α because S is contractive.

To show that the third condition holds, assume that $R\alpha\beta\gamma$ and $R\gamma\delta\epsilon$, that is, $\alpha\beta \overset{*}{\Longrightarrow} \gamma$ and $\gamma\delta \overset{*}{\Longrightarrow} \epsilon$. Setting $x = \alpha\delta$, we find: $x\beta \overset{*}{\Longrightarrow} \alpha\beta\delta \overset{*}{\Longrightarrow} \gamma\delta \overset{*}{\Longrightarrow} \epsilon$, so that $R\alpha\delta x$ and $Rx\beta\epsilon$.

Finally, to show that the fourth condition holds, assume that $R0\alpha x$ and $Rx\beta\gamma$; then $\alpha \overset{*}{\Longrightarrow} x$, so that $\alpha\beta \overset{*}{\Longrightarrow} x\beta \overset{*}{\Longrightarrow} \gamma$, that is, $R\alpha\beta\gamma$; the fifth condition is proved similarly. □

If Σ is a finite alphabet, we correlate distinct propositional variables with the elements of Σ. We write $P(\sigma)$ for the propositional variable correlated with the symbol σ.

If α is a string in Σ^*, we write $P(\alpha)$ for the propositional expression corresponding to α, where concatenation is represented by the fusion operator. Parentheses can be omitted in the propositional expression in view of the associative law for fusion. The expression t is correlated with the empty string.

Let S be a commutative, contractive semi-Thue system. The canonical model $\mathcal{M}(S)$ associated with S is the model defined on the model structure $M(S)$ by the valuation: $V(P(\sigma)) = \{\alpha \in \Sigma^* : \sigma \overset{*}{\Longrightarrow} \alpha \ (S)\}$, and $V(P) = \emptyset$ for uncorrelated variables.

LEMMA 2. *Let S be a commutative, contractive semi-Thue system, and γ, δ words of S. Then $\gamma \models P(\delta)$ in the canonical model $\mathcal{M}(S)$ if and only if $\delta \overset{*}{\Longrightarrow} \gamma$.*

Proof. If δ is a single symbol, then the lemma holds by definition. If δ is the empty word, then $\gamma \models P(\delta)$ if and only if $R00\gamma$, that is, $\delta \overset{*}{\Longrightarrow} \gamma$.

Assume that it holds for the words δ_1 and δ_2. Then $\gamma \models P(\delta_1\delta_2)$ if and only if there exist α and β so that $\alpha\beta \overset{*}{\Longrightarrow} \gamma$, $\delta_1 \overset{*}{\Longrightarrow} \alpha$ and $\delta_2 \overset{*}{\Longrightarrow} \beta$. This last condition is easily seen to be equivalent to $\delta_1\delta_2 \overset{*}{\Longrightarrow} \gamma$. □

Let S be a semi-Thue system, γ and δ words belonging to S. The formula $\Psi(S, \gamma, \delta)$, is defined as:

$$[P(\beta_1) \to P(\alpha_1) \land \ldots \land P(\beta_n) \to P(\alpha_n) \land t] \to .P(\delta) \to P(\gamma)$$

where $\alpha_1 \longrightarrow \beta_1, \ldots, \alpha_n \longrightarrow \beta_n$ are the proper productions of S.

LEMMA 3. *If S is a commutative contractive semi-Thue system, and γ, δ words belonging to S, then $R_{\to\land 0} \vdash \Psi(S, \gamma, \delta)$ if and only if $\gamma \overset{*}{\Longrightarrow} \delta \ (S)$.*

Proof. First, we show that if $\gamma \overset{*}{\Longrightarrow} \delta$ (S), then $\vdash \Psi(S, \gamma, \delta)$. If $\gamma \Rightarrow \delta$ (S), then the formula is provable by the axioms for conjunction, the theorem

$$(A \to B) \to .(A \circ C) \to (B \circ C),$$

and the associative, commutative and square increasing theorems for $\circ$. The general case then follows by Axiom 2, and transitivity of implication.

For the converse, let us assume that $\vdash \Psi(S, \gamma, \delta)$. Let $\alpha_k \longrightarrow \beta_k$ be a proper production of S. If $\gamma \models P(\beta_k)$ in the canonical model, then by Lemma 2, we have $\beta_k \overset{*}{\Longrightarrow} \gamma$, hence $\alpha_k \overset{*}{\Longrightarrow} \gamma$ so that $\gamma \models P(\alpha_k)$. Thus in the canonical model we have $0 \models P(\beta_k) \to P(\alpha_k)$. We have thus shown that the antecedent of $\Psi(S, \gamma, \delta)$ is true at 0 in the canonical model. It follows that the consequent $P(\delta) \to P(\gamma)$ is also true at 0. Hence, $\gamma \overset{*}{\Longrightarrow} \delta$ (S) by Lemma 2. □

4. COMPLEXITY THEORY

In this section, we review the basic notions of complexity theory required in the sequel. For a more complete treatment see [10].

An *off-line Turing machine* is defined to be a multi-tape Turing machine with a read-only input tape, a write-only output tape on which the head never moves left and a read-write work tape. Let Σ_1, Σ_2 be finite alphabets. A function $f : \Sigma_1^* \to \Sigma_2^*$ *reduces* a set $A \subseteq \Sigma_1^*$ to a set $B \subseteq \Sigma_2^*$ provided that $\alpha \in A \Leftrightarrow f(\alpha) \in B$ for all $\alpha \in \Sigma_1^*$.

If f reduces A to B, and in addition f is computable by a Turing machine which visits at most $log_2 \, n$ work tape squares during its computation on any word $\alpha \in \Sigma_1^*$ of length $n > 1$, then A is said to be *log-space reducible* to B; if in addition the length of $f(\alpha)$ is $O(length(\alpha))$, then A is *log-lin reducible* to B.

If A is log-lin reducible to B, then any procedure for deciding B can be converted, by means of the reduction, to a procedure for deciding A which uses space not much greater than that used by the first procedure. In particular, there is a $k > 0$ such that given a Turing machine which decides B in space c^n, one can find a Turing machine deciding A in space c^{kn}.

A set $A \subseteq \Sigma^*$ is said to be *decidable in space* $g : N \to N$ if there is a Turing machine which accepts A and visits at most $g(n)$ work tape squares during its computation on any word $\beta \in \Sigma^*$ of length n. A is decidable in *exponential space* if it is decidable in space g where $g(n) \le c^n$ for some $c > 1$.

A set A of words is *exponential space hard with respect to log-lin reducibility* if every set which is decidable in exponential space is log-lin reducible to A. If A itself is decidable in exponential space, then A is *exponential space complete with respect to log-lin reducibility*.

LEMMA 4. *If B is exponential space hard with respect to log-lin reducibility then there is a constant $c > 1$ such that any Turing machine accepting B uses space c^n for infinitely many inputs of length n.*

Proof. By the deterministic space hierarchy theorem [10, pp. 297–298], there is a set A decidable in space 3^n, but not 2^n. Since A is decidable in exponential space, it is log-lin reducible to B. Since A cannot be decided in space 2^n, it follows that B cannot be decided in space $2^{n/k}$. □

The preceding lemma shows that to prove an exponential space lower bound for decision procedures for $R_{\to \wedge \circ}$, it is sufficient to show that $R_{\to \wedge \circ}$ is exponential space hard with respect to log-lin reducibility. Since log-lin reducibility is transitive, this will follow provided we can show that a set known to be exponential space hard is log-lin reducible to $R_{\to \wedge \circ}$. In the following section, we exhibit such an exponential space hard set.

5. SPACE BOUNDED COUNTER MACHINES

A counter machine models a computer having a finite number of registers each of which can contain an arbitrary integer. The basic operations of the machine consist of adding 0, -1 or 1 to the current contents of a register, and branching to new states conditional upon a given register being empty or not. We now give a formal definition of this model.

A *3-counter machine* C consists of a finite set of states Q containing a pair of distinguished states q_0 (the initial state) and q_a (the accepting state), and a transition function

$$\delta : (Q \setminus \{q_a\}) \to (Q \times \{0, \pm 1\} \times I_3) \cup (Q \times Q \times I_3),$$

where $I_k = \{1, \ldots, k\}$. The *computation* of C is the (possibly infinite) sequence $c^0, c^1, \ldots$ of *instantaneous descriptions* $c^i \in Q \times Z^3$ where

(a) $c^0 = (q_0, 0, 0, 0)$;

(b)   If $i \in N, c^i = (q, z_1, z_2, z_3)$ and $\delta(q) = (q', d, k) \in Q \times \{0, \pm 1\} \times I_3$, then

$$c^{i+1} = (q', z'_1, z'_2, z'_3), \text{ where } z'_i = \begin{cases} z_i + d & \text{if } i = k \\ z_i & \text{otherwise;} \end{cases}$$

(c)   If $i \in N, c^i = (q, z_1, z_2, z_3)$ and $\delta(q) = (q', q'', k) \in Q \times Q \times I_3$, then

$$c^{i+1} = \begin{cases} (q', z_1, z_2, z_3) & \text{if } z_k = 0 \\ (q'', z_1, z_2, z_3) & \text{otherwise.} \end{cases}$$

The vector entry c^i_{k+1} is referred to as the contents of the k-th *counter* after i steps, for $k \in I_3$.

The machine C is said to *terminate* iff its computation contains the instantaneous description $(q_a, 0, 0, 0)$. This quadruple, if it occurs, is necessarily the last element in the computation. The *size* of a machine is the number of its states. The computation of a 3-counter machine is *bounded by* n if after any step in the computation the contents of all three counters are ≥ 0 and $\leq n$.

The following lemma can be derived from the results of [8]:

LEMMA 5. *The set* $ESC = \{C : C$ *is a terminating 3-counter machine whose computation is bounded by* $2^{2^{size(C)}}\}$ *is exponential space complete under log-lin reducibility.*

To prove an exponential space lower bound for the decision problem for $R_{\rightarrow \wedge \circ}$ we shall show how to construct from a given 3-counter machine a commutative contractive semi-Thue system so that we can reduce the problem ESC efficiently to the word problem for commutative contractive semi-Thue systems. In view of Lemma 3, this will prove an exponential space lower bound for the logical problem.

6. SUCCINCT SEMIGROUP PRESENTATIONS

Before giving the construction of the semi-Thue system, we first present a method used by Mayr and Meyer [15] to give succinct presentations of semigroups. A semigroup presentation is a Thue system, that is, a semi-Thue system in which the inverse of every production is included. We write $\alpha \equiv \beta$ for the two productions $\alpha \longrightarrow \beta$ and $\beta \longrightarrow \alpha$; we use the notation $\alpha \overset{*}{\equiv} \beta$ as an abbreviation for $\alpha \overset{*}{\Longrightarrow} \beta$ and $\beta \overset{*}{\Longrightarrow} \alpha$. We also employ the abbreviation e_n for 2^{2^n}.

For each $n \in N$, we define a commutative Thue system $\mathcal{P}_n$. The system $\mathcal{P}_n$ and its alphabet A_n are defined by induction on n. We define:

$$A_0 = \{s, f, c_1, c_2, c_3, c_4, b_1, b_2, b_3, b_4\}$$
$$\mathcal{P}_0 = \{sc_i \equiv fc_ib_i^2 : i \in I_4\}.$$

For $m > 0$, let $S, F, C_1, C_2, C_3, C_4, B_1, B_2, B_3, B_4$ be distinct symbols not in A_{m-1}. Then the alphabet of $\mathcal{P}_m$ is defined as:

$$A_m = A_{m-1} \cup \{S, F, C_1, C_2, C_3, C_4, B_1, B_2, B_3, B_4\}.$$

The elements of A_0 are of *level* 0, the elements of $A_m \setminus A_{m-1}$ of *level* m. As a notational convention, we use upper case letters $S, \ldots, B_4$ for the symbols of level m, lower case letters $s, \ldots, b_4$ for the corresponding symbols of level $m - 1$.

The Thue system $\mathcal{P}_m$ is defined as the system whose proper productions are those of $\mathcal{P}_{m-1}$ and the following equivalences:

$$\begin{array}{rll} S & \equiv sc_1 & \textit{(a)} \\ fc_1b_1 & \equiv sc_2 & \textit{(b)} \\ fc_2 & \equiv fc_3 & \textit{(c)} \end{array}$$

$$sc_3 b_1 \equiv sc_2 b_4 \qquad (d)$$
$$sc_3 \equiv fc_4 b_4 \qquad (e)$$
$$sc_4 \equiv F \qquad (f)$$
$$\text{and for } i \in I_4, \quad C_i f b_2 \equiv C_i B_i f b_3 \quad (g)\text{--}(j)$$

The definition of $\mathcal{P}_m$ is identical with that of Mayr and Meyer, except that for every level greater than 0, they include symbols $Q_1, \ldots, Q_4$. These symbols have been omitted because (as will be clear subsequently) they are redundant.

The Thue system $\mathcal{P}_n$ is designed to generate e_n B_i symbols from a single symbol C_i. This is accomplished by repeated squaring; each level represents a set of rules which squares the number of symbols given it as input from the previous level. Since $e_{n+1} = (e_n)^2$, this results in a set of rules of size $O(n)$ which generates e_n symbols.

LEMMA 6. *Let $S, F, C_i, B_i, for \ i \in I_4$ be of level n. Then*

$$SC_i \overset{*}{\equiv} FC_i B_i^{e_n} \ (\mathcal{P}_n), \text{ for } i \in I_4.$$

Proof. The lemma can be proved in a straightforward way by induction on n (for a full proof, see [15, Lemma 6]). □

7. SEMI-THUE SYSTEMS FROM COUNTER MACHINES

In the present section, we give the basic construction on which the lower bound is based. Let $C = (Q, \delta)$ be a 3-counter machine, where $n = |Q|$ is the size of C. In defining the semi-Thue system $\mathcal{S}_C$ associated with C, we shall leave the commuting and contracting rules tacit, giving only the proper rules of $\mathcal{S}_C$ explicitly.

The alphabet of $\mathcal{S}_C$ consists of the alphabet A_n of $\mathcal{P}_n$, together with the following added symbols:

(a)   Symbols h_1, h_2, h_3 (h_1, h_2 and h_3 serve as tokens indicating the contents of the counters in the machine);

(b)   For $q \in Q$, a symbol q in the semi-Thue alphabet;

(c)   For $q \in Q$ with $\delta(q) = (q', q'', k) \in Q \times Q \times I_3$, two additional symbols q_r and q_e;

(d)   For the initial state q_0, three additional symbols q_{02}, q_{03}, q_{04};

(e)   For the accepting state q_a, three additional symbols q_{a2}, q_{a3}, q_{a4}.

All of the symbols of $\mathcal{S}_C$ which are added to $\mathcal{P}_n$ are defined to be of level n. The symbols introduced by clauses 2 to 5 will be referred to as q *symbols*. In clause 2, we identify the symbols q with the corresponding states of the machine, so that we can write $q \in Q$, for example. In the last three cases, where new q symbols are added to the alphabet of $\mathcal{S}_C$, we associate the new q symbols with states in Q as follows: the symbol q_r has associated with it the state q, the symbol q_e the state q', the symbols q_{0i} the state q_0, and the symbols q_{ai} the state q_a.

The semi-Thue system $\mathcal{S}_C$ contains the following proper productions:

1.   All equivalences of $\mathcal{P}_n$;

2.   For $q \in Q$, with $\delta(q) = (q', d, k) \in Q \times \{0, \pm1\} \times I_3$:

   (a) $q \longrightarrow q'$ if $d = 0$
   (b) $qB_k \longrightarrow q'h_k$ if $d = 1$
   (c) $qh_k \longrightarrow q'B_k$ if $d = -1$

3.   For $q \in Q$ with $\delta(q) = (q', q'', k) \in Q \times Q \times I_3$:

   (a) $qh_k \longrightarrow q''h_k$
   (b) $q \longrightarrow q_r F C_k$
   (c) $q_r SC_k \longrightarrow q_e SC_k$
   (d) $q_e F C_k \longrightarrow q'$

4.   For q_0, the initial state of C,

   (a) $q_{02} F C_1 \longrightarrow q_{03} S C_2$
   (b) $q_{03} F C_2 \longrightarrow q_{04} S C_3$
   (c) $q_{04} F C_3 \longrightarrow q_0$

5.   For q_a, the accepting state of C,

   (a) $q_a \longrightarrow q_{a4} F C_3$
   (b) $q_{a4} S C_3 \longrightarrow q_{a3} F C_2$
   (c) $q_{a3} S C_2 \longrightarrow q_{a2} F C_1$.

The symbols belonging to $\mathcal{P}_n$ in the foregoing productions are all of level n. This completes the description of $\mathcal{S}_C$.

8. BASIC LEMMAS

The present section contains some unavoidable calculations. The purpose of these calculations is simple: to ensure that the productions corresponding to the zero-test capability of the 3-counter machine C work as intended, and that the number of occurrences of h_k, $k \in I_3$, never exceeds e_n. To accomplish this, it is necessary to define a number of numerical invariants.

So far, we have followed the development of Mayr and Meyer in [15] more or less literally. However, in proving the basic lemmas, we are compelled to diverge from their approach. Lemmas 7 and 8 of [15], which correspond to the lemmas of the present section, are syntactical in nature. However, this syntactical approach is not easy to use in the presence of the contraction rule.

To gain control over the problem, we need to define functions which assign values to the symbols in the words of $\mathcal{S}_C$. Symbols of different levels are assigned different values, because a single symbol of a higher level can be converted by the rules into a very large number of symbols of a lower level. We shall use the notation $\Phi(\alpha, \sigma)$ for the number of occurrences of symbol σ in the word α.

First, we define a function V_m^i on words of $\mathcal{S}_C$, where $-1 \leq m \leq n$ and $i \in I_4$. The function is defined by induction on m. $V_{-1}^i(\alpha) = 0$ for all $i \in I_4$. For $m \geq 0$, if the level m symbol $C_i \notin \alpha$ then $V_m^i(\alpha) = \Phi(\alpha, B_i)$; if the level m symbol $C_i \in \alpha$ then

$$V_m^i(\alpha) = \Phi(\alpha, B_i) + e_m \cdot \Phi(\alpha, S) + e_{m-1} \cdot V_{m-1}^1(\alpha) + V_{m-1}^2(\alpha),$$

where B_i and S are of level m.

Define the *height* $h(\alpha)$ of a word α of $\mathcal{S}_C$ as:

$$h(\alpha) = min\{m \in N : \Phi(\alpha, \sigma) > 0 \text{ for some } \sigma \text{ of level } m\}.$$

A word α of $\mathcal{S}_C$ is defined to be a *machine word* if it contains exactly one q symbol, which belongs to Q, $h(\alpha) = n$, and α contains no occurrences of F, S or C_i, $i \in I_4$. A word α of $\mathcal{S}_C$ is defined to be *regular* if it contains exactly one q symbol, and is either a machine word, or satisfies the conditions:

(1)   The q symbol is not in Q;

(2) $\sum_{i=1}^4 \Phi(\alpha, C_i) = \begin{cases} 1 & \text{if } C_1, \ldots, C_4 \text{ are of level } m, \\ & h(\alpha) \le m \le n, \\ 0 & \text{otherwise;} \end{cases}$

(3) $\Phi(\alpha, s) + \Phi(\alpha, f) = \begin{cases} 1 & \text{if } s, f \text{ are of level } h(\alpha) \\ 0 & \text{otherwise;} \end{cases}$

(4)   For $m < n$,

$$e_m \cdot V_m^1(\alpha) + V_m^2(\alpha) + V_m^3(\alpha) + e_m \cdot V_m^4(\alpha) \le e_{m+1}.$$

LEMMA 7.   *If $\alpha \xRightarrow{*} \beta$ $(\mathcal{S}_C)$, and α is regular, then β is regular.*

Proof. We begin by considering the equivalences in $\mathcal{P}_n$. If α is a machine word, then none of the productions in $\mathcal{P}_n$ can be applied, so we may assume that α satisfies the conditions (1) to (4). Since the rules of $\mathcal{P}_n$ leave the q symbol invariant, condition (1) is preserved.

In proving invariance for conditions (2) to (4), we shall consider the application of a production to a regular word α, which contains a symbol C_i of height $k = h(\alpha)$; the result of the production is β. If the production applied belongs to $\mathcal{P}_m$, and $V_m^i(\alpha) = V_m^i(\beta)$, for $i \in I_4$, then $V_j^i(\alpha) = V_j^i(\beta)$ for all j, $m \le j \le n$, since the production does not alter symbols of level above m.

For the rules in $\mathcal{P}_0$, it is easy to see that $V_0^i(\alpha) = V_0^i(\beta)$, $i \in I_4$, hence $V_m^i(\alpha) = V_m^i(\beta)$, for all m, $0 \le m \le n$.

We now consider the case where β is derived from α by a rule in $\mathcal{P}_m$, where $m > 0$.

If the rule applied is (a) $S \longrightarrow sc_1$, then by (3), α contains no symbols of level less than k, so that $V_{k-1}^1(\beta) = e_{k-1}$, hence $V_k^i(\alpha) = V_k^i(\beta)$, so that $V_m^j(\alpha) = V_m^j(\beta)$, for all $j \in I_4$, $m \ge k$. Hence, the conditions (2) – (4) are preserved.

If the rule applied is the converse production $sc_1 \longrightarrow S$, then $V_k^1(\alpha) \ge e_k$, hence by (4), $V_k^2(\alpha) = V_k^3(\alpha) = V_k^4(\alpha) = 0$. Thus, s and c_1 are the only symbols of level $h(\alpha)$, showing that (2) and (3) are preserved. Since $V^i_{k+1}(\alpha) = V^i_{k+1}(\beta)$, condition (4) is also preserved.

If the rule applied is one of the equivalences (b) – (e) or (g–j) then the level is invariant, and it is clear that conditions (2) and (3) are preserved. Since the rules in question alter only symbols of level $h(\alpha)$ or $h(\alpha) + 1$, it is sufficient to show that in each case the sum

$$e_j \cdot V^1_j(\alpha) + V^2_j(\alpha) + V^3_j(\alpha) + e_j \cdot V^4_j(\alpha)$$

for $j = k, k + 1$ is left fixed by these productions. This verification is an easy exercise, and is omitted.

If the production applied is (f) $sc_4 \longrightarrow F$, then, arguing as for the rule (a), the left-hand side of the production contains the only symbols of level $h(\alpha)$, so (2) and (3) are preserved, and clearly (4) is also preserved. If the production is the converse $F \longrightarrow sc_4$, then (2) and (3) are preserved, since F must be of level $h(\alpha)$, and condition (4) is also preserved. This completes the proof for the rules of $\mathcal{P}_n$.

In the case of the remaining productions 2(a) – 5(a), α must be either a machine word, or a word of level n, and it is easy to see from the form of the rules that regularity is preserved. □

LEMMA 8. *If α is regular and $\alpha \overset{*}{\Longrightarrow} \beta$ $(\mathcal{P}_m)$, then $V^i_m(\alpha) = V^i_m(\beta)$, for $i \in I_4, m \leq n$.*

Proof. The rules of $\mathcal{P}_m$ alter only symbols of level m or lower, so that to prove the conclusion of the lemma it is sufficient to show that $V^i_m(\alpha) = V^i_m(\beta)$, for all $i \in I_4$. The lemma is proved by induction on m.

For $m = 0$, the lemma follows immediately by the definition of V^i_0. Let $m > 0$. By induction hypothesis, we may assume that the production applied belongs to $\mathcal{P}_m \setminus \mathcal{P}_{m-1}$. If the production applied is (a) $S \longrightarrow sc_1$, then since α is regular, $h(\alpha) = m$. The equality $V^i_m(\alpha) = V^i_m(\beta)$ follows by definition. If the converse production $sc_1 \longrightarrow S$ is used, then by Lemma 7, β is regular, hence $h(\beta) = m$, so the equality again follows. If the production used is (f), then the word containing F has height m, and the value of V^i_m is not altered by the application of the production.

In the remaining cases, $h(\alpha) = h(\beta) = m - 1$, by regularity; the equation $V^i_m(\alpha) = V^i_m(\beta)$ is readily checked from the definition. □

We now define functions W^i, for $i \in I_3$:

$$W^1(\alpha) = V^1_n(\alpha) + \Phi(\alpha, h_1),$$
$$W^2(\alpha) = V^2_n(\alpha) + \Phi(\alpha, h_2) + e_n(\Phi(\alpha, q_{02}) + \Phi(\alpha, q_{a2})),$$
$$W^3(\alpha) = V^3_n(\alpha) + \Phi(\alpha, h_3) + e_n(\Phi(\alpha, q_{02}) + \Phi(\alpha, q_{03}) + \Phi(\alpha, q_{a2}) + \Phi(\alpha, q_{a3})).$$

LEMMA 9. *If* $\alpha \stackrel{*}{\Longrightarrow} \beta$ *($\mathcal{S}_C$), and α is regular, then* $W^i(\alpha) \geq W^i(\beta)$, *for* $i \in I_3$.

Proof. For the rules of $\mathcal{P}_n$, this follows from the previous lemma. For the rules which correspond to the rules of the counter machine C, the lemma is easy to check. Finally, since the value of W^i is monotone in the number of occurrences of symbols in a word, it is clear that the contraction rule can never increase the value $W^i(\alpha)$. □

Let α be a regular word in $\mathcal{S}_C$. Define the *state associated with* α, $state(\alpha)$, to be the state associated with the q symbol occurring in α. We associate with α an instantaneous description $D(\alpha)$, defined as follows:

$$D(\alpha) = (state(\alpha), \Phi(\alpha, h_1), \Phi(\alpha, h_2), \Phi(\alpha, h_3)).$$

LEMMA 10. *If* $q_{02}SC_1 = \alpha_0 \Rightarrow \cdots \Rightarrow \alpha_k = q_{a2}SC_1$ *is a derivation in* $\mathcal{S}_C$:

(1)   *For every* i, $0 \leq i < k$, *either* $D(\alpha_i) = D(\alpha_{i+1})$ *or* $D(\alpha_{i+1})$ *is derived from* $D(\alpha_i)$ *by a transition of* C;

(2) $\Phi(\alpha_i, h_j) \leq e_n$ *for all* $j \in I_3$.

Proof. First, observe that for $i \in I_3$, $W^i(q_{02}SC_1) = W^i(q_{a2}SC_1) = e_n$. It follows by Lemma 9 that for $i \in I_3$, $0 \leq j \leq k$, $W^i(\alpha_j) = e_n$, so that (2) follows immediately.

It is not hard to see that (1) holds for the rules of $\mathcal{S}_C$, with the possible exception of the productions corresponding to the zero-test capability of the counter machine, that is, the four productions 3(a) to 3(d) in the definition of $\mathcal{S}_C$. The crucial case is the production 3(c). If $\alpha_i \Rightarrow \alpha_{i+1}$ by this production, then $V_n^k(\alpha_i) = V_n^k(\alpha_{i+1}) = e_n$, hence $\Phi(\alpha_i, h_k) = \Phi(\alpha_{i+1}, h_k) = 0$. Thus condition (1) holds in this case.   □

THEOREM 1. *For a 3-counter machine* C,

$$C \in ESC \text{ if and only if } q_{02}SC_1 \stackrel{*}{\Longrightarrow} q_{a2}SC_1 \ (\mathcal{S}_C)$$

Proof. The implication holds left to right by the construction of $\mathcal{S}_C$, as can be easily verified. The implication holds right to left by Lemma 10.   □

THEOREM 2. (1) *The decision problem for* $R_{\rightarrow \wedge o}$ *is exponential space hard with respect to log-lin reducibility;* (2) *There is a constant* $c > 1$ *so that any Turing machine solving the decision problem for* $R_{\rightarrow \wedge o}$ *must use space* c^n *for infinitely many inputs of length* n.

Proof. The construction of the formula $\Psi(\mathcal{S}_C, q_{02}SC_1, q_{a2}SC_1)$ can be carried out in log-space, and its size is $O(size(C))$. The first part of the theorem now follows immediately from Lemma 5, Lemma 3 and Theorem 1. The second part follows from Lemma 4.   □

The preceding theorem shows that the decision problem for $R_{\to\wedge\circ}$ is very intractable. This intractability remains even if unlimited parallel processing is available as a computational resource. Let us represent the characteristic function of the set of theorems of $R_{\to\wedge\circ}$ as a family of Boolean functions, by encoding the formulas of $R_{\to\wedge\circ}$ as binary strings, and defining f_n to be the characteristic function of the set of theorems restricted to formulas having encodings of length n. Then a simple diagonal argument (see Wegener [23, pp. 140–141]) establishes that for infinitely many n, the number of logic gates in the smallest circuit computing f_n is bounded below by a function which is exponential in n.

9. OTHER LOGICS

In proving the lower bound, we made use of the constant t and the fusion operator $\circ$. However, the lower bound proved above also holds for the system $R_{\to\wedge}$. This system contains only the implication and conjunction connectives, and is axiomatized by omitting the axiom schemes 9 and 10 from $R_{\to\wedge\circ}$, and replacing the first two axiom schemes by the scheme $A \to A$.

To extend the lower bound to $R_{\to\wedge}$, we need to define an embedding of $R_{\to\wedge\circ}$ into $R_{\to\wedge}$ which reduces the first decision problem to the second. More precisely, we shall define a translation from the formulas of $R_{\to\wedge\circ}$ into the formulas of $R_{\to\wedge}$ which constitutes a log-lin reduction of the decision problem for $R_{\to\wedge\circ}$ to the decision problem for $R_{\to\wedge}$.

Let A be a formula of $R_{\to\wedge\circ}$, and let P_t and P_f be propositional variables not occurring in A. Define $\neg B$ as $(B \to P_f)$ and $(B \circ' C)$ as $\neg(B \to \neg C)$. Let A' be the result of replacing t by P_t and the operator $\circ$ by the defined operator $\circ'$. Then define $Trans(A)$ to be:

$$\bigwedge\{(\neg\neg P \to P)\wedge(P_t \to .P \to P) : P \text{ a variable in } A'\} \wedge P_t. \to .A'.$$

LEMMA 11.   If A is a formula of $R_{\to\wedge\circ}$, then $R_{\to\wedge\circ}\vdash A$ if and only if $R_{\to\wedge}\vdash Trans(A)$.

Proof. Assume that $R_{\to\wedge\circ}\vdash A$. Then A has a derivation in $R_{\to\wedge\circ}$ that contains only variables which occur in A. We can show by induction on the length of this derivation that if B is a formula in the derivation, then $Trans(B)$ is provable in $R_{\to\wedge}$. This is a straightforward exercise in the axiomatics of relevance logics; the details are left to the reader.

Conversely, assume that $R_{\to\wedge}\vdash Trans(A)$. Then $Trans(A)$ is provable in the full system R, with $\circ$, t and f as primitive symbols. Consider the formula which results from $Trans(A)$ by substituting t for P_t and f for P_f throughout. The antecedent of this formula is provable in R, hence the consequent is also provable in R. But the consequent is provably equivalent to A in R, since $(B \circ C)$ and $(B \to .C \to f) \to f$ are equivalent in R. Hence A is provable in R, and so $R_{\to\wedge\circ}\vdash A$, since R is a conservative extension of $R_{\to\wedge\circ}$.   □

With a little more work, we can extend the lower bound to $R_\rightarrow$, the pure implicational fragment of R. The only occurrences of conjunction in the formula $\Psi(S, \gamma, \delta)$ defined above are those displayed in the antecedent. If F is a set of formulas of $R_\rightarrow$, then $\bigwedge F \rightarrow A$ is provable in $R_{\rightarrow \wedge}$ if and only if a formula of the form $A_1 \rightarrow .A_2 \rightarrow \cdots A_k \rightarrow A$ is provable in $R_\rightarrow$, where $\{A_1, \cdots, A_k\} \subseteq F$. Using this observation, we can reduce the problem ESC to the decision problem for $R_\rightarrow$. In this case, the reduction does not belong to log-space, because there are exponentially many formulas to check for provability in general. However, the formulas are all of size $O(C)$, where C is the given 3-counter machine, so that the lower bound extends to $R_\rightarrow$ as well.

It is possible by means of appropriate translations to extend the lower bound to fragments of other relevance logics. R. K. Meyer and S. Giambrone [17] define an efficient embedding from the positive fragment of R into the positive fragment of the system of ticket entailment T ([4, p. 41f]). An examination of the embedding shows it to be a log-lin reduction of the decision problem for $R_{\rightarrow \wedge}$ to the decision problem for the implication-conjunction fragment of T. Since this constitutes a reduction to a proper subsystem of $R_{\rightarrow \wedge}$, we can state a general result.

THEOREM 3. *The decision problem for the implication-conjunction fragment of any logic intermediate between T and R is exponential space hard under log-lin reducibility.*

10. THE STRICT λ-CALCULUS

It is well known that valid schemes of implicational logic can be identified with the types of certain combinators ([7, pp. 312–315]). We can use this correspondence to transfer the lower bound to the appropriate form of the λ-calculus.

We consider the typed λI-calculus, formulated with infinitely many ground types $O_1, \cdots, O_n, \cdots$ (see Hindley and Seldin [9] for details). The restriction to λI-terms means that a term $\lambda x.F$ is well formed only if F contains a free occurrence of the variable x. If we correlate the variables of $R_\rightarrow$ bijectively with the ground types, then any implicational formula can be identified with a type, by interpreting $(A \rightarrow B)$ as the family of all functions from A into B.

THEOREM 4. *The problem of determining of an arbitrary type whether it is the type of a closed term of the λI-calculus is exponential space hard.*

Proof. It follows by the correspondence described by Curry and Feys [7] (see also Howard [11]) that for any type A, there is a closed term of type A if and only if A is provable in $R_\rightarrow$. $\square$

This result may be compared with the corresponding problem for the typed λ-calculus; this decision problem is polynomial-space complete (Statman [20]).

11. AN UPPER BOUND

In this final section, we discuss briefly the problem of providing an upper bound on the complexity of the decision problem for $R_{\to \wedge 0}$. The large gap between the upper and lower bounds is evidence of how far we are from a real understanding of the true complexity of these problems.

Ackermann's function is the function defined by Ackermann in 1928 [1] which eventually dominates any primitive recursive function.

THEOREM 5. *Kripke's decision procedure for $R_{\to \wedge 0}$ is primitive recursive in the Ackermann function.*

Proof. The decision procedure for $R_{\to \wedge 0}$ is described in [21, pp. 30–39](see also [4, pp. 136–139]). The fundamental strategy is to construct a proof search tree for a Gentzen-style formulation of $R_{\to \wedge 0}$, and then to show that in each case, the tree is finite.

The key lemma of Kripke which shows the tree to be finite ([4, pp. 138–139]) is essentially the same as the argument used in 1968 by Karp and Miller [12] to show that the reachability tree of a vector addition system (equivalently, Petri net or commutative semi-Thue system) is finite. McAloon in [14] analyses the lemma using non-standard models of arithmetic, and thereby provides an upper bound on the size of the reachability tree of a vector addition system. This bound is primitive recursive in the Ackermann function.

Because of the essential identity of the Kripke lemma and the Karp/Miller lemma, McAloon's arguments adapt directly to show that the size of the proof search tree is also primitive recursive in the Ackermann function. The procedure which consists in examining the proof search tree to see if it contains a proof of the given formula is primitive recursive in the size of the tree, so the bound holds for the entire procedure.   □

Although the lower bound proved above certainly shows the decision problem for $R_{\to \wedge 0}$ to be very intractable, the huge gap between upper and lower bounds is far from satisfactory. Which bound is closer to the truth?

Kripke in a letter of 1981 to Michael McRobbie is quoted ([21, p. 40]) as conjecturing that the decidability proof is unprovable in elementary recursive arithmetic. If this is so, then the upper bound may be closer to the truth than the lower bound; this seems quite appropriate, since it was Ackermann who not only invented the famous function, but also in his basic 1956 paper [2] founded the theory of entailment.

ACKNOWLEDGMENTS

I first discussed these problems in 1982 with Paul Thistlewaite, to whom I wish to express my thanks for his very stimulating conversation. It was Alan Ross Anderson and Nuel Belnap who taught me how to do logic. Thank you, Alan! Thank you, Nuel!

BIBLIOGRAPHY

[1] Ackermann, W. (1928): 'Zum Hilbertschen Aufbau der reellen Zahlen', *Mathematische Annalen* 99, pp. 118–133.

[2] Ackermann, W. (1956): 'Begründung einer strengen Implikation', *Journal of Symbolic Logic* 21, pp. 113–128.

[3] Anderson, A.R. and Belnap, N.D. Jr. (1958): 'A modication of Ackermann's 'rigorous implication.' *The journal of symbolic logic* 23, pp. 457–458. Abstract.

[4] Anderson, A.R. and Belnap, N.D. Jr. (1975): *Entailment: The Logic of Relevance and Necessity, Vol. 1*. Princeton University Press, New Jersey.

[5] Belnap, N.D. Jr. and Wallace, J.R. (1965): 'A Decision Procedure for the System E_I of Entailment with Negation' *Zeitschrift für mathematische Logik und Grundlagen der Mathematik* 11, pp. 277–289.

[6] Church, A. (1956): *Introduction to Mathematical Logic*. Princeton University Press, New Jersey.

[7] Curry, H.B. and Feys, R. (1968): *Combinatory Logic, Vol. 1*. North-Holland Publishing Company, Amsterdam.

[8] Fischer, P.C., Meyer, A.R., Rosenberg, A.L. (1968): 'Counter Machines and Counter Languages', *Mathematical Systems Theory* 2, pp. 265–283.

[9] Hindley, J.R. and Seldin, J.P. (1986): *Introduction to Combinators and λ-calculus*. Cambridge University Press, Cambridge.

[10] Hopcroft, J.E. and Ullmann, J.D. (1979): *Introduction to Automata Theory, Languages and Computation* Addison-Wesley Publishing Company, Reading, Massachusetts.

[11] Howard, W. 'The formulae-as-types notion of construction' in *To H. B. Curry, Essays on Combinatory Logic, Lambda Calculus and Formalism*, ed. by Hindley and Seldin, Academic Press, New York and London, pp. 479–490.

[12] Karp, R.M. and Miller, R. E. (1969): 'Parallel program schemata' *Journal of Computer and System Sciences* 3, pp. 147–195.

[13] Kripke, S. A. (1959): 'The Problem of Entailment', *Journal of Symbolic Logic* 24, p. 324. Abstract.

[14] McAloon, K. (1984): 'Petri nets and large finite sets', *Theoretical Computer Science* 32, pp. 173–183.

[15] Mayr, E. and Meyer, A. (1982): 'The Complexity of the Word Problems for Commutative Semigroups and Polynomial Ideals', *Advances in Mathematics* 46, pp. 305–329.

[16] Meyer, R.K. (1966): *Topics in Modal and Many-Valued Logic*. PhD thesis, University of Pittsburgh, Pennsylvania.

[17] Meyer, R.K. and Giambrone, S. (1980): 'R_+ is contained in T_+', *Bulletin of the Section of Logic, Polish Academy of Sciences* 9 (March 1980), pp. 30–32.

[18] Meyer, R.K. and Routley, R. (1973): 'An Undecidable Relevant Logic' *Zeitschrift für mathematische Logik und Grundlagen der Mathematik* 19, pp. 389–397.

[19] Routley, R. and Meyer, R.K. (1973): 'The Semantics of Entailment I', in Leblanc, H. (editor), *Truth, Syntax and Modality*. North Holland, Amsterdam.

[20] Statman, R. (1979): 'Intuitionistic propositional logic is polynomial-space complete' *Theoretical Computer Science* 9, pp. 67–72.

[21] Thistlewaite, P.B., McRobbie, M.A. and Meyer, R.K. (1988): *Automated Theorem-Proving in Non-Classical Logics*. Pitman, London; Wiley, New York and Toronto.

[22] Urquhart, A. (1984): 'The undecidability of entailment and relevant implication', *Journal of Symbolic Logic* 49, pp. 1059–1073.

[23] Wegener, I. (1987): *The Complexity of Boolean Functions*. B.G. Teubner, Stuttgart; John Wiley and Sons, Chichester.

J. MICHAEL DUNN

RELEVANT PREDICATION 3: ESSENTIAL PROPERTIES[1]

1. Introduction. I owe much to my thesis director Nuel Belnap, but I wonder if I can blame him for my recent idealist tendencies. The novelist Colin Wilson (1967) has a theory of ideas as infectious agents, much like viruses and needing hosts. It is interesting to speculate how the idealist infection was transmitted from Blanshard to Anderson and Belnap at Yale, and from them to me as their graduate student at Pittsburgh. Perhaps rather than being an infectious disease it is a hereditary one, linked in some complicated way with the intellectual genes for relevance logic, Platonism, and logical humor.

2. Background on Relevant Predication. In Dunn (1987) a certain definition of "relevant predication" was given in the context of first-order relevance logic with identity, and its formal properties were explored. This paper builds on that, but is more directly a continuation of Dunn (1990), which applied that theory to notions of intrinsic properties and internal relations. We here develop the idea that an essential property is not merely a necessary one, but also a relevant one (whether necessarily relevant, or relevantly necessary, is a subtlety to be explored). This idea can be exploited to solve a puzzle which will be raised about a certain asymmetry in essential relational properties.

But first we discuss the central definition of Dunn (1987) (carrying over the numbering to facilitate comparison), taking the opportunity to try to motivate it from a slightly different angle than previously.

(11) $(\rho x \varphi x)a =_{df} \forall x(x = a \rightarrow \varphi x)$ (Relevant Predication)

(This is read in "middle English" as "a relevantly has the property of being such an x that φx.")

The intuitive idea behind this definition can be grasped by contraposing it (quantifiers are dropped for visual clarity[2]). For relevant predication, we then have

$(11')$ $\sim \varphi x \rightarrow x \neq a.$

One way to think of this is that if an object failed to satisfy φ, it would on that account alone fail to be a. Metaphysically speaking, this invites us to consider what kind of a change φ makes in an object, *i.e.*, supposing that a is φ, then if any object (including a) were to fail to be φ, then on that account alone the object would be different from a.

---

[1] I will not repeat here all of the acknowledgements made in Dunn (1987, 1990), but many of those same people continue to have an effect on the present paper. Also I want to thank my new colleague Anil Gupta for some very helpful conversations.

[2] Throughout this paper individual symbols such as x, y, a, b are to be regarded as universally quantified in displayed formulas, unless clear indication is given to the contrary, as in secs. 3 and 4, where a and b are occasionally permitted to be definite descriptions.

J. M. Dunn and A. Gupta (eds.), Truth or Consequences, 77–95.
© 1990 *Kluwer Academic Publishers. Printed in the Netherlands.*

One's first reaction is that the change must be rather radical to assure that the difference in question is non-identity with a. If the difference in question had been mere "qualitative difference" one might say that φ is an intrinsic property, but not necessarily an essential one. But one is tempted to say that if the difference is numerical non-identity, then the property φ must be an essential one, for its loss produces a total disruption of the nature of the object in question. Natural though this temptation is, it is wrong, and the reason is that the kind of implication that $\rightarrow$ stands for is mere (contingent) relevant implication, not entailment (which also has the feature of necessity).

In symbols, what we are talking about is

(+) $\varphi a \rightarrow (\sim \varphi x \rightarrow x \neq a)$.

The thought is that if as a matter of mere contingent fact, a is φ, then as another matter of mere contingent fact, if x fails to be φ, then (relevantly) x fails to be identical to a. The non-identity of x with a does not follow with necessity from the fact that x fails to be φ, but derives from the contingent fact that a happens to be φ. This is just a version of the Indiscernibility of Identicals, and indeed if the formula above is contraposed in its consequent (a move valid in standard relevance logics), we get the following formula, which in Dunn (1987) was said to state that φ is *a formula of the kind that determines relevant properties.*

(*II*) $\varphi a \rightarrow (x = a \rightarrow \varphi x)$ (Relevant Property as a Kind).

This is even more clearly a version of the Indiscernibility of Identicals.

In that paper it was also shown that if φ is a formula of the kind that determines relevant properties, then so *is* $\sim \varphi$ (permute $x = a$ to the front, contrapose, reletter, and permute back). Thus we have this "negative" instance of (*II*):

(*NII*) $\sim \varphi a \rightarrow (x = a \rightarrow \sim \varphi x)$.

From (*NII*) we can get by contraposition (and double negation)

(−) $\sim \varphi a \rightarrow (\varphi x \rightarrow x \neq a)$.

The principles (+) and (−) (which are actually each equivalent to (*II*), as we have just seen) jointly say that φ "makes a difference" to an object. If a happens to be φ, then if an object fails to satisfy φ then on that count alone it fails to be a; and if a happens not to be φ, then if an object satisfies φ then on that count alone it fails to be a.

Things get more complicated when we consider a formula φ with two free variables x and y. This was explained in Dunn (1987) with reference to different versions of the Indiscernibility of Identicals. The issues are whether one has indiscernibility with respect to the x position, the y position, or both. And if this last, a further issue is whether the identity statements are nested:

$\varphi ab \rightarrow (x = a \rightarrow (y = b \rightarrow \varphi xy))$ (Relevant Relation as a Kind),

or conjoined:

$\varphi ab \rightarrow ((x = a \wedge y = b) \rightarrow \varphi xy)$ (Relevant Property of a Pair as a Kind).

If one has indiscernibility with respect to say the x position, Dunn (1987) spoke of a "relevant relational property," and similarly with respect to the y position. Facts 6 and 7 of Dunn (1987) combine to show that a formula φxy is of a kind that determines relevant relations iff it is of a kind that determines relevant relational properties in both the x and y positions. The issue of conjoined identities versus nested ones is a logical subtlety best understood by the initiates into relevance logic, but this last result gives us a metaphysical handle. Incidentally, I now think it is a mistake to speak of "relational properties" when indiscernibility is satisfied with respect to say just x (and not y). One should better speak say of "pseudo-relational properties" (because there is no relation, at least no relevant one). But I shall continue to speak of "relational properties" when indiscernibility is satisfied with respect to either position, reserving the epithet "pseudo" to make clear when we are talking of a case in which it is satisfied with respect to just one position.

We now have two different objects to which the formula φxy can "make a difference." There are the following alternatives.

Makes a difference to:

i) A specific one (only) of a and b: Relevant Pseudo-Relational Property.

ii) Each of a and b : Relevant Relation.

iii) One of a and b, but not a specific one: Relevant Property of a Pair.

iv) Neither of a or b : "External Relation."

The first three may be viewed as various species of "internal relation." The "relation" can reside in a particular one of a or b, or it can reside in each, or it can reside in the pair. The distinction between ii) and iii) is rather subtle when expressed in ordinary language. One is tempted to say in both instances that the "relation" resides in both, or in the pair, but in the case of ii) it resides distributively, and in the case of iii) it resides collectively.

Let us try to illustrate these with some relatively simple examples. These examples presuppose an ontology wherein spatial location is not an intrinsic property of an object, but rather consists of relations among objects (or is perhaps an intrinsic property of space). Further it presupposes a common sense physics wherein certain objects (e.g., those made of steel) are quite hard, with ordinary external contact not deforming them, whereas on the other hand some objects (e.g., those made of foam rubber) are easily penetrated and deformed, but perfectly resilient, returning to their shape once contact is removed.

Let us suppose then that we have two objects a and b, and that we somehow want to connect them. The weakest way would be to find some third item c, and use it to connect them in such a way that the objects a and b remain unchanged. This might be done for example by merely laying them down side by side on a table, or by tying them together with a string. Or supposing for a moment that a and b are steel pins, we might stick them both in the same foam rubber pin cushion. All of these produce no change in either a or b, and so should be considered mere external relations.

Suppose now that a is a steel pin, but that b is foam rubber pin cushion. One can connect them by poking a into b, and b is modified but not a (and also when they are disconnected and the hole in b vanishes under our hypothesis of perfect resiliency[3]). This is an example of a relevant pseudo-relational property.

Suppose again that both a and b are pins, and that one chooses to join them together by welding, thus intermingling their substance. This would produce a change in both a and b, and would be an example of a relevant (or "real") relation.

For some reason I have found it more difficult to come up with a familiar example from "the world of fasteners" to illustrate the notion of a relevant property of a pair. One has to tell a little bit of a story, which suggests that possibly there is still room for someone to make a lot of money by inventing a new kind of fastening system and finding the right application for it. More likely such a system already exists in some specialized application, and I would appreciate any reader who knows of such telling me about it.[4] One idea that comes to mind in this area is to make objects which are a combination of a pin cushion and pin, something like a thumb tack with a large foam area where the head usually is. Given two such objects a and b, they could then be connected together by inserting the pin part of a into the cushion part of b, or (and this is the important part) *vice versa*. If two objects are thus connected (or disconnected), one of a and b must change, but not a specific one. A property of the pair changes, but not necessarily a property of a specific item in the pair.

Another example of a relevant property of pairs, though it does not use literal fasteners, is the colors that the two objects have, say that *a is red and b is green*. In such a case one could "connect them", at least conceptually, by choosing to paint them both the same color, and (putting aside practical problems with which paint stores try to deal) one could do this by changing the color of either one.to match the other (and one could equally break the connection by changing the color of either one).

It was argued in Dunn (1990) that the doctrine of internal relations is best understood in many of its important variants as expressing the thought that at

---

[3] Remember that the foam rubber is postulated as truly resilient, so once the pin is pulled out it will return to its natural shape leaving no sign of the hole. This parenthetical material is important, since, as was made clear in the discussion above about the principle $(-)$ in the unary case, negative change is just as important as positive change. Coming to have the property should make a difference, but coming to lose it should just as well.

[4] My research assistant Monica Holland believes that she remembers from her childhood that the deluxe Tinker Toy sets came with some sticks that had the round pieces with holes permanently attached. Taking two of those, one then has a choice of how to join them. To make the story complete, one must remember that the ends of Tinker Toy sticks are split, so that the two sides of the split are pressed towards each other when one puts the stick in the hole. And one must imagine that the sides of the hole are not affected at all. Then when two such pieces are joined, the "stick" piece changes, while the "hole" piece does not, and either piece can be the "stick" piece or the "hole" piece.

least certain important relations reside "intrinsically" in their objects, and that this intrinsicality can be given formal expression using appropriate notions of relevant predication. It was argued that in the monadic case, assuming an ideal language, intrinsicality consists in the predicate modifying its argument (and nothing else since it is monadic). But in the dyadic case, there are various things one can mean by "intrinsicality," depending on whether one sees the predicate as modifying only a single position (relevant pseudo-relational property), each of both positions (relevant relation), or the pair (relevant property of the pair). Of course it was typical of the most radical wing of the tradition to argue that all (or at least all important) so-called relations are in fact internal, meaning by "internal" something like a relevant pseudo-relational property. This wing thus denies the reality of relations, stuffing a relation into but one of its terms, and thus ends up with, at the least, terms that behave much like Leibnizian monads, or perhaps even with but one term, "The Absolute."

But, as did Ewing (1934) before, I tend to think that the most reasonable sense of "internal relation" is that of Bosanquet (1888), wherein he says that "the phrase 'internal relations' seems to me to be not quite satisfactory as suggesting relations between parts within a given term. At least the view which to me appears reasonable would be better expressed by some such term as 'relevant relations', *i.e.*, relations that are connected with the properties of their terms, so that any alteration of relations involves an alteration of properties, and vice versa." This is a chilling anticipation of my notion of relevant relation, though I arrived at my notion and its connection to internal relations before I had read either Ewing or Bosanquet (hence more support for Wilson's theory of ideas as infectious diseases).

I want to make one qualification to the idea that a relevant predication involves a change in the terms. This is a nice intuitive handle on the notion, but "change" is sometimes more of a metaphor. What are we to say regarding terms that are necessarily existent and have all of their intrinsic properties necessarily (depending on your metaphysics, numbers, pure sets, properties, whatever)? Rather than "change" *per se*, in such cases we mean "modification" in its technical metaphysical sense, where attributes "modify" their subjects.

Ewing (1934) has examined ten different senses of the notion of "internal relation," and one of his preferred senses (his seventh) echoes ours. Thus he says (p. 131) "relations are internal in this sense means that, where two terms are related in some specific way, it is always true that they could not both be what they are without the relation being present." This sounds precisely like the principle of the Indiscernibility of Identicals, which we have taken to characterize relevant relations as a kind. Later (p. 133) he characterizes an actual internal relation holding between two objects a and b, saying "if 'x, y are a, b, then x and y are related by R', and from that follows—'if x and y were not related by R, then they would not be a, b,' *i.e.*, if the relations were absent both the terms could not be what they are."

Ewing has our same concern about unchangeable objects, for he says (pp. 130–131) that "this formula cannot be applied to relations between abstract universals, *e.g.*, the relation of equality between the pure number 4 and $2 + 2$, because we cannot speak of the possibility of an abstract universal being different from what it is, but only to relations between concrete terms." Clearly the problem that Ewing envisages is that his seventh sense would require (among other things) that

$$(D) \quad \sim aRb \rightarrow a \neq b.$$

But if aRb is a necessary relationship (for whatever reason—it does not really seem to matter whether a and b are abstract entities), then the above implication would hold for the usual reasons having to do with the paradox of strict implication which says that from an impossible proposition, anything follows.

But of course if we understand $\rightarrow$ as relevant implication in the sense of system **R** (or even as a strict relevant implication, or entailment in the sense of system **E**), then the formula (D) above is not trivialized just because aRb is necessary (and hence $\sim aRb$ is impossible).

To illustrate, it is proved as Fact 12 of Dunn (1987) that in R. K. Meyer's development of Relevant Peano Arithmetic, all formulas determine relevant properties and relations. The reason for this somewhat surprising result is that the formulas under discussion are all arithmetical formulas, and involve (besides logical notions) only the operations of successor, addition, and multiplication. Since the natural numbers are such a tight-knit lot (all being inductively generated from zero by successor), and since addition and multiplication are of course also traced back by axioms to successor and zero, the result is really not so mysterious. The key to the proof is the fact that one can get ("relevantly") from any natural number to any other by additions or subtractions, these last operations ultimately boiling down to successor.

3. Essential Properties. It has been fashionable, at least since Kripke (1963), (1972) to try to rehabilitate Aristotelian talk of essential properties, and connect it to modal logic. Of course, others, notably Quine (cf. *e.g.*, Quine (1956)), had earlier used this connection to say that modal logic is itself suspect. The idea put quickly is that "a has the essential property F" is to be analyzed as $\Box Fa$.

It has been noticed (cf. Marcus (1967), Parsons (1967)) that this analysis (at least if one does fine tune it with a "Chisholm") has the problem that all of us end up having many more essential properties than we might have thought. Thus, *e.g.*, Socrates not only has the property of being such that various excluded middles $Fx \lor \sim Fx$ hold of him (he is essentially either wise or not wise, a bicyclist or not a bicyclist, thought of by me or not thought of by me, etc.), but more generally, where P is any necessary truth (*e.g.*, a theorem of logic), Socrates has the property of being such that P. One might here be bothered by the fact that P need not even contain a free variable, and so not be the kind of formula that we ordinarily think of as determining a property. But one can use one of the devices mentioned in Dunn (1987) for dummying in free variables (and anyway, in classical logic, if P is a theorem it is equivalent to an arbitrary excluded middle $Fx \lor \sim Fx$). In a kind of miraculous way then each individual becomes a fount for all logical truths.

Marcus and Parsons try to discount such properties as in some obvious sense trivial, and they give other, more complicated definitions of essential properties, but there is still the feeling that something went awry at the start. Much can be gained by analyzing essential predication along the lines of necessary relevant predication (or should it be relevant necessary predication?).

It seems that it was intended by the tradition that essential properties should have an intimate connection with their bearers. They were after all supposed to be part of the very nature of their bearers. It seems paradoxical at best to say that besides humanity being a part of the nature of Socrates, say The Binomial Theorem is as well.

One proposal then is to analyze essential predication as

(*) $(\eta x\,\varphi x)a =_{df} \Box((\rho x\,\varphi x)a)$ (necessary relevant)[5].

Another proposal would be to analyze it as

(**) $(\eta x\,\varphi x)a =_{df} (\rho x\Box\,\varphi x)a$ (relevant necessary).

A third proposal, subtly different from each of the above, is to analyze relevant predication in the standard way, but to plug in the Anderson-Belnap entailment connective $\Rightarrow$ *in* place of their relevant implication connective $\rightarrow$. Thus where $\Rightarrow$ *is* entailment in the Anderson-Belnap system **E** we might define

(***) $(\eta x\,\varphi x)a =_{df} \forall x(x = a \Rightarrow \varphi x)$.

When contraposed, this has the form of G.E. Moore's (1922) definition of an internal relation as discussed in Dunn (1990) (identifying an internal relation with one that determines essential relational properties, as clearly seems to be Moore's intent), but of course Moore had in mind what we now call "strict implication."[6]

These definitions do not exactly amount to the same, for two somewhat subtle reasons. In the first place, Maksimova (1973) has shown that there is a problem in construing entailment in **E** as necessary relevant implication in **R**. My present mood is to think that given the subtle divergence of entailment from necessary relevant implication, the safest course is to put the definition (***) in terms of the arrow of **E** on the shelf, and understand it here as defined so that $\varphi \Rightarrow \psi$ is $\Box(\varphi \rightarrow \psi)$. Even then the formulas (*), (**), and (***) are still all non-equivalent.

In order to motivate the second reason, we must digress for a moment and discuss "the Barcan effect." It is well known from modal logic that the following two formulas are not always equivalent:

---

[5] One would like to use ϵ here (for "essential"), but Hilbert has already adopted it for his "indefinite description" operator. The use of η is a kind of "pun" based on its pronunciation ("eta," which almost picks up the "*e''*" sound of both "essential" and "entailment") and its appearance (it looks like an "*n,''*" which picks up both "nature" and "necessity").

[6] Though as Dunn (1990) points out, this may in large part be due to the poverty of logical technology at Moore's disposal then, and various discussions in Moore (1962) show that Moore did have some problems with the notion of entailment as strict implication.

(□∀) □∀x φx

(∀□) ∀x □φx.

Although in the modal logic S5 as usually formulated proof-theoretically (with a rule of generalization), they co-imply each other, it is not true in say S4 and weaker systems that (∀□) implies (□∀) (this implication is called "the Barcan formula"). Further, when the modal logic is formulated without a rule of generalization but instead takes generalizations of axioms as axioms, not even the Converse Barcan formula holds (that (□∀) implies (∀□)). It seems that one has all these options with respect to modal **R**. The system $R^\square$ has been traditionally formulated with S4 properties required of □ (cf. Anderson and Belnap (1975)), but there is no reason why one cannot play with different requirements, and some authors have. The system of first-order **R** was formulated in Meyer, Dunn, and Leblanc (1974) without a rule of generalization, but the formulation of Belnap (1967) has such a rule.

Now returning to our alternative contextual definitions of η, once we define $\varphi \Rightarrow \psi$ as $\square(\varphi \to \psi)$, then (***) amounts to

(***def) $\forall x \square (x = a \to \varphi x)$.

Further, if one works out the contextual definition of ρ in (*) and (**), one gets

(*def) $\square \forall x (x = a \to \varphi x)$, and

(**def) $\forall x (x = a \to \square \varphi x)$.

It is now clear that the three formulas above just express the different scope alternatives for □, and that the "Barcan effect" is operative , since in (*def) the quantifier is within the scope of the necessity operator, whereas in (**def) and (***def) it is the other way around. Moreover, it is easy to see that (***def) implies (**def), given the controversial assumption that true identities are necessary (distribute □ across → using a standard axiom of $R^\square$, and remove it from the antecedent by "transitizing" with the assumption in question: $x = a \to \square(x = a)$). The assumption amounts to restricting the individual terms to Kripke's well-known "rigid designators," a unrealistic restriction for many applications, but one we will make for the time being to see where it leads.

Moreover, in the usual formulation of $R^\square$, with generalization as a rule applied to arbitrary theorems (not just axioms), one can prove the Converse Barcan Formula, and then we have that (*def) implies (***def).

However, for a formulation of $R^\square$ with generalization restricted to axioms and where it is not postulated that identities are necessary, we can easily see that none of the three formulas above logically imply each other. We use the obvious fact that we are then dealing with a subsystem of a corresponding formulation of S4, and the well-known fact that these formulas are all logically distinct there.

It is interesting to note however that for formulas φ "of the kind that determine relevant properties" (cf. Dunn (1990)) it is arguable that we get the following chain of implications:

$(\rho x \square \varphi x)a \rightarrow \square \varphi a \rightarrow \square((\rho x \ \varphi x)a).$

The first implication holds quite generally for any formula φ, and is a simple instance of Fact 2 of Dunn (1990), which says, in rough English, that if a property holds relevantly of an individual, then it also just plain holds. In this case of course the property in question is not merely φ, but rather $\square \varphi$. This implication is in fact a theorem of standard first-order **R**, and hence $R^\square$, but its proof depends upon the universal instantiation axiom $\forall x \psi x \rightarrow \psi a$, which is a perfectly fine axiom for terms a that are rigid designators, but must be given up for if we add definite descriptions to our language for reasons familiar from modal logic. There will be more about this below.

The second implication is problematic, even for rigid designators, and at best holds only for formulas of the kind that determine relevant properties. To say of a formula that it is "of the kind that determines relevant properties," is just to say that it satisfies Indiscernibility of Identicals ((II) of sec. 2 above).

It was argued in Dunn (1987) that such a scheme is not to be regarded as a logical axiom in relevance logic, but rather to be taken as a proper axiom (for atomic φ anyway) precisely when φ is of the kind that determines relevant properties. Fact 1 of Dunn (1990) says of such formulas that

$\varphi a \rightarrow (\rho x \varphi x)a$

is a theorem, but we need to look at this more closely, since it is not a theorem of the logic alone, but rather a theorem of the theory gotten by adding appropriate instances of Indiscernibility of Identiticals as proper axioms.

The only issue is then whether one can prefix $\square$ to the above implication, since we can then get the second implication in the chain by distributing $\square$ across the implication of Fact 1.[7] Since modal distinctions were not at issue in Dunn (1990), the issue of the necessity of Fact 1 was not raised. It does seem plausible to argue that if a formula is of the kind that determines relevant properties, that this is not just a contingent fact but rather a necessary one. By this I do not mean that it is necessary that a particular predicate symbol be used to express the property, this is obviously quite arbitrary. But given that the symbol has the meaning that it has, the fact that it expresses a relevant property in general is not an accident.

This may seem hard to reconcile with the view expressed in Dunn (1987) that it is at least often the job of science to discover what the basic relevant properties are. But such a discovery would be at such a fundamental level, that it would not seem

---

[7] This question relates as well to the issue of whether formulas of the kind that determine relevant properties are closed under the necessity operator. (Facts 3 and 4 of Dunn (1987) investigate these questions for other connectives, finding that although such formulas are closed under negation without restriction, they are only closed in certain restricted ways under implication, conjunction, and disjunction.) There are two sub-issues. The first is the question just raised about whether one can put $\square$ in front of Indiscernibility of Identicals for such formulas. If one can put it there, then one can distribute it across both implications, ending up with $\square \varphi y \rightarrow (\square(x = y) \rightarrow \square \varphi x)$. The second sub-issue has also been discussed, and it is the issue whether $x = y \rightarrow \square(x = y)$ holds, which it plausibly does given that x and y are variables and hence can be treated as rigid designators.

odd to attach some degree of at least physical necessity to the fact so discovered.[8] I would additionally invoke Kripke's (1972) reasonably well-accepted category of the necessary *a posteriori*, which he invoked to argue science may discover through empirical investigations that a certain property is essential.[9]

We have barely begun to sort out all of the ramifications of the above considerations. As already said, given the subtle divergence of entailment from necessary relevant implication, the safest course seems to be to put the definition (***) on the shelf, at least for this occasion, and concentrate on the definitions (*) and (**).[10] With respect to distinguishing these, I do have two suggestions.

The first of these is to understand the distinction between (*) and (**) as at least roughly the traditional distinction between "*de dicto*" and "*de re*." A modal statement is said to be *de re* if the statement is somehow directly about a thing (or things), and to be *de dicto* otherwise, and the test as to whether a statement is *de re* is usually taken to involve Indiscernibility of Identicals (there are also most likely some syntactic markers). Thus the statement 'Necessarily nine is the square of three' is typically taken to be *de dicto* because it seems not to follow from it and the fact that the number of the planets is nine that necessarily the number of planets is the square of three.

On the other hand, 'Nine is such that it is necessarily the square of three' is a *de re* statement in that it seems to be talking directly of the number nine. Thomason and Stalnaker (1968, 1968a) have made good sense of this distinction using the lambda operator. Thus the first statement is symbolized by $\Box((\lambda x F x)a)$, whereas the second statement is symbolized by $(\lambda x \Box F x)a$.

---

[8] One might think that it is always the job of *a priori* metaphysics to establish such just what are the intrinsic properties. But it seems to me that science, in discovering the fundamental categories of the physical world, also has an important role to play. Consider for example the "fact" (in a reasonably common sense physics), that while shape is an intrinsic property of objects, color is not. Or for a more sophisticated example (which I owe to Anil Gupta), consider the distinction between inertial mass, which is presumably intrinsic, and gravitational mass (weight), which is not.

[9] It is somewhat frightening to imagine what some of the more sophisticated absolute idealists such as Blanshard might have done with a distinction such as the necessary *a posteriori*, in arguing for the position that causality is really a necessary or even logical relation. Consider Kripke's own claim that since natural kind terms function much like rigid designators, the identity

heat = the motion of molecules

is necessary but *a posteriori*. The statement that 'if there is heat in a thing, then there is heat in the thing' is a logical truth. But using the necessary identity above, one can obtain by substitution of identicals the statement 'if there is heat in a thing, then there is the motion of molecules in the thing', which is awfully close to establishing that 'heat causes the motion of molecules' is a logical truth.

[10] But (***def) may mark yet another important distinction, and this should be explored. Incidentally, Hintikka (1962, 1967) is an early example of someone trying to get the effect of scope distinctions using quantification and identity. Thomason and Stalnaker (1968) point out that this diverges from their own treatment using the lambda operator in the case of non-denoting singular terms. However, in the papers so far on relevant predication, I have been working with the standard formulation of **R**, with no descriptions and the "classical" assumption that all singular terms denote. I hope to have the opportunity to address these matters in a separate paper on existence and (relevant) definite descriptions, and there consider "liberated" versions of **R**.

In this connection, it is interesting to substitute ρ for λ in the above distinctions, and notice that we get (*) and (**) respectively. This suggests that they can be made roughly to do the same work.

The distinction between *de dicto* and *de re*, as explained above, would seem to depend upon having definite descriptions as first-class terms. If all of the terms are rigid designators, such as 'nine', '9', and 'IX', then it is difficult to make out any such distinction using the apparatus of modal logic alone. With this in mind, we can now discuss a bit more the familiar failure of universal instantiation for definite descriptions in the scope of necessity operators, but fine-tuned to our definitions.

Thus it is clearly arguable that when the term a is 'the number of the planets' and Fx abbreviates 'x is the square of 3', then $(\rho x \Box F x)a$—in English, the number of the planets (*i.e.*, 9) is such that it is necessarily the square of 3, and in more symbols:

$$\forall x(x = a \rightarrow \Box F x).$$

But universal instantiation would then yield,

$$a = a \rightarrow \Box F a,$$

and since $a = a$ is presumably a theorem even for non-rigid designators, we would have

$$\Box F a,$$

and yet this last is arguably false, since it is not necessarily the case that the number of planets is the square of 3—the number of planets might have been say only 8. The argument above is essentially the proof of Fact 2 in Dunn (1987), and we can see that it depends upon universal instantiation.

Within relevance logic (with modality) even without definite descriptions, we appear still to have a distinction which in English might be marked by saying that there is a difference between an object a necessarily relevantly having a property, and a relevantly having a necessary property. Since there has been a tendency in this series of papers to identify relevant predication with exemplification "properly so-called," this may amount to the difference between an object necessarily exemplifying a property, as opposed to its exemplifying a necessary property.

It would be nice at this point to trot out some metaphysical examples to sew up this distinction, and we shall ultimately attempt this in the next section, building upon a certain easily recognized but insufficiently discussed asymmetry in essential predication. But we first embark upon an interesting digression that was brought about by trying to think of examples from a somewhat different perspective, where the examples depend very much upon the "fine grained structure" of one's theory of objects.

The customary assumption regarding the semantics of modal logic, and one which I prefer, is that the very same object can be in the domain of two different possible worlds. But if we follow David Lewis (1968) in thinking that the very same object a cannot exist in two possible worlds, but only counterparts of it do, then one gets a relatively straightforward difference given certain plausible assumptions, including the identification of intrinsic and relevant predications in the monadic case (cf. sec. 2 of this paper, and Dunn (1990)). Thus at first blush it would seem that it would be very unlikely for a to intrinsically have a necessary property F, for this could not be the case without all the counterparts of a also having the property F. It would thus be the case that a's having $\Box F$ would not depend upon a alone, but also on its counterparts, and this would cancel out the thought that $\Box F$ is intrinsic to a. There undoubtedly are ways to define terms so that this consequence seems to be avoided, at least verbally. But this seems to be the straightforward consequence.

But maybe this seemingly straightforward consequence can be avoided, and not just verbally, by employing an observation from Dunn (1990) to the effect that other objects may be involved in the intrinsic properties of a thing, as long as that thing completely determines those objects and their required properties. The actual example was (non-Humean) causation. But at least on Lewis's view, possible worlds are completely causally isolated from each other, and so we cannot say that the thing a *causes* its counterparts in other worlds to have the property F.

But maybe there is some other, non-causal way in which a can be such that all by itself it determines that each of its counterparts in all of the other possible worlds be F. This situation might be described by saying that "a dictates to its counterparts." To take a homey example, it can be argued that it is intrinsic to Socrates, not only that he is human, but also that he is necessarily human—humanity is an essential property of Socrates. Now what this would mean regarding Socrates' counterparts is that nothing would be counted as similar enough to Socrates to be his counterpart if it lacked humanity. But it is not the case that Socrates *causes* his counterparts to have humanity, in anything like the way that Socrates and Xanthippe cause their children to have humanity. It is not as if Socrates somehow emanates humanity into his counterparts in the other worlds. The determination in question is more "semantic" than causal.

It seems as if a distinction is needed between two kinds of intrinsicality, one we might call "world local" and the other "world global." The former would not require inspection of objects in other possible worlds, whereas the latter would. And there are undoubtedly temporal, and even spatial analogs of this distinction as well, having to do with "another time, another place."[11]

---

[11] Thus with respect to the temporal analogy, can it be an intrinsic property of an object that it always was, or always will be square? One cannot tell by inspecting an object only here *and now* that this is the case. But if one understands the object to be a substance enduring as the same object over time, its having been square, or its going to be square, can both be viewed as intrinsic to the object itself, though perhaps not intrinsic to the object at this moment. On the other hand, if one views ordinary objects as constructions from momentary time slices or impressions, where these last are the real objects, then it seems unlikely that it can be an intrinsic property of one such momentary object that it was, or will be square, since this depends on what happens to other momentary objects in the past, or future. Of course if there is some strong (non-Humean) causal relation amongst such momentary objects, it would still be possible for a present monentary object to intrinsically have some future property that it determines (cf. Dunn (1990)), and presumably to have some past property too if objects have their origins essentially (cf. sec. 4 below).

4. Asymmetric Essential Predications. There is a phenomenon relating to essential predication and relations which I think has not been sufficiently highlighted in the literature. The phenomenon is the following. Take one of the standard examples of an essential property offered by Kripke: it is an essential property of Queen Elizabeth II that she had the parents she had. This has the asymmetric feature that while it is an essential property of QE II that she had the parents she had, it is presumably not an essential property of those particular individuals that they had QE II as a daughter. This by itself shows that one cannot symbolize "a has F essentially" as simply $\Box F a$.

One can multiply examples: According to various reputable philosophers, it is an essential property of the world that it was created by God, it is an essential property of the set $\{$Tom, Dick$\}$ that it has Tom as member, it is an essential property of Maine that it is north of Boston, it is an essential property of a particular table that it was made from a particular piece of wood. But in none of these cases does the converse seem to hold.[12]

Now one can get some handle on this using the standard semantics of modal logic. One can say, *e.g.*, that in every possible world in which say QE II exists (timelessly), her parents exist (*i.e.*, those particular individuals exist and stand to QE II in the parent relationship), but not vice versa. (Cf. Forbes (1985, p. 97): "an *essential property* of an object x is a property without possessing which x could not exist.") But this depends on at least one of the individuals in the relation being contingent and at least to this extent is *ad hoc*. Given the apparatus of relevant predication, it is entirely possible to have a formula φxy that determines a relevant predication in say the first position, but not the second (a psuedo-relational relevant property), and it thus appears that one can account for the asymmetries noted in essential predication. Thus on the first round through, it appears that for any of the "relations" in the examples above, one could have $\Box[(\rho x R x b)a]$, and yet fail to have $\Box[(\rho y R a y)b]$. This by itself would present a motivation for defining an essential property as a necessary relevant property.

Let us examine the examples above more closely, starting with one that supports the point. Given the standard theology, God is immutable, and hence not modifiable. So God's creating the world cannot make a difference to God, although it presumably makes a big difference to the world. This view of Aquinas's was used in Dunn (1987) to motivate the idea of relevant "relational properties" without relevant relations, what we are now calling relevant pseudo-relational properties. The asymmetry then that it is an essential property of the world that it was created by God, but not of God that the world was created by him, can be blamed on the asymmetry of the underlying "relation" of creation that it creates relational properties in one position, but not the other.

But consider QE II and her parents. Here the underlying relation (x and x' are the parents of y) does appear to be a relevant relation, making a difference to both

---

[12] One is tempted to conjecture that at least all typical examples of so-called "internal relations" on "The Modal Account" described in Dunn (1990) fit this asymmetric pattern.

the pair x, x' and also to y, and thus determining relational properties in both poles. If we perform a thought experiment and imagine that George VI and the Queen Mother Elizabeth were somehow not the parents of QE II, this presumably would mean a change in the properties of both QE II and her parents. The change in QE II is perhaps the most radical, for, at least on Kripke's view, QE II would not exist. But there would have to have been at least minor changes in either George VI, the Queen Mother, or both. Decency forbids our speculating too closely about those changes. Anyway the example can be made much simpler by imagining that people have but a single parent, being conceived by say parthogenesis. So let us make that assumption, symbolizing 'x is the child of y' as Rxy, and letting a and b be rigid designators for QE II and the Queen Mother, respectively.

The point is that we cannot understand the asymmetry as produced by the fact that Rxy determines relational properties in one of its poles, and not the other, because this is a relevant relation. Instead it is the case that the *modal* formula $\Box Rxy$ determines relational properties in one of its poles and not the other, and thus is not a relevant relation. More formally, the distinction is not that $\Box[(\rho x Rxb)a]$ holds, but not $\Box[(\rho y Ray)b]$, as with the world and God. It is rather with QE II and the Queen Mother that $(\rho x \,\Box Rxb)a$ holds, but not $(\rho y \,\Box Ray)b$.[13] The lesson here is that the asymmetry of essential predication cannot be blamed on the underlying relation. We thus cannot in this case understand essential predication as necessary relevant predication, but are forced to understand it instead as relevant necessary predication.

Let us now examine the set and its members. Tom could cease to be a member of the set {Tom, Dick} by virtue of Dick's non-existence, for then, on at least a standard intuition, the set would no longer exist. But this certainly produces a big change in the set. The only other way that the membership "relation" could fail to hold is for Tom not to exist, and this too would produce a change in the set. To recapitulate, if the membership "relation" were to fail to hold, this would require a change in the set, but it need not require a change in the member (in this case Tom). Thus membership determines relevant properties in only its second position.

While we have established this in particular only for sets whose members are contingent objects, it is natural to extend it to sets whose members are necessarily existent, and even to pure set theory, which is founded in the iterative conception on the empty set, and where every set has only sets as members. This shows at least potentially the advantage of a definition of essential property in terms of relevant predication, because at least on a natural metaphysics all the pure sets exist necessarily, and so a definition such as is found in Forbes (1985) (quoted above)

---

[13] There is the subtlety here as to whether when φxy is a formula of the kind that determines relevant relations, $(\rho x \,\varphi xb)a \leftrightarrow (\rho y \,\varphi ay)b$ is provable (we might call this the principle of equivalence between active and passive). In fact this has as easy proof, left to the reader, using the fact that we have Identical of Indiscernibilities in both positions. But there is a further subtlety as to whether the equivalence is necessary. If it is then we can prefix the equivalence with $\Box$, and then distribute it over the biconditional to obtain $\Box (\rho x \,\varphi xb)a \leftrightarrow \Box (\rho y \,\varphi ay)b$. The argument for the relevance of relations being a matter of necessity is the same as the argument in sec. 3 for the relevance of properties being a matter of necessity.

would be bound to have the consequence that for pure sets membership determines essential properties in both positions.

It is interesting to contrast membership with exemplification, which very plausibly determines relevant properties (though typically not necessary ones) only in its first position, at least given a common Platonic view of properties ("forms"). If Tom ceases to be triangular, this means that there was a change in Tom, but certainly not in the Platonic form triangularity.[14]

Now before we discuss the example concerning Maine and Boston, I must confess that I had initial difficulty in understanding what motivates it. I first had difficulty even in seeing that it is an essential property of Maine that it is north of Boston. I also had difficulty in seeing that 'x is north of y' determines relevant properties in either position, yet alone in an asymmetric way (and it did not seem to help much to put $\square$ in front of it). On the face of it relative direction is just the sort of relationship that seems external. Quite intuitively one could move an object, such as a railway car, from the south of Boston to its north, with no intrinsic change in the car.

So I had trouble making sense of this traditional example until we recently moved and I was reading through our property abstract. There I found that it appears to be a quite common practice to legally describe ("define") areas of land in terms of areas of land previously so described. Of course in principle the process must end somewhere, usually by reference to natural landmarks. I do not know the legal or historical situation with respect to Boston and Maine, but based on my knowledge that Maine was not one of the original Thirteen Colonies, it would not surprise me if some early surveyor gave a legal description of Maine that made reference to its being north of Boston. Of course Maine might have been established to the west of Boston, and this would make a big difference to Maine, given that areas of land are not the kinds of things that are routinely moved about. (Thus it would be a completely different region, with different topography, etc.). But this need not make any difference to Boston.

To make the point perfectly clear, let us suppose that the term 'Maine' is introduced as mere shorthand for the definite description 'the state whose lowermost southern boundary is so-and-so many miles north of Boston, etc.', where the "etc." is spelled out in surveryors' terms. Then of course 'being north of Boston' is a relevant property of Maine, for

$$\forall x(x = Maine \rightarrow x \ is \ north \ of \ Boston),$$

and furthermore this relevant predication is necessary, depending as it does simply upon the definition of 'Maine'.

---

[14] In the next paper in this series I plan to compare and contrast exemplification with membership, and in naive (type-free) systems of property-theory and set-theory respectively (even the pure versions of these theories, with no contingent objects) then use the argument of Russell's Paradox to show that neither exemplification nor membership is a relevant relation. One then has a choice as to which position fails to determine relevant properties, and it seems natural to make the choices as argued for above.

But of course if the name 'Maine' is a rigid designator, we no longer expect this result. Thus imagine that the term 'Maine' was introduced by a definite description like the one just above, fixing its reference to a certain region, but that the description is in no way the *meaning* of the term.[15] Then we no longer expect that being north of Boston is an essential, or even a relevant property of that region of land. If by some as yet unpredicted consequence of plate tectonics, Maine were to drift south of Boston, it does not seem as if that region of land would disappear, stop being Maine, or even necessarily change in any intrinsic way (we assume that enough of the land past its boundaries drifts with it so as to avoid the problem of the effects of rifts along its boundaries). Furthermore we no longer expect this result, for similar reasons, if we express the essential property as a relevantly necessary property (instead of, as in the formula above, as a necessarily relevant property).

There is an important moral to be learned from the example above, even if we are not sure of the details about how the actual example in English is to be analyzed. (Does 'Maine' function as a rigid designator, or is it rather legal shorthand for some definite description.) The point is that any formula φa can express a relevant property of a, as long as the term a is a definite description implying φ, for example, in the simplest case, 'the unique x such that φx'. And correspondingly, any formula ψab can express at least a relevant pseudo-relational property, given the right choice of a definite description a.[16]

But this does not by itself establish that the formulas φa and ψab establish relevant properties in the first position. That definition was done with terms that are rigid designators, and so has to do with the things themselves, and not their descriptions.

5. Kripke on Essentialness of Origins. When we come to the table and its origins, or to QE II and her parents, things rely on Kripiesque intuitions. Kripke (1972, p. 113) asks: "How could a person originating from different parents, from a totally different sperm and egg, be this very woman? ... It seems to me that anything coming from a different origin would not be this object."

Kripke (pp. 133–114) seems to want to generalize this to all objects.[17] Thus he talks of a particular table and asks:

---

[15] I believe it at least once was a common misconception of Kripke's "causal theory of proper names" that the original introduction had to be by a kind of "baptism," whereby the original user of the name was directly in causal contact, by perception, with the referent. But Kripke himself was always clear that the "causal" aspect had to do with the chain by which one user of the name passes it on to the next.

[16] It might appear more difficult, if not impossible, to get a formula φab to similarly express a relevant relation between a and b, merely in virtue of the definite descriptions a and b. This is because it might appear that the definite description a would have to involve b, and *vice versa*, in a kind of circularity. But consider 'The North Pole is north of the South Pole', where 'the North Pole' is defined something like 'the northernmost point', symmetrically for 'the South Pole', and of course north and south are converses.

[17] In note 56 (p. 114) Kripke says that "A principle suggested by these examples is: If an object has its origin from a certain hunk of matter, it could not have had its origin in any other hunk of matter. Some qualifications might have to be stated (for example, the vagueness of the notion of hunk of matter leads to some problems), but in a large class of cases the principle is perhaps susceptible of something like proof, using the principle of the necessity of identity for particulars." He goes on to say that "Strictly speaking

Now could this table have been made from a completely different block of wood, or even of water cleverly hardened into ice—water taken from the Thames River? We could conceivably discover that, contrary to what we now think, this table is indeed made of ice from the river. But let us suppose that it is not. Then, though we can imagine making a table out of another block of wood, or even from ice, identical in appearance with this one, and though we could have put it in this very position in the room, it seems to me that this is not to imagine this table as made of wood or ice, but rather it is to imagine another table, resembling this one in all external details, made of another block of wood, or even of ice.

It seems, on these intuitions, that if the table, which happens to be made from of a certain block of wood, somehow failed to be made from that wood, this would clearly produce a radical change in the table. For it would fail to exist, even though another table that looks just like it might exist, made from some other hunk of material. But this need not produce any change in the block of wood, at least as it was before it was made into a table.

There are two issues that must be distinguished, but which are easily confused. One is the issue of *origin* of a thing, and this is of course the issue with which Kripke is explicitly concerned. The other is the issue of the *material composition* of a thing. It is easy to lose track of this distinction when one is talking of a table being made from a hunk of wood. The origin is the hunk of wood, and so is the material. But with QE II, if we take her origins to be her parents, it seems clear that her origins are different than the stuff out of which she is composed.

If we tell a more scientific story, and say that her origins are a certain ovum and sperm, things get a bit more complicated, but in an instructive way. Then one might focus on the fact that some genetic material is passed on from her parents to her, but still we do not want to lose sight of the fact that by the time she is born and has grown a bit, most if not all of the material that makes up her body comes from sources outside of her parents. Even with the table, like with the ship of Theseus, one could replace a bit of it at a time. Then although its identity as a table could be traced to a particular piece of wood (*e.g.*, "the wood that George Washington told the woodwright to fashion into a trestle"), still it would no longer be composed of that particular material.

Kripke slides back and forth between the locutions "made from" and "made of." To my ear, the first smacks of origins and the second of composition, and these locutions might as well have been artfully chosen so as to disguise the underlying complexity of distinctions.

---

the 'proof' uses the necessity of distinctness, not of identity. However, the same types of distinctions that can be used to establish the latter can be used to establish the former. (Suppose $X \neq Y$; if X and Y were both identical to some object Z in another possible world, then $X = Z, Y = Z$, hence $X = Y$.)'' Incidentally, this last seems reminiscent of Blanshard's (1962) argument that distinctness is an internal relation (cf. Dunn (1990)).

It may be essential to the table that it is "made from" a certain block of wood, but is it also essential that it is "made of" the particular wood that is its substance (not just a type, like red maple, but a token, a particular bit of wood)? It would seem not, for as we have noted above the material of the table might be changed bit by bit over time. That the table is made of a particular material seems to be a relation of the whole-part kind. If the table is entirely wooden, then in fact it appears that the table is identical with the substance. And if the table is not entirely wooden (say it has a glass top), then at least the substance is identical to a part of the table. So what we have here is an example of an intrinsic relational property of the whole-part kind discussed in Dunn (1990), but not a necessary one.

6. Conclusion. This section is in fact mistitled, since the main point I wish to emphasize is that the discussion of this paper raises at least as many questions as it answers. I would be very pleased if these questions would be picked up by some of the skilled technicians from the essentialist industry.

BIBLIOGRAPHY

Anderson, A. R. and Belnap, N. D. *et al.* (1975): *Entailment: The Logic of Relevance and Necessity*, vol. 1, Princeton Univ. Press.

Belnap, N. D. (1967): "Intensional Models for First Degree Formulas," *The Journal of Symbolic Logic*, 32, pp. 1–22.

Blanshard, B. (1962): *Reason and Analysis*, La Salle, Illinois: Open Court Publishing Company.

Bosanquet, B. (1888): *Logic, or the Morphology of Knowledge*, 3 vols., Oxford Univ. Press, 2nd edition, 1911.

Dunn, J. M. (1987): "Relevant Predication 1: The Formal Theory," *Journal of Philosophical Logic*, 16, pp. 347–381.

Dunn, J. M. (1990): "Relevant Predication 2: Intrinsic Properties and Internal Relations," forthcoming in *Philosophical Studies*.

Ewing, A. C. (1934): *Idealism, A Critical Survey*, London: Methuen & Co., Ltd.

Forbes, G. (1985): *The Metaphysics of Modality*, Oxford: Clarendon Press.

Hintikka, J. (1962): *Knowledge and Belief*, Ithaca: Cornell University Press.

Hintikka, J. (1967): "Individuals, Possible Worlds, and Epistemic Logic," *Noûs*, 1, pp. 33–62.

Kripke, S. A. (1963): "Semantical Considerations on Modal Logic," *Acta Philosophica Fennica*, 16, pp. 83–94.

Kripke, S. A. (1972): *Naming and Necessity*, republished 1980 by Harvard University Press.

Lewis, D. K. (1968): "Counterpart Theory and Quantified Modal Logic," *The Journal of Philosophy*, 65, pp. 113–126.

Maksimova, L. (1973): "A Semantics for the Calculus E of Entailment," *Bulletin of the Section of Logic*, Polish Academy of Sciences, Institute of Philosophy and Sociology, 2, pp. 18–21.

Barcan Marcus, R. (1967): "Essentialism in Modal Logic," *Noûs*, 1, pp. 91–96.

Meyer, R. K., Dunn, J. M. and Leblanc, H. (1974): "Completeness of Relevant Quantification Theories," *Notre Dame Journal of Formal Logic*, 15, pp. 97–121.

Moore, G. E. (1922): "External and Internal Relations," in *Philosophical Studies*, New York: Harcourt, Brace & Co. Inc., pp. 253–275.

Moore, G. E. (1962): *Common-place Book 1919–1953*, ed. C. Lewy, London: George Allen & Unwin Ltd.

Parsons, T. (1967): "Grades of Essentialism in Modal Logic," *Noûs*, 1, pp. 156–174.

Quine, W. V. O. (1956): "Three Grades of Modal Involvement," in *The Ways of Paradox*, New York: Random House.

Thomason, R. H. and Stalnaker, R. C. (1968): "Modality and Reference," *Noûs*, 2, pp. 359–372.

Thomason, R. H. and Stalnaker, R. C. (1968a): "Abstraction in First-Order Modal Logic," *Theoria*, 34, pp. 203–207.

Wilson, C. (1967): *The Mind Parasites*, Oakland, California: Oneiric Press.

JAY L. GARFIELD

THE DOG: RELEVANCE AND RATIONALITY [1]

The Dog plays a curious role in the history of the disjunctive syllogism. His thoughts on the topic were reported and discussed
by such diverse authorities as Sextus Empiricus, the anonymous
medieval Bestiarists, and Samuel Taylor Coleridge. Two of these
reveal The Dog's proclivity for intensional senses of "or," and
the third shows that The Dog has astounding logical acumen,
despite The Man's attempt to muddy the analytical waters . . .
Sextus Empiricus wrote of the Real Dog as follows: . . . According to Chrysippus, who shows special interest in the irrational
animals, The Dog even shares in the far-famed "Dialectic." This
person, at any rate, declares that The Dog makes use of the fifth
complex indemonstrable syllogism when, on arriving at a spot
where three ways meet, after smelling at the two roads by which
the quarry did not pass, he rushes off at once by the third without
stopping to smell. For, says the old writer, The Dog implicitly
reasons thus: "The creature went either by this road, or by that,
or by the other: but it did not go by this road or by that: therefore
it went by the other." [296]

1. INTRODUCTION

One of the more intriguing asides in [Anderson & Belnap 1975] is §25.1 *The Dog*.
Here the invalidity of the classical disjunctive syllogism and the Relevant interpretation of disjunction are defended, and The Dog is redeemed from the charge of
classicism. Many of a classical persuasion find the Relevant treatment of the disjunctive syllogism among the most counterintuitive features of Relevance Logic. One
sometimes hears it urged that the failure to admit a rule with so much animal mag-
netism, particularly when the rule is *admissible* (the Meyer-Dunn argument [§25.2])
smacks of irrationality. Here I want to argue that despite this widespread counter-
intuition the Relevant interpretation of disjunction, and in particular its consequent
blocking of disjunctive syllogism, provides a better model for rational inference
than does its classical counterpart — that it is rational to reason Relevantly, but

[1] Thanks to G. Lee Bowie, Willem A. de Vries and Murray Kiteley for useful comments on an earlier
draft. Thanks also to the members of the Propositional Attitudes Task Force, particularly Bruce Aune,
Merrie Bergmann, G. Lee Bowie, Murray Kiteley, Janice Moulton, Tsenay Serequeberhan and Barry
Smith for a thorough and helpful discussion of a subsequent draft, and to James W. Garson for additional
advice and discussion. Thanks also to Richard Muller for invaluable technical assistance.

97

J. M. Dunn and A. Gupta (eds.), Truth or Consequences, 97–109.
© 1990 *Kluwer Academic Publishers. Printed in the Netherlands.*

irrational to reason classically. The argument will be primarily epistemological, rather than logical, but that is because rationality is, after all, an epistemological notion. My conclusion is hence that Relevance Logic is of quite general philosophical importance, and not merely of interest to logicians.

The proper role of logic in epistemology and psychology is now a hot topic of debate in philosophy and in cognitive science. Macnamara [1986] argues that logic constitutes a competence theory of human reasoning in just the way that Chomsky and his followers argue that a natural-language syntax constitutes a competence theory of human linguistic ability. I have criticized this view in [Garfield 1988], arguing that at best *some* logic could serve as a component of a normative theory of rationality (a view I will develop in more detail below). Harman [1986] on the other hand has argued that

> [T] here is no clearly significant way in which logic is specially relevant to reasoning. On the other hand immediate *implication* and immediate *inconsistency do seem important for reasoning, and so do implication and inconsistency* . . . But that is not to say that logical reasoning or logical inconsistency has any special status in human reasoning. [p. 20]

Cherniak's [1986] view is that a theory of "feasible" and "appropriate" logical inferences constitutes an important component of the theory of rationality but that an unconstrained logic is by itself irrelevant to the psychology and epistemology of reasoners. This debate — into which we will shortly plunge headlong — despite its complexity and despite the passion with which it is prosecuted, has as yet paid insufficient attention to two important questions: Which is the logic appropriate to a theory of rationality, however minimal or naturalized? Secondly, what is the appropriate ideal type for a theory of rational inference? I will argue that the answer to the first of these is "Relevance Logic," and to the second, "a fallible agent who reasons Relevantly." It is hence the prospect of reconstructing the theory of rationality on a Relevance foundation suggested by the need to answer these questions that will concern me in this paper.

This discussion takes place in the context of the movement known to its devotees by Quine's term "naturalized epistemology." This is the endeavor to engage in normative epistemology in cognizance of the facts emerging from the study of the psychology of reasoning, on the one hand, and to investigate the psychology of reasoning from a standpoint enriched by epistemological theory on the other. The idea is that we can better understand how we *ought* to reason by understanding how we *do* reason, and so by understanding the *factual constraints* on our reasoning imposed by our psychological constitution; and that we can better understand how we *in fact* reason by reflecting in part on what *would* constitute sound reasoning practices, and looking for them in the behavior of the human organism. (See [Kornblith 1986] for a number of excellent discussions of naturalized epistemology.) It is important in these discussions to be clear about just when one is making *psychological* claims and when one is making *conceptual* points. I am here engaging in normative epistemology — asking questions about how we *ought* to reason, regardless of whether we *in fact* reason that way — but this is epistemology which takes some general psychological facts seriously: We are imperfect; we have false beliefs; we have limited inferential powers; we have limited memory; we have sub-optimal belief fixations mechanisms; we inhabit an environment which does not go out of its way to deliver the truth to us, and in fact often goes out of its way to deceive us. I refer to this unfortunate state of inner and outer affairs as an "epistemically hostile environment."[2]

Epistemic hostility is important for epistemology. Too often characterizations of how we ought to reason, or what counts as justification for a belief, assume as a basis for theory that we live in an epistemically co-operative world — that we are perfect reasoners with infinite memory, infallible sensory apparatus, and that no-one is out to deceive us (see e.g. [Hintikka 1962]). This assumption is typically defended as an *idealization*. But there is idealization and idealization. When one idealizes away from everything interesting, one loses the most important theoretical insights: The ideal gas law idealizes away from the particularities of different gases and succeeds in capturing important theoretical generalizations; Hullian learning theory idealized away from differences in stimulus values of particular consequences to particular responses and so missed most of the complexity of learning [Bolles 1975]. If you idealize away from epistemic hostility, and so formulate a normative epistemology of agents inhabiting epistemically co-operative environments, you miss everything of interest to epistemology. That is simply because the whole point of being rational is to be able to navigate in epistemically hostile surroundings. If the world handed us knowledge and the means for extending it on a silver platter, any fool could acquire and extend it. But it doesn't. Perhaps for that reason we evolved as (more or less) rational. Rationality, in short, is our species' evolutionary response to epistemic hostility, just as fleetness is the rabbit's response to predatory hostility. Idealize away from *that* fact and normative epistemology becomes a subdiscipline of angelology.

Given this understanding of epistemology as the theory of how a rational agent should acquire, revise and extend its beliefs in the face of epistemic hostility, and given this understanding of logic as providing, inter alia, the formal theory of warranted inference, the question immediately arises, "Which logic provides the best recommendation for rational belief extension in the context of epistemic hostility?" The remainder of this essay will be devoted to arguing (by example — I will consider only disjunction) that the correct answer to this question is "Relevance Logic." I will begin by considering and rejecting several alternative, more classical proposals, and given the difficulties that emerge from these classical approaches I will characterize in more detail the place of logic in the theory of rationality. We will then be in a position to discuss disjunction directly. I will conclude by responding to several natural classical replies and defending The Dog as rational and Relevantly so.

---

[2] Here I follow Simon [1981] in referring to an organism's internal psychological mechanisms as part of its environment — as Simon calls it, the inner environment. For some purposes this may be counterintuitive, but here I think it is quite useful to emphasize the fact that in reasoning, potential sources of error are just that — potential sources of error, whether they are endogenous or exogenous.

2. RATIONALITY

There are a number of well-known difficulties encountered by unconstrained idealizations of rationality. Such idealizations typically impute a classical logic to the epistemic agent as the vehicle of belief extension and fixation. As a consequence, there is the possibility of belief-pollution attendant through classical disjunction-introduction $(p \rightarrow .p \vee q)$ in the environment of disjunctive syllogism, and through classical indirect proof $(p \wedge \neg p \rightarrow q)$, where error, inconsistency, or change of mind occur. As a consequence of these and related problems recent theorists in the naturalized epistemology movement have advised the replacement of this Hintikka-style idealization of rationality with a conception Cherniak has called "Minimal Rationality." Concepts of minimal rationality (for as we shall see there are varying approaches to constructing such concepts) are intended to provide us with idealizations of human inferential mechanisms, mechanisms designed for ideal functioning in epistemically hostile environments. The principal efforts on these lines, however, take for granted that the logic suitable for inclusion in such idealizations is classical, and that the task of the natural epistemologist is either to constrain the range of available classical inferences (Cherniak) or to reconceive the role of logic in the epistemic and psychological theory of belief revision (Harman). I will briefly characterize each of these attempts and argue that neither succeeds. Neither is without merit — but each fails to address the central questions about which logic to choose for epistemological purposes and the nature of appropriate idealization that lie at the heart of the theory of rational inference. I will then suggest that the reason for their failure is that they share with angelic epistemology a commitment to classical logic, and that there is reason to believe that replacing classical logic with Relevance logic is the first step to a useful epistemic theory of human inference.

Cherniak's theory of minimal rationality incorporates the following *minimal inference condition*:

> If A has a particular belief-desire set, A would make some, but not necessarily all, of the sound inferences from the belief set that are apparently appropriate. [p. 10]

and a *minimal consistency condition*:

> If A has a particular belief-desire set, then if any inconsistencies arose in the belief set, A would sometimes eliminate some of them. [p. 16]

These conditions, among others, are meant to steer a middle course between unreasonable demands of perfect consistency and completeness arising from an ideal conception of rationality on the one hand and an insufficiently constrained conception that describes transitions from state to state in such non-normative terms that characterizing these transitions as inferences or these states as propositional attitudes becomes vacuous on the other. The bulk of the theory, then, and for our purposes the important part, must be devoted to specifying which inferences, and which inconsistencies a minimally rational agent would draw or eliminate, and under which circumstances s/he would do so.

The demand of specifying the inferences that an agent must make in order to satisfy the demands of minimal rationality is met for Cherniak by a theory of *feasible inference*. A feasible inference is just an inference that is psychologically easy for an organism. For any minimally rational organism and any connective, there will be a ranking by difficulty of argument schemata involving that connective. The easy inferences are called *constitutive inferences*. More difficult inferences — hypothesized to be generally achieved by a chain of constitutive inferences — are expected of the organism in roughly inverse proportion to their complexity when constitutive inferences are taken as primitive computations. Cherniak is quite comfortable with the possibility of alternative feasibility orderings: For some connectives one organism might find inferences simple (easy) that for another would be extremely complex (difficult). This corresponds to a situation where the organisms in question have quite different natural deduction systems "wired in." But the point is that for an organism to count as employing a natural deduction system, it must count as using basic logical constants, and for it to use a logical constant in inference, there must be a set of inferences involving that constant that it makes quite reliably. But there need be no particular inferences that are made most reliably, and it is permissible, and indeed expected, that as the complexity of inferences increases (where this is measured by the number of constitutive steps required) successful inference becomes less frequent.

There is much to be said for such a theory of rationality. It manages to steer between the extremes of over-idealization and of merely descriptive psychology; it provides a plausible way of reconciling imperfection with rationality; it makes good a priori evolutionary sense — it makes sense to endow an organism with just those inference schemata in *ROM* that it needs to get by, and let it develop any extras as needed. But the theory is importantly incomplete in a respect critical for this discussion. Its deliberate logical ecumenism renders it incapable of addressing the important epistemological and logical question: What inferences ought a minimally rational organism make? Cherniak himself suggests — and I will dispute this suggestion below — that classical disjunctive syllogism is a plausible constitutive inference (though of course not a necessary one) for a minimally rational organism. But he explicitly urges that all that rationality requires is that some inferences be constitutive, and does not demand or proscribe any sound (by some standard or other) inferences per se. But while Cherniak's model is laudably motivated by a concern for the omnipresence of epistemic hostility, Cherniak fails to consider the possibility that epistemic hostility may make certain possible constitutive inferences bad moves. This is the possibility I will explore below.

Similar remarks can be made about Harman's remarkable and psychologically sensitive theory of belief revision and inference. While Harman argues persuasively that inference is a more general phenomenon than the use of logic, and that an understanding of the inferences of a rational agent demand attention to its psychology and to the demands placed on that psychology by the epistemically relevant facts concerning its environment, he neglects the possibility that particular inference schemata may be enjoined or proscribed by the demands of rationality in the context of hostility.

In Harman's case this omission is quite surprising. For in his discussion of the close connection between normative and descriptive issues in the epistemology of reasoning — particularly his discussion of undermining and belief revision — Harman argues persuasively that the normative question, "How ought an organism revise its belief corpus in response to new evidence?" can only be answered in light of an answer to the descriptive question, "What strategies for belief revision in fact lead to the most correct beliefs and the fewest false ones for this organism (given the facts about its psychology and environment)?" But the moral is drawn only for general strategies of belief revision, and for global justificatory strategies. Because of Harman's disdain for the role of logic in the normative theory of rationality Harman does not consider the question of what logics might be indicated by such facts.

I do not think that Harman's disdain for the centrality of logic in the theory of reasoning is entirely justified. In arguing for the conclusion that "logic does not have any special relevance to the theory of reasoning" [p. 11] Harman demonstrates that the following principles are defeasible:

> *Logical Implication Principle*: The fact that one's view logi-
> cally implies P can be a reason to accept P.

> *Logical Inconsistency Principle*: Logical inconsistency is to be
> avoided. [p. 11]

The first is defeasible because of the possibility of recognized error; the second because of the semantic paradoxes. Harman argues that logical implication and inconsistency are relevant to the theory of reasoning only as special cases of more general principles of implication-endorsement and inconsistency-avoidance that enjoin us to accept implications and avoid inconsistencies quite generally, whether those are logical, empirical, or of some other origin. This argument in turn depends on the dubious claim that (to paraphrase one of Harman's examples [p. 17]) such beliefs as *"X plays defensive tackle for the Philadelphia Eagles* implies *X weighs more than 150 pounds"* do not turn on any conception of logical implication. To the extent that a tacit use of logical inference rules is made (or ought to be made) by epistemic subjects in endorsing such implications, the argument against a central role for logic in at least the normative theory of inference fails. This much does emerge from Harman's discussion, though: A simpleminded view according to which classical propositional or first-order logic provides an adequate recipe for rational belief revision must be abandoned.

This is where Relevance comes in. One inescapable fact about our epistemic situation (over and above its lamentable and multifarious hostility) is the fact that the inferences on which our access to the truth, our successful actions, and often our lives depend require us to make use of all and only the information relevant to the conclusions we must draw. It hence might be that Relevance Logic is the appropriate logic for the normative theory of rationality. Before embarking on a small case study designed to show (by Baconian induction on a single case) that this is so, a few remarks are necessary in defense of the view that minimal rationality in the sense adumbrated is the appropriate sense of rationality for naturalized epistemology and in defense of the view that logic plays a role in the theory of such rationality.

Against these theories of admittedly minimal rationality, it might be urged by some of a more classical bent (see, e.g. [Hintikka op. cit.]) that these theories are at best armchair empirical theories of the unfortunately irrational actual reasoning of imperfect epistemic subjects. But, these objectors might urge, just as we expect of a theory of morality not an account of how actual imperfect moral agents behave but rather an account of how they *ought* to behave (even if such behavior is more than we could expect of actual persons) we should expect of an epistemological theory an account not of our actual, imperfect reasoning, but rather of our ideal reasoning (even if such behavior is more than we could expect of actual persons). Theories of minimal rationality, such an argument conclude, abdicate the responsibility assigned to the epistemologist.

There are at least two things to say against this line of argument: First, the analogy with ethics is a doubled-edged sword. For much recent ethical theory ([Care 1988], [Williams 1986]) has been devoted to arguing that it is critically important to consider not what the ideal quasi-Kantian moral agent ought to do in morally ideal circumstances, but rather what actual imperfect agents ought to do in actual imperfect moral circumstances given imperfect moral knowledge. This is not the place to evaluate this approach to moral theory. But if anything, the case seems clearer for such an approach in epistemology. Reasoning is, after all, a guide to the perplexed. It is of use to us precisely because our epistemic situation is one of hostility. A theory of knowledge for angels would not only be beside the point for understanding human knowledge, it would be trivial besides. But more importantly (and here the analogy with recent moral theory is also useful) such a theory is not, just in virtue of its attention to actual circumstances, empty of normative content. For such a theory is a theory of how one *ought* to reason in such circumstances — not a psychological theory of how we in fact *do* reason — and hence in the important sense involves an idealization. The Relevant ideal epistemic agent is — rather than a Hintikka-style angel — an ideal fallible human, in an appropriate sense of "ideal" — a sense that can only be grasped as the theory is articulated.

Given this conception of rationality, what is the place of logic in the theory thereof? A logic provides a characterization of (at least a large subset of) the arguments that we ought to endorse. A logic hence provides an account of how an ideal reasoner reasons. Distinct logics provide distinct characterizations, and hence a dispute among schools of logicians is not merely a dispute about mathematics, but a dispute about the appropriate ideal against which we should measure ourselves in epistemology. I will argue that while classical logic might be an appropriate ideal for angels (and so, as Kant would point out, it can at best provide not an imperative but rather a description) when we abandon that ideal for the one relevant for human reasoners, Relevance Logic provides a more epistemologically satisfactory account of the ideal reasoner.

3. DISJUNCTION AND RATIONAL BELIEF-EXTENSION

I shall now argue for a Relevant as opposed to a classical interpretation of disjunction in the theory of rationality. Suppose that you are a rational epistemic agent in an epistemically hostile environment: You are fallible (and you know it); you have false beliefs (and you know it — although of course you do not know which ones are false); both your belief acquisition mechanisms and your inference engine are flawed; you are inconsistent. But you try your best to believe only the true, to be consistent, and to hang onto beliefs only to the extent that they are justified. Now, suppose that one of the particularly menacing features of your epistemic environment is the presence of a certain very persuasive classical logician who convinces you of the soundness of classical disjunction introduction and the classical disjunctive syllogism. Suppose that in these unfortunate but all too common circumstances you come to believe on the misleading information of a normally reliable source (A) that Albuquerque is the capital of Arizona. Under the spell of the evil classical logician you freely disjoin (B) Belnap is a classical logician (with no relevance index, of course). Since A is justified, so is $A \lor B$. Now, suppose that a bit later your geographical source corrects himself, and you now come to believe $\neg A$. Now $\neg A$ and $A \lor B$ are both in your belief set, you have no positive reason to reject $A \lor B$, you are still classical, and so conclude B. B, of course, is manifestly false. What's more, from a suitably distant perspective (ours) you have no real reason to believe it. What went wrong? The answer is plain: you used classical disjunction rules.

Some might argue at this point that you do have a positive reason to reject $A \lor B$ — namely that its only justification was A, that A is now unjustified, and that you want to maintain only justified beliefs in your belief set. But this line of argument is uncompelling from the present perspective. For one thing, it is implausible (and much research indicates false as well [Harman op. cit.], [Nisbett & Ross 1980]) to suggest that we do keep track of the justifications of all of our beliefs and reject beliefs when their justifications are rejected. That is an apparently fixed feature of our psychological architecture, and one that makes good evolutionary-psychological sense — that is, it is itself a justified strategy for a rational agent with fixed reasoning resources and a lot to do. Again, we know that about ourselves (or we should), and that is an important component of epistemic hostility — one of the many respects in which we are fallible. The point of an epistemologically adequate logic is to give us good guidance in recognition of that fact. So, unless we have positive reason to reject $A \lor B$, we should assume that once it gains our assent, it remains there. And surely, $\neg A$ is insufficient reason by itself to reject it.[3]

---

[3] It might also be urged that the fault lies not with disjunction elimination, but with disjunction introduction — that what is epistemologically irresponsible is, in the first instance to go from A to $A \lor B$. This charge has some intuitive pull, especially when one focuses on these simplified cases, where the inference in question would be odd and unjustified indeed. But there are two important

Without classical disjunctive syllogism, you cannot get from $\neg A$ and $A \vee B$ to B. To get to B Relevantly from $\neg A$ you would need $\neg A \rightarrow B$. Now, while $\neg A \rightarrow B$ may be classically equivalent to $A \vee B$, it is, of course, not equivalent for the Relevance logician. And, of course, note two important epistemological facts: (1) You have no good reason (except for classical prejudice) to believe $\neg A \rightarrow B$; (2) If you *did* have good reason to believe it (as well as $\neg A$) you *would* be justified (on anybody's theory) in believing B by *modus ponens*. I conclude — especially given the frequency with which we believe and then later excise falsehood, and otherwise extend and then revise our defective belief corpus — that an acceptance of classical disjunctive syllogism in an epistemically hostile environment conduces to deriving unjustified and content-gratuitous conclusions, conclusions which would not be drawn by an agent using a Relevance logic. What better recommendation could a rational agent in a hostile environment want?[4] Of course more defense of this view is needed. The admissibility of disjunctive syllogism is in the background; the truth-preserving character of the rule remains to be disarmed; the non-equivalence of $\neg A \rightarrow B$ and $A \vee B$ must be defended epistemologically. The best way to do this is to consider the replies to the previous arguments offered by the classical logician.

---

things to say in reply, one formal, decisive and unsatisfying, and the other more epistemological, questionable and philosophically compelling: First, given the duality of disjunction- introduction and conjunction-elimination, one takes the latter and rejects the former only at the intolerable cost of a wildly counterintuitive or a uselessly weak system. This response may, of course, fail to satisfy the philosophical intuitions at stake. So, consider this: We typically belive theoretical claims on the basis of evidence. Often, our belief in a theory persists despite the discrediting of some early evidence in its favor, even when that evidence was originally responsible for our subscription to the theory in the first place. Some theories become so entrenched in our belief systems that they come to function virtually as axioms. (So, one might have been convinced of Galileo's claims about the solar system on the strength of his telescopic reports and then hold on to the theory for other reasons even after having learned that the telescopes weren't very good and that the observations were equivocal.) Now, suppose I believe that if the market Crashes, either the Accountants or the Bankers will leap from the windows. Suppose that this is a deeply held (or "axiomatic") belief. Suppose I also hold, as part of the same deeply held theory that Accountants leap only if the market Crashes. Now, suppose that I hear (from a mendacious source) that the Accountants are leaping. I come to believe that the market has Crashed (on the strength of A) and hence that $A \vee B$ (still only on the strength of A). I then learn, sometime later, once C is a stable belief, that in fact $\neg A$. Now, given this new belief and my now relatively stable belief in $A \vee B$, I infer B. This is still a "toy" case, but it is structurally similar to much of scientific inference: inference to theories on the basis of revisable data, and inference from theories to their consequences (which may be complex, and disjunctive) and, in light of new data, to further consequences. And it should be clear that there are hence cases where (1) a belief in $A \vee B$ may be grounded only in A (and "axioms" or their moral equivalents) and where (2) classical disjunctive syllogism consequently gets one in trouble.

[4] Similar epistemological arguments apply to classical vs. Relevant interpretations of the conditional. So, for instance, consider the two paradoxes afflicting the classical conditional: (i) $A \rightarrow .B \rightarrow A$ and (ii) $\neg A \rightarrow .A \rightarrow B$. Suppose one came to believe A mistakenly, then, since one believed (i) one came to believe $B \rightarrow A$ for some irrelevant B. One might then learn $\neg A$ and again infer, for no good reason, $\neg B$. Or, given (ii) and the false information that $\neg A$, one might, after storing $A \rightarrow B$, learn the falsity of $\neg A$, and then draw the unwarranted conclusion that B. Again, once we introduce epistemic hostility, replete with misinformation and cognitive limitations, classical logic, through inference rules that make no epistemological sense, wreaks havoc from which Relevance Logic can save us. The rational agent ought, therefore, in such circumstances, to reason relevantly.

4. THE RATIONAL CLASSICAL LOGICIAN, AND RELEVANT REJOINDERS

The rational classical logician may not be convinced. He may argue as follows: You (the Relevance logician) grant that $\neg A \rightarrow B$ and $\neg A$ together entail B. And surely, $\neg A \rightarrow B$ and $A \vee B$ are equivalent. Classically, they are, of course. Just as obviously, in R, E and their cousins, they are not. The question is, "Ought a rational agent in an epistemically hostile environment accept a logic according to which they are equivalent, or one according to which $\neg A \rightarrow B$ is not derivable from $A \vee B$?" When the question is put this way, the answer is clear. Knowledge is not stable. Its increase is not monotonic. Principles of belief extension and revision must be sensitive to this fact. To believe $\neg A \rightarrow B$ is to hold an "inference ticket" in Anderson and Belnap's terms. That ticket could survive one's change in mind with regard to A. The justification of the inference ticket is logically independent of the justification of A and of the justification of B. A belief in that entailment hence requires its own warrant, and not merely that of A or of B. epistemic hostility demands caution.

Anderson and Belnap make a closely related point, in a more modal frame of mind:

> The truth of $A \vee B$, with truth functional "or," is not sufficient for the truth of "If it were not the case that A, then it would be the case that B." Example: It is true that either Napoleon was born in Corsica or else the number of the beast is perfect (with truth functional "or"); but it does not follow that had Napoleon *not* been born in Corsica, 666 would equal the sum of its factors. On the other hand the intensional varieties of "or" which *do* support the disjunctive syllogism are such as to support corresponding (possibly counterfactual) subjunctive conditionals. When one says "that is either *Drosophila melanogaster* or *D. virilis*, I'm not sure which," and on finding that it wasn't *D. melanogaster*, concludes that it was *D. virilis*, no fallacy is being committed. But this is precisely because "or" in this context *means* "if it isn't one, then it is the other." [p. 176]

This remark about the semantic ambiguity of "or" between a straightforwardly disjunctive interpretation and an entailment-of-one- argument-by-the-falsity-of-the-other reading reflects a distinction between two epistemological situations: In the first, one has evidence for one or both disjuncts, and so for the disjunction. In the second, one has evidence for the relevance of the truth-value of one of the "disjuncts" for the truth-value of the other. Nothing could be more epistemically dissimilar. Were we angels, these circumstances might be coextensive. But we are not. And they are not.

"But," the classical logician pleads, "classical disjunctive syllogism is *truth-preserving*. And after all, all that we ask from a rule of inference — as opposed, say, to a rule of epistemic prudence — is that it never lead us from truth into falsehood.

What fault, therefore, can you find with this rule?" Again, the important thing for present purposes, is to ask this question from an epistemological point of view. And from that point of view, the answer is again clear: Since some of our beliefs are false, preservation of truth is not enough. A subject in an epistemically hospitable world would have only true beliefs; any old truth-preserving inference rule would be just fine for such a subject. But our world is not so obliging. In it, we need not only to preserve truth, but to avoid the gratuitous introduction into our belief sets of wild falsehood. We know that we entertain some false — and even some pairs of inconsistent — beliefs, and some of these may even be well-justified. In such circumstances, we have seen, admitting the disjunctive syllogism leads to the gratuitous insertion of irrelevant falsehood into our belief set.

The classical logician has one final argument: "Meyer and Dunn [1969][5] have demonstrated the admissibility of the disjunctive syllogism in E. So why not admit it?" The reply here is much the same as before. What Meyer and Dunn demonstrate is that if $\neg A$ and $A \vee B$ are theorems then so is B. That makes disjunctive syllogism harmless, as Anderson and Belnap note [314] for systems of pure logic. But that is cold comfort in the harsh world of epistemic hostility. In particular, while admission of the rule would not increase our stock of theorems, for any believer who believes more (and less) than logic requires or sanctions, admission will wreak havoc with the belief set. Where rationality is called for, Relevance makes a difference.[6]

5. SUMMING UP: THE RATIONAL DOG

We can now return to The Dog. If anybody lives in an epistemically hostile environment The Dog does. His best friend, after all (prior to his rescue by Anderson and Belnap) was the Man, who imputes to him the use of disjunctive syllogism. With friends like that . . . ? It hence behooves The Dog to reason Relevantly and not classically. The Man, as we have seen, charges the poor Dog with classicism. Anderson and Belnap ably defend a more charitable Relevant interpretation of The Dog's reasoning. They note that he may interpret the disjunction modally (hence as equivalent to $\neg A \rightarrow B$) in the recognition that the alternatives he considers are

---

[5] See also [Anderson and Belnap, 1975] pp. 300–321 for a detailed exposition of two alternative proofs.

[6] Here are two related considerations (both due to conversations with Lee Bowie): First, the admissibility of an inference rule does not in general entail the admissibility of what might be called a "conditional form" of that inference rule. So, for instance, where disjunctive syllogism is admissible, the following rule need not be: $(\vdash (C \rightarrow \neg A) \wedge \vdash (C \rightarrow (A \vee B))) \Rightarrow \vdash (C \rightarrow B)$ (where '$\vdash$' is read "is a theorem"). And since most of what we know we know conditionally (depending on evidence) introducing a classical disjunctive syllogism into our general cognitive apparatus (as opposed to our logical theorem generating mechanism) would have the effect of introducing a rule of the latter form. Second, and more epistemologically significant is the fact that we often assert distinct claims on the basis of distinct and mutually inconsistent sets of evidence. So, if I believe $A \vee B$ on the strength of evidence $E1$ and $\neg A$ on the strength of evidence $E2$ then it might well turn out that since $E1$ and $E2$ are inconsistent, I cannot rationally join them to get grounds for B. So, believing both $A \vee B$ and $\neg A$, where these are non-logical in general provides no reason for believing B. If our evidence was always consistent, admission of disjunctive syllogism might not be so bad. Our refusal to admit it recognizes the fact that sets of individually justified beliefs may not be jointly justified.

relevant to one another (in which case the disjunction cannot be introduced using a rule parallel to truth-functional disjunction introduction) and his inference is an instance of *modus ponens*. But we have yet to see why it could only be rational for him to do so.

In order to see why the rational Dog is the Relevant Dog, consider the parable of three Dogs who inhabit epistemically hostile environments. I leave it to the reader to judge which are rational: Dog_1 is told (by the mendacious Man) that The Man is off for a stroll on road A. He infers truth- functionally, in a moment of idle logical revery that The Man will go down either road A or road B (an unrelated highway to a distant place). The Dog, upon coming to the fork in the road whence A begins, picks up no scent of The Man (who is at home). He chuckles at the thought of inferring B from his available premisses $A \lor B$ and $\neg A$, and heads for home. Dog_2 is told by The Man that he will take either A or B — that if he is not down A, he will be down B. The Dog comes to the fork, finds no scent down A, quickly notes the relevance of the two alternatives, and from $\neg A \rightarrow B$ and $\neg A$ infers B, joining his best friend a few minutes later.

Dog_3, like Dog_1 is told that The Man will take A. Proud of his logical acumen, he infers, truth-functionally, $A \lor B$ for a suitably arbitrary B. Coming to A, he finds no trace of The Man (epistemic hostility being what it is) and sets off down B. He has never been heard from since.

BIBLIOGRAPHY

Anderson, A. & Belnap, N. (1975): *Entailment: The Logic of Relevance and Necessity*. Princeton: Princeton University Press.

Bolles, R. (1975): "Learning, Motivation and Cognition," in W. K. Estes (ed.) *Handbook of Learning and Cognitive Processes* vol. I. Hillsdale, NJ: Lawrence Earlbaum Associates.

Care, N. (1988): *On Sharing Fate*. Philadelphia: Temple University Press.

Cherniak, C. (1986): *Minimal Rationality*. Cambridge, MA: MIT Press/Bradford Books.

Garfield, J. (1988): "No Man's Land: Review of Macnamara's *A Border Dispute: The Place of Logic in Psychology*," *The Journal of Symbolic Logic* 53, pp. 314–317.

Harman, G. (1986): *Change in View: Principles of Reasoning*. Cambridge, MA: MIT Press/Bradford Books.

Hintikka, J. (1962): *Knowledge and Belief*. Ithaca, NY: Cornell University Press.

Kornblith, H. (1986): *Naturalizing Epistemology*. Cambridge, MA: MIT Press/Bradford Books.

Macnamara, R. (1986): *A Border Dispute: The Place of Logic in Psychology*. Cambridge, MA: MIT Press/Bradford Books.

Meyer, R.K. and M.J. Dunn (1969): "E, R and γ." *The Journal of Symbolic Logic* 34, pp. 460–474.

Nisbett, R. and L. Ross (1980): *Human Inference: Strategies and Shortcomings of Human Judgement*. Englewood Cliffs: Prentice-Hall.

Simon, H. (1981): *The Sciences of the Artificial*. Cambridge, MA: MIT Press.

Williams, B. (1986): *Ethics and the Limits of Philosophy*. Cambridge: Cambridge University Press.

JON BARWISE

CONSISTENCY AND LOGICAL CONSEQUENCE[1]

A personal note

During 1962-63, as a senior at Yale University, I had the good fortune to work as Nuel Belnap's research assistant. I was helping Nuel (at least he let me feel I was helping) investigate a certain fragment of the logic E of Entailment. Of those days I now recall mainly the excitement of collaboration, on which I have been hooked ever since, and the discovery of what it is like to do research. While I thoroughly enjoyed the experience, it was many years before I completely realized how important working with Nuel had been for me.

After graduation, I attended the Berkeley Model Theory Symposium on the way to graduate school at Stanford. I was quite taken with the elegance of the model-theoretic approach being pursued by the Tarski school, and soon became a convert. But I was never entirely comfortable about the conversion. I knew that Anderson, Belnap, and company were wrestling with very hard problems, but I didn't see how to fit their concerns into the model-theoretic world. And so I set them aside.

In recent years these worries have returned to haunt me, as I have begun to appreciate the enormous complexities of understanding the logic implicit in the languages people actually use, complexities that are idealized away in the usual formulation of first-order logic. In this paper, dedicated to my old teacher and friend, I would like to address one aspect of this complexity, one that has to do with two of Nuel's concerns: consistency and logical consequence.

This paper is divided into two parts. Section One contains a philosophical overview; Section Two is devoted to a more technical look at a particular case study.

Etchemendy's Problem

I think it is fair to say that since the pioneering work of Tarski and Gödel, the model-theoretic account of notions like consistency, logical truth, and logical consequence has been the dominant one in logic. For example, model theory has become the measuring stick of choice with which to judge deductive systems. A sentence is logically true, according to the model-theoretic analysis of the notion, just in case it is true in every model. The stature of a deductive system is judged by its ability to let us derive these sentences. At the very least, we require deductive systems to be

---

[1] This paper was written while the author was on leave from Stanford University at the Center for Advanced Study in the Behavioral Sciences, with support from the Center for the Study of Language and Information and the National Science Foundation (NSF #BNS87-00864). The author wishes to thank all these institutions for their support.

J. M. Dunn and A. Gupta (eds.), Truth or Consequences, 111–122.
© 1990 *Kluwer Academic Publishers. Printed in the Netherlands.*

sound, that is, to declare as derivable only sentences which are true in every model. And to really pass muster a deductive system must be complete: every sentence true in every model should be derivable.

This model-theoretic analysis has been so widely accepted that the adjective "model-theoretic" in "model-theoretic semantics" has become almost redundant. Nowadays many students of language and logic take semantics simply to be model-theoretic semantics. This identification is so wide-spread that critics of the predictions of the standard model-theoretic account of logical consequence often find themselves attempting to defend a syntactic account. It can seem like the only alternative.

This identification of semantics with model-theoretic semantics has been strongly challenged in Etchemendy (1990). Unlike most critics of the model-theoretic account, Etchemendy accepts the view that the notions of logical truth and logical consequence are fundamentally semantical in nature. The strength of Etchemendy's argument comes in part from his placing himself squarely within the semantical tradition. Accepting its premises, he argues persuasively that the Tarskian account in general fails to give anything like an adequate analysis of these fundamental notions. Not only does it fail to give an analysis of the notions – it is not even, according to Etchemendy, guaranteed to be extensionally correct. For example, he argues that the model-theoretic account of logical truth can, for particular languages, fail to declare as logically true sentences which are in fact logically true (he calls this problem "undergeneration"), or it can declare as logically true sentences which are not logically true ("overgeneration"), or both at once.

In this note I would like to put a slightly different slant on Etchemendy's claim, and discuss a real example that illustrates one of his main points.

Consistency

I find it helpful to recast Etchemendy's claim by focusing less on logical truth and logical consequence and more on a complementary pretheoretic notion, that of consistency. The intuitive notion of consistency that interests me is closely linked with the notion of possibility: a sentence S is consistent in this sense if it could be (or could have been) true.[2] More generally, a set T of sentences is consistent if it could be the case (or could have been the case) that all of the sentences in T are simultaneously true.

Proof theory derived its inspiration from the desire to understand logical truth and logical consequence. Model theory, on the other hand, focuses first and foremost on this notion of consistency. It starts from the above intuitive understanding and fleshes it out as follows. First, we note that there are several ways to put the intuitive condition that S could be true: that there is a possible configuration of the world

---

[2] In this paper, I follow tradition and ignore the important difference between sentences and statements made by particular uses of them. That is, I am ignoring the effects of context. Things become more subtle when context is taken into consideration, as we have learned from Kaplan (1978). The notions studied here really apply to statements. See Barwise and Etchemendy (1989) for a discussion and further references to the literature.

which would make S true, for example, or that there might be or might have been a set of circumstances which make S true.

All of these are couched in thoroughly modal terms, terms like "could be a ...," "might be a ..." or "a possible configuration." Model-theoretic semantics can be seen as at attempt to cash out these imprecise modal characterizations with precise non-modal characterizations.[3] The first step is to set up a mathematical framework for modeling the intuitive idea of a possible configuration of the world, or a possible set of circumstances. This is usually done by defining a class $\mathcal{V}$ of set-theoretic structures and quantifying over the structures in $\mathcal{V}$. Thus, we end up with a mathematical model of the intuitive notion: S is consistent if and only if there exists a structure in $\mathcal{V}$ in which S is true.

Model theory is supposed to connect up with logical truth and logical consequence by way of this notion of consistency. The basic assumption is that a sentence S is logically true if and only if its denial $\neg$S is not consistent, and similarly for logical consequence. So, given the above, we end up with the claim that S is logically true if and only if it is true in every structure in $\mathcal{V}$.

Looked at in this way, the model-theoretic analysis of logical truth can be factored into two parts. One is an assumption about the relationship between logical truth and consistency.[4] The other is a mathematical modeling of consistency. If either of these is flawed, then so is the resulting account of logical truth and logical consequence. Etchemendy calls both of these into question. Let's look at them in turn.

First, how confident are we in the proposed equation of the logical truth of S with the inconsistency of $\neg$S? One half of this is clearly unproblematic. If S is a logical truth, then there is simply no way that S could fail to be true, no matter how things were, so that $\neg$S must be inconsistent. But the other half of the biconditional seems far more problematic. What makes us think that if S is not a logical truth, then there is a possible configuration of the world in which S is false? Couldn't it be that S has to be true, for some reason or other, no matter how things are, but that the reason is not one of logic? That is, couldn't S be necessarily true for some reason without being logically true?

Etchemendy gives as an example the interpreted first-order language of number theory. Since this language is about the natural numbers, with the arithmetic operations, there is only one way things could be, the way they actually are, as given by the natural numbers. As a result, for this language the consistent sentences (i.e., the ones true in some possible configuration) coincide with the sentences that are true. Etchemendy argues convincingly that it is far less clear that our understanding of

---

[3] When I say that model-theoretic semantics can be seen in this way, I am opting for what Etchemendy calls "representational semantics." In doing so I am sluffing over (and accepting) a major argument in Etchemendy's book having to do with the difference between representational semantics and Tarskian semantics. In Barwise and Etchemendy (1989) we attempt a rational reconstruction of model-theoretic semantics as representational semantics.

[4] It should be noted that there is also a proof-theoretic notion of logical consistency: not having a blatant contradiction as a logical consequence. Another way to pose the question raised here is to ask about the relationship between these two notions of consistency.

logical truth commits us to the claim that every truth of arithmetic is a logical truth of the language of arithmetic.

But let us temporarily set the question of the relation between consistency and logical truth to one side. We can do this either by accepting the standard reduction of logical truth to consistency, or by simply setting aside logical truth, focusing instead on consistency itself. I choose the latter line. Thus, we ask ourselves, how sure can we be in general that the proposed model-theoretic analysis of this notion of consistency is right?

Etchemendy's answer is: In general, not at all. It can happen that a sentence is inconsistent but not declared so by the model theory. (This is the flip side of what Etchemendy calls "undergeneration.") This can happen only if some of the structures used to model possible circumstances do not in fact correspond to such circumstances.[5] And, conversely, it can happen that a sentence declared inconsistent by the model theory is in fact consistent (the flip side of Etchemendy's "overgeneration" problem). This can happen only if there is no model-theoretic structure to model the intuitively possible circumstances that would make the sentence true.

Logicians have recognized for some time that model theory can give us structures which don't actually model any set of possible circumstances. For example, if we are interested in the pretheoretic logical relations that arise in full second-order logic, but use Henkin models in our analysis, then the model-theoretic account will declare as consistent certain second-order sentences that seem, intuitively, to be impossible on the intended interpretation. Or, to look again at the language of arithmetic, non-standard models are models that do not model any possible way the numbers could really be. Such failures have not been taken as especially damning, though, since one could reply that in looking at arbitrary Henkin models and non-standard models of arithmetic, we were simply looking at unintended models. But Etchemendy's claim that the model-theoretic account can fail in the other direction, by characterizing as inconsistent sentences that are consistent, is a harder pill to swallow. In the reminder of this paper I argue that it is a problem we must absorb and learn how to respond to. It is this problem I refer to as "Etchemendy's Problem."

Etchemendy does give us one escape route from his problem. Re-examining an older observation of Kreisel, he looks at the significance of Completeness Theorems, when such theorems exist. He shows that a significant consequence of a Completeness Theorem can be to show that Etchemendy's Problem for that language will not be realized. For suppose some sentence S is declared inconsistent by a model theory for which we have a completeness result. Then, by completeness, there is a proof of ¬S. But, assuming each of the rules of inference is intuitively sound, then ¬S will be logically true, so that S is impossible. So in this case, Etchemendy's Problem goes away.

It is worth observing that this application of completeness does not depend on the rules in question being finitary. All that matters is that they preserve intuitive soundness. This sheds new light (at least new to me) on the significance of completeness results for infinitary systems, systems that use some infinitary rule like the ω-rule.

---

[5] In saying this, I am supposing that part of what it is to give a model of possible circumstances is to say what it means for a sentence to be true in it.

Database logic

The main purpose of this paper is to report a real example of Etchemendy's Problem. The example I have in mind comes from the study of databases, database languages, and database logic. In particular, it is inspired by Jacobs (1985), a book devoted to using model-theoretic methods to resolve some thorny issues in the study of databases. Just what the issues are is not relevant to the point of this note.

In order to be faithful to actual database practice, Jacobs has to enrich the traditional framework of first-order languages in certain ways. Intuitively, this extension seems unproblematic. However, it turns out that if we use as a metatheory the standard one used in doing first-order logic, ZFC, the model theory ends up declaring logically inconsistent various databases that seem not just consistent but in fact true. It is this phenomenon I claim to be an illustration of Etchemendy's Problem.

The basic problem comes from what are known as *non-hierarchical* databases. These are databases that contain circular data structures of a certain kind. In such a database, a table T may have some other table as an argument, and when you trace out the dependencies, you find that there are cycles in the relation given by: $T_1 \prec T_2$ if and only if the semantic content of T_1 is denoted by some term t that occurs in the table T_2. If one models the contents of these tables in anything like the standard manner then these cycles will end up generating infinite descending chains in the membership relation, something that is ruled out by the foundation axiom FA. And so sentences of database logic which are clearly intuitively consistent are declared inconsistent by the model theory.

As a very simple example of this, consider the database shown below.

If one models relationships in anything like the standard way, as Jacobs does, and if one represents this database with a conjunction of atomic sentences in database logic, and one works in the universe of wellfounded sets described by ZFC, then this database has no model, and so gets declared inconsistent by the model-theoretic account. But it is obviously not inconsistent. In fact, it is *true*.

We can boil the general problem down to its starkest case by considering atomic sentences of the form P(P). Do we want to rule such sentences *inconsistent* no matter what property the predicate P happens to express? What if P expressed the property of being a property?[6]

What does this mean for model-theoretic methods as applied to non-hierarchical database languages? Are they doomed? Of course not. Recall that model theory starts by trying to analyze the idea that a sentence S could be true in some set of circumstances. It provides a framework for modeling sets of circumstances as set-theoretic structures, and replaces the modal characterization by quantification over some collection $\mathcal{V}$ of structures. If the account goes wrong, then there are two places to adjust things. One is to change the way we model sets of circumstances. The other is to keep the standard representation of circumstances but to alter the

---

[6] Or, assuming the questionable identification discussed and set aside earlier, are we so sure that every sentence of the form ¬P(P) is a logical truth? It would surely be a surprising discovery if the sentence *The property of being a property is not itself a property* turned out to express a logical truth.

FatherOf

Father	Child
John	Max
Dan	David
Dan	Alisa

MotherOf

Mother	Child
Nancy	Max
Judith	David
Judith	Alisa

BrotherOf

Brother	Sibling
David	Alisa

SizeOf

Relation	Number
FatherOf	3
MotherOf	3
BrotherOf	1
SizeOf	4

collection of structures over which we quantify. What matters is that our modeling of sets of circumstances be close to intuitions, and that any intuitively possible set of circumstances be modeled, closely enough, within our collection of models, and conversely, that any model correspond to an intuitively possible set of circumstances.

In the next section I look at a version of database logic and provide a way out of the problem along the second line. I adjust the collection of structures by looking at a larger universe of sets. What I show is that if we keep the modeling scheme unchanged, but enlarge the collection of structures to those given to us by the anti-foundation axiom AFA, then the problem disappears: there are enough structures so that an intuitively sound deductive system is complete, and so every intuitively consistent set of sentences has a model.

Peter Aczel (private communication) has suggested an alternate modification, where the universe of sets is not altered, but where one complicates the representational scheme. Which approach would, if pursued, give rise to the most useful model theory is an open question. Both seem worth pursuing as a case study in how we can get around instances of Etchemendy's Problem.

Before turning to the more technical section, I want to return to the issue we set aside earlier, that of providing an analysis of the notion of logical truth and logical consequence.

Logical consequence

At first sight, it seems that if we follow Etchemendy in rejecting the reduction of logical consequence to that of consistency, then we are at a loss as to how to even begin to give a semantical analysis of logical consequence. However, there is also something quite liberating about this rejection. For it means that we are no longer forced to judge a deductive model of the consequence relation deficient if it fails to be model-theoretically complete. Indeed, in the case of the interpreted first-order language of arithmetic, this incompleteness would become an expected and desirable feature. It would allow us, for example, to distinguish between logical truths in the language or arithmetic, and those sentences that are true for genuinely number-theoretic reasons. It *might* be, for example, that the standard deductive systems provide the best model of logical consequence that we are going to get for this language. There is certainly some empirical evidence to support this view.

On the other hand, this is by no means certain. If we think of inference and logical consequence not in terms of relations among sentences, but in terms of information extraction, it could well be that there are valid methods of reasoning that one would want to say fall under the purview of logic, but which do not fit into standard deductive systems. The example I have in mind is symmetry arguments, especially in reasoning that uses visual representations (diagrams, pictures, and tables), described in Barwise and Etchemendy (1990a, 1990b). In the work reported in these papers, we have found symmetry arguments to be an especially powerful method of reasoning, one that is pretty much subject-matter independent (a good test for a principle of logic, perhaps), and one that is particularly hard to capture in the traditional deductive calculi.

Rejecting the standard reduction of logical consequence to consistency also frees us to study more fine-grained models of logical consequence, those that hew closer to the way people actually reason in various circumstances. Failures of completeness are no longer held against us. In particular, we can look at constructive reasoning in mathematics, or at the work of Anderson, Belnap and others on entailment and relevance, as examples of this enterprise. The three enterprises of studying truth, consequence, and consistency come to be seen as related but distinct endeavors.

CONSISTENCY IN DATABASE LOGIC: A CASE STUDY

In this section I am going to develop a simple non-hierarchical database language and use it to discuss some of the issues raised above in greater specificity, issues which only become clear with reference to specific examples. I could set this up within the framework developed by Jacobs, but I won't. While his languages do admit of circularity, they are not very well suited to my particular example, and would, besides, get us involved with a lot of irrelevant details. So instead I will develop a special purpose language for describing databases like the one exhibited in the table above. The main point I make with regard to this little language applies equally to Jacobs' languages.

The language

Our language is going to be a three-sorted language, with constants and variables for each sort. The three sorts are (1) people, (2) natural numbers, and (3) extensions of relations. For the sake of specificity, our language will have five binary relation symbols, FatherOf, MotherOf, SisterOf, BrotherOf, and SizeOf. The relation symbols are also considered constants of the third sort. We take the semantic content of these symbols to be the corresponding binary relations, *FatherOf, MotherOf, BrotherOf, SisterOf,* and *SizeOf*. The first four are to be understood as strict biological relations. These relations are thought of as primitive, not as sets of pairs.

Our language has individual constants Ken, Evelyn, ... standing for particular people, as well as individual constants 0, 1, 2, ... standing for the various natural numbers. Our language will also have variables of each sort: $x_1, x_2, \ldots$ to range over people; $n_1, n_2, \ldots$ to range over the natural numbers; and $Q_1, Q_2, \ldots$ to range over extensions of relations.

Terms of the first sort consist of names of people and the variables of that sort. Terms of the second sort consist of numerals and variables of that sort. Terms of the third sort consist of the five relation symbols and variables of the third sort.

The atomic sentences of our language are formed in the expected way. If R is any of the biological relation symbols and t_1, t_2 are terms of the first sort, then $R(t_1, t_2)$ is an atomic wff. If t_1, t_2 are terms of the second and third sort, respectively, then SizeOf(t_1, t_2) is an atomic wff. Finally, if t_1, t_2 are terms of the same sort, then $(t_1 = t_2)$ is an atomic wff.

Once we have the atomic wffs, we define the class of all wffs in the usual way, by closing under the propositional connectives and the quantifiers $\forall, \exists$ with respect to each sort. Thus we can express database constraints like the following:

- $\forall x \forall y \forall z [\text{FatherOf}(x, z) \land \text{FatherOf}(y, z) \rightarrow x = y \land \neg x = z]$
- $\forall x \forall y [\text{BrotherOf}(x, y) \rightarrow \neg \text{SisterOf}(x, y)]$
- $\forall u, v [\text{FatherOf}(u, v) \rightarrow \neg \text{SizeOf}(0, \text{FatherOf})]$

Intuitively, each of these will be true in any genuine set of circumstances. By contrast, the following will be true in some genuine circumstances, not in others. But each is, intuitively, a logical possibility.

- FatherOf(Jon, Claire)
- $\forall x \neg \text{FatherOf}(x, \text{Adam})$
- SizeOf(3, FatherOf)

By a *database* in this language we mean a conjunction of atomic sentences, i.e., a conjunction of atomic wffs with no free variables.

Database models

Let P be a set of people, including the people named by the names in our language. Our first job in giving a model-theoretic semantics for this language is to decide how we want to model the extension of relations. In order to avoid having distinct relations with the same extension, we keep track of the relations themselves.[7] Thus we define an *infon* to be a triple σ of the form $\langle R, a, b \rangle$ where R is a relation and a, b are objects of the appropriate sorts for the relation in question.[8] This infon is supposed to represent the possibility that a stands in relation R to b. The relation R is said to be the major constituent of the infon. By an *extension* for R we mean any finite set of infons with R as major constituent.

The reader may have noted that there is a circularity in this definition that needs to be clarified. The definition should be taken in the most liberal way possible. Thus we define the sets *Infons* and *Extensions$_R$* (one for each R) simultaneously to be the largest collections such that:

1. if $\sigma \in Infons$ then $\sigma = \langle R, a, b \rangle$ where either R is one of our biological relations and $a, b \in P$, or else R is the relation *SizeOf*, a is a natural number, and b is in *Extensions$_R$*, for some R; and
2. if r is in *Extensions$_R$*, then r is a finite set of infons, all having major constituent R.

By a *database model* for our language we mean a set $\mathcal{M}$ of R-extensions, one for each of our relations R. We write this as

$$\mathcal{M} = \{FatherOf^{\mathcal{M}}, MotherOf^{\mathcal{M}}, BrotherOf^{\mathcal{M}}, SisterOf^{\mathcal{M}}, SizeOf^{\mathcal{M}}\}$$

By a variable assignment in $\mathcal{M}$ we mean a function g from the variables of our language assigning people to variables of the first sort, natural numbers to variables of the second sort, and elements of $\mathcal{M}$ to variables of the third sort. This allows us to define, for any term t of our language, and any variable assignment g, the value of t in $\mathcal{M}$ relative to g, in the obvious manner. We write this $val(\text{t}, \mathcal{M}, g)$, noting that it is an object of the sort of the term t. We will omit the arguments $\mathcal{M}$ and g if they can be inferred from context.

Using this we define satisfaction of wffs in database models in the expected way. For example,

$$\mathcal{M} \models \mathsf{SizeOf}(\text{t}_1, \text{t}_2)[g] \quad \text{iff} \quad \langle SizeOf, val(\text{t}_1), val(\text{t}_2) \rangle \in SizeOf^{\mathcal{M}}.$$

The propositional connectives are treated classically. The range of the quantifiers is taken over the objects of the appropriate sort. In particular, the relation quantifiers range over $\mathcal{M}$, the extensions of the relations given by the database model.

---

[7] This still leaves us with an ambiguity about the empty extension, but that will not bother anything we say here.

[8] This term, meaning a unit of information, is borrowed from situation theory, but otherwise situation theory is not particularly in evidence here. One could also think of it as a datum or possible fact.

Inadequacies in the model theory

We are now in a position to discuss which sentences are judged consistent in virtue of being true in some database model. Are they the ones that seem, intuitively, to be consistent?

The answer, of course, is "No." Things go wrong in both directions. Lets start with the clearest and most interesting direction, the one that illustrates Etchemendy's Problem. Thus we want an example where the model theory fails by declaring inconsistent sentences which seem intuitively consistent. A simple example is the conjunction which represents the database displayed in the table in the first section of this paper. A simpler example would be any sentence of the form

$$\text{SizeOf}(k, \text{SizeOf}).$$

Whether this sentence is judged consistent by our model theory depends on the set-theoretical assumptions using in doing the model theory. To see this, let us define a *wellfounded database model* to be any such model in the universe of wellfounded sets.

LEMMA. *If $\mathcal{M}$ is wellfounded then $\mathcal{M} \models \forall n \neg \text{SizeOf}(n, \text{SizeOf})$.*

Proof. This follows from the way that ordered pairs and ordered triples are represented in set theory. It follows from this representation that each constituent of the triple $\langle x, y, z \rangle$ is a element of the transitive closure of the triple. Hence, if $\mathcal{M} \models \text{SizeOf}(k, \text{SizeOf})$, then $SizeOf^{\mathcal{M}}$ is an element of its own transitive closure, and so $\mathcal{M}$ is not wellfounded.

It follows of course that if we assume the foundation axiom, then the sentence above will not have a model, since any such model $\mathcal{M}$ would be non-wellfounded. On the other hand, if we use a more liberal set theory, say one that has the anti-foundation axiom AFA of Aczel, then this sentence will be consistent, since you can uses AFA to prove that this sentence has a model.

One can go further, and show that there is a deductive system with intuitively sound rules of inference which is complete for database models, provided one assumes something like AFA. This is, in fact, a version of an old Completeness Theorem due to Kanger (1955), discussed in Aczel (1988). Thus if we assume AFA, Etchemendy's Problem for this language is not a problem.

Finally, let us also turn to the other problem that model-theoretic accounts can exhibit. We claim that our model theory, with or without AFA, is in some ways too liberal, in that it declares consistent sentences which seem, intuitively, inconsistent. Consider for example the database

$$\text{FatherOf}(\text{Jon}, \text{Claire}) \land \text{SizeOf}(0, \text{FatherOf}).$$

This is inconsistent on our intuitive understanding of these sentences, but it does have a model. The trouble, of course, is that we have not insisted that the extension of the size relation be compatible with the rest of the database model. To do this, we need to restrict to models $\mathcal{M}$ which satisfy the following condition: if $\langle SizeOf, n, r \rangle$

is in $SizeOf^{\mathcal{M}}$ then $n = Card(r)$. If we do this, and still want a completeness theorem, then we are going to need to use some form of the ω-rule. Luckily, as we have noted, infinitary rules do not destroy the significance of completeness results when used to judge the soundness of the model theory.

For a somewhat more problematic example, consider the sentence

$$\exists x \exists (y \mathsf{BrotherOf}(x, y) \wedge \neg \mathsf{BrotherOf}(y, x) \wedge \neg \mathsf{SisterOf}(y, x)).$$

This too seems inconsistent, since being x's brother constrains x to be either your sister or your brother. This is just one of many constraints that hold in the real world that are not respected in our database models. This one seems very close to the surface of our intuitions about the language. We could, of course, simply restrict attention to models that satisfy this constraint.

For a still more problematic example, consider the sentence

$$\exists x \exists y (\mathsf{FatherOf}(x, y) \wedge \mathsf{FatherOf}(y, x)).$$

This is clearly impossible, but there will be database models where it is true. In this case, however, it is less clear whether this is a consequence of the meanings associated with the items in the language, or whether it is a biological impossibility. We could go on giving sentences which could not hold in any real set of circumstances, but where it becomes less and less clear that the fact is one about the language, as opposed to facts about the physical world. But these examples should make the point.

Conclusions

Examples like these lead me to think that if we are going to study consistency of real languages, languages where the predicates have meanings associated with them, then we are going to have to admit that there is a certain slack in the notion of consistency, a slack that can be fleshed out in different ways in the model theory. That is, we will end up with at best a relative notion of consistency, relative to a certain class of models, depending on just what sorts of configurations of the world we want to admit as possible for the purposes at hand. But really, given the modal character of the basic intuitions behind consistency, and the notorious vagueness of modal notions, it would have been a miracle if this were not so.

If this is so, it provides some cold comfort to those who have been attempting to model the complementary notion of logical consequence by means of deductive systems. A main complaint about such systems has been their relativity, as witnessed by the lack of a canonical deductive system. How can any one be the right one? But if we are right in the lesson drawn from Etchemendy's book, then we also lack a canonical model theory. It may just be that human language and thought is too complex to admit of simple, unique characterizations of notions like consistency and logical consequence. If so, logic is a lot richer than the old picture led some of us to suppose.

Bibliography

Aczel, Peter (1988): *Non-Well-Founded Sets*. CSLI Lecture Notes 14.

Barwise, Jon, and John Etchemendy (1989): Model-theoretic semantics, in Michael I. Posner, ed., *Foundations of Cognitive Science*, Cambridge, Mass: The MIT Press / A Bradford Book, pp. 207–243.

Barwise, Jon, and John Etchemendy (1990a): Visual information and valid reasoning. In *Visualization in Mathematics*, ed. W. Zimmerman. Mathematical Association of America, to appear.

Barwise, Jon, and John Etchemendy (1990b): Information, infons and inference. *Situation Theory and its Applications, I*, ed. R. Cooper, et al. CSLI Lecture Notes, to appear.

Etchemendy, John (1990): *The Concept of Logical Consequence*. Harvard University Press, to appear.

Jacobs, Barry (1985): *Applied Database Logic*. Prentice-Hall.

Kaplan, David (1978): On the logic of demonstratives. *Journal of Philosophical Logic*, 8, pp. 81–98.

Kanger, Stig (1957): *Provability in Logic*. Stockholm Studies in Philosophy 1. University of Stockholm: Almqvist and Wiksell.

DANIEL COHEN

ON WHAT CANNOT BE

A curious thing about the problem of counterpossibles is that for all its complexity it too can be put in Anglo-Saxon monosyllables: What is meant by 'if p then q' when 'p' could not be the case? Unfortunately, and despite some valiant attempts, the answer cannot be given in a word, and so the problem remains.

Indeed, the problem of counterpossible conditionals remains very near the center of philosophy, quickly involving, as it does, such central philosophical notions as necessity and possibility, conditionals and entailment, semantics and pragmatics, and most of the rest of the general run of topics from philosophical logic and philosophy of language. Still, for all the rich streams of philosophical enquiry at whose confluence the problem of counterpossibles stands, there are limits to what can intelligently said about about the class as a whole. I suspect that the philosophically interesting things that can be said about counterpossible conditionals are of interest more for what they say about philosophy rather than for what they say about the conditionals themselves.

The aim here is to make a relatively modest point about counterpossibles: Some counterpossibles — conditionals whose antecedents describe an impossibility — are not counterfactuals. This is not to say that the impossible might not be contrary to fact. I believe it always is. The consistency of the world is not the issue, however. Rather, it is simply to say that how counterpossibles are used and understood differs markedly from how more prosaic counterfactuals are used and understood. An adequate theoretical account has to make this difference manifest.

There are some additional, less modest points that are relevant and that I take to be true, but which, for reasons of space, are not developed here. Some counterpossibles are not counterfactuals — but some are. There are several different kinds of counterpossibles. The necessity for a pluralistic account of these conditionals shows, in a microcosm, that a complete semantics for natural languages would have to avail itself of a variety of tools, including proof-theory, possible worlds frameworks, and assertibility conditions. That is, the boundaries that are often drawn among pure grammar, proof-theory, semantics, and pragmatics (all broadly construed) are more nearly conventional than natural. Beyond that, because counterpossibles are, as it were, very near the limit of "what can be said," they should be very near the center of philosophical concern. The impossibility of a single logic here bespeaks of a similar impossibility for the larger philosophical enterprise. But, the lines of thought that lead to these conclusions re-affirm rather than call into question the centrality of logic for philosophy.

§1. Counterpossibles and counterfactuals. It seems natural to suppose that conditionals that entertain impossible conditions should be subsumed under a theory of counterfactuals. After all, what can't be, isn't. When the impossibility in question is historical or psychological or physical impossibility, this approach is fruitful. Just as "If kangaroos had no tails, they would topple over" can be read as asking us to

J. M. Dunn and A. Gupta (eds.), Truth or Consequences, 123–132.
© 1990 *Kluwer Academic Publishers. Printed in the Netherlands.*

consider a world with tailless kangaroos, so "If there were no gravity, objects would fly off the earth" apparently asks for consideration of a world without gravitation.

Logical impossibility might be thought to present a different sort of problem. If the impossible is also inconceivable, then a counterpossible would be asking us to do what cannot be done. It would be impossible to understand such a sentence.[1]

This line of reasoning comes a cropper on two counts. Whether or not the impossible is inconceivable, the locutions for counterfactuals do admit impossible conditions. Although the known falsity of the antecedent excludes most "open conditional" locutions,[2] the known impossibility of the antecedent of a conditional that is already a counterfactual does not have to change a thing. Even if "it can't be" normally precludes "what if" in a way that "it isn't" does not, the "what if" can always be pressed: "OK, so it's impossible. But *what if* it were true anyway?"

Beyond that, some impossibilities can indeed be entertained. Consider the following examples:

(1)   If there were a greatest prime, p, $p! + 1$ would be composite.

(2)   If there were a greatest prime, it would be eight.

(3)   If there were round squares, there might be round triangles, too.

(4)   Even if things could be red and blue at the same time, we wouldn't be able to register any such objects.

The temptation is to take the first of these as a paradigm. It answers to one step in Euclid's *reductio* argument against there being a greatest prime. Because of the connections between proofs and conditionals, the use of *reductio* argumentation presupposes the intelligibility of counterpossibles. This provides the strongest motivation for bothering with counterpossibles at all. The other examples are important, too, for what they show, viz., that the class of counterpossibles includes both truths and falsehoods (1 and 2), both woulds and mights (1 and 3),[3] and both full counterfactuals and semifactuals.[4] In short, counterpossibles seem to display all of the major characteristics of counterfactuals.

§2. Lewis on Counterpossibles. David Lewis is one who includes counterpossibles in his discussion of counterfactuals. The conclusion he reaches is that they can all be counted as true without harm.[5] In part this is because he thinks they are of only peripheral, system-completing interest. Besides, contradictions "materially" imply everything, and "strictly" speaking, this is also true: if one thing logically implies another it should counterfactually imply it also. Presumably, the linguistic data and more discriminating theories of implication are strictly immaterial.

There is a serious problem with Lewis's position. Initially, it concerns the interdefinability of would- and might-counterfactuals:

---

[1] Cf. Wittgenstein's remark at *Tractatus* 3.01ff. and Lewis 1986 pp. 6–7n.

[2] The term is from J. L. Mackie 1973.

[3] The difference between would- and might-counterfactuals is an important part of the account in Lewis 1973. It is also of moment to any probabilistic account of conditionals' truth or assertibility.

[4] This distinction, based on the (presupposed) truth-value of the consequent, was made by Goodman 1955. It becomes the cornerstone of the theory presented and developed in Kvart 1986.

[5] A more complete discussion of Lewis's reasons — and their shortcomings — can be found in Cohen 1988.

[P1] $A \square\!\!\rightarrow B \equiv \neg(A \diamondsuit\!\!\rightarrow \neg B)$

If all would-counterpossibles are true, then all might-counterpossibles would have to be false. As he admits, this is a bit counterintuitive. If anything, it would be more plausible to reverse the values, making all might-counterpossibles true and all would-counterpossibles false on the grounds that we simply could not say with certainty anything about how an impossible world would be. And so a second set of would- and might- counterfactual connectives are offered to reverse things. The problem remains but now in its negative image.

All the likely ways Lewis might alleviate the pressures caused by this misfit of theory and actual linguistic practice exacerbate matters, making it into more than the minor and isolated problem he would like it to be.

One option is "monster barring," the term used in Lakatos 1976 to characterize a rather obstinate attitude towards counterexamples to one's theory. Mostly, it involves a straightforward denial of the evidence, in this case, the apparent falsity of some counterpossibles (and the apparent truth of their might counterparts). This does not necessarily mean a merely partisan, knee-jerk defense of concept and theory. The data are not uncontroversial and well ought to be subject to scrutiny.

Monster barring does work well on occasion. For example, it is not at all unreasonable to question whether the counterpossible

(5)   If 2.1×3.4 is 71.4, then I'm a monkey's uncle

is really a conditional at all (and so provides an example of a counterpossible not in the subjunctive). There is no relevant logical connection between the antecedent and consequent states of affairs, there is no argument from the one to the other, and there is not even a pragmatic connection of the Austinian "If you're hungry, there are biscuits on the sideboard" sort. Perhaps (5) is best counted as a fancy locution for denying the antecedent, much as "That's a mistake if there ever was one" just asserts its consequence. One drawback to this approach is that it unnecessarily gets entangled with the question of which if-sentences are to count as conditionals without successfully answering it. (Example (5) does satisfy at least one proposal: the "then-transformation" test for conditionals proposed in Routley 1982, which successfully excludes such uses of "if" as "He is intelligent, if somewhat pedantic.") It is difficult to see how excluding unwanted if-sentences could be maintained without circularity. The semantics for conditionals do not precede their use.

Similarly, some putative counterpossibles might be discarded as not genuinely contrary to possibility. The monsters can, to stay with Lakatos' terminology, be "adjusted." For example,

(6)   If only 8×7 were 63, I'd have had an A on the test

has an impossible antecedent, and there are easily imagined circumstances in which it would (or would not) be assertible. However, it is plausibly read as an inexact expression of something like the more prosaic

(6')   If only the answer to problem five were 63, I'd have had an A.

The speaker is not really entertaining, nor asking the listener to entertain, the impossible situation that $8 \times 7 = 63$. While this sort of response works well enough for this example, it is less convincing when applied to any of (1)–(4).

Both of these options — denying that some apparent conditionals are real conditionals and denying that some apparently counterpossible conditionals are really contrary to possibility — have their legitimate applications. When taken as the only way to respond, they evade the issue rather than engage it.

A second and generally better line of response is, to resort to Lakatos' terminology yet again, "concept stretching." In this case, what needs to be stretched is the notion of "possible," and, derivatively, that of "possible worlds." Lewis does consider the inclusion of impossible worlds in the explicating framework:

> ... along with the *possible* possible worlds that differ from our world only in matters of contingent empirical fact, [we might add] some *impossible* possible worlds that differ from our world in matters of philosophical, mathematical, and even logical truth. (The pretense need not be taken very seriously to explain what happens in conversation; it just might be that this part of our conversational practice is founded upon a confused fantasy.) (1973, p. 24)

This route is rightly rejected by Lewis, but for all the wrong reasons. In the first place Lewis is content enough with a uniform treatment of counterpossibles for truth-valuational purposes. Beyond that, there is Lewis's realism with respect to possible worlds. He is not all that comfortable with the instrumentalist, "pretense" interpretation of even part of the formal semantics. Further, the introduction of distinct impossible worlds requires the abandonment of two-valued, truth-functional logic as the governing body. Lewis is not prepared to do this. Above all, this approach just does not fit with Lewis's overall understanding of counterfactuals as involving alternative ways the world it could be.

Each of these reasons for rejecting impossible counterfactual set-ups as explanatory devices for counterpossibles presupposes that all counterpossibles are indeed a subclass of counterfactuals for semantic purposes. This is suspect. Indeed, it is false. It may well be that "If kangaroos had no tails, they would topple over" can profitably be taken to mean that in any state of affairs in which kangaroos have no tails but which is otherwise as much like the actual as possible, kangaroos topple over; but it is harder to maintain that

(7)   If there were round squares, Euclidean geometry would be wrong,

should be given a parallel reading, i.e., that in any state of affairs which includes round squares but *which is otherwise as much like the actual as possible*, Euclid is wrong. What other details are permitted a state of affairs that has round squares? The similarity scale only goes so far. Resolutions of vagueness — standard or not — are not forthcoming.

There is an almost absolute resistance on the part of some counterpossibles to *any* resolution of vagueness. Pointing out the impossibility of a condition is germane, but it can also be knocking one's head against a wall: "But there *can't* be round squares!" "I know, but suppose there were anyway." The frustration is telling and what it tells us is to abandon the possible worlds framework for accommodating the antecedents of conditionals that are contrary to possibility.

The tactic Lewis actually adopts for explaining away the misfit between theory and linguistic practice is (no, not Lakatos' "method of proofs and refutations") an appeal to some additional, supplementary theoretical apparatus: pragmatics. Semantics, narrowly construed, is concerned solely with truth-conditions; pragmatics, understood as concerned with conversational implicatures and the like, can then account for the non-assertibility of certain truths, e.g., by being pointless in some contexts. The difference between (1) and (2) is read as a difference of assertibility, not truth-value.

Unfortunately, this option is not really open to Lewis. It is precluded for his particular account of counterfactuals by the relation he sees between semantics and pragmatics. In his view, an explanation is needed only for the truth of assertibles, not the falsehood of nonassertibles.[6] That is, truth is thought to be necessary but not sufficient for assertibility. This creates the problem for him already mentioned with respect to counterpossible might-conditionals. On his primary account, they are all false, a consequence of the vacuous truth granted all counterpossible woulds and the interdefinability of woulds and mights, [P1]. But they should none of them be assertible, if truth is a necessary condition for that. However, the assertibility of many, if not all, might-counterfactuals is admittedly established by the same arguments used for counterpossible woulds. The choice, then, comes down to changing the proof-theory or the semantics of the system, or else revising our understanding of the nature of the semantic-pragmatic relation.

The first options — changing the proof-theory or the semantics of the system — are not immediately palatable. They represent something of a choice of last resort for Lewis. Specifically, this would mean altering the interdefinability of would and might or else abandonning the vacuous truth of one or the other of the counterpossible pair.

The alternative also has its problems. The pressures caused by the misfit of truth and falsity with assertibilty and nonassertibility can be alleviated by simply severing the ties between the two. Confine the one distinction entirely to semantics and relegate the other completely to pragmatics. Truth need not be either necessary or sufficient for assertibility. But if assertibility is independent of semantics, then one or the other is otiose. Or, what's a theory of meaning for?

The recourse to extra-systemic considerations — pragmatics, in this case — is surely preferable to either ignoring, denying, or altering the data. Ultimately, however, it succeeds only in moving the troubles elsewhere. It is an attempt to sweep the semantic dust under the pragmatic rug.

§3. The Conditional Assertion Solution. The solution to Lewis's problem proposed in Cohen 1988 invokes Belnap's conditional assertion connective. The suggestion is that the relevant semantic clauses be reformulated using conditional

---

[6] The actual discussion of this is found on page 25 of Lewis 1973.

assertions as follows (using Aw to represent that A is true at the world w, and using the / symbol for conditional assertion):[7]

[S1] $A \square\!\!\!\rightarrow B$ is true (at a world, according to some system of spheres) iff
            $(\exists w)\{A_w/(ES)[w\text{is in}S/(x)(x\text{is in}S/(\neg A \vee B)_x)]\}$

[S2] $A \diamond\!\!\!\rightarrow B$ is true (at a world, according to some system of spheres) iff
            $(\forall w)\{A_w/(S)[w\text{is in}S/(\exists x)(x\text{is in}S/(A\&B)_x)]\}$

This solution can be fairly said to involve both a revision of the semantics insofar as it introduces a new connective (and truth-state) into the metalanguage, as well as a radical revision of the semantic-pragmatic relation in that the very possibility of conditional assertions obliterates the boundaries between them.

The advantages that this proposal has to offer Lewis are significant. It respects the interdefinability of would and might counterfactuals. At the same time, if there are to be no impossible worlds, no worlds in any sphere in which contradictory or inconceivable antecedents can be true, then both would and might counterpossibles are alike "nonassertive." Since nonassertive statements fail to say anything but nonassertiveness is a designated value in the logic of conditionals assertions,[8] this is the perfect formal counterpart to Lewis's desired "vacuous truth." Moreover, the implication from woulds to mights, which is so attractive, becomes a universal property of the system.[9]

[P2] $A \square\!\!\!\rightarrow B \Rightarrow (A \diamond\!\!\!\rightarrow B)$.

Previously, [P2] held only for "possible" counterfactuals.

For all the considerable advantages this solution has to offer Lewis, there are also drawbacks. Generally, these are determined by the overall methodological orientation, viz., using a possible worlds semantic framework for counterfactual conditionals. The solution remains viable but only within strict limits.

The primary shortcoming of the conditional assertion solution is that it is as "non-discriminating" as Lewis's own. But where Lewis assigned "true" to all counterpossibles — and "false" to their might counterparts — this assigns them all alike the same neither-true-nor-false "truth-value." The linguistic data once again rear their many heads. It was at this point that Lewis's theory was confounded by the supposed necessity of truth for assertibility and the falsity of counterpossible mights. Reading all counterpossibles as nonassertive statements, and so having a designated value, provides a way around this difficulty. The appeal to a complementary pragmatic filter now looks viable. Unfortunately, this is not so. This avenue is blocked because the relevant features have already been incorporated into the formulation of conditional assertions. They have, as it were, been co-opted.

---

[7] These translate roughly as "Some A–world is in a sphere, all of whose worlds are $(\neg A \vee B)$–worlds" and "Every A–world is only in spheres which have some $(A \wedge B)$–worlds," respectively. I believe these are equivalent to Lewis's original formulations. They have been recast in explicitly A–propositional and I–propositional form to exploit the Aristotelian connections recovered by the conditional assertion reading of quantification as developed in Belnap 1973.

[8] This is defended in Cohen 1986; van Fraassen 1975 disagrees.

[9] The only assumption needed to establish this, apart from principles of the logic of conditional assertion, is that the spheres be nested. Lewis insists on this anyway, in order to extract the relation of relative similarity.

Exactly how and why this is so becomes evident from a brief rehearsal of the development of the logic of conditional assertions. Belnap's conceptual prototypes for conditional assertions are conditional bets and questions. Accordingly, assertions are viewed both as acts and as contents inseparably. Thus, the semantic focus shifts from truth-conditions to assertibility-conditions right away. But the assertibility conditions for a conditional assertion, i.e., its non-falsity, are defined initially with reference to the satisfaction, i.e., truth, of its antecedent. The formalization — axiomatization cum formal semantics — of conditional assertions raised the question of generalizing with respect to antecedent nesting of conditional assertions: should nonassertive antecedents count as satisfied? The pragmatic spirit of the whole enterprise dictates an affirmative response.[10] The result is a conditional whose assertiveness depends on the nonfalsity, which is to say, assertibility, of its antecedent. In short, the *truth* conditions of the antecedent are conceptually relevant for determining the *assertibility* of the conditional assertion, while it is the *assertibility* conditions of the antecedent that are formally relevant for determining the full *truth* conditions of the conditional assertion.

The very presence of conditional assertions, even just their linguistic possibility, destroys any neat boundary between the semantic and the pragmatic (understanding the one as concerned only with truth-values and the other with the conventions governing assertibility and the speech act). Since pragmatic factors have already been incorporated into the account of conditional assertions, retreating to the pragmatic, as Lewis does, to make distinctions among counterpossibles, is not possible. Pragmatic considerations demand a non-uniform treatment, but the appropriate sort of pragmatic considerations have already been taken into account.

Appiah 1985 has a similar problem — and a solution worth exploring: in constructing a theory to explain how we use indicative conditionals, he reaches the conclusion that an impossible antecedent renders the entire conditional *una*ssertible. Any further distinctions that are needed can be explained by recourse to subjective features of the speech act: the speaker does not really understand what she or he is saying.

Appiah's proposal is not directly in conflict with either Lewis's proposal that counterpossibles all be true or the proposed solution calling for Belnapian nonassertiveness all around: Appiah is concerned only with the subclass of indicative conditionals. Should an impossible antecedent be used, he maintains, it can only be due to the speaker's own "computational imperfection." Were the impossibility of the condition recognized, the subjunctive would be used, the "monkey's uncle" example, given as (5) above, and other examples notwithstanding.[11]

However, whether or not Lewis adopts the conditional assertion solution to the primary counterpossible problem, he cannot avail himself of "pragmatic" considerations of this sort, i.e., of subjective rather than conversational determinants.

---

[10] The alternative path, however, has been explored and developed. See footnote 8.

[11] Another, perhaps better, example of an indicative counterpossible is "If there are any round squares, I've never seen one." This may be convertible into the "were-would" talk of subjunctive counterfactuals but not without some linguistic acrobatics. "Even if there were round squares, I still would not have seen them" says something a bit different, at least to my ears.

Counterfactual status is accorded conditionals according to the *presupposed* truth-value of the antecedent from the outset. That much of the subjective has already been taken into account.

If counterpossibles insist on being round square pegs, we will just have to resort to something besides possible worlds holes.

§4. Once upon a time we were advised of the appearance of the One True Logic in the guise of Pure Syntax, unencumbered by all the set-theoretic garbage of Semantics. No doubt this was all in accordance with some prophecy or relevation, possibly both. More recently, any original sins associated with that enterprise have been declared forgiven, even if only to highlight subsequent ones.[12] Without suggesting anything so grand as either a way to return to paradise or a way to hasten the establishment of the Kingdom of Rational Beings here in Departments of Philosophy, one might well take this much of the (anti-Papal?) Bull to heart: the accepted division and customary presentational forms of syntax and semantics have not been written in stone. Specifically, proof-theory can do some of the jobs normally reserved for semantics.

No one would suggest that the semantic apparatus is useless, but neither should it be supposed that a logic system without it is altogether without use. Some cases might just be like that fish without a bicycle. What, after all, is *the* purpose of providing a semantics for a logic? There can, of course, be any number of purposes, from formalizing and explicating the insights embodied in the system to seeking internal and external connections or just simply facilitating computation. Undoubtedly, there are others. There is no reason to suppose there is only one. What then is *the* purpose of a formal system? Again, there can be many purposes, with no need to suppose there can be only one. Further, these can include the tasks of formalization, explication, seeking connections, and computation. Undoubtedly, there are others. The semantic and proof-theoretic enterprises are not as separable as sometimes supposed.

When a formal system is itself a story told to help explication, that it should seem in need of further explication can only be a sign of failure, even if it is only a failure of nerve.

Counterpossibles need not all be forced into the counterfactual model. There are more hospitable ones available. For the most part, impossible antecedents are best understood as premises rather than either conditions of assertion or descriptions of other realities. That is just the point of so many counterpossibles. "If 8×7 were 63, then $8 \times 7 + 1$ would be 64" is an encapsulated argument. Anyone making the first computation but settling on 65, or even 57, for the final value would be in error a second time. That is part of what this says. No one is really expected to imagine seven eights totalling 63, let alone believe that that happens in some far-off, metaphysically exotic place.

None of this is meant to exclude the possibility of occasions asking for just that kind of world-making conceptual exercise. Some counterpossibles may well

---

[12] The introduction of these theological considerations into the literature of conditionals logics stems from Routley-Meyer 1973 and Meyer 1985.

function along those lines. Examples (3) and (4) are reasonable candidates for that sort of counterfactual reading, complete with recourse to impossible worlds. Other examples, transgressing whatever limits of conceivability and possibility happen to be conversationally permitted by a given context, are probably best read as non-assertions, as suggested by Lewis's "shrug defense" of vacuity and in line with the conditional assertion solution. In contrast to both of these, examples (5) and (7) require something else.

It is those counterpossibles which, like (5) and (7), function as encapsulations of arguments that are of primary logical and philosophical interest. Their very intelligibility is presupposed by *Reductio ad Absurdum* arguments. For these, an appreciable account can be provided. Moreover, that account can be "discriminating," in that both truth-values are used, as well as "realist," in that it assigns exactly one truth-value to each counterpossible falling within its range. All that is needed is some suitable bivalent filter. Unless one has fixed semantic preconceptions to the contrary, it simply needs be pointed out to be recognized that the deducibility relation is exactly that. The only appropriate way to clarify, explicate, or substantiate the locution that accommodates counterpossibles corresponding to the steps in *reductio* proofs is by providing sufficient proof-theoretic machinery for recovering the implied argument. A counterpossible of the form '$A > B$' is true just when $A \vdash_{CL} B$, where "CL" refers to some suitable "counterpossible," i.e., paraconsistent, logic.

It seems unlikely that the multiplicity ends with conditional assertion, impossible worlds, and counterpossible logic interpretations of conditionals with impossible antecedents. There are reasons for thinking that there might have to be a number of counterpossible logics on hand. Different circumstances call for the implementation — and suspension — of different logical laws. Consider the following Difficult Question:

(DQ)   If the failure of modus ponens implied the failure of modus tollens, and modus ponens were to fail, would modus tollens fail too?

Admittedly, this may well be a bit of irremediable nonsense with no answer safe from damning and definitive criticism. But logico-linguistic pathology aside, there is a point to be made: nothing is safe from the persistent 'what-if,' not even the logic of persistent 'what-ifs.' We have, after all, very sensibly asked what logic would be like without disjunctive syllogism. Some contexts call for the suspension of putative laws of logic; others do not, or call into question others.

The difference between Lewis's possible-worlds and the Routley-Meyer set-ups for relevant logics is not that the first are possible and the second are not, or that the first are "real possibilities" while the second have some less than really possible status. Rather, it is that they fill different functions. Explaining how and why failures of transitivity can occur for counterfactuals is not the same thing as generating a decision procedure for implications. Possible worlds turn out to be the wrong places to look to find the impossible. However, *if* the impossible were somehow possible, the possible-worlds framework would most assuredly be just the right context for semantic exploration. But, as it isn't, it ain't.

BIBLIOGRAPHY

Appiah, A. (1985): *Assertion and Conditionals*, Cambridge University Press.

Belnap, N. D. (1973): "Restricted Quantification and Conditional Assertion," in *Truth, Syntax, and Modality*, H. Leblanc, ed., North-Holland Publishing Co., Amsterdam, pp. 48–75.

Cohen, D. H. (1986): "A New Axiomatization of Belnap's Conditional Assertion," *Notre Dame Journal of Formal Logic*, vol. 27, pp. 124–132.

_____ (1988): "The Problem of Counterpossibles," *Notre Dame Journal of Formal Logic*, vol. 29, pp. 91–101.

Goodman, N. (1955): *Fact, Fiction, and Forecast*, Cambridge, Mass.

Kvart, E. (1986): *A Theory of Counterfactuals*, Hackett Publishing Company, Indianapolis.

Lakatos, I. (1976): *Proofs and Refutations*, J. Worrall and E. Zahar, eds., Cambridge University Press.

Lewis, D. (1973): *Counterfactuals*, Harvard University Press.

_____ (1986): *On the Plurality of Worlds*, Basil Blackwell, Oxford.

Mackie, J. L. (1973): *Truth Probability and Paradox*, Oxford University Press, New York.

Meyer, R. K. (1985): "A Farewell to Entailment," *Foundations of Logic and Linguistics, Problems and their Solutions*, G. Dorn and P. Weingartner, eds., Plenum Press, New York.

Routley, R. and Meyer, R. K. (1973): "The Semantics of Entailment I," *Truth, Syntax, and Modality*, H. Leblanc, ed., North-Holland, Amsterdam.

Routley, R. with Meyer, R. K., Plumwood, V. and Brady, R. T. (1984): *Relevant Logics and their Rivals I*, Ridgeview Publishing Co., Atascadero, California.

van Fraassen, B. C. (1975): "Incomplete Assertion and Belnap Connectives," *Contemporary Readings in Philosophical Logic and Linguistic Semantics*, Hockney, et al., eds., D. Reidel Publishing Co., Dordrecht, Holland, pp. 43–70.

Wittgenstein, Ludwig (1961): *Tractatus Logico-Philosophicus*, D. Pears and B. McGuinness, trans., Routledge & Kegan Paul, London.

RUTH MANOR

DURATIONS: TEMPORAL INTERVALS WITH GAPS AND UNDETERMINED EDGES[1]

1. Introduction and Overview

The study of the meanings of temporal expressions in natural language can proceed in two ways. The first consists of borrowing an ontological theory concerning how time "really" is, and then showing how temporal expressions are interpreted in this model. Let us call this the *physicalist* approach. The other approach is to start off by studying the temporal presuppositions employed in the language, and defining a model as the structure which satisfies these conditions. This approach we shall call the *analytist* approach. The two approaches share their goal, which is to provide a temporal model for natural language. However, they are driven by different motivations. The physicalist approach is ontology-driven. It views time as part of reality, and its structure as independent of linguistic considerations. It attempts to interpret the language in this model, possibly by adding assumptions about the language. The analytist approach, on the other hand, is language driven. It assumes that language "mirrors" reality to the extent in which it is describable in the language, and tries to define a temporal model based only on linguistic considerations. A theory is "complete", in a sense, if it combines both approaches and its (analytist) language-driven model can be constructed in a (physicalist) ontology-driven structure.

Most discussions of temporal logics and temporal semantics of natural language seem to follow the physicalist approach in providing a model based on a view that the primary temporal entities are instants i.e., points on a directed continuum. Some discussions assume that sentences are true (or false) at instants, while others argue that since certain processes "take time", the sentences describing them are not true at instants but at temporal intervals (Cresswell 1977, Kamp 1980, van Benthem 1983, Thomason, 1982). Yet, since these (open or closed intervals) are characterized in terms of their constituent points (or at least their end points), they are still viewed within an instant-based theory. I suppose that this approach is guided by Newtonian physics which assumes time to be a directed linear continuum.

The general idea in employing an analytist approach is to consider temporal structures presupposed by the language. Our temporal language presupposes the occurrence of certain events. Even the most common temporal expressions such as 'yesterday' or 'February 20 1986' can refer successfully only if we assume the

---

[1] This paper was supported in part by the National Science Foundation, grant number IST81-18393. It is based on an unpublished manuscript (Manor 1979). The current version is the result of much encouragement from Hans Kamp, Johan van Benthem, and Dov Gabbay who commented on the earlier version, and from Stanley Peters and Arthur Cody, who commented on and made several suggestions to improve the current version.

133

J. M. Dunn and A. Gupta (eds.), Truth or Consequences, 133–154.
© 1990 *Kluwer Academic Publishers. Printed in the Netherlands.*

occurrence of certain events. Hence, it seems reasonable to begin the discussion of temporal semantics by considering the *temporal reference* of event sentences, and the set of all temporal entities which are *identified* by event sentences. Roughly speaking, we say that an event sentence S describing the event e *refers temporally* to the time in which the event e allegedly takes place. An event sentence S *identifies* a temporal entity d, if S is true of d (i.e., the event described indeed takes place at time d) and S is untrue in any other time disjoint from d.

Here I start with an analytist approach by investigating the claim that the temporal reference of natural language sentences is to *durations* rather than to instants or intervals on a continuum. Unlike instants, durations are extended and contain proper subdurations. Unlike intervals, durations have undetermined (fuzzy) edges and they may contain gaps. Consider, for example,

(1)   John is smoking.

If this sentence is true at all, then it is true of a temporal interval rather than of a temporal instant, simply because smoking is a process which takes time. Moreover, although the sentence may be true of an interval and some of its subintervals, it could be false of some other (or all) of its subintervals. It is in this sense that the temporal reference of sentences such as (1) has gaps. Finally, the edges of this interval are undetermined. When we consider the event of John's smoking and the question when it starts, we have several equally good and mutually exclusive answers. For example, that his smoking starts when he is taking the cigarette from its pack, when he strikes the match, when he actually lights the cigarette, or when he starts inhaling, etc. There seems to be no compelling reason to prefer any one of these answers. Moreover, these answers themselves refer to extended time elements rather than to instants. This suggests that the assumption that there is a point which can serve to distinguish the time of John's smoking from the time of his non-smoking is unjustified. Rather, I suggest that the interval of which (1) is true, has undetermined edges.

The aim of the paper is to provide a duration model for natural language which is complete in that it combines the analytist and physicalist approaches. In Section 2 we consider some natural language examples which support the claim that temporal reference in natural language is to durations, and outline adequacy conditions for a duration model. In Section 3 we provide a formal characterization of a duration model for an event language E, containing no temporal expressions. This model is analytist in that we assume that every duration is identified by a sentence in the language. Its underlying temporal structure is minimal and can be defined in terms of a partial ordering and some existential assumptions. Finally, the model described is "temporally rich" in the sense that we can add to E temporal expressions and tenses and the resulting language is expressively complete.

In order to show the completeness of the approach, we show how a duration model can be constructed in terms of an instant-based model. This is motivated by two considerations. First, the instant-based model is supported by the physical view of events as occurring at instants. Second, though the event language does not contain temporal references to instants, educated natural language permits talk of instantaneous events used in discussion of classical physics. Hence in Section 4 we consider an extension L of the event language E which has expressions referring to instants. We describe an instant-based open intervals model for L, and use van Fraassen's (1969) method of supervaluations in generalizing over sets of instant-models, in order to define a four-valued supermodel.

In constructing this supermodel, we make use of Belnap's approach in constructing his (1977) four valued logic. It is therefore not surprizing that we can show that when we restrict our attention to a given temporal interval, the supermodel actually yields Belnap's four-valued logic, which is a model in which the "static" logical system of Tautological Entailments (Anderson and Belnap, 1975) is sound and complete. Moreover, the present temporal view provides an interesting application of Belnap's famous Four: When we consider the dynamic changes in the truth value of a sentence in an interval which is expanded or shrunk, the system has the properties of a duration model for the E fragment of L. In particular, the edges of an interval in which a sentence is true, may be undetermined and that interval may have subintervals in which the sentence is untrue.

These properties are used in Section 5 to show how a duration model for E can be constructed within the supermodel for L. In this model instants are equal citizens as durations are. Yet, while durations are identified by sentences in E, we do not assume that every instant is identifiable in terms of expressions of L.

2. Simple Temporal Reference

In this section, I will consider a few examples which suggest that the temporal references of sentences in natural language are durations, rather than instants or open or closed intervals on a temporal continuum. The choice of examples and their discussion serves to explain the motivation in the formal discussion in the later chapters.

We are concerned with the question of what time is and what entities it consists of. Assuming that events take place in time, we can suppose that any temporal entity is the time in which some unique event takes place. Namely, every temporal entity is identifiable by some event as the time in which the event takes place. Of course, more than one event may occur at any given time. Following the analytist approach, let us first consider only events which are describable in the language. We should not consider any description of an event as referring to a temporal entity, for it is possible to describe events which do not take place. Rather, we consider sentences which describe events truly. Consider, for example,

(2)   Mary ate a candy bar.

The *temporal reference* of this sentence is the times in which the event of Mary's eating a candy bar allegedly took place. If there are times in which that event actually takes place, then we say that they are the times *of which* the sentence is true. We should distinguish the temporal reference of an event sentence from the times *in which* its utterance is true. The temporal reference of (2) is the times *of* which the sentence is true, i.e., the times when Mary ate a candy bar . Since sentence (2) employs the past tense, the times *in* which the sentence is true, are times after that event.

Initially, we consider an event language E whose atomic sentences like (1) and (2) above, are simple event sentences which contain no temporal expressions and do not imply temporal relations among the events described. The following sentences, in contrast, do not have simple temporal references

(3)   Babies burp after eating.

(4)   He joined the Navy during World War II.

(5)   At the stroke of 12, Cinderella turned into a pumpkin.

(6)   She was born on April 5, 1970, at 4:05 PM.

(7)   Mrs. Jones was murdered between 3:00 and 5:00 PM.

(8)   She never sleeps long.

To support the claim that temporal references in natural language are durations, I first consider time to consist of the set of temporal references of simple event sentences, which are true of some time or another. That is, every temporal element is the time *of* which at least one sentence is actually true, and is "identifiable" by the sentence. Two further steps are then required. One is to show that these temporal references have undetermined edges and gaps, and the other is to show that this model is sufficient even for an extended language containing complex event sentences.

2.1 Intervals

Cresswell (1977) considers the following example

(9)   John is polishing every boot.

to argue that the temporal reference of some sentences involves intervals rather than instants. Suppose there are ten boots under consideration, and that John is polishing them one at a time. Then the idea is that any time in which the polishing process occurs, John is polishing at most one and not all ten boots. The point is not merely the process takes time, but also that (9) may be true *of* an interval without being true *of* all of its subintervals. Indeed, polishing a single boot also takes time, and hence the temporal reference of the sentence

(10)   John polishes a boot.

also involves intervals. However, we may want to claim that at any time during this interval John is polishing the boot namely, that (10) is true of all of its subintervals, while (9) is not. In (9) there is an implication of completion, so that its truth requires a the completion of a series of activities as described by (10).

2.2 Gaps

Let us consider this example further. The process of polishing a boot may not be continuous. Sentences (9) and (10) may both be true, even if when John polished the fifth boot, he took his lunch break and returned to polishing the same boot after lunch. In answer to the question "What are you doing now?", John can provide the following answers truly, depending on how he interprets 'now'.

(11a)   I am eating (and I am not polishing any boot).

(11b)   I am polishing the fifth boot.

(11c)   I am (in the process of) polishing every boot.

If the temporal reference of a sentence describing a process which is not continuous in time, then it must allow for "gaps": the sentence may be true of an interval and be non-true in some of its subintervals.

That this must be the case is also suggested by the following considerations. One of the puzzling aspects of the version of the Liar Paradox

(12)   I am (now) lying.

is that people actually use such expressions in every day language, without being considered as commiting themselves to a contradiction or a paradox. Indeed, students first exposed to this example have trouble seeing that there is a problem with the sentence and need to be told that 'now' refers to the time of utterance. Moreover, given that a speaker uttered this sentence and the hearers have no reason to assume that he intended to confuse them or contradict himself, the hearers can conclude — using a Gricean type of consideration (Grice, 1975) — that he meant to say that he was lying in a period ('now') which includes but is not identical to the time of utterance. Moreover, they can conclude that the time of utterance is a gap in that period. For otherwise, the speaker's utterance does lead to a contradiction. In other words, assuming that speakers can utter (12) sincerely and cooperatively, then the fact that (12) leads to a paradox proves indirectly that the 'now' interval refered to has a gap. But (12) is not a widely used sentence (possibly because people do not tend to admit to their lies so soon). But the same point applies to the following

(13)   John always surprizes me.

(14)   I'm (just) kidding you (or I'm always kidding).

If (13) is used to claim that John surprizes me even at the time of utterance, this gives rise to a version of the Surprize Exam Paradox, as it asserts the continuous expectation that John will act in an unexpected way. Similarly, (14) is normally *not* used as just another joke, but as a serious warning that the hearer not take the humorous comments made in the vicinity of the time of utterance too literally. If this analysis is correct, then the following sentences are not contradictory:

(15)   I am (now) lying, but not right now.

(16)   John always surprizes me, but right now he does not.

(17)   I am kidding you, but right now I'm quite serious.

There is indeed something strange in these sentences, and I suggest that this is because the but-clause is self evident, uninformative, and hence, redundant. In other cases, where no paradox arises, the explicit mention of a gap is not "strange":

(18)   I am polishing the fifth boot, but right now I am eating a sandwich.

2.3 Undetermined edges

Cresswell's analysis of the quantifier 'every' in (9) yields that there is a minimal interval (in the continuum) of which (9) is true. This implies that there is an instant distinguishing the polishing period from the periods after the polishing has been completed. But this assumption is not warranted by linguistic usage. Indeed, we do refer to the edges of the temporal reference of event sentences, by expressions like 'He stops polishing', 'He starts polishing', 'immediately after (before) polishing', etc. However, these typically refer to edge-intervals, rather than to instants. Vendler (1967), notes that certain verbs, "achievement verbs", as in the sentence

(19)   He reaches the top

do not have continuous tense, and explains this by the assumption that (19) is true of a unique and definite instant. This, again is not supported by linguistic usage. Sentence (19) indicates a comparison between connected periods (in which he is not yet at the top and when he is at the top). There is no linguistic reason to assume that there is a unique instant serving as the first instant in which he is at the top, or the last one before his being at the top.[2]

As a final argument, let us note that the examples in this section concern mainly the reference of 'now'. They indicate that 'now' (as well as 'right now', 'at this moment' etc.) may refer to a more or less extended inteval, it must contain or be identical to the time of utterance. Since, on the physical time line, any utterance takes time, 'now' can never refer to an instant on the continuum, but only to an interval. Assuming the flow of time is expressed in terms of the assumption that every temporal reference of an event sentence is simultaneous with some use of 'now', then it must have the same properties as some 'now' interval has. That is, it must be an extended period with undetermined edges and possibly with gaps.

3. A SYSTEM OF DURATIONS

3.1 The requirements of a duration system

Durations are temporal entities in which events, described by simple event sentences, take place. As such, they satisfy the following requirements:

R1.   Durations are partially ordered by the relation 'earlier than' ('before'), and a relation of 'inclusion' ('subduration'). Identity of durations and

---

[2] My point, in general is that linguistic considerations suggest that the temporal reference of event sentences are durations. We may *assume* that there are in our reality, instantaneous events, and this may justify our usage of expressions like "the temporal instant in which he reaches the top ...".

the intersection of durations can be defined in terms of these relations so that the following conditions hold:

a.   Durations have covers, namely, for any two durations there is a duration which includes both.

b.   Each duration is connected, i.e., if a duration is between two subdurations of d, then it is also included in d.

c.   If a duration is not a subduration of another, then the former has a subduration which is disjoint from the latter.

d.   For any two durations, either one is included in the other or one is earlier than the other.

R2.   Every duration has at least one event sentence which identifies it, i.e., the sentence is true of this duration and of no duration disjoint from it.

R3.   Durations are "intervals with undetermined edges", i.e., for every sentence which identifies a duration, there is another duration identifiedded by it, such that one is a proper subduration of the other.

R4.   An event sentence may be true of a duration, but non-true of some of its subdurations (i.e., the duration has "gaps"). In these subdurations, the event sentence is, in a sense, both true and false.

We now describe a duration system satisfying the above requirements. First, we describe the duration structure satisfying R1, as this requirement can be described independently of the relationships between event sentences and durations. The duration model describes these relationships.

3.2 D-structures

We start by characterizing a D-structure $\langle D, <, : \rangle$ which satisfies R1. We then construct a D-structure from a (linear) L-structure $\langle D, < * \rangle$. Intuitively, in a L-structure the temporal precedence relation '$< *$', "disjointly before", is assumed to hold between disjoint durations only, while in a D-structure the relation '$<$', "earlier than", holds between any mutually non-inclusive durations. Both '$<$' and '$:$' in a D-structure are defined in terms of the '$< *$' relation of the L-structure. (We use '$\neg$', '$\&$', 'or', '$\Rightarrow$', '$\Leftrightarrow$', '$\forall$' and '$\exists$' for the metalingustic negation, conjunction, disjunction, implication, equivalence, and the universal and existential quantifiers respectively.)

Def. 1: D-structure

The structure, $\langle D, <, : \rangle$ is a D-structure, where D is a non-empty set satisfying for all d's in D

D1   '$<$' is a transitive and anti-symmetric relation:

a. $d_1 < d_2 \ \& \ d_2 < d_3 \Rightarrow d_1 < d_3$

b. $d_1 < d_2 \Rightarrow \neg(d_2 < d_1)$

D2   ':' (inclusion) is a transitive relation:

$$d_1 : d_2 \ \& \ d_2 : d_3 \Rightarrow d_1 : d_3$$

D3   identity, '=', is defined by

$$d_1 = d_2 \Leftrightarrow_{df} d_1 : d_2 \ \& \ d_2 : d_1$$

intersection '∩' is defined conditionally by

$$(\exists d)(d : d_1 \ \& \ d : d_2) \Rightarrow$$
$$d_1 \cap d_2 = d_3 \Leftrightarrow_{df} d_3 : d_1 \ \& \ d_3 : d_2 \ \&$$
$$(\forall d)(d : d_1 \ \& \ d : d_2 \Rightarrow d : d_3)$$

Otherwise, we say that d_1 and d_2 are *disjoint* and we write

$$d_1 \cap d_2 = \text{empty}$$

(Note that 'empty' is not considered a duration)

D4   Cover duration

$$(\forall d_1, d_2)(\exists d_3)[d_1 : d_3 \ \& \ d_2 : d_3 \ \&$$
$$(\forall d)(d_1 : d \ \& \ d_2 : d \Rightarrow d_3 : d)]$$

D5   Connectedness

$$d_1 : d \ \& \ d_3 : d \ \& \ d_1 < d_2 < d_3 \Rightarrow d_2 : d$$

D6   Distinguishability

$$(\forall d_1, d_2)[\neg(d_1 : d_2) \Rightarrow (\exists d)(d : d_1 \& d \cap d_2 = \text{ empty})]$$

D7   Comparability (of non-inclusive durations)

$$(\forall d_1, d_2)(d_1 : d_2 \text{ or } d_2 : d_1 \text{ or } d_1 < d_2 \text{ or } d_2 < d_1)$$

D4–D7 correspond to the requirements R1a–R1d.

Note that we do not require that d_1 and d_2 be disjoint if $d_1 < d_2$. The idea is that since durations have fuzzy edges, we should not require their edges to "behave in a precise way". Graphically, $d_1 < d_2$ represents either

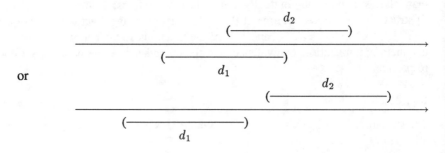

We now show how a D-structure can be defined in terms of a more minimal temporal structure, an L-structure, containing '$<^*$', "disjointly before" as the only temporal relation and satisfies the existence of a cover an intersection requirements.

Def. 2: L-structure

An *L*-structure is a structure $\langle D, < * \rangle$, where D is a non-empty set satisfying the following conditions:

L1   '$< *$' is a transitive and anti-symmetric relation:

      a. $d_1 < *d_2 \ \& \ d_2 < *d_3 \Rightarrow d_1 < *d_3$
      b. $d_1 < *d_2 \Rightarrow \neg(d_2 < *d_1)$

L2   Intersection (of incomparable durations)

$$\neg(d_1 < *d_2) \ \& \ \neg(d_2 < *d_1) \Rightarrow$$
$$(\exists c)(\forall d)[(d < *d_1 \text{ or } d < *d_2 \Leftrightarrow d < *c) \ \& $$
$$(d_1 < *d \text{ or } d_2 < *d \Leftrightarrow c < *d)]$$

L3   Cover

$$(\exists c)(\forall d)[(d < *d_1 \ \& \ d < *d_2 \Leftrightarrow d < *c) \ \& $$
$$(d_1 < *d \ \& \ d_2 < *d \Leftrightarrow c < *d)]$$

Given a *L*-structure, $L = \langle D, < * \rangle$, we now construct a *D*-structure, $\langle D, < , : \rangle$. First, we define inclusion, earlier, identity, and intersection and show that they have the desired properties.

Def. 3: inclusion

$$d_1 : d_2 \Leftrightarrow_{df} (\forall d)[(d < *d_2 \Rightarrow d < *d_1) \ \& \ (d_2 < *d \Rightarrow d_1 < *d)]$$

Roughly, d_1 is included in d_2 if d_2's "disjoint past" and "disjoint future" are respectively in d_1's "disjoint past and future".

Def. 4: earlier than

$$d_1 < d_2 \Leftrightarrow_{df} (\exists c_1, c_2)[c_1 : d_1 \ \& \ c_2 : d_2 \ \& \ c_1 < *d_2 \ \& \ d_1 < *c_2]$$

d_1 is earlier than d_2 if d_1 has a subduration in d_2's "disjoint past", and d_2 has a subduration in d_1's "disjoint future".

Def. 5: identity

$$d_1 = d_2 \Leftrightarrow_{df} (\forall d)[(d < *d_2 \Leftrightarrow d < *d_1) \& (d_2 < *d \Leftrightarrow d_1 < *d)]$$

Def. 6: intersection

$$(\exists c)(\forall d)[(d < *d_1 \text{ or } d < *d_2 \Leftrightarrow d < *c)\&$$
$$(d_1 < *d \text{ or } d_2 < *d \Leftrightarrow c < *d)] \Rightarrow$$

$$d_1 \cap d_2 = d_3 \Leftrightarrow_{df}$$

$$(\forall d)[(d < *d_1 \text{ or } d < *d_2 \Leftrightarrow d < *d_3)\&$$
$$(d_1 < *d \text{ or } d_2 < *d \Leftrightarrow d_3 < *d)]$$

Otherwise, we write $d_1 \cap d_2 =$ empty

THEOREM 1.   *An L-structure, with the definitions 3–6 as above is a D-structure.*

Constructing D-structures in terms of L-structures shows that our assumptions about time are minimal and intuitive. We assume only the partial order $< *$, that two $< *$-incomparable durations share a common subduration, and that any two durations have a cover duration.

3.3 Duration Models

Since we are concerned with the claim that temporal reference in (the event fragment of) natural language is only to durations, our model satisfies the condition (MR2) that every duration is determined by some sentence of the event language. This implies that the set of durations has at most countably many elements. However, it does not imply that time has only contably many elements, nor that we cannot refer to other temporal objects in some language. It means only that the set of temporal objects which are referents of event sentences have countably many elements.

Def. 7: duration model

Let E be an event language, with the (non-temporal) connectives '$\neg$','$\&$', and '$\vee$'. $M = \langle\langle D, <, :\rangle, V, \{T, U\}\rangle$ is a duration model for E, if D is a set of durations, $\{T, U\}$ is a set of values (corresponding to truth and untruth) and V a valuation function

$$V : E \times D \rightarrow \{T, U\}$$

satisfying (where $S, S_1, \ldots$ range over sentences of E, and $d, d_1, \ldots$ over durations in D)

V1	$V(S, d) = T \text{ or } V(S, d) = U$
V2	$V(S, d) = T \Rightarrow V(\neg S, d) = U$
V3	$V(S_1 \& S_2, d) = T \Leftrightarrow V(S_1, d) = V(S_2, d) = T$
V4	$V(S_1 \vee S_2, d) = T \Leftrightarrow V(S_1, d) = T \text{ or } V(S_2, d) = T$

and the following conditions obtain:

MR1 $\langle D, <, : \rangle$ is a D-structure

MR2 $(\exists S)[V(S, d) = T \ \& \ (\forall d_1)(d_1 \cap d = \text{empty} \Rightarrow V(S, d_1) = U)]$

          For any duration d, if S is a sentence satisfying the above, we write
          d/S, and we say that S *identifies* the duration d.

MR3 $d/S \Rightarrow (\exists d_1)[d_1/S \ \& \ \neg(d = d_1) \ \& \ (d : d_1 \text{ or } d_1 : d)]$

MR4 $(\exists S, d, d_1)(V(S, d) = T \ \& \ d_1 : d \ \& \ V(S, d_1) = U)$

Conditions MR1–MR4 consist of a formal representation of the conditions R1–R4
respectively.

Note that not every simple event sentence in natural language determines a
duration. Contradictions which are never true do not determine durations. Let us
call a model in which "all of time" is not a duration, a natural model. Namely, in
a natural model there is no duration which includes all durations as subdurations.
Tautologies, which are always true, and sentences which are periodically true, e.g.,

(20)   The sun is shining

do not determine a duration in any natural model. In an unnatural model, both
tautologies and periodic sentences determine the universal duration. However,
while tautologies are true in any duration, periodic sentences may not be true in
some durations. In other words, in unnatural models periodic sentences determine
the universal duration with gaps.

So far, we have outlined linguistic and philosophical considerations for supporting the claim that the temporal references of event sentences are durations, and
then formulated the conditions in terms of formal requirement on a duration model.
We now consider the extension ET of the event language, which is (temporally)
expressively complete and has expressions for temporal connectives and dates.

3.4 Adding temporal expressions to E.

In a D-structure, any two mutually non-inclusive durations are comparable with
respect to 'earlier'. This means that if we add to E the temporal connectives 'before'
and 'during' whose interpretations in the model are '$<$' and '$:$' respectively, then
the resulting language ET is expressively complete in the sense that any temporal
relations between durations in the model can be expressed in the extended language.

Let ET be a language obtained from E by adding two temporal connectives,
'before' and 'during', so that if S_1, S_2 are sentences of ET, so are

          S_1 before S_2

and

          S_1 during S_2.

Def. 8: Duration model for ET

Let E be an event language, and ET its extension obtained by adding 'before' and 'during' as two binary temporal connectives. Let M be a duration model for E, then M is a duration model for ET if its valuation V satisfies also

V5 $\quad V(S_1 \text{ before } S_2, d) = T \Leftrightarrow_{df} (\exists d_1, d_2 : d)(V(S_1, d_1) = T \,\&\,$
$\quad\quad\quad V(S_2, d_2) = T \,\&\, d_1 < d_2)$

V6 $\quad V(S_1 \text{ during } S_2, d) = T \Leftrightarrow_{df} (\exists d_1, d_2 : d)(V(S_1, d_1) = T \,\&\,$
$\quad\quad\quad V(S_2, d_2) = T \,\&\, d_1 : d_2)$

A system of dates can be defined in terms of a periodic event and a one-time event. For instance, given a specific clock we can define a day in terms of it by considering sentences like

(21) $\quad S_1$: The clock "strikes" 0:01 hour before it "strikes" 24, and not vice versa

describes a periodic event in that (by V5) S_1 is true of any 24 hour duration d_1 ending at midnight (give or take about a minute). The sentence

(22) $\quad S_2$: Guy was born

identifies a one-time event, assuming that it refers to my son, Guy. Thus, S_2 is going to be true of some duration d_2, and untrue of any duration disjoint from d_2. Thus, by V6,

(23) $\quad S_2 \text{ during } S_1$

is true of any duration which includes Guy's birth day, and hence

(24) $\quad S_1 \,\&\, (S_2 \text{ during } S_1)$

identifies Guy's day of birth. A complete system of dates can be constructed similarly. A duration model for E does not allow the set of durations to be the set of instants on a continuum. The assumption that durations are identifiable by sentences in E implies that there are at most countably many durations. Moreover, the condition that durations have undetermined edges precludes the possibility that there are minimal durations i.e., that a sentence can identify a unique duration.

4. INSTANT MODELS TO SUPERMODELS

We now turn to consider the physicalist approach. We assume that time consists of instants on the continuum, and events occur in time and this characterization is independent of what we can formulate in the language. Assuming such a structure, we can, of course, refer to temporal instants and intervals in natural language. The question we are facing now is whether we can coherently combine the two approaches. Given a language L which contains E as well as temporal expressions identifying instants, we need to show the consistency of the assumption that some sentences in L temporally refer to instants or intervals on a temporal continuum, while others refer to durations.

4.1 Instant structures and models

First we define an (instant) I-structure in the usual way, in terms of a linear and dense ordering on a set I of instants. An instant model assigns every sentence of L and every instant, either a true or a false truth value.

Def. 9: I-structure

$\langle I, < \rangle$ an instant-based structure (I-structure), if I is a non-empty set of instants and '$<$' is an ordering relation, satisfying

I1	$i_1 < i_2 \ \& \ i_2 < i_3 \Rightarrow i_1 < 12$
I2	$i_1 < i_2 \Rightarrow \neg(i_2 < i_1)$
I3	$i_1 < i_2$ or $i_2 < i_1$ or $i_1 = i_2$
I4	$i_1 < i_2 \Rightarrow (\exists i)(i_1 < i < i_2)$

To show how we can obtain a duration model, we first consider an instant model and its instantaneous valuation. The supervaluation needed to make the model a duration model is obtained as a generalization over sets of instantaneous valuations, i.e., a supervaluation.

Def. 10: instant model

Let L be a language with the connectives '$\neg$', '$\&$', and 'or'.
$IM = \langle I*, v, \{T, F\} \rangle$ is an instant model for L, if $I* = \langle I, < \rangle$ is an instant structure as above, $\{T, F\}$ are truth values, and v is an instantaneous valuation (i-valuation) function

$$v : L \times I \to \{T, F\}$$

satisfying (where S, S_1, and S_2 range over sentences of L, and i, i_1, and i_2 range over instants in I):

IV1	$v(S, i) = T$ or $v(S, i) = F$
IV2	$v(\neg S_1, i) = T \Leftrightarrow v(S_1, i) = F$
IV3	$v(S_1 \& S_2, i) = T \Leftrightarrow v(S_1, i) = v(S_2, i) = T$
IV4	$v(S_1 \text{ or } S_2, i) = T \Leftrightarrow v(S_1, i) = T$ or $v(S_2, i) = T$

4.2 Open Intervals

We define open intervals in the usual way, and prove that the set of open intervals over I is a D-structure.

Def. 11: open interval

t is an open intervals over I, if t is a subset of I satisfying

T1	$(\forall i_1, i_2, i)(i_1, i_2 \in t \ \& \ i_1 < i < i_2 \Rightarrow i \in t)$
T2	$(\forall i \in t)(\exists i_1, i_2 \in t)(i_1 < i < i_2)$
T3	$(\forall i \in t)(\exists i_1, i_2)(i_1 < i < i_2 \ \& \ \neg(i_1 \in t) \ \& \ \neg(i_2 \in t))$

(where '$\in$' is used as the metalinguistic membership sign).
T is the set of all open intervals over I.

Def. 12: meet interval

$$(\exists i)(i \in t_1, i \in t_2) \Rightarrow t_1 \cap t_2 =_{df} \{i : i \in t_1 \ \& \ i \in t_2\}$$

if there is no such instant, then we write $t_1 \cap t_2 = $ empty

Def. 13: interval inclusion

$$t_1 : t_2 \Leftrightarrow_{df} t_1 \cap t_2 = t_1$$

Def. 14: interval identity

$$t_1 = t_2 \Leftrightarrow_{df} t_1 : t_2 \ \& \ t_2 : t_1$$

Def. 15: interval disjoint ordering

$$t_1 < *t_2 \Leftrightarrow_{df} t_1 \cap t_2 = \text{empty} \ \& \ (\exists i_1 \in t_1)(\forall i_2 \in t_2)(i_1 < i_2)$$

THEOREM 2.
The structure $\langle T, < * \rangle$ is an L-structure.

Def. 16: interval ordering

$$t_1 < t_2 \Leftrightarrow_{df} (\exists r_1 : t_1, r_2 : t_2)(r_1 < *t_2 \ \& \ t_1 < *r_2)$$

THEOREM 3.
$\langle T, <, : \rangle$ *is a D-structure.*

THEOREM 4. *cover interval*
$Ct_1 - t_2 = t_3 \Leftrightarrow (\forall i)(i \in t_1 \text{ or } i \in t_2 \Rightarrow i \in t_3) \ \&$
$$[(\forall t, i)(i \in t_1 \text{ or } i \in t_2 \Rightarrow i \in t) \Rightarrow t_3 : t]$$

4.3 Valuation-set

We now have to define a model for intervals and in particular, to determine the truth value of sentences over open intervals. What we do is look at a family of instant models differing from each other only in their valuation functions, and satisfying certain "continuity requirements", as follows: Let L be a language closed under logical operations. Let $IM* = \langle I*, v*, \{T, F\} \rangle$ be a set of instant models for L, which differ from each other at most in their valuation, where $v*$ is the associated set of valuations, and let $\langle T, <, : \rangle$ be the interval structure constructed from it as indicated above.

Def. 17: model set and valuation set

$IM*$ is an interval model set, and $v*$ its valuation set, if it satisfies: (Where the t's range over intervals in T, S's range over sentences in L, v's range over valuations in $v*$, and i's range over instants in I)

TV1 $(\forall t, S)\{(\forall i \in t)(\exists v_1)(v_1(S, i) = T) \Rightarrow$
$\qquad (\exists v_2)(\forall i \in t)(v_2(S, i) = T)\}$

TV2 $(\forall S_1, S_2)(\forall i \in t)\{(\exists v_1)(v_1(S_1, i) = T) \ \&$
$\qquad (\exists v_2)(v_2(S_2, i) = T) \Rightarrow (\exists v)(v(S_1 \& S_2, i) = T)\}$

TV3 $(\forall t, S,)\{(\forall v, t_1 : t)(\exists i \in t_1)(v(S, i) = T \Rightarrow$
$\qquad (\exists v_1)(\forall i \in t)(v_1(S, i) = T)\}$

4.4 Supervaluation

Normally, when we refer to time instants, e.g., "the instant in which Johan became married" or "the stroke of 12", we *assume* that such a unique instant exists and we actually have no evidence that these moments are not (relatively small) intervals. However, for some purposes it is extremely important that we will be able to decide on "edge points" of processes and intervals. From a legal viewpoint, for example, it is important to determine a date in which a person stops being a minor and starts being considered an adult. Indeed, a legal system may have apparently contradictory interpretations of what a minor is. In California, the legal drinking age is 21, while the voting age is 18.

One could, of course assume that a minor-for-alcoholic purposes is a completely distinct concept from that of a minor-for-voting purposes. (i.e., that 'minor' is merely ambiguous). But the price we pay for such a decision is greater than our gain: both concepts share the idea that a minor is a person who cannot be held completely responsible for his action, is relatively easily manipulated, and should not be punished too severely.

Using this metaphor, a set of legistlative authorities can be viewed as a valuation set. That different authorities may have different considerations in deciding the critical age when a minor becomes an adult, can be viewed as a consequence of adopting a vague concept in an applicable legal system. The end result is that the precisely defined notion is somewhat arbitrary. E.g., there is really no reason, for instance, not to choose March 3 after one's 18th birthday as the age of voting, rather than the birthdate itself. Similarly, each of the valuations in a valuation set may be quite arbitrary. A supervaluation is then viewed as summarizing the values assigned by all the valuations in the set, as follows:

Def. 18: supervaluation

Let $v*$ be a valuation set as above, we define a supervaluation $V*$ as a function $V* : L \times T \to \{T, F, N, B\}$ satisfying for all S in L and t in T

$V*1 \qquad V * (S, t) = T \Leftrightarrow (\exists v)(\forall i \in t)(v(S, i) = T) \ \&$
$\qquad\qquad \neg(\exists v)(\forall i \in t)(v(S, i) = F)$

$V*2 \qquad V * (S, t) = F \Leftrightarrow (\exists v)(\forall i \in t)(v(S, i) = F) \ \&$
$\qquad\qquad \neg(\exists v)(\forall i \in t)(v(S, i) = T)$

$V*3 \qquad V * (S, t) = B \Leftrightarrow (\exists v)(\forall i \in t)(v(S, i) = T) \ \&$
$\qquad\qquad (\exists v)(\forall i \in t)(v(S, i) = F)$

$V*4 \qquad V * (S, t) = N \Leftrightarrow \neg(\exists v)(\forall i \in t)(v(S, i) = T) \ \&$
$\qquad\qquad \neg(\exists v)(\forall i \in t)(v(S, i) = F)$

Def. 19: supermodel

Let $IM* = \langle I*, v*, \{T, F\}\rangle$ be an interval model set and $V*$ a supervaluation defined for it, then we call the resulting model, $SM = \langle I*, V*, \{T, F, B, N\}\rangle$ a *supermodel* for L.

These definitions make use of Belnap's (1977) approach to a logic which enables one to draw conclusions from a set of possibly conflicting reports. Thus, we assume four values T, F, B, and N, standing respectively for True, False, Both, and Neither. The supervalue of S in interval t is T (True), if there is a valuation constantly verifying S over t and there is no valuation constantly falsifying S over t. S's supervalue in t is B (Both), if there is a valuation which constantly verifies S over t and there is a valuation which constantly falsifies S over t, and so on for the supervalues of F (False) and N (Neither). These definitions enable us to utilize Belnap's results, concerning the underlying "static" logic, obtained when we restrict our attention to a given interval, and "dynamic" logic, obtained when we consider "expanding" and "shrinking" the interval considered.

4.4.1 "Static" logic

If we consider a fixed time interval t, then the table of supervalues for negation, conjunction and disjunction are described by the following theorems.

Theorem 5.　*negation*

This definition yields the following supervalues for negation

$V*(S,t)$	T	F	B	N
$V*(\neg S,t)$	F	T	B	N

Theorem 6.　*meet and join*

a.　　　$V*(S_1 \& S_2, t) = \text{meet}\,\{V*(S_1,t), V*(S_2,t)\}$
b.　　　$V*(S_1 \vee S_2, t) = \text{join}\,\{V*(S_1,t), V*(S_2,t)\}$
　　　　where 'meet' and 'join' are the lattice operations in Belnap's (1977) lattice L4.

L4:

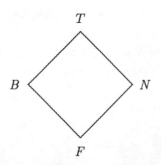

As a result, we inherit Belnap's (1977) completeness proof, namely that if we define valdity to be the lattice inclusion, then L4 is a complete model for Anderson's and Belnap's (1975) system of Tautological Entailments.

Def. 20: entailment

$$S_1 \vdash S_2 \text{ is } valid \text{ in } SM \Leftrightarrow_{df} (\forall t)(V * (S_1, t) \leq V * (S_2, t))$$
$$\text{where '}\leq\text{' is the L4 lattice-inclusion.}$$

THEOREM 7.   *completeness*

The logical system of Tautological Entailment (with '⊢' denoting entailment) is sound and complete in supermodels for L.

4.4.2 "Dynamic" Logic

Now consider what happens to the supervalue of a sentence if we extend or shrink the interval considered. In general, the results are not unique, and are represented by the following tables.

THEOREM 8.   *shrinking and extending*

Assuming that t_1 and t_2 are connected intervals, $\neg(t_1 \cap t_2 = \text{empty})$, then the supervalues, $V * (S, Ct_1 - t_2)$ and $V * (S, t_1 \cap t_2)$ are given by the following tables: (where the values are not unique, I have used '/' to distingush between the alternatives).

Extending	T	F	B	N	$V * (S, t_2)$
T	T	N	T	N	
F	N	F	F	N	
B	T	F	B	N	
N	N	N	N	N	
$V * (S, t_1)$		$[V * (S, Ct_1 - t_2)]$			

Shrinking	T	F	B	N	$V * (S, t_2)$
T	T/B	B	B	T/B	
F	B	F/B	B	F/B	
B	B	B	B	B	
N	T/B	F/B	B	$T/F/B/N$	
$V * (S, t_1)$		$[V * (S, t_1 \cap t_2)]$			

Or better, consider the lattice D4 obtained by turning L4[3]

---

[3] Interestingly, D4 is not identical but is the dual of Belnap's approximation lattice A4.

D4:

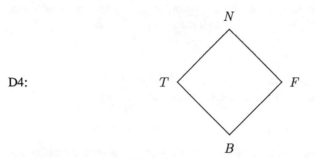

The value $V * (S, Ct_1 - t_2)$ is the A4 lattice "join" of $V * (S, t_1)$ and $V * (S, t_2)$. The value of $V * (S, t_1 \cap t_2)$ is not, however the (A4) "meet" of the corresponding values, but one of the values in the principal ideal generated by the greatest lower bound of $V * (S, t_1)$ and $V * (S, t_2)$.

4.4.3 Gaps and undetermined edges

The value N is given to a sentence S in an interval when there is no constant instantaneous valuation for S in the interval. In view of the condition TV3 on valuation set, it follows that the value N is given for a sentence in an interval iff there is a subinterval within which the sentence has the value T and there is a subinterval in which it has the value F.

> THEOREM 9.
> $$V * (S, t) = N \Leftrightarrow (\exists t_1 : t, t_2 : t)\{V * (S, t_1) = T \ \& \ V * (S, t_2) = F\}$$

We can now see in what sense an interval may have gaps and undetermined edges in a super-model. Consider again Cresswell's example

(9)   John is polishing every boot

Events:	John is not polishing	Polishing 1st boot	...	Polishing last boot	not polishing

```
        0    5    10   15   20   25   30   35   40   45   50
        |____|____|____|____|____|____|____|____|____|____|___→

Supervalue  (———F———) (——————————T——————————) (———F———)
of (9)      (——————————F——————————) (——T——) (——————————F——————————)
                  (—B—)                  (—B—)
                  (————————————————N————————————————)
```

I suggest that (9) is best represented as being true in the interval (15–40) during which John is polishing all the boots, as well as any subinterval in which he is polishing the last boots, in which he is completing the task (e.g., 25–35). In an interval before the polishing (such as 1–10) and after the polishing (40–50), (9) is false. In edge intervals (intersecting intervals in which the sentence is true and false respectively, e.g., 15–20, and 35–45) the value is both, while if we consider a cover of intervals in which the sentence is true and then false, 25–50, the supervalue is neither.

This analysis differs from Cresswell's and other open interval analyses in that it does not assume that the edge of an interval in which the sentence is true depends on a particular instant. Specifically, "the time in which John is polishing every boot", is described here as a time in which (9) is true and outside of which (9) is untrue. But if we consider that time to be an interval, it is not unique since both 15–40 and 25–35 satisfy this description. It is in this sense that durations have undetermined edges. But note that the above shows only that we can represent the indeterminacy of the edges. Whether the edges of durations are actually indeterminate, depends also on the richness of the language (used to identify durations) and the richness of the set of valuations.

That an interval has undetermined edges is defined relative to a sentence S. S is true of the interval and of some subinterval, and S has the value B in the edges.

Def. 21: undetermined edges

We say that S's interval has *undetermined edges* in t, if

$$(\exists t_1, t_2, t_3 : t)[t_1 < t_2 < t_3 \ \& \ V * (S, Ct_1 \neg t_3) = V * (S, t_2) = T$$
$$\& \ V * (S, t_1) = V * (S, t_3) = B]$$

Def. 22: generated intervals

We say that S generates an interval t, and we write S/t, if

$$V * (S, t) = T \ \& \ (\forall t')[t' \cap t = \text{empty} \Rightarrow \neg(V * (S, t') = T)]$$

Note that if S generates an interval t with undetermined edges, then S also generates another interval t_2, different from t_1.

5. Embedding a Duration Model in an Instant-based Supermodel

We show now that if L contains a sufficiently rich event language E, then we can embed a duration model of E in a supermodel of L.

Def. 23:

Let E be the event language fragment of L, and $SM = \langle I, T, <, :, V*, T, F, B, N \rangle$ a supermodel for L, we define a model $M = \langle T*, <, :, V, T, U \rangle$ as follows. Where $T*$ is a subset of T, V is the function

$$V : E \times T* \rightarrow \{T, U\} \text{ defined by}$$
$$V(S, t) = T \Leftrightarrow V * (S, t) = T \text{ and}$$

$$V(S, t) = U \Leftrightarrow \neg(V * (S, t) = T)$$

$T*$ is the set of all intervals of T, which are generated by the sentences in E and have undetermined edges.

(We have already noted that $\langle T, <, : \rangle$ is a D-structure. The requirement that the language E be sufficiently rich implies that it includes sufficiently many duration-generating sentences so that $\langle T*, <, : \rangle$ will be a D-structure.)

THEOREM 10. *requirement satisfaction*
Given that E is a sufficiently rich language, $M = \langle T*, <, :, V, \{T, U\} \rangle$ as defined above is a duration model for E.

We can now consider an extension of this model by adding for all S in L, t in T and i in I

$$V(S, t) = T \Leftrightarrow V * (S, t) = T$$
$$V(S, t) = U \Leftrightarrow \neg(V * (S, t) = T)$$

and

$$V(S, i) = T \Leftrightarrow (\forall v \in v*)(v(S, i) = T)$$
$$V(S, i) = U \Leftrightarrow \neg(V(S, i) = T)$$

The result yields truth values of every sentence in L in instants, open intervals and in durations. But what distiguishes durations from intervals is that E sentences are true of (and not merely in) durations. This extended model can thus be used to provide a common instant-based temporal interpretation for all the expressions of L.

CONCLUSION

This paper is concerned only with linear time, but I believe that the approach could be generalized and applied to branching time. In particular, we may start out with a set of E sentences which are possibly true, rather than those which are actually true at some time or another. In general, I believe that like durations, other objects — physical or theoretical — may have fuzzy boundaries.

This claim should be distinguished from the claim made by several proponents of fuzzy logic, that most natural language concepts are fuzzy (Goguen, 1970). The difference is ontological and depends on where we place the vagueness. Fuzzy logic characterizes vagueness in terms of degrees of set membership or degrees of truth. Hence, it associates vague terms (e.g., "bald") with precise objects (e.g., a set). This can succeed only if the reference relation itself is vague. However, this yields that the fuzzy edges of the terms "consume" the objects, in a sense. Consider the expression

(25)   The bald persons in the room.

Since according to fuzzy logic, we are all bald to a greater or lesser degree, (25) cannot (by itself) identify a proper subset of the people in this room. To refer sucessfully, the reference relation needs to be made precise, by specifying how degrees are assigned and what the cutpoint distinguishing "bald" from "not bald" is. But in doing this we take vague terms as precisely referring to precise objects, thereby ignoring the vagueness rather than interpreting it.

The present approach, in contrast, assumes that there are fuzzy objects, such as durations. A duration model interprets vague terms as precisely-referring to fuzzy objects. Thus, expressions like

(26)   When I finish writing this paper

refers precisely to a duration. That duration has fuzzy edges in the sense that its instantaneous edges are undetermined. If we insists that ultimately, the world is furnished with precise objects such as instants, then the present attempt shows how durations, which are fuzzy objects, can be constructed from them. This, without rendering the reference relation imprecise and without making all of us prematurely bald.

BIBLIOGRAPHY

Anderson, A. R. and Belnap, N. D. (1975): *Entailment: the Logic of Relevance and Necessity*, vol. 1, Princeton.

Åquist, L. and Guenthner, F. (1978): "Fundamentals of verb aspects and events within the setting of improved tense logic", *Studies in Formal Semantics*, F. Guenthner, C. Rohrer (eds.), North Holland.

Belnap, N. D. "A useful four valued logic", *Modern Uses Of Multiple Valued Logics*, J. M. Dunn, G. Epstein (eds.), Yale.

Cresswell, M. J. (1977): "Interval Semantics and logical words", *On the Logical Analysis of Tense and Aspect*, C. Rohrer (ed.), TBL Verlag.

Dowty, D. R. (1979): *Word Meaning and Montague Grammar*, Ch. 3, Synthese Language Library, D. Reidel.

Fine, K. (1975): "Vagueness, Truth and Logic", *Synthese* 30, pp. 265–300.

Goguen, J. (1970): "The logic of inexact concepts", *Synthese* 19, pp. 325–373.

Grice, H. P. (1975): "Logic and conversation", *Syntax and Semantics* vol.3, Cole, Morgan (eds.), Academic Press.

Kamp, J. A. W. (1980): "Some remarks on the logic of change, part I." *Time, Tense and Quantifiers*, C. Rohrer (ed.), Niemeyer Verlag.

Kasher, A. and Manor, R. (1980): "Simple present tense", *Time, Tense and Quantifiers*, C. Rohrer (ed.), Niemeyer Verlag.

Manor, R. (1979): "Intervals with undetermined edges", unpublished manuscript, Te Aviv University.

Rescher, N. and Urquhart, A. (1971): *Temporal Logic*, Springer Verlag.

Sanford, D. H. (1976): "Competing Semantics of Vagueness: Many Values Versus Super-Truth", *Synthese* 33, pp. 195–210.

Thomason, S. K. (1982): "On constructing instants from events", Research report no. 82–10, Simon Fraser University.

van Benthem, J.F.A.K. (1980): "Points and Periods", *Time, Tense and Quantifiers*, C. Rohrer (ed.), Niemeyer Verlag.

van Benthem, J.F.A.K. (1983): *The Logic of Time*, Reidel.

Vendler, Z. (1967): *Linguistics in Philosophy*, Cornell university Press.

van Fraassen, B. C. (1969): "Presuppositions, supervaluations and free logics", *The Logical Way of Doing Things*, K. Lambert (ed), Yale.

JAMES W. GARSON

CATEGORICAL SEMANTICS

0. INTRODUCTION

In "Tonk, Plonk and Plink" Belnap [1962] defended the claim that natural deduction rules define the meaning of a connective, provided at least that those rules form a conservative extension of the structural rules of deduction. In this paper we will investigate a stronger criterion of success for defining the meaning of a connective. Each connective comes with an intended interpretation, (for example, the intended interpretation of & is recorded by the truth table for &). For a set of rules to define the meaning of a connective, we would expect it to be categorical, i.e., we expect (roughly) that it force the intended interpretation of the connective on all its "models". To put it another way, rules define a connective when they are strong enough to eliminate any non-standard interpretations.[1]

In the domain of mathematical logic, from which we draw the concept of categoricity, the notion of a model of a sentence is straightforward. In the present application, however, we need the corresponding notion of a model of a rule. For this, McCawley [1981, pp. 61-69] chooses preservation of *truth*. He investigated whether a valuation which assigns the conclusion of a rule T provided it assigns the premises T would thereby be forced to obey the semantical conditions characteristic of a connective. We believe this approach is not adequately general, for it systematically eliminates intensional interpretations of the connectives. There are many rules, (for example Necessitation in modal logic, and Universal Generalization in quantificational logic) which do not preserve truth, and there are, correspondingly, intensional semantical conditions which cannot be expressed as local conditions on individual valuations. A fully general treatment will require that categoricity be defined via preservation of *validity* and that the conditions enforced be defined over *sets* of valuations. From this perspective, a set of rules is categorical when the semantical conditions for a connective are obeyed by any set of valuations V for which the rules preserve V-validity.

Categoricity entails an especially desirable form of completeness. When a set of rules is so strong that it allows no alternative interpretations for its connectives, we

---

[1] The demand that rules be categorical is a severe test for defining a connective. It is at least in the spirit, however, of Belnap's syntactic consistency and completeness conditions. It is not difficult to show that when a semantics $||S||$ obeys the (very weak) property that every atomic valuation has an extension in some set of valuations V obeying $||S||$, then any system categorical for $||S||$ meets Belnap's conservative extension requirement. It is also possible to show that as long as there is a set of valuations V obeying $||S||$ which is unique (in the sense that each atomic valuation has a unique extension in V) then any categorical system S defines unique roles of inference for the connectives. So our semantical requirements vindicate Belnap's purely syntactic requirements.

J. M. Dunn and A. Gupta (eds.), Truth or Consequences, 155–175.
© 1990 *Kluwer Academic Publishers. Printed in the Netherlands.*

expect (roughly) that any valuation for a consistent set of the system to be an intended model. As a result, any consistent set is satisfiable and the system is complete. But categoricity has a stronger consequence: the completeness is modular, i.e. the completeness of any pair of systems entails the completeness of their sum, so that one may confidently construct larger systems by adding together categorical logics.

Unfortunately, there are logics which are incomplete even though they are constructed from two (or more) complete subsystems. Past tense logic and future tense logic are complete, but their sum requires additional axioms to fix the relationships between the past tense and future tense operators. The system QS4 is composed of two complete systems: S4 and classical quantification theory, but it is incomplete (at least on one standard account of its semantics) because of the independence of the Barcan formula. Such behavior is a chronic annoyance in intensional logics. One satisfying feature of categoricity is that it insures modularity. When two systems are categorical, then their sum is always complete. When modularity fails, the blame lies with non–categoricity. The problem results from a mismatch between our intended interpretation for some logical constant and its *natural* interpretation, i.e., the semantical condition which *is* enforced by its rules. For this reason we will be interested in finding natural semantics for logical constants, for on these interpretations, modular completeness results are assured.

It turns out that natural semantics for many intensional logics approximates nicely their intended interpretations. The natural semantics for intuitionistic logic is its intensional S4 semantics, and the natural semantics for many modal logics reflect the corresponding semantical conditions in their canonical models. We will also find that the natural semantics for systems that accept Contraposition are related to the four–valued semantics for relevance logic. On the other hand, natural semantics for classical logic is intensional, and so differs from the intended interpretation. Natural semantics for classical propositional logic is related to supervaluation semantics, and the natural semantics for classical quantification differs from both the objectual and the substitution interpretation, though it is interesting none the less. We hope these results will sway the reader to respect natural semantics and to view intended interpretations which differ from the natural ones with suspicion.

1. Categoricity and Conjunction

Let us begin our discussion of categoricity with conjunction. Let $S\&$ be the system composed of the following natural deduction rules for $\&$:

$$\frac{\begin{array}{c} H \vdash A \\ H \vdash B \end{array}}{H \vdash A\&B} \qquad \frac{H \vdash A\&B}{H \vdash A} \qquad \frac{H \vdash A\&B}{H \vdash B}$$

together with the following system ($\vdash$) of structural rules for deduction:

($\vdash$ 1) $H \vdash A$ provided $A \in H$.

($\vdash$ 2)   If $H \vdash A$ for all $A \in H'$, and $H' \vdash B$ then $H \vdash B$.

To simplify our discussion, we consider the hypotheses H for these rules to be sets (rather than sequences) of sentences. However we use, for example, 'H, A' as an abbreviation for '$H \cup \{A\}$' so that we may present natural deduction rules in familiar sequent notation. We will assume, unless we say otherwise, that the systems we describe obey the structural rules.

Now let us formulate and answer the question as to whether these rules define the (truth tabular) meaning of &. Let a *valuation* v be a function from the set of sentences of a given language into the set $\{T, F\}$ of truth values which is *consistent*, i.e. v never assigns T to all the sentences. (It won't matter what the language is as long as it contains the binary connective &.) A set V of valuations (or a *model*) defines a corresponding notion of *V–validity* in the obvious way: $H \models_V C$ iff for all $v \in V$ if $v(H) = T$ then $v(C) = T$, where $v(H) = T$ means that $v(A) = T$ for each $A \in H$. Now suppose that $S\&$ preserves V-validity, that is, whenever the premises of one of these rules are V-valid then so is the conclusion. What does this tell us about the nature of V? The answer is satisfying, for preservation of V-validity entails $\|\&\|$, the truth condition for &:

$$\|\&\| \qquad \text{For all } v \in V, v(A\&B) = T \text{ iff } v(A) = T \text{ and } v(B) = T.$$

Let us say that V *is a model for a system of rules S* iff S preserves V-validity. Let V be *standard* (for $\|S\|$) iff V obeys the intended semantical conditions $\|S\|$ for S. What we have discovered is that every model of $S\&$ is standard. The rules force the models of $S\&$ to obey the intended interpretation of &. It is also easy to see that when V is standard for $\|\&\|$, V must be a model for $S\&$, for the system in question is sound. These desirable features of $S\&$ prompt the following definition: System of rules S is *categorical* (with respect to a semantical condition $\|S\|$ on a set of valuations) iff V is a model of S exactly when V is standard (for $\|S\|$). When S is categorical, S preserves V-validity iff V obeys $\|S\|$.

LEMMA 1. *$S\&$ is categorical for $\|\&\|$.*

Proof. From the soundness of $S\&$ it follows immediately that $S\&$ preserves V-validity if V obeys $\|\&\|$. For the other direction, assume that $S\&$ preserves V-validity, and show that V obeys $\|\&\|$. From our assumption, and $A, B \vdash_{S\&} A\&B$, $A\&B \vdash_{S\&} A$, and $A\&B \vdash_{S\&} B$, we know that $A, B \models_V A\&B$, $A\&B \models_V A$, and $A\&B \models_V B$. From this it follows immediately that V obeys $\|\&\|$. $\square$

2. Categoricity and Modular Completeness

Categoricity has a number of pleasing consequences. First, all categorical systems are complete, and this yields, for example, an instant proof of the completeness of $S\&$. Better yet, the completeness of categorical systems is modular, that is, categoricity of several systems entails the completeness of their sum.

To prove these results, we must first say a few words about the definitions of completeness and related notions. When we say that S is *complete for model V* (or V–complete for short) we mean that if $H \models_V C$ then $H \vdash_S C$. (Similarly S is V–consistent iff if $H \vdash_S C$ then $H \models_V C$, and S is V–adequate iff S is both V-consistent and V-complete.) These notions of completeness, consistency and adequacy will be useful in this paper, but they are not properly general since semantical conditions are not given by stipulating models, but rather by giving semantical conditions (such as $\|\&\|$) which are *properties* of models. Note that following the practice we established in the case of $\|\&\|$, we present such properties of models by giving corresponding (open) sentences containing the (free) metavariable V. A truly general account of completeness, consistency and adequacy of a system requires a definition of validity with respect to a semantics, i.e. a *property P* of models. The generalization we want is familiar from intensional logic. (Think of the valuations as possible worlds.) $H \models_P C$ iff $H \models_V C$ for every model V which obeys P. So S is *complete* (for $\|S\|$) iff if $H \models_{\|S\|} C$ then $H \vdash_S C$. (Similarly S is *consistent* (for $\|S\|$) iff if $H \vdash_S C$ then $H \models_{\|S\|} C$, and S is *adequate* (for $\|S\|$) iff S is both sound and complete (for $\|S\|$)).

The completeness proof for a categorical system S involves singling out a *canonical model* $|S|$ which respects the deductive behavior of S. Valuation v is *S-closed* iff if $H \vdash_S C$ and $v(H) = T$, then $v(C) = T$. A canonical model $|S|$ (for S) is the set of all S–closed valuations. We first show that any system S is adequate with respect to its canonical model.

Lemma 2.1. *S is $|S|$-adequate.*

Proof. For soundness, note that members of $|S|$ are deductively closed. For completeness, assume that $H \nvdash_S C$. Define valuation h as follows: $h(A) = T$ iff $H \vdash_S A$. Note that $h(C) = F$, so h is consistent. By ($\vdash$ 1), $H \vdash_S A$ for each $A \in H$, so we have $h(H) = T$. Function h is also S-closed, for suppose that $h(H') = T$ and $H' \vdash_S C'$. By the definition of h, we have that $H \vdash_S B$ for each $B \in H'$. By ($\vdash$ 2), $H \vdash_S C'$, and so $h(C') = T$ by the definition of h. So $h \in |S|$, $h(H) = T$ and $h(C) = F$, hence $H \nvDash_{|S|} C$. □

Lemma 2.2. *S preserves $|S|$-validity.*

Proof. By Lemma 2.1 we know S is $|S|$-adequate, so replace '$\vdash_S$' for '$\models_{|S|}$' in the statement of the rules to show that S preserves $|S|$-validity. □

When S is categorical for $\|S\|$, it follows by Lemma 2.2 that $|S|$ obeys $\|S\|$, Furthermore $|S|$ is the *largest* set of valuations that does so.

Lᴇᴍᴍᴀ 2.3. *If S is categorical for* $\|S\|$ *and V obeys* $\|S\|$, *then* $V \subseteq |S|$.

Proof. Suppose S is categorical for $\|S\|$ and V obeys $\|S\|$. It follows that S preserves V-validity, and so S is V-consistent. Suppose $H \vdash_S C$ and $v(H) = T$ for a given $v \in V$. By V-consistency, $v(C) = T$. So V contains only S-closed valuations and $V \subseteq |S|$. □

Next we show that the canonical model for S deserves its name. When S is categorical (for $\|S\|$), $\|S\|$-validity is equivalent to validity in the canonical model.

Lᴇᴍᴍᴀ 2.4. *If S is categorical for* $\|S\|$, *then* $H \models_{|S|} C$ *iff* $H \models_{\|S\|} C$.

Proof. Given that S is categorical, we know from Lemma 2.2 that $|S|$ obeys $\|S\|$. So if $H \models_{\|S\|} C$ then $H \models_{|S|} C$. For the other direction, assume $H \models_{|S|} C$, and let V be any set of valuations that obeys $\|S\|$. By Lemma 2.3, $V \subseteq |S|$, and so $H \models_V C$. Hence $H \models_{\|S\|} C$. □

This last feature of the canonical model yields the completeness result.

Tʜᴇᴏʀᴇᴍ 2.1. *If S is categorical, then S is complete.*

Proof. Immediate from Lemmas 2.1 and 2.4. □

That categorical systems are complete is relatively uninteresting. What is more important is that the completeness of categorical systems is modular. Let the sum $S + S'$ of two systems S and S' be the union of the sets of rules of both systems.[2] The semantics $\|S + S'\|$ for the resulting sum is the conjunction $\|S\| \& \|S'\|$ of their semantical conditions.

Lᴇᴍᴍᴀ 2.5. *The sum of any two categorical systems is categorical.*

Proof. Let S' and S'' be categorical systems with semantics $\|S'\|$ and $\|S''\|$ respectively. We must show that $S = S' + S''$ preserves V-validity iff V obeys $\|S\| = \|S'\| \& \|S''\|$. Suppose that S preserves V-validity. Then the rules of S' preserve V-validity and V obeys $\|S'\|$. Similarly, V also obeys $\|S''\|$, hence V obeys their conjunction $\|S' + S''\|$. Now suppose that V obeys $\|S\|$. Then V obeys $\|S'\|$ and $\|S''\|$, and so both S' and S'' preserve V-validity, hence so does S. □

It follows from this that categorical systems have modular completeness results.

---

[2] The reader might imagine that two systems S and S' are written in two different languages, in which case the language for the sum $S+S'$ differs from the language of S and S'. To avoid complications, however, we have assumed that a valuation assigns values to sentences of a single given language, with the result that S, S' and $S + S'$ must be already written in the same language. As a result, the language of S may contain connectives c' (which "really" belong to S' on the reader's way of thinking) which are absent from any rule of S or any clause of its semantics. Models of S assign arbitrary values to sentences $Ac'B$ when c' is a connective of this kind.

THEOREM 2.2. *The sum of any two categorical systems is complete.*

Proof. By Lemma 2.5 and Theorem 2.1.   □

3. CATEGORICITY FOR THE CONDITIONAL

The categoricity of $S\&$ is unusual. None of the other natural deduction rules for connectives of propositional logic is categorical. For example, the basic system $S\supset$ for the conditional is composed of $(\vdash)$ together with Modus Ponens and Conditional Proof.

Modus Ponens $\quad H \vdash A$ $\qquad$ Conditional Proof $\quad \dfrac{H, A \vdash B}{H \vdash A \supset B}$

$$\frac{H \vdash A \supset B}{H \vdash B}$$

Its classical semantics $\|\supset\|$ is simply the standard truth tabular property. (For simplicity in expressing this and future truth conditions, we assume variables 'v', 'v'', 'v''', etc. range over V.)

$\|\supset\| \qquad v(A \supset B) = T$ iff $v(A) = F$ or $v(B) = T$.

It is easy to see that $S\supset$ could not be categorical for this semantics.

LEMMA 3.1. $S\supset$ *is not categorical for* $\|\supset\|$.

Proof. We know by Theorem 2.1 that if $S\supset$ were categorical for $\|\supset\|$, then $S\supset$ would be complete for $\|\supset\|$. But $S\supset$ is incomplete on the truth tabular semantics for $\supset$ because of the independence of such sentences as Pierce's Law: $((A \supset B) \supset A) \supset A$.   □

It is interesting to locate the natural interpretation for $S\supset$, i.e. the semantics for which $\supset$ *is* categorical. Let us suppose that $S\supset$ preserves V-validity and try to determine what property this entails concerning the truth behavior of $\supset$. Because $A, A \supset B \vdash_{S\supset} B$, and since preservation of V-validity entails V-consistency, the following condition is met.

$\|\supset\|\rightarrow \qquad$ If $v(A \supset B) = T$, then if $v(A) = T$ then $v(B) = T$.

Condition $\|\supset\|\rightarrow$ insures that whenever $v(A) = T$ and $v(B) = F$, then $v(A \supset B) = F$. Since $B \vdash_{S\supset} A \supset B$, we also learn that whenever $v(B) = T$, $v(A \supset B) = T$. Together these conditions insure the truth behavior given in the first three rows of the truth table for $\supset$:

A	B	A⊃B
T	T	T
T	F	F
F	T	T
F	F	?

However, preservation of V-validity by $S\supset$ does not guarantee that if $v(A) = F$ and $v(B) = F$ then $v(A\supset B) = T$. It turns out however, that $S\supset$ is categorical for a truth condition $]\lbrack\supset]\lbrack$, which reminds us of the intuitionistic interpretation of $\supset$. (See, for example, Van Dalen [1986], p. 249.)

$]\lbrack\supset]\lbrack$ $\quad v(A\supset B) = T$ iff

for all v', if $v \subseteq v'$, then if $v'(A) = T$ then $v'(B) = T$.

Here we write $v \subseteq v'$ and say v' *is an extension of* v when $\lbrace A : v(A) = T\rbrace \subseteq \lbrace A : v'(A) = T\rbrace$. This clause is intensional; it is a property of V which cannot be expressed as a local restriction on the behavior of its individual members.

LEMMA 3.2. $S\supset$ *is categorical for* $]\lbrack\supset]\lbrack$.

Proof. The reader may verify that Modus Ponens and Conditional Proof preserve V-validity provided V obeys $]\lbrack\supset]\lbrack$. For the other direction, we must show that when $S\supset$ preserves V-validity, $]\lbrack\supset]\lbrack$ holds of V. To demonstrate $]\lbrack\supset]\lbrack$ from left to right, suppose $v(A\supset B) = T$ and $v \subseteq v'$. It follows that $v'(A\supset B) = T$ and hence that if $v'(A) = T$, then $v'(B) = T$ by $\|\supset\|\rightarrow$. (We explained why $\|\supset\|\rightarrow$ holds above.) To obtain $]\lbrack\supset]\lbrack$ from right to left, assume $v(A\supset B) = F$ and prove for some v', $v \subseteq v'$ and $v'(A) = T$ and $v'(B) = F$ as follows. Let $H_v = \lbrace B : v(B) = T\rbrace$. Note that from the contrapositive of the statement that Conditional Proof preserves V-validity we have:

If $v(H_v) = T$ and $v(A\supset B) = F$

then for some v', $v'(H_v, A) = T$ and $v'(B) = F$.

The antecedent of this conditional holds, and so the consequent follows:

for some v', $v'(H_v) = T$, $v'(A) = T$ and $v'(B) = F$.

This entails the desired result, for when $v'(H_v) = T$, $v \subseteq v'$. □

The moral of Lemma 3.2 is that the *classical semantics* for $\supset$ never was the interpretation generated by the classical rules. The natural interpretation of $S\supset$, is in fact, intuitionistic. This is to be expected since $S\supset$ yields the intuitionistic, not the classical, implication fragment.

4. CATEGORICITY AND NEGATION

It will come as no surprise that the classical rules for negation do not force the classical account of negation. In fact, the semantics for which the negation rules is categorical is intensional, and related again to intuitionistic semantics. Let us investigate the conditions enforced by the following classical negation rules.

Contradiction $A,\ \sim A \vdash B$ Indirect Proof $\dfrac{H,\ \sim A \vdash A}{H \vdash A}$

Let $S\sim$ be the result of adding these rules to the structural rules ($\vdash$), and let the classical semantics for $S\sim$ be $\|\sim\|$.

$\|\sim\|$ $v(\sim A) = T$ iff $v(A) = F$.

Notice that if $S\sim$ preserves V-validity, $A,\ \sim A \models_V B$, and for any $v \in V$, if $v(\{A,\ \sim A\}) = T$, then $v(B) = T$ for every sentence B. Since valuations are consistent, they may not assign T to every sentence B, and it follows that $v(\{A,\ \sim A\}) \neq T$. This yields $\|\sim\|\to$, the left to right portion of the classical truth condition $\|\sim\|$.

$\|\sim\|\to$ If $v(\sim A) = T$, then $v(A) = F$.

Unfortunately, that $S\sim$ preserves V-validity does not insure $\|\sim\|\leftarrow$, the truth clause in the other direction.

$\|\sim\|\leftarrow$ If $v(A) = F$, then $v(\sim A) = T$.

LEMMA 4.1. $S\sim$ *is not categorical for* $\|\sim\|$.

Proof. Note that by Lemma 2.2, $S\sim$ preserves $|S\sim|$–validity. So we need only find a member of $|S\sim|$ which violates the negation truth condition. Consider the valuation t which assigns T to all and only the *theorems* of $S\sim$. Clearly t is $S\sim$–closed, and it is also consistent, and hence a member of $|S\sim|$. When p is any atomic sentence, neither p nor $\sim p$ is a theorem of $S\sim$. So $t(p) = F$ and $t(\sim p) = F$ which violates the truth condition for negation.   □

So $S\sim$ allows interpretations of negation other than the standard one, interpretations where sentences are unexpectedly false. From one point of view, the existence of these non-standard valuations was predictable. Each of the non-standard valuations v corresponds to a partial valuation which leaves sentence A undefined exactly where negation misbehaves in v, (i.e. where $v(A) = v(\sim A) = F$). If $S\sim$ had been categorical for the classical semantics, there would have been "no room" for such weaker partial valuation semantics as supervaluations.[3]

---

[3] We may show that no partial valuation interpretation of $S\sim$ could exist if $S\sim$ were categorical for $\|\sim\|$ by the following argument. Because of the consistency of $S\sim$ with respect to supervaluation semantics, any set V of valuations which obeys that semantics is $S\sim$–closed and so a subset of $|S\sim|$. But given $S\sim$ is categorical for $\|\sim\|$, $|S\sim|$ would have to obey $\|\sim\|$, and so would V. Hence any V which obeyed supervaluation semantics would have to obey classical conditions, and so not contain any partial valuations.

$S\sim$ is not categorical for classical semantics, but $S\sim$ is categorical for $][\sim][$, the conjunction of $\|\sim\|\to$ with the intensional condition $][\sim][\leftarrow$.

$][\sim][\leftarrow$ If $v(A) = F$ then for some v', $v \subseteq v'$ and $v'(\sim A) = T$.

Although $][\sim][\leftarrow$ does not insure the classical behavior of $\sim$, it *does* say that when $v(A) = F$, there is an *extension* of v that behaves classically at A.[4]

LEMMA 4.2. *$S\sim$ is categorical for* $][\sim][$.

Proof. We will first assume that V obeys $][\sim][$, and show that Contradiction and Indirect Proof preserve V-validity. The case of Contradiction follows immediately from $\|\sim\|\to$. For Indirect Proof, assume that H, $\sim A \models_V A$, and suppose (for *reductio*) that $v(H) = T$ and $v(A) = F$ for some v. By $][\sim][$ we have a $v' \in V$ with $v \subseteq v'$, where $v'(\sim A) = T$. Since $v \subseteq v'$, $v'(H) = T$, and since H, $\sim A \models_V A$, $v'(A) = T$. But by $\|\sim\|\to$ we cannot have $v'(\sim A) = v'(A) = T$. Next we must show that if the rules of $S\sim$ preserve V-validity, $][\sim][$ holds. We have already explained why $\|\sim\|\to$ holds of V given A, $\sim A \models_V B$. To complete the demonstration, we need to show that when Indirect Proof preserves V-validity, $][\sim][\leftarrow$ holds. We begin with the contrapositive of the statement that Indirect Proof preserves V-validity:

$$\text{If } v(H) = T \text{ and } v(A) = F \text{ then for some } v',$$
$$v'(H, \sim A) = T \text{ and } v'(A) = F.$$

Now let $H_v = \{B : v(B) = T\}$. We obtain:

$$\text{If } v(A) = F \text{ then for some } v',$$
$$v'(H_v) = T, v'(\sim A) = T \text{ and } v'(A) = F.$$

But of course when $v'(H_v) = T$, $v \subseteq v'$, and so we obtain $][\sim][\leftarrow$.   □

Lemma 4.2 is not entirely satisfying, because $][\sim][$ does not have the form of a truth condition for negation: $v(\sim A) = T$ iff _____ . One might hope to find an equivalent version of $][\sim][$ in this standard form, for example something like the "intuitionistic":

$\|\neg\|$ $v(\sim A) = T$ iff for all v', if $v \subseteq v'$ then $v'(A) = F$.

Predictably, $\|\neg\|$ is weaker than $][\sim][$, for it does not insure the validity of the intuitionistically unacceptable rule Indirect Proof. It is interesting to note that while classical rules for negation do not force the classical interpretation of $\sim$, the intuitionistic system $S\neg$ for negation is categorical for $\|\neg\|$.

---

[4] $][\sim][$ expresses the germ of truth in the Lindenbaum Lemma. Let v^* be *maximal* iff if $v^* \subseteq v$ then $v^* = v$. Given $][\sim][\leftarrow$, we may prove that every valuation v has a maximal extension v^* by aping the familiar Lindenbaum argument. Note however, that such a maximal extension v^* need not be a member of V.

Lemma 4.3. $S\neg$ *is categorical for* $||\neg||$.

Proof. The reader may model the proof after Lemma 4.2. For rules of $S\neg$, take Contradiction and the intuitionistically acceptable form of Indirect Proof: $H, A \vdash \sim A \ / \ H \vdash \sim A$.						□

Lemma 4.3 (with Theorem 2.1) provides us with a quick completeness proof for $S\neg$. It also shows intuitionistic logic is well behaved, in the sense that $S\neg$ has a natural semantics in standard truth clause form. Not only that, the natural semantics for $S\neg$ is arguably its intended semantics. Since the relation $\subseteq$ is reflexive and transitive, $||\neg||$ is simply a special case of the famous S4 semantics for $S\neg$.

We do not know how to give a categorical semantics for classical logic in standard form, and we conjecture it cannot be done. We *can* show that $][\sim][$ is equivalent to the conjunction of $||\neg||$ with the additional, and seemingly *ad hoc*, stipulation $||\sim\sim||$:

$||\sim\sim||$		If $v(A) = F$, then for some v', $v \subseteq v'$ and for all v'', if $v' \subseteq v''$, then $v''(A) = F$.

This condition simply enforces validity of the intuitionistically unacceptable law of double negation.

Lemma 4.4. $][\sim][$ *is equivalent to* $||\neg|| \ \& \ ||\sim\sim||$.

Proof. To show that $||\neg|| \ \& \ ||\sim\sim||$ entails $][\sim][$, first note that $||\neg||$ entails $||\sim||\rightarrow$. To show that $||\neg|| \ \& \ ||\sim\sim||$ also entails $][\sim][\leftarrow$, assume $v(A) = F$ and use $||\sim\sim||$ to show that for some v', $v \subseteq v'$ and for all v'', if $v' \subseteq v''$ then $v''(A) = F$. But this amounts to: for some v', $v \subseteq v'$ and $v'(\sim A) = T$ by $||\neg||$. For the other direction, we show that $][\sim][$ entails both $||\neg||$ and $||\sim\sim||$. For $||\sim\sim||$, assume $v(A) = F$ and obtain: for some v', $v \subseteq v'$ and $v'(\sim A) = T$ by $||\sim||\leftarrow$. Hence by $||\neg||$, for some v', $v \subseteq v'$ and for all v'', if $v' \subseteq v''$ then $v''(A) = F$. For $||\neg||$ from left to right, suppose $v(\sim A) = T$ and $v \subseteq v'$. Hence $v'(\sim A) = T$, and so by $||\sim||\rightarrow$, $v'(A) = F$. For $||\neg||$, from right to left, assume $v(\sim A) = F$; then by $||\sim\sim||$, for some v', $v \subseteq v'$ and for all v'', if $v' \subseteq v''$ then $v''(\sim A) = F$. By $][\sim][\leftarrow$, it follows that for some v', $v \subseteq v'$ and $v'(A) = T$.						□

The classical stipulation $||\sim\sim||$ has an interesting interpretation from the point of view of intuitionistic semantics. Let us view $\subseteq$ as representing the process of extending our knowledge as new information becomes available. Let us say that a sentence A is undefined (not yet decided) at v when $v(A) = v(\sim A) = F$. It follows from $||\neg||$ that A is defined at v when it maintains its value in all extensions of v. So $||\sim\sim||$ says that every false sentence (even if undefined) becomes defined in some possible extension of our knowledge. This is exactly the bone of contention between classical and intuitionistic accounts. It is unfortunate for the classical logician that this stipulation cannot (as far as I know) be incorporated into a truth condition in standard form for which classical logic is categorical.

5. Four Valued Interpretations, Contraposition, and Relevance Logic

When negation behaves non-classically, there is a natural way, related to semantics for relevance logic [Dunn, 1986, p. 192], to define four "values" for any *two valued* valuation v as follows:

$v(A) = \uparrow$	(A is undefined)	iff	$v(A) = F$ and $v(\sim A) = F$.
$v(A) = \downarrow T$	(A is determined T)	iff	$v(A) = T$ and $v(\sim A) = F$.
$v(A) = \downarrow F$	(A is determined F)	iff	$v(A) = F$ and $v(\sim A) = T$.
$v(A) = \downarrow\downarrow$	(A is overdetermined)	iff	$v(A) = T$ and $v(\sim A) = T$.

Although the value $\downarrow\downarrow$ is impossible for a system of classical logic (since Contradiction is categorical for $\|\sim\|\rightarrow$), we may consider weaker systems which do not accept Contradiction, and so allow the fourth value. Such logics typically include Contraposition.

$$\text{Contraposition} \quad \frac{A \vdash B}{\sim B \vdash \sim A}$$

It is natural to wonder what the natural semantics for Contraposition is. We are interested in finding a semantical condition which is equivalent to the statement that Contraposition preserves V-validity. The condition $\|\leq\|$ which we are looking for says that V-validity corresponds to the ordering $\leq$ defined by the following famous lattice:

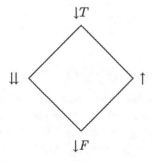

$$\|\leq\| \qquad A \models_v B \text{ iff for all } v \in V, v(A) \leq v(B)$$

(where $a \leq b$ iff a appears at or below b in the diagram).

LEMMA 5.1. *Contraposition is categorical for the condition* $\|\leq\|$.

Proof. First show that $\|\leq\|$ entails that Contraposition preserves V-validity. Assume that $A \models_V B$, and that $v(\sim B) = T$ and show that $v(\sim A) = T$ as follows. Given $A \models_V B$, we know by $\|\leq\|$ that $v(A) \leq v(B)$. Assume $v(B) = T$. Then $v(B) = \downarrow\downarrow$. Since $v(A) \leq v(B)$, we know that $v(A) = \downarrow\downarrow$ or $v(A) = \downarrow F$, but in either case $v(\sim A) = T$. Now assume $v(B) = F$. Then $v(B) = \downarrow F$, hence $v(A) = \downarrow F$, and $v(\sim A) = T$. Next we must show that if Contraposition preserves V-validity then $\|\leq\|$ follows. So assume that Contraposition preserves V-validity. For the proof of $\|\leq\|$ from left to right, assume $A \models_V B$. It follows that if $v(A) = T$ then $v(B) = T$, and if $v(\sim B) = T$ then $v(\sim A) = T$, i.e., if $v(\sim A) = F$ then $v(\sim B) = F$. We must show $v(A) \leq v(B)$ for all $v \in V$. The proof is by cases on the value of A.

Suppose $v(A) = \downarrow T$. Then $v(A) = T$ and $v(\sim A) = F$. So $v(B) = T$, $v(\sim B) = F$ and $v(B) = \downarrow T$, hence $v(A) \leq v(B)$.

Suppose $v(A) = \downarrow\downarrow$. Then $v(A) = T$ and $v(\sim A) = T$. So $v(B) = T$. If $v(\sim B) = T$, $v(B) = \downarrow\downarrow$, and if $v(\sim B) = F$ then $v(B) = \downarrow T$. Either way, $v(A) \leq v(B)$.

Suppose $v(A) = \uparrow$. Then $v(A) = F$ and $v(\sim A) = F$. So $v(\sim B) = F$.

If $v(B) = T$, $v(B) = \downarrow T$, and if $v(B) = F$, then $v(B) = \uparrow$. Either way, $v(A) \leq v(B)$.

Suppose $v(A) = \downarrow F$. Then $v(A) \leq v(B)$, since $\downarrow F \leq a$ for any value a.

For the proof of $\|\leq\|$ from right to left, assume for all $v \in V$, $v(A) \leq v(B)$. We will show $A \models_V B$. Assume $v(A) = T$. Then $v(A) = \downarrow T$ or $v(A) = \downarrow\downarrow$. In case $v(A) = \downarrow T$, $v(B) = \downarrow T$ and so $v(B) = T$. In case $v(A) = \downarrow\downarrow$, $v(B) = \downarrow\downarrow$ or $v(B) = \downarrow T$, but in either case $v(B) = T$.   □

Lemma 5.1 has interesting applications to relevance logic. It may be used to prove a four value characterization theorem for R with respect to R's canonical model $|R|$.

LEMMA 5.2. $\vdash_R A \rightarrow B$ *iff for all* $v \in |R|$, $v(A) \leq v(B)$.

Proof. Although R is not $|R|$-adequate (for we need the relevantly invalid structural rule ($\vdash 1$) to obtain Lemma 2.1), we can prove weak adequacy: $A \vdash_R B$ iff $A \models_{|R|} B$ using the strategy of Lemma 2.1, and $A \vdash_R A$. From this we know that Contraposition preserves $|R|$-validity. By Lemma 5.1, and the definition of categoricity, we know $\|\leq\|$ holds of $|R|$, that is, $A \models_{|R|} B$ iff for all $v \in |R|$, $v(A) \leq v(B)$. Putting these results together with the deduction theorem for R, we obtain: $\vdash_R A \rightarrow B$ iff for all $v \in |R|$, $v(A) \leq v(B)$.   □

The proof of Lemma 5.2 is very general, and says nothing about the semantical behavior of the connectives & or ∨. We would hope to show that $|R|$ is isomorphic to some better known semantical account for R so as to shed light, for example, on the four valued interpretation for first degree formulas [Dunn 1986, p. 187]. We are foiled, however, by the poor behavior of ∨ in $|R|$.[5] Still, the result is intriguing.

Notice that Lemma 5.2 would obtain for any logic which contains Contraposition and a conditional for which the (single premise) deduction theorem holds. So such four valued interpretations are in no way special to relevance logics, (though for classical logics they degenerate into three valued ones).

6. CLASSICAL CATEGORICITY

Apart from $S\&$, none of the systems for the propositional connectives is categorical for its classical interpretation. This failure of categoricity is not, however, a serious defect. A weaker notion of categoricity can be defined for systems with classical negation (i.e. systems which include $S{\sim}$) which has all the desirable features of categoricity proven in Section 2. So far we have demanded only that valuations be consistent, but we might also consider *classical models* whose valuations must also obey the classical truth condition $||{\sim}||$ for negation. Let us say that S is *classically categorical* (for $||S||$) iff V is a model of S just in case V obeys $||S||$ for all *classical models* V.

Although classical categoricity is weaker than categoricity in general, it obeys Theorems 2.1 and 2.2. So we know that the sum of any two classically categorical systems is complete. The reader may verify this by reviewing the proofs of all lemmas in section 2 with the understanding that valuations are all classical. The only change required is an appeal to the rules of $S{\sim}$ and the Lindenbaum Lemma in Lemma 2.1 to insure that the valuation h defined there is classical.

It is easy to prove that when V is a set of classical valuations, the intensional clauses $][\supset][$, and $][{\sim}][$ reduce to their extensional counterparts $||\supset||$ and $||{\sim}||$. It follows that $S\supset$ and $S{\sim}$ are classically categorical. It is also easy to verify that natural deduction systems for other connectives are classically categorical, provided that the rules of $S{\sim}$ are also available. We illustrate in the case of disjunction.[6] Let $S\vee$ be $S{\sim}$ plus the standard elimination and introduction rules for disjunction. Note the following facts about $S\vee$:

$$A, B \vdash_{S\vee} A \vee B$$
$$A, {\sim}B \vdash_{S\vee} A \vee B$$
$${\sim}A, B \vdash_{S\vee} A \vee B$$
$${\sim}A, {\sim}B \vdash_{S\vee} {\sim}(A \vee B)$$

---

[5] Although we know that $||\&||$, $][{\sim}][{\leftarrow}$, and $][\supset][$ hold in $|R|$, we do not see how to show the classical truth condition for ∨. We *can* show $v(A) = T$ or $v(B) = T$ entails $v(A \vee B) = T$, but the closest we know of for the reverse is: if $v(A \vee B) = T$ then for some v', $v \subseteq v'$ & ($v'(A) = T$ or $v'(B) = T$). This is something like, but not the same as, saying that every valuation has a prime extension.

[6] Another way to prove this is to first verify that ∨Out is categorical for the condition: if $v(A \vee B) = T$ then if $v(C) = F$ then for some v', $v \subseteq v'$ & ($v'(A) = T$ or $v'(B) = T$) & $v'(C) = F$. Then show that this condition reduces to the classical one in the case of maximal valuations.

If the rules of $S\lor$ preserve V-validity, each of these is V-valid, thus insuring members of V obey the semantical condition given by each row of the truth table for $\lor$. Similar arguments may be supplied for any other truth functional connective.

The classical categoricity of the rules for propositional logic connectives explains the modular completeness of its fragments. There is never a need to provide linking principles to guarantee the proper interaction between the connectives (provided the classical rules for negation are available). In the remainder of this paper we will be considering extensions of classical logic. So we will be primarily interested in classical categoricity, since it is a more useful measure of modular completeness.

7. CATEGORICITY IN PROPOSITIONAL MODAL LOGIC

Many propositional modal logics are categorical for conditions on V which resemble their standard semantics. Ordinarily, modal logic semantics involves the introduction of a frame $\langle W,R\rangle$ containing a set W of possible worlds and an accessibility relation R. It is easy enough, however, to let valuations play the role of the possible worlds, and to *generate* the accessibility relation R by the following definition.

(Def R) Rvv' iff for every wff A, if $v(\Box A) = T$, then $v'(A) = T$.

(Def R) is, in effect, the definition given to the accessibility relation in the canonical model for a propositional modal logic.

The advantage of (Def R) is that we will be able to develop modal logic semantics as a condition on V without introducing any independent structure such as frames. The truth condition for $\Box$ may be expressed entirely as a condition on sets of valuations V as follows:

$\|\Box\|$ $v(\Box A) = T$ iff for all v', if Rvv' then $v'(A) = T$.

The basic modal logic K is formed by adding rule (K) to PL.

(K) $\dfrac{H \vdash C}{\Box H \vdash \Box C}$
(where $\Box H$ is $\{\Box A : A \in H\}$)

LEMMA 7.1. (K) *is categorical for* $\|\Box\|$.

Proof. The reader can check that $\|\Box\|$ insures that (K) preserves V-validity. We must now show $\|\Box\|$ holds of V if (K) preserves V-validity. The direction from left to right in $\|\Box\|$ holds because of (Def R). For the other direction, we must show:

If $v(\Box A) = F$, then for some v', Rvv' and $v'(A) = F$.

Assume then that $v(\Box A) = F$. Let $\Box H$ be $\{\Box B : v(\Box B) = T\}$. Then we have that $v(\Box H) = T$ and $v(\Box A) = F$. By contraposing the statement that (K) preserves V-validity, we obtain:

If $v(\Box H) = T$ and $v(\Box A) = F$ then for some v', $v'(H) = T$ and $v'(A) = F$.

So there is a valuation v' with $v'(H) = T$ and $v'(A) = F$. Since $v'(H) = T$, Rvv', and so we have the desired result.   □

To develop semantics for modal logics stronger than K, we simply introduce the well known conditions on the accessibility relation R. Since each model V generates a frame $\langle V,R \rangle$ by (Def R), the familiar conditions on frames turn out to be simply conditions on V. The reader may worry that this approach varies from the more standard technique which introduces a frame as an independent structure. In the vast majority of modal logics, however, there is no difference. If a modal logic is *canonical*, (i.e. its classical canonical model meets the conditions on a frame for that logic) then whenever a set of sentences is satisfiable on a model which violates (Def R) it is also satisfiable in the canonical model, which obeys (Def R). So for canonical modal logics, notions of satisfiability (hence validity) are unaffected by our practice of generating frames from models.

Unfortunately, categoricity for stronger modal logics does not go as far as one would like. The systems $T (= K + (T): \Box A \vdash A)$ and S4 $(= T + (4): \Box A \vdash \Box\Box A)$, are categorical, but certain systems with rules involving $\sim$ (or $\Diamond$) such as B and S5 are not.

LEMMA 7.2. *If S is an extension of T such that $\nvdash_S p$ for some propositional variable p, then S is not categorical for any $\|S\|$ requiring symmetry of R.*

Proof. Assume the antecedent of the lemma and that $\|S\|$ insures R is symmetric. If S were categorical for $\|S\|$, then since Lemma 2.2 entails that S preserves $|S|$-validity, it would follow that the frame generated by $|S|$ is symmetric. But it is not by the following reasoning. Let v and v' be defined so that $v(A) = T$ iff $\vdash_S A$ and $v'(A) = T$ iff $\Box p \vdash_S A$. Clearly v and v' are members of $|S|$. If $v(\Box A) = T$ then $\vdash_S \Box A$, $\vdash_S A$, $\Box p \vdash_S A$, and $v'(A) = T$, so Rvv'. However $\nvdash_S p$, so $v(p) = F$, and $\Box p \vdash_S \Box p$, so $v'(\Box p) = T$, so not $Rv'v$.   □

Notice the proof of Lemma 7.2 uses valuations which are clearly not classical. When negation behaves classically, matters improve somewhat, for classical categoricity holds for all systems whose conditions $\|F\|$ on a frame are preserved under subset. (Condition C is *preserved under subset* iff if C holds of V and $V' \subseteq V$, then C holds of V'.) This includes B and S5, but excludes logics with conditions such as density or convergence.

LEMMA 7.3. *If S is an $\|S\|$-consistent extension of K, and $\|S\| = \|\Box\|$ & $\|F\|$, and $\|F\|$ is any property preserved under subset, then S is classically categorical for $\|S\|$.*

Proof. $\|S\|$-consistency insures that if V obeys $\|S\|$ then S preserves V-validity. Consider $|S|^*$, the set of all *classical* S-closed valuations. It is easy to verify that this is the canonical model for S, so it obeys $\|S\|$. Now assume that V is classical and S preserves V-validity. Then S is V-consistent, hence V is S-closed, and $V \subseteq |S|^*$. By Lemma 7.1, V obeys $\|\Box\|$. Since $\|F\|$ is preserved under subset, V obeys $\|F\|$. $\Box$

It is interesting to note that techniques for showing completeness for quantified modal logics often depend on the strength of the modal principles. (See Garson [1984].) Partial model techniques (which covertly use non-standard negation) run into difficulties with modalities as strong as B, while full model methods still run into problems for conditions on R that are not preserved under subset. (We are thinking, for example, of difficulties in establishing completeness, even for systems containing the Barcan formulas, of systems involving convergence.) We believe that these phenomena are directly related to the failure of the various forms of categoricity in the propositional modal systems. We might note that it is possible to improve on categoricity results for propositional logics by further weakening the notion of categoricity. If we insist that a set of valuations V only counts as a model when it contains an extension of every atomic valuation, then we can show (weakened) categoricity of all canonical modal logics. This has useful applications to completeness problems in quantified modal logic, a topic we leave to another paper.

8. CATEGORICITY IN QUANTIFICATIONAL LOGIC

Let us formulate classical quantification theory QL by adding the following rules to those of PL.

∀Out $\dfrac{H \vdash \forall x A}{H \vdash A}$

∀In $\dfrac{H \vdash A}{H \vdash \forall x A}$ provided x does not appear free in H.

t/xIn $\dfrac{H \vdash A}{H \vdash At/x}$ provided x does not appear free in H.

(At/x is the result of substituting the term t (properly) for each free occurrence of x in Ax.)

We have separated the traditional rule of Universal Instantiation into the two halves ∀Out and t/xIn on the grounds that rules that define a logical symbol ought to involve that symbol only. The traditional rule stipulates a relationship between two kinds of symbols: the quantifiers and the terms.

The obvious question to ask is whether QL is classically categorical. The answer is that it is not. To make this result official, we need to give the semantics for ∀. For smoothest connection with our treatment of valuations, we adopt Smullyan's

[1968, p. 46-47] device of substituting *objects* of a domain for *variables* in the quantifier truth clause. Let us begin with a domain D of objects. We assume that valuations are defined over both sentences and *pseudo-sentences*, i.e. results of replacing *objects* from D for free variables in sentences. The truth clause for the quantifier is now given by condition $||\forall||$ on sets of such valuations.

$||\forall|| \qquad v(\forall x A) = T$ iff for all $d \in D$, $v(Ad/x) = T$.

LEMMA 8.1. QL *is not classically categorical for* $||\forall||$.

Proof. By Lemma 2.1, QL is $|QL|$-adequate. So if QL were classically categorical for $||\forall||$ then $|QL|$ would obey $||\forall||$. However, we can construct a member of $|QL|$ which disobeys $||\forall||$. The set $\{At: t$ is a term$\} \cup \{-\forall x Ax\}$ is consistent in QL, and by the Lindenbaum Lemma, it has a maximal extension e, which cannot be omega complete, (i.e. it lacks the property that whenever At is a member for each term t, then $\forall x Ax$ is a member). The representing function for e is a classical valuation v which disobeys $||\forall||$ when the domain D is the set of terms. Clearly v is QL-closed and so a member of $|QL|$.   □

Lemma 8.1 shows that the intended interpretation for classical quantification theory goes beyond what is implicit in the quantifier rules. The same general strategy may be used to show that QL is not categorical for the objectual and substitution interpretations. We would like to know what the natural interpretation of QL is. Just as was the case for classical negation, we do not know how to give the natural semantics for QL in standard truth clause form.[7] However, we can give such a semantics for QL-, the result of deleting t/xIn from QL. We may then hope to develop a separate semantical condition for terms that corresponds to t/xIn. The natural semantics $][\forall][$ for QL- does without a domain and has (yet again) an intensional flavor.

$][\forall][\qquad v(\forall x A) = T$ iff for every v', if $v \subseteq_x v'$, then $v'(A) = T$.[8]

Here $v \subseteq_x v'$ means that v' is an extension of v save for formulas containing free x. More formally, $v \subseteq_x v'$ iff for every wff B which fails to contain free x, if $v(B) = T$ then $v'(B) = T$.

---

[7] The reader may wonder why QL is not categorical for the following clause for the quantifier.

$v(\forall x A) = T$ iff for all terms t not in A and all $v \subseteq_x v'$, $v'(At/x) = T$.

The problem is that $\forall$In does not preserve validity on this semantics.

[8] The reader may feel that this definition (and perhaps others we have presented) is circular. To calculate $v(\forall x A)$ one needs to know the relation $\subseteq_x$, and to know *that* we need to know values of all sentences on all valuations, and so the value of $v(\forall x A)$. This objection would be cogent if $][\forall][$ (and other conditions) were a recursive definition of the value of $\forall x A$. It is not. Remember, we are antecedently given a set V of valuations, and $\subseteq_x$ is therefore already given. Condition $][\forall][$ represents a requirement on V in order for V to obey a given semantics. The reader can verify that when V does obey this condition, then the value given by v to $\forall x A$ (for V) exists and is unique. As a result, enforcement of $][\forall][$ has the effect of a recursive stipulation of the value of $\forall x A$ even though it is not such a recursive definition itself.

LEMMA 8.2. QL- *is categorical for*][∀][.

Proof. Given that][∀][holds of V, it is easy to verify that ∀In and ∀Out preserve V-validity. For the other direction, we must show that][∀][holds of V assuming QL- preserves V-validity. To show][∀][left to right, assume that $v(\forall x A) = T$ and $v \subseteq_x v'$ for a given $v' \in V$. Since $\forall x A$ contains no free x, $v'(\forall x A) = T$. We have $\forall x A \vdash_{QL-} A$ hence $\forall x A \models_V A$, so $v'(A) = T$, the desired result. To show][∀][right to left, we prove][∀][← instead.

][∀][←   If $v(\forall x A) = F$ then for some v', if $v \subseteq_x v'$, then $v'(A) = F$.

So suppose that $v(\forall x A) = F$. Let $H_v = \{B: v(B) = T$ and B does not contain free $x\}$. Now consider the contrapositive of the claim that ∀In preserves validity.

If x is not free in H_v, then if $v(H_v) = T$ and $v(\forall x A) = F$, then $v'(H_v) = T$ and $v'(A) = F$ for some v'.

It follows that there is a valuation $v' \in V$ such that $v'(H_v) = T$ and $v'(A) = F$. So $v \subseteq_x v'$ and $v'(A) = F$ for this valuation v'.   □

][∀][is weaker than classical semantics for the quantifier because it does not validate t/xIn.

LEMMA 8.3. t/xIn *does not preserve*][∀][*-validity.*

Proof. It will suffice to show that $\forall x Fx \not\models_{][\forall][} Ft$, for $\forall x Fx \vdash Fx$ is clearly][∀][-valid, and $\forall x Fx \vdash Ft$ follows by t/xIn. Let V contain a single classical valuation v which assigns the following values to the atoms Fx and Ft: $v(Fx) = T$, $v(Ft) = F$. Let values for other atoms be arbitrary, and set the values of complex sentences using classical truth clauses for propositional logic and][∀][. Since the only valuation $v' \in V$ such that $v \subseteq_x v'$ is v, and $v(Fx) = T$, it follows that $v(\forall x Fx) = T$. So $v(\forall x Fx) = T$ and $v(Ft) = F$, and $\forall x Fx \not\models_V Ft$. Since V obeys][∀][, $\forall x Fx \not\models_{][\forall][} Ft$.   □

Lemma 8.3 shows that][∀][fails to insure that terms have existential import. In calculating $v(\forall x A)$, one searches only valuations v' *in* V such that if $v \subseteq_x v'$ then $v'(A) = T$. If V does not contain a valuation v' such that $v \subseteq_x v'$ and $v'(At/x) = T$, then $v(\forall x A) = T$ while $v(At/x) = F$. Under these circumstances, it is as if t did not denote in the virtual domain generated by V. It follows that QL-, the logic of][∀][, is not classical. It is not free logic either, since the same strategy given in the proof of Lemma 8.3 demonstrates $\forall x Ax \not\models_{][\forall][} \forall y Ay$. QL- is best understood as a system which has *separate* domains for each of the variables.

In order to generate a natural semantics for classical logic, we must supplement][∀][, with the condition][t/x][for which t/xIn is categorical.

][t/x][If $v(At/x) = F$ then for some v', $v \subseteq_x v'$ and $v'(A) = F$.

][t/x][insures the validity of $\forall x A \supset At/x$, and so says that all terms have existential import.

LEMMA 8.4. t/xIn *is categorical for* $][t/x][$.

Proof. The reader may verify that t/xIn preserves V-validity when $][t/x][$ holds of V. So all that remains is to show that $][t/x][$ holds assuming that t/xIn preserves V-validity. Suppose $v(At/x) = F$ and let $H_v = \{B : v(B) = T$ and B contains no free $x\}$. Use the contrapositive of the claim that t/xIn preserves V-validity to establish $v'(H_v) = T$ and $v'(A) = F$ for some $v' \in V$. Since $v'(H_v) = T$, $v \subseteq_x v'$.   □

It follows from Lemmas 8.2, 8.4 and 2.5 that the natural semantics for classical quantification theory is the conjunction of $][\forall][$ with $][t/x][$. We may also combine this result with results on categoricity for propositional modal logics and Theorem 2.2 to show completeness of quantified modal logics on the sentential interpretation. Results of this kind may then be strengthened to obtain completeness proofs for more traditional interpretations of the quantifiers. The situation is complicated, however, so we leave these matters for another paper.

In the case of classical valuations, $v \subseteq_x v'$ holds iff v and v' agree in value for all sentences containing no free x. Under these circumstances the only difference between $][\forall][$ and the objectual truth condition is that where the objectual condition would require that the two interpretations be identical save for what value they assign to the *variable* x, $][\forall][$ only requires they be identical save for the value they assign to *sentences* containing free x. Since $][\forall][$ involves values assigned to (open) sentences, we call the natural semantics for QL the *sentential interpretation* of the quantifier.

The sentential interpretation has not been discussed in the literature as far as I know. It is interesting for its formal applications, but it has philosophical merits as well. It provides a truth value semantics for $\forall$ without ontological commitment (since there is no explicit introduction of a domain of quantification), yet it avoids difficulties associated with the substitution interpretation. One of these is that unless one is careful in defining validity there, one validates the omega rule, with the result that strong completeness fails (because of a failure of compactness). Repairs are available, but they limit results on categoricity.[9] More importantly, the substitution interpretation is incompatible with a covert intention to quantify over uncountably infinite sets such as the real numbers (assuming at least that we allow only countably many terms). The sentential interpretation suffers from neither problem. It fails to validate the omega rule, and since the set of all *valuations* $v' \in V$ such that $v \subseteq_x v'$ may be uncountable, it is compatible with covert quantification over the reals.

The sentential interpretation may have gone unnoticed because of a failure to perceive the taxonomy of quantifier interpretations in the right way. The objectual

---

[9] One well known repair for the difficulty is to define validity via valuations over languages with possibly extra terms. From our perspective this requires the introduction of sets of valuations defined over varying languages. Such sets of valuations are isomorphic to sets of partial valuations over a universal language with sentences undefined when they do not exist in a given language. So the introduction of valuations over varying languages amounts from our point of view to adopting a non-classical account of negation. As a result, theorems on classical categoricity do not apply to the substitution interpretation, and completeness requires demonstration of (unweakened) categoricity. This limits application of our methods in quantified modal logic.

interpretation instructs us to check the value of $\forall x A$ at valuation v by looking at the value of A given *new valuations* of the variable x to members of the domain (valuations like v save at x). The substitution interpretation instructs us to check the values of *new sentences* At/x. This suggests that ontological commitment "goes with" the new valuations technique, while the new sentences method avoids it. Actually, Smullyan's interpretation already shows that it is possible to have ontological commitment with the new sentences method. The existence of the sentential interpretation shows that the choice between methods is completely orthogonal to the choice for or against ontological commitment. All four combinations are possible as is illustrated in the following chart.

Ontological Commitment	New Valuations Method	New Sentences Method
Yes	Objectual Interpretation	Smullyan's Interpretation
No	Sentential Interpretation	Substitution Interpretation

9. CONCLUSION

This paper explores a small sample of results which are possible using categorical semantics. We hope to have convinced the reader that natural semantics for the logical constants is philosophically revealing and formally useful. It has obvious applications in proving independence, and provides a powerful tool for exploring the pathological behavior that may result when an intended interpretation for a connective goes beyond its natural interpretation. The methods we have described provide handy new tools for establishing completeness and for appreciating better why completeness sometimes eludes us.

BIBLIOGRAPHY

Belnap, N. (1962): "Tonk, Plonk and Plink," *Analysis*, vol. 22, pp. 130–134.

Dunn, J. M. (1986): "Relevance Logic and Entailment," Ch. 3, vol. III of *Handbook of Philosophical Logic*, D. M. Gabbay and F. Guenthner (eds.) Reidel, pp. 117–224.

Garson, J.W. (1984): "Quantification in Modal Logic," Ch. 5, Vol. II of *Handbook of Philosophical Logic*, D.M. Gabbay and F. Guenthner (eds.) Reidel, pp. 249–307.

McCawley, J. D. (1981): *Everything that Linguists have Always Wanted to Know about Logic*, University of Chicago Press.

Smullyan, R. (1968): *First-Order Logic*, Springer-Verlag.

Van Dalen, D. (1986): "Intuitionistic Logic," Ch. 4, vol. III, of *Handbook of Philosophical Logic*, D. M. Gabbay and F. Guenthner (eds.) Reidel, pp. 225–339.

A. P. HAZEN

THE MYTH OF THE INTUITIONISTIC "OR"

There is a widespread impression that there is a special intuitionistic sense of disjunction, stronger than the classical sense. (There is a similar belief in a special intuitionistic sense of existential quantification; the fundamental issues involved are the same, as I hope to bring out.) The impression is mistaken — on the interpretation most favorable to the idea that there is a special intuitionistic disjunction, intuitionistic disjunction is weaker than classical — and it is philosophically pernicious. Early work by Belnap and some of his colleagues helps to show this.

Perhaps the most pernicious aspect of the view is the way in which it supports the larger misimpression that intuitionism — by which I mean the whole family of critical philosophies of mathematics of which Brouwer's and Bishop's are the best known — is about non-standard logic. It's not. Brouwer, at least, was quite explicit about it: formal logic is only an attempt to describe mathematical reasoning, and no such attempt can be considered final. Far from condemning non-constructive proofs for using the wrong logic, the critique of classical logic stems from the examination of informal proofs. Further, as David Nelson [1949] showed long ago, undoubtedly intuitionistic mathematics can be formalized in the framework of any of a variety of formal logics: Heyting's may be the most natural and was put forth by one of Brouwer's own countrymen, but Nelson's logic of "constructible falsity" can also claim to be an intuitionistic logic. To think of intuitionism as primarily concerned with logic, and the intuitionist as motivated by a peculiar and private vision of what is logically correct, is to misconstrue its philosophical direction totally. It obscures both the nature and the centrality to intuitionism of its critique of the idea of a completed infinity. (I am of the philosophical generation that read Quine as students and took "Logic and the Reification of Universals" as our guide to the positions in the philosophy of mathematics. I, at least, concentrated too much on logic, and on ontology as measured by Quine's logical criterion, and took years to appreciate the role of infinity in mathematical thought: the fundamental ontological disagreements are between positions that all accept quantification over abstract entities.) By deemphasizing the nonlogical core of intuitionism, it suggests that the mad position of the hypothetical *relevantist* is analogous to that of the intuitionist and equally deserving of philosophical respect.

The proper way to approach intuitionistic logic and its philosophical motivation, I think, is illustrated by Bas Van Fraassen's work on quantum logic and the semantic analysis of quantum theory (cf. [1974], [1975]). This emphasizes the idea of a domain of *propositions*: for quantum logic the important domain is that of quantum mechanical "observables"; for us it will be that of (intuitionistically meaningful) mathematical propositions. These propositions may be expressed by any of a variety of formal languages, but this is secondary: the nature of the propositions involved determines how appropriate a proposed linguistic representation will be, not the other way around. In particular, the sorts of logical connectives that can be introduced in

177

J. M. Dunn and A. Gupta (eds.), Truth or Consequences, 177–195.
© 1990 *Kluwer Academic Publishers. Printed in the Netherlands.*

a language expressing propositions from the domain is to be deduced from the facts about what operations this domain is closed under. In the case of quantum logic, Van Fraassen has shown how Reichenbach's three-valued logic and orthomodular logic reflect the structure of (parts of) the domain. They provide, he concludes, a fairly superficial semantic analysis of quantum theory. Their superficiality is perhaps in part due to the artificiality of considering the observables in isolation from the rest of quantum theory: here intuitionistic logic(s), claiming to describe the structure of the domain of *all* mathematical propositions, is a bit better off. When we look at the domain of intuitionistically admitted propositions and the various interpretations of intuitionism, however, we find that the natural disjunction and existential quantification operations behave like those of classical logic. On a certain interpretation of intuitionism, to be sure, we can argue that they are not quite identical to the classical operations, but they turn out on that interpretation to be weaker rather than stronger.

Most misimpressions rest on something. The fundamental observation giving rise to the notion of an intuitionistic "or" (and a corresponding intuitionistic "there is") is that intuitionists refrain from asserting disjunctions in certain situations where classical mathematicians are happy to. The classical mathematician says "Either there are seven consecutive sevens in the decimal expansion of π or there aren't;" the intuitionist refuses to. Conclusion: the intuitionists must mean something else by "or"; since their standards for asserting disjunctions are higher, their "or" must be logically stronger, perhaps related to classical disjunction in the way that strict implication is to material implication. The inference has obviously been tempting, but once it is stated the fallacy in it is equally obvious. It is, in fact, a cousin of the fallacy that leads so many people to think that "or," when it functions as a statement connective in ordinary English, has an exclusive sense. Some stubborn student comes up with it in every elementary logic class: "Either snow is white or else it's not white. That's true, but snow can't be both white and not white, so the case of both disjuncts being true is ruled out, so "or" must be exclusive." Patiently we try to point out that that case might be ruled out for other reasons, so that ruling it out need not be part of the job of "or," and we refer them to the discussion in section 1 of *Methods of Logic*, but they're never all convinced. (Anyone seriously interested in natural-language disjunction, by the way, should read Jennings [1986]: Jennings apparently believes that the classical languages are still common ground to all scholars, but the linguistic analysis is sophisticated and imaginative.) Similarly for the intuitionistic "or": we point out that instances of the law of excluded middle contain occurrences of negation as well as disjunction, and that there is independent reason (the failure of Double Negation Elimination, for example, in Heyting's logic) to think that intuitionistic negation differs from classical, and that there is thus no need to invoke a supposed intuitionistic disjunction to explain the intuitionists' unwillingness to assert excluded middles. Still, they're never all convinced. . ..

A more respectable argument notes something deeper about intuitionistic mathematical practice, the insistence on constructive proofs. An intuitionist demands constructive proofs of all theorems, but the requirement of constructivity has a particularly transparent form where disjunctions and existential quantifications are concerned. From a constructive proof of a disjunction a proof of one of the disjuncts can be extracted, and from a constructive proof of an existential quantification a proof of some instance may be extracted. Now we have, in modal logic, familiar examples of propositions that may be asserted if other propositions can be proven in special ways: thus $\Box P$ may be asserted if P can be derived from premises which are themselves all necessary truths. If one is approaching intuitionism from a classical point of view, therefore, it is tempting to regard the intuitionists' disjunctions and existential quantifications as involving special, quasi-modal, operators, and as being true only if a disjunct (instance) is not merely true, but constructively provable. This is, however, tempting only from such an external view-point, for it rests the distinction between the classical and intuitionistic logical operators on an un-intuitionistic distinction between the mere truth and the provability of mathematical propositions. It thus fails as an analysis disjunction and existential quantification *in intuitionistic mathematics*, for instead of considering what intuitionists regard as the domain of mathematical propositions, it looks only at the corresponding propositions in classical mathematics and tries to define "intuitionistic" logical operations on these classical propositions. (Or, as a devout and puritanical intuitionist might put it, tries to define intuitionistic logical operations on these meaningless pseudopropositions.) More conclusively, Dummett [1977] has argued that this classical interpretation does not even capture the correct formal logic (cf. pp. 21–22). Suppose, he argues, that we attempt to introduce constructive disjunction and existential quantification within classical mathematics where a constructive disjunction (existential quantification) is *true* only if one of its disjuncts (instances) is *provable*. Let F be a decidable predicate of natural numbers: we have an algorithm which, applied to any n, will produce either a proof of Fn or a proof of $\neg Fn$. We are thus, for any natural number n, in a position to prove the *constructive* disjunction of Fn with its negation. Now suppose that, as might be shown by presenting a counterexample but as might also be shown by *reductio*, F does not hold of every natural number. Then, reasoning classically, we may conclude that the *constructive* existential quantification, $\exists x \neg Fx$, will be true! We have, in fact, an algorithm for finding a counterexample: just apply the decision algorithm for F to each number in succession until, as is bound to happen sooner or later, we get a proof that F fails for one. Thus, working with the constructive disjunction and existential quantification we have defined within classical mathematics, we have Markov's Principle: if a predicate is decidable and does not hold of all natural numbers, there is (constructively) a number for which it fails. But Markov's Principle is not, in general, intuitionistically valid. To argue, after giving a *reductio* refutation of a universal hypothesis, that "sooner or later a counterexample will turn up," would be to give a paradigmatic example of the sort of thing intuitionists stigmatize as non-constructive proofs of existence.

Formal systems can be interpreted in each other in a myriad ways: that much is clear after about a century of modern logic. It shouldn't be too surprising, then, that some of the interpretations are suggestive. Some even look very much as if intuitionistic logic is a quasi-modal extension of classical logic. For instance, there are the various interpretations — when the detailed differences between them don't matter they all go by the generic title "Negative Interpretation" — of classical theories in intuitionistic ones that have been studied since Gödel and Gentzen almost simultaneously discovered their interpretations of classical first order arithmetic in intuitionistic (cf. Gödel [1933] and Gentzen [1933]). The trick is to look at formulas in which the only logical operators to occur are negation, conjunction, universal quantification and implication (Gödel overlooked implication, being perhaps more interested in the mere fact that an interpretation existed, but Gentzen, who seemed to be more intrigued by the detailed comparison of the systems, included it). Or, to put it another way, formulas in which the two operators under discussion, disjunction and existential quantification, don't occur. Classically, of course, every formula has an equivalent in this fragment of the language. If the atomic formulas of the theory under study are not (as those of arithmetic are) decidable, restrict your attention further to formulas in which every atomic subformula is doubly negated — again, in the classical theory this leaves us with a representative from each class of logically equivalent formulas. Now a miracle happens: for a goodly number of mathematically interesting theories, including axiomatizations of arithmetic and of set theory, a sentence in the fragment of the language under consideration is derivable from the axioms using classical logic if and only if it is derivable from them in Heyting's logic. In cases, like that of first order Peano Arithmetic, where the classical axioms themselves are intuitionistically plausible, this constitutes a reduction of the classical to the intuitionistic theories. (This result has been somewhat overshadowed by Gödel's and Gentzen's other feats, but by itself it was surely one of the most philosophically interesting technical observations of the period. In the 20's and 30's many people seem to have assumed that intuitionism was pretty much the same as the finitist standpoint of Hilbert's program — Herbrand, for instance, regularly used "intuitionniste" to mean finitist. The Negative Interpretation showed that this was a mistake, and, as Gödel pointed out at the end of his note, that intuitionism was more about set and function existence assumptions than about logic.)

The hypothesis suggests itself, then, that the intuitionists and the classicists really do agree about the disjunction- and existential quantifier-less fragment of the parts of mathematics covered by the Negative Interpretation. If we think of formulas as expressing the same proposition if they are logically equivalent, it looks as if we have an injection of the domain of classical arithmetic (etc.) propositions into the domain of intuitionistic ones, so why not identify them? (Well, for good philosophical reasons, I think, but reasons that would strike many mathematicians as irrelevant quibbles.) Intuitionistic arithmetic, etc., then turn out not to be fragments of the corresponding classical theories, but to include them and to be richer than them in structure. As Gentzen pointed out at the end of *his* note, the intuitionist draws more distinctions than the classical mathematician. These additional distinctions are drawn with the aid of special logical operators: the disjunction and existential quantification excluded from the Negative fragment of the language! Can't we then regard these operators as analogous to the modal logicians' operators, and the intuitionists as operating with something like a modal extension of the classical theory?

There are certain logical points telling against this interpretation of the Negative Interpretation. For one thing, in general not all of the propositions in the intuitionistic domain are obtainable from "classical" propositions by the use of disjunction and existential quantification. On any variant of the Negative Interpretation that calls for double negations to be inserted before atomic formulas or elsewhere, it will be necessary, not to add operators, but to *remove* these double negations in order to obtain sentences expressing some intuitionistic propositions. Removing a double negation, however, isn't obviously equivalent to any sort of modalization. Sentences may have logically equivalent double negations without themselves being logically equivalent. (Example: the double negation of any instance of the law of excluded middle is logically valid, but different excluded middles are generally not equivalent to each other.) When a sentence is logically equivalent to a double negation, there may be neither a strongest nor a weakest among the sentences whose double negations it is equivalent to. (Think of the double negations of conjunctions and disjunctions of excluded middles.) Given that modal logics typically admit substitution of logically equivalent formulas in modal contexts, we could summarize this by saying that there is no finite set of modal operators such that the full domain of intuitionistic propositions may be obtained by closing the domain of "classical" ones under those operators. The Negative Interpretation gives an injection of the classical propositions into the intuitionistic ones, so there is a sense in which the intuitionistic conceptual scheme is an expansion of the classical one. It is not, however, a modal expansion of it, nor — unless propositions are very finely individuated — its closure under any propositional operators.

But this argument can at most render slightly less attractive the view that intuitionistic disjunction and existential quantification are operators added to a Negative language shared by intuitionists and classicists. A more fundamental criticism is that the identification of classical propositions with their images under the Negative injection is in no way forced on us. The situation is comparable to the one diagnosed by Benacerraf in his classic "What Numbers Could Not Be" [1965]. Each of the "reductions" of arithmetic to set theory gives us an injection of the domain of arithmetic propositions into that of set theoretic ones. This by itself, however, does not justify the identification of the arithmetic proposition with its set theoretic image. Indeed, given the multiplicity of reductions, identification could lead to outright contradiction, though this is a bit delicate. Suppose we consider only reductions that live in a common set theoretic environment: those provided by the Zermelo and Von Neumann numbers, for example, as opposed to the Frege-Russell reduction, which needs a different axiom of infinity. Then, if we are willing to accept equivalence within set theory as a sufficient condition for two sentences of the language of set theory to express the same proposition, we can consistently identify arithmetic *propositions* with their images under both reductions: for any sentence of arithmetic, the sentences about Zermelo numbers and about Von Neumann numbers corresponding to it will be equivalent within set theory. The arithmetic quantifiers, "there is a natural number such that" and "every natural number is such that" correspond, however, to different operators on set theoretic propositions on the different reductions, so inconsistency would result at this level. (This is, of course, just a reformulation of the familiar point that the different reductions can give differing truth values to such mixed sentences as "There is a natural number which has two distinct members.")

The corresponding objection to the Negative Interpretation is that there are other ways of injecting more or less extensive parts of the domain of classical mathematical propositions into that of intuitionistic ones. They do not all give equivalent propositions as images of the classical propositions they are defined for, and, when the mappings of propositions are extended in the most natural way to a mapping of classical logical operations to intuitionistic ones (this will depend on the details of the way each injection is defined), they will associate very different propositional operations with the classical logical operators.

The Negative Interpretation does map a large and, from the point of view of the usual languages and axiomatizations, natural collection of classical propositions into intuitionistic ones, but it is not an interpretation of the whole of classical mathematics. Other interpretations may map incomparable sets of classical propositions into intuitionistic ones, and I know of no principled argument that the Negative Interpretation's definition over the whole of, for example, first order arithmetic gives it any conceptual priority. As for the interpretations it provides for the classical logical operations, the only thing that can be said for the identification of classical disjunction (existential quantification) with intuitionistic negated conjunction of negations (negated universal quantification of negation) is that the logical behavior of the image operations is similar to that of the sources.

Actually, the similarity of logical behavior is by no means exact with the simpler versions of the Negative Interpretation. The translations of classically valid *formulas* are intuitionistically provable, but not all classical *inferences* (sequents), even between Negative formulas, are intuitionistically valid: it is not in general valid to infer even a formula in the Negative fragment from its double negation. Now, this defect can be patched up to some degree by complicating the translation. Since, for example, a negation follows intuitionistically from a triple negation, inference by double negation elimination can be saved by a version of the Negative Interpretation that inserts enough extra double negations in the course of producing its image of a classical formula. (The Hilary Putnam of the late 1970's was very impressed by this. *That* Putnam was influenced by Michael Dummett's verificationist generalization of intuitionism, and used a Negative Interpretation to argue that one could be an intuitionist in one's heart but still speak and even argue with the vulgarly classical: cf. his [1978], pp. 25–27.) Even at its best, however, the imitation of classical logic works only in the subdomain of propositions expressed by Negative formulas. Neither negated conjunction of negations nor any variant interpretation of disjunction known to me allows one to mimic classical logic when the operators are applied to arbitrary intuitionistic propositions.

When, moreover, we look at the way the Negative Interpretation translates the various classical logical operators, it appears that those least affected include negation, implication, and universal quantification: the most clearly "intensional" of the intuitionistic operators, both in the sense that Heyting's own explanations of their sense made the most essential use of the notion of operations on constructions and in the sense that, in the familiar modal interpretations of intuitionistic logic (discussed below), the necessity operator occurs essentially in their translations. This ought by itself to raise suspicions about the faithfulness of the Negative Interpretation to the meanings of the classical logical operators it supposedly captures. It is at this point that Belnap and his associates enter the picture. Belnap's teacher Frederic Fitch was, as far as I know, the first to discover an intuitionistic interpretation of a part of classical mathematics which preserved the extensional operators, conjunction, disjunction, and existential quantification. His work, starting in the 1940's, on "Basic Logic" can be seen as defining a formal system for a certain fragment of first order arithmetic (cf. his [1942] and subsequent papers). The language of the system permits the definition of all recursively enumerable predicates and allows conjunction, disjunction and existential quantification in the formation of complex formulas. (A bit tendentiously, but mainly for brevity, I shall henceforth refer to &, ∨, and ∃ as the *extensional* operators, and to ⊃, ¬, and ∀ as the *intensional*.) Proofs within the system are intuitionistically acceptable and its theorems therefore intuitionistically valid, but on the other hand any classically provable formula in the language of his system is provable within it. (Fitch is, I think, one of the most under-rated figures in twentieth-century philosophy. His formulations were often idiosyncratic, with the result that his logical work is often dismissed as simply oddball, even when it is relevant to important and fashionable topics.) A few years later John Myhill extended these ideas, and perhaps tried to make them more accessible, in his intriguingly titled [1950]. Completeness was claimed in a very strong sense: any classically *true* sentence in the language of the theory was provable in it, and, of course, this sort of completeness could only be obtained in a theory of restricted expressive power. The language of Myhill's theory did not contain any of the intensional operators: completeness would no longer have been obtainable if any of them had been added. On the other hand, it did have the three extensional operators, and, again, its theorems are all intuitionistically acceptable. Put neutrally, what Fitch and Myhill showed was that, in a certain fragment of arithmetic containing the recursively enumerable predicates and allowing the three extensional logical operators, classical truth, classical provability, and intuitionistic provability coincide. Put in the terms of the present discussion: for a certain part of the domain of classical mathematical propositions — those that can be expressed in the formal languages under discussion — there is a particularly simple injection into the domain of intuitionistic propositions, an injection defined by what Quine calls the "homophonic translation scheme."

Recall that the main selling point for the Negative Interpretation was that, where it works, the logical behavior of the (complex) intuitionistic logical operators mimics that of the classical operators they translate. If the "Homophonic Interpretation" can make the same claim, no motive will remain for identifying classical disjunction with intuitionistic negated conjunction of negations, and so no motive stemming from the Negative Interpretation for distinguishing intuitionistic and classical disjunction. The results so far described don't quite achieve this: not all classically invalid quantificational schemata have counterexamples with recursively enumerable predicates (it's a near miss), so the coincidence of classical and intuitionistic provability for an arithmetic language containing all recursively enumerable predicates doesn't by itself show that the operators occurring in the language have the same logic intuitionistically and classically. Belnap (working with Leblanc and Thomason — cf.

Belnap and Thomason [1963] and Belnap, Leblanc, and Thomason [1963]), however, showed something even stronger by proof-theoretical means: not only within the Fitch-Myhill fragment where the Homophonic Interpretation works but quite generally, the logic of disjunction and conjunction is the same intuitionistically as classically. Any classically valid inference whose validity turns on the conjunction-disjunction structure of the premisses and conclusion can be shown valid by the use of intuitionistically acceptable rules. Actually, the result is a bit stronger still: since they study sequent calculi (it's a pity that Anderson and Belnap's term *consecution* didn't catch on, but it didn't), the theorem is that any classically valid argument schema whose premisses and conclusion are formulas in conjunction and disjunction *or (first degree) implications of such formulas* can be shown valid using only intuitionistic rules of inference. Their discussion is in terms of calculi with at most a single formula in the succedent of each sequent, but they remark (end of Belnap and Thomason [1963]) that the "results easily generalize to Gentzen systems with multiple constituents on the right." Note that intuitionistic logic can accommodate a considerable relaxation of Gentzen's restriction to sequents with at most one succedent formula. The only rules that have to be restricted in this way are those for the introduction, in the succedent, of the three intensional operators. (This is easily seen: think of a sequent as meaning the same as the corresponding implicational formula with the conjunction of the sequent's antecedent formulas as antecedent and the disjunction of its succedent formulas as consequent. Then all of Gentzen's other rules are valid intuitionistic inferences even with multiple succedent. Allow multiple succedents in one of those three rules, however, and we can easily derive excluded middle, that a disjunction implies at least one of its disjuncts, or the "Constant Domain" rule that $\forall x(P \vee Fx)$, with x not free in P, implies $(P \vee \forall x Fx)$. This means that, as long as we restrict our attention to sequents containing only the extensional operators, the usual primitive rules for classical logic are all intuitionistically valid.

Belnap and Thomason's result also extends to cover existential quantification, though their proof doesn't generalize all that easily. To see that the result holds, note first that, since Cut is an intuitionistically valid rule, there is no problem about getting from one sequent to another obtained from it by substituting an intuitionistically equivalent formula for one of its antecedent or succedent formulas. Thus, given suitable intuitionistic normal forms, we can restrict our attention to arguments whose premisses and conclusions contain only formulas in them. Now, it is the intensional operators that get in the way of the prenexing operations in intuitionistic logic and, for that matter, that bollix the reductions to conjunctive and disjunctive normal form in intuitionistic propositional logic. As long as we have only the extensional operators, every formula is intuitionistically equivalent to a prenex formula, and every quantifier-free formula both to one in conjunctive normal form and to one of disjunctive normal form.

If we were only interested in arguments having *formulas* as premisses and conclusion, or equivalently in provable sequents, this would be enough to allow an easy proof that classical and intuitionistic logic agreed when only the extensional operators are involved. In the propositional case, classical and intuitionistic logics both amount to distributive lattice theory. By Gentzen's strengthened *Hauptsatz*, a prenex sequent has a proof in which all uses of propositional rules are earlier than any use of a quantificational rule — a proof in which, there is a quantifier-free propositionally valid *midsequent* whose antecedent formulas are all instances of antecedent formulas of the prenex sequent desired, whose succedent formulas are all instances of the its succedent formulas, and from which the prenex sequent can be obtained by use of the quantifier and Contraction rules. Now consider such a proof of a classically valid prenex sequent in which only the extensional operators appear. By the coincidence of the two propositional logics on the conjunction-disjunction fragment, the midsequent of a proof of this sequent will be provable intuitionistically. The existential quantifier and contraction rules, however, are the same for the two logics.

As it happens, the formula corresponding to an extensional sequent, since there are no universal quantifiers in its antecedent formulas, is intuitionistically equivalent to a prenex formula (with either an AE or an EA prefix), but this argument does not extend to cover inferences between sequents: prenexing the formula corresponding to such an inference would involve pulling a universal quantifier out of the antecedent of a conditional, and that's one of the operations that doesn't work intuitionistically. Formulas in the extensional operators, however, have another normal form — essentially what Hintikka calls a *distributive normal form* — which does allow us to extend the Belnap-Thomason result. Consider a formula in the extensional operators. It has (intuitionistically) a prenex normal form. The matrix of this normal form, in turn, can be put into disjunctive normal form. Existential quantifiers, however, distribute across disjunction, so the original formula is equivalent to a disjunction of existentially quantified conjunctions. (Call an existentially quantified conjunction of atoms an *inventory*; the claim is that any extensional formula is intuitionistically equivalent to a disjunction of inventories.) Since we have conjunction and disjunction, we can replace any sequent with an equivalent one with singular antecedent and succedent. Thus any *rule*, in the sense of Belnap and Thomason, is equivalent to one having as premisses and conclusion sequents each having a disjunction of inventories for antecedent and succedent. Implication between inventories is, however, the same classically as intuitionistically, and decidable to boot: where N is the number of variables in the premiss or conclusion (whichever has more), consider the types of N-tuples of objects describable by a conjunction of atomic predications, and check whether all those which satisfy the premiss satisfy the conclusion. But we know by Belnap and Thomason's result that arguments having sequents with disjunctions in the antecedent and succedent don't cause any problems. Putting it all together: given an argument with extensional sequents as premisses and conclusion, start by replacing it with an equivalent argument in which each sequent has a disjunction of inventories as antecedent and succedent. Replace each distinct inventory with a distinct propositional variable; any time one inventory implies another, add the sequent having the corresponding variables as antecedent formula and succedent formula as an additional premiss. The resulting argument is (classically and intuitionistically) valid if and only if the original was. To obtain a proof of the original argument from the standard intuitionistic rules (assuming it was valid): appeal to Belnap and Thomason for an intuitionistic proof of the corresponding propositional argument, replace the propositional variables with the inventories they stand for, plug in the proofs of implication between the inventories above the added premisses, and, finally, do whatever you have to in order to get the formulas in the premisses and conclusion out of normal form and back to what you were given.

To summarize: the formal logic of the extensional operators is the same intuitionistically as classically. (And, incidentally, implication between extensional sequents is a solvable case of the *Entscheidungsproblem*.) At least at this level, if you want a logic with a nonclassical "or," you'll have to go further afield than intuitionism — perhaps to (Hilary Putnam's favorite) Orthomodular Quantum Logic, whose conjunction-disjunction fragment corresponds to the theory of certain nondistributive lattices.

There remain the modal interpretations, not, this time, the idea attacked above that intuitionistic "or" is a quasi-modal operator added to classical logic, but the interpretations of the intuitionistic systems in classical systems with modal operators. Whereas the earlier idea was to identify certain classical propositions with a subdomain of the intuitionistic ones, this interpretation goes in the other direction: the propositions of intuitionistic mathematics are to be identified with certain modalized classical propositions. (This isn't an altogether unproblematic formulation: given the radically "anti-realist" orientation of the philosophy underlying intuitionistic mathematics, it is not clear that any identification of intuitionistic with classical propositions can be ultimately satisfactory to a believing intuitionist. We are talking, however, about a classical interpretation of intuitionism and talking from a classical standpoint.) The modal operator can be thought of as expressing some such notion as provability — Shapiro and Goodman and their co-workers speak of it as an "epistemic" operator — and should be governed by a modal logic not too far away from S4. For our problem, however, the usual versions of the modal interpretation aren't much help. The intuitionistic disjunction of two intuitionistic propositions is identified either with the classical disjunction of the modal propositions they are identified with, or with something equivalent in S4 to this disjunction. The opportunities for distinguishing classical and intuitionistic disjunction seem slim. Still, the standard modal interpretations don't seem entirely satisfactory. Shapiro and Goodman are interested solely in recapturing within a classical context the distinctions intuitionistic mathematics makes; they are not sympathetic to the critical and anti-realist side of intuitionism as a philosophy of mathematics. It would be nice, however, if a technical interpretation could give at least some suggestion of this side of things, if only to help understand why intuitionistic *mathematics* (including logic) should be thought of as congenial to intuitionistic philosophy. Maybe some variant. . . .

There is a variant on the well-known modal interpretations of intuitionistic mathematics — one using a deontic rather than an alethic/epistemic modal logic — which seems more perspicuous, in various conceptual ways, than the usual versions. In particular, whereas the usual modal interpretations bring out the importance of provability to intuitionism in a way that may help the classically minded to gain a feel for it, they do not adequately suggest the way in which intuitionism views infinite totalities (such as that of the natural numbers) as at best *potential*. The use of a deontic modal logic allows us, in the "possible worlds" semantics of the modal language, to make do with worlds having finite domains of objects, even in interpreting theories like arithmetic whose axioms imply the existence of infinitely many objects. The constructive meaning of such a model theory is far from clear, but one is permitted to hope that it will be, at least, suggestive.

Neither the modal interpretation of intuitionistic theories nor the modal interpretation of the notion of potential infinity is new. Gödel [1933a] announced the modal interpretation of Heyting's propositional calculus, incidentally giving the first "Lemmon-style" axiomatization of a modal logic (S4) as an extension of two-valued logic. Kripke mentions the interpretation of intuitionistic systems as an application at the end of his [1963] and begins his [1965] with a note to the effect that it was inspired by the combination of his earlier work on modal logic with the familiar modal interpretations of intuitionistic systems. It is at least moderately familiar that the interpretation of Heyting's logic will go through on a wide variety of translations (Gödel mentions several alternatives in a footnote, the one most used today not among them) and some variety of modal logics. Thus, though S4 is the modal logic most usually cited in this connection, the interpretation of at least the propositional calculus will work for such weaker logics as $K4 + 4c$ (terminology after Chellas [1980]), and Goldblatt [1978] shows that a logic stronger than S4 (having a natural provability interpretation) can be used.[1] The present writer first encountered the suggestion that something like intuitionistic logic can be obtained from an interpretation in a system of specifically deontic character in a paper by a sometime colleague of Belnap's: Fogelin [1968]. On the other front, Abraham Robinson proposed a modal analysis of a notion of potential existence or potential truth in an appendix to his [1965]; similarly, Charles Parsons, in his [1977], [1981], and [1983], uses modal formulations in an attempt to analyze the sense in which the set-theoretic universe is conceived of as potential. The two uses of modal notions, however, have not quite made contact with each other. Robinson does not, in his appendix, specify a modal object language (though in the body of his essay he suggests that modal forms of reasoning may be appropriate in foundational studies), but the model theory he describes has "possible worlds" forming a directed set under a relation of "accessibility"; such a constraint on the accessibility relation validates a modal logic stronger than S4, known as S4.2. Similarly, Parsons remarks that the interpretation of classical set theories in his modal ones depends on a modal logic at least as strong as S4.2. S4.2, however, is *not* one of those used in the modal interpretation of Heyting's logic; when non-modal propositional calculus is interpreted in modal in the usual ways, the use of S4.2 as an underlying logic yields a derived propositional calculus properly extending Heyting's. Enter deontic logic and a new translation.

We start by considering the translation of intuitionistic into modal arithmetic used in Shapiro [1985] and Goodman [1984]. Atomic formulas are translated by their own necessitations. (Recall that in standard formulations of elementary arithmetic, atomic formulas are decidable: thus there is no distinction between the truth and the

---

[1] Lloyd Humberstone and Krister Segerberg have mentioned to me that Leo Esakia has shown that this logic, S4Grz, is the strongest modal logic which will do. They did not have the exact citation, but from the review, Esakia [1979] sounds as if it might be the relevant paper.

188   THE MYTH OF THE INTUITIONISTIC "OR"

provability of their instances from either the classical or the intuitionistic standpoint.)
Letting A*,B* stand for the translations of A,B we have

$$(A \& B)* = (\Box A * \& \Box B*)$$
$$(A \vee B)* = (\Box A * \vee \Box B*)$$
$$(A \supset B)* = \Box(\Box A* \supset \Box B*)$$
$$(\neg A)* = \Box \sim \Box(A*)$$
$$(\forall x A)* = \Box \forall x(A*)$$
$$(\exists x A)* = \exists x \Box(A*)$$

(cf. Shapiro [1985] p. 25). Taking as their modal logic a form of quantified
S4 with the Converse Barcan Principle but not the Barcan Principle (that is, the
version of quantified S4 yielded by the traditional axiomatization and characterized
in the Kripke semantics by models in which the domain of a world is a subset
of the domain of any world accessible from it), and for non-logical axioms the
translations of the usual axioms of Heyting Arithmetic, Shapiro and Goodman
have, between them, shown that a sentence of first-order arithmetic is a theorem of
Heyting Arithmetic if and only if its translation is a theorem of the modal system.
A non-realist interpretation of the modal system is not possible, however, since the
(non-modal) sentences saying, *e.g.*, that the natural numbers are strictly linearly
ordered by *greater than* and that for every natural number there is a greater, are
provable: any model of the system must have an infinite domain (indeed, since
the necessitations of these sentences are also provable, an infinite domain for each
"possible world"). An anti-Platonist modal interpretation of arithmetic seems to
call for a deontic logic of $\Box$: one appropriate to a reading of the modal operator
as *ought*, interpreted so as to allow us to say that mathematical principles ought
to be true (but sometimes aren't true of the real world) and, in particular, that the
existential claims of arithmetic have this feature. Every number, we want to say,
ought to have a successor, but there is no guarantee that the real world contains
any infinite series of objects. Even if we weaken our modal logic to D4 (Chellas's
KD4), however, the axioms obtained by the translation suggested above come close
to having infinitary existential consequences. The problem lies in the translation of
existential quantifications, which, unlike the other operators, don't get an additional
initial $\Box$. We will, therefore, have a theorem to the effect that it ought to be the
case that (the natural numbers are strictly linearly ordered and every number has a
successor). Thus, though there is no longer the implication that there must be an
infinite series of numbers in the real world, a "possible worlds" model for the deontic
system will have an infinite domain in any "ideal world" — a result painfully close
to the Platonic conception of the infinite series actually existing (not here but) in a
sort of abstract heaven.

Existential quantifications must be given a modalized translation. Robinson and
Parsons, in their modal theories of mathematical potentiality, treated the existence of
mathematical objects as possible existence: in effect defining $(\exists x A)*$ as $\Diamond \exists x(A*)$.
At this point, however, the recovery of standard mathematical theories from the

modal formulations required a stronger modal logic. Natural numbers ought to have unique successors, but a formulation with this treatment of existence would allow a number to have one successor in one "possible world" and another, with different properties, in another. Given that the successors have their mathematical properties necessarily, this is ruled out by adopting the logic S4.2, on which the worlds form a directed set under accessibility. Once we have adopted a deontic modality, on which "necessary" existence does not imply actual existence, we are free to adopt the translation $\Box\exists x(A*)$. With this translation of existential quantification, the 4.2 principle ($\Diamond\Box A \supset \Box \Diamond A$) is no longer needed, so we may use a logic in which Heyting's logic can be faithfully interpreted. We may state this as

THEOREM I. *The Shapiro-Goodman result, that a sentence of first order arithmetic is a theorem of Heyting Arithmetic if and only if its translation is a theorem of their Epistemic Arithmetic, will (provided that the modified translation of existential quantifications is adopted) continue to hold when the modal logic in Epistemic Arithmetic is weakened from S4 to K4+4c (or to a logic, such as the deontic KD4+4c, intermediate between K4+4c and S4).*[2]

Note that, since most arithmetic functions (including successor) will not be everywhere defined in a finite linearly ordered model, we will have to consider a rather unconventional formulation of Heyting Arithmetic in which predicate symbols are used in place of function symbols. Each **n**-adic function symbol in the usual formulation will be replaced with an **(n+1)**-adic relation symbol, and the recursion equations (suitably reformulated as conditionals) will be supplemented with axioms asserting the existence and uniqueness of values for the functions. We may keep the individual constant 0. (Examples of suitable axioms may be found in Smorynski [1973].) It is easy to see that the resulting theory is a "version" of Heyting Arithmetic. When the new relations are defined in terms of the old functions and identity in the obvious way, the new axioms are trivial theorems, and, in the other direction, the old axioms are trivially proven when the functions are contextually defined in the Russellian manner from the new relations. (The general theory of definite descriptions is not as simple in the context of intuitionistic as in that of classical logic, but we are taking the fulfillment of their existence and uniqueness presuppositions as axiomatic.)

To prove Theorem I in the right to left direction, note that the translation of an existential quantification into Epistemic Arithmetic implies its own necessitation (and, indeed, would continue to do so even if the propositional modal logic were weakened to K4). Thus, in the context of Shapiro and Goodman's own system, with S4 as modal logic, their translation of an existential quantification is equivalent to ours, and their result would still hold for their Epistemic Arithmetic if our translation were adopted. Goodman's [1985] proof that no modal translation of a sentence of first order arithmetic is provable in Epistemic Arithmetic unless the sentence itself is

---

[2] Wim Blok points out that, if you are willing to insert enough extra squares in your tranlation, the 4 ($\Box A \supset \Box\Box A$) and 4c ($\Box\Box A \supset \Box A$) principles can be weakened: we need only require that, for some positive N, a block of N squares is equivalent to one of $N + 1$. So it may be that there is no weakest modal logic permitting a translation of intuitionistic logic.

provable in Heyting Arithmetic immediately implies the corresponding result for the weaker systems obtainable from Epistemic Arithmetic by weakening its underlying modal logic.

Left to right, the proof is by an elementary verification that inferences permitted by Heyting's logic translate into inferences permitted by the modal logic. It is of some interest to see how particular modal principles are used in verifying the translations of different rules of Heyting's logic. The modal schema 4, or (what is equivalent to it in a natural deduction formulation of modal logic like that of Fitch [1952] or [1966]) the permission to reiterate necessitations into strict subordinate proofs without dropping their initial squares, is needed in deriving the introduction rules for the various logical operators of Heyting's logic. In the other direction, if we operate within K4 (or even KD4), we will be left with extra squares in front of the conclusions of instances of most of the elimination rules. To get rid of them we need the converse of 4, which Chellas calls 4c. (4c is of course trivially available in the alethic system S4.) The specific deontic principle ($\Box A \supset \Diamond A$) might (from the standpoint of a provability interpretation of the square) be thought of as expressing the consistency of mathematical intuition and will be valid in the "finite-world" models to be described below, but does no work in the derivation of the principles of Heyting's logic.

With regard to the question of an intuitionistic "or," note that, whereas the Shapiro-Goodman translation of a formula with one of the intensional operators as main operator *is* a necessitation (and properly stronger in S4 than the formula that would be obtained by dropping the initial $\Box$), their translations of formulas governed by extensional operators are *not* necessitations. They are, however, equivalent in S4 to their own necessitations, a fact we have appealed to in the proof of Theorem I. The Shapiro-Goodman translation of a conjunction is equivalent to its own necessitation even in $K4 + 4c$, but that of a disjunction implies but is not implied by its own necessitation in the weaker logics. There is thus a choice to be made. In what follows we will assume a further modification of the Shapiro-Goodman translation (for which Theorem I will still hold): we will take $(A \lor B)^*$ to be $\Box(\Box A * \lor \Box B*)$.

The modal logics K4+4c (which we will henceforth, following Chellas, call K4!) and KD4+4c (D4!) have relational possible worlds semantics: they are characterized by frames in which the accessibility relation is transitive, dense (in the sense that if a world C is accessible from a world A, then there is some world B such that B is accessible from A and C is accessible from B), and, for D4!, serial (for every world there is at least one world accessible from it). This semantics is not suitable for our modal representation of potential infinity. No world with a finite domain, in our treatment, will verify all "necessary" truths: no such world, to use the terminology of deontic logic, is *ideal*. Thus no relational model (other than a trivial K4! model on which every necessitation is true) can consist solely of finite worlds. We adopt, therefore, a version of *neighborhood* semantics. Our models will be *trees* of worlds, with the worlds below a given world being extensions of it with enlarged domains, each branch of the tree being infinite in length. The neighborhoods of a world will be those sets of worlds which *bar* it (and which are "solid" below the barrier): that is, the necessitation of a given formula will be true at a world if and only if every path of the tree through the given world ultimately gets to a point after which it consists solely of worlds at which the given formula itself is true. We will describe the applications of models with finite worlds after stating the usual semantic metatheorems of modal logic for the general case of neighborhood models on trees of the sort described.

THEOREM II. *The propositional modal logic D4! is sound and complete with respect to neighborhood models on trees of the sort described, even if we restrict ourselves to models in which no world is ideal (that is, no world has true at it all the formulas whose necessitations are true at it).*

Proof (soundness): By the results stated in Chapter 7 (especially sections 7.2 and 7.4, with the validity of 4c being extracted from the result of exercise 7.38) of Chellas, neighborhood models of the sort described validate all the principles of D4!.

Proof (completeness): Given a set of formulas consistent in D4!, the Henkin methods usual in modal logic can be used to define a verifying model of the sort described. Let the initial node of the tree be a maximal consistent superset of the given set. Given a node of the tree, let it have as successors on the next level down maximal consistent sets containing each set composed of (a) one formula whose possibilitation is in the given node and (b) all formulas whose necessitations are in the given node. Let an atomic formula, as usual, be true at a node if and only if it is a member of that node, define neighborhoods as described above, and it is easy to see that any formula is true at a world if and only if it is a member of it. The only unfamiliar point is the role of 4c. By it, $\diamond \diamond A$ will belong to any node containing $\diamond A$, with the result that any node containing $\diamond A$ will have at least one successor containing $\diamond A$. There will therefore be at least one node below it *at every level* containing A, so the set of nodes at which A is false cannot bar the original node, ensuring that $\diamond A$ is true at it. To show that we can require that no world in a model be ideal, let there be a denumerable series of propositional variables not occurring in the original consistent set and add, to every node at the n-th level of the tree, $\sim P$ and $\Box P$ for the n-th and later such variables P, P and $\Box P$ for any earlier ones.

Any such model for D4! generates a Beth model for Heyting's propositional logic: let an atomic formula of Heyting's logic be true at a node in the tree if and only if its translation (*i.e.*, its necessitation) is true at that node in the modal model, and evaluate compound formulas by Beth's rules. Then every formula of Heyting's logic is true at a node if and only if its translation is true at that node in the modal model. Further, the transformation between modal models and Beth models works in both directions: take a Beth model, thought of as a tree with atomic formulas true at some of its nodes, and treat it as a modal model. The modal translation of a formula of Heyting's logic will be true at a node if and only if the Heyting formula was true at that node in the Beth model.

Suppose, now, that we consider the quantified logic obtained by grafting standard axiomatizations of D4! and first order logic together, that is, the quantified version of D4! in which the Converse Barcan Principle holds but the Barcan Principle itself does not. If we require that every world have as its domain a superset of the domains of the worlds above it in the tree, the above Henkin-style completeness proof goes through with minimal changes, giving us

THEOREM III. *Theorem II extends to the case of quantified D4! with Converse Barcan Principle, given that worlds lower on the tree have as domains supersets of the domains of higher worlds.*

Proof: straightforward generalization of that for the propositional case. Although the models in which every world has a finite domain require expanding domains as in Theorem II, it is of some interest, in view of the familiar fact that with relational models constant domains validate the Barcan Principle, that the Barcan Principle can be falsified in neighborhood models defined on trees as described, with all the nodes of the tree sharing a common domain. Suppose that the domain is denumerably infinite, let the predicate F be false of all elements of the domain at the origin of the tree and true of the first **n** elements of the domain, but false of all later ones, at any node on the **n**-th level below the origin. Thus for each element of the domain, if we go down far enough we reach a level at which the origin is barred by worlds at which F is true of that element, making $\forall x \Box F x$ true at the origin. On the other hand, there is no node at which F is true of all elements in the domain; *a fortiori* the origin is not barred by a set of nodes at which it is true of all elements, so $\Box \forall x F x$ is false at the origin, falsifying the Barcan Principle. D4! with only the Converse Barcan Principle is not, however, complete for the constant domain version of the present semantics, for a relative of the Barcan Principle, $\forall x \Box A x \supset \Box \forall x \Box A x$, is valid on it. (We *do* have completeness for a more general kind of constant-domain neighborhood model.)

Even without completeness, the soundness of D4!+CnvBP for constant-domain models allows us to extend the remark made above about Beth models to predicate logic, giving us

THEOREM IV. *The translation given of Heyting's logic into D4!+CnvBP is faithful: a formula is a thesis of Heyting's logic if and only if its translation is a thesis of the modal system.*

Proof: The only if direction is established by the case by case verification mentioned for Theorem I; the if direction follows from the remark above about Beth models. For suppose a formula is not a thesis of Heyting's logic. Then a falsifying Beth model can be given that can be converted into a falsifying constant domain neighborhood model on a tree for the modal translation, showing that the translation is not a thesis of D4!+CnvBP.

I am not altogether sure what the significance of this is. The deontic interpretation of intuitionistic systems strikes me as conceptually attractive and deserving of further investigation, both technical and conceptual. From the point of view of our current topic, however, it has a clear relevance: if we think of intuitionistic mathematical propositions as corresponding to propositions in a classical context whose expression ought to start with an *ought*, then we finally have an interpretation on which the intuitionistic "or" differs from the classical. Let A and B be two intuitionistic propositions. We identify them with a pair of ought-propositions. Their intuitionistic disjunction in turn gets identified with the proposition that one or the other of these ought-propositions *ought* to be true. But that, given D4! as our logic of ought, is properly weaker than the classical disjunction of the two ought-propositions. When we interpret intuitionism deontically, intuitionistic propositions are identified with classical ones to which either classical disjunction or (the interpretation of) intuitionistic disjunction can be applied. The results differ, but in the opposite direction to that usually supposed.

194   THE MYTH OF THE INTUITIONISTIC "OR"

BIBLIOGRAPHY

Belnap, N. and Thomason, R. (1963): "A Rule-Completeness Theorem," *Notre Dame Journal of Formal Logic* 4, pp. 39–43.

——————, H. Leblanc, and Thomason, R.: "On Not Strengthening Intuitionistic Logic," *Notre Dame Journal of Formal Logic* 4, pp. 313–320.

Benacerraf, P. (1965): "What Numbers Could Not Be," *Philosophical Review* 74, pp. 47–73; reprinted in Benacerraf and Putnam, pp. 272–294.

Benacerraf, P., and Putnam, H. (eds.) (1983): *Philosophy of Mathematics: selected readings*, (second edition) Cambridge (Cambridge U.P.)

Chellas, B. (1980): *Modal Logic*, Cambridge (C.U.P.).

Dummett, M. (1977): *The Elements of Intuitionism*, Oxford (O.U.P.).

Esakia, L. (1979): "On the Variety of Grzegorczyk Algebras" (in Russian), in *Studies in Nonclassical Logics and Set Theory* (Russian), Moscow (Nauka), pp. 257–287; rev. *Mathematical Reviews* 81j:03097.

Fitch, F. (1942): "A Basic Logic Fitch's Basic Logic," *Journal of Symbolic Logic* 7, pp. 105–114.

—————— (1952): *Symbolic Logic: an introduction*, New York (Ronald).

—————— (1966): "Natural Deduction Rules for Obligation," *American Philosophical Quarterly* 3, pp. 27–38.

Fogelin, R. (1968): "Wittgenstein and Intuitionism," *American Philosophical Quarterly* 5, pp. 267–264.

Gentzen, G. (1933): "On the Relation Between Classical and Intuitionistic Arithmetic"; first published (in English) in M. Szabo, ed., *Collected Papers of Gerhart Gentzen/*, Amsterdam (North-Holland), 1969.

Gödel, K. (1933): "On Intuitionistic Arithmetic and Number Theory," *Ergebnisse eines mathematischen Kolloquiums* 4, pp. 34–38; Eng. tr. in M. Davis, ed., *The Undecidable*, Hewlett NY (Raven).

—————— (1933a): "An Interpretation of the Intuitionistic Sentential Logic," *Ergebnisse eines mathematischen Kolloquiums* 4, pp. 39–40; Eng. tr. in J. Hintikka, ed., *Philosophy of Mathematics*, Oxford (O.U.P.) 1969, pp. 128–129.

Goldblatt, R. (1978): "Arithmetical necessity, Provability and Intuitionistic Logic," *Theoria* XLIV, pp. 38–46.

Goodman, N. (1984): "The Knowing Mathematician," *Synthese* 60, pp. 21–38.

—————— (1985): "Epistemic Arithmetic is a Conservative Extension of Intuitionistic Arithmetic," *Journal of Symbolic Logic* 49, pp. 192–203.

Jennings, R. (1986): "The Punctuational Sources of the Truth-Functional "Or"," *Philosophical Studies* 50, pp. 237–257.

Kripke, S. (1963): "Semantical Considerations on Modal Logic," *Acta Philosophica Fennica* XVI, pp. 83–94.

—————— (1965): "Semantic Analysis of Intuitionistic Logic I," in J. Crossley and M. Dummett, eds., *Formal Systems and Recursive Functions*, Amsterdam (North-Holland), pp. 92–130.

Myhill, J. (1950): "A Complete Theory of Natural, Rational and Real Numbers,"*Journal of Symbolic Logic* 15, pp. 185–196.

Nelson, D. (1949): "Constructible Falsity," *Journal of Symbolic Logic* 14, pp. 16–26.

Parsons, C. (1977): "What is the Iterative Conception of Set?" in R. Butts and J. Hintikka, eds., *Logic, Foundations of Mathematics, and Computability Theory*, pp. 335–367; repr. in Parsons (1983a), pp. 268–297, and in Benacerraf and Putnam, pp. 503–529.

—————— (1981): "Modal Set Theories (abstract)," *Journal of Symbolic Logic* 46, pp. 683–4.

—————— (1983): "Sets and Modality," in Parsons (1983a), pp. 298–341.

—————— (1983a): *Mathematic in Philosophy*, Ithaca (Cornell U.P.).

Putnam, H. (1978): *Meaning and the Moral Sciences*, London (Routledge).

Robinson, A. (1965): "Formalism '64," in Y. Bar-Hillel, ed., *Logic, Methodology, and Philosophy of Science: Proceedings of the 1964 Conference*, Amsterdam (North-Holland), pp. 228–246.

Shapiro, S. (1985): "Epistemic and Intuitionistic Arithmetic," in S. Shapiro, ed., *Intensional Mathematics*, Amsterdam (NorthHolland), pp. 11–45.

Smorynski, C. (1973): "Applications of Kripke Models," in A. Troelstra, ed., *Metamathematical Investigations of Intuitionistic Arithmetic and Analysis* (LNM # 344), Berlin (Springer-Verlag), pp. 324–391.

Van Fraassen, B. C. (1974): "The Labyrinth of Quantum Logic," in R. Cohen and M. Wartofsky, eds., *Logical and Epistemological Problems in Contemporary Physics (Boston Studies in the Philosophy of Science* 13), Dordrecht (Reidel); repr. in C. Hooker, ed., *The Logico-Algebraic Approach to Quantum Mechanics I*, Dordrecht (Reidel), 1975.

——————— (1975): "Semantic Analysis of Quantum Logic," in C. Hooker, ed., *Contemporary Research in the Foundations and Philosophy of Quantum Theory*, Dordrecht (Reidel).

VIRGINIA KLENK

WHAT MATHEMATICAL TRUTH NEED NOT BE[1]

I might have titled this paper "In Defense of Eidophobia", eidophobes, in
Belnapese, being those who, for one reason or another, find the idea of abstract
entities distasteful. Since Nuel himself is an eidophile, I occasionally found myself
at philosophical odds with him. But one of the best things about being a student of
Nuel's was that he had no need for eidological clones. So in a sense perhaps the
greatest tribute I could render to his pedagogy is this paper, which makes it very clear
that my eidophobia has remained intact. Studying with Nuel Belnap, one never had
to fear that the spirit of independent (even eidocidal) inquiry might be compromised.

Much recent work in the philosophy of mathematics has accepted fairly uncritically a number of assumptions which taken together constitute what I shall call
"holism". (I use this term because the position reflects so closely the views of W.V.O.
Quine, and centers around the thesis that the formal and empirical sciences fall upon
a continuum.) Jointly these assumptions seem to entail mathematical platonism,
the view that mathematical objects such as sets and numbers exist independently
of human creation, that mathematical statements refer to such objects, and that in
doing mathematics we are making discoveries about these objects analogously to
the way in which we make discoveries about the elementary particles of physics.[2]
Indeed, one of the fundamental theses of the holist doctrine is that the traditional
distinction between the empirical sciences and the "apriori" disciplines of logic and
mathematics is unfounded, and that no sharp line can be drawn between synthetic
and analytic statements.

Briefly, the holist argument for platonism runs as follows: because of the
continuity between the formal and empirical sciences, whatever theory of *truth*
holds for one should also hold for the other, so that truth conditions for sentences
in the various disciplines should be parallel.[3] In particular, since for a singular or
an existential statement to be true in, say, geography, there must exist objects of a
certain sort, such as cities, so for mathematical existential and singular statements
to be true there must be mathematical objects such as numbers. Furthermore, it is
argued, given the indispensable role of statements such as "there is a limit of the
sequence $(1 + n)^{\frac{1}{n}}$ as n goes to 0" in physical science, we must suppose that such

---

[1] I would like to thank Michael D. Resnik for extensive comments and criticisms of an earlier draft.
I would also like to thank Theodore Drange, Pieranna Garavaso, Stephen C. Hetherington, Lila Luce,
and Michael Resnik for very helpful comments on this version.

[2] This is not the only possible characterization of platonism. A more recent version claims only
that what the statements of classical mathematics say is correct, without giving a referential account of
"correct". To these versions of mathematical platonism my remarks are irrelevant, but there is a long and
continuing version of platonism in which mathematical statements refer to mathematical objects, and it
is this version I am addressing here. In fact, I think it is highly debateable whether the term "platonism"
is appropriate for disquotational views, or methodological platonism, but this is an issue I do not wish to
debate here.

[3] This is made very explicit by Paul Benacerraf in "Mathematical Truth", *Journal of Philosophy*,
Vol. LXX, No. 19; Nov. 8, 1973, pp. 662.

J. M. Dunn and A. Gupta (eds.), Truth or Consequences, 197–208.
© 1990 *Kluwer Academic Publishers. Printed in the Netherlands.*

statements are true. Thus we must conclude that there are mathematical objects, that a platonist account of mathematics is correct.

In what follows I will try to show that this argument for platonism is unsound, primarily because the rationale for a referential semantics in mathematics — the supposed continuity between formal and empirical studies — cannot be maintained. Hence the title of the paper: mathematical truth need not be construed on a correspondence model because there is no particular reason to think that mathematics is epistemologically similar to, or continuous with, the natural sciences.

Part I is a negative argument, showing only that the above widely regarded argument for platonism does not succeed. This in itself would not, of course, be the end of platonism; other arguments might be forthcoming. In Part II I provide additional reasons for rejecting a correspondence theory of truth for mathematics, and with it, platonism. I point out some undesirable consequences of the correspondence theory that have been overlooked, and some reasons for thinking that, if not false, it is at least empty. Mathematical truth not only *need* not be construed as correspondence; it *should* not be.

I. THE HOLIST DOGMA

The best possible reason for accepting an assertion is that it is the consequence of a valid deductive argument whose premises are all true. Although few would claim such an enviable position for mathematical platonism, many believe that the following argument comes close to establishing platonism as a philosophical fact.

What I shall call the "holist dogma" consists of the following theses, which seem to lead inexorably to a platonist conclusion:[4]

1) We have some scientific knowledge.

2) What we know is true.

3) Mathematics, including some mathematical existence claims (such as the statement that there is a limit to a certain convergent series), is essential to scientific knowledge.

4) There is no non-arbitrary way to draw a clear line between mathematical propositions and the propositions of physical science. Thus, if we want to predicate truth of statements in physical science we should be prepared to do the same for the statements of mathematics.

5) Therefore, in doing physical science we are committed to the truth of some mathematical existence claims.

6) The correct account of truth for existence claims is in terms of the referential interpretation of the quantifiers, so that an existential statement is true if and only if there are objects of the appropriate sort.

7) Thus we are committed, if we accept the claims of physical science, to the existence of whatever mathematical entities are required for

---

[4] The argument I give below combines arguments found in various places in the writings of W.V.O. Quine and Paul Benacerraf.

the truth of the mathematical existence claims used in that science. This is generally taken to be at least the set of all real numbers and real number functions, a non-denumerable infinity.

This reconstruction represents what many have taken to be the strongest, or even the only, good argument for the existence of mathematical objects. Thus, if it can be shown to be inconclusive, mathematical platonism will be seriously undercut. It should be noted that if even one of the premises 1, 2, 3, 4, or 6 is indefensible (steps 5 and 7 are inferences from previous steps), then the argument fails.

What I will do in the following pages is to argue that premise 2, though it appears to be almost analytic, is only plausible if we reject premise 6, and that premise 4, the central dogma of holism, is not plausible at all, at least in any sense that lends support to a referential account of mathematical statements. Although my primary attack will be against premise 4, what we may call epistemological holism, I will first raise some questions about premises 2 and 6. It should be noted that my comments here are merely suggestive; they are intended only to provide a backdrop, rather than a deep or definitive analysis of the issues involved.

On one reading of premise 2, it is a mere truism. (I will not take issue at all with premises 1 or 3). If by knowledge we *mean* knowing *that*, knowing some proposition, and if a proposition is defined as something which must be either true or false, then, since presumably we don't know anything false, it follows by elementary reasoning that what we know must be true.

We should not accept uncritically, however, the claim that all knowledge is propositional, or the implications of that claim for mathematical platonism. There are lots of things we know, like the rule of Modus Ponens and the outcome of the 1988 presidential election, which are not in propositional form. It might be objected that we can *put* the outcome of the 1988 presidential election into propositional form, and that the result is a true statement. It is not at all clear that we can thus recast all types of knowledge, however, and just to assume that we can do so is to beg the question about mathematics. It may be that our knowledge of mathematics is more akin to rules of inference than to statements of fact, so that a simple propositional analysis is inappropriate.[5]

One might reply that we can also put our knowledge of *rules* into propositional form: we can say "The consequent of a conditional follows from the conditional and its antecedent", and of course this statement is true. The question now, however, is the appropriate analysis of the predicate "true", and whether the truth of statements *about* logical inference commits us to the existence of logical or mathematical entities. This is a very large topic, and I can only sketch an answer here. In the first place, no one believes, I think, that the correctness or the use of Modus Ponens, for instance, commits us to the existence of logical objects corresponding to the rule. M.P. can be seen as a *pre*scription, not a *de*scription, and thus it is descriptive of nothing. A good case can be made that mathematical "statements" are similarly prescriptive, rather than descriptive, so that the question of corresponding entities is

---

[5] Ludwig Wittgenstein suggests this in *Remarks on the Foundations of Mathematics*.

out of place.[6] Thus, even if for practical reasons we ascribe truth to mathematical propositions (perhaps just to distinguish correct procedures from incorrect ones) the ascription of truth need carry with it no ontological implications.

One might argue that the *meta*linguistic statements about logic and mathematics do carry ontological commitments, at least to infinite sets of formulas. However, if rules in the *object* language have no ontological significance, one could reasonably maintain that the logic of the metalanguage (including the logic of existence), which so exactly parallels that of the object language, also has no ontological import. It should be noted as well that physics and mathematics themselves have little need or use for such metastatements. Mathematics and physics proceeded without any metamathematics at all until the 20th century, and even now most working mathematicians are indifferent to, or even oblivious of, metamathematical considerations. And the claim of the holist is that the only mathematics we need be concerned with is that required by the sciences. Although there are certainly questions about what is "required" in the sciences (we will raise this issue later), it does seem that metamathematics is not required by physics in the same way that the calculus is required.

I would argue, then, that in the case of mathematics what we have are not propositions, descriptions, but *pre*scriptions, so that premise 2 — that what we know is true — should be rejected on the grounds that prescriptions are neither true nor false. If the reply be that rules can be put into the form of propositions as well, I would argue that the concept of "true" as applied to such propositions is not defined in terms of correspondence, so that premise 6 should be rejected. Truth for such statements can be interpreted just in terms of the correctness of the rule.

Premise 6, in any case, is suspect. As a *general* account of truth for existence claims, it is not terribly plausible. We make all kinds of truth claims, in all kinds of contexts — in ethics, aesthetics, logic, and even within the framework of literature. (It is true that David Copperfield had two wives.) To what do literary or ethical truths correspond? There may *be* some way of analyzing these on a correspondence model, but the analysis is likely to be rather complex, and will not give us any *simple* correspondence between statements and objects, as seems to be required by a referential version of truth. Of course, we might just *posit* certain objects — ethical facts, or values — to correspond with our true statements. The *ad hoc*ness of such a move, however, is unattractive, and tends to suggest that the problem is really the generalized correspondence theory of truth in the first place.

The correspondence theory, however, does appear eminently plausible when we consider the world of "ordinary" space-time objects and empirical science, and it is possible to set aside ethics and aesthetics as pathological cases (or simply as very difficult), and to take the referential view as the paradigm meaning of "truth", and empirical science as the paradigm of knowledge. The burden would then fall on the non-referentialist to show why ethical or mathematical language, say, should not be subject to analysis along correspondence lines. Many contemporary philosophers have taken this tack. Quine, for instance, has argued that there is only one meaning

---

[6] Wittgenstein, *op. cit.*

of "there is," and that this meaning is best explicated by means of a referential, objectual interpretation of the quantifiers, in which an existential sentence is true if and only if there are *objects* of a certain sort.[7] Benacerraf has also argued for a uniform semantics for the various parts of our language, and in particular, a referential semantics. An adequate theory of truth he suggests, "should . . . provide similar truth conditions for similar sentences."[8]

But presumably a uniform semantics would not be called for, and ontic commitments in mathematics could be avoided, if we could show that the sentences of mathematics are *not* similar to ordinary empirical sentences in the relevant sense of "similar". We are not entitled to conclude that true mathematical statements correspond with some mathematical reality unless we can show that empirical statements and mathematical statements are sufficiently like in kind. In other words, the call for semantic holism is not well- motivated without an argument to the effect that empirical and mathematical statements are semantically alike.

Quine's arguments for what we might call "epistemological holism" — the claim that no sharp line can be drawn between the mathematical and the empirical (premise 4 of the holist argument for platonism) — are supposed to fill this gap. If mathematics and empirical science do indeed form a continuum, then it would seem that they are like in kind, so that if we accepted referential truth conditions for one, we would also, in good conscience, have to accept them for the other, and would be compelled to accept the existence of mathematical objects on a par with the existence of neutrinos.

This epistemological holism, the continuity claim, has achieved nearly the status of a paradigm in philosophy. "Any statement can be held true come what may" and "No statement is immune to revision"[9] have become as entrenched as anything gets in philosophy, which is puzzling given now little evidence there is for them. In what follows I shall argue that these claims of continuity are not well-founded and that even if they were, they would not entail (even given the rest of the holist argument) a parallel semantics or mathematical platonism.

There is in their favor, of course, the fact that attempts to *define* "analytic" and "synthetic" have come up short, but this is irrelevant to the claims at hand. For one thing, the terms "analytic" and "synthetic" are not synonymous with "mathematical" and "empirical", and it is the latter pair that is at issue here. Furthermore, the lack of a formal definition does not mean we cannot sort items into one class or the other, and that is all that is required. If we know what enterprises are mathematical and what are empirical, as we certainly do, then we can draw a line between them, despite the lack of a formal definition. To claim, as Quine does, that a *de facto* distinction is just the result of arbitrary disciplinary boundaries is simply to beg the question. It is much more likely that the disciplinary boundaries are the consequence of real differences in kind.

There are, in fact, significant methodological differences between mathematics and empirical science that argue against the continuity hypothesis. It is a truism that

[7] See, for instance, "On What There Is" and "Existence and Quantification."
[8] Benacerraf, *op. cit.*
[9] W.V.O. Quine, "Two Dogmas of Empiricism".

mathematics is an armchair science, and proceeds by proof, whereas in empirical science some kind of physical observation of "what is out there" is essential. An obvious objection might be that mathematicians are also making observations, but of a different, abstract, kind of entity. For a dualist or idealist this is an option; there is no reason not to claim that (some) human beings are capable of directly observing mathematical objects. This approach is not available to the typical holist, however, who generally holds a kind of naturalism with regard to creatures of the space-time world. The direct apprehension account, in fact, is really unintelligible given the assumptions about mathematical objects and human beings that most holists want to make. Human beings, they will claim, are physical entities; mathematical objects are abstract, which means among other things that they are not in space-time and have no causal interactions with physical entities. Thus there is no way for abstract mathematical objects to affect our generally recognized faculties for acquiring perceptual knowledge. There is simply no way of directly connecting up the abstract entities of mathematics with our presumably physical knowing apparatus.[10] Thus, we must reject the suggestion that mathematicians are observing their subject matter in much the same way as physicists.

It might be argued that mathematics uses empirical methods because mathematical discoveries are often made by seeing what happens in a large number of cases — a kind of induction — or by use of a physical apparatus, the computer. Checking a large number of mathematical cases, however, is still mathematics if, as is presumed, the checking is done by mathematical methods rather than, say, telescopes. Furthermore, even the use of computers does not take us out of the realm of mathematics. A computer is not designed to detect objects — even such elusive objects as neutrinos — but to compute, to do the same thing we could do with pencil and paper if we could write fast enough and live long enough. But no one has ever argued that the use of pencil and paper makes mathematics an empirical science; no more does the use of computers.[11]

It could be argued, however, that these methodological differences in the context of *discovery* are insignificant beside the essential affinity of mathematics and empirical science in the context of *justification*. Mathematics, it is said, is so intertwined with physical theory, so embedded in that theory, that it is *tested* in the same way: by confrontation with what we observe. The metaphor of a mesh or web of knowledge, in which no thread is independent of the others, has been compelling, and it contains more than a grain of truth: physics would not exist without mathematics, and a good bit of mathematics would not exist without physics. The question is whether this kind of interdependence has anything to say about the ontology of mathematics.

---

[10] This point is made by Benacerraf, in "Mathematical Truth".

[11] The questions raised by the recent use of high-powered computers in the proof of, say, the four-colored theorem, are not questions about the epistemological status of mathematics as a whole, but only about the archival status of particular claims in mathematics and about what constitutes a proof. No one has suggested that the use of computers transmutes the four-color conjecture into a statement of physical science, but only that such use many *not* transmute it into a theorem. The question is whether it has really been proved.

The argument seems to be that the semantics for mathematics should parallel the semantics for physical theory because of the continuity between mathematics and physics. The continuity claim seems to be based upon the embeddedness of mathematics in physical theory. I shall argue that this embeddedness in no way implies that mathematics is ontologically similar to physics, that it is *about* numbers as physics is about neutrinos.

In the first place, it is difficult to see why the use of mathematics in the verification, of, say, the existence of distant planets or the approach of a submarine, should be any evidence that *non*-physical objects exist. Why should the fact that mathematics helps us find out all sorts of *physical* things be any evidence whatsoever that mathematical statements describe a *non*-physical universe? At the very least we would need some kind of metaphysical theory detailing the relationship between the non-physical objects — abstract forms — and the physical objects. For Plato, of course, abstract forms could be detected through the observation of physical objects because the former inhered in the latter. Even Plato seems not to have been completely satisfied with this account — the third man problem is unsolved — and certainly a holist would be loath to make such a theory any part of the world picture. But without it, the *use* of mathematics in physics tells us exactly nothing about the relationship between mathematical statements and mathematical objects.

Furthermore, although mathematics is used in deriving empirical results, the converse is not the case. Symmetry fails. As noted earlier, the use of computers cannot be compared to the use of telescopes. The fact that mathematical theorems are derived without the help of physical apparatuses should at least suggest that we have here two different kinds of operation. In any case, the mere use of mathematics in physics is no argument for structural and semantic similarity. Logic is also used in physics, yet no one takes that as an argument for the existence of logical objects.

The most interesting holist claim, perhaps, is that mathematics is *tested* through physical theory. The mathematical statement is embedded in a physical theory, which is then compared with the physical world. If the physical theory is confirmed then so is the mathematics, which is inextricably intertwined with it.[12] The holist conclusion, then, is that because the means of ascertaining the truth of mathematical and physical statements are the same, the statements themselves must be semantically similar.

But it is patently false that mathematical theories are tested in the context of physical theory. The criterion for acceptance of a mathematical theory has nothing whatsoever to do with the success of any physical theory in which it happens to be used. (Mathematicians have invariably, in my experience, reacted with incredulity when confronted with this account of mathematical verification.) If mathematics were confirmed by physical theory, then it would also be disconfirmed by the failure of a physical theory, but this just does not happen. Physical theories incorporating a great deal of mathematics have failed by the score, but never has mathematics been considered to be the source of the problem or been discarded as a result.[13] Mathematical theories are simply never declared false when the physical theories

---

[12] This is found in various places in the writing of W.V.O. Quine.

[13] At least not mathematics that has been done correctly. Physical theories may, of course, encounter difficulties through outright mathematical errors such as miscomputation.

that incorporate them are rejected. Mathematics is neither falsified nor verified in physical theory.

(There is a nice irony here in the use of the purported corrigibility of mathematics (and hence its similarity to physics) in the holist argument to establish platonism. It is quite likely that *originally* the existence of abstract, eternal objects was proposed to explain precisely the *in*corrigibility of mathematics. One could explain the eternal truths of mathematics only by reference to immutable, eternal objects, which contrasted with the ever-changing physical world.)

It might be argued that even though at present mathematical theories are not confirmed through physical application, originally, when our basic number systems were developed, it was success empirically that led to their survival. This may well be true, but does not contribute to an argument for platonism. If we consider just finitary arithmetic, there is no argument for abstract entities; a formalist or even empiricist account will do. If the issue is infinitary mathematics, then no claim can be made of empirical confirmation, since we have no experience empirically of infinite collections. One might rejoin that infinitary mathematics is confirmed *through* its finite applications, just as a universal law in physics is confirmed (on this very simple model) through specific instances. The analogy is inapt, however. In the physical example we proceed from particular observations about whales, e.g., to a general *law* about whales, where the singular propositions and the general statements are about the same kind of thing. In the suggested mathematical confirmation, however, we would be going from instances of mathematical statements applied to, say, whales, to *general* mathematical claims not about whales or any other physical thing, but about *abstract* entities, a very different kettle of fish. The reply here might be that the *singular* mathematical statements, even though confirmed though physical objects, are yet *about* abstract objects, the numbers. But then again, the difficulty lies in explaining how the existence of *physical* objects can serve to confirm or provide evidence for the existence of *non*-physical objects.

In any case, whatever the origins of our basic number systems, there doesn't really seem to be much doubt that at *this* point in our linguistic history they have a different epistemological status than physics or biology. Mathematics and logic simply have a different *role* in our language than empirical theories, and it is part of that role that they remain fixed. No examples have been forthcoming of formal theories being declared false on the basis of empirical observation. In fact, a good bit of philosophy of mathematics historically has been devoted to explaining *why* mathematics is thus fixed, the fixity, rightly, being accepted as a given. Mathematics just does have a special status, and the fact that it is used in physical theory (as is logic) does not mean that it is *like* physics (anymore than logic) in any semantic or ontological sense, and it certainly is no reason for thinking that it is empirically corrigible.

What then of the widely accepted claims that "Any statement can be held true come what may" and "No statement is immune to revision."? Their plausibility, perhaps, is due to a failure to examine the status of such claims. As empirical statements, and on a purely individual basis, they are perhaps true. Some people believe the earth is flat, despite all evidence to the contrary. But individual intellectual pathology is not the point. What is no doubt meant is that among rational people collectively, statements may come and go; no statement has absolute epistemological privilege. But again, taken as an empirical claim, it is supported by no evidence whatsoever. On the contrary, all the evidence points to the fact that we *do* hang on to what has traditionally been considered mathematics and logic "come what may" in the empirical world. Of course, errors are sometimes discovered in proofs, so that statements previously considered to be theorems have to be demoted to mere conjectures, or even rejected in the face of counter-examples, but these are *mathematical* refutations, and not disconfirmations by means of empirical observations. Even with the discovery of non-Euclidean geometry, Euclidean geometry was not taken to have been refuted, but was simply said not to be the geometry of physical space. I can see no reason why we should accept the hypothesis that logical and mathematical systems can be falsified on the basis of empirical experience; no evidence has ever been provided for this claim, and we should not be expected to accept it on faith.

A possible interpretation of the epistemological continuity hypothesis is to take it not as a statement of fact, but as a *prescription*, a claim to the effect that we *ought* to be willing to give up any scientific theory, formal or empirical, in the face of contrary evidence. But for one thing, this is already to assume that formal theories are open to empirical refutation, that they are the sorts of theories which *can* be inconsistent with empirical observations. Thus such an interpretation would be question-begging. Again, the continuing acceptance and use of Euclidean geometry, after the discovery of the application of non-Euclidean geometry to physical space, indicates that mathematicians do not think of mathematical theories as empirically corrigible. More importantly, if the epistemological continuity claim is simply that we *ought* to consider them as corrigible, then it cannot play the role in the holist argument that it is supposed to play. If not exactly a decision, it amounts to an exhortation to a decision not to draw a sharp line between the empirical and analytic. But such an exhortation cannot serve as a premise in a proof, and thus cannot be used to buttress an argument for platonism.

In any case, even if we were to accept as a fact the claim that no statement is immune to revision, this would not contribute to showing that mathematical objects exist on a par with physical objects. It is highly likely that if any "analytic" statements are given up, they will be *logical* claims, such as the law of excluded middle, rather than mathematical statements such as "$2 + 3 = 5$". But surely no one would claim that the corrigibility of the law of excluded middle requires us to accept a referential semantics for logic or the existence of logical objects. If possible rejection of logical claims does not imply the existence of logical objects then possible rejection of mathematical claims should not imply the existence of mathematical objects.

The holist argument for platonism thus fails. Premise 2, that *whatever* we know is true, is plausible only if we reject premise 6, that truth for singular and existential statements is always to be defined in terms of reference. Even if we grant that truth for *empirical* statements depends on reference, the argument that mathematical statements also correspond to some real domain depends on premise 4, which asserts a continuity between the formal and empirical sciences. But as we have seen, the arguments *for* continuity and *from* continuity are flawed. Continuity has not been established, and even if it had, platonism would not be the consequence. Thus the holist argument has not demonstrated that we must take mathematical statements to be true in the sense of correspondence with a world of mathematical objects.

II. Referential Incapacity

The argument above is directed primarily against the continuity thesis, which is supposed to provide the rationale for using parallel semantics — a referential semantics — for physical theory and mathematics. If, as I maintain, this continuity is a myth, then any argument for platonism that relies on the purported continuity will fail. Platonists with the courage of their convictions, however, will have noted that the continuity thesis was needed only because premise 6 was deemed implausible, without much argument, and because mathematical statements were construed as rules, with even less argument. Why should not a platonist simply rejoin that mathematical statements *are* declarative and that grammatically similar sentences *should* have similar semantics?

As we shall see, the answer to the second is that a correspondence theory of truth for mathematics has awkward consequences. This in turn is one reason for supposing that the grammar of mathematical statements is not so straightforward as it might appear. In any case, it has been amply demonstrated in the last 30 years that the surface structure of a sentence may not reflect its deep structure. Sentences that are grammatically questions may in fact function as commands, or even assertions. So even if mathematical sentences are *prima facie* assertions, we need not assume that that is their real role in the language. In any case, "$2 \times 18 = 36$" is not, to my mind, *prima facie* an assertion. So there are reasons to be doubtful that mathematical sentences are declarative, and even more reasons to suppose that their truth is not determined by correspondence with abstract objects.

One of the reasons often given for a referential or "literal" account of truth for mathematics is that it explains the usefulness of mathematics in applications. If mathematical statements were not (literally) true, it is claimed, it would be hard to account for their utility. I will argue, on the contrary, that it is the referential account that has trouble explaining the practical use of mathematics and that, in fact, reference to abstract objects plays no role in utility.

According to the referential view, a mathematical statement is true if and only if there are objects corresponding to the singular terms and existential quantifiers that actually do have the properties and relations ascribed to them by the statements. Now, in general, we verify a mathematical proposition by finding a proof, not by direct observation of the entities denoted by the terms of the statement. But this means that *the requisite correspondence is not what is established*, so that we are not justified in affirming the *truth* of a mathematical proposition when we find a proof. But are we ever then in a position to establish the truth of mathematics, and if so, how? If not, how can we claim that mathematics is useful only because it is (literally) true? Does it make sense to assert this when we can never know whether the mathematics we use is true? The literal truth of mathematics appears to be wholly irrelevant to its generation and thus to its usefulness in applications.

One might object (since we are no longer discussing the holist argument specifically) that we *do* have direct apprehension of mathematical objects, and that this is how we establish truth. But then we need to ask whether we could be wrong about some of the mathematics we find useful, and what would be the consequence. Somehow, it seems highly unlikely that *by direct apprehension* we would find that we were mistaken about, say, the claim that $\frac{1}{4} + \frac{1}{3} = \frac{7}{12}$. Given how embedded our current use of fractions is, it is almost inconceivable that we would say it was false just on the basis of "intuition". And even if we did, it is even more unlikely that we would give up this mathematical result in practice. We would almost certainly continue as before, since our system of fractions has served us so well.[14] But then, again, literal truth — correspondence — really has nothing to do with practice, and so can do nothing to *explain* the practical success of mathematics.

A rather interesting consequence of the correspondence view is that it would require us to jettison essential portions of our mathematics — all the singular and existential statements — if it turned out that a certain *philosophical* view, mathematical platonism, was false. If the mathematical singular or existential statement is true just in case there are objects of a certain sort, then if there are no such objects, these statements are false, and since we would not want to accept false statements, we would have to throw out, e.g., the claim that $2 + 2 = 4$! We would have to abandon that entire portion of our mathematical theory just as we abandoned the phlogiston theory when it appeared there was no such thing as phlogiston. But the extreme unlikelihood of our giving up "$2 + 2 = 4$" even if mathematical objects were shown not to exist indicates that their existence is not what leads us to accept that statement in the first place, and that the notion of correspondence is empty and irrelevant. Why suppose at all that there is a world of mathematical objects corresponding to our mathematical formulas, when their absence would make no difference at all to our mathematical practice?

There are still other reasons to doubt the literal truth of mathematical statements. There are many mathematical theories, perhaps most, to which mathematicians do not attribute truth, such as the axioms for various kinds of geometries and group theories. The enterprise is to see what follows from the various sets of axioms, without supposing that the axioms are *true*. Mathematicians themselves take an "if-thenist" approach to some parts of mathematics. But if not all mathematical theories need be taken as true, then it is not clear why *any* mathematical theory should be so construed. (And if all consistent theories *are* taken as true, then one might as well *define* truth as consistency and so eliminate all reference to mathematical objects.)

The existence of such a two-tiered system of mathematics — some theories taken as (literally) true and others as just uninterpreted axiom sets — is not seen as a problem by everyone. Quine, for instance, explicitly states that truth should be attributed only to those portions of mathematics that find a use in physical theory.

---

[14] Ludwig Wittgenstein makes this point in *Remarks on the Foundations of Mathematics.*

But there are real difficulties with this reply. First, it seems quite arbitrary to draw a line in this fashion between mathematical theories which are supposed to be true, and those which are only treated in a hypothetical manner, especially when we remember that it is not eternally fixed which parts of mathematics are required for physical science. Almost everyone would grant that the mathematics of real numbers is necessary for physics, but other cases are not so clear. Group theory is now widely used in biology; is it *required* for biology? Could we do everything we want to do without it? What about probability theory and applied statistics in the social sciences? (Or are they not really sciences?) Various mathematical disciplines are used in various sciences, and new and unexpected applications keep cropping up. Where do we draw the line? Shall we say that a mathematical theory is true when it has an application? *Becomes* true when an application is found? This seems a very odd way of using the concept "true".

One might reply that we only *discover* that mathematical theories are true when we find an application, but that their actual truth status does not change. But then we should be prepared to grant literal truth to *any* consistent theory, since we never know ahead of time which mathematical theories are going to find applications. Some which were at one time considered completely abstract, and useless outside of mathematics itself, have found physical interpretations. Group theory is just one example. But again, if we are willing to grant truth to any consistent theory, then we might as well just *define* truth in terms of consistency. A referential account is otiose. Even worse, it is again not clear why the discovery of an application of a mathematical theory to the *physical* world should render it true in the sense of correspondence with *abstract* mathematical objects.

To conclude, an account of mathematical truth based on correspondence with abstract objects has no real function, and in addition, it has unacceptable consequences. And the one supposedly good reason for accepting this version of truth, the claimed continuity between mathematics and empirical science, is seen to be a mirage. The argument for a referential semantics is unsound, and the consequences of such a semantics are unhappy. Truth as correspondence for mathematics should be laid to rest, and with it platonism.

GARREL POTTINGER

A TOUR OF THE MULTIVARIATE LAMBDA CALCULUS [1]

1. INTRODUCTION

We discuss a lambda calculus in which a single λ may bind an arbitrary finite sequence of variables. This introduces terms of the form $\lambda x_0 \ldots x_{n-1} \cdot X$ which are *not* the result of performing n univariate abstractions. For example, we have $\lambda xy \cdot x \neq \lambda x \cdot \lambda y \cdot x$. Redexes have the form $(\lambda x_0 \ldots x_{n-1} \cdot X)Y_0 \ldots Y_{n-1}$, and such a redex contracts to the result of simultaneously substituting $Y_0, \ldots, Y_{n-1}$ for $x_0, \ldots, x_{n-1}$ in X.

The multivariate lambda calculus really is different from the ordinary univariate calculus. Note, for example, that $(\lambda xy \cdot x)X$ will be normal, but $(\lambda x \cdot \lambda y \cdot x)X$ will not. Thereby hangs a tale which will be told briefly now and fully in the sequel.

In some ways, the multivariate lambda calculus is quite similar to the ordinary univariate calculus. The foremost similarity is that both calculi have the Church-Rosser property — if X converts to Y, then, for some Z, X reduces to Z and Y reduces to Z [Pot88a, Theorem 5.8].

The Church-Rosser theorem implies that the multivariate lambda calculus is a conservative extension of the ordinary univariate lambda calculus and allows us to conclude that the behavior of normal forms is what we would expect from our experience with the ordinary lambda calculus. That is, following [Chu41], we define X to be *β-normal* if, and only if, no Y is the result of contracting a redex in X, and we specify that Y is a *β-normal form of* X if, and only if, X converts to Y and Y is β-normal. Then, using the Church-Rosser (and dropping the β's to simplify notation), we can prove: (1) if Y is a normal form of X, then X reduces to Y and (2) if Y_1 and Y_2 are normal forms of X, then $Y_1 = Y_2$.

Having said a bit about what the multivariate lambda calculus and the ordinary lambda calculus have in common, we turn to pointing out how they differ.

To begin with, consider S, K, and I. It would be nice to be able both to say that the usual reduction rules for these combinators characterize them completely and to identify them with lambda terms. This is possible in the multivariate lambda calculus, but not in the ordinary lambda calculus (Section 6). The same thing works for all other familiar combinators, such as B, C, W, and so on.

This provides one piece of evidence that it is sensible to take combinators to be closed terms of the multivariate lambda calculus which contain no constants. One can also use a simply described (but, of necessity, infinite) set of such terms to analyze binding *via* a definition of bracket abstraction (Section 7), and it is possible

[1] Acknowledgment of Sponsorship: The research which produced the information contained in this document was sponsored, in whole or in part, by the U.S. Air Force Systems Command, Rome Air Development Center, Griffiss AFB, New York 13441–5700 under Contract No. F30602–85–C–0098.

J. M. Dunn and A. Gupta (eds.), Truth or Consequences, 209–229.
© 1990 *Kluwer Academic Publishers. Printed in the Netherlands.*

to give a Curry-style axiomatization of conversion by using the terms in question (Section 8). Thus, the multivariate lambda calculus provides a satisfying answer to the question "What is a combinator?"

In contrast with the univariate lambda calculus, the multivariate lambda calculus also contains normal fixed-point combinators (Section 9). And, by using such combinators, it is possible to give an elegant representation of the recursive functions in which the functions are represented by normal terms [Pot87].

There is a price to be paid for these interesting and useful features of the multivariate lambda calculus — the distinction between multivariate binding and iterated univariate binding which provides them is inconsistent with η-conversion (Section 10). On the other hand, the semantical techniques of [Mey82] can be extended to the multivariate calculus (Section 11), so giving up η-conversion is not a terrible sacrifice.

Besides these novelties, we base our treatment of the multivariate calculus on a new account of terms which avoids the niggling involved in dealing with α-conversion by getting rid of that relation. We begin the body of the paper by explaining how this works.

2. Abstract syntax

We take terms to be objects existing in certain algebraic structures the postulates of which are arranged so that terms which would ordinarily be said to α-convert to one another turn out to be the *same* term. In the definition which follows (and everywhere else in this paper), "=" denotes *identity*.

A *term structure* is a quintuple $\mathcal{S} = (\mathcal{T}, \mathcal{V}, \mathcal{C}, (\_1 \_2), (\lambda\_1. \_2))$ which satisfies conditions (1)–(6), below.

The sets $\mathcal{T}$, $\mathcal{V}$, and $\mathcal{C}$ contain the terms, variables, and constants of $\mathcal{S}$. As usual, $\mathcal{V}^*$ is to be the set of finite sequences $\sigma, \sigma_1, \ldots$ of elements of $\mathcal{V}$. Also, ν is to be a constant or a variable. In order to simplify notation, we define $\sigma_1 \sigma_2 = \sigma_1 \frown \sigma_2$ and $\sigma_1 \nu \sigma_2 = \sigma_1 \frown \langle \nu \rangle \frown \sigma_2$. And we don't use angle brackets and commas in writing notations for terms when names of the variables in binding sequences are used to display the sequences.

(1) $\mathcal{V}$ is denumerable, $\mathcal{V}$ and $\mathcal{C}$ are disjoint, and $\mathcal{T}$, $\mathcal{V}$, and $\mathcal{C}$ are disjoint from $\mathcal{V}^*$.

(2)   Application is defined for pairs of terms and yields terms as values. But application never yields a constant, a variable, or an object in the range of abstraction as a value.

(3)   Abstraction is defined for pairs which have an element of $\mathcal{V}^*$ as their first component and a term as their second component. The operation yields terms as values, but never yields a constant, a variable, or an object in the range of application.

(4) $\mathcal{T}$ is the smallest set which contains $\mathcal{C}$ and $\mathcal{V}$ and is closed under application and abstraction with respect to arbitrary elements of $\mathcal{V}^*$.

(5) $X_1 X_2 = X_1' X_2'$ if, and only if, $X_1 = X_1'$ and $X_2 = X_2'$.

(6) $\lambda\sigma \cdot X = \lambda\sigma' \cdot X'$ if, and only if, σ and σ' are the same length, and one of (a)–(c) holds.

(a) For some ν and ν', $X = \nu$, $X' = \nu'$, and either

 (i) ν is not a component of σ, ν' is not a component of σ', and $\nu = \nu'$, or

 (ii) σ has the form $\sigma_1 \, \nu \, \sigma_2$, σ' has the form $\sigma'_1 \, \nu' \, \sigma'_2$, σ_2 and σ'_2 are the same length, ν is not a component of σ_2, and ν' is not a component of σ'_2.

(b) X has the form $X_1 X_2$, X' has the form $X'_1 X'_2$, $\lambda\sigma \cdot X_1 = \lambda\sigma' \cdot X'_1$, and $\lambda\sigma \cdot X_2 = \lambda\sigma' \cdot X'_2$.

(c) X has the form $\lambda\sigma_1 \cdot X_1$, X' has the form $\lambda\sigma'_1 \cdot X'_1$, and $\lambda\sigma \, \sigma_1 \cdot X_1 = \lambda\sigma' \, \sigma'_1 \cdot X'_1$.

Taken in conjunction with (1)–(5), (6) (b) and (c) reduce identity conditions for terms which arise *via* abstraction to the case where the terms on which abstraction is performed are constants or variables. Condition (6) (a) provides a simple criterion of identity for abstracts of the latter sort.

An example illustrating how this works is in order. Consider $\lambda x \cdot \lambda y \cdot xy$, $\lambda y \cdot \lambda x \cdot yx$, and $\lambda x \cdot \lambda y \cdot yx$. We should be able to show that $\lambda x \cdot \lambda y \cdot xy = \lambda y \cdot \lambda x \cdot yx$ and that $\lambda x \cdot \lambda y \cdot xy \neq \lambda x \cdot \lambda y \cdot yx$. (From now on, it is assumed that distinct notations for variables denote distinct variables, unless the context indicates the opposite.)

We have $\lambda xy \cdot x = \lambda yx \cdot y$ and $\lambda xy \cdot y = \lambda yx \cdot x$, by condition (6) (a) (ii). Condition (6) (b) implies that $\lambda xy \cdot xy = \lambda yx \cdot yx$, and this and condition (6) (c) lead to $\lambda x \cdot \lambda y \cdot xy = \lambda y \cdot \lambda x \cdot yx$.

On the other hand, conditions (3), (4), and (6) (a) imply that $\lambda xy \cdot x \neq \lambda xy \cdot y$. Applying these conditions again and then using condition (5), we may infer that $\lambda xy \cdot xy \neq \lambda xy \cdot yx$. This and condition (6) (c) imply that $\lambda x \cdot \lambda y \cdot xy \neq \lambda x \cdot \lambda y \cdot yx$.

Term structures make sense because it is sensible to regard $\lambda\sigma \, \sigma_1 \cdot X_1$ as being less complex than $\lambda\sigma \cdot \lambda\sigma_1 \cdot X_1$. In fact, using the induction principle licensed by condition 4, it can be shown that there is a unique function, *Complex*, which has $\mathcal{T}$ as its domain and satisfies the following conditions: (1) *Complex* $\nu = 1$, (2) *Complex* $X_1 X_2 = (Complex\ X_1) + (Complex\ X_2)$, and (3) *Complex* $\lambda\sigma \cdot X = (Complex\ X) + (Length\ \sigma) + 1$.

So, we have:

$$Complex\ \lambda\sigma \cdot \lambda\sigma_1 \cdot X_1$$
$$= (Complex\ X_1) + (Length\ \sigma_1) + 1 + (Length\ \sigma) + 1$$
$$= (Complex\ X_1) + (Length\ \sigma\ \sigma_1) + 2$$
$$> (Complex\ X_1) + (Length\ \sigma\ \sigma_1) + 1$$
$$= Complex\ \lambda\sigma\ \sigma_1 \cdot X_1$$

There is a subtlety here which is worth remarking on — the description of *Complex* given in the preceding paragraph cannot really be regarded as a definition. This is so because, in the abstraction case, the value *seems* to depend on σ. It can be shown that, in fact, there is no such dependence, but this must be proved. The correct formal procedure is to define *Complex* as a relation and then show that it is a function, and this unfamiliar pattern is frequently encountered in a formal treatment of the multivariate lambda calculus based on term structures [Pot88a].

Note that the problem described in the preceding paragraph would arise even in a treatment of the univariate lambda calculus, if the treatment employed the sort of abstract syntactic description we are discussing (*e.g.*, [Pot88b]). This is the price we pay for getting rid of bound variables and α-conversion. And, as far as theoretical discussion of the lambda calculus is concerned, we really *have* gotten rid of bound variables. In Section 3 we will see how to make sense of talking about free variables in this sort of setting. But nothing similar can be done for talk about bound variables. To see this, consider the question "Which variables are bound in $\lambda x \cdot x$?" The only possible answers are "All variables" or "No variables", if terms are thought of in the abstract way described here, and this means that the question is nonsense.

3. Substitution

The notion of a term structure gives us a way of talking about lambda terms which divorces questions of term identity from questions about substitution. Of course, we do need a substitution operation in order to define reduction and conversion. The business of this section is to define substitution in the abstract setting provided by term structures.

First, we must explain how talk about free variables is to be construed in dealing with an arbitrary term structure. An induction based on the measure *Complex* can be used to show that there is a unique function FV defined for members of $\mathcal{T}$ which satisfies the following conditions, where c is a member of $\mathcal{C}$ and $^{Vr}\sigma$ is the set of variables which are components of σ: (1) $FV\ c = \emptyset$, (2) $FV\ x = \{x\}$, (3) $FV\ X_1 X_2 = (FV\ X_1) \cup (FV\ X_2)$, (4) $FV\ \lambda\sigma \cdot \nu = (FV\ \nu) - (Vr\ \sigma)$, (5) $FV\ \lambda\sigma \cdot X_1 X_2 = (FV\ \lambda\sigma \cdot X_1) \cup (FV\ \lambda\sigma \cdot X_2)$, and (6) $FV\ \lambda\sigma \cdot \lambda\sigma_1 \cdot X = FV\ \lambda\sigma\ \sigma_1 \cdot X$.

An induction based on *Complex* also will show that we always have $FV\ \lambda\sigma \cdot X = (FV\ X) - (Vr\ \sigma)$, so FV tells us correctly which variables are free in a given term.

Now we are ready to consider how to explain substitution formally. Where τ is a finite sequence of terms which has the same length as σ, we wish to define *Sub* $[\tau/\sigma/X]$ so that it will be the result of subsituting the components of τ, respectively and simultaneously, for the components of σ in X. As usual, in order to do this correctly we must avoid variable conflicts when the definition requires us to interchange *Sub* and λ. Also, if a variable turns up more than once in σ, we must specify which component of τ is to be substituted for it.

We solve the second problem by substituting the component of τ which matches the right-most occurrence of a given variable in σ for that variable. The following three definitions allow us to explain exactly what must be avoided in order to solve the first.

Where τ and σ are the same length, Y is a *conflict term for* τ, σ, and X if, and only if, τ has the form $\tau_1 \ Y \ \tau_2$, σ has the form $\sigma_1 \ x \ \sigma_2$, τ_2 and σ_2 are the same length, x is not a component of σ_2, and $x \in FV \ X$.

The set of *conflict variables for* τ, σ, and X is the union of the sets $FV \ Y$ such that Y is a conflict term for τ, σ, and X.

And τ, σ, X and σ_1 *conflict* if, and only if, some component of σ_1 is a member of the set of conflict variables for τ, σ, and X.

Thus, τ, σ, X and σ_1 conflict if identifying $Sub \ [\tau/\sigma/\lambda\sigma_1 \cdot X]$ and $\lambda\sigma_1 \cdot Sub \ [\tau/\sigma/X]$ is certain to involve variable capture.

It can be shown that there is a unique function Sub, defined for sequences of terms and variables of the same length and arbitrary terms, which satisfies the following conditions.

(1)   If ν is not a component of $\sigma^\dagger$, then $Sub \ [\tau/\sigma^\dagger/\nu] = \nu$.

(2)   If $\sigma^\dagger$ has the form $\sigma_1^\dagger \ x \ \sigma_2^\dagger$, τ has the form $\tau_1 \ Z \ \tau_2$, $\sigma_2^\dagger$ and τ_2 are the same length, and x is not a component of $\sigma_2^\dagger$, then $Sub \ [\tau/\sigma^\dagger/x] = Z$.

(3) $Sub \ [\tau/\sigma^\dagger/X_1 X_2] = Sub \ [\tau/\sigma^\dagger/X_1] Sub \ [\tau/\sigma^\dagger/X_2]$

(4)   If no component of $\sigma^\dagger$ is a member of $FV \ \lambda\sigma \cdot \nu$, then $Sub \ [\tau/\sigma^\dagger/\lambda\sigma \cdot \nu] = \lambda\sigma \cdot \nu$.

(5)   If some component of $\sigma^\dagger$ is a member of $FV \ \lambda\sigma \cdot \nu$ and τ, $\sigma^\dagger$, ν, and σ do not conflict, then $Sub \ [\tau/\sigma^\dagger/\lambda\sigma \cdot \nu] = \lambda\sigma \cdot Sub \ [\tau/\sigma^\dagger/\nu]$.

(6)   If $Sub \ [\tau/\sigma^\dagger/\lambda\sigma \cdot X_1] = \lambda\sigma \cdot X_1'$ and $Sub \ [\tau/\sigma^\dagger/\lambda\sigma \cdot X_2] = \lambda\sigma \cdot X_2'$, then $Sub \ [\tau/\sigma^\dagger/\lambda\sigma \cdot X_1 X_2] = \lambda\sigma \cdot X_1' X_2'$.

(7)   If $Sub \ [\tau/\sigma^\dagger/\lambda\sigma \ \sigma_1 \cdot X_1] = \lambda\sigma \ \sigma_1 \cdot X_1'$, then $Sub \ [\tau/\sigma^\dagger/\lambda\sigma \cdot \lambda\sigma_1 \cdot X_1] = \lambda\sigma \cdot \lambda\sigma_1 \cdot X_1'$.

The virtue of the foregoing explanation of substitution is that worries about variable capture are confined to clause (5). However, it is not even clear that a function has been defined, and, even if there is nothing wrong as far as that goes, it certainly is not obvious that Sub will behave as we know a substitution operation ought to. We indicate briefly how to deal with these problems.

As in the case of the explanation of *Complex* given in Section 2, it is not immediately clear that the foregoing conditions on Sub define a function, since the value specified in clause (5) seems to depend on σ and similar worries arise in the cases of clauses (6) and (7). In order to overcome this problem, first one uses an induction based on *Complex* to show that if $\sigma_1^\dagger \ \sigma_2$ and $\sigma_1^{\dagger\dagger} \ \sigma_2$ are the same length and no component of $\sigma_1^\dagger$ or $\sigma_1^{\dagger\dagger}$ is a member of $(FV \ X) - (Vr \ \sigma_2)$, then $\lambda\sigma_1^\dagger \ \sigma_2 \cdot X = \lambda\sigma_1^{\dagger\dagger} \ \sigma_2 \cdot X$. A further induction on *Complex* Y then shows that $Sub \ [\tau/\sigma^\dagger/Y]$ has at most one value. The lemma stated in the preceding sentence is applied (with σ_2 empty) if $Y = \lambda\sigma \cdot \nu$ and some component of $\sigma^\dagger$ is a member of $FV \ \lambda\sigma \cdot \nu$. The other cases of the induction are routine.

It must also be shown that Sub always has at least one value for appropriate triples of arguments. For this purpose and, also, in order to show that this formal notion behaves as our pretheoretic understanding of substitution tells us it should, we must establish a sufficient condition for interchanging Sub and λ and show that this condition can always be met.

We would like to prove that if the components of σ are neither components of $\sigma^\dagger$ nor free in any component of τ, then $Sub\,[\tau/\sigma^\dagger/\lambda\sigma \cdot X] = \lambda\sigma \cdot Sub\,[\tau/\sigma^\dagger/X]$. And we would also like to show that the antecedent of this proposed lemma can always be satisfied, given arbitrary τ and $\sigma^\dagger$ and an arbitrary term of the form $\lambda\sigma \cdot X$. Then a simple induction on the structure of terms would show that Sub is defined when it ought to be, and, in the process of proving this, we would also have shown that the constraints imposed by our pretheoretic understanding of substitution are satisfied. All this can be done in the following way.

Let us say that a *change of bindings* is an injection of $\mathcal{V}$ into $\mathcal{V}$ and, where Ch is a change of bindings, define Ch to be a *change of bindings for* X if, and only if, the range of Ch does not intersect $FV\ X$. Also, where $\sigma = \langle x_0,\dots,x_{n-1}\rangle$, let $Ch\ \sigma = \langle Ch\ x_0,\dots,Ch\ x_{n-1}\rangle$. We can show *via* an induction based on *Complex* that if Ch is a change of bindings for $\lambda\sigma\cdot X$, then, for some X', $\lambda\sigma\cdot X = \lambda(Ch\ \sigma)\cdot X'$. Obviously, given a finite set of variables, we can always produce a change of bindings the range of which is disjoint from the set in question. So, given arbitrary τ and $\sigma^\dagger$ and an artibrary term of the form $\lambda\sigma \cdot X$, we may assume without loss of generality that the components of σ are neither components of $\sigma^\dagger$ nor free in any component of τ. Given this, we can show that the rule for interchanging Sub and λ proposed above is correct by means of another induction based on *Complex* (it turns out that we need to know that the antecedent of the interchange rule can always be satisfied in order to show that the rule is correct) and then finish off the project of showing that Sub really is substitution according to the plan of the preceding paragraph.

It must be admitted that the arguments just sketched are not simple when written out in detail [Pot88a]. But they are certainly no more complicated than those which must be given in order to establish the basic properties of univariate substitution in traditional treatments of the lambda calculus [CF58], and, since α-conversion need not be considered in the present setting, the overall theoretical description of terms and substitution is actually simpler than traditional accounts of these concepts for the univariate lambda calculus.

4. Reduction and Conversion

We begin our discussion of reduction and conversion by introducing a compact notation for iterated application. Where $\tau = \langle X_0,\dots,X_{n-1}\rangle$ $(n \geq 0)$, let $X\ \$\ \tau = XX_0\ \dots\ X_{n-1}$. Given this, we specify that $(\lambda\sigma \cdot X)\ \$\ \tau$ is a *β-redex* if, and only if, σ and τ are the same length. And, of course, a β-redex $(\lambda\sigma \cdot X)\ \$\ \tau$ *β-contracts* to $Sub\,[\tau/\sigma/X]$.

The multivariate β-contraction just defined includes ordinary β-contraction — if σ is of length 1, we are back on familiar turf. On the other hand, $\lambda \cdot X$ β-contracts to X and $(\lambda xy \cdot x)X$ is not a β-redex. How this affects reduction and conversion will be explained in what follows, but first we must give official definitions of these relations.

Where $contr_\beta$ is the relation of β-contraction defined above, let $red_{1\beta}$ be the smallest relation satisfying:

(1) $contr_\beta \subseteq red_{1\beta}$,

(2) $X\,red_{1\beta}\,Y \Rightarrow ZX\,red_{1\beta}\,ZY$ $\&XZ\,red_{1\beta}\,YZ$, and

(3) $X\,red_{1\beta}\,Y \Rightarrow \lambda\sigma \cdot X\,red_{1\beta}\,\lambda\sigma \cdot Y$.

β-reduction is the transitive, reflexive closure of $red_{1\beta}$, and *β-conversion* is the transitive closure of the symmetric closure of β-reduction. In what follows we use "red_β" and "$conv_\beta$" as shorthand for "β-reduction" and "β-conversion". For the most part, these are the only reduction and conversion relations discussed below, so we will also drop the β's and simply write "red", "$conv$", and so on, unless the context involves explicit mention of other reduction and conversion relations.

5. SOME GENERAL REMARKS ABOUT COMBINATORY LOGIC

Combinatory logic is usually thought of as the study of two different sorts of calculi — calculi of combinators and lambda calculi. Combinators are taken to be terms built up from certain basic combinators by means of application, and basic combinators are regarded as constants without internal structure. Lambda calculi, on the other hand, involve terms built up from variables (and, perhaps, some constants) by means of the lambda operator, which is a variable binding operator, and application.

It has been clear since the publication of [Ros35a, Ros35b] that calculi of combinators and lambda calculi are equivalent, but working out the details of this equivalence has proved to be a complex, delicate, and rather vexing job, as one can see from [CF58, Chapter 6] and [CHS72, Chapter 11].

The traditional method for attempting to work out the details of the equivalence between calculi of combinators and lambda calculi is to show that the rules postulated for the basic combinators allow us to simulate the lambda operator, on the one hand, and to show that certain lambda terms behave as the basic combinators do, on the other.

If attention is restricted to lambda calculi involving only univariate bindings, the minimum requirement for simulating the lambda operator by means of combinators is to show how to define $[x] \cdot X$ so that (1) the variables of $[x] \cdot X$ are just those of X less x and (2) $([x] \cdot X)Y$ converts to $Sub\,[Y/x/X]$. It turns out that this minimum requirement can be met using finite sets of basic combinators for which only very simple algebraic rules are postulated.

Unfortunately, satisfying the minimum requirement for a simulation of the lambda operator is not enough — known methods of defining bracket abstraction when only simple algebraic rules are postulated for the basic combinators do not allow us to conclude that $[x] \cdot X$ converts to $[x] \cdot Y$, given that X converts to Y. Following Curry, let us call this property (ξ).

Property (ξ) is *important*. It tells us that we may operate with defined functions inside the scopes of other function definitions, and this is done freely and often in the functional computations of ordinary mathematics. Consider, for example, partial derivatives. If D is the functional which maps unary functions on the reals to their derivatives and $f = \lambda x \cdot \lambda y \cdot x^2 + y^2$, then the partial derivative of f with respect to its first argument is $g = \lambda y \cdot D \lambda x \cdot fxy$. In order to show that $g = \lambda y \cdot \lambda x \cdot 2x$, we replace f by its definiens to obtain $g = \lambda y \cdot D \lambda x \cdot (\lambda x \cdot \lambda y \cdot x^2 + y^2)xy$, reduce the right hand side to $\lambda y \cdot D \lambda x \cdot x^2 + y^2$, and apply the basic rules for differentiating polynomials. But if the reduction is prohibited, we can't even get started.

Curry showed how to solve this problem by introducing additional postulates for the basic combinators, but introducing these new postulates raises questions for which traditional methods have not provided satisfactory answers.

First, one is left wondering how to regard the basic combinators of the original, unextended calculus of combinators. This is an important question both because we must understand such calculi in order to see clearly what is going on in combinatory logic [CHS72, pp. 22ff] and because such calculi have interesting applications in computer science [Tur84].

Second, although the theory of conversion for combinatory calculi extended by postulates designed to make bracket abstraction provide a full simulation of the lambda operator is well-behaved, the theory of reduction (i.e., strong reduction) for such calculi is much less satisfactory. For example, the theory of conversion is insensitive to the choice of basic combinators, but the theory of reduction is *extremely* sensitive to this [HS86, p. 85].

6. What Combinators Are

The multivariate lambda calculus provides a different way of looking at the question of the relation between calculi of combinators and lambda calculi. Let us say that a term of the multivariate lambda calculus is *pure* if, and only if, it can be built up without using constants. Formally, we take a *combinator* to be a pure closed term of the multivariate lambda calculus. Of course, this amounts to proposing a formal explication for "combinator", and we must argue that the proposal is reasonable.

To begin with, we show that combinatory calculi based on simple algebraic postulates of reduction — theories of weak reduction in the terminology of [CF58] — can be regarded as subsystems of the full multivariate lambda calculus. This provides a simple answer to the question how the combinators of weak combinatory calculi should be regarded, and since all ordinary pure closed terms are terms of the multivariate lambda calculus, we may still regard all such terms as combinators according to the formal explication for "combinator" proposed above. So we are about to show that the proposed explication enables us to explain something which certainly needs to be explained without doing violence to the ordinary usage of "combinator".

In order to show how to embed calculi of weak reduction in the multivariate lambda calculus, we consider the most familiar of all such calculi — the calculus of weak reduction based on S, K, and I. After dealing with this example, we indicate how to obtain such an embedding for an arbitrary calculus of weak reduction. We also show that, assuming plausible conditions on the desired embedding, restricting attention to ordinary lambda terms rules out the the possibility of achieving an embedding for the weak *SKI* calculus.

We want to identify the weak combinators S, K, and I with pure closed terms of the multivariate lambda calculus in such a way that, on the class of terms built up from variables, constants, and the terms identified with the weak combinators, red_β and $conv_\beta$ coincide with the reduction and conversion relations generated by postulating the rules (S), (K), and (I) — i.e., postulating that $SXYZ$ contracts to $XZ(YZ)$, KXY contracts to X, and IX contracts to X. The following identifications will do the job: (1) $S = \lambda xyz \cdot xz(yz)$, (2) $K = \lambda xy \cdot x$, and (3) $I = \lambda x \cdot x$.

Observe that if X is a term of the weak *SKI* calculus, X' is the corresponding multivariate lambda term, and $X' red_{1\beta} Y'$, then Y' corresponds to a term obtained by performing one reduction step on X in the weak *SKI* calculus. It follows that if X' is the multivariate lambda term corresponding to the term X of the weak *SKI* calculus and $X' red_\beta Y'$, then Y' corresponds to a term Y of the weak *SKI* calculus and X reduces to Y in that calculus.

Now consider arbitrary terms X and Y of the weak *SKI* calculus, and let X' and Y' be the corresponding multivariate lambda terms. It is obvious that $X' red_\beta Y'$ if X reduces to Y, and given the remarks of the preceding paragraph, we see that X reduces to Y if $X' red_\beta Y'$. As for conversion, it is evident that if X converts to Y in the weak *SKI* calculus, then $X' conv_\beta Y'$. For the converse, suppose $X' conv_\beta Y'$ and, applying the Church-Rosser theorem, let $X' red_\beta Z'$ and $Y' red_\beta Z'$. Invoking the remarks of the preceding paragraph again, we have X reduces to Z and Y reduces to Z, where Z is the term to which Z' corresponds. It follows that X converts to Y in the weak *SKI* calculus.

Although we have been discussing S, K, and I, the method involved in producing the desired embedding is completely general. Let us say that σ is *irredundant* if, and only if, no variable occurs twice in σ. Using ι to refer to irredundant sequences of variables, we specify that a *rudimentary* combinator is a term of the form $\lambda \iota.X$, where X is built up from the components of ι by means of application alone. Then, given a weak calculus of combinators, we can produce an embedding into the multivariate lambda calculus by simply mapping each weak combinator to the rudimentary combinator determined by the basic contraction rule for that weak combinator.

Now we consider the prospects for embedding the weak *SKI* calculus into a target consisting of ordinary lambda terms. Besides requiring that the contraction rules (S), (K), and (I) for the weak combinators must hold as properties of red_β for the lambda terms with which the weak combinators are to be identified, it seems reasonable to require that the lambda terms be normal and that the target of the embedding be closed under red_β. Call the last mentioned condition $(CL\ SKI)$.

There is no problem about I, so we look for ordinary terms S_1 and K_1 to play the roles of S and K.

In view of (K), we must have $K_1 xy\ red_\beta x$. Since K_1 is to be ordinary, β-normal, and closed, K_1 must have the form $\lambda x \cdot X$, where X is β-normal. It follows that $K_1 x contr_\beta X$, so, since $K_1 xy\ red_\beta x$, we must also have $Xy\ red_\beta x$, where X

is β-normal. Since $y \neq x$ (as we have been assuming tacitly), y is not free in X. From this we can show that $X = \lambda y \cdot Y$, where Y is normal and $(\lambda y \cdot Y)y$ $red_\beta x$. But $(\lambda y \cdot Y)y$ $contr_\beta Y$, so we must have $Y = x$ and $K_1 = \lambda x \cdot \lambda y \cdot x$.

We also have $K_1 I$ $red_\beta \lambda y \cdot I = \lambda y \cdot \lambda x \cdot x$, so $(CL\ SKI)$ fails. It follows that no ordinary terms meet the proposed standard for behaving as they should, if the weak combinators S, K, and I are to be identified with them.

Although the argument does not require it, note that if S_1 is ordinary, closed, and β-normal and S_1 satisfies (S), then we must have $S_1 = \lambda x \cdot \lambda y \cdot \lambda z \cdot xz(yz)$. Thus $S_1 I$ $red_\beta \lambda y \cdot \lambda z \cdot z(yz)$, so $(CL\ SKI)$ must also fail if we attempt to take the weak combinator S to be an ordinary term.

7. Bracket Abstraction

Of course, S_1 and K_1 are interesting and important, despite what has just been shown. It is well known that every ordinary lambda term converts to a term built up from $\lambda x \cdot \lambda y \cdot x$, $\lambda x \cdot \lambda y \cdot \lambda z \cdot xz(yz)$, variables, and constants by means of application alone. This is enough to explain why S_1 and K_1 are worthy of the intensive study they have received.

Let us say that a set of terms, s, *generates* X if, and only if, X converts to a term built up from members of s, variables, and constants by means of application alone. As we have just noted, $\{S_1, K_1\}$ generates every ordinary term. But it is easy to show that *no* finite set of terms generates every term of the multivariate lambda calculus. To see this, consider a finite set of terms s, and let n be the maximum of the lengths of variable sequences involved in abstractions used to build up terms in s. No term built up by means of application alone from terms in s, variables, and constants can reduce to $\lambda x_1 \ldots x_{n+1} \cdot x_{n+1}$, because the bound n is preserved by reduction. Since $\lambda x_1 \ldots x_{n+1} \cdot x_{n+1}$ is normal, it follows that, in fact, no such term converts to it.

One of the main traditional aims of combinatory logic is to use combinators to explain variable binding [CF58, pp. 1–11], and besides constituting a traditional and worthwhile part of the subject matter of combinatory logic, such explanations play an important role in efforts by computer scientists to implement satisfactory functional programming languages [Tur84]. Consequently, as part of the process of arguing that the explication of "combinator" proposed above is reasonable, we need to show that the negative result of the preceding paragraph does not make such an analysis impossible. This will now be done.

Since S, K, and I are also interesting and important, it would be nice to show that it is possible to use combinators to analyze binding by means of an argument in which S, K, and I play a central role. Bearing this in mind, we begin by reminding ourselves why $\{S_1, K_1\}$ generates every ordinary term.

First, we have $S_1 K_1 K_1$ red $\lambda z \cdot K_1 z(K_1 z)$ red I. Now, where X is built up from variables, constants and combinators by means of application, define $\langle\!\langle x \rangle\!\rangle_1 \cdot X$ as follows [CF58, algorithm (abcf), p. 193]:

(a) $\langle\!\langle x \rangle\!\rangle_1 \cdot X = K_1 X$, if $x \notin FV\ X$,

(b) $\langle\!\langle x\rangle\!\rangle_1 \cdot x = I$,

(c) $\langle\!\langle x\rangle\!\rangle_1 \cdot Xx = X$, if $x \notin FV\ X$, and

(f) $\langle\!\langle x\rangle\!\rangle_1 \cdot XY = S_1(\langle\!\langle x\rangle\!\rangle_1 \cdot X)(\langle\!\langle x\rangle\!\rangle_1 \cdot Y)$, if $Y \neq x$ or $x \in FV\ X$.

Let $\langle\!\langle x\rangle\!\rangle \cdot X$ be defined similarly, but using S and K in place of S_1 and K_1. Also, let $\langle x\rangle_1 \cdot X = (\langle\!\langle x\rangle\!\rangle_1 \cdot X)x$, and let $\langle x\rangle \cdot X = (\langle\!\langle x\rangle\!\rangle \cdot X)x$.

It is easy to show that if X is built up from variables, constants, and combinators by means of application, then $FV\ \langle\!\langle x\rangle\!\rangle \cdot X = (FV\ X) - \{x\}$ and $\langle x\rangle \cdot X\ red\ X$. A *fortiori*, the same thing is true for x, $\langle\!\langle x\rangle\!\rangle_1 \cdot X$ and $\langle x\rangle_1 \cdot X$, since only the definitions of $\langle\!\langle x\rangle\!\rangle \cdot X$ and $\langle x\rangle \cdot X$ and (S), (K), and (I) need to be used in the induction on construction of terms which proves the preceding statement.

Now let $A = \lambda x \cdot \lambda y \cdot xy$. Note that $A(SKK)\ red\ I$. Also, where X is built up from variables, constants, and combinators, we have $\lambda x \cdot X\ conv\ \lambda x \cdot \langle x\rangle \cdot X = \lambda x \cdot (\langle\!\langle x\rangle\!\rangle \cdot X)x\ conv\ (\lambda y \cdot \lambda x \cdot yx)\langle\!\langle x\rangle\!\rangle \cdot X = A\langle\!\langle x\rangle\!\rangle \cdot X$, and, similarly, $\lambda x \cdot X\ conv\ A\langle\!\langle x\rangle\!\rangle_1 \cdot X$.

Let $[x] \cdot X = A\langle\!\langle x\rangle\!\rangle \cdot X$, and let $[x]_1 \cdot X = A\langle\!\langle x\rangle\!\rangle_1 \cdot X$. Using this definition of univariate bracket abstraction, we can easily show that $\{A, S, K\}$ and $\{A, S_1, K_1\}$ generate all ordinary terms. We also have $\lambda x \cdot \lambda y \cdot xy\ conv\ S_1(S_1(K_1S_1)(S_1(K_1K_1)I))(K_1I)$. Since $\{S_1, K_1\}$ generates I, it follows that $\{S_1, K_1\}$ generates every ordinary term.

So far, so good. We have established the familiar result that $\{S_1, K_1\}$ generates every ordinary term and, at almost no extra cost, have shown that $\{A, S, K\}$ also does the job. Along the way, a sufficient explanation for our interest in S, K, and I has been given. It remains to show that some reasonable set of combinators generates all terms. This will be done by replacing A by a set of combinators which can be described in a simple, uniform way and then generalizing the definition of bracket abstraction to multivariate bracket abstraction.

An *applicator* is a combinator of the form $\lambda x \cdot \lambda\iota \cdot x\ \$\ \iota$, where x does not occur in ι and the length of ι is at least 1. Let $\mathcal{A}$ be the set of applicators and, for $i \geq 1$, let A_i be the applicator $\lambda x \cdot \lambda\iota \cdot x\ \$\ \iota$ such that the length of ι is i. (So, for example, $A = A_1$.) We will show that $\mathcal{A} \cup \{S, K\}$ generates every term.

First, we note that we can choose bindings in such a way that every term in the range of the abstraction operation has the form $\lambda\iota \cdot X$. This is so because an induction based on *Complex* can be used to show that if neither x nor x' is a member of $(FV\ X) - (Vr\ \sigma_1)$, then $\lambda\sigma\ x\ \sigma^\dagger \cdot X = \lambda\sigma\ x'\ \sigma^\dagger \cdot X$.

Now, where X is a term built up from variables, constants, and combinators by means of application and $\langle\!\langle x\rangle\!\rangle \cdot X$ is defined in the way specified above, define $\langle\sigma\rangle \cdot X$ by: (1) $\langle\sigma\rangle \cdot X = X$, if σ is empty, and (2) $\langle\sigma\rangle \cdot X = (\langle\sigma_1\rangle \cdot \langle\!\langle x\rangle\!\rangle \cdot X)x$, if $\sigma = \sigma_1\ x$.

Thus, $\langle\sigma\rangle \cdot X$ will have the form $X'\ \$\ \sigma$, where no variable of σ is free in X' and $X'\ \$\ \sigma\ red\ X$. Let $\langle\!\langle\sigma\rangle\!\rangle \cdot X$ be the X' in question, and define: (1) $[\sigma] \cdot X = X$, if σ is empty, and (2) $[\sigma] \cdot X = A_i\langle\!\langle\iota\rangle\!\rangle \cdot X$, where $\lambda\sigma \cdot X = \lambda\iota \cdot X$ and the length of ι is i, if σ is not empty.

Clearly, we have $[\sigma] \cdot X\ conv\ \lambda\sigma \cdot X$, for terms X built up from variables, constants, and combinators by means of application, so an induction on construction of terms will show that $\mathcal{A} \cup \{S, K\}$ generates every multivariate lambda term (*cf.* the definition of *Bracket* , below).

8. An algebraic treatment of conversion

Definitions of bracket abstraction which operate on many variables at the same time are also considered in [Cur33] and [Abd76], but these papers provide no information relating the defined abstraction and the lambda operator. The preceding account of bracket abstraction certainly provides such information, but, since it is given by making direct use of the multivariate lambda calculus, it remains to recast this account of bracket abstraction in the form of a Curry-style theory of combinators. We show how to do so.

Let *CONV* be the smallest relation on terms built up from applicators, S, K, variables, and constants by means of application which satisfies the following conditions: $[\rho]$ X *CONV* X, $[\sigma]$ X *CONV* Y $\Rightarrow$ Y *CONV* X, $[\tau]$ X *CONV* Y & Y *CONV* Z $\Rightarrow$ X *CONV* Z, $[\mu]$ X *CONV* Y $\Rightarrow$ ZX *CONV* ZY, $[\nu]$ X *CONV* Y $\Rightarrow$ XZ *CONV* YZ, $[S]$ $SXYZ$ *CONV* $XZ(YZ)$, $[K]$ KXY *CONV* X, $[A_n]$ for $n \geq 1$, $[A_n\ 1]$ $A_n XY_1 \ldots Y_n$ *CONV* $XY_1 \ldots Y_n$, $[A_n\ 2]$ AA_n *CONV* A_n, and $[A_n\ 3]$ $Xy_1 \ldots y_n$ *CONV* $Yy_1 \ldots y_n$ $\Rightarrow$ $A_n X$ *CONV* $A_n Y$ provided $y_1, \ldots, y_n$ are distinct and not free in X and Y, $[A_3 S]$ $A_3 S$ *CONV* S, and $[A_2 K]$ $A_2 K$ *CONV* K.

Note that the foregoing definition of *CONV* does not involve λ — as far as the definition is concerned, we can consider S, K, and the applicators to be structureless constants.

It is easy to show that the postulates used to define *CONV* hold for *conv*. Consequently, if X *CONV* Y, then X *conv* Y. We sketch a proof that, for X and Y in the field of *CONV*, the converse holds.

For arbitrary multivariate lambda terms, define *Bracket* by:

(1)   *Bracket* $\nu = \nu$,
(2)   *Bracket* $XY = ($ *Bracket* $X)($ *Bracket* $Y)$, and
(3)   *Bracket* $\lambda\sigma \cdot X = [\sigma] \cdot$ *Bracket* X.

First, we will show that if X *conv* Y, then *Bracket* X *CONV* *Bracket* Y. Then we will show that, for X in the field of *CONV*, *Bracket* X *CONV* X.

Until further notice, it is assumed that all terms being discussed are in the field of *CONV*.

Postulates $[\rho]$ through $[\tau]$ assert that *CONV* is an equivalence relation, and $[\mu]$ and $[\nu]$ provide the expected replacement properties. Taken together with $[S]$ and $[K]$, this will allow us to show that $(\langle\!\langle\sigma\rangle\!\rangle \cdot X)\ \$\ \tau$ *CONV* *Sub* $[\tau/\sigma/X]$, provided σ and τ are the same length. Given this and $[A_n\ 1]$, it follows that, for such sequences, we will also have $([\sigma] \cdot X)\ \$\ \tau$ *CONV* *Sub* $[\tau/\sigma/X]$.

The methods of [HS86, Chapter 2] can be used to show: $\langle\!\langle \mathbf{a} \rangle\!\rangle$ if ι and ι' are the same length and no component of ι' is free in X, then $\langle\!\langle\iota\rangle\!\rangle \cdot X = \langle\!\langle\iota'\rangle\!\rangle \cdot$ *Sub* $[\iota'/\iota/X]$, and $\langle\!\langle \mathbf{b} \rangle\!\rangle$ if τ and σ are the same length and the variables occuring in ι are neither components of σ nor free in any component of τ, then $Sub\ [\tau/\sigma/\langle\!\langle\iota\rangle\!\rangle \cdot X] = \langle\!\langle\iota\rangle\!\rangle \cdot Sub\ [\tau/\sigma/X]$.

Clearly, bracket abstraction will inherit these properties, which gives us: **[a]** if ι and ι' are the same length and no component of ι' is free in X, then $[\iota] \cdot X = [\iota'] \cdot Sub\ [\iota'/\iota/X]$, and **[b]** if τ and σ are the same length and the variables occuring in ι are neither components of σ nor free in any component of τ, then $Sub\ [\tau/\sigma/[\iota] \cdot X] = [\iota] \cdot Sub\ [\tau/\sigma/X]$.

Given $[\rho]$ through $[\tau]$, $[\mu]$, $[\nu]$, $[S]$, and $[K]$, we can also show that $X\ CONV\ \langle\iota\rangle \cdot X$. It follows that if $X\ CONV\ Y$, then $\langle\iota\rangle \cdot X\ CONV\ \langle\iota\rangle \cdot Y$. Also, $\langle\iota\rangle \cdot X = (\langle\!\langle\iota\rangle\!\rangle \cdot X)\ \$\iota$, and $\langle\iota\rangle \cdot Y = (\langle\!\langle\iota\rangle\!\rangle \cdot Y)\ \$\ \iota$. Consequently, by $[A_n\ 3]$ and the definition of bracket abstraction, we have: **[c]** $X\ CONV\ Y \Rightarrow [\sigma] \cdot X\ CONV\ [\sigma] \cdot Y$.

Now consider arbitrary X and Y. It follows from the foregoing that if $X\ conv\ Y$, then $Bracket\ X\ CONV\ Bracket\ Y$.

In order to prove that $Bracket\ X\ CONV\ X$, for X in the field of $CONV$, it will suffice to show that: **[d]** $[x] \cdot [y_1\ \ldots\ y_n] \cdot xy_1\ \ldots\ y_n\ CONV\ A_n$, **[e]** $[xyx] \cdot xz(yz)\ CONV\ S$, and **[f]** $[xy] \cdot x\ CONV\ K$.

We have $[x] \cdot [y_1\ \ldots\ y_n] \cdot xy_1\ \ldots\ y_n = AA_n$, $[xyz] \cdot xz(yz) = A_3 S$, and $[xy] \cdot x = A_2 K$, so **[d]**–**[f]** follow from $[A_n\ 2]$, $[A_3 S]$, and $[A_2 K]$.

This completes the proof of the second lemma and, therewith, the argument that, for X and Y in the field of $CONV$, if $X\ conv\ Y$, then $X\ CONV\ Y$. Thus, we have shown that, for such X and Y, $X\ conv\ Y$ if, and only if, $X\ CONV\ Y$.

Due to the form of $[A_n\ 3]$, the preceding argument is not quite enough to justify the claim that an algebraic treatment of conversion has been given. We tie up this loose end by showing how to replace $[A_n\ 3]$ with an infinite set of postulates of the form $X\ CONV\ Y$, where X and Y are closed.

To begin with, note that $[A_n\ 3]$ is a special case of **[c]**. Define $[\sigma\ x]^* \cdot X$ by: (1) σ is empty $\Rightarrow [\sigma]^* \cdot X = X$ and (2) $[\sigma\ x]^* \cdot X = [\sigma]^* \cdot [x] \cdot X$.

Now consider the postulate: **[c^{++}]** $X\ CONV\ Y \Rightarrow [\iota']^* \cdot [\iota] \cdot X\ CONV\ [\iota']^* \cdot [\iota] \cdot Y$, provided $(FV\ X) \cup (FV\ Y) \subseteq (Vr\ \iota') \cup (Vr\ \iota)$.

We will show that **[c]** can be derived from the set of postulates obtained replacing $[A_n\ 3]$ with **[c^{++}]**, and then we will show that, in turn, **[c^{++}]** can be replaced by: **[c$^+$]** $[\iota']^* \cdot [\iota] \cdot X\ CONV\ [\iota']^* \cdot [\iota] \cdot Y$, provided $X\ CONV\ Y$ is an instance of $[S]$, $[K]$, or $[A_n\ 1]$, ι' and ι have no components in common, and $(FV\ X) \cup (FV\ Y) \subseteq (Vr\ \iota') \cup (Vr\ \iota)$, and **[g]** $([x] \cdot [y] \cdot [\iota']^* \cdot [\iota] \cdot x\ \$\ \iota'\ \$\ \iota\ (y\ \$\ \iota'\ \$\ \iota))([\iota']^* \cdot [\iota] \cdot X)([\iota']^* \cdot [\iota] \cdot Y)\ CONV\ [\iota']^* \cdot [\iota] \cdot XY$, provided ι' and ι have neither x nor y as components and have no components in common, and $(FV\ X) \cup (FV\ Y) \subseteq (Vr\ \iota') \cup (Vr\ \iota)$.

In order to show that **[c^{++}]** yields **[c]**, we first observe that $[A_n\ 3]$ is not needed in proving $([\sigma] \cdot X)\ \$\tau\ CONV\ Sub\ [\tau/\sigma/X]$. Consider X and Y such that $X\ CONV\ Y$, choose ι so that $[\iota] \cdot X = [\sigma] \cdot X$ and $[\iota] \cdot Y = [\sigma] \cdot Y$, and let $Vr\ \iota' = ((FV\ X) \cup (FV\ Y)) - (Vr\ \iota)$. By **[c^{++}]**, we have $[\iota']^* \cdot [\iota] \cdot X\ CONV\ [\iota']^* \cdot [\iota] \cdot Y$, so $([\iota']^* \cdot [\iota] \cdot X)\ \$\ \iota'\ CONV\ ([\iota']^* \cdot [\iota] \cdot Y)\ \$\ \iota'$ follows *via* $[\nu]$.

Using the remark at the beginning of the preceding paragraph, the way ι was chosen, $[\sigma]$, and $[\tau]$, we obtain $[\sigma] \cdot X = [\iota] \cdot X = Sub\,[\iota'/\iota'/[\iota] \cdot X]$ $CONV\,Sub\,[\iota'/\iota'/[\iota] \cdot Y] = [\iota] \cdot Y = [\sigma] \cdot Y$, as required.

Now consider the problem of deriving $[\mathbf{c}^{++}]$ from $[\mathbf{c}^{+}]$ and $[\mathbf{g}]$. Since imposing the condition that ι' and ι have no components in common does not weaken $[\mathbf{c}^{++}]$, it suffices to establish this modified form of $[\mathbf{c}^{++}]$. Also, although $[\mathbf{c}^{+}]$ has only been postulated for instances of $[S]$, $[K]$, and $[A_n\ 1]$, $[\mu]$ can be used to extend $[\mathbf{c}^{++}]$ to $[A_n\ 2]$, $[A_3S]$, and $[A_2K]$, because all terms involved in these postulates are closed. Since instances of $[\mathbf{c}^{+}]$ and $[\mathbf{g}]$ do not involve terms containing free variables, it follows that, in fact, if $X\,CONV\,Y$ can be derived from $[S]$, $[K]$, $[A_n\ 1]$, $[A_n\ 2]$, $[\mathbf{c}^{+}]$, $[\mathbf{g}]$, $[A_3S]$, and $[A_2K]$ by means of $[\mathbf{c}^{++}]$, then $X\,CONV\,Y$ can be derived from these postulates by means of $[\mu]$.

In order to complete the derivation of $[\mathbf{c}^{++}]$ from $[\mathbf{c}^{+}]$ and $[\mathbf{g}]$, we must show that the modified version of $[\mathbf{c}^{++}]$ also holds if $X\,CONV\,Y$ is derived from $[S]$, $[K]$, $[A_n\ 1]$, $[A_n\ 2]$, $[\mathbf{c}^{+}]$, $[\mathbf{g}]$, $[A_3S]$, and $[A_2K]$ by means of one of $[\rho]$ through $[\nu]$. We may assume inductively that the version of $[\mathbf{c}^{++}]$ in question applies to the conversion statements involved in the antecedents of $[\sigma]$ through $[\nu]$.

Clearly, an instance of $[\rho]$ or $[\sigma]$ will be transformed into an instance of the same postulate by applying $[\mathbf{c}^{++}]$ to all conversion statements involved in the instance. Given the inductive hypothesis, this suffices to finish the argument in these cases.

Suppose we are dealing with an instance of $[\tau]$, where $X\,CONV\,Y$ and $Y\,CONV\,Z$ are the conversion statements of the antecedent and $X\,CONV\,Z$ is the consequent. Let the consequent of the instance of $[\mathbf{c}^{++}]$ under consideration be $[\iota']^* \cdot [\iota] \cdot X\ \ CONV\ [\iota']^* \cdot [\iota] \cdot Z$, and let $Vr\ \iota'' = FV\,[\iota']^* \cdot [\iota] \cdot Y$. The inductive hypothesis yields $[\iota''\ \iota']^* \cdot [\iota] \cdot X\ \ CONV\ [\iota''\ \iota']^* \cdot [\iota] \cdot Y$, and $[\iota''\ \iota']^* \cdot [\iota] \cdot Y\ CONV\ [\iota''\ \iota']^* \cdot [\iota] \cdot Z$, so $[\tau]$ leads to $[\iota''\ \iota']^* \cdot [\iota] \cdot X\ \ CONV\ [\iota''\ \iota']^* \cdot [\iota] \cdot Z$. We can use $[\nu]$ to derive $([\iota''\ \iota']^* \cdot [\iota] \cdot X)\ \$\ \iota''\ \ CONV\ ([\iota''\ \iota']^* \cdot [\iota] \cdot Z)\ \$\ \iota''$.

Since $[A_n\ 3]$ is not needed in proving that $([\sigma] \cdot X)\ \$\tau\ CONV\,Sub\,[\tau/\sigma/X]$, the desired conclusion follows.

This leaves us $[\mu]$ and $[\nu]$ to deal with. We treat $[\nu]$.

Let $X\,CONV\,Y\ \Rightarrow\ XZ\ \ CONV\,YZ$ be the given instance of $[\nu]$, and let $[\iota']^* \cdot [\iota] \cdot XZ\ \ CONV\ [\iota']^* \cdot [\iota] \cdot YZ$ be the conversion statement we must derive. The inductive hypothesis gives us $[\iota']^* \cdot [\iota] \cdot X\ \ CONV\ [\iota']^* \cdot [\iota] \cdot Y$, so $[\mu]$, $[\rho]$, and $[\nu]$ yield $([x] \cdot [y] \cdot [\iota']^* \cdot [\iota] \cdot x\ \$\ \iota'\ \$\ \iota\ (y\ \$\ \iota'\ \$\ \iota))([\iota']^* \cdot [\iota] \cdot X)([\iota']^* \cdot [\iota] \cdot Z)$ $CONV\ ([x] \cdot [y] \cdot [\iota']^* \cdot [\iota] \cdot x\ \$\ \iota'\ \$\ \iota(y\ \$\ \iota'\ \$\ \iota))([\iota']^* \cdot [\iota] \cdot Y)([\iota']^* \cdot [\iota] \cdot Z)$, where ι and ι' have neither x nor y as components. The desired conversion statement follows from $[\mathbf{g}]$, $[\sigma]$, and $[\tau]$.

The argument that $[\mathbf{c}^{+}]$ and $[\mathbf{g}]$ suffice as substitutes for $[A_n\ 3]$ is now complete. And since it is easy to show that $[\mathbf{c}^{+}]$ and $[\mathbf{g}]$ hold for our original postulate system, given the equivalence result for $conv$ and $CONV$, it follows that this change of postulates does not alter $CONV$.

The developments of Sections 5 through 8 are enough to show that the explication of "combinator" proposed in Section 6 is both reasonable and illuminating. From now on, we take the explication for granted and consider other interesting properties of the multivariate lambda calculus.

9. FIXED–POINT COMBINATORS

A *fixed-point combinator* is a combinator F such that for all X, FX *conv* $X(FX)$. If we think of terms as representing functions, a fixed-point combinator represents a function which maps arbitrary functions of the sort represented by terms to fixed-points thereof.

There are ordinary terms which are fixed-point combinators. Consider, for example, *Turing's combinator* [Tur37] $T = (\lambda x \cdot \lambda y \cdot y(xxy))(\lambda x \cdot \lambda y \cdot y(xxy))$. Turing's combinator is a fixed-point combinator. In fact, we have: $(\lambda x \cdot \lambda y \cdot y(xxy))$ $(\lambda x \cdot \lambda y \cdot y(xxy))$ *red* $\lambda y \cdot y((\lambda x \cdot \lambda y \cdot y(xxy))(\lambda x \cdot \lambda y \cdot y(xxy))y)$. Consequently, TX *red* $(\lambda y \cdot y(Ty))X$ *red* $X(TX)$.

The existence of ordinary terms which are fixed-point combinators is noteworthy for two reasons. First, if we think of terms as representing functions, it follows that, within the classes of functions considered, there exist functions which uniformly crank out fixed-points, for each function in such a class. This feature of the ordinary lambda calculus prevented formal semantical understanding of that calculus until Dana Scott taught us how to accomodate it. Second, fixed-point combinators can be used in a very natural way in proving that the recursive functions are representable in the ordinary lambda calculus [Bar84, pp. 127–134]. (According to [CHS72, p. 225], the use of fixed-point combinators to treat primitive recursion originated in [Ros50].)

The version of Scott's methods developed in [Mey82] will be modified to cover the multivariate lambda calculus in Section 11. The present order of business is to point out a difference in the behavior of fixed-point combinators available in the multivariate lambda calculus and fixed-point combinators available in the ordinary lambda calculus. We also discuss briefly how this difference allows us to represent the recursive functions, using fixed-point combinators, in a much more pleasant way than is possible in the ordinary lambda calculus.

Neither T nor any other ordinary term which is a fixed-point combinator has a normal form. To see this, suppose, for *reductio*, that X is an ordinary lambda term which is both normal and a fixed-point combinator. Since X is a fixed-point combinator, Xx *conv* $x(Xx)$. By the Church-Rosser theorem, there is a Z such that Xx *red* Z and $x(Xx)$ *red* Z, and such a Z must have the form xZ_1. Evidently, $Z \neq Xx$, so, since X is closed and normal, it follows that X has the form $\lambda x \cdot X_1$, where X_1 is normal. Consequently, $Z = X_1$, and $x(Xx)$ *red* X_1. But we also have $x(Xx) = x((\lambda x \cdot X_1)x)$ *red* xX_1, where xX_1 is normal. Since $x(Xx) \neq X_1 = Z$ and xX_1 is the only term other than itself to which $x(Xx)$ reduces, we must have $Z = xX_1$. This is impossible, since we have already deduced $Z = X_1$.

In contrast with this, there are normal fixed-point combinators in the multivariate lambda calculus. Define: $T_2 = (\lambda xy \cdot y(xxy))(\lambda xy \cdot y(xxy))$. Clearly, T_2 is normal, and T_2X contracts to *Sub* $[(\lambda xy \cdot y(xxy))\ X/x\ y/y(xxy)]$, which is $X(T_2X)$. Hence, T_2 is a normal fixed-point combinator.

[Pot87] shows how to modify the proof of [Bar84, pp. 127–134] so as to produce a representation of the general recursive functions in the multivariate lambda calculus which uses a fixed-point combinator but, nevertheless, represents the functions by means of normalizable terms. (Another modification of essentially the same proof which yields ordinary normal terms representing the functions is given in [Bar76, pp. 241–242]. But, of course, fixed-point combinators are not used in the modified proof.) Before proceeding witn the rest of the present paper, we pause to explain why this representation is interesting.

We need not (and do not) claim that terms without normal forms are meaningless, or anything of the sort, in order to prefer a representation which uses only normalizable terms. The advantage is practical — terms which have normal forms are easier to deal with computationally than those that do not.

Furthermore, it is not news that a representation which proceeds by means of normalizable terms can be given. One can produce normal terms representing the recursive functions by working in the λI-calculus [Kle36], and, as was noted above, a λK-representation which uses normal terms is given in [Bar76]. What *is* news is that in the multivariate lambda calculus, one can give a representation of this kind which makes use of fixed-point combinators. Since fixed-point combinators provide a very elegant and satisfying way of handling recursion and minimization, this is a plus for the multivariate lambda calculus.

10. The Rejection of η-conversion

What has been said since Section 5 is enough to make it clear that the multivariate lambda calculus is, in some ways, quite different from the ordinary lambda calculus. Furthermore, the differences we have surveyed are interesting and useful. We now note one more — the distinction between multivariate binding and iterated univariate bindings, on which all this depends, is *incompatible* with η-conversion.

To see this, suppose we were to postulate that $\lambda x \cdot Xx$ converts to X, provided x is not free in X, and let λ^* indicate iterated univariate bindings (where, for the sake of uniformity, we define $\lambda^* \langle \rangle \cdot X = X$). Where $\lambda \sigma \cdot X = \lambda \iota \cdot X'$, we have: $\lambda^* \sigma \cdot X \ conv_\beta \lambda^* \iota \cdot (\lambda \iota \cdot X') \ \$ \ \iota$. The new postulate would also give us: $\lambda \sigma \cdot X \ conv \ \lambda^* \iota \cdot (\lambda \iota \cdot X') \ \$ \ \iota$. Together, these yield: $\lambda \sigma \cdot X \ conv \ \lambda^* \sigma \cdot X$. Thus, the distinction we have been trading on collapses.

Note also that extending the multivariate lambda calculus by simply postulating η-reduction would produce a calculus which does not have the Church-Rossser property — $A = \lambda^* xy \cdot xy$ would convert to $\lambda xy \cdot xy$, but A would reduce only to itself and I, while $\lambda xy \cdot xy$ would be normal.

This could be "fixed" by postulating that $\lambda x \ y \ \sigma \cdot X$ reduces to $\lambda x \cdot \lambda y \ \sigma \cdot X$, which, in effect, is what we have been doing ever since Church began thinking about lambda terms. Of course, there is good reason to assume this if we want to deal with η-reduction and η-conversion, but, as we have seen, simply introducing the contraction mentioned in the preceding sentence destroys much that is of interest. We will now argue that this destruction is profitless by showing how to modify the semantical treatment of the ordinary $\lambda \beta$-calculus given in [Mey82] to fit the multivariate lambda calculus. In order to simplify the discussion, we assume that C is empty.

11. What a Model of the Multivariate Lambda Calculus Is

We begin by rehearsing how to use certain retracts as environment models of the ordinary lambda calculus.

Described concretely, a *retract* is a quadruple $(D, [D \to D], r, i)$ such that:

(1) D is a set,
(2) $[D \to D] \subseteq D^D$,
(3) $r : D \to [D \to D]$,
(4) $i : [D \to D] \to D$, and
(5) $\forall f \in [D \to D], (r \circ i)f = f$.

Given a retract $\mathcal{R} = (D, [D \to D], r, i)$, we explain application as the binary operation $\bullet$ defined for $d, d_1 \in D$ by: $d \bullet d_1 = (rd)d_1$.

An $\mathcal{R}$-*valuation* is a mapping from $\mathcal{V}$ into D. We specify that $\mathcal{R}$ is an *ordinary environment model* if, and only if, D is non-empty and, for every ordinary X and every $\mathcal{R}$-valuation V, the function *Eval*, defined as follows, has a value.

CASE 1: X is a variable: Then *Eval* $\mathcal{R} \, XV = VX$.
CASE 2: $X = YZ$: Then *Eval* $\mathcal{R} \, XV = (\, Eval \, \mathcal{R} \, YV) \bullet (\, Eval \, \mathcal{R} \, ZV)$.
CASE 3: $X = \lambda x \cdot Y$: Let f be defined for $d \in D$ by $fd = \, Eval \, \mathcal{R} \, YV[d/x]$, where $V[d/x]$ is the valuation obtained from V by setting $(V[d/x])x = d$. Then *Eval* $\mathcal{R} \, XV = if$.

Some remarks about the intuitive background of these definitions are in order, before generalizing this account of ordinary environment models to provide environment models for the multivariate lambda calculus.

First, note that clause (5) of the definition of retracts implies that i is an injection and r is a surjection. So, on the one hand, r allows us to view each object in D as a way of representing a function from D to D, and this representation exhausts $[D \to D]$. And, on the other, i specifies which object in D is the canonical representation of a member of $[D \to D]$. Given this way of looking at things, the definition of *Eval* is quite natural and so is the requirement that, in a model, *Eval* must always have a value — this closure condition amounts to saying that we can always interpret abstraction, which, after all, is the aim of the enterprise.

Now consider the problem of generalizing the concept of an ordinary environment model to the multivariate lambda calculus. Clearly, what we need to do is introduce a way of viewing members of D as functions from D^n into D $(n \geq 1)$ and choose canonical representatives of such functions in a fashion which does *not* compel us to use the same object as the value of $\lambda x \cdot \lambda \sigma \cdot X$ and $\lambda x \cdot (\lambda x \, \sigma \cdot X)x$. (We must be able to avoid such an identification of values, because, for example, both $\lambda x \cdot \lambda y \cdot x$ and $\lambda x \cdot (\lambda xy \cdot x)x$ are normal.)

Given a retract $\mathcal{R} = (D, [D \to D], r, i)$, we can achieve the first goal of the preceding paragraph by means of the following definitions. For $d \in D$ and $\delta = (d_1, \ldots, d_n) \in D^n$ $(n \geq 1)$, define $d \odot \delta$ by:

(1) $n = 1 \Rightarrow d \odot \delta = d \bullet d_1$ and
(2) $n > 1 \Rightarrow d \odot \delta = (d \odot (d_1, \ldots, d_{n-1})) \bullet d_n$.

Also, let:

(1) $f_d^n = \{(\delta, d \odot \delta) | \delta \in D^n\}$,

(2) $[D^n \to D] = \{f_d^n | d \in D\}$, and

(3) $r^n d = f_d^n$.

Then, for every $n \geq 1$ and every $d \in D$, r^n specifies which member of $[D^n \to D]$ is represented by d, and this representation exhausts $[D^n \to D]$.

A *frame* is a quadruple $(D, \{[D^n \to D]\}_{n \geq 1}, \{r^n\}_{n \geq 1}, \{i^n\}_{n \geq 1})$ satisfying: (1) $\mathcal{R} = (D, [D^1 \to D], r^1, i^1)$ is a retract, $D \neq \emptyset$, and no member of D is an ordered pair, and (2) for $n > 1$, (a) $[D^n \to D]$ and r^n are the function spaces and mappings defined from $\mathcal{R}$ in the manner of the preceding paragraph, (b) $i^n : [D^n \to D] \to D$, and (c) $\forall f \in [D^n \to D]$ $(r^n \circ i^n)f = f$.

As usual, we consider n-tuples to be built up by nesting pairs, so it follows that the function spaces of a frame are all disjoint. Let us also take it that the nesting used in building n-tuples associates to the right and define $f @ d_1$, for $f \in [D^n \to D]$ and $d_1 \in D$, as follows: (1) $n = 1 \Rightarrow f @ d_1 = fd_1$ and (2) $n > 1 \Rightarrow f @ d_1 = \{(\delta, f(d_1, \delta)) | \delta \in D^{n-1}\}$.

For $n > 1$, we will have $r^{n-1}(d \bullet d_1) = (r^n d) @ d_1$, so, as far as application is concerned, we are dealing with a version of the usual notion of currying. On the other hand, since we have not stipulated that, for $n > 1$ and $f \in [D^n \to D]$, $(i^n f) \bullet d_1 = i^{n-1}(f @ d_1)$, we will not be compelled to give $\lambda x \cdot \lambda \sigma \cdot X$ and $\lambda x \cdot (\lambda x \ \sigma \cdot X)x$ the same value in those frames which will count as environment models.

Generalizing the foregoing definition of ordinary environment models, we specify that a frame $\mathcal{F}$ is an *environment model* if, and only if, for every X and every $\mathcal{F}$-valuation V, the following definition furnishes a value for *Eval*. (Of course, as above, an *$\mathcal{F}$-valuation* is a mapping from $\mathcal{V}$ into D.)

Case 1 X is a variable: Then $Eval\, \mathcal{F} X V = V X$.

Case 2 $X = YZ$: Then $Eval\, \mathcal{F} X V = (\, Eval\, \mathcal{F} Y V) \bullet (\, Eval\, \mathcal{F} Z V)$.

Case 3 $X = \lambda \sigma \cdot Y$: There are two subcases.

Case 3.1 $X = \lambda \cdot Y$: Then $Eval\, \mathcal{F} X V = Eval\, \mathcal{F} Y V$.

Case 3.2 $X = \lambda x_1 \ \ldots \ x_n \cdot Y$, where $n \geq 1$: Given $d_1, \ldots, d_n \in D$, let $V[d_1 \ \ldots \ d_n / x_1 \ \ldots \ x_n]$ be defined by setting: $(V[d_1 \ \ldots \ d_n / x_1 \ \ldots \ x_n])x_i = d_j$, where $j = \max \{k | 1 \leq k \leq n \ \& \ x_i = x_k\}$. Also, define f for $(d_1, \ldots, d_n) \in D^n$ by: $f(d_1, \ldots, d_n) = Eval\, \mathcal{F} Y V[d_1 \ \ldots \ d_n / x_1 \ \ldots \ x_n]$. Then $Eval\, \mathcal{F} X V = i^n f$.

It is not difficult to show that if X *conv* Y, then $Eval\, \mathcal{M} X V = Eval\, \mathcal{M} Y V$, for every environment model $\mathcal{M}$ and every $\mathcal{M}$-valuation V. We indicate how to prove the converse by constructing a term model.

Let $[X] = \{Y | X \ conv \ Y\}$, and let $D_T = \{[X] | X \in T\}$. Also, let $[(X_1, \ldots, X_n)] = ([X_1], \ldots, [X_n])$, and define $r_T^n[X]$ $(n \geq 1)$ as follows: $r_T^n[X] = \{([\tau], [X \$ \tau]) | \tau \in T^n\}$.

Now let $[D_T^n \to D_T] = \{r_T^n[X] | X \in T\}$, and define i_T^n as follows, for $f = r_T^n[X]$: $i_T^n = [A_n X]$.

One can easily show that $\mathcal{M}_T = (D_T, \{[D_T^n \to D_T]\}_{n\geq 1}, \{r_T^n\}_{n\geq 1}, \{i_T^n\}_{n\geq 1})$ is an environment model. Also, where $x_0, \ldots, x_{n-1}$ $(n \geq 0)$ are the distinct free variables of X and $[X_0], \ldots, [X_{n-1}]$ are their respective values under the $\mathcal{M}_T$-valuation V, one can show: $Eval\ \mathcal{M}_T\ XV = [Sub\ [X_0 \ldots X_{n-1}/x_0 \ldots x_{n-1}/X]]$.

Consequently, where X does not convert to Y and V is the $\mathcal{M}_T$-valuation defined by $Vx = [x]$, for all x, one has $Eval\ \mathcal{M}_T\ XV = [X] \neq [Y] = Eval\ \mathcal{M}_T\ YV$. It follows that if X and Y have the same value under every valuation in every environment model, then $X\ conv\ Y$.

A *combinatory model* is a quintuple $(D, \bullet, s, k, \{a_n\}_{n\geq 1})$ which satisfies the following conditions, where $\bullet$ associates left, and the various d's involved are members of D: $[s]\ s \bullet d_1 \bullet d_2 \bullet d_3 = d_1 \bullet d_3 \bullet (d_2 \bullet d_3)$, $[k]\ k \bullet d_1 \bullet d_2 = d_1$, $[a_n]$ for $n \geq 1$, $[a_n 1]\ a_n \bullet d \bullet d_1 \bullet \ldots \bullet d_n = d \bullet d_1 \bullet \ldots \bullet d_n$, $[a_n 2]$ $a_1 \bullet a_n = a_n$, and $[a_n 3]\ \forall d_1, \ldots, d_n \in D\ d \bullet d_1 \bullet \ldots \bullet d_n = d' \bullet d_1 \bullet \ldots \bullet d_n \Rightarrow$ $a_n \bullet d = a_n \bullet d'$, $[a_3 s]\ a_3 \bullet s = s$, and $[a_2 k]\ a_2 \bullet k = k$.

In what follows, we consider only combinatory models in which no member of D is an ordered pair.

Where $\mathcal{M}$ is a combinatory model, V is an $\mathcal{M}$-valuation, and X is a term built up from S, K, applicators, and variables, define $Eval$ as follows: (1) $X = S \Rightarrow Eval\ \mathcal{M}\ XV = s$, (2) $X = K \Rightarrow Eval\ \mathcal{M}\ XV = k$, (3) $X = A_n \Rightarrow Eval\ \mathcal{M}\ XV = a_n$, (4) $X = x \Rightarrow Eval\ \mathcal{M}\ XV = Vx$, and (5) $X = YZ \Rightarrow Eval\ \mathcal{M}\ XV = (Eval\ \mathcal{M}\ YV) \bullet (Eval\ \mathcal{M}\ ZV)$.

We define $Eval$ for arbitrary terms by:

$$Eval\ \mathcal{M}\ XV = Eval\ \mathcal{M}\ (Bracket\ X)V.$$

Consider an environment model

$$\mathcal{M} = (D, \{[D^n \to D]\}_{n\geq 1}, \{r^n\}_{n\geq 1}, \{i^n\}_{n\geq 1}),$$

and, where X is closed, let $Eval\ \mathcal{M}\ X$ be the element d of D such that, for some $\mathcal{M}$-valuation V, $d = Eval\ \mathcal{M}\ XV$. The *associated combinatory model* of $\mathcal{M}$ is $(D, \bullet, Eval\ \mathcal{M}\ S, Eval\ \mathcal{M}\ K, \{Eval\ \mathcal{M}\ A_n\}_{n\geq 1})$.

Now, given a combinatory model $\mathcal{M} = (D, \bullet, s, k, \{a_n\}_{n\geq 1})$ and $d \in D$, define f_d^n from $\bullet$ as as we did in explaining what a frame is, and define $[D^n \to D]$ and r^n similarly. Let $i^n f_d^n = a_n \bullet d$.

It can be shown that $(D, \{[D^n \to D]\}_{n\geq 1}, \{r^n\}_{n\geq 1}, \{i^n\}_{n\geq 1})$ is an environment model. This environment model is the *associated environment model* of the combinatory model $\mathcal{M}$.

And, as in the treatment of [Mey82], it can also be shown that the two transformations just defined are inverses which preserve $Eval$. Thus, the notion of a combinatory model provides an analysis of the closure condition imposed on the function spaces employed in environment models by reqiring that $Eval$ have a value for every valuation in every such model.

In closing, we remark that, of course, there is a great deal more to do here. In particular, nothing has been said about how the apparatus of complete partial orderings and continuous functions might be extended to the setting provided by the sorts of models we have introduced. It remains to be seen what can be done along these lines. But it does seem fair to say that we have provided a reasonable semantics for the multivariate lambda calculus, which is sufficient for present purposes.

BIBLIOGRAPHY

[Abd76]   Abdali, S. K. (1976): "An Abstraction Algorithm for Combinatory Logic", *Journal of Symbolic Logic* 41, pp. 222–224.

[Bar76]   Barendregt, H. P. (1976): "A Global Representation of the Recursive Functions in the λ-calculus", *Theoretical Computer Science* 3, pp. 225–242.

[Bar84]   Barendregt, H. P. (1984): *The Lambda Calculus: Its Syntax and Semantics*, North-Holland Publishing Company, Amsterdam, New York, and Oxford.

[CF58]   Curry, Haskell Brooks and Feys, Robert (1958): *Combinatory Logic*, vol. 1, North-Holland Publishing Company, Amsterdam. Reprinted 1968 and 1974.

[CHS72]   Curry, Haskell Brooks and Hindley, J. Roger and Seldin, Jonathan P. (1972): *Combinatory Logic*, vol. 2, North-Holland Publishing Company, Amsterdam and London.

[Chu41]   Church, Alonzo (1941): *The Calculi of Lambda Conversion*, Princeton University Press, Princeton.

[Cur33]   Curry, Haskell Brooks (1933): "Apparent Variables from the Standpoint of Combinatory Logic", *Annals of Mathematics* 34, pp. 381-404.

[HS 86]   Hindley, J. Roger and Seldin, Jonathan P. (1986): *Introduction to Combinators and λ-calculus*, Cambridge University Press.

[Kle36]   Kleene, Stephen Cole (1936): "λ-definability and Recursiveness", *Duke Mathematical Journal* 2, pp. 340–353.

[Mey82]   Meyer, Albert R. (1982): "What is a Model of the Lambda Calculus?", *Information and Control* 52, pp. 87–122.

[Pot87]   Pottinger, Garrel (1987): "Lambda Binding without Bound Variables", *Technical Report* TR 11-4. Revised January 1988.

[Pott88a] Pottinger, Garrel (1988): "Enriched Lambda Calculi", *Odyssey Research Associates*. The first version of this document was actually written in the fall of 1985 and privately circulated.

[Pott88b] Pottinger, Garrel (1988): "Ulysses: Logical Foundations of the Definition Facility", *Technical Report* TR 11-9.

[Ros35a] Rosser, J. B. (1935): "A Mathematical Logic without Variables I", *Annals of Mathematics* 36, pp. 127-150.

[Ros35b] Rosser, J. B. (1935): "A Mathematical Logic without Variables II", *Duke Mathematical Journal* 1, pp. 328–355.

[Ros50]   Rosenbloom, P. C. (1950): *The Elements of Mathematical Logic*, New York.

[Tur37]   Turing, Alan M. (1937): "The p-function in λ-K-conversion", *Journal of Symbolic Logic* 2, p. 164.

[Tur84]   Turner, David (1984): "Combinator Reduction Machines", in *International Workshop on High-level Computer Architecture*, Department of Computer Science, University of Maryland.

STORRS McCALL

CHOICE TREES

The title of this paper comes from what is at the time of writing Nuel Belnap's most recent work, "Some concepts for choice trees" (September 1988). This is not a finished paper, more like thinking-out-loud for future writing, but it's fascinating, insightful and, in my opinion, seminal work. Its companion pieces are "Seeing to it that: a canonical form for agentives" (written jointly with Mickey Perloff, June 1988), and "Declaratives are not enough" (May 1988).

Before I launch into trees and choices, I want to say a little about Nuel. I arrived at the University of Pittsburgh in September 1963, two months after Nuel, and my office was next to his in the old Schenley Hotel, with a communicating door between. For eleven years, tolerating and even actively supporting my frequent visits to Uganda, Nuel kept me on the straight and narrow path in logic, at the same time encouraging innovative ideas. He exercised the same benign influence on the thinking of his graduate students, as the papers in this volume testify. When I first arrived in 1963, the hunt was on to find a Gentzenization of relevance logic, and not only his graduate seminars but mine too got caught up in the search. Over the years the objectives changed but the enthusiasm remained, and the arrival of Alan Anderson in 1965 made the wheel turn faster, and the lights burn brighter. Tragically, Alan's light went out in 1973, and we are all the poorer for that, but Nuel's has continued to shine ever since, as with the help of successive generations of students he has put together volume two of *Entailment.* Enough said. This paper is intended as a tribute to you, Nuel, from an old friend whose philosophical interests have run parallel to yours and who will always be indebted to you for help, stimulus and enlightenment.

Now for choice trees. What Belnap does in his thinking-aloud paper is to present a beautiful "metaphysics of choice", a metaphysics that I predict will become more and more important and interesting as philosophers discover more and more in it. Already it is rich and complex. The fundamental ideas are those of *tree* and *choice*.

A tree consists of *moments*, i.e. complete instantaneous world states, partially ordered by the relation $\leq$, denoting weak temporal precedence. Thus if $m \leq n$ we say loosely that m *precedes* or *lies in the past of* n, reserving the asymmetric relation $<$ for "properly precedes". We also say that m is a *lower bound* for n, and that n is an *upper bound* for m. Two moments m and n are *incomparable* if neither $m \leq n$ nor $n \leq m$. What distinguishes a tree from other partially ordered sets is (i) that any two moments have a common lower bound, and (ii) that incomparable moments have no common upper bound, or equivalently that any two lower bounds of a given moment must themselves be comparable.

Although his intention is to analyze the notion of "seeing to it", or "bringing it about", by the use of choice trees as semantic model structures, Belnap is apparently not averse to allowing choice trees to stand as literal metaphysical pictures of the world. Thus moments can be regarded as instantaneous space-like slices or

J. M. Dunn and A. Gupta (eds.), Truth or Consequences, 231–244.
© 1990 *Kluwer Academic Publishers. Printed in the Netherlands.*

hyperplanes in Minkowski spacetime, in which case a tree is a branched spatio-temporal structure which branches along the time axis (not along one of the spatial axes). Each branch or "history" of this structure is a complete Minkowski continuum: a maximal chain of moments. For semantic purposes, in computing truth-values, it is often convenient to resort to simpler models and treat trees as finite, or as consisting of discrete sets of moments, or to regard histories as one-dimensional. But the full metaphysical impact of Belnap's insights is realized only once his tree-models are interpreted as pictures of a concrete world of space and time, in which agents like ourselves live and make decisions.

The most interesting parts of a tree are its branch points, and Belnap devotes a fair amount of space to discussing what goes on there. Let's begin with the one-dimensional case. Depending on whether the set of moments in a tree has the order type of the integers, the rationals, or the reals, we get different varieties of branch point:

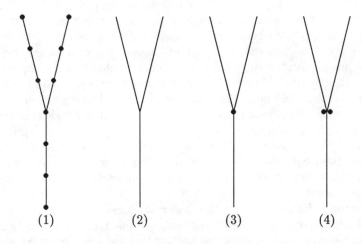

(1)   (2)   (3)   (4)

In case (1), the tree consists of discrete nodes. It can be broken down into three sets of moments, the trunk and the two branches, which have just one element in common, the branch point. ("Branch" as used here has a different meaning from "history".) In case (1), the trunk contains its own least upper bound and the branches each contain their own greatest lower bound. Belnap would call a branching or split of this kind a *jump*.

In case (2), the set of moments comprising the tree has the order type of the rational numbers. For example, the trunk might consist of all moments the time of which was less that $\sqrt{2}$, and each branch might consist of moments the time of which was greater than $\sqrt{2}$. The trunk would not contain its own least upper bound, nor would any of the branches contain their own greatest lower bound. (The lub and glb would not belong to the tree.) Belnap calls a split of this kind a *gap*.

The order type of the moments in cases (3) and (4) is that of the reals, with the consequence that the least upper bound of the trunk and the greatest lower bound of each branch all belong to the tree. What distinguishes (3) from (4) is that in the former case the trunk contains its own lub but neither branch contains its own glb, while in the latter case each branch contains its own glb but the trunk does not contain its own lub. Belnap calls a branching of type (3) a *lower cut*, and a branching of type (4) an *upper cut*. An interesting feature of case (4) is that the trunk possesses two distinct incomparable least upper bounds. This is not a contradiction, but shows we have moved from number analysis to topology.

Belnap points out that if the set of moments constituting a tree is a lower semi-lattice, meaning that any two moments not only have a lower bound, but have a greatest lower bound, then any branching of histories which are continua will automatically be of type (3) rather that type (4). Furthermore, a tree which is a lower semi-lattice has the attractive property that any two moments or elements a and b uniquely determine their meet $a \wedge b$, with the result that $a \leq b$ is definable as $a \wedge b = a$ and the tree can be regarded as a species of commutative semigroup. But, despite the temptation of such logical simplifications, Belnap rightly prefers not to assume that choice trees are lower semi-lattices, so that type (4) branching remains a possibility. The axioms characterizing the moments of a tree are therefore the following:

1. $a \leq a$
2. $(a \leq b \ \& \ b \leq c) \supset a \leq c$
3. $(a \leq b \ \& \ b \leq a) \supset a = b$
4. $(\exists c)(c \leq a \ \& \ c \leq b)$
5. $(a \leq c \ \& \ b \leq c) \supset (a \leq b \vee b \leq a)$.

If in addition the lower semi-lattice requirement is imposed, axiom 4 is replaced by the stronger axiom 6:

6. $(\exists c)(d)((d \leq a \ \& \ d \leq b) \equiv d \leq c)$.

Up to this point trees have been considered as sets of moments, or instantaneous world-states, ordered by the relation "$\leq$". But more primitively, a choice tree X may be viewed as a *topological space*, i.e. a set of space-time points, the topology of which is defined by a set U of open subsets of X. As before, the branches of X may be one-dimensional or, more realistically, four-dimensional space-time continua. It turns out that the topology of branched spaces (of which trees are just one species) is a fascinating and as yet unexplored subject.

Consider for simplicity's sake a single one-dimensional, two-branched tree, in the shape of a "Y". There exists no continuous one-one mapping of this topological space onto a straight line. A "Y" is not homeomorphic with a straight line, and (like a circle) must be treated as a distinct variety of topological space. The same goes for two and higher dimensional branched spaces, the distinctive qualities of which we shall investigate.

See Ray Douglas, *Times Arrows Today*, pp. 180, 184.
A "Y" is not locally Euclidean. At the branch point there are neighborhoods not homeomorphic with R^1, the real line.

As was stated above, the most interesting part of a branched space is the area where it branches. There are three different possibilities here, which are most easily stated if we consider a (binary) tree as a topological space X consisting of three disjoint sets of points, the trunk T and the two branches A and B. We define a *neighborhood* Nx of a point x as an open set that contains x, and a *limit point* of a set S as a point y such that every neighborhood Ny of y contains a point in S which is distinct from y. (A limit point of S may or may not be in S.) Let S' denote the set of all limit points of S. Two non-empty sets S and T are said to be *separated* if $S \cap T = S \cap T' = S' \cap T = 0$, i.e. if neither contains any limit points of the other. Finally, a set is *connected* if it is not the union of two separated sets.

Using these definitions, the three different types of branching can be described topologically. The first, which can be passed over quickly, corresponds to a "gap". Here the three sets T, A and B, comprising the trunk and the two branches, are all separated from one another, with the result that the tree is a disconnected space. The other two types, where the tree is connected, are more interesting.

In the first connected case, corresponding to a "lower cut", there is a unique branch point or set of branched points serving as the common limit point or boundary between the trunk and the two branches. If we stipulate that this branch point or boundary belongs to the trunk, we may say that the trunk is "closed at the split", while the branches are "open at the split". The second connected case is the reverse of this, with the trunk being open at the split and the two branches both being closed at the split. This case corresponds to an "upper cut", and differs from the first in that branchings of this kind lack a unique branch point or "branch surface".

In type one or lower cut branchings, where there is a branch surface, the dimensionality of the surface depends on the dimensionality of the tree. The branch surface of a one-dimensional tree is a point, of a two-dimensional tree is a line, of a three-dimensional tree is a plane, and of a four-dimensional tree is a volume. If the tree is four-dimensional and branches in time, the branch point is a space-like hyperplane, a three-dimensional instantaneous state of the world. In upper cut branchings, the trunk is open at the split and there is no unique instantaneous branch point.

It was stated above that branched spaces are topologically distinct from unbranched spaces, and in the case of upper cut branched spaces a simple, basic and purely topological characterization of this difference can be given. The same can be done for lower cut spaces, but there the differences are more complicated.

The principal difference between upper cut branched spaces and standard topological spaces is that the former are not Hausdorff spaces. Hausdorff spaces are topological spaces which satisfy a condition known as the Hausdorff separation axiom.

Hausdorff axiom: Given any two distinct points x and y of a topological space X, there exist disjoint neighborhoods Nx and Ny of x and y.

Almost all spaces studied by topologists satisfy the Hausdorff axiom, which is considered to be a relatively mild extra condition to impose on a topological space.[1]

---

[1] J.R. Munkres, *Topology*, Englewood Cliffs 1975, p. 99.

Yet the existence of two distinct incomparable limit points to the trunk of an upper cut branched space violates the Hausdorff condition:

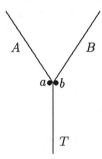

Any open set containing a contains points of T, as does any open set containing b, so that no two neighborhoods Na and Nb will be disjoint. There is, however, a weaker separation axiom due to Fréchet, known as the T_1 axiom, which upper cut spaces do satisfy:

T_1 *axiom.* Given any two distinct points x and y of X, there exists a neighborhood Nx of x such that $y \notin Nx$.

This condition is met by the points a and b in the figure above. Furthermore, the T_1 axiom is strong enough to permit the derivation of an important property of Hausdorff spaces, the fact that in them all finite point sets are closed.[2] Upper cut spaces are therefore not Hausdorff spaces, but are instead T_1-spaces.

Lower cut branched spaces, which *are* Hausdorff spaces, differ fundamentally from upper cut spaces. The differences can be brought out by examining the two spaces from the standpoint of path-connectedness.

Given a topological space X, a *path* in X from x to y is a continuous function $f : [a, b] \rightarrow X$ of some closed interval in the real line into X, such that $f(a) = x$ and $f(b) = y$. A space X is said to be *path connected* if every pair of points of X can be joined by a path in X. Now lower cut spaces and upper cut spaces are both path-connected, but with a difference. Consider a path from a point x on one branch of a one-dimensional upper cut space X to a point y on the other:

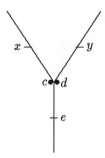

Let c and d be the greatest lower bounds of the two branches. The path from x to y cannot go directly from c to d without intermediate points, since if it did the path would be the union of two closed subsets $[x, c]$ and $[d, y]$. The only way this union could be the image under a function f of $[a, b]$ in the real line would be for the two distinct points c and d to be the images of the same real point, i.e. for there to be a $z \in [a, b]$ such that $f(z) = c$ and $f(z) = d$. But this is impossible, f being a function. Hence the path from c to d must contain intermediate points belonging to X's trunk.

Suppose the path contains all points between c and some intermediate point e. Then it must contain e itself, since if it merely contained the open interval (c, e), followed by the open interval (e, d), its inverse image under f would be the union of two open subsets U and V of the real line:

Here $f(U) = (c, e)$ and $f(V) = (e, d)$, and since the function f is continuous U and V must be open, being the inverse images of open sets. But the real line is not the union of two open sets. Hence the path from c to d must contain a point e on the trunk of the upper cut space X, the point $f^{-1}(e)$ being the common limit point of U and V. Furthermore, the path from c to e to d must traverse some points twice, meaning that a small object moving along the path would occupy the same points on two different occasions.

It would appear, therefore, that what distinguishes an upper cut space from a lower cut space, or indeed from any other topological space, is that some paths in upper cut spaces double back on themselves, forcing those who follow them to retrace their steps. The cash value of this metaphor in topology is that a "doubled path" is a continuous function of the real line, the inverse of which is not a function, whereas an "undoubled path" is a continuous one-one function. The difference between "path", "doubled path", and "undoubled path" in a space X can be summed up in the following table, where $f : [a, b] \to X$ is a function of some closed interval of the real line into X:

	f	f^{-1}
path	continuous	
doubled path	continuous	not a function
undoubled path	continuous	(continuous)

For an undoubled path, the inverse function f^{-1} may be continuous, in which case the path is homeomorphic with the real line, or it may not, but in either case f^{-1} must be a function.

Let us say that a topological space is *strongly path connected* if every pair of points in X can be joined by an undoubled path in X. Then a (one-dimensional) upper cut space UC is path connected but not strongly path connected, whereas a lower cut space LC is strongly path connected. The two dimensional analogues of these spaces, $UC \times R$ and $LC \times R$, also differ in that the union of any two branches plus the branch point in $LC \times R$ is homeomorphic with the real plane $R \times R$, whereas the (connected) union of two branches of $UC \times R$ is not. As those who have tried to press flowers between the pages of a book will appreciate, the attempt to flatten out two adjacent branches of an upper cut space always leaves a ridge, which no amount of cutting or paring can eliminate.

So far we have stressed the particular qualities of upper cut branched spaces, and shown how they differ from other topological spaces. But lower cut spaces have their own peculiarities as well, and it is possible to give a topological characterization of them which, though not based on such fundamental differences as those distinguishing upper cut spaces, nevertheless mark them off from other topological spaces in a clear way.

The central idea is this. In a lower cut branched space every path which links a point on the trunk with a point on one of the branches, or which links two points on different branches, also passes through at least one point in a given unbranched connected set; the "branch surface". The occurrence of the word "unbranched" in the previous sentence requires, in order to make the distinction between branched and unbranched spaces rigorous, that we proceed inductively, beginning with one-dimensional spaces and moving upwards.[3] That we are able to do this depends on the fact that the "branch surface" of an $n + 1$-dimensional branched space is n-dimensional.

The basis of the inductive definition of a branched toplogical space is as follows. X is a *one-dimensional binary branched space* if there exist distinct points x, y, z, and w of X such that the following holds:

(1) Every path in X which joins any two of x, y and z passes through w:

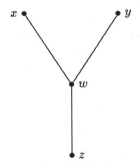

If X is unbranched, it is impossible to find four distinct points which satisfy (1).

For the induction step, replace the point w by an unbranched connected subset W of X. X is then an $n + 1$-*dimensional binary branched space* if there exist

---

[3] A concise way of defining dimensionality in topological spaces may be found under the entry "Topology" in the *McGraw-Hill Encyclopedia of Science and Technology*, vol. 18 p. 422.

distinct points x, y and z of X, and a connected, unbranched, simply connected n-dimensional subset W of X, where $x, y, z \notin W$, such that:

(2) Every path in X which joins any two of x, y and z passes through at least one member of W:

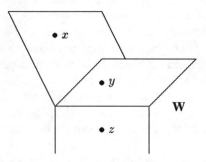

If X is unbranched, there exists no W which divides triples of distinct points in this way. However, if W itself were branched then (2) might hold even though X were unbranched:

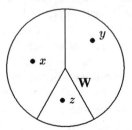

For this reason, the definition of a branched $n + 1$-dimensional space depends upon the prior definition of a branched n-dimensional space. Similarly, if W were not simply connected (a space is simply connected if any closed path in it can be continuously contracted to a point) then (2) might also hold:

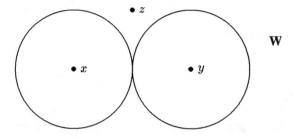

Summing up, what distinguishes a lower cut branched space from an unbranched space is the presence of a connected set of branch points which separates branches from trunk and branches from branches. In a lower cut space, trunk and branches are interchangeable in the sense that the union of any two branches plus the branch point, or the trunk and any branch, constitute a space which is homeomorphic with R, or R^2, or R^3, ... In the case of upper cut spaces, as we saw, this is not so. There the union of the trunk and any branch is the same as with a lower cut space, but the union of any two branches is either disconnected or is itself an upper cut space not homeomorphic with R, or R^2, or R^3, ... This asymmetry is pleasing to those who would like to find some objective feature in nature that distinguishes the trunk of a choice tree from its branches.

Turning now from trees to choices, Belnap states that at each moment n there is a set of choices open to each agent α, represented by a partition, choice$_\alpha(n)$, of all the n-histories (all the histories that pass through n). For a single agent a and a single moment m, there might for example be three choices open to a at m, represented diagrammatically as follows:

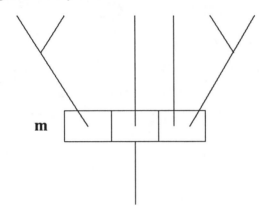

The diagram is less than perfect, since it should show both a smooth split at m and the three partitions of the m-histories, but I don't see how it can be improved on. Using the notion of choice, Belnap states his main result, which is to provide truth-conditions for statements ascribing agency. In the earlier paper, "seeing to it that: a canonical form for agentives", Belnap and Perloff propose that the canonical form of such statements should be $[\alpha \ldots p]$, where α is an agent and p is a declarative sentence. The intention is that the square-bracket sentence should be true entirely because of a choice of the agent; thus

[Belnap . . . the second volume of *Entailment* is completed]

is true entirely because of a prior choice or decision of Belnap's. English locutions which could go in place of the . . . are "brings it about that", "causes it to be the case that", "is responsible for the fact that", "takes steps in order that", "sees to it that", etc., and the authors fix on "stit" as an abbreviation for the last of these. The canonical form thus becomes $[\alpha$ stit $p]$.

The truth-conditions are as follows. Suppose we are evaluating $[\alpha$ stit $p]$ at a moment n on a history h. Then the first condition for the truth of $[\alpha$ stit $p]$ is that p be true on history h at moment n. (One would not wish "α sees to it that the boat is launched" to be true if the boat is not launched.) Secondly, there must be a prior moment m also on h where α had a choice. That is, the m-histories are partitioned by choice$_\alpha(m)$. For $[\alpha$ stit $p]$ to be true at n, the authors require that (i) every m-history which belongs to the same member of choice$_\alpha(m)$ as h must have p true at the same "level" or time as n, and (ii) p must be false on some m-history at the same level or time as n. (If $[\alpha$ stit $p]$ is true, every m-history on which p is false must of course belong to a different member of choice$_\alpha(m)$ from the member to which h belongs.) There are in short three ways in which $[\alpha$ stit $p]$ can fail to be true at n, represented diagrammatically as follows:

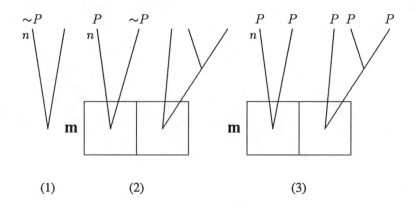

(1)   (2)   (3)

In (1), p is false at n. In (2), p is false at some m-history which belongs to the same partition as h, (so that α's choice was not efficacious in making p true). In (3), p is true on all m-histories (so that p was inevitable and α's choice added nothing). Failing all these ways of being false, $[\alpha$ stit $p]$ is true at n.

   These truth-conditions seem right. If in choosing to finesse the queen I make it inevitable that my partner and I lose the rubber, and if there were ways of winning it by not finessing the queen, then I was responsible for losing it; I saw to it (however inadvertently) that we lost. Wise parents see to it that their children are protected against measles by vaccination, meaning that with vaccination measles never occur, but without it they may. The truth-conditions are retrospective, looking back to a prior choice by the agent.

   Belnap's notion of a choice is tied to a single moment: choice$_\alpha(n)$ is a partition of all histories that pass through the moment n. But in order for an agent to be faced with a choice, the important thing is not a unique moment but a branching or splitting of histories, and as was seen earlier a split can be either a lower cut or an upper cut. If it is a lower cut then there is a unique moment — the limit point of the trunk — to serve as the n of choice$_\alpha(n)$, but if the branching is an upper cut there is no such single moment. Instead there is a multiplicity of incomparable moments -

the limit points of the different branches - and hence no way of defining the partition choice$_\alpha(n)$.

This is a difficulty, certainly, but I don't think it's an insuperable one. In addition to the concept of a moment, Belnap also defines the concept of an *instant* as a set of moments on different histories. Intuitively, an instant is the set of all moments on all histories which occur at the same time:

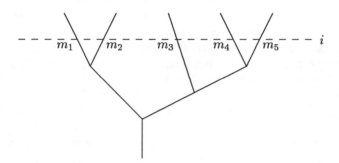

Each moment m_1-m_5 belongs to the same instant i, and the ordering of instants is identical to the ordering of the corresponding moments on each history. Using the notion of an instant, we can redefine choices as partitions of the set of histories which split off a given history at a given instant, in the following way.

Suppose h is a history, i an instant, and suppose that there is a lower cut branching of h at i, meaning that there is a unique moment $m \in h$, $m \in i$ which is the greatest lower bound of the set of histories $H(h, i)$ which branch off h at i. Now suppose that the branching of h at i is upper cut rather than lower cut. The obvious picture here is that over some open interval earlier than i the history h is unbranched, but that at i itself every history which branches off h has its separate, incomparable moment which serves as its lower bound. The set of histories of this upper cut branching is again $H(h, i)$, and an agent's choice at (h, i) can be defined as a partition of $H(h, i)$, whether the branching is a lower cut or an upper cut.

Belnap says that at each moment there is a set of choices open to each agent ("Some concepts", p. 8). But I do not think he can mean this literally. Take my own case. (Philosophers love to take themselves as examples, presumably on the principle that nothing else is better known to them.) I am sitting here writing "Choice trees", and it's true that I am making choices, and that I *stit* the right words are on the paper. Perhaps in a couple of hours I make hundreds of small decisions of this kind. But a decision *every moment*? I doubt it. A decision or a choice seems to me to be a conscious affair, and my consciousness couldn't cope with a choice every moment. Most of the time, with respect to most of the things I do, I am on "automatic pilot". My breathing, for example, is on automatic pilot, except for the rare moments when I consciously choose to take a breath. My sitting in the chair is on automatic pilot. This is not to say that I couldn't get up and walk around the room. But I don't, because with regard to sitting I'm on automatic pilot, meaning that I just keep on doing what I'm doing without thinking about it. My not getting up in these circumstances is on quite a different basis from my consciously deciding not to get up when the idea of having a cup of coffee occurs to me.

Choices and decisions, then, are for me affairs of consciousness.[4] There is no such thing as an unconscious choice. It's true that we do say things like "After sleeping on it, Peter realized that unconsciously he had chosen to remain and face the music", but such a "choice" is always subject to conscious ratification or revision. In the absence of conscious ratification not even Peter would be prepared to admit that a choice had been made. But if choices are conscious, then the number of choices made by an average agent on an average day is far from astronomical. The important question concerning choice trees is, should an agent's daily choices be fewer in number than the branchings he faces on the tree? Or should the two be the same?

Here's an argument for saying there should be more branchings than choices. I'm sitting in my chair writing, and the last thing on my mind is changing my position to lying on the floor. But despite this, there is a chance that next moment I may find myself on the floor. I may have a seizure or a stroke, or a brick may fly in through the window and knock me down. Some of these events that land me on the floor may be caused by amplification of quantum events, so that they are indeterministic and unpredictable in principle. The natural way to represent them is by indeterministic branching of histories, in which case it would appear that there should be more branchings than choices.

I'm not sure what Belnap would say about this. Probably he would say that my ending up on the floor is something that happens to me, rather than something I do. However, Belnap's model can accomodate such happenings with relatively little change. The change would allow choice trees, or more accurately "universe" trees in which the branched courses of events represent all that is physically possible, to branch in the absence of choice, and indeed in the absence of agents. In the days before the appearance of life, when choices were non-existent, there were still quantum possibilities which could be represented by branched courses of events. However, these branches would lack the partitioning into choice sets which marks the presence of an agent. If that were so, the existence of a partition of branches would constitute a formal difference between choice and non-choice situations. In the case of my sitting in my chair, there could still be branches in which a moment later I was lying on the floor, but in the absence of a partition I would not be lying there by choice.

Before I stop, there is a further possible extension of Belnap's metaphysical model of choice that I would like to mention, an extension that yields interesting results. Belnap has worked out novel and profound truth-conditions for sentences of the form [α stit p]. But perhaps we could look ahead and see what kind of analysis would be appropriate for [α decides that p], or [α chooses p]. Belnap's truth-conditions for [α stit p] are retrospective in that they appeal to a prior choice by the agent. By the time [α stit p] is a candidate for evaluation, the choice on which its truth-conditions are based has already been made. But this isn't the case

---

[4] "Decision", *Canadian Journal of Philosophy*, 17 (1987), pp .261–288.

with [α decides that p], or [α chooses p]. Here the choice is contemporaneous with the truth-conditions. To devise appropriate analyses for these locutions involves a substantial change in Belnap's choice trees, one that I would hesitate to propose were the gains in getting clear about choice and decision not potentially great.

For Belnap choice$_\alpha(n)$, or choice$_\alpha(h, i)$, is a partition of all n-histories, or of all histories that branch off from h at instant i. This breaking up of a set of histories into disjoint subsets, of which the agent chooses one, accurately represents the *range of choice* facing the agent at a moment or instant. But what feature of the metaphysical model corresponds to the *choice made by the agent*? "Range of choice", and "choice made", are two different things. How can our model accomodate both?

To begin with we must distinguish between *deciding to do something* (when that thing may lie in the future), and *implementing our decision*, i.e. acting on it. I can decide, in January, to visit Pittsburgh in March, but between decision and action many things may intervene. Something may prevent my visit, or I may die, or forget, or change my mind, or lack the firmness of purpose to actually purchase a ticket. These things I named "impedances" in my 1987 paper in the CJP. But for the moment let's ignore decisions taken beforehand and concentrate on cases where there is no temporal gap between decision and implementation. For example, walking along the street I may suddenly decide to take a bus and step into one waiting at a stop. Or I may reach out and choose a bottle of wine from among ten different labels at the liquor commission. Or I may vote "yes" at a meeting by raising my hand. In these cases, the truth-conditions of [α decides that p] or [α chooses p] require (i) that there be an instant t at which the decision or the choice is made, (ii) that at t there be two or more alternatives facing α, in at least one but not all of which p holds, and (iii) that p be true at some instant later than t.

The additional feature needed for these truth-conditions, which may be added to Belnap's model, is a feature which picks out one and only one moment on the choice tree as the actual moment. Such a device could be regarded as a little pointer, like one displayed on maps at botanical gardens and art museums for the convenience of vistors, saying "you are here". It's a way of finding where we are located on the choice tree. Given this device, or something equivalent to it, suitable truth-conditions for [α decides that p], or [α chooses p], the verbs of which are in the present tense, can be constructed.

Suppose we have located ourselves on the choice tree, meaning that we have identified our "moment" on it: - a space-like hyperplane, or instantaneous world state, in some reference frame or other. This moment, call it m_o, is the *actual state* of the world. Let the time of m_o (the instant to which m_o belongs) be t_o. There are two possibilities of interest in connection with [α decides that p]. Either m_o is a lower cut branch point, i.e. is the glb of two or more distinct histories, or m_o is not a branch point, but is one of an open set of moments with an upper cut branching immediately above it. We consider these two possibilities separately.

In the first case the truth-conditions for [α decides that p], or [α chooses p], are the following. (i) The agent α makes her decision or choice at t_o. (ii) The histories which branch off at m_o are partitioned into two sets, the p-histories and the *not* p-histories, and α's choice consists in selecting the set of p-histories. So far these truth-conditions are not dissimilar to those for [α stit p]. But condition (iii) is different. Condition (iii) stipulates that, given any instant t_1 later that t_o, the actual or you-are-here moment m_1 which corresponds to t_1 is located on a p-history. (It is necessary that the you-are-here moment should not jump arbitrarily about the tree with the passage of time, but move smoothly and continuously up it.) What condition (iii) does is to ensure that α's choice is *effective*; that her decision to bring about p results in p's being actually true an instant later. The "actual truth" of p, in turn, at some instant later than t_o, is ensured by the fact that the you-are-here arrow, at all times later than t_o, indicates a moment on a p-branch rather than on a *not* p-branch. To find out whether p is true or false, in the actual world, look for the you-are-here arrow on the tree.

If m_o is not a branch point, but is followed by an upper cut branching an instant later, say at t_1, then the truth-conditions of [α decides that p] are as follows. (i) α makes her decision or choice at t_o. (ii) The histories which branch off at t_1, each of which possesses its own incomparable glb at t_1, are partitioned into the p-histories and the *not* p-histories, and α's choice, at t_o, consists in selecting the set of p-histories. (iii) At t_1, the moment indicated by the you-are-here arrow is the glb of a p-branch. As before, condition (iii) ensures that α's choice is effective; that p, as a result of α's choice, is true in the actual world. Which of the many branches at t_1 represents the actual world is indicated, of course, by the arrow.

I hope that the role played in the truth-conditions for [α decides that p] by the you-are-here arrow, or the actuality-arrow, is clear. I don't know of any other way of getting the right truth-conditions. There are other devices besides the arrow, certainly, that could be used in place of it. The feature I personally favour is the selection of one and only branch at each branch point or upper cut branching as the actual branch, and the vanishing of all the rest. This results in a dynamic choice tree or universe tree which is being continuously pruned: in this model the top of the trunk indicates the "present", which works its way, either stochastically or as a result of people's choices, up the tree. But whether we employ branch attrition, or a you-are-here arrow, is not important as far as the truth-conditions of [α decides that p] are concerned. The essential thing is that there should be some way of picking out, at each instant, the actual state of affairs from amongst the many possible states of affairs on the choice tree.

ALDO BRESSAN

THE EXTENSIONAL BUT HYPER-INTENSIONAL CALCULUS C_α WITH ORDERLESS CONSTANTS AND VARIABLES

1. INTRODUCTION

(A). *Background and main results of this work*

The present paper is written from the same point of view as [3] to [5] and [8] to [11]. Briefly, this differs from the views of Quine, Church and Parsons — see [12], [13], [15], and [16] — in that no semantical notions such as the *sense of* ... needs to be primitive in $\mathcal{L}''_\alpha$ or $\mathbf{L}_\alpha$, and in that these languages have Fregean semantics.[1]

In [8] the interpreted modal sense language $\mathcal{SL}^\nu_\alpha$ is introduced. In it, strongly iterated belief sentences can be constructed. Furthermore it contains, among other things, descriptions, nonlogical operators and wfes (i.e., well formed expressions) having both types of all finite levels and sense orders represented by all ordinals $< \alpha$, a possibly transfinite ordinal.

An axiom system valid in $\mathcal{SL}^\nu_\alpha$ is represented in [9]. In order to improve it, the author considered, for the sake of simplicity, the extensional part $\mathcal{L}_\alpha$ of $\mathcal{SL}^\nu_\alpha$ deprived of nonlogical operators; and he changed the semantics of $\mathcal{L}_\alpha$, in two steps: $\mathcal{L}'_\alpha$ and $\mathcal{L}''_\alpha$ — see [11], §11, §12.

Any variable [constant] of $\mathcal{L}''_\alpha$ (i.e. of $\mathcal{L}_\alpha$) has the form v^β_{tn} $[c^\beta_{t,\mu}]$ where $t(\in \tau_\nu)$ is its type, $n[\mu]$ is its index, and $\beta(< \alpha)$ is its (sense) order. In the present work, first, an analogue $\mathbf{L}_\alpha$ of $\mathcal{L}''_\alpha$ is constructed, in which the variables and constants, v_{tn} and $c_{t\mu}$, are orderless; sense orders are kept in effect only in operators. Second, a logical calculus $\mathbf{C}_\alpha$ based on $\mathbf{L}_\alpha$ and having the axioms A8.1–30, is presented. By $\mathbf{L}_\alpha$'s orderless features, this presentation practically needs the expressions in $\mathbf{L}_\alpha$ itself, of several basic semantical notions — see the metalinguistic definitions (7.3–13) and the (semantical) Theorem 7.1. The analogues for $\mathcal{L}''_\alpha$ of these expressions and axioms are easily induced; and several of these analogues are new and interesting.[2]

For more detail on the content of this work see subsection (D).

---

[1] For more details on the comparison of Bressan's views with those of Quine, Church, and Parsons [those of Bealer in [2]] see the 1st part of §1 [see §4] in [11].

[2] A few among the basic semantical notions for $\mathcal{L}_\alpha$ are expressed within $\mathcal{L}_\alpha$ itself in [9]. Since the variables of $\mathcal{L}_\alpha$ have sense orders, these expressions are much easier to determine than the expressions (7.3–13) belonging to $\mathbf{L}_\alpha$. Similar considerations hold for the axioms for $\mathcal{L}_\alpha$ presented in [9]. Furthermore $\mathcal{L}_\alpha$ is turned in $\mathcal{L}''_\alpha$ — see [11], §§11,13 — to increase the validity range of some among those axioms.

J. M. Dunn and A. Gupta (eds.), Truth or Consequences, 245–265.
© 1990 *Kluwer Academic Publishers. Printed in the Netherlands.*

(B). *Some leading ideas of the present work*

In the semantics of, e.g., $\mathcal{L}''_\alpha$ or $\mathbf{L}_\alpha$ every wfe Δ has a HQE (hyper-quasi-extension), $\overline{\Delta} = \text{des}_{\mathcal{I}\mathcal{V}}(\Delta)$ at every c-valuation $\mathcal{I}(\in I^\alpha)$ and v-valuation $\mathcal{V}(\in V^\alpha)$ — where any $\mathcal{I} \in I^\alpha$ [$\mathcal{V} \in V^\alpha$] assigns values to constants [variables]. This HQE represents the (hyper-)extension (or object) denoted by Δ (at $\mathcal{I}$ and $\mathcal{V}$). Furthermore Δ has a QS (quasi-sense) $\check{\Delta} = \text{sens}_{\mathcal{I}\mathcal{V}}(\Delta)$, which represents its sense. The semantics of $\mathcal{L}''_\alpha$ and $\mathbf{L}_\alpha$ are based on the same HQE's and QS's.

Now regard $1, 2, 3 \ldots$ as primitive notions, for the sake of simplicity. Any entity Δ, e.g. $lg_2\, 8(= 3 = 6/2)$ is considered to have an extension, 3 (the one of the entities 3 and 6/2), and to have a sense (different from those of 3 and 6/2). The sense of the entity 3 (any definition of 3 being disregarded in §1) is considered as ostensive — see §10 in [5] for more details.

In order to render HQE's and QS's easier to deal with, *(technical sense)* is used here and in e.g. [8] to [11], according to the following intuitive idea.[3]

DEFINITION 1.1.   *The (technical) sense of an entity Δ is Δ's ordinary sense in case this is non-ostensive, and Δ's (hyper-extension) otherwise.*

In the ordinary [hyper-intensional] modal language ML^ν [$S\mathcal{L}^\nu_\alpha$] introduced in [7] [in [8]], the identity (or equality) sign = denotes contingent (or extensional) identity. In the extensional languages $\mathcal{L}_\alpha$, $\mathcal{L}''_\alpha$, and $\mathbf{L}_\alpha$ it likewise denotes extensional identity. As is customary in logic, the equality $F = G$, where F and G are predicates, means in those languages that F and G hold for the same entities: briefly $(\forall x) \cdot F(x) = G(x)$, where for the sake of simplicity the nonexisting object is identified with the empty set $\emptyset$. Therefore, roughly speaking, the hyper-intensionality axiom

$$(1.1) \qquad F = G \equiv (\forall x).\, F(x) \equiv G(x)$$

is stated for $\mathcal{L}_\alpha$ and $\mathcal{L}''_\alpha$ (in various ways).[4] This practically forces us to assign QS's to variables, and to study the conditions on F's and G's hyper-extensions that are necessary and sufficient for the equivalence $F(x) \equiv G(x)$ to hold for every hyper-intensional choice of x; and in case F and G are predicates of $\mathcal{L}_\alpha$ with different sense orders, these conditions are not trivial, as the examples considered in [11] §§10–11 show. Furthermore, thus certain revisions of the notion of hyper-extensions for predicates are induced. I think the interest that they may have is independent of, e.g., the way in which = is used or meant; and this interest is related with the fact that, so to speak, sense are constructed, step by step, by the expressions of the language being considered.

In, e.g., $\mathcal{L}_\alpha$ or $\mathbf{L}_\alpha$ the (extensional) identity $F = G$ assures the interchange-ability of F and G only in extensional contexts. The analogue for general contexts

---

[3] The use of *sense* in [8] to [11] is also justified in [11], §6 and the last paragraph of §4.

[4] Axiom 1.1 and its analogues for relations and functions hold in e.g. the *ordinary* $\mathcal{L}''_\alpha$ — see at the end of subsection (B) — provided certain conditions on orders are satisfied; but it does not hold in the *refined* $\mathcal{L}''_\alpha$.

is assured by the synomyny — i.e. the hyperintensional identity — of F and $G : F \asymp G$. This relation can in effect be defined within any of the languages $\mathcal{SL}_\alpha^\nu$, $\mathcal{L}_\alpha$, $\mathcal{L}_\alpha''$, and $\mathbf{L}_\alpha$. Therefore by a general result attained by A. Zanardo and Cinzia Bonotto in [6], no completeness theorem based on *general* models can hold for them.

In [11] two versions of $\mathcal{L}_\alpha''$ are considered: the *ordinary* $\mathcal{L}_\alpha''$ and the *refined* $\mathcal{L}_\alpha''$. In the former the nonexisting attribute (or function) a_ϑ^* (of type ϑ) is regarded to be $\emptyset$, and (1.1) holds. In the latter version $a_\vartheta^* \neq \emptyset$ is assumed and (1.1) has a more complex version, as well as its analogues for relations and functions — see A8.11 for $\mathbf{L}_\alpha$ and especially axiom (13.1) in [11] for $\mathcal{L}_\alpha''$.

(C). *An ordinary way of avoiding truth paradoxes. Consequences for* $\mathcal{L}_\alpha''$ *and* $\mathbf{L}_\alpha$

In order to avoid (truth) paradoxes connected with belief sentences, the believing relation is considered only in the forms $B^\beta(\mathcal{M}, p)$, $\mathcal{M}$ believes that p (holds), at a sense order $\leq \beta$, for $0 < \beta < \alpha$ — see [11], §2 — where B^β is regarded as sensitive to p only in case p's order is $< \beta$. Generally logicians use the relation $B^\beta(\mathcal{M}, p)$ — which strictly speaking is outside ordinary languages — only in the last case, and for very low values of β. Instead, in e.g., $\mathcal{L}_\alpha$, $\mathcal{L}_\alpha''$ or $\mathbf{L}_\alpha$ $B^\beta(\mathcal{M}, p)$ is well formed whenever $\mathcal{M}$'s and p's orders are $< \alpha$. This is done for the sake of generality and uniformity (an analogue is considered below, for ordinary extensional languages) and it is particularly useful for $\mathbf{L}_\alpha$ by its orderless-properties — see below.

The above well-formedness property of B^β is in effect an extension of the way B^β is generally considered by logicians. Analogously material implication, $\supset$, is an extension of ordinary (extensional) implication (if $1 = 2$, then Rome is in America). This extension contains something strange; and it strongly induces the same on the ordinary entailment relation, as it appears from Anderson and Belnap's well known and great work [1] on relevance logic, just performed to avoid the strange (non-relevant) features of ordinary entailment. Therefore it is not very unlikely that some features of $B^\beta(\ldots)$'s extension, mentioned above and described below, may appear arbitrary and even strange, in spite of the author's efforts to base it on reasonable criteria.

In an ordinary extensional language, for any predicate P, e.g. $P(3)$ is true iff so is $P(lg_2\, 8)$. More generally, if a and Δ are expressions of a same object and (only) the former is ostensive, then $P(a)$ and $P(\Delta)$ are equivalent. In $\mathcal{L}_\alpha''$ (or $\mathbf{L}_\alpha$) this situation is generalized as follows, roughly speaking.

(a)   If (at given c- and v-valuations) P is a predicate of sense order β, a and Δ are expressions of a same object, δ_a and δ_Δ are their respective orders, a is ostensive, and $\delta_a \leq \beta \leq \delta_\Delta$, then $P(a)$ and $P(\Delta)$ are equivalent.[5]

Note that δ_a can be > 0; in fact, e.g., the expression B^β can be regarded (at a natural c-valuation) as both ostentive and of order $\beta(> 0)$. However, if $\delta_a < \beta$ and $\delta_\Delta < \beta$, then $P(a) \equiv P(\Delta)$ can be false.

---

[5] If p is ostensive, i.e. p denotes a truth value, then $B^\beta(\mathcal{M}, p)$ is reasonably false. Consequently, by (a) $B^\beta(\mathcal{M}, q)$ is false when q's sense order is $\geq \beta$, which is satisfactory.

(D). *More details on the content of this paper*

After having stated the formation rules for $\mathbf{L}_\alpha$ in §2, in §3 it is briefly explained while the non-existing object of any type t is identified with the truth value $\mathbf{F}$ (false), in e.g. $\mathcal{L}''_\alpha$ and $\mathbf{L}_\alpha$ — for more details see [11], §4. Furthermore, in §3, $\overline{\Delta} = des_{\mathcal{I}\mathcal{V}}(\Delta)$ is determined for the ordinary extensional segment $\mathbf{L}_1$ of $\mathbf{L}_\alpha$. In §4 $\breve{\Delta} = sens_{\mathcal{I}\mathcal{V}}(\Delta)$ is determined in the general case. The same is done for $\overline{\Delta}$ in §6, after having introduced the HQEs for $\mathbf{L}_\alpha$ directly, in §5. Note that the HQEs are constructed in [11] for $\mathcal{L}''_\alpha$, in two steps. The semantics for $\mathbf{L}_\alpha$, as well as the one for $\mathcal{L}''_\alpha$, is based on the set QE_t^β of the QEs (or HQEs) of orders $\leq \beta$ and type $t(\in \tau_\nu)$ — briefly the $QE_t^\beta s-$, on the $QS_t^\beta s$ (i.e., the QSs of orders $\leq \beta$ and type t), and on the sets $A_t^\beta = (\cup_{\delta<\beta} QS_t^\delta) \cup QE_t^\beta$. In §6 certain relations among these sets — in part already presented in [11] — are written, in order to justify the validity in $\mathbf{L}_\alpha$ of axioms A8.21–26.

In §7 some basic semantical notions for $\mathcal{L}''_\alpha$ and $\mathbf{L}_\alpha$ are expressed within $\mathbf{L}_\alpha$ itself. This is practically necessary to write several axioms of the logical calculus C_α valid in $\mathbf{L}_\alpha$, in connection with the fact that $\mathbf{L}_\alpha$'s variables and constants are orderless. That the above expressions have the required meanings is assured by Theorem 7.1, the main semantical theorem of this paper. In §8 a rich axiom system is presented. It consists of 30 axioms plus the mutually incompatible axioms $(8.2)_{1-2}$ which distinguish the *ordinary* C_α from the *refined* C_α. The afore-mentioned expressions and axioms have rather obvious and generally easier counterparts in $\mathcal{L}''_\alpha$. Most of these have never been written, in spite of the interest that these analogues may have.

2. FORMATION RULES FOR THE INTERPRETED LANGUAGE $\mathbf{L}_\alpha$
EXTENSIONAL BUT HYPERINTENSIONAL

As well as $\mathcal{L}''_\alpha$ ($\mathcal{SL}^\nu_\alpha$, $\mathcal{L}_\alpha$, and $\mathcal{L}'_\alpha$) — see [11], §3 — where $\alpha(> 0)$ is a possibly transfinite ordinal, the language $\mathbf{L}_\alpha$ being introduced is based on the *individual types* 1 to ν, the *propositional type* 0, and more thoroughly on the type system τ_ν, i.e. the least set τ_ν for which (i) $\{0, \ldots, \nu\} \subseteq \tau_\nu$ and (ii) if $t_0, \ldots, t_n \in \tau_\nu$, then the $(n+1)$-tuple $\langle t_1, \ldots, t_n, t_0 \rangle \in \tau_\nu$.

For $t_0 = 0$ $[t_0 \neq 0]$ $\langle t_1, \ldots, t_n, t_0 \rangle$ is used as an attribute [function] type and, following Carnap, is denoted by $(t_1, \ldots, t_n)$ $[(t_1, \ldots, t_n; t_0)]$.

The primitive symbols of $\mathbf{L}_\alpha$ are those of $\mathcal{L}''_\alpha$ (or $\mathcal{L}_\alpha$), except that variables and constants have no sense-order suffixes; they are the variables $v_{t,n}$ and constants $c_{t,\mu}$, of type t and index n or μ respectively, for $t \in \tau_n$, $n \in \mathbb{N}_* =_D \mathbb{N} - \{0\}$, and $0 < \mu < \alpha + \omega$, where ω is the first transfinite ordinal; furthermore left and right parentheses, the connectives $\sim$ and $\supset$, the all sign $\forall$, the identity sign $=$, the symbol 1 for descriptions, and the one λ for lambda-expressions.

The class E_t of $\mathbf{L}_\alpha$'s wfes of type t is defined recursively by rules (φ_{1-8}) below, regarded as holding for (i) $m, n \in \mathbb{N}_*$, (ii) $t, t_0, \ldots, t_n \in \tau_\nu$, and (iii) β and δ_1 to δ_m ordinals $< \alpha$. The recursion concerns the lengths of wffes; and rule (φ_r)

equals in effect the r-th of the formation rules (φ_{1-8}) for $\mathcal{L}_\alpha$ (up to sense-order suffixes) only for $r = 1$ to 5.

(φ_1) $\qquad v_{t,n}, c_{t,\mu} \in E_t (n \in \mathbf{N}_*, 0 < \mu < \alpha + \omega)$.

(φ_2) $\qquad$ If $\Delta_i \in E_{t_i}$ $(i = 1, \ldots, n)$ and $\Delta_0 \in E_{\langle t_1, \ldots, t_n, t_0 \rangle}$, then
$\qquad\quad \Delta_0(\Delta_1, \ldots, \Delta_n) \in E_{t_0}$.

(φ_3) $\qquad$ If $\Delta_1, \Delta_2 \in E_t$, then $(\Delta_1 = \Delta_2) \in E_0$.

(φ_{4-5}) $\quad$ If $p, q \in E_0$, then $\sim p$, $(p \supset q) \in E_0$.

(φ_{6-7}) $\quad$ If $p \in E_0$, then $(\forall v_{tn}, c_{0\beta})p \in E_0$ and $(1 v_{tn}, c_{0\beta})p \in E_t$.

(φ_8) $\qquad$ If x_1 to x_m are m (distinct) variables, $x_1 \in E_{t_1}, \ldots, x_m \in E_{t_m}$, and
$\qquad\quad \Delta_0 \in E_{t_0}$, then $(\lambda x_1, \ldots, x_m, c_{0\delta_1}, \ldots, c_{0\delta_m})\Delta_0 \in E_{\langle t_1, \ldots, t_m, t_0 \rangle}$.

CONVENTION 2.1. *We simply write* $(\forall v_{tn}, \beta)$ p, $(1 v_{tn}, \beta)$ p, *and* $(\lambda x_1, \ldots, x_m, \delta_1, \ldots, \delta_m)\Delta_0$ *for the wfes introduced by rules* (φ_{6-8}) *respectively; and for* $\delta_1 = \ldots = \delta_m = \beta$, $(\lambda x_1, \ldots, x_m; \beta)\Delta_0$ *stands for the above* λ-*expression.*

DEFINITION 2.1. (a) *We call* β *the order of the above operators* $(\forall v_{tn}, \beta)$, $(1 v_{tn}, \beta)$, *and* $(\lambda x_1, \ldots, x_m, \delta_1, \ldots, \delta_m)$ *with* $\beta = max(\delta_1, \ldots, \delta_m)$.

(b) *The order* Δ^{ord} *of any wfe* Δ *(of* $\mathbf{L}_\alpha$*) is defined to be the maximal of the orders of the operators occurring in it, if these exist, and zero otherwise.*

If $\mathcal{A}^{<\delta}$ is a class $\forall \delta < \beta$ $[\forall \delta \leq \beta]$, then we set $(2.1)_1$ $[(2.1)_{2-3}]$ below.

$$(2.1) \qquad \mathcal{A}^{<\beta} = \bigcup_{\delta < \beta} \mathcal{A}^\delta, \quad \mathcal{A}^{\leq \beta} = \bigcup_{\delta \leq \beta} \mathcal{A}^\delta, \quad \mathcal{A}^{\beta \dagger} = \mathcal{A}^\beta - \mathcal{A}^{<\beta},$$

$$E_t^\delta = \{\Delta \in E_t \mid \Delta^{\mathrm{ord}} \leq \delta\}, \quad \mathrm{wfe}^\delta = \bigcup_{t \in \tau_\nu} E_t^{\delta \dagger} \quad (\delta < \alpha).$$

CONVENTION 2.2. *By* $x, y, z, x_1, \ldots$, *by* $p, q, r, r_1, \ldots$, *and by* $\Delta, \Delta_1, \ldots$ *arbitrary variables, wffs (well formed formulas), and wfes of* $\mathbf{L}_\alpha$ *are denoted respectively.*

CONVENTION 2.3. *Every expression of* $\mathbf{L}_\alpha$ *used in the sequel is assumed to be well-formed.*

3. ON THE NON-EXISTING OBJECT a_t^ν. SEMANTICS FOR THE ORDINARY EXTENSIONAL SEGMENT $\mathbf{L}_1$ OF $\mathbf{L}_\alpha$

The present theory for $\mathbf{L}_\alpha$ — like the one for $\mathcal{L}_\alpha''$ in [11] — has been constructed looking forward to extensions of $\mathbb{L}_\alpha$ to typeless and modal languages. Especially from this point of view it is technically useful to identify the truth value false, $\mathbf{F}$, with the non-existing object a_t^ν of type t — which is the designatum of the descriptions of type t that fail to satisfy their conditions of exact uniqueness:

$$(3.1) \qquad a_t^\nu = a_0^\nu = \mathbf{F} \qquad\qquad\qquad \forall t \in \tau_\nu.$$

Likewise the set of points is identified, in projective geometry, with the set formed by both (ordinary) points and directions. The identification (3.1) is also useful for $\mathbf{L}_\alpha$ itself, in that it favours a unified treatment of attributes and functions, without requiring the use of a three-valued PC (propositional calculus). We must use this PC, if we both assume $a_0^\nu \notin \{\mathbf{F}, \mathbf{T}\}$ ($\mathbf{T}$ being the truth value true) and use descriptions based on propositional variables such as $(1v_{0n}, \beta)\Delta$.

The identification (3.1) is specified and discussed in [11], §4. Now let us only note that, first,

(a)   in a modal extension of $\mathbf{L}_\alpha$ probability functions can be dealt with; some arguments of them are propositional; hence the use of descriptions such as $(1v_{0n}, \beta)p$ becomes natural. Furthermore

(b)   in a typeless (and modal) extension of $\mathbf{L}_\alpha$, variables range over both objects and propositions, so that $(3.1)_1$ is practically mandatory and $(3.1)_2$ is required by a two-valued PC — see below (4.2) in [11].

Let $\mathbf{L}_\lambda$ be $\mathbf{L}_\alpha$'s λ-th segment, i.e. the language formed by $\mathbf{L}_\alpha$'s wfes that contain none of the constants $c_{t\mu}$ with $\mu \geq \lambda$ (and $t \in \tau_\nu$), so that their orders are $< \lambda$. One could state the semantics of $\mathbf{L}_\alpha$ directly for any $\lambda = \beta + 1 < \alpha$. However, for the sake of clarity it is preferable to introduce, first, $\mathbf{L}_1$'s semantics, especially because of identity (3.1) (and because of the definition (5.8) of $QE_{(t_1,\ldots,t_m,t_0)}^\beta$). The sets $\mathcal{D}_1$ to $\mathcal{D}_\nu$ are regarded as *proper individual domains* if

$$(3.2) \qquad \mathbf{F} \notin \mathcal{D}_i, \ \mathcal{D} \neq \varnothing \text{ for } i = 1,\ldots,\nu \qquad\qquad (\mathbf{F} \text{ is elementless}).$$

Furthermore, let us set

$$(3.3) \qquad \mathcal{D}_0 = \{\mathbf{T}\}, \ D_j = \mathcal{D}_j \cup \{\mathbf{F}\} \qquad\qquad (j = 0,\ldots,\nu).$$

Hence D_i is the set of possibly non-existing individuals of type i for $i \in \{1,\ldots,\nu\}$. The domain [counterdomain] of any function f is denoted by $\mathcal{D}_f$ (or $\mathcal{D}f$) [$\mathcal{CD}_f$]. For any classes A and B,

$$(3.4) \qquad \begin{bmatrix} A \to B \\ A \rightarrowtail B \end{bmatrix} =_D \left\{ f \mid f \text{ is a function}, \mathcal{D}_f \begin{bmatrix} = A \\ \subseteq A \end{bmatrix}, \mathcal{CD}_f \subseteq B \right\}$$

One wants to gradually define the class QE_t^β of the HQEs (hyper-quasi-extensions or ordered QEs) of sense orders $\leq \beta$ and type t, as well as the class QS_t^β of the QSs of orders $\leq \beta$ and type t $(0 \leq \beta < \alpha, t \in \tau_\nu)$.

For $t \in \tau_\nu$, QE_t^0 is determined by clauses (3.5–7) below with $\beta = 0$, which in effect are clauses (5.4), (11.1) for $\beta = 0$, and (5.6) in [11].

$$(3.5) \qquad QE_t^\beta = D_t \qquad\qquad\qquad\qquad (t = 0, \ldots, \nu),$$

$$(3.6) \qquad EQ_{\langle t_1, \ldots, t_n, t_0 \rangle}^0 = [(EQ_{t_1}^0 \times \ldots \times EQ_{t_n}^0 \rightarrowtail QE_{t_0}^0)] \times \{0\}] \cup \{\mathbf{F}\}$$
$$(t_0, \ldots, t_n \in \tau_\nu),$$

QE_t^β being the class of *proper* EQ_t^βs:

$$(3.7) \qquad QE_t^\beta = QE_t^\beta - \{\mathbf{F}\}, \text{ hence } QE_t^\beta = QE_t^\beta \cup \{\mathbf{F}\} \ (t \in \tau_\nu, \beta < \alpha).$$

For $0 < \lambda \leq \alpha$ $V^\lambda[I^\lambda]$ will denote the set of *v-valuations* [*c-valuations*] for $\mathbf{L}_\lambda$, to be determined below: $V \in V^\lambda$ $[I \in I^\lambda]$ iff V $[I]$ is a function defined only on the variables [constants] of $\mathbf{L}_\alpha$ for which the first [second] of the relations

$$(3.8) \qquad V(v_{tn}) \in A_t^\beta, \ I(c_{t\mu}) \in A_t^\beta \text{ with } A_t^0 = QE_t^0$$
$$(t \in \tau_\nu, \ \beta < \lambda, \ n \in \mathbb{N}_*, \ 0 < \mu < \beta + \omega)$$

holds, where A_t^β (the set of entities assignable to v_{t1}^β by the v-valuations for $\mathbf{L}_{\beta+1}$) is defined by $(3.8)_3$ and (5.2) below. By $(3.8)_3$ V^1 and I^1 are already determined.

Let us define the c-valuations $I_*^\lambda \in I^\lambda$ and I_* by

$$(3.9) \qquad I_*^\lambda(c_{t\mu}) = \mathbf{F} \ (\lambda \leq \alpha, \ t \in \tau_\nu, \ 0 < \mu < \beta + \omega); \ I_* = I_*^\alpha.$$

For every wfe Δ of $\mathbf{L}_\lambda$, its *(hyper)-quasi extensional designatum* (or HQE-designatum) $des_{IV}(\Delta)$ at any $I \in I^\lambda$ and $V \in V^\lambda$ $(0 < \lambda \leq \alpha)$ will be defined in such a way that, for some $t \in \tau_\nu$,

$$(3.10) \qquad \overline{\Delta} = des_{IV}(\Delta) \Rightarrow \overline{\Delta} \in QE_t^{<\lambda} \qquad (\Delta \in E_t^{<\lambda}, \ I \in I^\lambda, \ V \in V^\lambda).$$

As well as in [11], (3.11–13), we state the conventions

$$(3.11) \qquad f(\xi_1, \ldots, \xi_n)^\dagger = \begin{cases} f(\xi_1, \ldots, \xi_n) & \text{if } f \text{ is a function and} \\ & \langle \xi_1, \ldots, \xi_n \rangle \in \mathcal{D}_f; \\ \mathbf{F} & \text{otherwise,} \end{cases}$$

$$(3.12) \qquad (c)_1 = a_1 \text{ for } c = \langle a_1, a_2 \rangle,$$

and, in case $0 < \lambda \le \alpha$ while $\mathcal{V}, \mathcal{V}' \in V^\lambda$,

$$(3.13) \qquad \mathcal{V}' = \mathcal{V}\left(\begin{matrix} x_1, \dots, x_m \\ \xi_1, \dots, \xi_m \end{matrix}\right)$$

$$\text{iff } \mathcal{V}'(x) = \left[\begin{matrix} \xi_i & \text{for } x = x_i \ (i = 1, \dots, m); \\ \mathcal{V}(x) & \text{otherwise.} \end{matrix}\right.$$

For $\lambda = 1$, rules (H_{1-8}) below define $(3.10)_1$ recursively under assumptions (i) to (iii) and (3.14–16) below. Rule (H_r) coincides in effect with the r-th of the analogous rules (h_{1-8}) for $\mathcal{L}_\alpha$ (and hence for $\mathcal{L}''_\alpha$), written in [11] §§5,12, only for $r = 1, \dots, 5$.

(i) $\qquad n = m + 1$, $\Delta_j \in E^\lambda_{t_j}$ with $t_j \in \tau_\nu$ $(j = 0, \dots, n)$ — see $(2.1)_4$,
(ii) $\qquad x_1$ to x_m are m variables in E_{t_1} to E_{t_m} respectively, and
(iii) $\qquad \mathcal{V} \in V^\lambda, \mathcal{I} \in I^\lambda$ and δ_1 to δ_m are ordinals $< \alpha$.

$$(3.14) \qquad \overline{\Delta}_j = \mathrm{des}_{\mathcal{I}\mathcal{V}}(\Delta_j) \qquad\qquad\qquad (j = 0, \dots, n).$$

$$(3.15) \qquad \overline{\Delta}'_n = \mathrm{des}_{\mathcal{I}\mathcal{V}'} \ \text{ where } \mathcal{V}' = \mathcal{V}\left(\begin{matrix} x_1, \dots, x_m \\ \xi_1, \dots, \xi_m \end{matrix}\right) \qquad (n = m + 1).$$

$$(3.16) \qquad f = \{\langle \xi_1, \dots, \xi_n \rangle \mid \langle \xi_1, \dots, \xi_m \rangle \in QE^0_{t_1} \times \cdots \times QE^0_{tm},$$
$$\mathbf{F} \ne \xi_n = \overline{\Delta}'_n\} \qquad\qquad\qquad \text{— see (3.13,15).}$$

Rule	If Δ is	then $\overline{\Delta} = \mathrm{des}_{\mathcal{I}\mathcal{V}}(\Delta)$ is
(H_1)	$v_{tn}[c_{t\mu}]$,	$\mathcal{V}(v_{tn})\ [\mathcal{I}(c_{t\mu}]$.
(H_2)	$\Delta_0(\Delta_1, \dots, \Delta_n)$,	$(\overline{\Delta}_0)_1(\overline{\Delta}_1, \dots, \overline{\Delta})^\dagger$ — see (3.11–12).
(H_3)	$\Delta_1 = \Delta_2(t_1 = t_2)$,	$\mathbf{T}$ if $\overline{\Delta}_1 = \overline{\Delta}_2$; $\mathbf{F}$ otherwise.
(H_4)	$\sim \Delta_1(t_1 = 0)$,	$\mathbf{F}\ [\mathbf{T}]$ if $\overline{\Delta}$ is $\mathbf{T}\ [\mathbf{F}]$.
(H_5)	$\Delta_1 \supset \Delta_2(t_1 = t_2 = 0)$,	$\mathbf{T}$ if $\overline{\Delta}_1$ is $\mathbf{F}$ or $\overline{\Delta}_2$ is $\mathbf{T}$; $\mathbf{F}$ otherwise.
(H_6)	$(\forall x_1, 0)\Delta_2(t_2 = 0)$,	$\mathbf{T}$ if $\overline{\Delta}'_2 = \mathbf{T}\ \forall \xi_1 \in EQ^0_{t_1}$ — see (3.15) for $n = 2$; otherwise $\mathbf{F}$.
(H_7)	$(1 x_1, 0)\Delta_2(t_2 = 0)$,	ξ_1, if ξ_1 is the unique element of QE^0_t such that $\overline{\Delta}'_2 = \mathbf{T}$ — see (3.15) for $n = 2$; otherwise $\mathbf{F}$.
(H_8)	$(\lambda x_1, \dots, x_m; 0)\Delta_n$,	$\langle f, 0 \rangle$ — see (3.16).

By (3.6, 7, 16), $\langle f, 0 \rangle$ is an element of $Q\mathcal{E}_{t_0}$; and conversely every such element has that form.

4. RULES OF QS-DESIGNATION FOR $\mathbf{L}_\lambda$ WITH $0 < \lambda \leq \alpha$

First, fix $\lambda = \beta + 1$ $(0 < \lambda \leq \alpha)$ and assume that, for $t \in \tau_\nu$, we know $A_t^\beta = QS_t^{<\beta} \cup QE_t^\beta$ — see $(3.8)_3$ and (5.2) below — as well as — see (3.8) —

$$(4.1) \qquad \overline{\Delta} = des_{\mathcal{I}V}(\Delta)[\check{\Delta} = sens_{\mathcal{I}V}(\Delta)] \text{ for } \mathcal{I} \in I^\lambda, V \in V^\lambda,$$

$$\text{and } \Delta \in E_t^\beta \, [\Delta \in E_t^{<\beta}].$$

We want to define $\check{\Delta}$ for $\mathbf{L}_\lambda$, i.e. for $\Delta \in E_t^\beta (t \in \tau_\nu)$, in analogy with $\check{\Delta}$'s definition stated for $\mathcal{L}''_\alpha$ in [11], §12. To attain this goal, first we consider, besides (4.1), the conditions (i) to (iii) in §3 (for $\lambda = \beta + 1$) and the definitions (4.2–3) below.

$$(4.2) \qquad \check{\Delta}_j = sens_{\mathcal{I}V}(\Delta_j) \qquad\qquad\qquad (j = 0, \ldots, \nu).$$

$$(4.3) \qquad g =_D \{\langle \xi_1, \ldots \xi_n\rangle \mid \langle \xi_1, \ldots, \xi_m \rangle \in A_{t_1}^{\delta_1} \times \ldots \times A_{t_m}^{\delta_m},$$

$$\xi_n = sens_{\mathcal{I}V'}(\Delta_n)\} \qquad\qquad \text{— see (3.13).}$$

Then we state the rules of QS-designation $(\mathcal{E}_{1-8})$ below, regarded to hold for all entities that satisfy the aforementioned conditions. Among these rules $(\mathcal{E}_r)$ coincides in effect with the r-th of the corresponding rules for $\mathcal{L}''_\lambda$ — see [11], §12 — only for $r = 1, \ldots, 5$.

Rule	If Δ is	then $\check{\Delta} = sens_{\mathcal{I}V}(\Delta)$ is
$(\mathcal{E}_1)$	$v_{tn} \, [c_{t\mu}]$,	$\mathcal{V}(v_{tn}) \, [\mathcal{I}(c_{t\mu})]$.
$(\mathcal{E}_2)$	$\Delta_0(\Delta_1, \ldots, \Delta_n)$,	$\langle \check{\Delta}_0, \ldots, \check{\Delta}_n \rangle$.
$(\mathcal{E}_3)$	$\Delta_1 = \Delta_2 (t_1 = t_2 = 0)$,	$\langle =, \check{\Delta}_1, \check{\Delta}_2 \rangle$.
$(\mathcal{E}_{4-5})$	$\sim \Delta_1, \Delta_1 \supset \Delta_2 (t_1 = t_2 = 0)$,	$\langle \sim, \check{\Delta}_1, \rangle, \langle \supset, \check{\Delta}_1, \check{\Delta}_2 \rangle$ respectively.
$(\mathcal{E}_{6-7})$	$(\forall x_1, \delta_1)\Delta_2, (1x_1, \delta_1)\Delta_2(\delta_2 = 0)$,	$\langle \forall, g \rangle, \langle 1, g \rangle$ respectively — see (4.3) for $n = 2$.
$(\mathcal{E}_8)$	$(\lambda x_1, \ldots, x_m; \delta_1, \ldots, \delta_m)\Delta_n$,	$\langle \lambda, g \rangle$ — see (4.3).

Remark that the ordinals δ_1 to δ_m do not appear explicitly in the QSs $\langle \forall, g \rangle$ to $\langle \lambda, g \rangle$ assigned to Δ by rules $(\mathcal{E}_{6-8})$ respectively, in spite of their presence in Δ's main operator. However δ_1 to δ_m are taken there into account implicitly, in that any of those QS's determines the corresponding ordinal through g. In fact, by (4.3), this ordinal can be recognized by looking at $\mathcal{D}_g$.

The class QS_t^β of the QSs of type $t(\in \tau_\nu)$ and orders $\leq \beta$ can be defined by any of the mutual equivalent equalities $(4.4)_{1-2}$ below.

$$(4.4) \qquad QS_t^\beta = \left\{ sens_{\mathcal{I}V}(\Delta) \mid V \in V^{\beta+1}, \right.$$

$$\left. \begin{bmatrix} \mathcal{I} \in I^{\beta+1} \\ \mathcal{I} = \mathcal{I}_*^{\beta+1}, \quad \Delta \text{ is constantless} \end{bmatrix} \right\} \qquad \text{— see (3.9).}$$

The considerations made for $\mathcal{L}_\alpha$ in [11], below (8.7), also hold for $\mathbf{L}_\alpha$. In particular, see Theorem 8.1 (c) and (8.10) in [11], we have the following.

THEOREM 4.1. *If* $\mathcal{I}_r \in I^\lambda$, $\mathcal{V}_r \in V^\lambda$, *and* Δ_r *is a wfe$^{<\lambda}$ ($r = 1, 2$), then*

$$(4.5) \qquad sens_{\mathcal{I}_1 \mathcal{V}_1}(\Delta_1) = sens_{\mathcal{I}_2 \mathcal{V}_2}(\Delta_2) \Rightarrow des_{\mathcal{I}_1 \mathcal{V}_1}(\Delta_1) = des_{\mathcal{I}_2 \mathcal{V}_2}(\Delta_2).$$

Therefore, for every $\sigma \in QS^{<\lambda}$, *we can define* σ's *extension by requiring that e.g. for some constantless wfe$^{<\lambda}$* Δ *and some* $\mathcal{V} \in V^\lambda$ *we should have*

$$(4.6) \qquad \sigma^E = des_{\mathcal{I}\mathcal{V}}(\Delta), \; \sigma = sens_{\mathcal{I}\mathcal{V}}(\Delta) \; (\mathcal{I} = \mathcal{I}_*^{\beta+1}) \qquad \text{— see (3.9)}.$$

Assume now that λ is a limit ordinal and we know — of $\mathsf{L}_{\beta+1}$'s semantics — both A_t^β and the objects (4.1) $\forall \beta < \lambda$. Then QS_t^β too is determined for $\beta < \lambda$. Hence we know L_λ's semantics.

DEFINITION 4.1. *If (a)* $\xi \in QE_t^\delta$ [$\sigma \in QS_t^\delta$], *then the least value of* δ *for which (a) holds is called the order of* ξ [σ], *briefly* ξ^{ord}[σ^{ord}].

One has

$$(4.7) \qquad \xi^{\text{ord}} \leq \sigma^{\text{ord}} \text{for } \sigma \in QS_t^{<\alpha} \text{and } \xi = \sigma^E.$$

5. QEs FOR $\mathsf{L}_{\beta+1}$ WITH $0 < \beta < \alpha$

In [11], §7, first the directions (α) and (β) below are considered in order to assign a HQE (hyper–quasi-extension) to any functional or relational expression $\Delta_0(\Delta_1, \ldots, \Delta_n)$ of e.g. $\mathcal{L}_\alpha$, of order 1.

(α)   Use the QS $\check{\Delta}_i$ of the argument Δ_i, if $(\check{\Delta}_i)^{\text{ord}} < \Delta_0^{\text{ord}}$ ($i = 1, \ldots, n$) and

(β)   Use the HQE $\overline{\Delta}_i$ of Δ_i otherwise ($i = 1, \ldots, n$).

After some considerations supporting (α) and (β), the following reasonable alternative for (α) — which also modifies (β) — is considered in [11], §7.

(α')   Use $\check{\Delta}_i$ whenever $(\check{\Delta}_i)^{\text{ord}} < (\overline{\Delta}_0)^{\text{ord}}$ ($i = 1, \ldots, n$).

The languages $\mathcal{L}_\alpha'$ and $\mathcal{L}_\alpha''$ conforming with (α') and (β), have nicer axioms than $\mathcal{L}_\alpha$ which conforms with (α) and (β). Therefore the latter directions are used to construct L_α.

The semantics for $\mathcal{L}_\alpha'$ and $\mathcal{L}_\alpha''$ are constructed in [11], §11 and §12, on the basis of some examples exhibited in [11], §10. Roughly speaking, the latter semantics is obtained from the former by reducing the set QS_ϑ^β for $\vartheta \in \tau_\nu - \{0, 1 \ldots, \nu\}$ and $0 < \beta < \alpha$. This reduction is carried out technically in [11], §12, first, by adding the objects (i) to (iv) below to the versions for $\mathcal{L}_{\beta+1}'$ of the sets QE_t^β, A_t^β, and QE_t^β:

(i)   the set PQE_ν^β of the pre-QEs (pre-quasi-extensions) of type $\vartheta \in \tau_\nu - \{0, \ldots, \nu\}$ and orders $\leq \beta$.

(ii) σ's δ-equivalent QS, briefly $\sigma^{E\delta}$ or $\psi_{\beta\delta}(\sigma)$, for any QS σ and $\delta < \beta$,

(iii)   the β-mate $m^\beta(\xi)$ of any $\xi \in EQ_\vartheta^{<\beta}$, and

(iv)   the set $LQE(\zeta)$ of the lower order QEs (of type ϑ) corresponding to
             any $\zeta \in PQE_t^\beta$, which set is at most a singleton.

Second, in [11], §12, one defines, for $\mathcal{L}''_{\beta+1}$, the resulting objects

(5.1) $QE_t^\beta,\ Q\mathcal{E}_t^\beta,\ A_t^\beta,\ PQE_t^\beta,\ \psi_{\beta\delta}(\cdot),\ m^\beta(\cdot),\ LQE_\vartheta(\cdot)$

$$(t \in \tau_\nu,\ \vartheta \in \tau_\nu - \{0,\ldots,\nu\})$$

by recursion on t and ϑ. The analogue can be done for L_λ with $\lambda = \beta + 1 < \alpha$ by
means of clauses (3.5) and (3.7) — which yield EQ_r^β and $\mathcal{E}Q_t^\beta$ for $r \in \{0,\ldots,\nu\}$,
$t \in \tau_\nu$, and $0 \leq \beta < \alpha$ — and by clauses (5.2–4), Definition 5.1, and clauses (5.7–8)
below.

(5.2) $A_t^\beta =_D QS_t^{<\beta} \cup QE_t^\beta$ $(t \in \tau_\nu)$.

(5.3) $\sigma^{E\delta} =_D \psi_{\beta\delta}(\sigma) =_D \left[\begin{matrix} \sigma^E \\ \sigma \end{matrix} \text{ if } \sigma \left[\begin{matrix} \notin \\ \in \end{matrix} \right. A_t^\delta \text{ for } \sigma \in QS_t^{<\beta} \ (t \in \tau_\nu, \delta < \alpha).$

By Definition 4.1, for $\sigma \in QS_t^{<\beta}$, $\sigma \in QS_t^{<\delta}$ iff $\sigma^{\mathrm{ord}} < \delta$. Furthermore, by (5.3)
and rule (H_6) below, any $\sigma \in QS_t^{<\alpha}$ equals $\sigma^{E\delta}$ whenever σ can be assigned to v_{t1}
by the quantifier $(\forall v_{t1}, \delta)$ of $\mathcal{L}_{\delta+1}$. For any QS σ, $\sigma^{E\delta} = (\sigma^{E\delta})^{E\delta}$. Furthermore
$\sigma^{E\delta} = \sigma = \sigma^E$ for $\sigma \in QE_t^{\delta\dagger}$.

Incidentally remark that by the directions (α') and $\beta)$ above — conformed with
by rules (H_{1-8}) below — $\rho = \sigma^{E\delta}$ iff ρ is the one with the least order among the
QS's σ_* that are equivalent to σ in connection with σ's effect on any predicate Δ_0
whose extension $\overline{\Delta}_0$ has the order δ. More precisely, the above QS's σ_* are the
QS's that render $\Delta_0(\Delta_*)$ equivalent to $\Delta_0(\Delta_1)$ whenever $(\overline{\Delta}_0)^{\mathrm{ord}} = \delta$, $\check{\Delta}_1 = \sigma$,
and $\check{\Delta}_* = \sigma_*$.[6]

(5.4) $PQE_\vartheta^\beta =_D \{f \in (A_{t_1}^\beta \times \ldots \times A_{t_m}^\beta \rightarrowtail Q\mathcal{E}_{t_0}^\beta) \mid f \neq \emptyset\} \times \{\beta\}$

$$(\vartheta = \langle t_1, \ldots, t_m, t_0 \rangle)$$

so that $PQE_\vartheta^\beta \cap QE_\vartheta^{<\beta} = \emptyset$.

---

[6] Assume $0 \leq \delta < \beta < \alpha$, $t \in \tau_\nu$, and $\sigma \in QS_t^{<\beta}$; use x, y, and F for v_{t1}, v_{t2}, and $v_{(t)1}$,
respectively; and set, for $\mathcal{I} = \mathcal{I}_*^\beta$ — see (3.9) —,

$$\textstyle\sum_{\beta t} = \{\sigma_* \in QS_t^{<\beta} \mid \mathrm{des}_{\mathcal{I}\mathcal{V}}[(\forall F, \delta)F(x) = F(y)] = \mathbf{T}$$

$$\text{for all } \mathcal{V} \in V^\lambda \text{ such that } [\mathcal{V}(F)^E]^{\mathrm{ord}} = \delta,\ \mathcal{V}(x) = \sigma,\ \mathcal{V}(y) = \sigma_*\}.$$

Call $\sigma^{E\delta}$ or $\psi_{\beta\delta}(\sigma)$ the unique $\rho \in \sum_{\lambda t}$ such that $\rho^{\mathrm{ord}} \leq \sigma_*^{\mathrm{ord}}$ for all $\sigma_* \in \sum_{\beta t}$. Obviously (a)
$\mathcal{D}\psi_{\beta\delta} = \sum_\beta =_D \bigcup\{\sum_{\beta t} \mid t \in \nu_\nu\}$. Furthermore (b) for $\beta < \gamma < \alpha$, $\psi_{\gamma\delta}$ is an extension of $\psi_{\beta\delta}$
to $\sum_\gamma$.

DEFINITION 5.1. *For $\delta < \beta < \alpha$ and $\eta = \langle \eta_1, \delta \rangle \in QE_\vartheta^\delta$ — see $(5.4)_2$ —, we say that ζ is η's β-mate in case $\zeta = \langle \zeta_1, \beta \rangle (\in PQE_\vartheta^\beta)$, where ζ_1 is the m-ary function such that, first, $\langle \sigma_1, \ldots, \sigma_m \rangle \in \mathcal{D}\zeta_1$ iff, for some $\langle \rho_1, \ldots, \rho_m \rangle \in \mathcal{D}_\eta$, $(\mathcal{A}_i)$ either $\sigma_i \in A_{t_i}^\delta$ and $\rho_i = \sigma_i (= \sigma_i^{E\delta})$ or $\sigma_i \in QS_{t_i}^{<\beta} - A_{t_i}^\delta$, $\rho_i \in QE_{t_i}^\delta$, and $\sigma_i \neq \rho_i = \sigma_i^E (= \sigma_i^{E\delta})$ $(i = 1, \ldots, m)$, i.e.*

$$(5.5) \qquad \mathcal{D}\zeta_1 = \{\sigma \in QS_{t_1}^{<\beta} \times \ldots \times QS_{t_m}^{<\beta} \mid \sigma^{E\delta} \in \mathcal{D}\eta_1\}$$

$$(\sigma^{E\delta} = \langle \sigma_1^{E\delta}, \ldots, \sigma_m^{E\delta} \rangle);$$

and second, the holding of the alternatives $(\mathcal{A}_1)$ to $(\mathcal{A}_m)$ (i.e. $\sigma \in \mathcal{D}\zeta_1$) implies

$$(5.6) \qquad \zeta_1(\sigma) = \eta_1(\sigma^{E\delta}) \qquad\qquad (\sigma \in \mathcal{D}\zeta_1).$$

Furthermore for $\vartheta \in \langle t_1, \ldots, t_m, t_0 \rangle \in \tau_\nu$ we set

$$(5.7) \qquad LQE(\zeta) =_D \{\eta \in QE_\nu^{<\beta} \mid \zeta = m^\beta(\eta)\} \qquad (\forall \zeta \in PQE_\vartheta^\beta)$$

and

$$(5.8) \qquad QE_\vartheta^\beta =_D QE_\vartheta^{<\beta} \cup \{\zeta \in PQE_\vartheta^\beta \mid LQE(\zeta) = \emptyset\}.$$

THEOREM 5.1.   *For $\zeta \in PQE_\vartheta^\beta$ — see (5.4) — $LQE(\zeta)$ is at most a singleton.*

This can be proved exactly like the assertion (γ) at the end of §12 in [11].

6. RULES OF QE-DESIGNATION AND SEMANTICS FOR $\mathbf{L}_\lambda$ $(1 < \lambda \leq \alpha)$

In order to define $\overline{\Delta} = \mathrm{des}_{\mathcal{I}\mathcal{V}}(\Delta)$ for any wfe Δ of $\mathbf{L}_\lambda$ with $1 < \lambda \leq \alpha$ (and $\lambda = \beta + 1$) at any $\mathcal{I} \in I^\lambda$ and $\mathcal{V} \in V^\lambda$, in accordance with the directions (α') and (β) in §5, we assume (i) to (iii) above (3.14), and the definitions (3.15), (4.2), and (6.1–2) below;

$$(6.1) \qquad \overline{\Delta}_j = \mathrm{des}_{\mathcal{I}\mathcal{V}}(\Delta_j) \qquad\qquad (j = 0, \ldots, n),$$

$$(6.2) \qquad \hat{\Delta}_i = \begin{bmatrix} \check{\Delta}_i & \text{if } (\check{\Delta}_i)^{\mathrm{ord}} < (\overline{\Delta}_0)^{\mathrm{ord}}; \\ \overline{\Delta}_i & \text{otherwise} \end{bmatrix} \qquad (i = 1, \ldots, n);$$

and — see (3.15) — we set

$$(6.3) \qquad f =_D \{\langle \xi_1, \ldots, \xi_n \rangle \mid \langle \xi_1, \ldots, \xi_m \rangle \in A_{t_1}^{\delta_1} \times \ldots \times A_{t_m}^{\delta_m}, \xi_n = \overline{\Delta}'_n \neq \mathbf{F}\}.$$

Incidentally, as can be checked by rules $(\mathcal{E}_{1-8})$ in §4, (4.4), and rules (H_{1-8}) below, by (4.3) and (6.3) we have that

$$(6.4) \qquad \begin{bmatrix} f \\ g \end{bmatrix} \in (A_{t_1}^{\delta_1} \times \ldots \times A_{t_m}^{\delta_m}) \longmapsto \begin{bmatrix} QE_{t_n}^{d_f\dagger} \\ QS_{t_n}^{\delta_g\dagger} \end{bmatrix} \text{ with } d_f \leq \delta_g < \lambda,$$

where

$$(6.5) \qquad \begin{bmatrix} d_f \\ \delta_g \end{bmatrix} =_D sup \left\{ \begin{bmatrix} f(\xi)^{\text{ord}} \\ g(\xi)^{\text{ord}} \end{bmatrix} \middle| \xi \in \begin{bmatrix} \mathcal{D} f \\ A_{t_1}^{\delta_1} \times \ldots \times A_{t_m}^{\delta_m} \end{bmatrix} \right\}.$$

Furthermore, by $(6.4)_1$ and (5.4)

$$(6.6) \qquad \langle f, d_f \rangle \in PQE_\vartheta^{d_f} \qquad\qquad (\vartheta = \langle t_1, \ldots, t_m, t_0 \rangle).$$

In connection with the correctness of the inductive procedure used here to define $\mathbf{L}_\lambda$, note that g is not used in rules (H_{1-8}) below. Furthermore note that, by Definition 4.1 and (6.4–5) — *when Δ is given by rule $(\mathcal{E}_r)$ in §4 with $r \in \{6, 7, 8\}$, we have*

$$(6.7) \qquad \check{\Delta}^{\text{ord}} = \delta_g \text{— see (6.5), where } g \text{ is defined by (4.3)}$$

with n replaced by 2, 2, and n itself respectively.

Among the rules (H_{1-8}) below (for $\mathbf{L}_\lambda$) (H_r) coincides in effect with the r-th of the QE-designation rules (h_{1-8}) for $\mathcal{L}_\alpha''$ — see [11], §12 — only for $r = 1, \ldots, 5$. The same rules below define $\overline{\Delta}$ by an induction on Δ's length ℓ_Δ.

Rule	If Δ is	then $\overline{\Delta} = \text{des}_{\mathcal{I}\mathcal{V}}(\Delta)$ is
(H_1)	$v_{tn} [c_{t\mu}]$,	σ^E, where $\sigma = \mathcal{V}(v_{tn})[\sigma = \mathcal{I}(c_{t\mu})]$, if $\sigma \in QS_t^{<\beta}$ — see (4.6); σ otherwise.
(H_2)	$\Delta_0(\Delta_1, \ldots, \Delta_n)$	$(\overline{\Delta}_0)_1 (\hat{\Delta}_1, \ldots, \hat{\Delta}_n)^\dagger$ — see (6.2) and (3.11–12).
(H_3)	$\Delta_1 = \Delta_2 (t_1 = t_2)$	$\mathbf{T}$ if $\overline{\Delta}_1 = \overline{\Delta}_2$; $\mathbf{F}$ otherwise.
(H_4)	$\sim \Delta_1 (t_1 = 0)$	$\mathbf{F}$ [$\mathbf{T}$] if $\overline{\Delta}_1$ is $\mathbf{T}$ [$\mathbf{F}$].
(H_5)	$\Delta_1 \supset \Delta_2 (t_1 = t_2 = 0)$	$\mathbf{T}$ if $\overline{\Delta}_1 = \mathbf{F}$ or $\overline{\Delta}_2 = \mathbf{T}$; $\mathbf{F}$ otherwise.
(H_6)	$(\forall x_1, \delta_1)\Delta_2 (t_2 = 0)$	$\mathbf{T}$ if $\overline{\Delta}_2' = \mathbf{T}$ for all $\xi_1 \in A_{t_1}^{\delta_1}$ — see (3.15) for $n = 2$; $\mathbf{F}$ otherwise.

(H_7) $(1x_1, \delta_1)\Delta_2(t_2 = 0)$ η, if η is the unique element of $QE_{t_1}^{\delta_1}$ such that, for some $\xi_1 \in A_{t_1}^{\delta_1}$, we have both $\overline{\Delta}'_2 = \mathbf{T}$ — see (3.15) for $n = 2$ — and either $\xi_1^{\text{ord}} = \beta$ and $\eta = \xi_1$, or $\xi_1^{\text{ord}} < \beta$ and $\eta = \xi_1^E$ — see (4.6); $\mathbf{F}$ otherwise.

(H_8) $(\lambda x_1, \ldots, x_m, \delta_1, \ldots, \delta_m)\Delta_n$ $\langle f, d_f \rangle$ if the set $LQE(\langle f, d_g \rangle)$ is empty; its unique element otherwise — see (6.3), (6.5)$_1$, (6.6), (5.7), and Theorem 5.1.

Incidentally, the two alternatives in (H_7) are written in order to have a correct recursive definition of $\mathbf{L}_\lambda$. When the definition of $\mathbf{L}_\alpha$ is at hand, one can easily check that assertion (H_7) simplifies into

$(\overline{H}_7)$ If Δ is $(1x_1, \delta_1)\Delta_2$, then (i) $\overline{\Delta} = \eta$ if η is the unique element of $QE_{t_1}^{\delta_1}$ such that both $\eta = \xi_1^E$ — see (4.6) — and $\overline{\Delta}'_2 = \mathbf{T}$ — see (3.15) with $n = 2$ — for some $\xi_1 \in A_{t_1}^{\delta_1}$ and (ii) $\overline{\Delta} = \mathbf{F}$ if such a unique η fails to exist.

Consider any ordinal λ ($0 < \lambda \leq \alpha$) and assume $\mathbf{L}_\delta$ as known for $\delta < \lambda$. In case $\lambda = \beta + 1$ for some β, the objects (5.1) are defined by recursion on t (and ϑ) in §3, for $\beta = 0$, and in §5 for $\beta > 0$.

In case λ is a limit ordinal, i.e. $\lambda = \cup\lambda \neq 0$ — see Theorem 10.3 (ii) in [14], p. 76 — the objects (5.1) and $QS_t^\beta (t \in \tau_\nu)$ are known for $\beta < \lambda$; consequently so are $QE_t^{<\lambda}, A_t^{<\lambda}$, and $QS_t^{<\lambda}$ ($t \in \tau_\nu$).

No matter what kind of ordinal λ is, we can define the objects (1) I^λ and V^λ by (3.8)$_{1-3}$, (2) f by (6.3), (3) $des^\lambda(= des)$ by rules (H_{1-8}) in §3 [§6] for $\lambda = 1[\lambda > 1]$ (and by induction on ℓ_Δ), (4) g by (4.3), (5) $sens^\lambda(= sens)$ by rules $(\mathcal{E}_{1-8})$ in §4 (and by induction on ℓ_Δ), (6) QS_t^β by (4.4) if $\lambda = \beta + 1$ (for $\lambda = \cup\lambda$, $QS_t^{<\beta}$ is known), and σ^E for any $\sigma \in QS_t^{<\beta}$ by (4.6).

Thus the semantics for $\mathbf{L}_\lambda$ is determined. Hence by transfinite induction on λ, the one for $\mathbf{L}_\alpha$ is defined.

The relations (9.3–4) in [11], proved to hold for $\mathcal{L}_\alpha$ and $\mathcal{L}''_\alpha$, also hold for $\mathbf{L}_\alpha$:

(6.8) $\begin{cases} QE_r^\beta = QE_r^0, \ QE_r^\beta = QE_r^0 & (r = 0, \ldots, \nu; \ \beta < \alpha), \\ QE_\vartheta^\delta \subset QE_\vartheta^\beta, \ Q\mathcal{E}_\vartheta^\delta \subset Q\mathcal{E}_\vartheta^\beta & (t \in \tau_\nu - \{0, \ldots, \nu\}; \delta < \beta < \alpha), \\ QS_t^\delta \subset QS_t^\beta & (t \in \tau_\nu, \ \delta < \beta < \alpha), \end{cases}$

where $\subset$ excludes identity; furthermore, *for $\delta < \beta < \alpha$ and $t \neq t' (\in \tau_\nu)$*

(6.9) $QE_t^\delta \cap QE_{t'}^\beta = \begin{bmatrix} \mathbf{F} \\ \{\mathbf{F}, \emptyset\} \end{bmatrix}$ *and*

$Q\mathcal{E}_t^\delta \cap Q\mathcal{E}_{t'} = \begin{bmatrix} \emptyset & \text{for } \{t, t'\} \cap \{0, \ldots, \nu\} \neq \emptyset, \\ \{\emptyset\} & \text{otherwise.} \end{bmatrix}$

Let us add that by (5.2), (6.8)$_{1-3}$, and (4.4), we have that for $t \in \tau_\nu$, $r \in \{0,\ldots,\nu\}$, $\vartheta \in \tau_\nu - \{0,\ldots,\nu\}$, and $\beta = \cup\beta < \alpha$

$$(6.10) \qquad EQ_t^\delta \subseteq A_t^\delta \subset QS_t^\delta, \; A_t^{<\beta} = QS_t^{<\beta}, \; QS_r^\beta = A_r^\beta, \; QS_\vartheta^{<\beta} \subset A_\vartheta^\beta.$$

DEFINITION 6.1. *If (3.2) holds, $\mathcal{I} \in I^\alpha$, and $\mathbf{I} = \langle \mathcal{D}_1,\ldots,\mathcal{D}_\nu,\mathcal{I}\rangle$, then $\mathbf{I}$ is said to be an interpretation of $\mathbf{L}_\alpha$.*

7. SOME BASIC SEMANTICAL NOTIONS FOR $\mathbf{L}_\alpha$ EXPRESSED IN $\mathbf{L}_\alpha$ ITSELF

CONVENTION 7.1. *Instead of* $(\forall x_1, \delta_1)\ldots(\forall x_m, \delta_m)$ *we may write* $(\forall x_1,\ldots,x_m, \delta_1,\ldots,\delta_m)$ *and even* $(\forall x_1,\ldots,x_m; \beta)$ *in case* $\delta_1 = \ldots = \delta_m = \beta$. We use the rather customary definitions

$$(7.1) \qquad (\exists x, \beta)p \equiv_D \sim (\forall x, \beta) \sim p,$$
$$(\exists^{(1)} x, \beta)p \equiv_D (\forall x, y; \beta).p \wedge p[x/y] \supset x = y,$$
$$(\exists_1 x, \beta)p \equiv_D (\exists x, \beta)p \wedge (\exists^{(1)} x, \beta),$$
$$a_t^* =_D (1v_{t1}, 0)v_{t1} \neq v_{t1}.$$

We now introduce certain (eleven logical) wffs (or better wff-schemes) $\Delta \in \mathcal{E}_t^\beta$ to $\Delta \in \mathcal{OS}_t^{\beta\dagger}$ of $\mathbf{L}_\alpha$, in order to express in $\mathbf{L}_\alpha$ itself certain basic semantical properties of the entity expressed by $\mathbf{L}_\alpha$'s arbitrary wfe Δ, at the arbitrary $\mathcal{I} \in I^\alpha$ and $\mathcal{V} \in V^\alpha$. These wffs are determined briefly by the metalinguistic definitions (7.3–13) below[7] where conditions (i), (ii), and (7.2) below are assumed.

(i) $\qquad \beta < \alpha; t \in \tau_\nu; \Delta, \Delta_1, \Delta_2 \in E_t; \mathcal{I} \in I^\alpha$; and $\mathcal{V} \in V^\alpha$.

(ii) $\qquad x, y, F$, and G are distinct variables that do not occur in Δ, Δ_1, or Δ_2.

$$(7.2) \qquad d_\Delta^\gamma =_D (1x, \gamma)(\forall G, \gamma) \cdot G = G \wedge x = \Delta \; (\gamma < \alpha);$$
$$x, y \in E_t; \; F, G \in E_{(t)}.$$

Here are the aforementioned definitions where, roughly speaking, $\mathcal{E}, \mathcal{S}, \mathcal{O}$ and $\mathcal{NO}$ stand for extension, sense, ostensive, and nonostensive respectively.

$$(7.3) \qquad \Delta \in \mathcal{E}_t^\beta =_D (\exists F, \beta)F(\Delta).$$

---

[7] By "briefly" we refer to the fact that e.g. (7.5) stands for the definition $\Delta \in \mathcal{E}_t^{<\beta} \equiv_D \Delta \in \mathcal{E}_t^\beta \wedge \sim \Delta \in \mathcal{E}_t^{\beta\dagger}$, which determines the meaning of the wff $\Delta \in \mathcal{E}_t^{<\beta}$.

(7.4) $\Delta \in \mathcal{E}_t^{\beta\dagger} \equiv_D \Delta \in \mathcal{E}_t^\beta \wedge (\forall x, y, F; \beta).\Delta = x = y \wedge F(x) \supset F(y).$

(7.5–6) $\mathcal{E}_t^{<\beta} =_D \mathcal{E}_t^\beta - \mathcal{E}_t^{\beta\dagger}, \ \Delta_1 \asymp^\beta \Delta_2 =_D \Delta_1 \asymp_{<\beta} \Delta_2$
$\equiv_D (\forall F, \beta).F(\Delta_1) \equiv F(\Delta_2) \ (\asymp_\beta =_D \asymp^{\beta+1}).$

(7.7) $\Delta \in \mathcal{NOS}_t^{<\beta} \equiv_D \sim (\Delta \asymp^\beta d_\Delta^\beta).$

(7.8) $\Delta \in \mathcal{S}_t^{<\beta} \equiv_D (\exists F, \beta) \cdot F(\Delta) \in \mathcal{NOS}_0^{<\beta}.$

(7.9–10) $\mathcal{OS}_t^{<\beta} =_D \mathcal{S}_t^{<\beta} - \mathcal{NOS}_t^{<\beta}, \ \mathcal{S}_t^\beta =_D \mathcal{S}_t^{<\beta+1}.$

(7.11) $\mathcal{S}_t^{\beta\dagger} =_D \mathcal{S}_t^\beta - \mathcal{S}_t^{<\beta}.$

(7.12–13) $\mathcal{OS}_t^{\beta\dagger} =_D \mathcal{OS}_t^\beta - \mathcal{S}_t^{<\beta}, \ \mathcal{A}_t^\beta =_D \mathcal{S}_t^{<\beta} \cup \mathcal{OS}_t^\beta.$

Any wfe Δ that contains some constant or free variable, can have a QS $\check{\Delta}$ of order greater than any fixed $\beta(< \alpha)$, at some $\mathcal{I} \in I^\alpha$ and $\mathcal{V} \in V^\alpha$. Furthermore it is easy to prove the following

LEMMA. *Conditions* (i), (ii), *and* (7.2) *imply that*

(7.14) $\xi^{\mathrm{ord}} = max(\gamma, \check{\Delta}^{\mathrm{ord}})$ for $\check{\Delta} = sens_{\mathcal{I}V}(\Delta)$ and $\xi = sens_{\mathcal{I}V}(d_\Delta^\gamma).$

The meanings of the logical wffs (7.3–13) appear from the following:

THEOREM 7.1. *Choose arbitrarily* $\Delta \in E_t$, $\mathcal{I} \in I^\alpha$, *and* $\mathcal{V} \in V^\alpha$. *Furthermore, for* $r = 3, \ldots, 13$ *consider* $\mathbf{L}_\alpha$'s *wff* $(\Delta \in \ldots)$ *or* $(\Delta \ldots \Delta_1)$ *briefly determined by Definition* (7.r) — *see footnote 7. Its truth conditions are given by the translation relation* $(\ldots \approx \ldots)$ *written as formula* (7.12 +r) *below, in which* $\overline{\Delta} = des_{\mathcal{I}V}(\Delta)$, $\check{\Delta} = sens_{\mathcal{I}V}(\Delta)$, *and* $\check{\Delta}_1 = sens_{\mathcal{I}V}(\Delta_1)$, *and for which some possible readings are suggested below* (7.25).

(7.15–17) $\Delta \in \mathcal{E}_t^\beta \approx \overline{\Delta} \in QE_t^\beta, \ \Delta \in \mathcal{E}_t^{\beta\dagger}[\mathcal{E}_t^{<\beta}] \approx \overline{\Delta} \in QE_t^{\beta\dagger}[QE_t^{<\beta}].$

(7.18) $\Delta_1 \asymp^\beta \Delta_2 \approx \begin{cases} \text{(a)} & \check{\Delta}_1 = \check{\Delta}_2 \in QS_t^{<\beta} - QE_t^\beta \text{ or} \\ \text{(b)} & \overline{\Delta}_1 = \overline{\Delta}_2 \text{ and } (\mathcal{A}_i)\check{\Delta}_i = \overline{\Delta}_i \text{ or} \\ & \check{\Delta}_i^{\mathrm{ord}} \geq \beta \ (i = 1, 2). \end{cases}$

(7.19–20) $\Delta \in \mathcal{NOS}_t^{<\beta} \approx \check{\Delta} \in QS_t^{<\beta} - QE_t^\beta, \ \Delta \in \mathcal{S}_t^{<\beta} \approx \check{\Delta} \in QS_t^{<\beta}.$

(7.21) $\Delta \in \mathcal{OS}_t^{<\beta} \approx \check{\Delta} \in QE_t^{<\beta}.$

(7.22–23) $\Delta \in \mathcal{S}_t^\beta[\mathcal{S}_t^{\beta\dagger}] \approx \check{\Delta} \in QS^\beta[QS^{\beta\dagger}].$

(7.24–25) $\Delta \in \mathcal{OS}_t^{\beta\dagger}[\mathcal{A}_t^\beta] \approx \check{\Delta} \in QE_t^{\beta\dagger}[A_t^\beta].$

E.g. (7.16–17) can be read as (α) *the wff* $\Delta \in \mathcal{E}_t^{\beta\dagger}$ $[\Delta \in \mathcal{E}_t^{<\beta}]$ *holds* — i.e. has $\mathbf{T}$ as QE — *designatum* — *at* $\mathcal{I} \in I^\alpha$ *and* $\mathcal{V} \in V^\alpha$ iff (β) $\overline{\Delta} \in QE_t^{\beta\dagger}$ $[\overline{\Delta} \in QE_t^{<\beta}]$, or iff (β') *the entity* Δ (*of type* t) *has an extension of order* $= \beta$ $[< \beta]$.

Furthermore (7.18) can be read as $\Delta_1 \asymp^\beta \Delta_2$ means that the entities Δ_1 and Δ_2 (of type t) are β-*synonymous*, i.e. that they behave as synonymous entities for predicates of extensional orders $\leq \beta$, in that either (a) they have the same nonostensive sense of order $< \beta$, or (b) they have the same extension and the sense of each of them is either ostensive or of order $\geq \beta$. Furthermore, by (7.19) [(7.21)]

$\Delta \in \mathcal{NOS}_t^{<\beta}$ [$\check{\Delta} \in \mathcal{OS}_t^{<\beta}$] means that Δ has a nonostensive [ostensive] (technical) sense of order $< \beta$ — see Definition 1.1.

Brief Proof of Theorem 7.1. Thesis (7.15) is obvious; and each of theses (7.17, 20–25) too, when the preceding theses are taken into account. To prove thesis (7.16) assume that (a) $\Delta \in \mathcal{E}_t^{\beta\dagger}$ holds. Then $\Delta \in \mathcal{E}_r^\beta$ too is true by (7.4); hence by (7.15), (b) $\overline{\Delta} \in QE_t^\beta$.

Assume now (c) $\overline{\Delta} \in QE_t^{<\beta}$. Then we can choose $\mathcal{V}'$ satisfying $(3.15)_2$ for $\langle x_1, \ldots, x_m \rangle = \langle x, y, F \rangle$, $\xi_1 = \overline{\Delta}$, $\xi_2 \in QS_t^{<\beta}$, $\xi_2 \neq \xi_2^E = \xi_1$, and $\xi_3 = \langle f, \beta \rangle$ with $\mathcal{D}f = \{\xi_1\}$, so that $\xi_3 \in QS_t^{\beta\dagger}$. Then the wff $\Delta_4 \equiv_D \Delta = x = y \wedge F(x) \wedge \sim F(y)$ holds at $\mathcal{I}$ and $\mathcal{V}'$. Then $(\forall x, y, F; \beta) \cdot \Delta = x = y \wedge F(x) \supset F(y)$ is false at $\mathcal{I}$ and $\mathcal{V}$, which by (7.4) contrasts with (a). Hence (c) is false. Then (b) implies (d) $\overline{\Delta} \in QE_t^{\beta\dagger}$. We conclude that (a) $\Rightarrow$ (d).

The converse implication is easy to prove in that this can be done by using $\mathbf{L}_\alpha$, in effect, as an ordinary extensional language. Thus (7.16) holds.

To prove (7.18) note that by (7.6) $\Delta_1 \asymp^\beta \Delta_2$ is true iff (e) for all $\xi \in A_{(t)}^\beta$ the wff $F(\Delta_1) \equiv F(\Delta_2)$ holds at $\mathcal{I}$ and $\mathcal{V}' = \mathcal{V}\begin{pmatrix} F \\ \xi \end{pmatrix}$ — see (3.13). By rule (H_2) in §6, condition (e) is equivalent to the alternative (a) or (b) in (7.18). Thus thesis (7.18) holds.

To prove (7.19), note that by (7.7), the truth of the wff (f) $\Delta \in \mathcal{NOS}_t^{<\beta}$ is equivalent to the falsity of (g) $\Delta_1 \asymp^\beta \Delta_2$, being assumed that Δ_1 is Δ and Δ_2 is d_Δ^β. Thus $\overline{\Delta}_1 = \overline{\Delta}_2 \neq \check{\Delta}_2 \neq \check{\Delta}_1$ and $\check{\Delta}_2^{\text{ord}} \geq \beta$. Hence by (7.18), (g) is true iff either $\check{\Delta}_1 = \overline{\Delta}_1$ or $\check{\Delta}_1^{\text{ord}} \geq \beta$. Then (g) is false iff both $\overline{\Delta} \neq \check{\Delta}$ and $\check{\Delta}^{\text{ord}} < \beta$, i.e. iff $\Delta \in QS_t^{<\beta} - QE_t^\beta$. Thus thesis (7.19) holds. $\square$

8. A LOGICAL CALCULUS $\mathbf{C}_\alpha$ VALID IN $\mathbf{L}_\alpha$

THE ORDINARY AND REFINED VERSIONS OF $\mathbf{L}_\alpha$ AND $\mathbf{C}_\alpha$

We want to introduce the lower predicate calculus with identity and descriptions $\mathbf{LPCID}_\alpha$ based on $\mathbf{L}_\alpha$, and more generally the logical calculus $\mathbf{C}_\alpha$. Therefore we take definitions (7.3–13) (and Conventions 2.1–3) into account and we assume that

(i) $\beta < \alpha, \gamma < \alpha, \delta < \alpha, t \in \tau_\nu, \Delta \in E_t, m \in \mathbb{N}_*, r \in \{0, \ldots, \nu\}$, and $\langle t_1, \ldots, t_m, t_0 \rangle \in \tau_\nu$,

(ii) x, y and z are three (distinct) variables of type t, of which x and y fail to occur free in Δ, and

(iii) x_1 to x_m are m variables in E_{t_1} to E_{t_m} respectively, while f and g are two functional or attribute expressions.

Then, first the wffs A8.1–10 below are valid in $\mathbf{L}_\alpha$ — i.e., $\mathbf{T}$ is their HQE-designatum at all $\mathcal{I} \in I^\alpha$ and $\mathcal{V} \in V^\alpha$. Furthermore they are regarded as the axioms of the $LCPID_\alpha$.

A8.1–3. $(p \supset .q \supset r) \supset .(p \supset q. \supset .p \supset r); \quad \sim q \supset \sim p. \supset (\sim q \supset p. \supset q); \quad p \supset .q \supset p.$

A8.4. $\Delta \in \mathcal{A}_t^\beta \lor p[x/\Delta] \in \mathcal{S}_t^\gamma . \land (\forall x, \delta)p \supset p[x/\Delta]\, (\beta \leq \delta, \, \gamma \leq \delta).$[8]

A8.5. $(\forall x, \beta)(p \supset q) \supset .p \supset (\forall x, \beta)q$ *where x does not occur free in p.*

A8.6–7. $x = x, \quad x = y \land y = z \supset z = x.$

A8.7–8. $p = q \equiv .p \equiv q, \quad \sim p \equiv p = a_0^*.$

A8.10. (a) $\Delta \in \mathcal{A}_t^\beta \lor p[x/\Delta] \in \mathcal{S}_t^\gamma . \land (\exists^{(1)}x, \delta)p \land p[x/\Delta] \supset \Delta = (1x, \delta)p \ (\beta \leq \delta, \, \gamma \leq \delta),$

   (b) $\sim (\exists_1 x, \delta)p \supset (1x, \delta)p = a_t^*$ — see $(7.1)_4$.

In analogy with the considerations on $\mathcal{L}_\alpha''$ in [11] below (13.15) we now specify the ordinary [refined] (version of $\mathbf{L}_\alpha$ by requiring the HQE $\mathbf{F}$ of the non-existing object to equal [not to equal] the HQE $\langle \emptyset, 0 \rangle$ of the empty attribute or function $\emptyset_\vartheta$ of any type $\vartheta \in \tau_\nu - \{0, \dots, \nu\}$.

The following metalinguistic definition of $\emptyset_\vartheta$ is adequate in any version of $\mathbf{L}_\alpha$ — see $(7.1)_4$.

(8.1) $\emptyset_\vartheta =_D (1f, 0).f \neq a_\vartheta^* \land (\forall y_1, \dots, y_m).f(y_1, \dots, y_m) = a_{t_0}^*$

— see (i) — where y_r is $v_{t_n, r}\ (r = 1, \dots, m)$. Instead the 1st $[2^{nd}]$ of the wffs

(8.2) $\emptyset_\vartheta = a_\vartheta^*, \quad \emptyset_\vartheta \neq a_\vartheta^* \qquad\qquad (\vartheta = \langle t_1, \dots, t_m, t_0 \rangle \in \tau_\nu)$

is valid only in the ordinary [refined] $\mathbf{L}_\alpha$. The $LPCID_\alpha$ added with it will be called the *ordinary [refined]* $LPCID_\alpha$. The analogous stipulations will be regarded as stated for the logical calculus $\mathbf{C}_\alpha$.

The deduction rules for the $LPCID_\alpha$ (or $\mathbf{C}_\alpha$) are *modus ponens* $(p, p \supset q \vdash q)$ and the *generalization rule for axioms*:

GRA. *If A is an axiom and $\beta < \alpha$, then* $\vdash (\forall v_{tn}, \beta)A.$

In order to state the axioms A8.11–30 below for the extension $\mathbb{C}_\alpha$ of the $LPCID_\alpha$, we now define the β-n-tuple $\{\Delta_1, \dots, \Delta_n\}_\beta\ (\beta < \alpha)$, which is even empty in case $\Delta_i \in \mathcal{E}_{t_i}^{\delta_i \dagger}$ holds for $\delta_i > \beta\ (i = 1, \dots, m)$:[9]

(8.3) $\{\Delta_1, \dots, \Delta_n\}_\beta =_D (\lambda x, \beta) \bigvee_{i=1}^n x = \Delta_i$

$$(x \text{ fails to be free in } \Delta_1 \text{ to } \Delta_n).$$

The *refined* version of the hyper-intensionality axiom — relevant even for the ordinary extensional segment $\mathbf{L}_1$ of $\mathbf{L}_\alpha$, see footnote 15 in [11], §13 — reads

---

[8] The analogue of A8.4 for $\mathcal{L}_\alpha''$ is axiom (14.1) in [11]. The alternative $\Delta \in \mathcal{A}_t^\beta$ with $\beta \leq \delta$ $[p[x/\Delta] \in \mathcal{S}_t^\gamma$ with $\gamma \leq \delta]$ in A8.4 corresponds to the cases (ii) and (iii) [to the case (i)] considered for the latter axiom (below it) in [11].

[9] $\bigvee_{i=1}^n p_i \equiv_D p_1 \lor \dots \lor p_n; \quad \bigwedge_{i=1}^n p_i \equiv_D p_1 \land \dots \land p_n.$

A8.11. $f, g \in \mathcal{E}_\vartheta^\beta \supset .(f = g \vee \{f, g\}_0 = \{a_\vartheta^*, \emptyset_\vartheta\}_0)$
$\equiv (\forall x_1, \ldots, x_m, \delta_1, \ldots, \delta_m) f(x_1, \ldots, x_m)$
$= g(x_1, \ldots, x_m) \quad (\beta \leq \delta_i < \alpha \text{ for } i = 1, \ldots, m)$ — see (iii).

In the ordinary $\mathbf{C}_\alpha$, by $(8.2)_1$ and A8.13 below, A8.11 yields its *ordinary* version — obtainable from A8.11 by replacing $(f = g \vee \ldots)$ with $f = g$.

Here is the existence axiom — or building axiom, see [14], p. 16 — for attributes and functions.

A8.12. $\Delta \in \mathcal{S}_t^\beta \supset (\exists f, \beta)(\forall x_1, \ldots, x_m; \delta_1, \ldots, \delta_m).f(x_1, \ldots, x_m) = \Delta.$
A8.13–14. $\Delta = a_\vartheta^* \supset \Delta(\Delta_1, \ldots, \Delta_n) = a_{t_0}^*, \quad (\exists x, 0)x \neq a_t^* \ (t = 0, \ldots, \nu).$

By (3.2), A8.14 is obviously valid (and for $t \in \tau_\nu$).

The axiom for λ-expressions reads

A8.15. $\bigwedge_{i=1}^{m} \Delta_i \in \mathcal{A}_{t_i}^{\delta_i} \supset .p[x_1/\Delta_1, \ldots, x_m/\Delta_m]$
$\equiv [(\lambda x_1, \ldots, x_m, \delta_1, \ldots, \delta_m)](\Delta_1, \ldots, \Delta_m).$

The axioms below are more related to $\mathbf{L}_\alpha$'s peculiar hyper-intensional features than the preceding axioms.

A8.16–17. $(\forall v_{t1}, \beta)v_{t1} \in \mathcal{A}_t^\beta, \quad \Delta \in \mathcal{E}_r^0 \text{for } \Delta \in E_r.$
A8.18. $\Delta_0 \in \mathcal{E}_\vartheta^\beta \wedge x \in \mathcal{OS}_t^{\delta_i\dagger} \wedge \Delta_i \notin \mathcal{E}_i^{<\beta} \wedge x = \Delta_i \supset .p \equiv p[x/\Delta_i],$
where $i \in \{1, \ldots, m\}$ *and* p *is obtained from* $\Delta_0(\Delta_1, \ldots, \Delta_m)$
$(= p[x/\Delta_i])$ *by replacing* Δ_i *with* x — *see* (i).
A8.19. $\Delta \in \mathcal{E}_t^\beta \supset (\exists x, \beta).x = \Delta \wedge x \in \mathcal{OS}_t^\beta.$
A8.20–21. $\mathcal{A}_t^0 = \mathcal{OS}_t^{0\dagger}, \mathcal{E}_r^\beta = \mathcal{E}_r^0$ see footnote 7.
A8.22–23. $\mathcal{E}_\vartheta^\delta \subset \mathcal{E}_\vartheta^\beta \ (\delta < \beta), \quad \mathcal{A}_t^\beta \subset \mathcal{S}_t^\beta$ — see (i) and footnote 7.

In case β *is a limit ordinal,*

A8.24–26. $\mathcal{S}_t^{<\beta} = \mathcal{A}_t^{<\beta}(=_D \mathcal{A}_t^\beta - \mathcal{E}_t^{\beta\dagger}), \mathcal{S}_r^\beta = \mathcal{A}_r^\beta, \mathcal{S}_\vartheta^{<\beta} \subset \mathcal{A}_\vartheta^\beta \ (\beta = \cup\beta \neq 0).$

The validities of A8.21–26 follow from the six relations $(6.8)_{1,3}$ and $(6.10)_{1-4}$ respectively.

Now assume that, for $s = 2$ to 8, $\Delta_{(s)}$ is the wfe $\Delta_{(s)}$ exhibited in rule $(\mathcal{E}_s)$ (in §4). Furthermore, in case $s \leq 5$ call Δ_1' to Δ_k' those among the wfes Δ_0, $\Delta_1, \Delta_2, \ldots, \Delta_n$ that occur in $\Delta_{(s)}$ explicitly (and let Δ_1' to Δ_k' be variables, if preferred). Then — see footnote 7.

A8.27. (a) $\bigwedge_{i=1}^{k} \Delta_i' \in \mathcal{S}_{t_i}^{<\beta} \supset \Delta_{(s)} \in \mathcal{S}_t^{<\beta} \ (s = 2, \ldots, 5),$

(b) $(\forall x_1, 0)(\Delta_2 \in \mathcal{S}_0^{\delta_1}) \supset .\Delta_{(6)} \in \mathcal{S}_0^{\delta_1} \wedge \Delta_{(7)} \in \mathcal{S}_t^{\delta_1},$

(c) $(\forall x_1, \ldots, x_m; 0)(\Delta_n \in \mathcal{S}_t^{<\beta}) \supset \Delta_{(8)} \in \mathcal{S}_t^{<\beta}$
$(\beta > max(\delta_1, \ldots, \delta_m)).$

Thus the recursive clauses for $\mathcal{S}_t^{<\beta}$ are stated.

The remaining axioms concern (basic) synonymy (i.e., roughly speaking, the maximum synonymy relation to be considered) — other synonymy relations are dealt with in [5], sections 10–11.

A8.28. $\Delta \in \mathcal{S}_t^{<\beta} \supset .\Delta \asymp_\beta \Delta_1$ if Δ_1 is an equivalent of Δ.[10]

A8.29. $\Delta \in \mathcal{A}_t^\beta \equiv (\exists x, \beta)x \asymp_\beta \Delta$,

A8.30. $x \in \mathcal{S}_t^{<\beta} \supset .\Delta \asymp^\beta \Delta' \wedge \Delta_1 \asymp^\beta \Delta_2 \equiv \Delta[x/\Delta_1] \asymp^\beta \Delta'[x/\Delta_2]$
         where $\Delta_1, \Delta_2 \in E_t$, and x occurs free in both Δ and Δ'.

---

[10] Roughly speaking, Δ_1 is obtained from Δ by (certain) well known changes of bound variables, that render the wff $\Delta = \Delta_1$ valid — see Definition 3.1 in [8].

BIBLIOGRAPHY

[1]   Anderson, A. R. & Belnap, N. (1975): Entailment. The logic of relevance and necessity. Princeton University Press, 543pp.

[2]   Bealer, G. (1982): Quality and Concept, Claredon Press, Oxford, 311pp.

[3]   Bonotto, C. (1981/82): Synonymy for Bressan's modal calculus MC^ν. Part 1: A synonymy relation for MC^ν. Part 2: A sufficient criterium for non-synonymy, *Atti Istituto Veneto di Scienze, Lettere ed Arti*, 140, pp. 11–24, pp. 85–99.

[4]   Bonotto, C. & Bressan, A. (1983/84): On a synonymy relation for extensional first order theories. Part 1: A notion of synonymy. Part 2: A sufficient criterium for non-synonymy. Applications. Part 3: A necessary and sufficient condition for synonymy. *Rend. Sem. Math.*, Univ. Padova 69 (1983), pp. 63–76, 70 (1983), pp. 13–19, 71 (1984), 1–13.

[5]   Bonotto, C. & Bressan, A. (1984): On generalized synonymy notions and corresponding quasi-senses. *Memoir in Atti Acc. Naz. Nincei*, (VIII), 17, pp. 163–208.

[6]   Bonotto, C. & Zanardo, A. (1989): A non-compactness phenomenon in logics with hyperintensional predication. *Journal of Philosophical Logic*, 18, pp. 383–398.

[7]   Bressan, A. (1972): A general interpreted modal calculus. Yale University Press, New Haven, 327pp.

[8]   Bressan, A. (1985): On the interpreted sense calculus SC_α^ν. In "Foundations of Logic and Linguistics" edited by G. Dorn and P. Weingartner (Plenum Publishing Corporation), pp. 427–463.

[9]   Bressan, A. (1984): Axiom system for the sense language $S\mathcal{L}_\alpha^\nu$. In *Atti Ist. Veneto di Scienze, Lettere ed Arti*, 147, pp. 19–30.[11]

[10] Bressan, A. (1985): On the logic of senses. An anomalous use of belief sentences. Its rigorous formal treatment. Atti degli Incontri di Logica Matematica, Vol. 3 (Siena 1985, Padova 1985, Siena 1986) Scuola di specializzazione in Logica Mat., Dipart, di Mat., Univ. di Siena.

[11] Bressan, A.: New semantics for the extensional but hyper-intensional part $\mathcal{L}_\alpha$ of the modal sense language $S\mathcal{L}_\alpha^\nu$. Forthcoming in the *Notre Dame Journal of Formal Logic*.

[12] Church, A. (1954): Intensional isomorphism and identity of belief. *Philosophical Studies*, 5, pp. 65–72.

[13a] Church, A. (1951): A formulation of the logic of sense and denotation. In "Structures, Method, and Meaning, Essays in Honour of H. M. Sheffer". New York, pp. 3–24.

[13b] ——————— : Outline of a revised formulation of the logic of sense and denotation. *Noûs* 7 (1973), 24–33, 8 (1974), 135–156.

[13c] ——————— : A revised formulation of sense and denotation.

[14] Monk, D. (1969): Introduction to set theory. McGraw-Hill, New York.

[15] Parsons, C. (1982): Intensional logic in extensional language. *J.S.L.*, 47, pp. 289–328.

[16] Quine, W. Van Orman (1960): Word and object. The technology press of the MIT or Wiley & Sons, Inc., New York and London, 294pp.

---

[11] The work [9], presented at the 1st International Conference on Systems Research, Information and Cybernetics, 1984, Baden-Baden, ought to be printed in the proceedings of that conference; however, in November 1988 the printing work of these proceedings had not yet been started.

JOHN F. HORTY

A SKEPTICAL THEORY OF MIXED INHERITANCE

1. INTRODUCTION

This paper is concerned with the problem of providing a semantic account for inheritance networks capable of representing both strict and defeasible information. The importance of representing defeasible information in a knowledge base — particularly, in a frame- or network-based inheritance reasoner — has been widely recognized ever since the publication of Minsky's original paper on frames [11]. Although early systems designed to allow defeasible inheritance reasoning, such as FRL [12] and NETL [6], were subject to semantic difficulties in their treatment of cancellation, these problems by now are essentially solved. In fact, there exist today a number of well-defined and intuitively attractive theories of defeasible inheritance, including those of Touretzky [15], Sandewall [13], and Horty et al. [8]. The variety of these theories does not seem to indicate any kind of instability or chaos in our understanding, but instead, the presence of a range of options in the design space for defeasible inheritance reasoners; some of these options are surveyed in Touretzky et al. [16].

It has been suggested, however, by Brachman [3, 4] and Israel [10], that this intense concern with the issue of representing defeasible information has obscured some of the more general problems exhibited by network formalisms capable of representing only defeasible information. Unless a formalism is able to represent strict or indefeasible information as well, it cannot express the important analytic or definitional relations among concepts. A system capable of representing only defeasible information cannot capture, for example, the necessary subsumption of Indian elephants under elephants; it can represent, without any kind of inconsistency, the fact that some particular Indian elephant might just happen not to be an elephant.

One way of responding to these difficulties is to abandon the project of encoding defeasible information in an inheritance reasoner, concentrating instead on definitional relations among richly structured concepts. This approach, which has been explored by those working in the tradition of KL-ONE and its descendants, has led to a number of useful results, including the design of classification algorithms for the automatic placement of complex concepts in a semantic network. However, the approach also carries with it the disadvantage of forcing defeasible information, which must be represented somewhere in the knowledge base, to be represented outside of the inheritance reasoner — perhaps, as suggested by Brachman and Schmolze [5], in a separate collection of default rules. The problem with this idea, of course, is that it is hard to see how a system could actually use the defeasible information if it were represented in this way: theorem proving in default logic is not a realistic possibility.

An alternative possibility is to explore ways in which strict and defeasible taxonomic information might be combined in a single inheritance network. This paper

J. M. Dunn and A. Gupta (eds.), Truth or Consequences, 267–281.

presents a first step along these lines: a theory of inheritance for semantic networks containing strict or defeasible, positive or negative IS-A links, all mixed together. The analysis of mixed inheritance described here is itself a mixture, combining the theory of strict inheritance from Thomason et al. [14] with the skeptical theory of defeasible inheritance provided by Horty et al. [8].

2. BASIC CONCEPTS

2.1 Links and nets

Letters from the beginning of the alphabet (a through d) refer only to objects or individuals; letters from the middle of the alphabet (m through t) refer only to properties or kinds. Letters from the end of the alphabet (u through z) range over both objects and properties.

The link types $x \Rightarrow p$ and $x \not\Leftrightarrow p$ represent positive and negative *strict* statements. If x is a property, these positive and negative strict links are equivalent to quantified conditionals: the link $q \Rightarrow p$ represents a statement of the form 'Every Q is a P'; the link $q \not\Leftrightarrow p$ represents a statement of the form 'No Q is a P'. If x is an object, these positive and negative strict links are equivalent to atomic and neg-atomic statements from ordinary logic: $a \Rightarrow p$ and $a \not\Leftrightarrow p$ represent the statements Pa and $\neg Pa$.

The link types $x \rightarrow p$ and $x \not\rightarrow p$ represent positive and negative *defeasible* statements. If x is a property, these defeasible links correspond to ordinary generic statements: $q \rightarrow p$ and $r \not\rightarrow p$, for example, might stand for the statements 'Birds fly' and 'Mammals don't fly'. There is nothing in classical logic very close in meaning to generic statements like these. For example, 'Birds fly' does not mean that all birds fly, since it is true even in the presence of exceptions. Instead, it seems to mean that "typical birds" fly — or that for any given bird a, it is most natural to suppose that a flies. If x is an object, it is more difficult to find a simple reading for these defeasible links; but we will assume that $a \rightarrow p$ and $a \not\rightarrow p$, respectively, mean something along the lines of 'It is most natural to suppose that Pa' and 'It is most natural to suppose that $\neg Pa$'.

Capital Greek letters represent *networks* — finite graphs, with nodes and link types as described. Networks are themselves classified as *strict* if they contain only strict links, or *defeasible* if they contain no strict links emanating from property nodes. *Mixed* networks can contain both strict and defeasible links emanating from property nodes.

2.2 Paths

Lower case Greek letters refer to *paths* — special sequences of links. Often, it is convenient to refer to an arbitrary path in a way that displays some of the nodes it passes through without displaying the particular link types connecting those nodes. For this purpose, we adopt a notation according to which '$\pi(x, \sigma, y)$' refers to an arbitrary positive path, and '$\bar{\pi}(x, \sigma, y)$' likewise to an arbitrary negative path, from x through σ to y. As a convention governing this π-notation, we assume that adjacency of node symbols entails adjacency of nodes on the paths symbolized. Thus, for example, '$\bar{\pi}(x, u, \sigma, y)$' refers to a negative path beginning with a direct link of any type from x to u, and then moving through σ to y.

Paths are classified as simple or compound, strict or defeasible, positive or negative. The simple paths are just the direct links — classified as strict or defeasible, positive or negative, along with the links themselves. Compound paths are defined inductively, as follows.

(1) If $\pi(x, \sigma, p)$ is a strict positive path, then: $\pi(x, \sigma, p) \Rightarrow q$ is a strict positive path; $\pi(x, \sigma, p) \not\Leftrightarrow q$ is a strict negative path; $\pi(x, \sigma, p) \rightarrow q$ is a defeasible positive path; and $\pi(x, \sigma, p) \not\rightarrow q$ is a defeasible negative path.

(2) If $\bar{\pi}(x, \sigma, p)$ is a strict negative path, then: $\pi(x, \sigma, p) \Leftarrow q$ is a strict negative path.

(3) If $\pi(x, \sigma, p)$ is a defeasible positive path, then: $\pi(x, \sigma, p) \Rightarrow q$ is a defeasible positive path; $\pi(x, \sigma, p) \not\Leftrightarrow q$ is a defeasible negative path; $\pi(x, \sigma, p) \rightarrow q$ is a defeasible positive path; and $\pi(x, \sigma, p) \not\rightarrow q$ is a defeasible negative path.

(4) If $\bar{\pi}(x, \sigma, p)$ is a defeasible negative path, then: $\pi(x, \sigma, p) \Leftarrow q$ is a defeasible negative path.

It follows from this definition than an individual can occur in a path only as its initial node. Let us define a *negative segment* as a strict or defeasible negative link, possibly followed by a reverse positive strict path — that is, as a link sequence either of the form $x_1 \not\rightarrow x_2 \Leftarrow \cdots \Leftarrow x_n$ or of the form $x_1 \not\Leftrightarrow x_2 \Leftarrow \cdots \Leftarrow x_n$. Then it follows from this definition also that if a negative segment occurs in a path, it can occur only at the very end.

2.3 Inheritance

Intuitively, paths represent arguments, which *enable* certain statements as their conclusions. A positive path of the form $\pi(x, \sigma, y)$ enables the statement $x \Rightarrow y$ if it is strict or x is an individual, and the statement $x \rightarrow y$ if it is defeasible and x is a kind; likewise, a negative path of the form $\bar{\pi}(x, \sigma, y)$ enables $x \not\Leftrightarrow y$ if it is strict or x is an individual, and $x \not\rightarrow y$ if it is defeasible and x is a kind. Given a network Γ, the purpose of an inheritance theory is to specify the set of statements *supported* by Γ — that is, the set of statements we can reasonably conclude from the statements contained in Γ. We arrive at this specification in a roundabout way, defining a statement as supported by Γ just in case it is enabled by a path that Γ permits. It remains only to define the paths *permitted* by Γ — intuitively, the arguments sanctioned in the context of Γ.

3. MOTIVATION

Since our approach to mixed inheritance combines the theory of strict inheritance from [14] with the theory of defeasible inheritance from [8], we first summarize these two theories, and then explain how they fit together.

3.1 Strict inheritance

For strict networks, our definition of permitted paths is very simple. According to the theory of [14], a strict network Γ permits exactly the paths it contains — that is, Γ permits σ just in case σ is a path entirely composed of links contained in Γ. In the case of Γ_1 (Figure 1), for example, the permitted paths include $a \Rightarrow s \Rightarrow r$ and $p \Rightarrow q \not\Rightarrow r \Leftarrow s$. Suppose we interpret the nodes in this net so that p = starlings, q = birds, r = mammals, s = dogs, and a = Rover. Then the first of these paths shows us how Γ_1 supports the conclusion that Rover is a mammal ($a \Rightarrow r$); the second shows how it supports the conclusion that no starlings are dogs ($p \not\Rightarrow s$). The net does not permit, for example, the path $p \Rightarrow s \Rightarrow r$, since the link $p \Rightarrow s$ is not contained in Γ_1. Likewise, $q \not\Rightarrow r \Leftarrow s \Leftarrow a$ is not permitted, even though all its links are contained in Γ_1, since it is not a path.

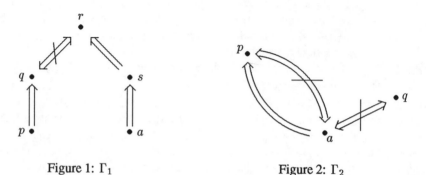

Figure 1: Γ_1 Figure 2: Γ_2

It is important to note that this analysis of strict inheritance, although straightforward, is not the standard view. Strict networks contain only strict links, each of which is equivalent, as explained above, to a formula of classical logic. It may seem natural, then, to use classical logic itself to provide a semantics for such a network — by identifying the network with the set of formulas that translate its links, and then defining a statement as supported by the network just in case it belongs to the deductive closure of that set. This idea, which we take to be the standard view, is due originally to Hayes [7]. To see that it is different from the theory of [14], consider, for example, the net Γ_2 (Figure 2). This network would be translated into the set $\{Pa, \neg Pa, \neg Qa\}$. Since the set is inconsistent, any statement at all belongs to its classical deductive closure; so according to the standard view, Γ_2 should be taken to support every statement — including, say, Qa. According to the analysis of [14], however, Γ_2 does not support Qa, since it permits no positive path from a to q, and in fact provides uncontested evidence that $\neg Qa$.

It is, in some ways, a delicate matter to decide between the analysis of strict inheritance provided by [14] and the traditional analysis of [7]. One is always free to regard a strict network simply as a notational variant of some classical theory, so that the analysis of [7] would be appropriate. Still, there seems to be some value in taking seriously the graph-based nature of inheritance reasoners, which derive conclusions corresponding only to actual paths. The problem is then to see whether we can make logical sense of such a reasoner by designing an appropriate logic, rather than by forcing the reasoner to conform to the standards of an already-existing logic. This task is carried out for strict networks in [14], which provides both a Gentzen-style proof theory for path-based inheritance reasoning and an interpretation of the resulting logic in a four-valued model based on that explored by Belnap [1, 2] and Dunn [6].

The proof theory of [14] is a calculus in the style of Gentzen [8] for proving sequents of the form $\Gamma \vdash A$, where Γ is a set of statements (a net) and A a statement (a link). Informally, such a sequent is supposed to mean that A is derivable from Γ. The sequent calculus contains as its *structural rule* the schema

$$A \vdash A,$$

where A is atomic — that is, of the form $a \Rightarrow p$ or $a \not\Rightarrow p$. This gives us our axioms. In addition, we have the following *logical rules*, for introducing both $\Rightarrow$ and $\not\Rightarrow$, on the right and on the left of the turnstile.

$$\frac{\Gamma^a, a \Rightarrow p \vdash a \Rightarrow q}{\Gamma^a \vdash p \Rightarrow q} \quad \vdash\Rightarrow$$

$$\frac{\Gamma \vdash a \Rightarrow p \qquad \Delta, a \Rightarrow q \vdash A}{\Gamma, \Delta, p \Rightarrow q \vdash A} \quad \Rightarrow\vdash$$

$$\frac{\Gamma \vdash a \not\Rightarrow q \qquad \Delta, a \not\Rightarrow p \vdash A}{\Gamma, \Delta, p \Rightarrow q \vdash A} \quad \Rightarrow\vdash'$$

$$\frac{\Gamma^a, a \Rightarrow p \vdash a \not\Rightarrow q}{\Gamma^a \vdash p \not\Rightarrow q} \quad \vdash\not\Rightarrow$$

$$\frac{\Gamma \vdash a \Rightarrow p \qquad \Delta, a \not\Rightarrow q \vdash A}{\Gamma, \Delta, p \not\Rightarrow q \vdash A} \quad \not\Rightarrow\vdash$$

$$\frac{\Gamma \vdash a \Rightarrow q \qquad \Delta, a \not\Rightarrow p \vdash A}{\Gamma, \Delta, p \not\Rightarrow q \vdash A} \quad \not\Rightarrow\vdash'$$

In the rules $\vdash\Rightarrow$ and $\vdash\not\Rightarrow$, Γ^a is supposed to represent a collection of formulas not containing a. We do need both the rules $\Rightarrow\vdash$ and $\Rightarrow\vdash'$ to capture the meaning of $\Rightarrow$ on the left of the turnstile; neither will do alone. Likewise, both $\nRightarrow$ $\vdash$ and $\nRightarrow$ $\vdash'$ are necessary.

We provide here a sample proof, of the sequent $p \Rightarrow q, q \nRightarrow r \vdash p \nRightarrow r$, simply in order to illustrate these rules.

$$
\frac{\dfrac{a \Rightarrow p \vdash a \Rightarrow p \qquad a \Rightarrow q \vdash a \Rightarrow q}{a \Rightarrow p, p \Rightarrow q \vdash a \Rightarrow q} \rightarrow\vdash \qquad a \nRightarrow r \vdash a \nRightarrow r}{\dfrac{p \Rightarrow q, q \nRightarrow r, a \Rightarrow p \vdash a \nRightarrow r}{p \Rightarrow q, q \nRightarrow r \vdash p \nRightarrow r} \vdash\nRightarrow} \nRightarrow\vdash'
$$

It is shown in [8] that this logic is both sound and complete with respect to the notion of permission for strict nets: the sequent $\Gamma \vdash A$ is provable just in case Γ enables A.

The interpretation of this logic relies on the set $T = \{\{T\}, \{F\}, \emptyset, \{T, F\}\}$ as truth values. Following Belnap and Dunn, we identify these values with the four information states of a database with respect to a proposition: (i) the state of possessing evidence for the proposition, and no evidence to the contrary; (ii) the state of possessing evidence against the proposition, and no evidence to the contrary; (iii) the state of possessing no evidence either for or against the proposition; (iv) the state of possessing evidence both for the proposition and against it well. These explanations should suggest why it is natural to take the power set of $\{T, F\}$ as the set of truth values: if X is one of the values from T, '$T \in X$' means that there is evidence for any proposition bearing the truth value X, and '$F \in X$' means that there is evidence against such a proposition.

A *valuation* v on the language of strict links can be defined as follows. Relative to a domain D, the valuation assigns an individual $v(a)$ in D to each individual term a of the language, and a function $v(p)$ from D to T to each generic term p. Where v is a valuation, $v^d a$ is the valuation like v for all terms other than a, but which assigns the value d to a. The following rules extend v to the entire language.

- $v(a \Rightarrow p) = [v(p)](v(a))$.
- $v(a \nRightarrow p) = Not(v(pa))$, where $Not(\{T\}) = \{F\}$, $Not(\{F\}) = \{T\}$, $Not(\emptyset) = \emptyset$, and $Not(\{T, F\}) = \{T, F\}$.
- $v(p \Rightarrow q) = \{T\}$ if for all $d \in D$, we have $T \in v^d a(qa)$ if $T \in v^d a(pa)$ and $F \in v^d a(pa)$ if $F \in v^d a(qa)$; and $v(p \Rightarrow q) = \emptyset$ otherwise.
- $v(p \nRightarrow q) = \{T\}$ if for all $d \in D$, we have $F \in v^d a(qa)$ if $T \in v^d a(pa)$ and $F \in v^d a(pa)$ if $T \in v^d a(qa)$; and $v(p \nRightarrow q) = \emptyset$ otherwise.

Given this interpretation, the notion of semantic implication is defined in the usual way: Γ *semantically implies* A just in case, for all valuations v, if $T \in v(B)$ for all

$B \in \Gamma$, then $T \in v(A)$. It is shown in [16] that this kind of four-valued implication characterizes the notion of strict inheritance, in the sense that a net Γ enables a statement A just in case Γ semantically implies A. From this it follows, of course, that the implication relation characterizes also the the sequent calculus presented above: $\Gamma \vdash A$ is provable just in case Γ semantically implies A.

3.2 Defeasible inheritance

Defeasible inheritance is more complicated than strict inheritance, primarily because defeasible networks, unlike their strict counterparts, do not permit all the paths they contain. The distinction derives from the different role played in the two kinds of networks by conflicting paths. Any strict network containing conflicting paths is inconsistent, though — as the theory of [16] shows — the effects of the inconsistency can be localized. But defeasible networks can contain conflicting paths without even local inconsistency. Consider, for example, Γ_3 (Figure 3). Although this net contains conflicting paths, it is not inconsistent: it admits interpretations under which all of its links represent true statements — including the well-known interpretation with $a =$ Nixon, $q =$ Quakers, $r =$ Republicans, and $p =$ pacifists. Since the net is consistent, no reasonable theory of defeasible inheritance would say that it permits both of the conflicting paths $a \Rightarrow q \rightarrow p$ and $a \Rightarrow r \not\rightarrow p$ at once. Any such theory would allow us to draw inconsistent conclusions — for example, that Nixon both is a pacifist ($a \Rightarrow p$) and that he isn't ($a \not\Rightarrow p$) — from consistent information.

Theories of defeasible inheritance differ among themselves in their treatment of conflicting paths. One kind of theory associates with each network containing conflicting paths a number of different extensions, corresponding to different resolutions of the conflicts. Because each extension supports a maximal set of conclusions (subject to certain constraints) we describe these theories as *credulous*; an example is the theory of Touretzky [15]. The present paper is based on an alternative approach to defeasible inheritance, developed in [16], which has the advantage of associating with any given network only a single extension. We describe this alternative as a *skeptical* approach — since it embodies the broadly skeptical idea that conflicting arguments, represented in networks by conflicting paths, tend to neutralize each other. Applied to Γ_3, for example, the skeptical approach tells us that neither of the conflicting paths should be permitted.

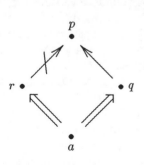

Figure 3: Γ_3

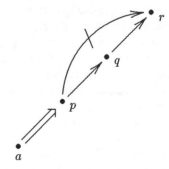

Figure 4: Γ_4

In fact, the theory of [8] is not thoroughly skeptical: its skepticism is restricted to compound paths, and even compound paths can be neutralized only by those conflicting paths that are not themselves, as we say, preempted. The first of these restrictions has the effect that, even in the face of conflicts, any non-compound path contained in a network — that is, any direct link — will be permitted by that network. As explained in [8], this principle is well-motivated, particularly against the background of the four-valued logic; but it is not a crucial feature of the theory.

The second restriction, however, is crucial. Preemption is the mechanism by which, in case of conflicts, arguments based on more specific information are allowed to override arguments based on less specific information. For example, consider Γ_4 (Figure 4) — with, say, a = Tweety, p = penguins, q = birds, and r = flying things. Since this net contains the two conflicting paths $a \Rightarrow p \rightarrow q \rightarrow r$ and $a \Rightarrow p \not\rightarrow r$, an unrestricted skepticism would permit neither. However, it seems in this case that the latter of these paths *should* be permitted, because it represents an argument based on more specific information. The second restriction above reflects this intuition. We say that a path of the form $\pi(x, \tau, v) \rightarrow y$ is *preempted* in a net Γ just in case there is a node z such that (i) Γ permits a path $\pi(x, \tau_1, z, \tau_2, v)$, so that z provides "more specific" information than v about x, and (ii) $z \not\rightarrow y \in \Gamma$, so that z gives us "direct" information contrary to that provided by v. (The definition of preemption for negative paths is symmetrical.) According to the theory of [8], even a conflicted path will be permitted if the only paths with which it conflicts are themselves preempted; so, for example, $a \Rightarrow p \not\rightarrow r$ will be permitted by Γ_4, since $a \Rightarrow p \rightarrow q \rightarrow r$ is preempted.

3.3 Mixed inheritance

The theory of [14] tells us, then, that a strict network permits exactly the paths it contains; the theory of [8] tells us that a defeasible network permits a path it contains just in case that path is either a direct link, or any other path with which it conflicts is itself preempted. Now, to combine these two theories into an account of inheritance for mixed networks, we first carry over entirely the analysis of strict inheritance from [14], and then modify the analysis of defeasible inheritance from [8] to accommodate the presence of strict links. Since it incorporates the analysis of [14], the resulting theory tells us that a mixed network permits exactly the strict paths it contains. Likewise, since it is based on the analysis of [8], the resulting theory also embodies the skeptical idea that a compound defeasible path is neutralized by any conflicting path that is not itself preempted. However, in order to develop this idea in a mixed context, we need to modify slightly our conception of the kind of paths that represent conflicts, as well as our understanding of the preemption relation among conflicting paths.

In defeasible networks, all conflicts share a simple form: they involve paths with identical initial nodes, identical end nodes, and opposite polarity. But the presence of strict links introduces the possibility of less direct conflicts, even among defeasible paths. As an illustration, consider Γ_5 (Figure 5). Here it seems reasonable, in light of the strict segment $r \Rightarrow s \Rightarrow t$, to regard $p \rightarrow q \rightarrow r$ and $p \rightarrow u \rightarrow v \not\rightarrow t$ themselves as conflicting paths, even though they do not share an end node. Imagine, for example, that r = dogs, s = mammals, and t = animals, so that the strict segment tells us that *all* dogs are animals. In the context of Γ_5, then, the path $p \to q \to r$, which represents an argument to the effect that p's are dogs, carries with equal force the conclusion that p's are animals; so it conflicts with $p \to u \to v \not\to t$, which represents an argument that p's are not animals.

What this example shows is that two defeasible paths can represent conflicting arguments, even if they have different end nodes, when one of the paths clashes with a strict consequence of the other. Of course, such strict consequences can themselves be classified as positive or negative. Let us define

$$\kappa_\Gamma(x) = \{x\} \cup \{y : \Gamma \ contains \ a \ strict \ positive \ path \ from \ x \ to \ y\},$$
$$\bar\kappa_\Gamma(x) = \{y : \Gamma \ contains \ a \ strict \ negative \ path \ from \ x \ to \ y\},$$

so that $\kappa_\Gamma(x)$ and $\bar\kappa_\Gamma(x)$ represent the positive and negative strict consequences attributed to x by Γ — the set of properties that x must possess, according to Γ, and the set of properties that x cannot possess. It is then natural to extend our conception of conflicting defeasible paths so that, in addition to the ordinary kinds of clashes, a path of the form $\pi(x, \sigma, u) \to y$ will be said to conflict in a net Γ with any path of the form $\pi(x, \tau, v) \not\to m$ where $m \in \kappa_\Gamma(y)$, and also with any path of the form $\pi(x, \tau, v) \to m$ where $m \in \bar\kappa_\Gamma(y)$. Our general skeptical attitude regarding conflicting paths will then have to apply to these new kinds of conflicts as well. In Γ_5, for instance, neither $p \to q \to r$ nor $p \to u \to v \not\to t$ will be permitted, since each is neutralized by its conflict with the other.

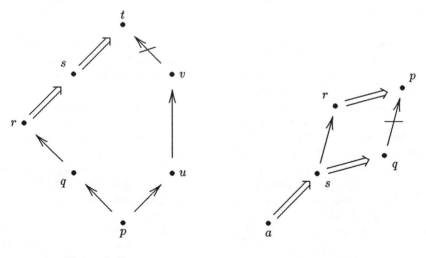

Figure 5: Γ_5 Figure 6: Γ_6

Just as the presence of strict links allows for the possibility of new kinds of conflicts, however, it provides also for the possibility of new relations of preemption. To see this, consider the network Γ_6 (Figure 6), supplied with an interpretation under which a = Hermann, p = persons born in America, q = native speakers of German, r = persons born in Pennsylvania, and s = native speakers of Pennsylvania Dutch. Under this interpretation, Γ_6 tells us is that Hermann is a particular speaker of Pennsylvania Dutch, that every speaker of Pennsylvania Dutch speaks German (since Pennsylvania Dutch is a dialect of German), that German speakers tend not to be born in America, that speakers of Pennsylvania Dutch tend to be born in Pennsylvania, and that everyone born in Pennsylvania is born in America.

According to our new, extended conception, the paths $a \Rightarrow s \rightarrow r$ and $a \Rightarrow s \Rightarrow q \not\rightarrow p$ now represent conflicting arguments in the context of Γ_6, since $p \in \kappa_{\Gamma_6}(r)$. Of course, we would not want to remain skeptical in this case. The path $a \Rightarrow s \Rightarrow q \not\rightarrow p$, representing the argument that Hermann was not born in America since he is a native speaker of German, should be *preempted* in Γ_6: the fact that his dialect is Pennsylvania Dutch provides a more specific argument to the contrary. Without modification, however, the treatment of preemption from [8] does not give us this result. A path can be preempted only if there is more specific and direct information to the contrary; and, although s does provide "more specific" information than q, the path $s \rightarrow r \Rightarrow p$ does not represent "direct" information to the contrary — at least, not according to the standards of [8], which holds that direct information can be carried only by direct links.

Evidently, it is this last requirement concerning the nature of direct information that needs to be modified in the present context. In the context of defeasible networks, it makes good sense to say that direct information can be carried only by direct links: any compound path represents an argument that can itself be undermined. In the context of mixed nets, however, certain kinds of compound paths *can* legitimately be thought to carry direct information — namely, compound paths consisting of a single defeasible link followed by a strict end segment, of any length. In Γ_6, for example, the path $s \rightarrow r \Rightarrow p$ should be thought of as telling us directly that speakers of Pennsylvania Dutch are born in America: for even by the standards of [8], $s \rightarrow r$ counts as a direct statement of the fact that speakers of Pennsylvania Dutch are born in Pennsylvania, and the strict extension $r \Rightarrow p$ simply tells us that *everyone* born in Pennsylvania is born in America.

Adjusting our definition of preemption to account for this new notion of direct information, we say now that a negative path $\pi(x, \tau, v) \not\rightarrow m$ is preempted in a mixed network Γ if there exist nodes z and n such that Γ permits a path $\pi(x, \tau_1, z, \tau_2, v)$ with $z \rightarrow n \in \Gamma$ and $m \in \kappa_\Gamma(n)$. This new definition allows us to conclude, as it should, that $a \Rightarrow s \Rightarrow q \not\rightarrow p$ is preempted in Γ_6; so the net does end up supporting the conclusion that Hermann was born in America. It is a bit more complicated to formulate mixed preemption for positive paths, although no new ideas are involved, simply because direct information to the contrary can now take the form either of a positive defeasible link followed by a negative strict extension, or of a negative defeasible link followed by a reverse positive strict extension. Formally, we say that a positive path $\pi(x, \tau, v) \rightarrow m$ is preempted in a mixed network Γ if there exist nodes z and n such that Γ permits a path $\pi(x, \tau_1, z, \tau_2, v)$ with either (i) $z \rightarrow n \in \Gamma$ and $m \in \bar{\kappa}_\Gamma(n)$ or (ii) $z \not\rightarrow n \in \Gamma$ and $n \in \kappa_\Gamma(m)$.

4. DEFINING MIXED INHERITANCE

In this section, we assemble our motivational ideas into a rigorous definition of the permission relation for mixed networks; we use the symbol ' ⊳ ' to stand for the permission relation, so that 'Γ ⊳ σ' means that the net Γ permits the path σ.

4.1. Mixed degree

Like that of [8], the present definition is inductive. Our first step, then, is to assign a measure of "complexity" to each path σ in a net Γ in such a way that it can be decided whether Γ ⊳ σ once it is known whether Γ ⊳ σ' for each path σ' less complex in Γ than σ itself.

In order to arrive at the appropriate notion of path complexity, we proceed through a number of auxiliary ideas. As we recall, a path is a joined sequence of links containing a negative segment, if at all, only at the very end. Let us say, then, that a *generalized path* is a sequence of links joined like an ordinary path, except that it can contain negative segments anywhere, and perhaps more than one. (Example: $p \not\rightarrow q \Leftarrow r \not\rightarrow s \Leftarrow t$ is a generalized path, but it is not a path, since its negative segment $p \not\rightarrow q \Leftarrow r$ is not an end segment.) Next, let us define the *defeasible length* of a generalized path as follows: if the generalized path does not contain a strict initial segment, then its defeasible length is simply the number of defeasible links in the path; if the generalized path does contain a strict initial segment, then its defeasible length is the number of defeasible links in the path augmented by one. (Example: the generalized path $r \rightarrow s \Rightarrow t \rightarrow u$ has a defeasible length of two, since it contains two defeasible links and no strict initial segment; the generalized path $p \Rightarrow q \Rightarrow r \rightarrow s \Rightarrow t \rightarrow u$ is three, since it contains a strict initial segment along with two defeasible links.)

Using these ideas, we can now define the *degree* of a path σ in a net Γ — written, $deg_\Gamma(\sigma)$ — as the greatest defeasible length of any acyclic generalized path in Γ from the initial node of σ to its end node. (Example: $deg_5(p \rightarrow q \rightarrow r) = 3$, since the acyclic generalized path from p to r in Γ_5 whose defeasible length is greatest is $p \rightarrow u \rightarrow v \not\rightarrow t \Leftarrow s \Leftarrow r$, with a defeasible length of 3.) In order to insure that the assignment of degree to the paths in a network has the appropriate properties, we need to restrict the application of our theory, as in [8], to paths free from certain kinds of defeasible cycles (a defeasible cycle is a cyclic generalized path containing at least one defeasible link); for the present, we limit will our attention, even more severely than necessary, to networks which are either entirely acyclic, or which contain only strict cycles.

The notion of degree defined here is a straightforward generalization of the notion defined in [8]. However, it is not quite appropriate as a measure of path complexity for an inductive definition of the permission relation; in the present context, the measure of complexity needs to carry just a bit more information. Basically, we want our measure of a path's complexity to tell us, in addition its degree, whether or not the path possesses a strict end segment. Therefore, we define the *mixed degree* of a path σ in a net Γ as a pair $\langle n, v \rangle$. The first component of the pair tells us the degree of σ in Γ: $n = deg_\Gamma(\sigma)$. The second component tells us, simply, whether or not σ possesses a strict end segment: by convention, we let

$v = 0$ if σ does not possess a strict end segment, and $v = 1$ if it does. We define a lexical ordering on the mixed degrees by giving priority to the first component: $\langle n, v \rangle < \langle n', v' \rangle$ iff either $n < n'$ or $n = n'$ and $v < v'$. The idea behind this ordering is that degree is the primary measure of path complexity — but of two paths identical in degree, one with and one without a strict end segment, the path lacking the strict end segment is classified as less complex.

4.2. The definition

Our definition of the permission relation has the overall structure of a definition by cases. Any path σ from a mixed network can be divided into the subpaths $\mu(\sigma)$ and $\delta(\sigma)$, where $\mu(\sigma)$ is the maximal strict end segment of σ, and $\delta(\sigma)$ is the result of truncating $\mu(\sigma)$ from σ. (Example: if σ is $x \Rightarrow y \rightarrow p \not\Rightarrow r \Leftarrow s$, then $\mu(\sigma)$ is $p \not\Rightarrow r \Leftarrow s$ and $\delta(\sigma)$ is $x \Rightarrow y \rightarrow p$.) Using this notation, then, we specify the conditions under which $\Gamma \models \sigma$ in three separate cases, depending on the form of σ. Our first case deals with defeasible paths possessing strict end segments.

Case A: $\sigma \neq \delta(\sigma)$ and $\sigma \neq \mu(\sigma)$. Then $\Gamma \models \sigma$ iff $\Gamma \models \delta(\sigma)$ and $\Gamma \models \mu(\sigma)$.

The next case deals with strict paths.

Case B: $\sigma = \mu(\sigma)$. Then $\Gamma \models \sigma$ iff each link in σ is contained in Γ.

Finally, we deal with the case of paths ending in defeasible links — which itself divides into subcases, as such paths may be simple or compound.

Case C-I: $\sigma = \delta(\sigma)$ and σ is a direct link. Then $\Gamma \models \sigma$ iff $\sigma \in \Gamma$.

Case C-II: $\sigma = \delta(\sigma)$ and σ is a compound path. Two subcases to consider.

1. σ is a positive path, of the form $\pi(x, \sigma_1, u) \rightarrow y$. Then $\Gamma \models \sigma$ iff
   (a) $\Gamma \models \pi(x, \sigma_1, u)$;
   (b) $u \rightarrow y \in \Gamma$;
   (c) For $m \in \kappa_\Gamma(y)$, $x \not\rightarrow m \notin \Gamma$ and $m \notin \bar{\kappa}_\Gamma(x)$;
   (d) For $m \in \bar{\kappa}_\Gamma(y)$, $x \rightarrow m \notin \Gamma$ and $m \notin \kappa_\Gamma(x)$;
   (e) For all v, m, τ such that $\Gamma \models \pi(x, \tau, v)$ with $v \not\rightarrow m \in \Gamma$ and $m \in \kappa_\Gamma(y)$, there exist z, n, τ_1, τ_2 such that either (i) $z = x$ or (ii) $\Gamma \models \pi(x, \tau_1, z, \tau_2, v)$, with (iii) $z \rightarrow n \in \Gamma$ and $m \in \kappa_\Gamma(n)$;
   (f) For all v, m, τ such that $\Gamma \models \pi(x, \tau, v)$ with $v \rightarrow m \in \Gamma$ and $m \in \bar{\kappa}_\Gamma(y)$, there exist z, n, τ_1, τ_2 such that either (i) $z = x$ or (ii) $\Gamma \models \pi(x, \tau_1, z, \tau_2, v)$, with either (iii) $z \rightarrow n \in \Gamma$ and $m \in \bar{\kappa}_\Gamma(n)$ or (iv) $z \not\rightarrow n \in \Gamma$ and $n \in \kappa_\Gamma(m)$.

2. σ is a negative path, of the form $\pi(x, \sigma_1, u) \not\rightarrow y$. Then $\Gamma \models \sigma$ iff
   (a) $\Gamma \models \pi(x, \sigma_1, u)$;
   (b) $u \not\rightarrow y \in \Gamma$;
   (c) For m such that $y \in \kappa_\Gamma(m)$, $x \rightarrow m \notin \Gamma$ and $m \notin \kappa_\Gamma(x)$;
   (d) For all v, m, τ, such that $\Gamma \models \pi(x, \tau, v)$ with $v \rightarrow m \in \Gamma$ and $y \in \kappa_\Gamma(m)$, there exist z, n, τ_1, τ_2 such that either (i) $z = x$ or (ii) $\Gamma \models \pi(x, \tau_1, z, \tau_2, v)$, with either (iii) $z \rightarrow n \in \Gamma$ and $m \in \bar{\kappa}_\Gamma(n)$ or (iv) $z \not\rightarrow n \in \Gamma$ and $n \in \kappa_\Gamma(m)$.

It should be clear that this definition, although structured as a definition by cases, is properly an induction on mixed degree. Case A defines permission for a path σ of mixed degree $\langle n, 1 \rangle$ in terms of the path $\delta(\sigma)$ of mixed degree $\langle n, 0 \rangle$ and the path $\mu(\sigma)$ of mixed degree $\langle 1, 1 \rangle$ — both inductively simpler. Cases B and C-I are basis cases, defining permission respectively for paths of mixed degree $\langle 1, 1 \rangle$ and $\langle 1, 0 \rangle$. Finally, Case C-II defines permission for paths of mixed degree $\langle n, 0 \rangle$ with $n > 1$ in terms of paths of mixed degree $\langle n', v' \rangle$ — where v' may be either 0 or 1, but $n' < n$ so that the overall measure of mixed degree is simpler.

It is evident from Case B that our treatment of mixed inheritance agrees with the treatment of [14] when it is applied to strict networks. It agrees also with the treatment of [8] when it is applied to purely defeasible networks — and the proof of this fact is reassuringly simple. If Γ is a defeasible network, then the mixed degree of any path in Γ as defined here is simply $\langle n, 0 \rangle$, where n is its ordinary degree as defined in [8]; so the two inductive definitions move through paths in the same order. If Γ is purely defeasible, then only the Cases C-I and C-II are used in determining permission. Case C-I is identical to the corresponding clause in the definition from [8]. Since Γ is defeasible, it turns out that for every node x we have $\kappa_\Gamma(x) = \{x\}$ and $\bar{\kappa}_\Gamma(x) = \emptyset$. Under these conditions, the extra clauses (d) and (f) in Case C-II.1 disappear (become logical truths), and the remaining clauses in both Case C-II.1 and C-II.2 are logically equivalent to the corresponding clauses in the definition from [8].

5. CONCLUSION

By combining the analysis of strict inheritance from [14] with the skeptical analysis of defeasible inheritance from [8], we have developed a well-defined and intuitively attractive theory of inheritance for semantic networks containing both strict and defeasible links. Although these matters are not discussed here, this theory does satisfy the crucial properties of *soundness* and *atomic stability* defined in [8]. At this point, the topic that stands out as the most important area for further research concerns the application of this work to the representation of complex concepts, such as Brachman and Israel's "three-legged elephant" or the traditional "unmarried man." In order to represent such concepts along with defeasible information in a taxonomic reasoner, it is necessary, first, to develop a theory of inheritance allowing for the expression of both strict and defeasible relations. The present paper presents such a theory — but it does not go on to address the problem of dealing with complex concepts within this framework.

ACKNOWLEDGMENTS

This material is based on work supported by the National Science Foundation under Grant No. IRI-8700705, and by the Army Research Center under Grant No. DAAL-03-88-K0087.

The account of mixed inheritance described here was worked out in conjuction with Richmond Thomason, who has developed an equivalent approach to the same problem; it was first presented in [10]. I am very grateful to Thomason, and also to David Touretzky, both for sparking my interest in the topic of inheritance, and for many illuminating discussions.

This paper is dedicated with respect and affection to Nuel Belnap.

BIBLIOGRAPHY

[1] Belnap, N. (1977): How a computer should think. In G. Ryle (ed.), *Contemporary Aspects of Philosophy*. Oriel Press, pp. 30–56.

[2] Belnap, N. (1977): A useful four-valued logic. In J. Dunn and G. Epstein (eds.), *Modern Uses of Multiple-valued Logic*. D. Reidel, pp. 8–37.

[3] Brachman, R. (1983): What IS-A is and isn't: an analysis of taxonomic links in semantic networks. *Computer*, vol. 16 (October, 1983), pp. 67–73.

[4] Brachman, R. (1985): "I lied about the trees" or, defaults and definitions in knowledge representation. *The AI Magazine*, vol. 6 (Fall, 1985), pp. 80–93.

[5] Brachman, R. and Schmolze, J. (1985): An overview of the KL-ONE knowledge representation system. *Cognitive Science*, vol. 9, pp. 171–216.

[6] Dunn, J. M. (1976): Intuitive semantics for first degree entailments and "coupled trees." *Philosophical Studies*, vol. 29.

[7] Fahlman, S. (1979): *NETL: a System for Representing and Using Real-world Knowledge*. The MIT Press.

[8] Gentzen, G. (1934): Untersuchungen über das Logische Schliessen. *Mathematische Zeitschrift* 39, pp. 176–210, 405–431. Translated in M. Szabo (ed.), *The collected papers of Gerhard Gentzen*, North-Holland, 1969, pp. 68–131.

[9] Hayes, P. (1979): The logic of frames. In *Frame Conceptions and Text Understanding*, D. Metzing (ed.), Walter de Gruyter and Co., pp. 46–61. Reprinted in *Readings in Knowledge Representation*, R. Brachman and H. Levesque (eds.), Morgan Kaufmann (1985), pp. 287–297.

[10] Horty, J. and Thomason, R. (1988): Mixing strict and defeasible inheritance. In *Proceedings of AAAI-88*, Morgan Kaufmann.

[11] Horty, J., Thomason, R. and Touretzky, D. (1990): A skeptical theory of inheritance in nonmonotonic semantic networks. In *Artificial Intelligence*, vol. 42, pp. 311–348. A preliminary version appears in *Proceedings of AAAI-87*, Morgan Kaufmann, pp. 358–363.

[12] Israel, D. and Brachman, R. (1984): Some remarks on the semantics of representation languages. In *On Conceptual Modelling: Perspectives from Artificial Intelligence, Databases, and Programming Languages*, M. Brodie, J. Mylopoulos, and J. Schmide (eds.), Springer-Verlag.

[13] Minsky, M. (1974): A framework for representing knowledge. MIT Artificial Intelligence Laboratory Memo No. 306. Reprinted without appendix in *The Psychology of Computer Vision*, P. Winston (ed.), McGraw-Hill (1975), pp. 211–277.

[14] Roberts, R. and Goldstein, I. (1977): *The FRL Manual*. AI Memo No. 409, MIT Artificial Intelligence Laboratory.

[15] Sandewall, E. (1986): Non-monotonic inference rules for multiple inheritance with exceptions. *Proceedings of the IEEE*, vol. 74, pp. 1345–1353.

[16] Thomason, R., Horty, J., and Touretzky, D. (1986): A calculus for inheritance in monotonic semantic nets. Technical Report CMU-CS-86-138, Computer Science Department, Carnegie Mellon University, 24 pp.

[17] Touretzky, D. (1986): *The Mathematics of Inheritance Systems*. Morgan Kaufmann.

[18] Touretzky, D., Horty, J., and Thomason, R. (1987): A clash of intuitions: the current state of nonmonotonic multiple inheritance systems. In *Proceedings of IJCAI-87*, Morgan Kaufmann, pp. 476–482.

ROBERT L. BIRMINGHAM

THE LOGIC OF *MITCHILL V. LATH*[1]

The logician imagines that lawyers know too little logic to err interestingly. Nevertheless in *Mitchill v. Lath*,[2] decided in 1928, when Kurt Gödel was young and Nuel Belnap not born, a distinguished court, the Court of Appeals of New York, made a logical mistake that Hans Reichenbach later made too and that L. Jonathan Cohen is making right now.

The mistake of the court of appeals concerned the parol evidence rule. That rule prevents proof of some promises in contract actions. If we let judges do logic beyond their comprehension or at least beyond their training and expressive powers, we interpret *Mitchill*'s 'p, therefore q', in which 'p' and 'q' apply different forms of the parol evidence rule, not as a non sequitur but as omitting premises. To supply the premises illuminates the rule.

I.

In *Mitchill v. Lath*, Catherine C. Mitchill sued Charles and Fred Lath, brothers. The litigants' names, and that of plaintiff's husband, 'R. Milton Mitchill, Jr.', already inform. *Mitchill* would have been a different case had plaintiff styled herself 'Cathy'. The addresses of counsel from the record reinforce our nascent understanding: attorney for the Laths, "96 Main Street, Beacon, N.Y."; for Mrs. Mitchill, "63 Wall Street, New York City."[3]

"The middle-class wife," Thorstein Veblen wrote in 1899,

> still carries on the business of vicarious leisure, for the good name of the household and its master. . . . The head of the middle-class household has béen reduced by economic circumstances to turn his hand to gaining a livelihood by occupations which often partake largely of the character of industry, as in the case of the ordinary business man of today. . . . It is by no means an uncommon spectacle to find a man applying himself to work with the utmost assiduity, in order that his wife may in due form render for him that degree of vicarious leisure which the common sense of the time demands.[4]

---

[1] The author thanks Nancy Dunham for help writing this essay and Sharon Jones and Kathleen Moore for help editing it. Tom Malnati suggested Figure 8.

[2] 247 N.Y. 377, 160 N.E. 646 (1928).

[3] Record at title page.

[4] T. Veblen, "The Theory of the Leisure Class," in *The Portable Veblen* 122–23 (M. Lerner, ed. 1976.)

J. M. Dunn and A. Gupta (eds.), Truth or Consequences, 283–305.
© 1990 *Kluwer Academic Publishers. Printed in the Netherlands.*

If we extrapolate pardonably, that form of life underlies *Mitchill*. The Mitchills, in Mrs. Mitchill's name, bought a small farm, consisting of a house and perhaps thirty acres, from the Laths. They remodelled the house for a summer home. There Mrs. Mitchill could in that season render vicarious leisure. Their investment in the property above the purchase price was $23,000.[5] The sum suggests the level at which they consumed. "[T]he Lath boys,"[6] local residents whom, incidentally, the Mitchills hired to help landscape the property, conspicuously consumed nothing.

Two hundred sixty-three feet from the farm house, on adjacent land, lay the object of the litigation: an ice house, shown in Figure 1.[7] Defendants did not own the land, but owned and operated the ice house, and had the right to remove it. This appreciation of a machine-made spoon is a benchmark against which to measure the effect of an ice house: "[T]he consumption, or even the sight of such goods, is inseparable from an odious suggestion of the lower levels of human life, and one comes away from their contemplation with a pervading sense of meanness that is extremely distasteful and depressing to a person of sensibility."[8] At least Mrs. Mitchill testified she spoke thus to Charles and Fred Lath:

> The Witness: . . . I said [to Charles Lath], "It would be impossible for me to live as I am accustomed to live with that ice house in front of me, not only because the place is unsightly, but because I can't live close to an ice house, and if we decide to buy the place, we will only decide to buy it with the condition that you will remove this ice house before we take possession of the property. Will you do this?" . . .
>
> . . . .
>
> A. I said [to Fred Lath], ". . . [Y]ou must realize that we can't live here with this ice house here, on account we can't live here comfortably, the way we intended to live, and the way we want to live, and the way we were used to living . . . ."[9]

On various occasions, among them that of the quoted question, the Laths promised to remove the ice house.[10]

They broke their promise. The loss to Mrs. Mitchill was in the first instance aesthetic. In her complaint, she described the ice house, with some restraint, as "of ungraceful and unattractive design."[11] Veblen in the late nineteenth century remarked an increasing "predilection for the rustic and the natural."[12] Mrs. Mitchill lacked the predilection. Imagine a large plastic deer.

---

[5] Record at 146.

[6] *Id.* at 110, 117, 190.

[7] J. Dawson, W. Harvey & S. Henderson, *Cases and Comment on Contracts* 450 (5th ed. 1987). For a picture of the farm house see *id.* at 453.

[8] T. Veblen, *supra* note 4, at 191.

[9] Record at 78, 82.

[10] *See infra* Figure 10.

[11] Record at 5.

[12] T. Veblen, *supra* note 6, at 107.

THE ICE HOUSE

Figure 1

Besides aesthetic distress, caused by the mere local persistence of the ice house, Mrs. Mitchill suffered aural injuries from the Laths operating the ice house "in a loud, boisterous and offensive manner."[13] Mr. Mitchill testified:

> Q. Will you state, with reference to the disturbance to the community or to your peace and the occupancy of your dwelling, in what manner this ice business was conducted? A. Well, the ice business is conducted in this way: A certain number of times a week, maybe three, maybe four times a week, this ice truck comes there in the morning anywhere from seven, seven-fifteen, seven-thirty, after which hour there is no sleeping.

> Mr. Meyer: Now, I object, and ask that "after which hour there is no sleeping" be stricken from the record.
> The Court: Yes, strike it out.

> The Witness: They are there, possibly, depending on the amount of ice they are going to take, anywhere from an hour to an hour and a half. They have to go in the icehouse — they first have to open the doors; there are long doors on the icehouse that require some kind of hammering to open them, because they are fastened in some way, how I don't know, probably by cleats, and the men go inside, get the ice, bring it to the top of this entrance where they have a long chute to which their truck is backed up right to the bottom of that chute, and down goes the

---

[13] Record at 51.

ice. Every time a cake goes down, crash, crash, crash, until the truck is filled.[14]

The behavior was the more infractious by happening in the morning, when a wife engages in leisure most conspicuously, since at that time people like the Laths work. About especially the offensiveness:

> Q. Mr. Mitchill, what do you use the pond across the way from that icehouse for?

>> Mr. Meyer: That is objected to as incompetent and irrelevant. There is no claim here that there was any particular restriction or privilege as to his putting a pond or that anything should not be put there.
>> The Court: Overruled.
>> Mr. Meyer: Exception.

> The Witness: That pond was built by us primarily and used by us for swimming. It has always been our desire to have a place with a swimming pool on, where we could swim when we wanted to, and that is what we built it for.

> Q. Does the loading of these trucks interfere with the use of that pool for swimming?

>> Mr. Meyer: That is objected to as calling for a conclusion, improper and irrelevant.
>> Mr. Dominick: I will withdraw the question.
>> The Court: I will sustain that.

> Q. Mr. Mitchill, will you state what occurred to your knowledge, when you or members of your family or guests have been endeavoring to use that pond as a swimming pool? A. Why, when we were swimming, and the ladies were there, if at any time we were swimming and this truck happened to be loading at the icehouse, why, there was much conversation by the type of people who were loading up about the women, remarking about their bathing suits, snickering. It is that feeling that you are just being talked about; the absolute lack of privacy and decency.[15]

The situation reminds the modern reader slightly of *Straw Dogs*. Consequently *Mitchill* is a model of the law monopolizing force and of recourse to law displacing violent self-help.

---

[14] *Id.*

[15] *Id.* at 54–55.

II.

Mitchill looks to the logician like an easy case: one ought to keep one's promises. As if to confirm the lay understanding, the trial court decided for Mrs. Mitchill and New York's intermediate appellate court affirmed. Improbably, however, the court of appeals reversed. The decision of the court of appeals on the face of it contradicts the Marxist insight "that law protects property, social inequality, and class domination."[16] Surely, one thinks, the leisure class lost out here. Nevertheless, the decision, read reflectively, does not refute Marxist teaching, since it affirms the parol evidence rule, itself not neutral between classes.

Mitchill is not just any parol evidence rule case but the outstanding one, the classic statement of the rule. In contracts casebooks, it likely appears first in the chapter on that rule,[17] the rest of the chapter trying to live it down. Nobody likes it, but for its result, not its logic. The rule addresses this situation: there is a document or writing that otherwise expresses (or is) the parties' contract; a party alleges that the parties intended as part of their contract an additional promise the other made, usually orally but at least outside the writing. The rule if it applies prevents triers of fact from learning about that additional promise or enjoins them to disregard it.

Mrs. Mitchill could not have prevailed merely by proving the promise plus the injury. A promise, standing alone, lacks consideration. Oversimply, 'bargain' being a technical term, such a promise does not belong to a bargained-for exchange, consequently a court will not enforce it. Sometimes a court will enforce a promise because the promisee has relied; but not the New York court the Laths' promise in 1928. Because the promise alone would not be enforced, Mrs. Mitchill pleaded the contract to convey the farm house. The Mitchills' promise to pay the Laths then could be consideration for the Lath's promises to convey the farm house *and* to remove the ice house. But so pleading invited the Laths to invoke the parol evidence rule.

Cases in which defendant invokes the parol evidence rule paradigmatically are tried to a jury. In these cases, plaintiff tells the judge out of the hearing of the jury she intends to prove defendant's parol promise. The judge applies the rule to find out whether she may. If so, she presents her evidence, defendant rebuts, and the jury decides the truth. If not, the jury learns nothing of the promise; and if that is her case, plaintiff loses.

By a Marxist reading, inconsequential for the logic of *Mitchill*, the exploitation enters thus. Predominantly, jurors are the Laths of this world; by and large, its Mitchills get promises in writing. The parol evidence rule prevents jurors from contravening the writing. They might do this by empathetically finding falsely that defendant promised; or by finding truly that she did.

Mitchill differed, having been tried to the court, Seeger, J., presiding, not to a jury. The apparatus of objecting to evidence is still in place though. It is as if

[16] Kamenka, "Law," in *A Dictionary of Marxist Thought* 275 (T. Bottomore ed. 1983).

[17] *See, e.g.*, J. Dawson, W. Harvey & S. Henderson, *supra* note 9, at 449; L. Fuller & M. Eisenberg, *Basic Contract Law* 559 (4th ed. 1981); F. Kessler, G. Gilmore & A. Kronman, *Contracts* 837 (3rd ed. 1986) (in which, however, *Mitchill* is the third case); R. Scott & D. Leslie, *Contract Law and Theory* 472 (1988); R. Summers & R. Hillman, *Contract and Related Obligation* 646 (1987).

attorney Meyer is playing at being a lawyer. Theoretically, Seeger did two things diachronically. First, in his role as interpreter of law, he decided the parol evidence rule did not apply, consequently admitted the evidence. Second, in his role as trier of fact, he found on that evidence that the Laths "promised and agreed, in consideration of the purchase of the farm by the plaintiff, to remove the said ice house."[18] The Laths did not forget; hence if Seeger is right, they lied.

III.

Logic enters *Mitchill* primarily at the lower left node of the tree in Figure 2. First, the court of appeals decided only whether Seeger rightly admitted the Mitchills' testimony that the Laths promised. The subsequent issue, who told the truth, is one of fact, hence unreviewable on appeal, except as to whether or not a reasonable person *could have* resolved it as did the trial court. An appellate court "is in no position to cope with factual disputes";[19] a reason it is not appears later.[20] The logician may ignore the far right node.

Second, the issue of admissibility has two parts: what is the rule?; and did Seeger correctly apply it? Andrews, J., wrote for the court; Lehman, J., dissented, another judge joining him. So it was 5-2. The majority and dissenting opinions agree on the rule, join issue on how to apply it. Their disagreement over application matters to the logician no more than whether there are two or three apples on the table mattered to Whitehead and Russell at the end of the couple hundred pages by which they proved '1 + 1 = 2'. We have followed the left branch of the tree to 'rule'.

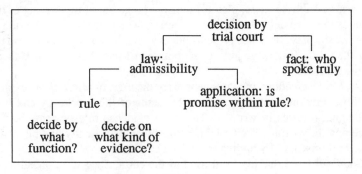

Figure 2

[18] Record at 302.
[19] Branion v. Gramly, 855 F.2d 1256, 1261 (7th Cir. 1988).
[20] *See infra* at 23.

Third, a parol evidence rule viewed simply is a function from evidence, pieces of language, like the writing or Mrs. Mitchill's testimony, 'Charles Lath told me ... ',[21] into the set of performatives {'Exclude', 'Admit'}. It requires, though, that one specify the *kind* of evidence used to calculate a value of this function. One profitably interprets the specification to define the argument places of the function. The three prominent specifications, named nostalgically after eminent, dead contracts scholars who advocated them, are: a judge may consider "the writing alone" (*strict Williston*); "the writing in the light of surrounding circumstances — excluding, however, the most vital circumstance of all, the evidence of the prior negotiations themselves" (*lenient Williston*); "all circumstances, including the evidence of the prior negotiations"(*Corbin*).[22] Consequently, depending on which specification a court adopts, the arguments of the function are only the document, that and a description of the circumstances, etc.

That leaves, fourth, the lower left node of Figure 2, the function itself. Lehman in dissent best described it.

> [T]he question we must decide is whether or not, *assuming* an agreement was made for the removal of an unsightly ice house from one parcel of land as an inducement for the purchase of another parcel, the parties would ordinarily or naturally be expected to embody the agreement for the removal of the icehouse in the written agreement to convey the other parcel.[23]

But Andrews agreed on it. If a court answers the question 'Yes', it excludes the evidence; otherwise, it admits it. The court's description is logically interesting. It also is significant for legal practice, since it recurs often.[24]

Lehman himself italicized 'assuming'. Hence the rule is intentionally conditional. Like a counterfactual it directs: 'Go to the possible world most like the actual world except that at it the Laths promised. Inspect the writing. If it contains the promise, exclude the evidence; if it does not, admit it.' The rule is not truly counterfactual since the world most like the actual world etc. may *be* the actual world. Separately, one profitably reads Lehman's language "would ordinarily or naturally be expected" as a lawyer's oblique demand for a particular probability.

Hence,

> *Rule 1* (Mitchill's *Rule*): Exclude the evidence of the parol promise if $P(W|M) > p$; otherwise admit it.

---

[21] *See infra* Figure 10.

[22] E. Farnsworth, *Contracts* § 7.3 (1982).

[23] 247 N.Y. at 386, 160 N.E. at 649.

[24] *See, e.g.*, Braten v. Bankers Trust Co., 60 N.Y.2d 155, 162, 456 N.E.2d 802, 805, 468 N.Y.S.2d 861, 864 (1983) ("the oral agreement fails ... because... the parties could have been expected to embody it in th[e] writing"); Lee v. Joseph E. Seagram & Sons, 552 F.2d 447, 451 (2d Cir. 1977) ("the overarching question is whether, in the context of the particular setting, the oral agreement was one which the parties would ordinarily be expected to embody in the writing").

The influential Restatements of Contracts adopts it. *Restatement (Second) of Contracts* § 216 (1981); *Restatement of Contracts* § 240 (1933). So does the modern, authoritative treatise, E. Farnsworth, *supra* note 24, § 7.3.

'P($W|M$)' abbreviates, say, 'the probability that the writing contains the promise, on the condition that the promise was made'; p is the greatest lower bound of what would ordinarily and naturally be expected. As a plausible reading of 'expect', one expects an event only if it is more likely than not to occur. Maybe it must be significantly more likely: in a 100-ticket lottery, do we expect that one of tickets 1-51 will win, despite that being more likely than not? If not, $.5 < p$ is a necessary not a sufficient condition on p.

IV.

Rule 1 should perplex the lay or professional reader, because its purposes are opaque. She sees that the parol evidence rule works a compromise between two values. First, contracting parties should be secure in their *written* agreements: able to exhibit all their promises so that neither party need fear the other will perjure herself to add to or contradict them. Second, the court should enforce all and only the promises the parties made — including the parol promises — because those are what the parties agreed to.

Call the values that the rule arbitrates between 'security' and 'justice'. Let 'P(M)' represent the posterior probability defendant promised. On the one hand, to maximize *justice*, a court must admit evidence defendant promised if P(M) > .5, exclude that evidence if P(M) < .5.[25] To maximize *security*, a court must exclude all parol evidence, regardless of P(M). Then in those cases where P(M) > .5, which ought to be a lot of cases, and which pretty clearly include *Mitchill*, the values conflict.

Figure 3 illustrates the tradeoff, the rates of exchange, between security and justice. Along the y-axis plot the threshold probability q — the greatest lower bound of the P(M)'s for which the court admits the evidence. q is a good index of security: the higher it is, the more security; $q = 0$ is none at all; $q = 1$ is total security. For a Bayesian 1 or 0 is not, C. I. Lewis to the contrary not withstanding,[26] an empirical probability, because evidence cannot revise it: if the antecedent or prior probability is 0, multiplying it by anything, as a Bayesian must do to get the posterior probability, will not alter it. Neither will a Bayesian, beginning with an intermediate probability, reach a posterior probability of 0 or 1. The y-axis starts at .5 because a lower value is inferior in *both* security and justice.

---

[25] If the jury is reliable and P(M) as the court finds it is slightly below .5, it might best let the jury decide; I will disregard this refinement.

[26] *See infra* note 39.

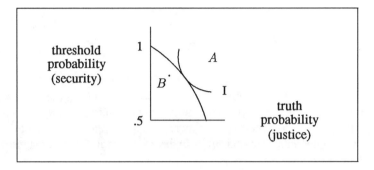

Figure 3

Along the x-axis of Figure 3 plot the quantity of justice: the probability the court admits evidence of actual, excludes evidence of feigned promises. The x-axis as well as the y-axis starts at .5, since if actual and feigned promises are equally likely, a court that excludes evidence randomly with any probability expects to do that well. We do not know cardinally this second probability unless we know how possible cases are distributed along the y-axis. Still, for any distribution, this second probability, considered ordinally, is greatest at $q = .5$.

Also the *expected* loss of justice from excluding evidence of a promise whose probability of having been made is .99, relative to excluding evidence of a promise whose probability of having been made is .51, is large. Between the two cases, the *actual* loss, if it occurs, is constant or varies just randomly; the probability of escaping it, however, increases 49-fold.

Contract law "produces" jointly security and justice. It must exchange more security to get an additional unit of justice as justice increases and conversely. If the possible cases are uniformly distributed along the y-axis, the production frontier is a quarter circle, or — depending on the scales of the axes — a quarter ellipse. The law optimizes at point A in Figure 3. There indifference curve I, whose satisfaction is the highest attainable, is tangent to the production frontier.

We get:

> *Rule 2 (Best Rule)*: Exclude the evidence of the parol promise
> if $P(M) < q$; otherwise admit it.

Rule 2 is really the set of rules having $.5 \leq q \leq 1$. As q varies, Rule 2 traces out the production frontier. Any rule different from Rule 2 sometimes puts the community at a point like B inside this frontier. Substituting Rule 2, for some q, for this different rule, the community achieves more of one value, holding the other constant: it can move vertically or horizontally from B to the production frontier.

Rule 2 consequently is the sole *efficient* rule; only efficiency matters, since Rule 2's with different q's can strike any balance between security and justice.

V.

So we have an efficient rule, Rule 2; and a rule, Rule 1, that so far does not fit in. They differ since only Rule 1 invokes possible worlds. At least that is how things look at this stage of the dialectic. Why ought the probability the promise *would be* in the writing, *if* it had been made, matter? It appears metaphysical in the law's sense: inconsequential for adjudication. In the law "identity" and "existence" often are "metaphysical questions."[27]

The answer is straightforward if we make that conditional probability 1. Then if the promise is not in the writing, we know the promise was not made. The parol evidence rule of the Uniform Commercial Code, read literally, exploits that relationship – if we may translate its word 'certainly' by '$p = 1$'. The Code requires that if a promise would, if made, "certainly have been included in the document in the view of the court," and it is not included, then evidence of its "alleged making must be kept from the trier of fact."[28] That is safe enough, although 1 is, again, a pretty high probability. Surely *Mitchill* did not contemplate $p = 1$.

One presumes Andrews and Lehman decided efficiently, which comes down to their having applied an efficient rule. Rule 1 insofar as it differs from Rule 2 is not efficient, hence something is wrong. Maybe the *Mitchill* court decided not inefficiently but arbitrarily. The facts being clear, French judges would cast a die if the law was uncertain.[29] That is sensible if a court must decide some way and has no idea which.

An arbitrary parol evidence rule might be *Exclude the evidence if the die turns up 1–4; admit it if the die turns up 5 or 6*. Its security is that of Rule 2 with $q = .67$ but it has only the justice of the y-axis, .5. Still it may be optimal if cheap. It costs nothing to cast a die; or to take an actual rule, that minors may void their contracts, a court or contracting parties inexpensively find out the age of a person, although what matters is her competence, for which age is an imperfect surrogate. Rule 1 is not cost effective. Often it is expensive to find out what it turns on. Hence Andrews and Lehman would have chosen an arbitrary rule differently.

Story 1 is the *Mitchill* court did not see that Rules 1 and 2 differ. Two passages in Andrews' opinion lend it credence but they will support other stories too.

The parol promise, Andrews wrote,

> must be one that parties would not ordinarily be expected to em-
> body in the writing; *or put in another way* an inspection of the
> written contract, read in the light of surrounding circumstances

---

[27] G. Plamer, *Mistake and Unjust Enrichment* 46 (1962).

[28] UCC § 202, Official Comment 3.

[29] M. Screech, *Rabelais* 268–72 (1979).

must not indicate that the writing appears "to contain the engagement of the parties, and to define the object and measure the extent of such engagement."[30]

Up to the semicolon, the passage states Rule 1; thereafter it states Rule 2 in that rule's lenient Williston form. The emphasized connective "or put in another way" seems to relate the statements as linguistic variants of one rule.
  Also,

> an inspection of this contract shows a full and complete agreement, setting forth in detail the obligations of each party. On reading it one would conclude that the reciprocal obligations of the parties were fully detailed. Nor would his opinion alter if he knew the surrounding circumstances. The presence of the ice house, even the knowledge that Mrs. Mitchill thought it objectionable would not lead to the belief that a separate agreement existed with regard to it. Were such an agreement made it would seem most natural that the inquirer should find it in the contract.[31]

Sentences 1 and 2 apply the strict Williston form of Rule 2; 3 and 4 apply its lenient Williston form; 5 applies Rule 1. That no transitional phrase connects sentences 4 and 5 suggests the court in 5 did not intend to change the rule.
  Williston's "magisterial"[32] treatise has the same seeming discontinuity. It says,

> [T]he test of admissibility is much affected by the inherent probability of parties who contract under the circumstances in question, simultaneously making both the agreement in writing which is before the court, and also the alleged parol agreement. The point is not merely whether the court is convinced that the parties before it did in fact do this, but whether parties so situated generally would or might do so.[33]

That is Rule 2. Its footnote 4, intended to support this passage, invokes *Mitchill*:

> In a leading case, Mitchill v. Lath, 247 NY 377, 160 NE 646, 68 ALR 239, the court laid down the following tests to be used in determining the admissibility of parol evidence to prove a separate and collateral agreement: '... (3) [the agreement] must be one that parties would not ordinarily be expected to embody in the writing.'[34]

That is Rule 1. Williston's footnotes were often faulty and it looks like note 4 is that too.

---

[30] 247 N.Y. at 381, 160 N.E. at 647 (emphasis added).
[31] *Id.* at 381–82, 160 N.E. at 647.
[32] G. Gilmore, *The Death of Contract* 6 (1974).
[33] 4 S. Williston, *Contracts* § 638 (3d ed. 1961).
[34] *Id.* at n.4.

VI.

I will, however, proceed as if everyone is logically astute, and reject story 1. Then Andrews must have derived or imagined he could derive one rule from the other.

Part IV, if right, makes evident the *direction* of the derivation. Rule 2's '$P(M) < q$' implies 'Exclude the evidence', which is where we want to finish, while Rule 1's '$P(W|M) > p$' implies no such thing. Hence the *Mitchill* court argues or imagines it might argue as in Figure 4. At best the argument is awfully enthymematic. I will retrieve the implicit premises, working back from '$P(M) < q$', in four steps, the first three themselves arguments, the first two uncontroversial.

$$P(W|M) > p$$
.
.
.

$$P(M) < q$$

Exclude the evidence

Figure 4

First, modus ponens. Nothing is less controversial than that. The argument is as in Figure 5. For our purposes, its first premise is a notational variant of 'If $-W$, then $P(M) < q$'. Its second premise, in natural language, '(that) the writing does not contain the parol promise', appears analytic: the promise would not be parol if the writing contained it. Of course we are trying to talk about the world. Putting 'alleged' before 'parol', we make an empirical claim perhaps as certain as a claim that there is not a rhinoceros in the room. If W, what are the litigants *doing* here? Also, Andrews et al. could have just inspected the writing and *seen* $-W$.

$$P(M|-W) < q$$
$$-W$$
$$P(M) < q$$

Figure 5

Second, excluded middle. Figure 6's argument is valid too, an instance or generalization of '$P(A) + P(-A) = 1$': 'the sum of the probabilities of anything and its not being the case is 1'. Already,[35] by stipulating $.5 < p$ and $.5 \leq q$, we have restricted p and q enough for the argument to succeed.

$$P(-M \mid -W) > p$$
$$.5 < p$$
$$.5 \leq q$$
$$P(M \mid -W) < q$$

Figure 6

VII.

Third, Reichenbach's mistake. Reichenbach made it in a "celebrated"[36] debate with Nelson Goodman[37] and especially C. I. Lewis.[38]

> Now if there exist probability implications between phenome-nal sentences, they establish a concatenation between such sen-tences; and this concatenation works in both directions, from the past to the future as well as from the future to the past. If the phenomenal sentence a, in a certain context, makes the phenomenal sentence b highly probable, whereas non-a would make non-b highly probable, then conversely, the verification of b will make a highly probable, whereas the verification of non-b would make a highly improbable.[39]

The second of Reichenbach's sentences supplies the required argument. One translates to *Mitchill* using the correspondences 'a' = 'M', 'b' = 'W', and 'is high' = '$> p$'. Figure 7 exhibits the result.

---

[35] *See supra* at 8, 10.

[36] van Cleve, "Probability and Certainty: A Reexamination of the Lewis-Reichenbach Debate," *Phil. Stud.*, 32 (1977), p. 323.

[37] Goodman, "Sense and Certainty," *Phil. Rev.*, 61 (1952), p. 160.

[38] Lewis, "The Given Element in Empirical Knowledge," *Phil. Rev.*, 61 (1952), p. 168.

[39] Reichenbach, "Are Phenomenal Reports Absolutely Certain?," *Phil. Rev.*, 61 (1952), p. 153. The presuppositions of the debate, especially Reichenbach's contribution to it, are those of logical empiricism, quaintly pre-Sellars.

Lewis, a foundationalist, wanted that *some* observation sentences be absolutely certain. He dis-qualified sentences of the physical object language, because e.g. a whinny in the indefinite future might make doubtful or refute 'Here is a Holstein'. Lewis believed, however, that phenomenal sentences — replace 'Here is a Holstein' by 'I see a black-and-white expanse' — could be thus certain; I might err about there having been a cow, but still I saw the expanse.

Reichenbach thought Lewis mistaken because expanses or whatever are causally related too: a black-and-white expanse at t_0 may affect the probability of that or a different expanse at t_1. Consequently one can predict phenomena from phenomena; and retrodict too.

$$P(W|M) > p$$
$$P(-W| - M) > p$$
$$P(-M| - W) > p$$

Figure 7

The first premise of this argument is likewise that of Figure 4's argument, so we are getting somewhere. Its second premise, like '$-W$', is transparently true. What it asserts, often occurring in a nonactual world, is not very observable. But the probability of 'If $-M$, then $-W$' approaches 1; the Laths, with presumed peasant cunning,[40] would not sign a document that recited they promised, if they did not promise. Thus, its premises true or posited, if Reichenbach's argument is valid, the proof of Figure 4 is complete.

To construct a counterexample to the argument, to show it is invalid, imagine that a patient, X, has one of two diseases, D_0 and D_1. View them symmetrically: they are equally serious; X's physician (Y, who later is also the hospital administrator) cannot treat simultaneously for both diseases; the probabilities the treatments will succeed are identical; etc. Hence Y treats for D_0 or D_1 depending on which X more probably has.[41]

The test that distinguishes between the diseases is right with probability .8 in this sense: P(test diagnoses $D_0|X$ has D_0) = P(test diagnoses $D_1|X$ has D_1) = .8. That probability is high: at law it approaches being beyond a reasonable doubt.[42] We execute people who are not much more probably guilty than this. Hence $P(b|a) = P(-b| - a) =$ high, and the hypothetical case satisfies the premises of Reichenbach's argument.

But the argument's conclusion may still be false, because Reichenbach does not control for the antecedent or prior probability that X has a particular disease. If D_0 is 19 times as common as D_1, that probability is .95. Then if the test reports D_1, it misdiagnoses more often (out of 100 possible cases: $95 \times .2 = 19$) than not ($5 \times .8 = 4$); P(X has $D_1|$ test diagnoses D_1) = .17 ($4/(19 + 4)$).

Figure 8 shows the situation geometrically. $P(-a| - b) < .5$ if the area of the long, narrow rectangle along the left side, that represents $-a$ & $-b$, is less than the area of the wider rectangle across most of the top, that represents a & $-b$. The first

---

[40] Trotsky once started a speech in New York: "Workers and peasants of the Bronx . . . ."

[41] Cohen, "Can Human Irrationality be Experimentally Demonstrated?," *Behavioral & Brain Sci.*, 4 (1981), p. 329. The usual counterexample, e.g. in Bar-Hillel & Margalit, "In Defense of the Classical Notion of Evidence," *Mind*, 88 (1979), pp. 579–80, involves taxis.

[42] *See* Simon & Mahan, "Quantifying Burdens of Proof: A View from the Bench, the Jury, and the Classroom," *Law & Soc'y Rev.*, 5 (1971), p. 328.

rectangle's area, as I have drawn it, certainly is less. In this case, then, Reichenbach's conclusion, that "the verification of non-b" makes "a highly improbable," is false.

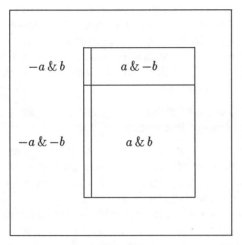

Figure 8

Stopping here, a likely place, gives a second story of *Mitchill*. By it Andrews and Lehman, in this narrow instance as good logicians as Reichenbach, understood Rules 1 and 2 differ, but derived Rule 2 from Rule 1. They made an interesting mistake, disregarding a prior; but still they made a mistake.

VIII.

Fourth, the principle of insufficient reason. One may eliminate a counterexample, if so inclined, by adding a premise that bars it. L. Jonathan Cohen states the medical counterexample in the course of arguing that everybody always behaves rationally. That is tautological for economists. "Many" physicians, however, in the circumstances of the counterexample, asked which disease they would treat for, reply 'D_1.'[43] Since that looks irrational, P(X has D_1 | test diagnoses D_1) being .17, Cohen must explain.

Oddly, Cohen adds an argument place to get a predicate or open sentence 'For ___, P(X has D_1 | test diagnoses D_1) = ___'. He fills the first place by 'X' or 'Y', giving '.17' or '.8' respectively at the second place. The academic literature says '.17' for everybody, X and Y, but so much the worse for it. Cohen says

---

[43] Gärdenfors, "Probabilistic Reasoning and Evidentiary Value," in *Evidentiary Value* 52 (P. Gärdenfors, B. Hansson & N. Sahlin eds. 1983).

censoriously: "[T]he literature is propagating an analysis that could increase the number of deaths from a rare disease of this kind."[44]

Cohen continues:

> Admittedly, the standard statistical method would be to take the prior frequency into account here, and this would be absolutely right if what was wanted was a probability for any patient considered not as a concrete particular person, not even as a randomly selected particular person, but simply as an instance of a long run of patients.[45]

No good is going to come of distinguishing between X as "a concrete particular person" and as "an instance" in a sequence.

> The administrator [Y] who wants to secure a high rate of diagnostic success for his hospital at minimal cost would be right to maximize just that probability, and therefore to dispense altogether with the tests. But a patient is concerned with success in his own particular case, not with stochastic success for the system. So he needs to evaluate a propensity-type probability, not a frequency-type one, and the standard statistical method would then be inappropriate.[46]

This is silly. X and Y have the same interest: to treat X for the disease she more probably has. The "minimal cost" is a red herring; one only regards the cost of a test, balances cost against benefit, if there is some benefit, and so far there is none here. Any cost > 0 is too much.

Imagine the conversation:

> X: Treat me for D_0; the probability is .83 I have it.
> Y: No, I will treat you for D_1; the probability is .8 you have it.
> *Cohen (attending as a medical ethicist)*: You are both right.

Well, they cannot both be right. That sort of thing works in ethics, if 'A is good' abbreviates 'I like A', but not here. Y builds her rate of success one case at a time. The probabilities are epistemic, in the sense that ultimately X has one disease or the other, and X and Y get something different from 0 or 1 because they do not know everything. The probabilities, however, cannot differ unless X and Y conditionalize on different evidence, and they do not.

Cohen explains:

> [T]he prior probabilities have to be appropriate ones, and there is no information about you personally that establishes a greater predisposition in your case to disease [D_0] than to disease [D_1]. We have to suppose equal predispositions here, unless told that

---

[44] Cohen, *supra* note 44, at 329.
[45] *Id.*
[46] *Id.*

the probability of $[D_0]$ is greater (or less) than that of $[D_1]$
among people who share all your relevant characteristics, such
as age, medical history, blood group, and so on.[47]

Here is Cohen defending his explanation: "What I actually suggested was that in the absence of information determining appropriate prior probabilities here the subjects did right to 'suppose equal predispositions' . . . ."[48]

That is okay. There are many prior probabilities, e.g. the probability that an orange was grown in California, that are contextually inappropriate in the medical hypothetical case, and the .95 might be one. It is Cohen's example. Then, however, the prior probability is inappropriate for Y's calculations as well as X's.

Independently, something is wrong with the last quoted sentence, unless Cohen is just using 'relevant' tendentiously, since the prior probability would be 1 or 0 if the members of the reference class shared all X's relevant characteristics, reading 'relevant' oppositely from 'metaphysical'.[49]

Still, Cohen's explanation provides the *Mitchill* court the premise that bars the counterexample. To get a prior of .5, Cohen, directing that we "suppose equal predispositions," uses the principle of insufficient reason, Pascal's principle. It "asserts that when the conditions permit two or more different outcomes, yet we have no evidence favoring any particular outcome over any other, we ought to assign the same probability to each outcome."[50]

It is not the best principle in the world. It lacks a canonical way to individuate hypotheses among which to divide the probability. For instance, 'Charles Lath promised' and 'Fred Lath promised', set against 'Nobody promised', yield a prior probability that the Laths promised, $P(M_0)$, of .67, not .5, as would 'The Laths (one or both of them) promised'. And although dividing the probabilities seems intuitively right, what justifies it?

The principle of insufficient reason is, however, "traditional."[51] It commends itself to lawyers, who respect precedent, as having been used before. We make valid Figure 7's version of Reichenbach's argument if, using the principle, we add a premise '$P(M_0) = .5$'.[52] We can keep Reichenbach from making a mistake in the

---

[47] *Id.*

[48] Cohen, "Author's Response: Are There Any A Priori Constraints on the Study of Rationality?," *Behavioral & Brain Sci.*, 4 (1981), p. 365.

[49] *See supra* at 10.

[50] Harsanyi, "Bayesian Decision Theory, Subjective and Objective Probabilities, and Acceptance of Empirical Hypotheses," *Synthese*, 57 (1983), p. 341.

[51] Niniluoto, "L. J. Cohen Versus Bayesianism," *Behavioral & Brain Sci.*, 4 (1981), p. 349.

[52] We are just applying Bayes' theorem. Write

$$O(M \mid -W) = \frac{P(-W \mid M)}{P(-W \mid -M)} \, O(M_0),$$

where $O(X)$, the odds that X, is the probability that X divided by the probability that $-X$. Then with $P(M_0) = .5$, so that $O(M_0) = 1$, and with $P(-W \mid -M) = 1$, it is plausibly almost that large,

$$O(M \mid -W) = 1 - P(W \mid M).$$

debate by adding a like premise. It or something weaker, e.g. 'The prior probability is not extremely high or low', may covertly be there.[53]

IX.

Story 3, then, is that the completed proof of Figure 9 is the court's argument in *Mitchill*. I will discuss the advantage to a court of using it and compare the kind of evidence a court using it admits with the kind it usually admits.

The big discontinuity between kinds of evidence separates the lenient Williston and the Corbin views.[54] Take the writing first. Nobody doubts its *physical properties*, which one might inspect because it is before the court. Typically, Mrs. Mitchill did not dispute its *authenticity*, say by denying her signature. Its *meaning* is trickier. Plaintiff in *Trident Center v. Connecticut Gen. Ins. Co.*[55] sought to prepay a loan despite the contract saying: "Maker shall not have the right to prepay . . . ."[56] *Trident* "presents the question whether parties in California can ever draft a contract that is proof against parol evidence," the court said. "Somewhat surprisingly, the answer is no."[57] So much for security which seems stuck at 0.

The *Trident* court, however, would admit parol evidence only to find out what the writing meant. It sent the case back to the trial court to ascertain this. It is going to be hard or impossible for plaintiff to prove it meant the quoted passage, less the word 'not'. The reader should recognize that the result has conceptually nothing to do with the parol evidence rule but might subvert it.

A court's finding out the writing's meaning precedes its applying the parol evidence rule. As is evident from Lehman's statement the rule,[58] the parol evidence

---

If $P(W|M) = 1$, as in the Uniform Commercial Code's parol evidence rule, $P(M| - W) = 0$; if $P(W|M) = 0$, hence that the promise is not in the writing reveals nothing, it would not be there in any case, and $P(M| - W) = P(M_0) = .5$; if $P(W|M) = .5$, then $-W$ excludes .25 of the possible cases, those in which the promise is in the writing, so that, there remaining twice as many cases without the promise as with it, $P(M| - W) = .33$.

[53] A footnote two sentences after the passage quoted from Reichenbach, *see supra* at 15, conceivably cures its defect:

> From the existence of a probability $P(a, b)$ alone we cannot infer that a probability $P(b, a)$ exists; see my "Theory of Probability" (Berkeley, 1949), pp. 109–110. But this inference can be made if, in addition, the probabilities $P(a)$ and $P(-a, b)$ exist; this follows from formula (9) (*ibid.*, p. 92), when the general reference class A is omitted. I may add the remark that all these considerations, of course, belong in what I have called advanced knowledge.

Reichenbach, *supra* note 39, at 153–54 n.5. Reichenbach reads '$P(a, b)$' as I have read '$P(b|a)$': 'the probability of b, on condition that a'. The footnote, then, says that the prior matters. It does not, however, say how it matters, or quite say that it matters to the argument two sentences back. Seeing Reichenbach's *Theory of Probability* does not help.

[54] *See supra* at 7.
[55] 847 F.2d 564 (9th Cir. 1988).
[56] *Id.* p. 566.
[57] *Id.* p. 565.
[58] *See supra* at 7.

$$P(W|M) > p$$
$$P(-W|-M) > p$$
$$P(M_0) = .5$$
$$P(-M|-W) > p$$
$$.5 < p$$
$$.5 \leq q$$
$$P(M|-W) < q$$
$$-W$$
$$P(M) < q$$

Exclude the evidence

Figure 9

rule uses the writing's meaning. So prior to applying the rule a court must decide this semantic property. *Trident* is just an extreme statement of a court's license to do so, by a federal court petulantly applying state law, as a federal court must when as in *Trident* it hears a case because the parties reside in different states. *Trident*, however, makes conceptually possible, although not yet practically threatening, a court's avoiding the parol evidence rule by, for instance, finding that by 'The Laths will convey the farm' the parties *meant* 'The Laths will convey the farm and remove the ice house'.

Neither do contracting parties often dispute the circumstances. Andrews stated the circumstances in *Mitchill* as "the presence of the ice house" and "that Mrs. Mitchill thought it objectionable."[59] Still, also typically, the Laths did not come to court asking, "What ice house?"; anyhow Mrs. Mitchill had pictures.

Who said what, however, the negotiations, often are vigorously disputed. Seeger in *Mitchill* heard the testimony in Figure 10. The mere inquiry unsettles. Thayer described a "lawyer's paradise" where "a lawyer, having a document referred to him, may sit in his chair, inspect the text, and answer all questions without raising his eyes."[60] The contracting parties may like that too.

A way to see the loss of security from letting in evidence of the negotiations is to take $P(W|M)$, in the strict Williston view, and less convincingly in the lenient Williston view, as a property of the writing. On these views the court will look at

---

[59] *See supra* at 11.
[60] J. Thayer, *A Preliminary Treatise on the Law of Evidence* 428–29 (1898).

```
For Mitchill:

    The Witness [Mr. Mitchill]: ...I said, "I
think we will buy the place, and the price is all right,
but if we buy it, it is understood that the icehouse
must be removed before we come up the following spring."
That was then the fall of 1923; that before we moved
up the following spring, it was understood that the
icehouse must be removed.  Charles Lath then assured me
that it would be.


    Q.  What did he say?  A.  Charles Lath told me
in so many words that the ice house would be removed.
(Record at 31.)


    The Witness [Mrs. Mitchill]: ...I said,
"Well, of course, if we should decide to buy the place,
we would only buy it with the consideration that you
would remove this ice house," and [Charles Lath] said
surely, they would do that ... .  (Record at 78.)


    Q.  What did [Charles Lath] say?  A.  [Mr.
Gillespie] He said he would remove the ice house.
(Record at 96.)


For the Laths:

    Q.  Did you ever tell Mrs. Mitchill or Mr.
Mitchill, either one of them, that you would ever remove
this ice house?  A.  [Charles Lath] No.  (Record at
158.)


    Q.  Did you promise Mr. Mitchill or Mrs.
Mitchill that that ice house would be removed?  A.
[Fred Lath] No, sir.  (Record at 201.)
```

Figure 10

the writing and maybe the surrounding circumstances and estimate $P(W|M)$. The circumstances are fixed, the parties' testimony will agree on them. The writing the contracting parties control. So if they can think like the court, by manipulating the writing *they can themselves set* $P(W|M)$. That they must think like the court significantly qualifies, since $P(W|M)$ is opaque. A Corbin court's argument place for testimony of negotiations, however, throws off the parties' calculations. Who knows what a party will testify to?

Evidence of the negotiations is of vanishingly small significance for deciding $P(W|M)$, just as the outcome of a particular coin toss matters hardly at all to the probability the coin lands heads. Ideally, what matters is the limit, in an infinite sequence of tosses, of the ratio of heads; a single toss is a small proportion of that sequence. Or so the argument goes. Actually, we can get a good empirical probability with finitely many tosses, the same small proportion. The judges, however, are going to get $P(W|M)$ by introspection, not by sampling.

On the other hand, the best evidence for $P(M)$, if a court calculates it, rather than infers it, is that of the negotiations. The logic of *Mitchill* lets a court get $P(M)$ without going through the best, but controverted, evidence.

Rule 1 does not make sense for a Corbin court. The camel that the logic of *Mitchill* elaborately tries to keep out is for it already inside the tent. So it might as well straight out calculate $P(M)$. A Marxist interpretation of Corbin's parol evidence rule is that it simply filters the evidence through the judge, herself an instrument of exploitation, who if she decides $P(M) < q$ keeps the issue of whether the Laths promised from the jury.

X.

A sentence quoted earlier from Professor Williston, "The point is not merely whether the court is convinced that the parties before it did in fact do this, but whether parties so situated generally would or might do so,"[61] marks the difference between a hands-on and a statistical $P(M)$. Ordinarily the law abhors the latter, as in the forbidden inference of Figure 11.

Illustratively, imagine 20 prisoners in a compound. A guard among them falls, knocking himself unconscious. One prisoner goes off to a corner of the compound; the other 19 deliberate. Prisoners' deliberating is ordinarily ominous: "Surely the administrators of Pontiac do not believe that prison gangs meet ... to discuss the *The Critique of Pure Reason* ...."[62] They, the 19 of them, kill the guard.[63]

A second, distant guard witnesses the killing, and the proportion of participants, and is the state's sole witness at the trial of a randomly selected prisoner, P_{17}, for the murder. The evidence establishes a probability of guilt of .95. But that is insufficient, as a matter of law, consequently the case does not get to the jury. The probability is, however, high enough; its statistical character somehow disqualifies it. That disqualification is just the opposite of what happens with the parol evidence rule, which excludes the direct, embraces the statistical evidence.

The result is hard to explain. Here are two insufficient explanations, the second better than the first, and a third that mostly succeeds. First, statistical proofs, like the example, are such that anybody can calculate them. So the jury process loses its unobservability, and the lay person confronts the law's willingness to incur some risk of killing somebody innocent. This invoking of lay sensibilities fails since the paradox is in civil law too. Imagine a plaintiff struck by a bus. That is all she knows. She offers to prove that X company buses are 19 times as frequent at that

---

[61] *See supra* at 12.

[62] David K. v. Lane, 839 F.2d 1265, 1278 (7th cir. 1988) (Easterbrook, J., dissenting).

[63] Nesson, "Reasonable Doubt and Permissive Inferences: The Value of Complexity," *Harv. L. Rev.*, 98 (1979), p. 1193.

$$\boxed{\begin{array}{c}
\text{P(a prisoner is guilty} \mid \\
\text{19 of 20 prisoners are guilty)} \\
= .95. \\[4pt]
\text{19 of 20 prisoners are guilty} \\[4pt]
P_{17} \text{ is a prisoner} \\[4pt]
\text{P}(P_{17} \text{ is guilty}) = .95
\end{array}}$$

Figure 11

place as buses of Y company, the only other source of buses. So the probability is .95 X company did it. She has no case;[64] yet the lay person faces with equanimity that a probability only marginally above .5 satisfies the civil burden of proof by a preponderance of the evidence.

Second, the .95 probability may be unresilient, that is, responsive to new evidence.[65] P_{17} having been hanged, P_4 might come forward to say, "She was innocent." That would discomfit the administration of justice and not do much for the dead defendant either. The idea goes back to Peirce, who recognized that a .5 probability of drawing a white bean from a bag, got by drawing and replacing two beans, one black, one white, differs from a .5 probability after many draws.[66] But Peirce's limiting case of infinitely many draws is itself statistical. And even if we rule out other evidence, every prisoner but P_{17} being dead etc., the legal intuition is that still we cannot convict.

Third, there must be an evidentiary mechanism that works.[67] That is, the event complained of must cause the evidence that it occurred. P_{17}, if guilty, did not cause *much* of the evidence, since without her the probability a prisoner is guilty drops only from .95 to .947. The parol evidence rule not only does not demand this causal connection; its Williston versions forbid it. They require that a case be decided by statistical evidence that, except most strikingly in some cases of employment discrimination, elsewhere in the law is by itself insufficient.

---

[64] Sargent v. Massachusetts Accident Co., 307 Mass. 246, 29 N.E. 2d 825 (1940).

[65] B. Skyrms, *Causal Necessity* 12 (1980); Skyrms, "Resiliency, Propensities and Causal Necessity," *J. Phil.*, 74 (1977),p. 704.

[66] C. Peirce, "The Probability of Induction," in 2 *Collected Papers of Charles Sanders Peirce* 420–26 (1932). *See also* J. Keynes, "A Treatise on Probability," in 8 *The Collected Writings of John Maynard Keynes* 77 (1973).

[67] Sahlin, "How to Be 100% Certain 99.5% of the Time," *J. Phil.*, 83 (1986), p. 91; *see generally Evidentiary Value* (P. Gärdenfors, B. Hannson & N. Sahlin eds. 1983).

CONCLUSION

There is, finally, something of Hume's essay *Of Miracles* in the parol evidence rule. There Hume let the statistical evidence that establishes a law of nature override the evidentiary mechanism of eyewitnesses of a miracle, as always more reliable. The parol evidence rule disqualifies the direct evidence, not because it is unreliable, but to protect the repose of a contracting party.[68]

---

[68] D. Hume, "Of Miracles," in *Enquiries Concerning the Human Understanding and Concerning the Principles of Morals* 109 (2d L. Selby-Bigge ed. 1902) (1st ed. 1777).

HUGUES LEBLANC AND PETER ROEPER

WHAT ARE ABSOLUTE PROBABILITIES A FUNCTION OF?

Truth-value semantics was born twice on the same day, at a conference on Free Logic held at Michigan State University in June of 1967. On that day J. Michael Dunn and I read consecutive papers, each of them an account of logical truth and logical implication that exploited the substitution interpretation of the quantifiers and discarded models in favor of truth-value assignments. Dunn's piece, written in collaboration with Nuel D. Belnap, was published in 1968 as [4]; mine was published the same year as [6]. By then Bas C. van Fraassen had informed Belnap, Dunn and me that a truth-value account of logical truth was in Evert W. Beth's *Foundations of Mathematics* of 1959; and soon thereafter I noticed that a truth-value account of first-order logical truth, and more generally of ω-order logical truth, was in Karl Schütte's "Syntactical and Semantical Properties of Simple Type Theory" of 1960. The accounts of first-order implication in [4] and [6] may, however, have been new. They differed from each other in one important respect, Dunn and Belnap adding new names or terms, while I merely reindexed the old ones. The first trick, as Dunn and Belnap indicated, was in imitation of one in Leon Henkin's "The Completeness of the First-Order Functional Calculus" of 1949; the other was a suggestion to me by K. Jaakko Hintikka. So the semantics born in East Lansing on that day was a many-fathered thing after all.[1]

Nuel, who eventually disowned the adding of terms and concluded instead that first-order logic is strongly incomplete when interpreted the truth-value way, lost interest in the matter. But Michael made a later contribution to truth-value semantics when in [3] he offered for propositional modal logic an account of logical truth that discarded possible worlds in favor of truth-value assignments; and, with Robert K. Meyer, he used the substitution interpretation of the quantifiers to prove in [14] that the relevance logic RQ is weakly complete. As for myself, I have remained fascinated by truth-value semantics. This co-authored paper, for proof, does for probability what [4] and [6] did for truth. It is with much affection for Nuel and much admiration for his work that it is contributed to the present *Festschrift*.

Hugues Leblanc

---

[1] The appellation "truth-value semantics" was suggested to me by Quine.

J. M. Dunn and A. Gupta (eds.), Truth or Consequences, 307–325.

SECTION I

Suppose first that the statements of a language L are compounded from given atomic statements by means of just '$\sim$' and '$\wedge$'. Then the truth-value of a statement A of L is a function of the truth-values of the atomic components of A in L, i.e. of those atomic statements of L that A is compounded from. As for the sets of statements of L, suppose they are constructed *conjunctively* and their atomic components in L are taken to be those of their various members. Then the truth-value of a set S of statements of L is likewise a function of the truth-values of *its* atomic components in L.

Suppose next that the components of L are compounded from given atomic statements by means of '$\sim$', '$\wedge$', *and* '$\forall$'; suppose L has 't_1', 't_2', ... as its *denumerably many* terms; and suppose quantifications are construed *substitutionally*. Then talk is of *substatements* rather than *components*,[2] and the truth-value of a statement A of L is a function of the truth-values of the atomic substatements of A in L, i.e. of those atomic statements of L that A is compounded from. As for the sets of statements of L, suppose they are again construed conjunctively and their atomic substatements are taken to be those of their various members. Then the truth-value of a set S of statements of L is likewise a function of the truth-value of the atomic substatements of S in L.

Our concern here, a generalization of earlier concerns of Belnap's, Dunn's and Leblanc's with truth-values, is with absolute probabilities,[3] more specifically, with the absolute probabilities of sets of statements of L. Individual statements of L, as opposed to sets of them, are not forgotten in the process: the absolute probability of statement A of L *is* that of the unit set $\{A\}$ of A. But focusing on sets of statements has its dividends. Thanks to it, the account in section II of first-order probability has the same *separation property* as Gentzen's account of first-order provability. And, thanks to it, the question our title poses can be sharply answered. Let S be a set of statements of L, and $ASS(S)$ consist of the atomic substatements of S in L. The truth-value of S, we just noted, is a function of the truth-values of the *members* of $ASS(S)$. The absolute probability of S, contrastingly, is a function of the absolute probabilities of countably many finite *subsets* of $ASS(S)$. Proof of the result, and proof that it cannot be improved upon, are in section III.

Expectedly, when a set S of statements in L is inconsistent, its truth-value cannot but be F, and its absolute probability cannot but equal 0. Proved in [12] is that when S — though consistent — is not *instantially consistent in the sense of* [12], its truth-value is also sure to be F and its absolute probability also sure to equal 0. Fortunately, however, when denumerably many new terms are added to L, the set becomes instantially consistent at once, its truth-value may again be T as well as F,

---

[2] To be more exact, talk is of *subformulas* rather than *components*, but we prefer the appellation 'substatements'.

[3] A generalization in that absolute probability functions with just 0 and 1 as their values are truth-value functions and vice-versa. Proof of the fact is in [7].

and its absolute probability may again exceed as well as equal 0. We take up these matters in section IV.[4]

SECTION II

The language L under consideration here is a first-order language of the customary sort. It has as its logical operators '$\sim$', '$\wedge$', and '$\forall$', and as its terms the denumerably many 't_1', 't_2', . . . listed earlier. Its statements are the customary ones except in this respect: $(\forall X)A$ counts as a statement of L only if the result $A(t_1/X)$ of putting 't_1' everywhere in A for X does. Consequently, identical quantifiers cannot overlap in a statement of L; and, when $(\forall X)A$ is a vacuous quantification, X does not occur at all in A. $A(t_1/X)$ is of course one of the (substitution-) instances of $(\forall X)A$ in L, the others being $A(t_2/X), A(t_3/X), \ldots$. We refer to the set of them by means of '$I((\forall X)A)$'. As is customary but worth repeating here, (i) each statement of L is a substatement of itself in L, (ii) A is a substatement of $\sim A$ in L, (iii) each of A and B is a substatement of $(A \wedge B)$ in L, (iv) each instance of $(\forall X)A$ in L is a substatement of $(\forall X)A$ in L, and (v) if A is a substatement of B in L and B is a substatement of C in L, then A is a substatement of C in L. The substatements in L of a set S of statements of L are the substatements in L of its various members; and, as indicated earlier, we refer to the set of the atomic ones among them by means of '$ASS(S)$'. Lastly, we presume the statements of L to come in some alphabetic order; the one in [13], due to R.M. Smullyan, will do.

Further prerequisites of section III are these notions: *the operator-complexity* $oc(A)$ and *the quantifier-height qh(A) of a statement A of L*, *the operator-complexity* $oc(S)$ and *the quantifier-height qh(S) of a finite set S of statements of L*, and *the rank r(S) of such an S*. Our account of $r(S)$ may be new: we take $r(S)$ to be the pair $\langle qh(S), oc(S') \rangle$, where S' consists of all and only the members of S that are of quantifier-height $qh(S)$.

(1)   Let A be an arbitrary statement and S be an arbitrary finite set of statements in L. Then $oc(A)$ is inductively defined thus, 't_1' in the fourth clause being the alphabetically first term of L:

$$oc(A) = \begin{cases} 0 & \text{for } A \text{ an atomic statement} \\ oc(B) + 1 & \text{for } A \text{ a negation } \sim B \\ oc(B) + oc(C) + 1 & \text{for } A \text{ a conjunction } B \wedge C \\ oc(B(t_1/X)) + 1 & \text{for } A \text{ a quantification } (\forall X)B, \end{cases}$$

and $oc(S)$ is defined thus, $A_1, A_2, \ldots, A_n$ in the second clause being in alphabetic order the various members of S:

---

[4] To anticipate some, a set S of statements of L is said to be *instantially consistent* if no contradiction can be gotten from S by means of the customary rules of proof for L *plus* one allowing proof of a universal quantification of L from the set of its substitution instances *in L*. This extra rule is an extension to terms *generally* of the *omega-rule* of *omega-logic* for *numerical* terms.

$$oc(S) = \begin{cases} 0 & \text{for } S \text{ empty} \\ \sum_{i=1}^{n} oc(A_i) & \text{otherwise.} \end{cases}$$

(2)   Let A and S be as in (1). Then $qh(A)$ is inductively defined thus, 't_1' in the fourth clause being as before:

$$qh(A) = \begin{cases} 0 & \text{for } A \text{ an atomic statement} \\ qh(B) & \text{for } A \text{ a negation } \sim B \\ \max(qh(B), qh(C)) & \text{for } A \text{ a conjunction } B \wedge C \\ qh(B(t_1/X)) + 1 & \text{for } A \text{ a quantification } (\forall X)B, \end{cases}$$

and $qh(S)$ defined thus, $A_1, A_2, \ldots, A_n$ in the second clause being as before:

$$qh(S) = \begin{cases} 0 & \text{for } S \text{ empty} \\ \max(qh(A_1), qh(A_2), \ldots, qh(A_n)) & \text{otherwise.} \end{cases}$$

(3)   Let S be a finite set of statements of L. Then $r(S)$ is defined thus:

$$r(S) = \langle qh(S), oc(\{A : A \in S \text{ and } qh(A) = qh(S)\})\rangle,$$

and of two finite sets S and S' of statements of L we say that
$$r(S) < r(S')$$
if (i)
$$qh(S) < qh(S')$$
or (ii)
$$qh(S) = qh(S'),$$
but then
$$oc(\{A : A \in S \text{ and } qh(A) = qh(S)\})$$
$$< oc(\{A : A \in S' \text{ and } qh(A) = qh(S')\}).$$

Together with the definition of an absolute probability function for L, this lemma will deliver our main result:

LEMMA 1. *Let S be an arbitrary finite set of statements of L, A be the alphabetically latest member of S of quantifier-height $qh(S)$, and S' be $S - \{A\}$.*

CASE 1. *A is a negation $\sim B$. Then*
$$r(S') < r(S) \text{ and } r(S' \cup \{B\}) < r(S).$$

CASE 2. *A is a conjunction $B \wedge C$. Then*
$$r(S' \cup \{B\} \cup \{C\}) < r(S).$$

CASE 3.1. *A is a vacuous quantification $(\forall X)B$. Then*
$$r(S' \cup \{B\}) < r(S).$$

CASE 3.2. *A is a non-vacuous quantification $(\forall X)B$. Then*
$$r(S' \cup S'') < r(S)$$
for every finite subset S'' of $I(A)$.

Proof

Case 1: Suppose *first* that

$$qh(S') < qh(S),$$

in which case $\sim B$ is the only member of S of quantifier-height *qh(S)*. Then of course

$$r(S') < r(S).$$

Suppose *next* that

$$qh(S') = qh(S).$$

Then

$$oc(\{A : A \in S' \text{ and } qh(A) = qh(S')\})$$
$$= oc(\{A : A \in S' \text{ and } qh(A) = qh(S)\}).$$

But

$$oc(\{\sim B\}) > 0.$$

So

$$oc(\{A : A \in S' \text{ and } qh(A) = qh(S')\})$$
$$< oc(\{A : A \in S' \cup \{\sim B\} \text{ and } qh(A) = qh(S)\}).$$

So

$$r(S') < r(S).$$

As for $S' \cup \{B\}$,

$$qh(S' \cup \{B\}) = qh(S)$$

and hence

$$oc(\{A : A \in S' \cup \{B\} \text{ and } qh(A) = qh(S' \cup \{B\})\})$$
$$= oc(\{A : A \in S' \cup \{B\} \text{ and } qh(A) = qh(S)\}).$$

But

$$oc(\{\sim B\}) > oc(\{B\}).$$

So

$$oc(\{A : A \in S' \cup \{B\} \text{ and } qh(A) = qh(S' \cup \{B\})\})$$
$$< oc(\{A : A \in S' \cup \{\sim B\} \text{ and } qh(A) = qh(S)\}).$$

So

$$r(S' \cup \{B\}) < r(S).$$

Case 2:

$$qh(S' \cup \{B\} \cup \{C\}) = qh(S).$$

So

$$oc(\{A : A \in S' \cup \{B\} \cup \{C\} \text{ and } qh(A) = qh(S' \cup \{B\} \cup \{C\})\})$$
$$= oc(\{A : A \in S' \cup \{B\} \cup \{C\} \text{ and } qh(A) = qh(S)\}).$$

But

$$oc(\{B \wedge C\}) > oc(\{B\}) \cup \{C\}).$$

So

$$oc(\{A : A \in S' \cup \{B\} \cup \{C\} \text{ and } qh(A) = qh(S' \cup \{B\} \cup \{C\})\})$$
$$< oc(\{A : A \in S' \cup \{B \wedge C\} \text{ and } qh(A) = qh(S)\}).$$

So

$$r(S \cup \{B\} \cup \{C\}) < r(S).$$

Case 3.1: Suppose *first* that

$$qh(S') < qh(S),$$

in which case $(\forall X)B$ is the only member of S of quantifier-height $qh(S)$. Then

$$qh(S' \cup \{B\}) < qh(S)$$

and hence

$$r(S' \cup \{B\}) < r(S).$$

Suppose *next* that

$$qh(S') = qh(S)$$

and hence

$$qh(S' \cup \{B\}) = qh(S).$$

Then

$$oc(\{A : A \in S' \cup \{B\} \text{ and } qh(A) = qh(S' \cup \{B\})\})$$
$$= oc(\{A : A \in S' \cup \{B\} \text{ and } qh(A) = qh(S)\}).$$

But

$$qh(\{B\}) < qh(S).$$

So

$$oc(\{A : A \in S' \cup \{B\} \text{ and } qh(A) = qh(S' \cup \{B\})\})$$
$$= oc(\{A : A \in S' \text{ and } qh(A) = qh(S)\}).$$

But

$$oc(\{(\forall X)B\}) > 0.$$

So

$$oc(\{A : A \in S' \cup \{B\} \text{ and } qh(A) = qh(S' \cup \{B\})\})$$
$$= oc(\{A : A \in S' \cup \{(\forall X)B\} \text{ and } qh(A) = qh(S)\}).$$

So

$$r(S' \cup \{B\}) < r(S).$$

Case 3.2: Letting S'' be an arbitrary finite subset of $I(A)$, suppose *first* that

$$qh(S') < qh(S).$$

Since

$$qh(S'') < qh((\forall X)B)$$

and hence

$$qh(S'') < qh(S),$$

we have

$$\max(qh(S'), qh(S'')) < qh(S),$$

hence

$$qh(S' \cup S'') < qh(S),$$

and hence

$$r(S' \cup S'') < r(S).$$

Suppose *next* that

$$qh(S') = qh(S)$$

and hence

$$qh(S' \cup S'') = qh(S).$$

Then

$$oc(\{A : A \in S' \cup S'' \text{ and } qh(A) = qh(S' \cup S'')\})$$
$$= oc(\{A : A \in S' \text{ and } qh(A) = qh(S)\}).$$

But

$$qh(S'') < qh(S).$$

So

$$oc(A : A \in S' \cup S'' \text{ and } qh(A) = qh(S' \cup S'')\})$$
$$= oc(\{A : A \in S' \text{ and } qh(A) = qh(S)\}).$$

But

$$oc(\{(\forall X)B\}) > 0.$$

So

$$oc(\{A : A \in S' \cup S'' \text{ and } qh(A) = qh(S' \cup S'')\})$$
$$< oc(\{A : A \in S' \cup \{(\forall X)B\} \text{ and } qh(A) = qh(S)\}).$$

So

$$r(S' \cup S'') < r(S)$$

again.   □

SECTION III

In this, our cumulative account of the probability functions for L,[5] Σ_0 consists of all the finite sets of atomic statements of L, Σ_f consists of all the finite sets of (atomic and compound) statements of L, and Σ_ω consists of all the (finite and infinite) sets of statements of L. Also '$S \subset_f S'$' is short for 'S is a *finite* subset of S''.

(1)   Let P_0 be an arbitrary real-valued function on Σ_0, and let F_{P_0} be the function on $\Sigma_0 \times \Sigma_0$ defined thus, A in the second clause being the alphabetically latest member of S_2:

$$F_{P_0}(S_1, S_2) = \begin{cases} P_0(S_1) & \text{for } S_2 \text{ empty} \\ F_{P_0}(S_1, S_2 - \{A\}) - F_{P_0}(S_1 \cup \{A\}, S_2 - \{A\}) & \\ & \text{otherwise.} \end{cases}$$

Then P_0 constitutes *a probability function for L of type 0* if it meets these two constraints:

(i) $P_0(\emptyset) = 1$.
(ii) $0 \le F_{P_0}(S_1, S_2)$, *where* $S_1 \cap S_2 = \emptyset$ *and* $S_1 \cup S_2 \ne \emptyset$.[6]

(2)   Let P_0 be an arbitrary probability function for L of type 0. Then *the extension of P_0 to Σ_f* is the function P_f on Σ_f defined thus, A in the last three clauses being the alphabetically latest member of S that is of quantifier-height $qh(S)$ and S' being $S - \{A\}$:

$$P_f(S) = \begin{cases} P_0(S) & \text{for } r(S) = \langle 0,0 \rangle \\ P_f(S') - P_f(S' \cup \{B\}) & \text{for } r(S) > \langle 0,0 \rangle \text{ and} \\ & A \text{ of the sort } {\sim}B \\ P_f(S' \cup \{B\} \cup \{C\}) & \text{for } r(S) > \langle 0,0 \rangle \text{ and} \\ & A \text{ of the sort } B \wedge C \\ \inf\{P(S' \cup S'') : S'' \subset_f I(A)\} & \text{for } r(S) > \langle 0,0 \rangle \text{ and} \\ & A \text{ of the sort } (\forall X)B \end{cases}$$

(3)   A real-valued function P_f on Σ_f constitutes *a probability function for L of type f* if there exists a probability function P_0 for L of type 0 of which P_f is the extension to Σ_f.

(4)   Let P_f be an arbitrary probability function for L of type f. Then *the extension of P_f to Σ_ω* is the function P_ω on Σ_ω defined thus:

---

[5] Relative (= conditional) probability functions are not under consideration here. So we hereafter drop the qualifying 'absolute'.

[6] Suppose S_1 is $\{A_1, A_2, \ldots, A_n\}$ and S_2 is $\{A_{n+1}, A_{n+2}, \ldots, A_{n+m}\}$, and suppose P_f is what we understand in (2) by the extension of P_0 to P_f. Then $F_{P_0}(S_1, S_2)$ is tantamount to $P_f(\{A_1, A_2, \ldots, A_n, {\sim}A_{n+1}, {\sim}A_{n+2}, \ldots, {\sim}A_{n+m}\})$, i.e., to the probability of a state-description in Carnap's sense or that of a proper subset of one. Carnap in [2] would have '<' where with Popper in [15] we have '$\le$'. The function F_{P_0} is studied in [10].

$$P_\omega(S) = \begin{cases} P_f(S) & \text{for } S \text{ finite} \\ \inf\{P_f(S') : S' \subset_f S\} & \text{otherwise.} \end{cases}$$

(5)   A real-valued function P_ω on Σ_ω constitutes *a probability function for L of type ω* if there exists a probability function P_f for L of type f of which P_ω is the extension to Σ_ω.

For brevity's sake we hereafter talk of probability functions *tout court* rather than probability functions of type ω, and refer to them by means of 'P' rather than 'P_ω'.

And now the main result of this paper:

THEOREM 1. *Let P be an arbitrary probability function for L, and S be an arbitrary set of statements of L. Then there exist countably many finite subsets $S_1, S_2, \ldots$ of ASS(S) and a numerical function f on $P(S_1), P(S_2), \ldots$ such that*

$$P(S) = f(P(S_1), P(S_2), \ldots).^7$$

Proof

CASE I: S is finite. The proof is by transfinite induction on the rank $r(S)$ of S.

Basis: $r(S) = \langle 0, 0 \rangle$. Then S is empty or is a finite set of atomic statements in L, and in either case there exists a finite subset S_1 of $ASS(S)$ (S itself) and a numerical function f on $P(S_1)$ (the identity function) such that

$$P(S) = f(P(S_1)).$$

Inductive Step: $r(S) > \langle 0, 0 \rangle$. Let A be the alphabetically latest member of S of quantifier-height $qh(S)$, and S' be $S - \{A\}$. The proof is by cases.

Case 1: A is a negation $\sim B$. Then, by the definition of P,

(1) $P(S) = P(S') - P(S' \cup \{B\})$.

But, by *Lemma 1*,

$$r(S') < r(S)$$

and

$$r(S' \cup \{B\}) < r(S).$$

So, by the hypothesis of the induction, there exist countably many finite subsets $S_1', S_2', \ldots$ of $ASS(S')$, hence of $ASS(S)$, and a numerical function f' on $P(S_1'), P(S_2'), \ldots$ such that

$$P(S') = f'(P(S_1'), P(S_2'), \ldots),$$

---

[7] Note that, having countably many members, $ASS(S)$ has countably many finite subsets. Note further that when any member of S has a non-vacuous quantification as a substatement, $ASS(S)$ has denumerably many finite subsets.

and there exist countably many finite subsets $S_1'', S_2'', \ldots$ of $ASS(S' \cup \{B\})$, hence of $ASS(S)$, and a numerical function f'' on $P(S_1''), P(S_2''), \ldots$ such that

$$P(S' \cup \{B\}) = f''(P(S_1''), P(S_2''), \ldots).$$

So, by (1),

$$P(S) = f'(P(S_1'), P(S_2'), \ldots) - f''(P(S_1''), P(S_2''), \ldots)$$
$$= f(P(S_1'), P(S_1''), P(S_2'), P(S_2''), \ldots).$$

Case 2: A is a conjunction $B \wedge C$. Then, by the definition of P,

(2) $$P(S) = P(S' \cup \{B\} \cup \{C\}).$$

But, by *Lemma 1*,

$$r(S' \cup \{B\} \cup \{C\}) < r(S).$$

So, by the hypothesis of the induction, there exist countably many finite subsets $S_1, S_2, \ldots$ of $ASS(S' \cup \{A\} \cup \{B\})$, hence of $ASS(S)$, and a numerical function f on $P(S_1), P(S_2), \ldots$ such that

$$P(S' \cup \{B\} \cup \{C\}) = f(P(S_1), P(S_2), \ldots).$$

So, by (2),

$$P(S) = f(P(S_1), P(S_2), \ldots).$$

Case 3.1: A is a vacuous quantification $(\forall X)B$. Then, by the definition of P,

(3.1) $$P(S) = P(S' \cup \{B\}).$$

But, by *Lemma 1*,

$$r(S' \cup \{B\}) < r(S).$$

So, by the hypothesis of the induction, there exist countably many finite subsets $S_1, S_2, \ldots$ of $ASS(S' \cup \{B\})$, hence of $ASS(S)$, such that

$$P(S' \cup \{B\}) = f(P(S_1), P(S_2), \ldots).$$

So, by (3.1),

$$P(S) = f(P(S_1), P(S_2), \ldots).$$

Case 3.2: A is a non-vacuous quantification $(\forall X)B$. Then, by the definition of P,

$$(3.2) \qquad P(S) = \inf\{P(S' \cup S'') : S'' \subset_f I(A)\}.$$

Now, let $S''_1, S''_2 \ldots$ be in any order you please the finite subsets of $I(A)$. By *Lemma 1*,

$$r(S' \cup S''_i) < r(S)$$

for each i from 1 on. So, by the hypothesis of the induction, there exist for each such i countably many finite subsets $S'''_{i_1}, S'''_{i_2}, \ldots$ of $ASS(S' \cup S''_i)$, hence of $ASS(S)$, and a numerical function f_i on $P(S'''_{i_1}), P(S'''_{i_2}), \ldots$ such that

$$P(S' \cup S''_i) = f_i(P(S'''_{i_1}), P(S'''_{i_2}), \ldots).$$

So, by (3.2),

$$\begin{aligned} P(S) &= \inf\{f_i(P(S'''_{i_1}), P(S'''_{i_2}), \ldots) : i = 1, 2, \ldots\} \\ &= f(P(S'''_{1_1}), P(S'''_{1_2}), P(S'''_{2_1}), P(S'''_{2_2}), \ldots). \end{aligned}$$

CASE II: S is infinite. Then, by the definition of P,

$$(4) \qquad P(S) = \inf\{P(S') : S' \subset_f S\}.$$

Now, let $S'_1, S'_2, \ldots$ be in any order you please the finite subsets of S.[8] By Case I there exist for each i from 1 on countably many finite subsets $S''_{i_1}, S''_{i_2} \ldots$ of $ASS(S'_i)$, hence of $ASS(S)$, and a numerical function f_i on $P(S''_{i_1}), P(S''_{i_2}), \ldots$ such that

$$P(S'_i) = f_i(P(S''_{i_1}), P(S''_{i_2}, \ldots)).$$

So, by (4),

$$\begin{aligned} P(S) &= \inf\{f_i(P(S''_{i_1}), P(S''_{i_2}), \ldots) : i = 1, 2, \ldots\} \\ &= f(P(S''_{1_1}), P(S''_{1_2}), P(S''_{2_1}), P(S''_{2_2}), \ldots). \end{aligned}$$

$\square$

So, with $P(A)$ understood as $P(\{A\})$:

COROLLARY 1. *Let P be an arbitrary probability function for L, and A be an arbitrary statement of L. Then there exist countably many finite subsets $S_1, S_2, \ldots$ of $ASS(\{A\})$ and a numerical function f on $P(S_1), P(S_2), \ldots$ such that*

$$P(A) = f(P(S_1), P(S_2), \ldots).$$

As remarked earlier, *Theorem 1* cannot be improved upon. Suppose A_1, A_2, A_3 are three atomic statements of L. When P has but 0 and 1 as its values and hence is but a truth-value function, $P(\{A_1, A_2\})$ is sure to be a numerical function of $P(\{A_1\})$ and $P(\{A_2\})$, and $P(\{A_1, A_3\})$ is sure to be a numerical function of $P(\{A_1\})$ and $P(\{A_3\})$. Not so, however, when P has three or more values. As readers of Carnap know, the function P in Table I readily extends to a total probability function for L:

---

[8] Note that, having countably many members, S has countably many finite subsets.

TABLE I

$$P(\{A_1\}) = 1/2 \begin{cases} P(\{A_1, A_2\}) = 1/8 \begin{cases} P(\{A_1, A_2, A_3\}) = 1/16 \\ P(\{A_1, A_2, \sim A_3\}) = 1/16 \end{cases} \\ P(\{A_1, \sim A_2\}) = 3/8 \begin{cases} P(\{A_1, \sim A_2, A_3\}) = 3/16 \\ P(\{A_1, \sim A_2, \sim A_3\}) = 3/16 \end{cases} \end{cases}$$

$$P(\{\sim A_1\}) = 1/2 \begin{cases} P(\{\sim A_1, A_2\}) = 3/8 \begin{cases} P(\{\sim A_1, A_2, A_3\}) = 3/16 \\ P(\{\sim A_1, A_2, \sim A_3\}) = 3/16 \end{cases} \\ P(\{\sim A_1, \sim A_2\}) = 1/8 \begin{cases} P(\{\sim A_1, \sim A_2, A_3\}) = 1/16 \\ P(\{\sim A_1, \sim A_2, \sim A_3\}) = 1/16 \end{cases} \end{cases}$$

All three of $P(\{A_1\})$, $P(\{A_2\})$, and $P(\{A_3\})$ equal 1/2. Yet $P(\{A_1, A_3\})$ equals 1/4, whereas $P(\{A_1, A_2\})$ equals 1/8. So there cannot be a numerical function f on $P(\{A_1\})$, $P(\{A_2\})$, and $P(\{A_3\})$ such that both:[9]

$$P(\{A_1, A_2\}) = f(P(\{A_1\}), P(\{A_2\}))$$

and

$$P(\{A_1, A_3\}) = f(P(\{A_1\}), P(\{A_3\})).$$

SECTION IV

With '⊃' defined in terms of '∼' and '∧' as is customary, let *the axioms of L* be the statements of L of the following six forms:

A1. $A \supset (A \wedge A)$
A2. $(A \wedge B) \supset A$
A3. $(A \supset B) \supset (\sim(B \wedge C) \supset \sim(C \wedge A))$
A4. $A \supset (\forall X)A$
A5. $(\forall X)A \supset A(T/X)$
A6. $(\forall X)(A \supset B) \supset ((\forall X)A \supset ((\forall X)B)),$

plus the statements of L of the form $(\forall X)(A(X/T))$, where A is an axiom of L and T is a term of L. Given a statement A of L and a set S of statements of L, one would acknowledge as a *proof of A from S* (in the standard sense) any *finite* sequence of statements of L whose last entry is A, and every one of whose entries is (i) a member of S, (ii) an axiom of L, or (iii) the consequent C of a conditional $B \supset C$ of L, and both B and $B \supset C$ occur earlier in the sequence;[10] and one would then say that A is *provable from S* (in the standard sense), for short

$$S \vdash A,$$

---

[9] The example is from [9].
[10] The rule applied here to get C is of course *Modus Ponens*.

if there exists a proof of A from S (in the standard sense).

A *proof of A from S in the instantial sense,* on the other hand, would be any *countable, possibly transfinite,* sequence of statements of L whose last entry is A, and every one of whose entries is as (i)–(iii) above *or* is (iv) a quantification $(\forall X)B$ of L, and all the members of $I((\forall X)B)$ occur earlier in the sequence;[11] and one would say that A is *provable from S in the instantial sense,* for short

$$S \vdash_i A,$$

if there exists a proof of A from S in the instantial sense. This done, one would say that a set S of statements in L is *consistent* (in the standard sense) if there exists no statement A of L such that both $S \vdash A$ and $S \vdash \sim A$, that and S is *instantially consistent* if there exists no statement A of L such that both $S \vdash_i A$ and $S \vdash_i \sim A$. By way of illustration, these two sets, though clearly consistent, are not instantially consistent:

and
$$S_1 = \{F(T) : \text{for any term } T \text{ of } L\} \cup \{\sim(\forall x)F(x)\}^{12}$$

$$S_2 = \{F(T, T') : \text{for any two terms } T \text{ and } T' \text{ of } L\}$$
$$\cup \{\sim(\forall x)(\forall y)F(x, y)\}.$$

As indicated in Section I, [12] has proof that if a set S of statements of L is *not* instantially consistent, then the truth-value of S is sure to be F on every truth-value assignment to the members of $ASS(S)$. Since truth-value assignments are but two-valued absolute probability functions, it follows from the result in question that if S is *not* instantially consistent, then $P(S)$ is sure to equal 0 for every *two-valued* probability function P for L. Generalizing, we go on to show that if S is *not* instantially consistent, then $P(S)$ is sure to equal 0 for *every* probability function P for L. Needed for this are two lemmas. The proof of *Lemma 2* is simple enough, but as it is lengthy we do not reproduce it.

LEMMA 2. *Let P be an arbitrary probability function for L, and S and S' be arbitrary sets of statements of L.*

(a)   If $P(S) = 0$, then $P(S \cup S') = 0$;
(b) $P(S \cup S') = \inf\{P(S \cup S'') : S'' \subset_f S'\}.$

LEMMA 3. *Let P be an arbitrary probability function for L, let S and S' be arbitrary sets of statements of L, and let A be an arbitrary statement of L.*

(a)   If $P(S) = P(S \cup \{A\})$, then $P(S \cup S') = P(S \cup S' \cup \{A\})$;
(b)   If $P(S) = P(S \cup \{A\})$ and $P(S) = P(S \cup S')$,
        then $P(S) = P(S \cup S' \cup \{A\})$;
(c)   If $P(S) = P(S \cup \{B\})$ for every member B of S',
        then $P(S) = P(S \cup S')$.

---

[11]   The rule applied here to get $(\forall X)B$ is of course the one discussed in note 4. In the presence of it, (ii) in this account may be weakened to read: (ii) an axiom of L of one of the six forms $A1$-$A6$.

[12]   A set S of statements of L is said in [12] to be *term-consistent* if there exists no quantification $(\forall X)A$ of L such that $S \vdash A(T/X)$ for each and every term T of L and yet $S \vdash \sim(\forall X)A$. S_1 is not term-consistent, but — intriguingly — S_2 is. See [12] for more on this.

Proof

(a) Suppose

$$P(S) = P(S \cup \{A\}).$$

Then, by the definition of P,

$$P(S \cup \{\sim A\}) = 0.$$

Hence, by *Lemma 2(a)*,

$$P(S \cup S' \cup \{\sim A\}) = 0.$$

So, by the definition of P,

$$P(S \cup S') = P(S \cup S' \cup \{A\}).$$

(b) By (a).

(c) Suppose

$$P(S) = P(S \cup \{B\})$$

for every member B of S.

Case 1: S' is finite. The proof of (c) is by mathematical induction on the number n of members of S'.

Basis: $n = 1$. Then (c), trivially.

Inductive Step: $n > 1$. Let C be an arbitrary member of S'. Then, by the hypothesis of the induction,

$$P(S) = P(S \cup S' - \{C\}).$$

But, by the hypothesis on P,

$$P(S) = P(S \cup \{C\}).$$

So, by (b),

$$P(S) = P(S \cup S').$$

Case 2: S is infinite. Then, by *Lemma 2(b)*,

$$P(S \cup S') = \inf\{P(S \cup S'') : S'' \subset_f S'\}.$$

But, by Case 1,

$$P(S \cup S'') = P(S)$$

for every finite subset S'' of S'. So

$$P(S \cup S') = P(S). \qquad \square$$

THEOREM 2.   *Let P be an arbitrary probability function for L, S be an arbitrary set of sentences of L, and A be an arbitrary statement of L. If $S \vdash_i A$, then $P(S) = P(S \cup \{A\})$.*

Proof

Suppose $S \vdash_i A$. We show by transfinite induction that

$$P(S) = P(S \cup \{A'\})$$

for every entry A' in the proof of A from S.

Case (i): A' belongs to S. Then trivially

$$P(S) = P(S \cup \{A'\}).$$

Case (ii): A' is an axiom of L. Then, by *Theorem 4.41* in [8],

$$P(\emptyset \cup \{A'\}) = 1.$$

But, by the definition of P,

$$P(\emptyset) = 1.$$

So, by *Lemma 3(a)*,

$$P(S) = P(S \cup \{A'\}).$$

Case (iii): A' is the consequent of a conditional $B \supset A'$ (i.e. $\sim(B \wedge \sim A')$), and both B and $B \supset A'$ occur earlier in the proof of A from S. Then, by the hypothesis of the induction,

$$P(S) = P(S \cup \{\sim(B \wedge \sim A')\}).$$

Hence, by the definition of P,

$$\begin{aligned} P(S) &= P(S) - P(S \cup \{B\} \cup \{\sim A'\}) \\ &= P(S) - P(S \cup \{B\}) + P(S \cup \{B\} \cup \{A'\}). \end{aligned}$$

But, by the hypothesis of the induction,

$$P(S) = P(S \cup \{B\}).$$

So

$$P(S) = P(S \cup \{B\} \cup \{A'\}).$$

But, by the hypothesis of the induction again and *Lemma 3(a)*,

$$P(S \cup \{A'\}) = P(S \cup \{B\} \cup \{A'\}).$$

So

$$P(S) = P(S \cup \{A'\}).$$

Case (iv): A' is a quantification $(\forall X)B$, and all the members of $I((\forall X)B)$ occur earlier in the proof of A from S. Then, by the hypothesis of the induction,

$$P(S) = P(S \cup \{B(T/X)\})$$

for every member $B(T/X)$ of $I((\forall X)B)$. Hence, by *Lemma 3(c)*,

$$P(S) = P(S \cup I((\forall X)B)).$$

But

$$P(S \cup I((\forall X)B)) = \inf\{P(S \cup S'') : S'' \subset_f I((\forall X)B)\}$$

by *Lemma 2(b)*, and hence

$$P(S \cup I((\forall X)B)) = P(S \cup \{(\forall X)B\})$$

by the definition of P. So

$$P(S) = P(S \cup \{A'\}). \qquad \qquad \square$$

So:

COROLLARY 2. *If a set S of statements of L is not instantially consistent, then $P(S) = 0$ for every probability function P for L.*

Proof

Suppose S not instantially consistent. Then there exists at least one statement of L such that both

$$S \vdash_i A$$

and

$$S \vdash_i \sim A.$$

Suppose P an arbitrary probability function for L. Then, by *Theorem 2*,

$$P(S) = P(S \cup \{A\})$$

and

$$P(S) = P(S \cup \{\sim A\}).$$

So, by the definition of P,

$$P(S) = 0. \qquad\qquad \square$$

There is also proof in [12] that any set of statements of L that is consistent (in the standard sense) and *infinitely extendible* is instantially consistent, a set being infinitely extendible if denumerably many terms of L are foreign to it. Now let L^+ be any first-order language that is exactly like L except for having denumerably many new terms besides those of L. Any statement of L counts of course as a statement of L^+, and hence any set of statements of L counts as a set of statements of L^+, an infinitely extendible one at that, since the denumerably many terms of L^+ that are new with L^+ are perforce foreign to it. So, *in its capacity as a set of statements of L^+*, any set of statements of L that is consistent is sure to be instantially consistent. But *Lemma 1* holds true with S there an arbitrary finite set of statements of L^+, and so does *Theorem 1* with P there an arbitrary probability function for L^+ and S an arbitrary set of statements of L^+. So, in particular, the probability of a set S of statements of L is a function of the probabilities of countably many finite subsets of $ASS^+(S)$, $ASS^+(S)$ *the set of the atomic substatements of S in L^+*. And, when S is consistent, that probability is sure to exceed 0 for one or more probability functions for L^+.[13]

---

[13] We thank George Weaver with whom we discussed the phrasing and proof of Theorem 1, and Opher Etzion who prepared the text for publication. Hugues Leblanc held a Summer Research Grant from Temple University while this paper was written.

BIBLIOGRAPHY

[1]   Beth, E.W. (1959): *The Foundations of Mathematics*, Amsterdam: North-Holland.
[2]   Carnap, R. (1950): *Logical Foundations of Probability*, Chicago: University of Chicago Press.
[3]   Dunn, J.M. (1973): "A Truth-Value Semantics for Modal Logic", in *Truth, Syntax, and Modality*, H. Leblanc, ed., Amsterdam: North-Holland, pp. 87–100.
[4]   Dunn, J.M. and N. D. Belnap, Jr. (1968): "The Substitution Interpretation of the Quantifiers", *Noûs*, Vol. 2, pp. 177–185.
[5]   Henkin, L. (1949): "The Completeness of the First-Order Functional Calculus", *The Journal of Symbolic Logic*, Vol. 14, pp. 159–166.
[6]   Leblanc, H. (1968): "A Simplified Account of Validity and Implication for Quantificational Logic", *The Journal for Symbolic Logic*, Vol. 33, pp. 231–235.
[7]   Leblanc, H. (1982): "Popper's 1955 Axiomatization of Absolute Probability", *Pacific Philosophical Quarterly*, Vol. 63, pp. 133–145.
[8]   Leblanc, H. (1983): "Alternatives to First-Order Semantics ", in *Handbook of Philosophical Logic, Volume I*, Reidel Publishing Company, pp. 189–274
[9]   Leblanc, H. (1984): "A New Semantics for First-Order Logic, Multivalent and Mostly Intensional", *Topoi*, Vol. 3, pp. 55–62.
[10] Leblanc, H. and P. Roeper, (1986): "Absolute Probability Functions: A Recursive and Autonomous Account", in *The Tasks of Contemporary Philosophy, Proceedings of the 19th International Wittgenstein Symposium*. Vienna: Verlag Holder-Pichler-Tempsky, pp. 484–494.
[11] Leblanc, H. and P. Roeper: *Absolute Probability Functions and their Semantic Payoff*, in preparation.
[12] Leblanc, H., P. Roeper, M. Thau, G. Weaver: "Henkin's Completeness Proof: Forty Years Later", *Notre Dame Journal of Formal Logic*, forthcoming.
[13] Leblanc, H., and W.A. Wisdom, (1976): *Deductive Logic*, revised edition, Boston: Allyn and Bacon.
[14] Meyer, R. K., J. M. Dunn, and H. Leblanc, (1974): "Completeness of Relevant Quantification Theories", *Notre Dame Journal of Formal Logic*, Vol. 14, pp. 97–121.
[15] Popper, K. R. (1959): *The Logic of Scientific Discovery*, New York: Basic Books.
[16] Schütte, K. (1960): "Syntactical and Semantical Properties of Simple Type Theory", *The Journal of Symbolic Logic*, Vol. 25, pp. 305–326

PATRICK MAHER

HOW PREDICTION ENHANCES CONFIRMATION [1]

> But in establishing axioms by this kind of induction, we must
> also examine and try whether the axiom so established be framed
> to the measure of those particulars only from which it is derived,
> or whether it be larger and wider. And if it be larger and wider,
> we must observe whether by indicating to us new particulars it
> confirm that wideness and largeness as by a collateral security;
> that we may not either stick fast in things already known, or
> loosely grasp at shadows and abstract forms; not at things solid
> and realised in matter.
>
> Francis Bacon [1, cvi]

1. THE PREDICTIVIST THESIS

Since the scientific revolution, there have been persistent endorsements, both by scientists and philosophers of science,[2] of the view that predictions have special value in confirming hypotheses. According to this view, evidence which was used in formulating a hypothesis does not confirm the hypothesis as strongly as it otherwise would. I shall call this view *the predictivist thesis*.

The predictivist thesis can be formulated in Bayesian terms. Let H be a hypothesis, and let E be some evidence for H. Let M_H denote that method M generated a hypothesis which entails H. (I will say more about methods shortly.) Let O denote that evidence E was available to M when it generated H, and let $\bar{O}$ be the negation of H. If $M_H.E.\bar{O}$ holds, we can say evidence E was *predicted* by M; and if $M_H.E.O$ holds, E was *accommodated* by M. Let P be the subjective probability function of some rational person who has not yet learned the truth values of M_H, E and O. Then the predictivist thesis asserts that

$$(1) \qquad P(H|M_H.E.\bar{O}) > P(H|M_H.E.O).$$

---

[1] Because it uses formal tools to illuminate scientific reasoning, this paper seemed suitable to honor Nuel Belnap. I got to know Nuel when I was a graduate student at the University of Pittsburgh. His modal logic seminar was a highpoint of my graduate studies. He gave enthusiastic support when I decided to enroll in the math department; this paper draws on what I learned there.

This paper was written while I was a fellow with the Michigan Society of Fellows, and on leave from the University of Illinois at Urbana-Champaign. The research reported here was supported in part by the National Science Foundation under grant SES-8708168.

[2] Including Huygens [9, preface], Whewell [24, vol. 2, p. 64f.], Peirce [17], Duhem [5, ch. II, §5], Popper [18, p. 241f.], and Kuhn [12, p. 154f.] The physicist S. Chandrasekhar has recently cited, as one of the main reasons to be confident in the general theory of relativity, that "it does not violate the laws of other branches of physics not contemplated in its formulation, such as thermodynamics or quantum theory" [4, pp. 151f.].

J. M. Dunn and A. Gupta (eds.), Truth or Consequences, 327–343.
© 1990 *Kluwer Academic Publishers. Printed in the Netherlands.*

It is easy to see that the predictivist thesis does not hold universally. For example, consider two tosses of a fair coin, which we will denote toss 1 and toss 2. Let E be the proposition that toss 1 lands heads, and let H be the proposition that tosses 1 and 2 both land heads. Let M be the method of randomly guessing the outcomes of coin tosses. (I am assuming that M is known to have only a random chance of making a successful prediction.) Then a very natural assignment of probabilities will give

$$P(H|M_H.E.\bar{O}) = P(H|E) = 1/2,$$

and

$$P(H|M_H.E.O) = P(H|E) = 1/2.$$

This is a counterexample to the predictivist thesis.

Some philosophers of science[3] have opposed the predictivist thesis, and maintained that whether evidence was predicted or accommodated is irrelevant to confirmation. According to this position, it is always the case that

(2) $\qquad P(H|M_H.E.\bar{O}) = P(H|M_H.E.O).$

But this equality also has counterexamples. At the end of section 2.2 below, I will give an example in which H and E are as above, but the reliability of M is unknown; and in that example, $P(H|M_H.E.\bar{O}) = 2/3$, while $P(H|M_H.E.O) = 1/2$. Since $P(H) = 1/4$, we have in this example

(3) $\qquad P(H|M_H.E.\bar{O}) > P(H|M_H.E.O) > P(H),$

which violates (2).

Some of those who have held the predictivist thesis have maintained that accommodated evidence cannot confirm (or corroborate) a hypothesis to any degree.[4] A Bayesian formulation of this position would be that

(4) $\qquad P(H|M_H.E.O) = P(H).$

But the two examples discussed above are both counterexamples to (4). Furthermore, (3) makes it clear that the predictivist thesis does not entail (4).

Although (1), (2) and (4) all fail in some situations, it still might be the case that one of them holds under the sorts of conditions that usually obtain in scientific inquiry. And in fact, I shall argue in this paper that the predictivist thesis (1) is indeed true under those conditions. Since (1) and (2) are inconsistent, it follows that (2) is false under the same conditions. I believe that (4) is false in almost all contexts, though I shall not argue for that here.

[3] Mill [16, bk. III, ch. 14], Keynes [10, p. 305], Rosenkrantz [21, p. 169f.], Horwich [8, pp. 108–117]. The arguments which some of these authors have offered are criticized in [15].

[4] Popper [19, p. 418], Lakatos [13, p. 123], Redhead [20, p. 357], Giere [6, pp. 159–161].

Of previous attempts to explain why the predictivist thesis should be true, the most explicit and detailed are those of Campbell and Vinci [2, 3]. If either of those accounts had been satisfactory, the account I shall offer would not be needed. But in fact, these accounts are both vitiated by fallacies, as pointed out in [15, note 5].

My account is based on the idea that a successful prediction normally confirms the reliability of the method by which a hypothesis was generated, whereas accommodation of the same evidence normally provides less (if any) reason to believe that method is reliable. Since confirmation of the reliability of a method also confirms the hypotheses generated by the method, it follows that the predictivist thesis normally holds.[5]

Before turning to my account, let me clarify the central notion of a *method* of generating hypotheses. From a formal point of view, a method of generating hypotheses can be regarded as a function which maps a set A of propositions onto the set of probability distributions over a set B of propositions. In the intended interpretation, each element of A is a possible body of evidence that might be input to the method, and each element of B is a hypothesis that might be generated by the method. The probability distribution which is the value of the method for a given argument $A \in A$ is interpreted as giving the probability with which the method would generate the various elements of B, given that the evidence input to the method is A. (If the method is deterministic, the probability measures in its counterdomain will all be degenerate 0–1 distributions.)

To see how this formalism may be applied to a concrete case, let M be Mendeleyev's method of generating hypotheses about the chemical elements. Here A will consist of propositions describing various possible bodies of evidence about the chemical elements (and perhaps other relevant facts). One element A of A describes the evidence which was actually available to Mendeleyev in 1871. The set B consists of various possible hypotheses about the elements, and one element B of B asserts the existence of the elements in Mendeleyev's periodic table of 1871. M maps A onto a probability distribution over B, representing the probability of Mendeleyev asserting the various hypotheses in B given the available evidence A. Although we know Mendeleyev did in fact assert B on the basis of A, most of us would be largely ignorant of this probability distribution. We probably have even less idea of what hypothesis Mendeleyev would have proposed if his evidence had been substantially different to what it in fact was. But such ignorance does not prevent us from successfully referring to the method, or making inferences about its properties (such as its reliability).

After these preliminaries, I turn to the account of why the predictivist thesis is true, when it is.

---

[5] I put forward this idea in [15], where a formal Bayesian analysis was also given. But that analysis made a number of unrealistic simplifying assumptions; in particular, I there assumed that the hypothesis generating method is believed to be either completely reliable, or else random. The present paper will give a more general analysis, and eschew such unrealistic assumptions.

2. Special case: Predicting tosses of a fair coin

I begin by analyzing the somewhat special case of predicting tosses of a fair coin. The symmetries involved in this example allow the main features of the analysis to be exhibited without complicating details, and the concrete interpretation should help intuition. Later I will give a more general analysis, which is intended to be applicable to confirmation of hypotheses in science.

We have already seen that if hypotheses about the tosses of a fair coin are generated by a method that is known to have only a random chance of success, then the predictivist thesis is violated. What I will show here is that if the reliability of the method is not known for certain, and provided some other plausible conditions hold, then the predictivist thesis holds.

2.1. Assumptions

As before, we consider two tosses of a fair coin, denoted toss 1 and toss 2. E is a hypothesis about the outcome of toss 1 (e.g. that it lands heads), and E' is a hypothesis about the outcome of toss 2 (e.g. that it too is heads); H is the conjunction of E and E'. M is some method of generating hypotheses about the outcome of these coin tosses. For any proposition A, M_A will denote that M has generated a proposition which entails A. We take it as given throughout that the truth value of E' has not been input to M.

I assume that there is believed to be some chance (or objective probability) R that a prediction by M, concerning either coin toss, will be correct. That is, there is thought to be some chance R that E will be true, given that M has predicted E; and also the same chance that E' will be true, given that M has predicted E'. (If the method has only a random chance of making a successful prediction, then $R = 1/2$.) Since E is predicted by M just in case $M_E.\bar{O}$ holds, and E' is predicted by M just in case $M_{E'}$ holds, R can also be described as the conditional chance of E given $M_E.\bar{O}$, and of E' given $M_{E'}$. It is therefore natural to suppose that the following principle of direct inference holds for all $r \in [0, 1]$:

$$(5) \qquad P(E|M_E.\bar{O}.R = r) = P(E'|M_{E'}.R = r) = r.$$

In order for (5) to be meaningful, we need a suitable definition of conditional probability. According to the classical definition,

$$(6) \qquad P(A|B) = \frac{P(A.B)}{P(B)}.$$

On this definition, $P(A|B)$ is undefined if $P(B) = 0$. But we want to allow R to have a continuous probability distribution, in which case $P(R = r) = 0$ for all r, and (6) would entail that the conditional probabilities in (5) are undefined. To avoid this, we introduce the following definition:

DEFINITION: Let A and C be events, with $P(C) > 0$. A conditional probability of A given C and $R = r$, denoted $P(A|C.R = r)$, is a function $q(r)$, defined on the reals, such that for all Borel sets B,

$$(7) \qquad P(A.R \in B|C) = \int_B q(r) \, dF(r|C),$$

where $F(\cdot|C)$ is the probability distribution of R conditioned on C.

The probabilities conditioned on C which appear in this definition are defined by (6). It follows from the Radon-Nikodym theorem that $P(A|C.R = r)$ exists, and is unique up to a set of probability 0.[6]

Provided that $M_E.\bar{O}$ and $M_{E'}$ both have positive probability, the conditional probabilities appearing in (5) are now well defined. They are not, however, unique; we will therefore interpret (5) as asserting that the function $q(r) = r$ is one function which satisfies the definitions of both $P(E|M_E.\bar{O}.R = r)$ and $P(E'|M_{E'}.R = r)$.

I shall assume that $P(M_H.E.\bar{O})$ and $P(M_H.E.O)$ are both positive. This entails the proviso of the preceding paragraph; and it is an unobjectionable assumption in the present context.

When we know the chance of an event, our subjective probability for that event is *resilient*, in the sense that it is insensitive to certain further information [23, 14]. For example, if you know that a coin is fair, then your subjective probability for it landing heads on the next toss will be 1/2, regardless of what you know about the outcome of previous tosses. Similarly, in our prediction example, it is reasonable to assume that if the value of R is known, then information about M's success in predicting the first toss will not alter the subjective probability of it successfully predicting the second toss. More precisely, I assume that for all $r \in [0, 1]$,

$$P(E'|M_{E'}.M_E.E.\bar{O}.R = r)$$
$$= P(E'|M_{E'}.M_E.E.O.R = r) = r.$$

I will likewise assume that when R is known, the (subjective) probability of the method successfully predicting the first toss is unaffected by knowledge of what the method predicts concerning the second toss; that is,

$$P(E|M_E.\bar{O}.M_{E'}.R = r) = r.$$

---

[6] The integral in (7) is a Lebesgue-Stieltjes integral. For an account of this, and of the Radon-Nikodym theorem, see Kolmogorov and Fomin [11]. The application of the Radon-Nikodym theorem in the present context requires that $P(A.R \in B|C)$, considered as a function of B, be absolutely continuous with respect to the Lebesgue-Stieltjes measure corresponding to $F(\cdot|C)$. This condition follows from the fact that, for any real number r,

$$P(A.R \le r|C) \le P(R \le r|C) = F(r|C).$$

Since H is equivalent to the conjunction of E and E', and M_H is equivalent to the conjunction of M_E and $M_{E'}$, the preceding two equalities simplify to

(8) $\qquad P(E|M_H.\bar{O}.R = r) = r.$

(9) $\qquad P(H|M_H.E.\bar{O}.R = r) = P(H|M_H.E.O.R = r) = r.$

Since E and E' concern the outcome of tosses of a fair coin, it is not unreasonable to expect that the propositions $M_H.\bar{O}$ and $M_H.E.O$ are each by themselves probabilistically independent of R. For $M_H.\bar{O}$ says that M has predicted E and E', but not whether these predictions were successful; and $M_H.E.O$ says that M has accommodated E and predicted E', but does not say whether the prediction was successful. We then have

(10) $\qquad F(r|M_H.\bar{O}) = F(r|M_H.E.O) = F(r) \qquad\qquad 0 \le r \le 1.$

(If the coin were not fair, then (10) would not hold. For example, if the coin were known to be biased for tails, and if H asserts that tosses 1 and 2 land heads, then M_H would be evidence that M is unreliable. I have assumed that the coin is fair in order to be able to make the simplifying assumption (10).)

Finally, I assume that the reliability of M is not known with certainty. Formally:

(11) $\qquad P(R = r) < 1 \qquad\qquad\qquad\qquad\qquad\qquad 0 \le r \le 1.$

For example, if M is a method based on observing (a) the orientation of the coin before it is tossed, and (b) the height to which the coin rises as it is tossed, then one might well be uncertain of M's reliability.

Apart from (11), I assume nothing else about the probability distribution of R. In particular, I allow that the probability distribution of R may be discrete, continuous, or a mixture of discrete and continuous distributions.

I will now show that the predictivist thesis (1) follows from the foregoing assumptions.

2.2. Derivation of the predictivist thesis

We have

$$
\begin{aligned}
(12) \quad F(r|M_H.E\bar{O}) &= (R \le r|M_H.E\bar{O}) & \text{by definition} \\
&= \frac{P(E.R \le r|M_H.\bar{O})}{P(E|M_H.\bar{O})} & \text{by (6)} \\
&= \frac{P(E.R \le r|M_H.\bar{O})}{P(E.R \le 1|M_H.\bar{O})} & \text{since } P(R \le 1) = 1 \\
&= \frac{\int_0^r P(E|M_H.\bar{O}.R = x)\, dF(x|M_H\bar{O})}{\int_0^1 P(E|M_H.\bar{O}.R = x)\, dF(x|M_H\bar{O})} & \text{by (7)}
\end{aligned}
$$

$$= \frac{\int_0^r P(E|M_H.\bar{O}.R = x)\, dF(x)}{\int_0^1 P(E|M_H.\bar{O}.R = x)\, dF(x)} \qquad \text{by (10)}$$

$$= \frac{\int_0^r x\, dF(x)}{\int_0^1 x\, dF(x)} \qquad \text{by (8)}$$

$$= \frac{\int_0^r x\, dF(x)}{\mathcal{E}(R)},$$

where $\mathcal{E}(R)$ is the expected value of R. It follows [7, Theorem 32.B] that for any finite-valued function φ for which $\int_0^1 \varphi(r)\, dF(r|M_H.E.\bar{O})$ is defined,

$$(13) \qquad \int_0^1 \varphi(r)\, dF(r|M_H.E.\bar{O}) = \frac{1}{\mathcal{E}(R)} \int_0^1 r\varphi(r)\, dF(r).$$

I now apply this result to the evaluation of $P(H|M_H.E.\bar{O})$. We have

$$(14) \qquad P(H|M_H.E.\bar{O})$$

$$= P(H.R \leq 1|M_H.E.\bar{O})$$

$$= \int_0^1 P(H|M_H.E.\bar{O}.R = r)\, dF(r|M_H.E.\bar{O}) \qquad \text{by (7)}$$

$$= \int_0^1 r\, dF(r|M_H.E.\bar{O}) \qquad \text{by (9)}$$

$$= \frac{1}{\mathcal{E}(R)} \int_0^1 r^2\, dF(r) \qquad \text{by (13)}$$

$$= \frac{\mathcal{E}(R^2)}{\mathcal{E}(R)}.$$

Turning now to the other probability which figures in the predictivist thesis, we obtain

$$(15) \qquad P(H|M_H.E.O)$$

$$= P(H.R \leq 1|M_H.E.O)$$

$$= \int_0^1 P(H|M_H.E.O.R = r)\, dF(r|M_H.E.O) \qquad \text{by (7)}$$

$$= \int_0^1 r\, dF(r|M_H.E.O) \qquad \text{by (9)}$$

$$= \int_0^1 r\, dF(r) \qquad \text{by (10)}$$

$$= \mathcal{E}(R).$$

From (14) and (15), we have that (1) holds if and only if

$$(16) \qquad \mathcal{E}(R^2) > [\mathcal{E}(R)]^2.$$

This would be an instance of Jensen's inequality [22, p. 63] except that the inequality here is strict, not weak. However, a proof of Jensen's inequality is easily modified to yield strict inequality in the present case, using the facts that the square function is *strictly* convex, and our assumption (11) that the probability distribution of R is not concentrated on a point. Thus (16) holds, and hence the predictivist thesis (1) does also.

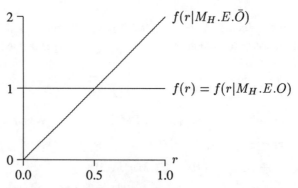

The case of a uniform prior for R

In order to visualize how successful prediction adds to the confirmation of H, consider the special case in which $F(r) = r$, $0 \leq r \leq 1$. That is, we are considering the case in which R has the uniform prior density function $f(r) = 1$. Then $\mathcal{E}(R) = 1/2$. Differentiating (10) and (12) respectively gives

$$f(r|M_H.E.O) = f(r) = 1;$$
$$f(r|M_H.E.\bar{O}) = r/\mathcal{E}(R) = 2r.$$

These density functions are plotted in the figure. We see that $M_H.E.\bar{O}$ increases the probability density of values of R greater than $\mathcal{E}(R)$, and reduces that of values of R less than $\mathcal{E}(R)$. So the expected value of R is increased; in fact, $\mathcal{E}(R|M_H.E.\bar{O}) = 2/3$. On the other hand, $\mathcal{E}(R|M_H.E.O.) = \mathcal{E}(R) = 1/2$. Thus $M_H.E.\bar{O}$, but not $M_H.E.O$, has confirmed the reliability of M, thus increasing the probability of the prediction E' made by M.

3. The general case

I now proceed to generalize the account of the preceding section. The more general account given here is intended to be applicable, in particular, to the case where H is a scientific hypothesis, and E is some evidence for H. As before, I will first describe the assumptions to be made, and later show that these assumptions entail the predictivist thesis.

3.1. Assumptions

I will assume again that

$$(17) \qquad P(M_H.E.\bar{O}) > 0 \qquad \text{and} \qquad P(M_H.E.O) > 0.$$

This assumption could probably be removed by further generalizing the definition of conditional probability; but since (17) is a plausible assumption when E is scientific evidence, such a refinement will not be pursued here.

It will be convenient to assume that H entails E. This is not a substantive assumption. For suppose that E is evidence for a hypothesis H^- which does not entail E. Let H be the conjunction of H^- and E. The situations which the predictivist thesis compares are both situations in which M_E and E hold; and under these circumstances, M_{H^-} and H^- are equivalent to M_H and H, respectively. We can therefore substitute H for H^-, without changing the situation in any way that would make a difference to the predictivist thesis. And of course, H entails E.

Let E' be the union (or disjunction) of H and $\bar{E}$. Since H entails E, this definition has the consequence that H is the intersection (or conjunction) of E and E'. Intuitively, E' represents that part of the content of H which goes beyond E.

I will continue to assume that there is believed to be a chance (objective probability) of E being true given that M has predicted E, and similarly for E'. Now in the context where E is some scientific evidence, and H is a scientific hypothesis, E and E' need not describe events which can in any natural sense be regarded as repeatable. Nevertheless, the notion of chance is meaningful in this context: someone who thinks that there is an unknown chance of an event occurring has a subjective probability function which is a mixture of the possible chance distributions; and these chance distributions are characterized by resiliency.

In the special case of the preceding section, we were able to assume that the chance of E, given that it was predicted by M, is the same as that of E'. But in general, this assumption will not hold. For example, if a coin is biased 2/3 for heads, and if E states that a toss of this coin lands heads, and if E' states that another toss lands tails, and if M is the method of randomly predicting coin tosses, then the chance of E given that it was predicted by M is 2/3, while the chance of E' given that it was predicted by M is 1/3.

I shall denote these two chances by R_1 and R_2 respectively. We can say that R_1 is the reliability of M in regard to a prediction of E, and R_2 is M's reliability in regard to a prediction of E'. The principle of direct inference, analogous to (5), is then that for all $r \in [0, 1]$,

$$(18) \qquad P(E|M_E.\bar{O}.R_1 = r) = r;$$
$$(19) \qquad P(E'|M_{E'}.R_2 = r) = r.$$

I have already mentioned the resilience of subjective probabilities when the chance of the event is known. Applying that general idea to the present case, I shall assume that when the value of R_2 is known, then the subjective probability of E' given $M_{E'}$ is insensitive to both $M_E.E.\bar{O}$ and $M_E.E.O$. This assumption together with (19) gives

$$P(E'|M_{E'}.M_E.E.\bar{O}.R_2 = r) = P(E'|M_{E'}.M_E.E.O.R_2 = r)$$
$$= r.$$

Using the fact that H is equivalent to the conjunction of E and E', we then obtain

(20) $$P(H|M_H.E.\bar{O}.R_2 = r) = P(H|M_H.E.O.R_2 = r) = r.$$

Equations (18) and (20) correspond to (8) and (9) in section 2.1.

Let F_i be the probability distribution of R_i, $i = 1, 2$. An analog of (10) for our general case would be

$$F_1(r|M_H.\bar{O}) = F_1(r|M_H.E.O) = F_1(r) \qquad 0 \le r \le 1.$$

But as I have already remarked, these identities cannot be expected to hold in general. If H is improbable relative to its alternatives, its prediction by M will be evidence that M is unreliable. However, we can plausibly assume that

(21) $$F_1(r|\bar{O}) = F_1(r) \qquad 0 \le r \le 1.$$

For one would need to have unusual background information to have the fact that E was not input to M confirm (or disconfirm) M's reliability as a predictor of E.[7] Also, it seems safe to assume that in the sorts of situations which would normally prevail in science,

(22) $$F_1(r|M_E.E.O) = F_1(r).$$

For $M_E.E.O$ merely asserts that M has accommodated E, and any method likely to be used in science can be expected to be successful in accommodating the evidence input to it.

If $r < s$, and if E is thought less probable than its alternatives, one might very well have

$$P(M_E|\bar{O}.R_1 = r) > P(M_E|\bar{O}.R_1 = s).$$

Under these circumstances, $M_E.\bar{O}$ would confirm $R_1 = r$, and disconfirm $R_1 = s$. That is, the mere fact that M predicted E would be reason to believe that M is unreliable. While I do not wish to rule out this phenomenon, we need to put some bound on it, or else even a successful prediction would not necessarily confirm a method's reliability. The assumption I shall make is that

(23) $$rP(M_E|\bar{O}.R_1 = r) < sP(M_E|\bar{O}.R_1 = s) \qquad 0 \le r < s \le 1.$$

---

[7] For an example of such unusual background information, see [15, p. 277].

This allows $P(M_E|\bar{O}.R_1 = r)$ to exceed $P(M_E|\bar{O}.R_1 = s)$ by an amount which depends on the difference between r and s. Of course, (23) also permits $P(M_E|\bar{O}.R_1 = r)$ to be less than $P(M_E|\bar{O}.R_1 = s)$, in which case no limit is imposed on the size of the difference. I suggest that this is a reasonably mild condition which we could expect to be satisfied in realistic contexts.

I will also assume that the true value of R_1 is not known with certainty, i.e.

(24) $P(R_1 = r) < 1$ $0 \leq r \leq 1.$

The assumptions made to this point entail that successful prediction of E increases the expected value of R_1—as will be shown below. I will now make two further assumptions which enable me to move from that result to the predictivist thesis.

When E and E' are on related topics (as they will be if the hypothesis H which entails them both is not an arbitrary conjunction), then evidence for the reliability of M as a predictor of E would normally also be evidence for M's reliability as a predictor of E', provided the evidence bears on R_2 only via its relevance to R_1. Now when $M_E.E$ is given, the further information $\bar{O}$ would normally be relevant to R_2 only via its relevance to R_1; so we can assume:

(25)   If $\mathcal{E}(R_1|M_E.E.\bar{O}) > \mathcal{E}(R_1|M_E.E.O)$,
            then $\mathcal{E}(R_2|M_E.E.\bar{O}) > \mathcal{E}(R_2|M_E.E.O)$.

No doubt it would be possible to derive (25) from more fundamental assumptions, along the lines of the informal discussion just given. But since I expect that (25) will not be controversial, I shall simply adopt it as a primitive assumption.

For the sorts of reasons which we have already discussed in connection with (10) and (23), it can very well be the case that the prediction of E' disconfirms the reliability of M as a predictor of E', so that

$$\mathcal{E}(R_2|M_H.E.\bar{O}) < \mathcal{E}(R_2|M_E.E.\bar{O}).$$

But it is hard to think of any plausible reason why the degree of any such disconfirmation would depend on whether E had been predicted or accommodated. It therefore seems reasonable to expect that

$$\frac{\mathcal{E}(R_2|M_H.E.\bar{O})}{\mathcal{E}(R_2|M_E.E.\bar{O})} = \frac{\mathcal{E}(R_2|M_H.E.O)}{\mathcal{E}(R_2|M_E.E.O)}.$$

But for our purposes, it will suffice to assume only the weaker inequality

(26) $$\frac{\mathcal{E}(R_2|M_H.E.\bar{O})}{\mathcal{E}(R_2|M_E.E.\bar{O})} \geq \frac{\mathcal{E}(R_2|M_H.E.O)}{\mathcal{E}(R_2|M_E.E.O)}.$$

The next section will show that when these assumptions hold, so does the predictivist thesis.

3.2. Derivation of the predictivist thesis

We have

$$
\begin{aligned}
&F_1(r|M_E.\bar{O})\\
&= P(R_1 \leq r|M_E.\bar{O})\\
&= \frac{P(M_E.R_1 \leq r|\bar{O})}{P(M_E|\bar{O})} &\text{using (6) and (17)}\\
&= \frac{1}{P(M_E|\bar{O})} \int_0^r P(M_E|\bar{O}.R_1 = x)\, dF_1(x|\bar{O}) &\text{by (7)}\\
&= \frac{1}{P(M_E|\bar{O})} \int_0^r P(M_E|\bar{O}.R_1 = x)\, dF_1(x) &\text{by (21).}
\end{aligned}
$$

It follows that for any finite–valued function φ for which $\int_0^1 \varphi(r)\, dF_1(r|M_E.\bar{O})$ is defined,

$$
\begin{aligned}
(27) \quad &\int_0^1 \varphi(r)\, dF_1(r|M_E.\bar{O})\\
&= \frac{1}{P(M_E|\bar{O})} \int_0^1 \varphi(r) P(M_E|\bar{O}.R_1 = r)\, dF_1(r).
\end{aligned}
$$

Now

$$
\begin{aligned}
F_1(r|M_E.E.\bar{O}) &= P(R_1 \leq r|M_E.E.\bar{O})\\
&= \frac{P(E.R_1 \leq r|M_E.\bar{O})}{P(E.|M_E.\bar{O})} &\text{using (6) and (17)}\\
&= \frac{P(E.R_1 \leq r|M_E.\bar{O})}{P(E.R_1 \leq 1|M_E.\bar{O})} &\text{since } P(R_1 \leq 1) = 1\\
&= \frac{\int_0^r P(E|M_E.\bar{O}.R_1 = x)\, dF_1(x|M_E.\bar{O})}{\int_0^1 P(E|M_E.\bar{O}.R_1 = x)\, dF_1(x|M_E.\bar{O})} &\text{by (7)}\\
&= \frac{\int_0^r x\, dF_1(x|M_E.\bar{O})}{\int_0^1 x\, dF_1(x|M_E.\bar{O})} &\text{by (18)}\\
&= \frac{\int_0^r x P(M_E|\bar{O}.R_1 = x)\, dF_1(x)}{\int_0^1 x P(M_E|\bar{O}.R_1 = x)\, dF_1(x)} &\text{by (27).}
\end{aligned}
$$

So for any finite–valued function φ for which $\int_0^1 \varphi(r)\, dF_1(r|M_E.E.\bar{O})$ is defined,

$$
\begin{aligned}
(28) \quad &\int_0^1 \varphi(r)\, dF_1(r|M_E.E.\bar{O})\\
&= \frac{\int_0^1 \varphi(r) r P(M_E|\bar{O}.R_1 = r)\, dF_1(r)}{\int_0^1 r P(M_E|\bar{O}.R_1 = r)\, dF_1(r)}.
\end{aligned}
$$

Therefore

$$\mathcal{E}(R_1|M_E.E.\bar{O}) = \int_0^1 r \, dF_1(r|M_E.E.\bar{O}) \qquad \text{by definition}$$

$$= \frac{\int_0^1 r^2 P(M_E|\bar{O}.R_1 = r) \, dF_1(r)}{\int_0^1 r P(M_E|\bar{O}.R_1 = r) \, dF_1(r)} \qquad \text{by (28).}$$

We also have

$$\mathcal{E}(R_1|M_E.E.O) = \int_0^1 r \, dF_1(r|M_E.E.O)$$

$$= \int_0^1 r \, dF_1(r) \qquad \text{by (22).}$$

So $\mathcal{E}(R_1|M_E.E.\bar{O}) > \mathcal{E}(R_1|M_E.E.O)$ if and only if

$$(29) \qquad \int_0^1 r^2 P(M_E|\bar{O}.R_1 = r) \, dF_1(r)$$

$$> \int_0^1 r P(M_E|\bar{O}.R_1 = r) \, dF_1(r) . \int_0^1 r \, dF_1(r).$$

Equation (29) corresponds to equation (16) of Section 2.2. However, unlike (16), (29) cannot be proved by a simple modification of the proof of Jensen's inequality. So the next task is to give a proof of (29).

Let f, g and h be the functions defined on $[0, 1]$ by

$$f(r) = r^2 P(M_E|\bar{O}.R_1 = r)$$
$$g(r) = r P(M_E|\bar{O}.R_1 = r)$$
$$h(r) = r.$$

Then (29) can be expressed as

$$\mathcal{E}(f) > \mathcal{E}(g).\mathcal{E}(h).$$

For each positive integer n, let Π_n^f be the following partition of $[0, 1]$:

$$\left\{ f^{-1}\left[\frac{i-1}{n}, \frac{i}{n}\right) : i = 1, \ldots, n-1 \right\} \bigcup \left\{ f^{-1}\left[\frac{n-1}{n}, 1\right] \right\}.$$

Define Π_n^g and Π_n^h similarly. Also let a and b be numbers such that $a < b$, $P(0 \leq R_1 \leq a) > 0$, and $P(b \leq R_1 \leq 1) > 0$. The existence of such a and b follows from (24). Let $\Pi_{ab} = \{[0, a], (a, b), [b, 1]\}$, and let $\emptyset$ denote the empty set. We define

$$\Pi_n = \{A \cap B \cap C \cap D : A \in \Pi_n^f, \ B \in \Pi_n^g, \ C \in \Pi_n^h, \ D \in \Pi_{ab}\} \setminus \emptyset.$$

Thus II_n is also a partition of $[0,1]$, and all its elements are nonempty. Since the functions f, g and h are measurable, the elements of II_n are measurable sets.

Let $\text{II}_n = \{A_1, \ldots, A_k\}$, and choose $r_i \in A_i$, $i = 1, \ldots, k$. We define functions f_n, g_n and h_n on $[0,1]$ as follows (where I_{A_i} is the indicator function of the set A_i):

$$f_n(r) = \sum_{i=1}^{k} r_i^2 P(M_E | \bar{O}.R_1 = r_i) I_{A_i}(r)$$

$$g_n(r) = \sum_{i=1}^{k} r_i P(M_E | \bar{O}.R_1 = r_i) I_{A_i}(r)$$

$$h_n(r) = \sum_{i=1}^{k} r_i I_{A_i}(r).$$

These definitions ensure that $|f_n(r) - f(r)|$, $|g_n(r) - g(r)|$ and $|h_n(r) - h(r)|$ are all no more than $1/n$, for all $r \in [0, 1]$. Thus $\{f_n\}$, $\{g_n\}$ and $\{h_n\}$ converge uniformly to f, g and h respectively.

Now we show that there exists $\varepsilon > 0$ such that 1

(30) $\mathcal{E}(f_n) - \mathcal{E}(g_n)\mathcal{E}(h_n) \geq \varepsilon$ for all positive integers n.

Let $P_i = P(M_E | \bar{O}.R_1 = r_i)$. Then

$$\mathcal{E}(f_n) - \mathcal{E}(g_n)\mathcal{E}(h_n)$$

$$= \sum_{i=1}^{k} r_i^2 P_i P(A_i) - \sum_{i=1}^{k} r_i P_i P(A_i) . \sum_{i=1}^{k} r_i P(A_i)$$

$$= \sum_{i=1}^{k} r_i P_i P(A_i) \left[r_i - \sum_{j=1}^{k} r_j P(A_j) \right]$$

$$= \sum_{i=1}^{k} r_i P_i P(A_i) \left[r_i - r_i P(A_i) - \sum_{j \neq i} r_j P(A_j) \right]$$

$$= \sum_{i=1}^{k} r_i P_i P(A_i) \left[r_i P(\bar{A}_i) - \sum_{j \neq i} r_j P(A_j) \right]$$

$$= \sum_{i=1}^{k} r_i P_i P(A_i) \left[r_i \sum_{j \neq i} P(A_j) - \sum_{j \neq i} r_j P(A_j) \right]$$

$$= \sum_{i=1}^{k} r_i P_i P(A_i) \left[\sum_{j \neq i} P(A_j)(r_i - r_j) \right]$$

$$= \sum_{i=1}^{k} \sum_{j \neq i} r_i P_i P(A_i) P(A_j)(r_i - r_j).$$

For each term of the form $r_i P_i P(A_i)P(A_j)(r_i - r_j)$, there is another with i and j interchanged. Adding two such terms gives

$$r_i P_i P(A_i)P(A_j)(r_i - r_j) + r_j P_j P(A_i)P(A_j)(r_j - r_i)$$
$$= P(A_i)P(A_j)(r_i - r_j)(r_i P_i - r_j P_j).$$

Thus we can write

$$\mathcal{E}(f_n) - \mathcal{E}(g_n)\mathcal{E}(h_n) = \sum_{i=1}^{k}\sum_{j=1}^{i-1} P(A_i)P(A_j)(r_i - r_j)(r_i P_i - r_j P_j).$$

Hence

$$\mathcal{E}(f_n) - \mathcal{E}(g_n)\mathcal{E}(h_n) \geq \sum_{r_i \geq b}\sum_{r_j \leq a} P(A_i)P(A_j)(r_i - r_j)(r_i P_i - r_j P_j).$$

At this point it is convenient to let P_a denote $P(M_E | \bar{O}.R_1 = a)$, and similarly for P_b. Then by (23), $r_j P_j \leq a P_a$ for all $r_j \leq a$, and $r_i P_i \geq b P_b$ for all $r_i \geq b$. Hence

$$\mathcal{E}(f_n) - \mathcal{E}(g_n)\mathcal{E}(h_n)$$
$$\geq \sum_{r_i \geq b}\sum_{r_j \leq a} P(A_i)P(A_j)(b - a)(b P_b - a P_a)$$
$$= P(0 \leq R_1 \leq a)P(b \leq R_1 \leq 1)(b - a)(b P_b - a P_a)$$
$$= \varepsilon, \text{ say.}$$

The quantity ε does not depend on n. Our choice of a and b, together with (23), entail that $\varepsilon > 0$. Thus (30) has been proved.

Now choose n such that

$$\sup_{r\in[0,1]} max\ \{|f_n(r) - f(r)|, |g_n(r) - g(r)|, |h_n(r) - h(r)|\} < \frac{\varepsilon}{4}.$$

Then

$$\mathcal{E}(f) - \mathcal{E}(g)\mathcal{E}(h)$$
$$> \mathcal{E}(f_n) - \frac{\varepsilon}{4} - [\mathcal{E}(g_n) + \frac{\varepsilon}{4}][\mathcal{E}(h_n) + \frac{\varepsilon}{4}]$$
$$\geq \mathcal{E}(f_n) - \mathcal{E}(g_n)\mathcal{E}(h_n) - \varepsilon \qquad \text{since } \mathcal{E}(g_n), \mathcal{E}(h_n), \varepsilon \leq 1$$
$$\geq 0 \qquad\qquad\qquad\qquad\qquad\qquad\qquad \text{by (30).}$$

So (29) holds, and hence

(31) $\qquad \mathcal{E}(R_1 | M_E.E.\bar{O}) > \mathcal{E}(R_1 | M_E.E.O).$

Equations (25) and (31) entail that

$$\mathcal{E}(R_2|M_E.E.\bar{O}) > \mathcal{E}(R_2|M_E.E.O).$$

This together with (26) gives

$$(32) \qquad \mathcal{E}(R_2|M_H.E.\bar{O}) > \mathcal{E}(R_2|M_H.E.O).$$

Now

$$(33) \qquad \mathcal{E}(R_2|M_H.E.\bar{O})$$

$$= \int_0^1 r\, dF_2(r|M_H.E.\bar{O})$$

$$= \int_0^1 P(H|M_H.E.\bar{O}.R_2 = r)\, dF_2(r|M_H.E.\bar{O}) \qquad \text{by (20)}$$

$$= P(H.R \le 1|M_H.E.\bar{O}) \qquad\qquad\qquad \text{by (7)}$$

$$= P(H|M_H.E.\bar{O}).$$

Similarly,

$$(34) \qquad \mathcal{E}(R_2|M_H.E.O) = P(H|M_H.E.O).$$

Equations (32)–(34) yield the predictivist thesis (1).

4. Conclusion

I have demonstrated that certain conditions are sufficient for the predictivist thesis to hold. While these conditions can conceivably fail, I have suggested that they would normally hold in scientific contexts. If that is right, then it follows that the predictivist thesis normally holds in scientific contexts. The demonstration also provides insight into *why* the thesis should hold: Under the assumed conditions, successful prediction confirms the reliability of the method by which the hypothesis was generated, while successful accommodation gives less, if any, confirmation to the method's reliability. This difference translates into a difference in the probability of the hypothesis generated by the method; for reason to believe a method reliable is reason to believe the hypotheses it generates.

BIBLIOGRAPHY

[1]   Bacon, Francis (1620): *Novum Organum*, English translation in Spedding, Ellis and Heath eds.,
      The Works of Francis Bacon, London 1860, vol. IV.
[2]   Campbell, Richmond and Vinci, Thomas (1982): "Why are Novel Predictions Important?",
      Pacific Philosophical Quarterly, 63 pp. 111–121.
[3]   Campbell, Richmond and Vinci, Thomas (1983): "Novel Confirmation", *British Journal for the
      Philosophy of Science*, 34 pp. 315–341.
[4]   Chandrasekhar, S. (1987): *Truth and Beauty*. University of Chicago Press.
[5]   Duhem, Pierre (1914): *La Théorie Physique: Son Objet, Sa Structure*. Marcel Rivière & Cie.
      Second edition. Translated by P.P. Wiener as *The Aim and Structure of Physical Theory*, Prince-
      ton: Princeton University Press (1954).
[6]   Giere, Ronald N. (1984): *Understanding Scientific Reasoning*. Holt, Rinehart and Winston.
      Second edition.
[7]   Halmos, Paul R. (1950): *Measure Theory*. Van Nostrand.
[8]   Horwich, Paul (1982): *Probability and Evidence*. Cambridge University Press.
[9]   Huygens, Christiaan. (1690): *Traite de la Lumiere*. Pierre vander Aa. Translated by S.P. Thomp-
      son as *Treatise on Light*, London: Macmillan (1912).
[10] Keynes, John Maynard (1921): *A Treatise on Probability*. Macmillan.
[11] Kolmogorov, A. N. and Fomin, S. V. (1970): *Introductory Real Analysis*. Prentice-Hall. Reprinted
      Dover 1975.
[12] Kuhn, Thomas S. (1970): *The Structure of Scientific Revolutions*. University of Chicago Press.
      Second edition.
[13] Lakatos, Imre (1970): "The Methodology of Scientific Research Programmes", in I. Lakatos
      and A. Musgrave (eds.) *Criticism and the Growth of Knowledge*. Cambridge University Press,
      pp. 91–196.
[14] Lewis, David (1980): "A Subjectivist's Guide to Objective Chance", in R. C. Jeffrey (ed.) *Studies
      in Inductive Logic and Probability*, volume 2. University of California Press, pp. 263–293.
[15] Maher, Patrick (1988): "Prediction, Accommodation, and the Logic of Discovery", *PSA 1988*
      volume 1, pp. 273–285.
[16] Mill, John Stuart (1872): *A System of Logic*. Longmans, Green and Co. Eighth edition.
[17] Peirce, Charles S. (1883): "A Theory of Probable Inference", in Charles S. Peirce (ed.) *Studies
      in Logic*. Little, Brown, pp. 126–181.
[18] Popper, Karl R. (1965): *Conjectures and Refutations*. Harper and Row. Second edition.
[19] Popper, Karl R. (1968): *The Logic of Scientific Discovery*. Harper and Row. Second edition.
[20] Redhead, Michael (1978): "Ad Hocness and the Appraisal of Theories", *British Journal for the
      Philosophy of Science* 29 pp. 355–361.
[21] Rosenkrantz, Roger D. (1977): *Inference, Method and Decision*. D. Reidel.
[22] Rudin, Walter (1974): *Real and Complex Analysis*. McGraw-Hill. Second edition.
[23] Skyrms, Brian (1980): *Causal Necessity*. Yale University Press.
[24] Whewell, William (1847): *The Philosophy of the Inductive Sciences*. Parker. Second edition.

BAS C. VAN FRAASSEN

FIGURES IN A PROBABILITY LANDSCAPE[1]

1. THE PRIMARY LOGIC OF JUDGEMENT

In general, our opinion is certainly not expressible in precise numerical probabilities. But in some cases it is, and in the case of a small field of propositions — e.g. a field generated by a single proposition — my opinion may be exactly represented by a single probability function. Therefore I shall begin with the fiction that it is always so.

Expression of a judgement is a partial expression of one's opinion. Examples are accordingly:

(a)	It seems more likely than not that A
(b)	It seems twice as likely that A than that B
(b′)	It seems at least as likely that A as that B
(c)	It seems π times more likely that A than not, on the supposition that C

The semantic notion needed is that of a probability function which satisfies a given judgement. It is easy to see what that means for this example. For example, p satisfies (a) exactly if $p(A) > p(-A)$.

Epistemic logic has been misguided when it investigated the relation

John believes that . . . $\Vdash$ John believes that _____
In John's opinion, (b) $\Vdash$ In John's opinion, (b′)

which holds if the situation which satisfies the former must also satisfy the latter (*truth preservation*). This led to triviality, because for any example of this relationship we can imagine a moron who is a counter- example. Instead we should look for the significant relationship

$$(b) \Vvdash (b')$$

which should hold intuitively if any rational opinion partially expressed through (b) must also be expressible in part by (b′). On our fiction, this means that any probability function which satisfies the former also satisfies the latter.

---

[1] I am very glad to have this opportunity to honor my teacher, and eventual colleague and friend, Nuel Belnap. In my first year as a graduate student I had Nuel's seminar on the logic of judgement, which took us on an exploration of the riches of formal semantics — greater than the fabled treasures of the Indies and the Spanish Main to my eyes. Questions, it turned out, needed a great deal for their understanding: semantics, the technique of consistency and completeness proofs, modal logic, and most of all, the enlargement of philosophical logic beyond the realm of declarative factual statements. That was the beginning; tautological entailment, relevance, algebraic techniques, and much more were to follow. It is easy and pleasant to recall those days, and perhaps most of all Nuel's gentle and unpolemical spirit, always ready to laugh a little at his own and our shared excitement.

J. M. Dunn and A. Gupta (eds.), Truth or Consequences, 345–356.
© 1990 *Kluwer Academic Publishers. Printed in the Netherlands.*

Brian Ellis (1979) investigated this subject for non-probabilistic judgements; see my (1980).

This sets the primary subject for investigation. We can immediately note a useful reduction of the forms of judgement, in terms of the statistical notion of expectation ("expectation value").

A *space* is a couple $S = \langle K, F \rangle$ with $\Lambda \neq K \in F$ and F a field of subsets of K (the *events* or *propositions*). The probability functions on S are defined by the conditions

(P1) $0 = p(\Lambda) \leq p(A) \leq p(K) = 1$
(P2) $p(A \cup B) + p(A \cap B) = p(A) + p(B)$

A *random variable* (*rv*) on K is a function $g : K \rightarrow R$ (real numbers) which is "measurable" with respect to F, that is

(RV) $g^{-1}(E) \in F$ for all Borel sets E

where the Borel sets are the countable unions and intersections of intervals ((half-) open, (half-) closed) of real numbers. I shall restrict the discussion to rv with finite range which I shall call simple rv. Then (RV) amounts to

(RV simp) $g^{-1}(r) \in F$ for all real numbers r.

Intuitively, g is a quantity which has a numerical value in each possible state of affairs, and its value can be described by means of field F of propositions.

For given probability function p, the *expectation* $Ep(g) = \Sigma p(A)g_A$ where A ranges over the *characteristic partition* X_g of rv g, which has the members required by (RV simp), and I use the notation

for $A = g^{-1}(r)$, write $g_A = r$.

Example. g measures the daily rainfall in inches, and K is a finite set of days. Then for a person with subjective probability p, the number $E_p(g)$ is the *expected* number of inches of rain — which means, the possible daily amounts of rain, averaged in terms of his probabilities for those amounts.

Let our standard forms of judgement now be all Boolean combinations of

$E(f \geq a)$ satisfied by p iff $E_p(f) \geq a$
$E(f \leq a)$ satisfied by p iff $E_p(f) \leq a$

This is already redundant, since $E(f \leq a)$ is the same as $E(-f \geq -a)$. We can further abbreviate:

$$E(f = a) \ = E(f \geq a) \,\&\, E(f \leq a)$$
$$E(f, [a, b]) = E(f \geq a) \,\&\, E(f \leq b)$$
$$E(f > a) \ = {}^{\sim}E(f \leq a)$$
$$E(f, (a, b]) = E(f > a) \,\&\, E(f \leq b)$$

and so forth. But we can also reduce the other forms of judgement, by using the *indicators* of propositions: $I_A(x) = 1$ if x is in A (A is true at x) and $= 0$ otherwise. Then

$$p(A) = r \text{ iff } E_p(I_A) = r$$

$$p(A) : p(B) = r \text{ iff } E_p(I_A - rI_B) = 0$$
$$p(A|B) = r \text{ iff } E_p(I_{A \cap B} - rI_B) = 0$$

provided $p(B) \neq 0$

because expectation is *linear*:

$$E_p(af + bg) = aE_p(f) + bE_p(g)$$

We can now rewrite our original examples as:

(a) $P[A < -A] = E(I_A - I_{-A} < 0)$

(b) $P[A = rB] = E(I_A - rI_B = 0)$

(b') $P[A \geq B] = E(I_A - I_B \geq 0)$

(c) $P[A = \pi - A|C] = E\big((I_{A \cap C} - (\pi/\pi + 1)I_C) = 0\big)$

so that the now defined family of judgements comprises a large variety. There are however intuitively possible judgements which are not so expressible, such as that A and B seem independent (which is satisfied by p exactly if $p(A)p(B) = p(A \cap B)$).

2. STATES OF OPINION: VAGUE PROBABILITY

If a person has numerically precise probabilities, the judgements he or she expresses will convey only part of that. The difference between that fiction and ourselves, I propose as improved hypothesis, is that in our case a finite and even small number of judgements may convey all there is to our opinion. But then there is a large class of probability functions which satisfy just those judgements, hence which are compatible with the person's state of opinion. Call that his or her *representor* (*class*).

Suppose my entire state of opinion can be expressed by means of the judgement $P[A \geq 0.5]$ or equivalently $E(I_A, [0.5, 1])$. Then we may equally say *either* that my probability for A is *vague*, with lower and upper bounds 0.5 and 1, *or* that I am *ambivalent* between or about the probability functions p such that $0.5 \leq p(A) \leq 1$. This modelling of vagueness as ambivalence — the "supervaluation" way — is familiar from the general literature on that subject (Fine (1975), Kamp (1977), van Fraassen (1968, 1970) are among the earliest discussions). It certainly has its limits, which have to do with the well-known "vagueness of vagueness", and this subject continues to be explored (see e.g. Tappenden (1989)).

The logic and semantics of vague probability was worked out satisfactorily over several decades (see especially Smith (1961), Levi (1974), Spielman (1976), Williams (1976), Suppes and Zanotti (1977), Jeffrey (1983)). In my opinion the results are perfectly summed up in Theorem 1 of Gaifman (1988). I will explain how his models work, and then develop the generalized theory applying to vague expectation judgements.

An ordinary statement, such as "It rains" is meant to represent some member of the field of propositions on which our probabilities are defined. Each such proposition is represented by a class of situations in which it is true. What about the judgement that it seems as likely as not that it will rain? Its semantic value is the set of probability functions which give 0.5 to that proposition. But we may also wish to consider the proposition *that it is* (*was, will be*) *my opinion that rain seems as likely as not*. To have this proposition to think about, it needs to belong to that field. That in turn means that we must think of each situation as including me having some state of opinion or other. Well, that is quite possible. We can think that way without circularity. Here is, roughly, how Gaifman handles it:

> There exists for the space $\langle K, F \rangle$ a function P such that for each A in F and interval $[a, b] \subseteq [0, 1]$, there is a member B of F such that $P(A, [a, b]) = B$, and this function P is moreover such that ...

I will not go into the details, for Gaifman then gives the representation theorem which establishes that this is equivalent to:

> There exists for the space $\langle K, F \rangle$ a function p mapping K into the probability functions defined on F, and such that $P(A, [a, b]) = \{x \in K : a \leq p(x)(A) \leq b\}$ belongs to F for all A in F, and for all a, b in $[0, 1]$.

How exactly does such a structure model my opinion? *First* of all we may think of F as having a subfield for each definite "ordinary" topic on which I have opinions — for instance, the field of propositions about the weather tomorrow, or over the next year, or the tosses of a given die or dice. *Secondly*, we can see my representor class in this structure: the set $RC = \{p(x) : x \in K\}$ is the set of probability assignments (to the whole of F) compatible with my opinion.

There is a problem which I must discuss here, if only briefly. The model represents also opinions about my own opinion. There must be criteria of rationality for those too. Suppose that my opinion about whether it will rain is vague, and completely expressed by the judgement

(1) $P[rain, [0, 0.5]]$

What opinion might I have concerning the autobiographical proposition which is true exactly if (1) expresses my opinion about rain completely? Could I give probability 0.8 to the statement that my probability for rain is greater than 0.5? If I do, my opinion has some defect; the question is only whether it is a factual error or a logical one. Am I like someone who believes that Hitler was a misunderstood good man, or like someone who believes that a square with the same perimeter as a certain circle, has a greater area than that circle? The latter is incoherent, even if he does not realize it. In this paper I shall discuss only opinion "of first order".

If we call such a combination $\langle K, F \rangle$ and P (or p) a model, the general logic of judgements has found an image in a restricted logic of propositions. For example

$$P[A = x], P[B = y], P[A \cap B = z] \mathbin{|\!|\!\vdash} P[AB = x + y - z]$$

is called correct *because*

$$P(A, [x]) \cap P(B, [y]) \cap P(A \cap B, [z]) \subseteq P(A \cup B, [x + y - z])$$

in *all* models, and hence also, if the left hand side is K in such a model, then so is the right hand side.

3. STATES OF OPINION: VAGUE EXPECTATION

The outline of a theory of vague expectation, along the above lines, is now clear enough. The main first desideratum will be a representation theorem, formulated in such a way that we have a clear and complete axiomatization of the theory. To this end I define the two notions of VEX ("Vague Expectation") model and structure. I will use Greek letters to range over closed real number intervals.

$\langle K, F, p \rangle$ is a *VEX model* iff $\Lambda \neq K \in F$;
F is a field of subsets of K; and
$p : K \rightarrow \{$probability functions with domain $F\}$ such that

$$E(f, \delta) = \{x \in K : E_{p(x)}(f) \in \delta\}$$

is in F for each closed interval δ and every simple rv f of the space $\langle K, F \rangle$.

$\langle K, F, E \rangle$ is a *VEX structure* iff $\Lambda \neq K \in F$;
F is a field of subsets of K, and
$E : \{$simple $rv\} \times \{$closed intervals$\} \rightarrow F$ such that

Ive. $E(f, [inf(f), sup(f)]) = K$
        $E(f, \Lambda) = \Lambda$
IIve. $E(kf, [a, b]) = E(f, [ka, kb])$ if $k \neq 0$
IIIve. $\cap E(fi, \delta i) \subseteq E(\Sigma f_i, C)$
        where C is the least closed interval that contains all δ_i
IVve. $E(f, [a, b]) \cap E(h, [c, d]) \subseteq E(g, [min(a, c), max(b, d)])$
        if $f \leq g \leq h$.
Vve. $E(f, \delta \cap \delta') = E(f, \delta) \cap E(f, \delta')$
VIve. $E(f, \delta \cup \delta') = E(f, \delta) \cup E(f, \delta')$
        if $\delta \cup \delta'$ is a closed interval.

In IIIve. I have left the index set indefinite; this should be finite in the present context, but could be countable if we require all the probability functions in question to be probability measures (i.e. countably additive).

We should note that all the other forms of judgement discussed are available to us here. Since a simple rv f has a minimum f_-, for example, $E(f \leq b) = E(f, [f_-, b])$, and of course $E(f > b) = K - E(f \leq b)$, and so forth.

THEOREM 1. *If $\langle K, F, p \rangle$ is a VEX model, and E is defined by $E(f, \delta) = \{x \in K : E_{p(x)}(f) \in \delta\}$ then $\langle K, F, E \rangle$ is a VEX structure.*

The proof is elementary, by inspection of the "axioms" Ive.-VIve.

THEOREM 2. *If $\langle K, F, E \rangle$ is a VEX structure, then for each simple rv f of space $\langle K, F \rangle$ and for each set $\Lambda \neq Y \subseteq K$ there are numbers a_f^Y, b_f^Y such that:*

$$Y \subseteq E(f, \delta) \qquad \text{if and only if} \qquad [a_f^Y, b_f^Y] \subseteq \delta$$

COROLLARY. *If $\langle K, F, E \rangle$ is a VEX structure, then there is for each x in K and each simple rv f of space $\langle K, F \rangle$ a unique number r_f^x such that:*

$$x \in E(f, \delta) \qquad \text{if and only if} \qquad r_f^x \in \delta.$$

THEOREM 3. *If $\langle K, F, E \rangle$ is a VEX structure and p, p' are defined by*

$$p(x)(A) = inf\{z : x \in E(I_A, [0, z])\}$$
$$p'(x)(A) = sup\{z : x \in E(I_A, [z, 0])\}$$

then $p = p'$ and $\langle K, F, p \rangle$ is a VEX model.

It is easy to see how Theorem 3 will follow from the preceding ones. Applying the Corollary to $f = I_A$ we see at once that $p = p'$ because both pick out r_f^x for each x in K. The "axioms" in the definition of VEX structures give the ordinary characteristics of expectation when the intervals are degenerate; using E' for neutrality:

$$\begin{aligned} E'(f \leq a) &= \{x \in K : E_{p(x)}(f) \leq a\} \\ &= \{x \in K : r_f^x \leq a\} \\ &= \{x \in K : [r_f^x] \subseteq [a_f^K, a]\} \\ &= \{x \in K : \{x\} \subseteq E(f, [a_f^K, a])\} \\ &= \{x \in K : x \in E(f, [a_f^K, a])\} \\ &= E(f \leq a) \end{aligned}$$

and so this set will be in F as required.

So this ends the proof of Theorem 3 from the Corollary. The latter follows from Theorem 2 by setting $Y = \{x\}$. Writing then a_f^x, b_f^x accordingly, we consider the equation

$$E(f, [a_f^x, b_f^x]) = E(f, [a_f^x, r]) \cup E(f, [r, b_f^x])$$

which is true for $a_f^x \leq r \leq b_f^x$. But then, if this interval is not degenerate, x must lie in one of those two parts, and $[a_f^x, b_f^x]$ is not minimal in the required sense — contrary to supposition.

There remains Theorem 2. It will suffice that for $\Lambda \neq X \subseteq K$ there is a smallest closed interval δ such that $X \subseteq E(f, \delta)$. It is already part of the supposition that we have a VEX structure, that this set $E(f, \delta)$ is in the field of propositions.

The rv f is simple, so its range falls inside a closed interval $[f_-, f_+]$ and $E(f, [f_-, f_+]) = K$ by Ive. Consider the family of closed subintervals δ of this interval such that, for given $X \neq \Lambda$, $X \subseteq E(f, \delta)$. By Ive, IVve, Vve this is a proper filter, and since $[f_-, f_+]$ is compact, it follows that this filter has a non-empty intersection. (Cf. e.g. Gaal (1964), Ch. III, sections 1 and 2.) Call it E. This must itself be a closed interval, for if δ is in the family, and $E \subseteq \delta$ then also the least closed interval containing E is contained in δ, for all δ in this filter, and hence part of, and therefore identical with E. This ends the proof.

4. CONDITIONALIZING A VEX

The next obvious question to ask is: how does a person's opinion change with time? There are philosophical disputes and also nice general results in this area, which I have discussed elsewhere (1984, 1986, 1987). At least from a *technical* point of view the old rule of Conditionalization

(COND) prior p, evidence $E \rightarrow$ posterior $p' = p(-|E)$

plays a central role almost everywhere. So that is what I shall take up here.

Suppose a person's opinion is vague, equivalently, that his or her opinion is ambivalent on a whole set of probability functions. Suppose in addition that he thinks in a certain case that a certain rule such as COND is applicable. Then it would seem that his posterior opinion should be in effect ambivalence on the new set, formed from the original one by applying the rule to each of its members. This leads us to the definition:

> If $M = \langle K, F, p \rangle$ is a VEX and B in F such that $E(I_B = 0) \neq K$, then the conditionalization of M on B is the structure
>
> $$M_B = \langle K^B, F^B, p^B \rangle$$
>
> where
>
> $$K^B = K \cap E(I_B > 0)$$
> $$F^B = \{A \cap E(I_B > 0) : A \in F\}$$
> $$p^B(x)(Q) = p(x)(Q|B)$$
>
> for all x in K^B, and Q in F^B.

Our suppositions entail at once that $K^B \neq \Lambda$ and that F^B is a subfield of F.

Some violence is done here to the range of envisaged possible situations if, for example, these include ones in which Santa Claus exists, and all the latter are ones in which the precise opinion associated assigns *zero* to B. So it looks as if we are confusing the conditionalization of opinion on B — "learning" that B, taking B as one's total new evidence, with "learning" — taking as one's total new evidence — that one's own opinion *really is* such as to give B a positive probability.

But I think this case does not arise if we make up the VEX in the way it should be made up. Suppose $\langle K^0, F^0 \rangle$ represents only possible situations logically independent of my present opinion, but that opinion is vague on the set Q of probability functions on F^0. Then we should build our VEX starting with $K = K^0 \times Q$ — in other words, in such a way that the association of probability functions is used purely and solely to represent our present opinion. But $\langle K^0, F^0 \rangle$ itself could be made up of VEXs, say ones that represent in part our possible *future* states of opinion — that makes for no difficulty.

Theorem 4. *A conditionalization of a VEX is a VEX.*

I chose a VEX model to focus on, because there we see at once that p^B does indeed assign probability functions on F^B. The rest is not so obvious, because there is no definition of conditional probability in terms of expectation. To prove the theorem, I shall first prove a lemma for all VEX models, which concerns a surrogate for conditionalization. Let us define for $M = \langle K, F, p \rangle$:

$$E/_x^B(f) = \sum \{p(x)(A|B)f_A : A \in X_f\}$$

$$\text{if } x \in E(I_B > 0) \text{ and undefined otherwise;}$$

and then prove the

Lemma. *if $x \in E(I_B > 0)$ then $E/_x^B(f) \in [a, b]$ if and only if x belongs to the two propositions $E(h - aI_B \geq 0)$ and $E(h - bI_B \leq 0)$.*

To prove this assume x is indeed in $E(I_B > 0)$ in which case the following are equivalent:

1. $E/_x^B(f) \in [a, b]$
2. $a \leq \sum \{p(x)(A|B)f_A : A \in X_f\} \leq b$
3. $a \leq 1/p(x)(B) \sum \{p(x)(A \cap B)f_A : A \in X_f\} \leq b$
4. $ap(x)(B) \leq E_x(f.I_B) \leq bp(x)B$

because $f.I_B$ defined by $f.I_B(x) = f(x).I_B(x)$ takes value f_A on $A \cap B$ and *zero* elsewhere for exactly the members A of X_f. But 4 is equivalent to the conjunction:

5. $E_x(aI_B) \leq E_x(f.I_B)$ and $E_x(f.I_B) \leq E_x(bI_B)$
6. $x \in E(f.I_B - aI_B \geq 0)$ and $x \in E(f.I_B - bI_B \leq 0)$

as the lemma asserts.

But we see now that there is a close relationship between E^B and its surrogate $E/^B$ partially defined on M. If g is an *rv* of $\langle K^B, F^B \rangle$ define $g+$ to be the *rv* on $\langle K, F \rangle$ such that

$$g+_A = g_A \text{ for } A \text{ in } X_g \text{ and } g+_{K-K^B} = 0$$

then we have

7. $E/_x^B(g) = E_x^B(g)$ for all x in K^B
8. $\{x \in K^B : E/_x^B(g) \in [a, b]\} = K^B \cap \{x \in K :$
$$E/_x^B(g+) \text{ is defined and in } [a, b]\}$$

9. $$= K^B \cap E(g + .I_B - aI_B \geq 0) \cap$$
$$E(g + .I_B - bI_B \leq 0)$$

which is certainly in F, and hence, in view of the definition, also in F^B. This ends the proof.

5. PRESERVATION OF FIGURES: FINITE DESCRIBABILITY

We are finite beings. Some of us are also small-minded. Anyone who can be simulated on a computer surely is that. But as long as we are finite then, even if we are not small-minded, with respect to any well-defined field of propositions our expressible opinion must be expressible in a finite number of judgements — so in that respect we are just the same.

Within this context therefore the representor of my state of opinion too is a finite intersection of propositions $E(f \geq 0)$ — let us call such a set a *figure*. (Obviously $E(f \geq a) = E(f - a \geq 0)$ etc.; we are not losing generality here.) The *complexity* of a figure is the least number of such propositions of which it is an intersection.

To say that my representor is a figure means that it is a figure in the set of all probability functions on a given space. If a certain VEX $\langle K, F, p \rangle$ then models my state of opinion, that means that $\{p(x) : x \in K\}$, which is my representor, is a figure in the set of probability functions with domain F.

Question (essentially raised earlier by Gilbert Harman — see my (1987)):

  — is this property of being a figure preserved under conditionalization?
  — if so, does its complexity decrease, or increase and if the latter, by how much?

It is easy to see why this is of interest: having opted for a representation we believe adequate — partly in its observance of human limitations — we shouldn't like it to be one which becomes inadequate if the state of opinion is changed by something so apparently elementary as conditionalization. But the answer to the first part is *yes*, and the answer to the second is that the complexity *increases at most by a little*, and *often decreases*.[2]

Let X be the set of probability functions on a given domain. A *figure* (in X) — a finitely describable subset — is equivalently the intersection of finitely many "half-spaces" defined by bounded expectation values:

$$E(f \geq a) = \{r : E_r(f) \geq a\}$$
$$E(f \leq a) = \{r : E_r(f) \leq a\}$$

where f is a random variable on the domain. I shall use p, q, r as variables ranging over the probability functions on that domain. Abbreviation:

$$|B| = E(I_B = 1) = E(I_B \geq 1) \cap E(I_B \leq 1)$$
$$= \{r : r(B) = 1\}$$

---

[2] With thanks to John Broome for a helpful discussion.

where I_A is the *indicator* taking value 1 on A and 0 on $-A$.

For any subset S of X define:

$$S_B = \{p(-|B) : p \in S \text{ and } p(B) > 0\}$$

the *conditionalization* of S on B in X.

Theorem 5. *If S is a figure in X, so is S_B*

To prove this, note that p has a ("orthogonal") decomposition in terms of B, if $0 < p(B) < 1$:

$$p = cp^+ + (1-c)p^-$$
$$\text{where } 0 < c \leq 1, p^+ = p(-|B); p^- = p(-|K - B).$$
$$\text{So also } E_p(f) = cE_{p^+}(f) + (1-c)E_{p^-}(f).$$

Lemma. $(D \cap E)_C = D_C \cap E_C$.

Obvious from the definition. Hence we need only look at a single half space. I'll do it for $E(f \geq a)$.

Lemma. $E(f \geq a) = E(f - a > 0)$.

So let us take $S = E(g \geq 0)$. Noting that if p^+ exists then $p(B) > 0$, we argue:

$$q \in S_B \text{ iff } q = p^+ \text{ for some } p \in S$$
$$\text{i.e. such that } E_p(g) \geq 0$$
$$\text{i.e. such that } cE_{p^+}(g) + (1-c)E_{p^-}(g) \geq 0$$
$$\text{i.e. such that } cE_{p^+}(g) \geq -(1-c)E_{p^-}(g)$$

Hence: $q \in S_B$ iff $q \in |B|$ and there is r in $|K - B|$ and number $0 < c \leq 1$ such that

$$(^*) \qquad E_q(g) \geq \frac{(c-1)}{c}E_r(g)$$

We have two cases:

Case 1:   for some r in $|-B|$, $E_r(g) > 0$. Then the RHS of $(^*)$ has no lower bound (as c goes to 0 it goes to negative infinity), so $S_B = |B|$

Case 2:   for all r in $|-B|$, $E_r(g) \leq 0$. In that case, the RHS of $(^*)$ ranges from 0 to positive infinity, so then the LHS need only be non-negative, and $S_B = |B| \cap E(g \geq 0)$.

In both cases S_B is a figure, as was to be proved.

Example. Let S be the set of probability functions on a given domain that give A a probability $> .5$. The rv is then $I_A - .5$, and this has positive expectation for some r in $|-B|$. So the above implies that $S_B = |B|$. Indeed — suppose p gives 1 to B; then $p = p^+$ and whatever $p(A)$ is, we can mix p with a p^- so that the resultant is in S, i.e. gives A a probability $> .5$, while also giving B a non-negative probability.

This was enough to show that the property of being a figure is preserved. Let us now look at the complexity. Conditionalization will transform each half space into either $|B|$ or its intersection with $|B|$. In other words for each relevant rv we either keep the information that its expectation is non-negative or else lose it altogether — while of course gaining the information involved in the new certainty of B. The latter corresponds to the intersection of two half-spaces. Therefore the new complexity is *at most two more* than the old, and generally even less than it was.

THEOREM 6. *The complexity of a figure increases by at most two under conditionalization.*

This sums up all the preceding, for it implies preservation of figurehood.[3]

---

[3] The author thanks the National Science Foundation for research support.

BIBLIOGRAPHY

Achinstein, P. and Hannaway, O. (eds.) (1985): *Observation, Experiment, and Hypothesis in Modern Physical Science.* Cambridge, MA: Bradford, MIT Press.

Earman, J. (ed.) (1983): *Testing Scientific Theories; Minnesota Studies in the Philosophy of Science,* vol. X. Minneapolis: University of Minnesota Press.

Ellis, Brian (1979): *Rational Belief Systems.* Oxford: Blackwell.

Fine, Kit (1975): "Vagueness, Truth and Logic". *Synthese* 30.

Gaal, S.A. (1964): *Point Set Topology.* New York: Academic Press.

Gaifman, H. (1988): "A Theory of Higher Order Probabilities", pp. 191–219 in Skyrms and Harper, vol. I.

Jeffrey, R.C. (1985): "Probability and the Art of Judgement" in Achinstein and Hannaway, pp. 95–126.

Jeffrey, R.C. (1983): "Bayesianism with a Human Face", pp. 133–156 in Earman (1983).

Kamp, Hans (1977): "Two Theories about Adjectives" in Keenan.

Keenan, E.L. (ed.) (1977): *Formal Semantics of Natural Language.* Cambridge: Cambridge University Press.

Levi, I. (1974): "On Indeterminate Probabilities", *Journal of Philosophy* 71, pp. 319–418.

Martin, R. (ed.) (1970): *The Paradox of the Liar.* New Haven: Yale University Press.

Rescher, N. (ed.) (1987): *Scientific Inquiry in Philosophical Perspective.* Lanham, MD: University Press of America.

Skyrms, B. and Harper W. (eds.) (1988): *Causation, Chance, and Credence,* 2 vols. Dordrecht: Kluwer.

Smith, C.A.B. (1961): "Consistency in Statistical Inference and Decision" *Journal of the Royal Statistical Society* B23, pp. 1–25.

Spielman, S. (1976): "Bayesian Inference with Indeterminate Probabilities" pp. 185–196 in Suppe and Asquith (1976), vol. I.

Suppe, F. and Asquith, P. (1976): *PSA,* in two volumes. East Lansing, MI: Philosophy of Science Association 1976–77.

Suppes, P. and Zanotti, M. (1977): "On Using Random Relations to Generate Upper and Lower Probabilities", *Synthese* 36, pp. 427–440.

Tappenden, J. (1989): Doctoral dissertation, Princeton University.

van Fraassen, Bas C. (1968): "Presupposition, Implication, and Self-Reference", *Journal of Philosophy* 65.

_____ (1978): "Rejoinder: On a Kantian Conception of Language", in Martin.

_____ (1980): "Critical Study of Brian Ellis, Rational Belief Systems", Canadian *Journal of Philosophy* 10, pp. 497–511.

_____ (1987): "Symmetries of Personal Probability Kinematics", in Rescher.

Williams, P. (1967): "Indeterminate Probabilities", pp. 229–246 in Przelewski et. al.

NUEL BELNAP: CURRICULUM VITAE

PRESENT POSITION: Alan Ross Anderson Distinguished Professor of Philosophy, Professor of Sociology, Professor of History and Philosophy of Science, and Professor of the Intelligent Systems Program, University of Pittsburgh.

PERSONAL: born Evanston, Illinois, May 1, 1930.

EDUCATION: B. A., University of Illinois, 1952; M. A., Yale University, 1957; Ph. D., Yale University, 1960.

EMPLOYMENT:
Yale University, Department of Philosophy, Instructor, 1958–1960; Assistant Professor, 1960–1963.
University of Pittsburgh, Department of Philosophy, Associate Professor, 1963–1966; Professor, 1966 to date; Professor of Sociology, 1967 to date; Professor of History and Philosophy of Science, 1971 to date; Alan Ross Anderson Lecturer, 1983–84; Alan Ross Anderson Distinguished Professor, 1984 to date; Professor in the Intelligent Systems Program, 1988 to date.
University of California at Irvine, Visiting Professor of Philosophy, Winter, 1973.
Indiana University, Visiting Oscar R. Ewing Professor of Philosophy, Fall, 1977, Fall, 1978, and Fall, 1979.

PROFESSIONAL ASSOCIATIONS: American Philosophical Association; Association for Symbolic Logic (Program Committee Chairman, 1961; Executive Committee, 1970–1973; representative to Section L of the AAAS, 1974–84; Committee on reviews policy, 1974–1976; Oversight Committee 1988–1989; Nomination Committee 1989); American Association for the Advancement of Science; Society for Exact Philosophy (Vice president, 1971–1974; President, 1974–1976; Program coordinator, 1978; treasurer, 1979–80); Mind Association (U. S. treasurer, 1974 to date).

FELLOWSHIPS AND PRIZES:
Predoctoral: Tew Prize, Yale, 1955; Sterling Junior Fellow, Yale, 1955–1956; Fulbright Fellow, Louvain, Belgium, 1957–1958.
Postdoctoral: Morse Research Fellow, 1962–1963; Guggenheim Fellow, 1975–1976; National Endowment for the Humanities Fellow (declined), 1975–1976; Center for Advanced Study in the Behavioral Sciences Fellow (partially funded by the National Endowment for the Humanities), 1982–1983; Fellow, American Academy of Arts and Sciences, 1988–.

EDITORIAL BOARDS: *American Philosophical Quarterly*, 1966–1978; *Journal of Philosophical Logic*, 1970 to date (treasurer, 1970–1976; vice president, 1976–82; chairman of the Board of Governors, 1982–1988); *Notre Dame Journal of Formal Logic*, 1970 to date; *Philosophy of Science*, 1975 to date; *Studia Logica*, 1976 to date; *Philosophical Research Archives*, 1976 to date.

GRANTS, CONSULTANTSHIPS, AND RESEARCH FELLOWSHIPS:
Director of a program of Summer Undergraduate Research and Independent Study, sponsored by the National Science Foundation (National Science Foundation Grants 11848 and G21871), 1960–63.

Consultant, Office of Naval Research (Group Psychology Branch) Contract SAR/Nonr–609(16), "Problem solving and social interaction," 1960–63.

Consultant, System Development Corporation, Santa Monica, California, c. 1961–1967.

Associate investigator, National Science Foundation Grant No. GS–190, "An investigation of some non-classical systems of mathematical logic," 1963–65.

Consultant, University of Pittsburgh Knowledge Availability Center, 1963–66.

Senior research associate, Center for the Philosophy of Science, University of Pittsburgh, 1964–1978; Fellow, 1979 to date.

Principal investigator, National Science Foundation Grant No. GS–689, "An investigation of some non-classical systems of mathematical logic," 1965–68.

Co-designer, under a grant from International Business Machines to the University of Pittsburgh, of a course on the use of computers for research in the humanities, 1965–67.

Working Group 2.2 (Formal Description of computer languages), International Federation of Information Processors, 1967–1976. Travel to meetings in Vienna (1967), Sardinia (1968), Copenhagen (1968), and Vienna (1969) was supported by the University of Pittsburgh.

Senior Research Fellow, Programming Research Group, Oxford University, Hilary Term, 1970. Sabbatical from Pittsburgh.

Principal investigator, National Science Foundation Grant GS–28478, 1971–1976.

Visiting Fellow, Australian National University, January–March, 1976.

Consultant, Westinghouse Research Laboratory, May, 1981.

NUEL BELNAP: DOCTORAL STUDENTS

Giannoni, Carlos	1966	*Conventionalism in logic*
Meyer, Robert	1966	*Topics in modal and many-valued logics*
Dunn, J. Michael	1966	*The algebra of intensional logics*
Woodruff, Peter	1969	*Foundations of three-valued logic*
Garson, James	1969	*The logics of space and time*
Wilson, Kent	1969	*Are modal statements really metalinguistic?*
Grover, Dorothy	1970	*Topics in propositional quantification*
Manor, Ruth	1971	*Conditional forms: Assertion, necessity, obligation, and commands*
Urquhart, Alasdair	1972	*The semantics of entailment*
Pottinger, Garrel	1972	*A theory of implications*
Broido, Jonathan	1974	*Generalization of model theoretic notions and the eliminability of quantification into modal contexts*
Vandernat, Arnold	1974	*First-order indefinite & generalized semantics for weak systems of strict-implication*
Birmingham, Robert L.	1976	*Law as cases*
Helman, Glen	1977	*Restricted Lambda Abstraction and the interpretation of some non-classical logics*
Parks, R. Zane	1977	*Studies in philosophical logic & its history*
Gupta, Anil	1977	*The logic of common nouns: an investigation in quantified modal logic*

Cohen, Daniel	1983	*The logic of conditional assertion* (Indiana University; J. Michael Dunn, co-director)
Horty, John	1986	*Some aspects of meaning in non-contingent language*
Garfield, Jay	1986	*Cognitive science and the ontology of mind*
Kremer, Michael	1986	*Logic and truth*

NUEL BELNAP: PUBLICATIONS

Articles (except reprintings) are *'d. Monographs and books
are **'d. Unmarked items are abstracts, reviews, reprints, etc.

1955
*1. "Two components of existence," *Ideas*, vol. 5 (1955), pp. 21–26.

1958
2. "A modification of Ackermann's 'rigorous implication'" [by A. R. Anderson
   and NDB] (abstract), *Journal of symbolic logic*, vol. 23 (1958), pp. 457–458.

1959
*3. "EQ and the first order functional calculus," appendix to *Completeness-
   theorems for the systems E of entailment and EQ of entailment with quantification* by A. R. Anderson, Technical report No. 6, Office of Naval Research
   (Group Psychology Branch) Contract SAR/Nonr-609(16), New Haven, 1959,
   pp. 25–27. Also appears in *Zeitschrift für mathematische Logik*, vol. 6 (1960),
   pp. 217–218.
*4. "Modalities in Ackermann's 'rigorous implication'" [by A. R. Anderson and
   NDB], *Journal of symbolic logic*, vol. 24 (1959), pp. 107–111.
5. "Pure rigorous implication as a 'Sequenzen-kalkül'" (abstract), *Journal of symbolic logic*, vol. 24 (1959), pp. 282–283.
6. "A proof of the Löwenheim-Skolem theorem" [by A. R. Anderson and NDB]
   (abstract), *Journal of symbolic logic*, vol. 24 (1959), pp. 285–286.
7. "Tautological entailments" (abstract), *Journal of symbolic logic*, vol. 24 (1959),
   p. 316.
*8. "A simple treatment of truth functions" [by A. R. Anderson and NDB], *Journal
   of symbolic logic*, vol. 24 (1959), pp. 301–302.
9. "A simple proof of Gödel's completeness theorem" [by A. R. Anderson and
   NDB] (abstract), *Journal of symbolic logic*, vol. 24 (1959), pp. 320–321.

1960
**10. *A formal analysis of entailment*, Technical report No. 7, Office of Naval Re-
   search (Group Psychology Branch) Contract SAR/Nonr-609(16), New Haven,
   1960, pp. viii, 107.
*11. "Independent axiom schemata for the pure theory of entailment" [by A. R.
   Anderson, NDB and J. R. Wallace], *Zeitschrift für mathematische Logik*, vol. 6
   (1960), pp. 93–95.

12. Book note: *Axiomatic set theory* (New York, 1960) by P. Suppes, *Review of metaphysics*, vol. 14 (1960–61), p. 175.
13. Review of "Existential presuppositions and existential commitments" (*Journal of philosophy*, 1959) by J. Hintikka, *Journal of symbolic logic*, vol. 25 (1960), p. 88.
14. Review of "Nondesignating singular terms" (*Philosophical review*, 1959) by H. Leblanc and T. Hailperin, *Journal of symbolic logic*, vol. 25 (1960), pp. 87–88.
15. Review of "Towards a theory of definite descriptions" (*Analysis*, 1959) by J. Hintikka, *Journal of symbolic logic*, vol. 25 (1960), pp. 88–89.
*16. "Entailment and relevance," *Journal of symbolic logic*, vol. 25 (1960), pp. 144–146.
17. "First degree formulas" (abstract), *Journal of symbolic logic*, vol. 25 (1960), pp. 388–389.

1961

*18. "First degree entailments" [by A. R. Anderson and NDB], Technical report No. 10, Office of Naval Research (Group Psychology Branch) Contract SAR/Nonr-609(16), New Haven, 1961, pp. iv, 35.
*19. "A decision procedure for the system EI- of entailment with negation" [by NDB and J.R. Wallace], Technical report No. 11, Office of Naval Research (Group Psychology Branch), Contract SAR/Nonr-609(16), New Haven, 1961, pp. 31.
20. Book note: *Leviathan: a simulation of behavioral systems, to operate dynamically on a digital computer* (Santa Monica, 1959) by B. K. Rome and S. C. Rome, *Review of metaphysics*, vol. 15 (1961–62), p. 195.
21. Book note: *Formal representation of intentionally structured systems* (Santa Monica, 1959) by B. K. Rome and S. C. Rome, *Review of metaphysics*, vol. 15 (1961–62), p. 195.
22. Book note: *Markov learning models for multiperson interactions* (Stanford, 1960) by P. Suppes and R. C. Atkinson, *Review of metaphysics*, vol. 15 (1961–62), p. 196.
*23. "Enthymemes" [by A. R. Anderson and NDB], *Journal of philosophy*, vol. 58 (1961), pp. 713–723.
*24. "Tonk, Plonk and Plink," *Analysis*, vol. 22 (1961–62), pp. 130–134.

1962

*25. "Tautological entailments" [by A. R. Anderson and NDB], *Philosophical studies*, vol. 13 (1962), pp. 9–24.
*26. "Intuitionism reconsidered" [by H. Leblanc and NDB], *Notre Dame journal of formal logic*, vol. 3 (1962), pp. 79–82.
*27. "The pure calculus of entailment" [by A. R. Anderson and NDB], *Journal of symbolic logic*, vol. 27 (1962), pp. 19–52.

1963

28. "First degree entailments" [by A. R. Anderson and NDB], *Mathematische Annalen*, vol. 149 (1963), pp. 302–319. A slightly revised version of item 18.

29. Review of *Computers and common sense* (Columbia University Press, 1961) by M. Taube, *Modern uses of logic in law*, March 1963, pp. 34–38.

*30. "A rule-completeness theorem" [by NDB and R. H. Thomason], *Notre Dame journal of formal logic*, vol. 4 (1963), pp. 39–43.

**31. *An analysis of questions: preliminary report*, System Development Corporation, Santa Monica, California, 1963, pp. 160.

32. Review of *Natural deduction* (Wadsworth, 1962) by J. M. Anderson and H. W. Johnstone, Jr., *American mathematical monthly*, 1963.

33. Review of "The number of classes of invertible boolean functions" (*Journal ACM*, 1963) by M. A. Harrison, *Computing reviews*, vol. 4 (1963), p. 138.

34. Review of *Truth-functional logic* (The Free Press of Glencoe, New York, 1962) by J. A. Faris, *Computing reviews*, vol. 4 (1963), p. 229.

*35. "On not strengthening intuitionistic logic" [by NDB, H. Leblanc and R. H. Thomason], *Notre Dame journal of formal logic*, vol. 4 (1963), pp. 313–320.

36. "On not strengthening intuitionistic logic" [by NDB, H. Leblanc and R. H. Thomason] (abstract), read at December 1963 meeting of the Association for Symbolic Logic, *Journal of symbolic logic*, vol. 28 (1963), p. 297.

1964

37. Review of "A logic of questions and answers" (*Philosophy of Science*, 1961), *Communication: A logical model* (The M.I.T. Press, 1963), and "A model for applying information and utility functions" (*Philosophy of Science*, 1963) by D. Harrah, *Journal of symbolic logic*, vol. 29 (1964), pp. 136–138.

1965

38. Review of "A measure of subjective information" by R. Wells, *Structure of language and its mathematical aspects, Proceedings of symposia in applied mathematics*, vol. 12, American Mathematical Society, 1961, pp. 237–244, and "Comments" by J. D. Sable and R. Wells, *ibid.*, pp. 267–268. *Journal of symbolic logic*, vol. 30 (1965), pp. 244–245.

39. "A decision procedure for the system EI- of entailment with negation" [by NDB and J. R. Wallace], *Zeitschrift für mathematische Logik*, vol. 11 (1965), pp. 277–289. A revision of item 19.

1966

40. "Questions, answers, and presuppositions," *Journal of philosophy*, vol. 63 (1966), pp. 609–611. Abstract of a paper read at the 1966 meeting of the Eastern Division of the American Philosophical Association.

41. Combined review of three articles by B. Sobocinski and six articles by I. Thomas, all on Lewis-like modal logics, *Journal of symbolic logic*, vol. 31 (1966), pp. 498–500.

*42. "Intensionally complemented distributive lattices" [by NDB and J. Spencer], *Portugaliae Mathematica*, vol. 25 (1966), pp. 99–104.

1967

*43. "Intensional models for first degree formulas," *Journal of symbolic logic*, vol. 32 (1967), pp. 1–22.

44. "Special cases of the decision problem for entailment and relevant implication," *Journal of symbolic logic*, vol. 32 (1967), pp. 431–432. Abstract of a paper read at the 1967 meeting of the Association for Symbolic Logic.

45. "Homomorphisms of intentionally complemented distributive lattices" [by J. M. Dunn and NDB] (abstract), *Journal of symbolic logic*, vol. 32 (1967), p. 446.

*46. "Comments on H. Simon's 'The logic of heuristic decision making,'" *The logic of decision and action*, ed. N. Rescher, University of Pittsburgh Press, 1967, pp. 27–31.

47. "Tonk, Plonk and Plink," *Philosophical logic*, ed. P. F. Strawson, Oxford, 1967, pp. 132–137. A reprinting of item 24.

1968

*48. "Homomorphisms of intensionally complemented distributive lattices" [by J. M. Dunn and NDB], *Mathematische annalen*, vol. 176 (1968), pp. 28–38.

49. "Entailment" [by A. R. Anderson and NDB], *Logic and Philosophy*, ed. G. Iseminger, New York, 1968, pp. 76–110. A version of item 27, with some revisions, deletions, and additions. Also contains a portion of item 25.

*50. "The substitution interpretation of the quantifiers" [by J. M. Dunn and NDB], *Noûs*, vol. 2 (1968), pp. 177–185.

51. Reviews of three articles by C. A. Meredith and A. N. Prior, one by A. F. Bausch, and one by M. J. Cresswell, *Zentralblatt für Mathematik und ihre Grenzgebiete*, vol. 146 (1968), pp. 8–9.

1969

*52. "Åqvist's corrections-accumulating question-sequences," *Philosophical logic*, ed. J. W. Davis, D. J. Hockney, and W. K. Wilson, Reidel, 1969, pp. 122–134.

*53. "Questions: their presuppositions, and how they can fail to arise," *The logical way of doing things*, ed. K. Lambert, Yale University Press, 1969, pp. 23–37.

1970

*54. "Every functionally complete m-valued logic has a Post-complete axiomatization" [by NDB and S. McCall], *Notre Dame journal of formal logic*, vol. 11 (1970), p. 106.

*55. "Conditional assertion and restricted quantification," *Noûs*, vol. 4 (1970), p. 1–13.

56. Review of "A propositional logic with subjunctive conditionals" (*Journal of symbolic logic*, 1962) by R. B. Angell, *Journal of symbolic logic*, vol. 35 (1970), pp. 464–465.

1972

*57. "*S-P* interrogatives," *Journal of philosophical logic*, vol. 1 (1972), pp. 331–346.

58. "Foreword" to *A general interpreted modal calculus* by A. Bressan, Yale University Press, 1972, pp. xiii–xxv.

1973

*59. "Quantifying in and out of quotes" [by NDB and D. L. Grover], *Truth, syntax, and modality*, ed. H. Leblanc, North-Holland, 1973, pp. 17–47.

*60. "Restricted quantification and conditional assertion," *Truth, syntax, and modality*, ed. H. Leblanc, North-Holland, 1973, pp. 48–75.

1974

61. "A memorial note on A. R. Anderson," *Metaphilosophy*, vol. 5 (1974), pp. 73–75.

1975

*62. "A prosentential theory of truth" [by D. L. Grover, J. L. Camp, Jr. and NDB], *Philosophical Studies*, vol. 27 (1975), pp. 73–125.

63. "A useful four-valued logic" (abstract), *Proceedings of the 1975 International Symposium on Multiple-valued Logic*, eds. N.B. Cocchiarella, J.M. Dunn, G.E. Epstein, and S. Shapiro, available from IEEE Computer Society, Long Beach, California, p. 399.

*64. "Grammatical propaedeutic," *The logical enterprise*, ed. A. R. Anderson, R. B. Marcus, and R. M. Martin, Yale University Press, 1975, pp. 143–165.

**65. *Entailment: the logic of relevance and necessity*, vol. I [by A. R. Anderson and NDB], Princeton University Press, 1975, pp. xxxii, 542.

*66. "Testing matrix claims interactively on a computer," *Cirpho*, vol. 3 (1975), pp. 7–9.

1976

**67. *The logic of questions and answers* [by NDB and T. B. Steel and with a Bibliography of the theory of questions and answers by U. Egli and H. Schleichert], Yale University Press, 1976, pp. vi, 209.

*68. "The two property," *The relevance logic newsletter*, vol. 1 (1976), pp. 173–180.

*69. "How a computer should think," *Contemporary aspects of philosophy*, ed. G. Ryle, Oriel Press, 1976, pp. 30–55.

1977

70. "Relevant analytic tableaux" [by M. A. McRobbie and NDB] (abstract), *The relevance logic newsletter*, vol. 2 (1977), pp. 46–49.

71. "Entailment (vol. 1) errata," *The relevance logic newsletter*, vol. 2 (1977), pp. 176–182.

*72. "A useful four-valued logic," *Modern uses of multiple-valued logic*, ed. J. M. Dunn and G. Epstein, D. Reidel, 1977, pp. 8–37.

1978

*73. "BINDEX: a book indexing system," *Scholarly publishing*, vol. 9 (1978), pp. 167–170.

74. A reprinting of item 24. *Contemporary Philosophical Logic*, ed. I. M. Copi and J. A. Gould, St. Martin's Press, pp. 44–48.

1979

*75. "Rescher's hypothetical reasoning: an amendment," *The philosophy of Nicholas Rescher: discussion and replies*, ed. E. Sosa, D. Reidel, 1979, pp. 19–28.
*76. "Relevant analytic tableaux" [by M. A. McRobbie and NDB], *Studia Logica*, vol. 38 (1979), pp. 187–200.

1980

*77. "A consecution calculus for positive relevant implication with necessity" [by NDB, A. Gupta, and J. M. Dunn], *Journal of philosophical logic*, vol. 9 (1980), pp. 343–362. (By error the title appeared as "A consecutive... .")
*78. "Modal and relevance logics: 1977," *Modern logic—a survey*, ed. E. Agazzi, D. Reidel, 1980, pp. 131–151.

1981

79. Photograph: inside dust cover of *Mind design*, ed. J. Haugeland, Bradford Books, Montgomery, VT, 1981.
*80. "Entailment and the disjunctive syllogism" [by NDB and J. M. Dunn], *Contemporary philosophy. A new survey.*, vol. 1, Martinus Nijhoff, The Hague/Boston/London, 1981, pp. 337–366.
*81. "*Logica docens* and relevance," *Teaching philosophy*, vol. 4 (1981), pp. 419–427.
82. Russian translation of item 67: *Logika voprosov i otvetov* [by NDB and T. Steel, Jr.], translated by G. E. Krejdlin, edited and with foreword and notes by V. A. Smirnov and V. K. Finn, Progress Publishers (17 Zubovsky Blvd., Moscow 119021), 1981, pp. 288. Also included are translations of items 69 (pp. 208–239) and 72 (pp. 240–267).
83. Russian translation of item 43. *Semantika modal' nix i intensional' nix logik*, compiled, edited and with an introductory essay by V. A. Smirnov, Progress Publishers (17 Zubovsky Blvd., Moscow 119021), 1981, pp. 325–362. The translation is by A. L. Nikiforov.

1982

*84. "Questions and answers in Montague grammar," *Processes, beliefs, and questions*, ed. S. Peters and E. Saarinen, D. Reidel, 1982, pp. 165–198.
85. Reprintings of items 26 and 35. *Existence, truth and provability* by H. Leblanc, State University of New York Press, Albany, 1982, pp. 385–389 and pp. 390–396.
*86. "Display logic," *Journal of philosophical logic*, vol. 11 (1982), pp. 375–417.
*87. "Gupta's rule of revision theory of truth," *Journal of philosophical logic*, vol. 11 (1982), pp. 103–116.
*88. "Approaches to the semantics of questions in natural language (II)," *Philosophical essays dedicated to Lennart Åqvist on his fiftieth birthday*, ed. T. Pauli, University of Uppsala, Sweden, 1982, pp. 16–33.

1983

*89. "Approaches to the semantics of questions in natural language (I)," *Meaning, use, and interpretation of language*, ed. R. Bäuerle, C. Schwarze, and A. von Stechow, Walter de Gruyter, 1983, pp. 22–29.

*90. "Symbolization trees," unit 25 of *Understanding symbolic logic* by V. Klenk, Prentice-Hall, 1983, pp. 402–411.

91. "Display logic" (abstract), *Journal of symbolic logic*, vol. 48 (1983), p. 907.

1984

*92. "Proof tableau formulations of some first-order relevant ortho-logics" [by M. A. McRobbie and NDB], *Bulletin of the section of logic*, Polish Academy of Sciences, Institute of Philosophy and Sociology, vol. 13 (1984), pp. 233–240.

1986

93. "Approaches to the semantics of questions in natural language: part I," *From models to modules: studies in cognitive science from the McGill Workshops*, eds. I. Gopnik and M. Gopnik, Ablex Publishing Corporation, Norwood, NJ, 1986, pp. 257–284. In spite of the agreement of this title with that of item 89, this is essentially a reprinting of a combination of items 88 and 89.

1987

*94. "A note on extension, intension, and truth," [by A. Gupta and NDB] *Journal of philosophy*, pp. 168–174, 1987.

95. "Foreword" to *Imperatives* by C. L. Hamblin, Basil Blackwell, 1987.

96. German translation of item 62. *Der Wahrheitsbegriff: Neue Erklärungsversuche*. Edited by L. B. Puntel. (Darmstadt: Wissenschaftliche Buchgesellschaft), 1987. The translation is by I. Dumitriv and V. Winko.

1988

*97. "Seeing to it that: a canonical form for agentives" [by NDB and M. Perloff], *Theoria*, vol. 54 (1988) pp. 175–199.

INDEX OF NAMES

INDEX OF SUBJECTS